THE

LIFE AND WORK

OF

ST. PAUL

THE

LIFE AND WORK

OF

ST. PAUL

BY

F. W. FARRAR, D.D., F.R.S.

Late Fellow of Trinity College, Cambridge
Canon of Westminster
and Chaplain in Ordinary to the Queen

VOLUME II

NEW YORK
E. P. DUTTON & COMPANY
31 WEST 23D STREET
1903

TABLE OF CONTENTS.

Book IX.
EPHESUS.

CHAPTER XXXI.
PAUL AT EPHESUS.

St. Paul leaves Corinth—Nazarite Vow—Ephesian Jews—Fourth Visit to Jerusalem—Cold Reception—Return to Antioch—Confirms Churches of Galatia and Phrygia—Re-visits Ephesus—Its Commerce, Fame, and Splendour—Its Great Men—Roman Rule—Asylum — Temple of Artemis — The Heaven-fallen—Megabyzi—Ephesian Amulets—Apollonius of Tyana—Letters of the Pseudo-Heraclitus—Apollos—Disciples of John—School of Tyrannus—"Handkerchiefs and Aprons"—Discomfiture of the Beni Sceva—Burning of Magic Books—Trials and Perils at Ephesus—Bad news from Corinth—The Ephesia—Exasperation of the Artisans—Artemis—Demetrius—Attempt to seize Paul—Riot in the Theatre—Gaius and Aristarchus—Speech of the Recorder—Farewell to the Church at Ephesus—Present Condition of Ephesus 1

CHAPTER XXXII.
FIRST LETTER TO THE CHURCH AT CORINTH.

Difficulties of Converts from Heathenism—Letter from Corinth—Various Enquiries—Disputes in the Church—Apollos' Party—Petrine Party—The Judaic Teacher—Disorderly Scenes in Church Assemblies—The Agapæ—Desecration of the Eucharistic Feast—Condonation of the Notorious Offender—Steps taken by St. Paul—Sends Titus to Corinth—Dictates to Sosthenes a letter to the Corinthians—Topics of Letter—Greeting—Thanksgivings—Party-spirit—True and False Wisdom—Sentence on the Notorious Offender—Christ our Passover—Christian and Heathen Judges—Lawful and Unlawful Meats—Marriage—Celibacy—Widows—Divorce—Meats offered to Idols—Digression on his Personal Self-abnegation, and Inference from it—Covering the Head—Disorder at the Lord's Supper—Glossolalia—Charity—Rules about Preaching—The Resurrection—Practical Directions—Salutations—Benediction 45

CHAPTER XXXIII.

SECOND LETTER TO THE CHURCH AT CORINTH.

Anxiety of St. Paul—Short Stay at Troas—Meeting with Titus—Effect of First Letter on the Corinthians—Personal Opposition to his Authority—Return of Titus to Corinth—Trials in Macedonia—Characteristics of the Epistle—Greeting—Tribulation and Consolation—Self-defence—Explanations—Metaphors—Ministry of the New Covenant—Eloquent Appeals—Liberality of the Churches of Macedonia—Exhortation to Liberality—Sudden change of Tone—Indignant Apology—Mingled Irony and Appeal—False Apostles—Unrecorded Trials of his Life—Vision at his Conversion—Proofs of the Genuineness of his Ministry—Salutation—Benediction 88

CHAPTER XXXIV.

SECOND VISIT TO CORINTH.

Second Sojourn in Macedonia—Brief Notice by St. Luke—Illyricum the furthest point of his Missionary Journey—Institution of the Offertory—His Fellow Travellers in the Journey to Corinth—His Associates at Corinth—Condition of the Church—Two Epistles written at Corinth 119

CHAPTER XXXV.

IMPORTANCE OF THE EPISTLE TO THE GALATIANS.

Judaising Opponents among the Galatian Converts—Galatian Fickleness—Arguments against St. Paul—Circumcision the Battle-ground—Christian Liberty at Stake—Instances of Proselytes to Circumcision among the Heathen Royal Families—Courage and Passion of St. Paul's Argument—The Epistle to the Galatians, the Manifesto of Freedom from the Yoke of Judaism 129

CHAPTER XXXVI.

THE EPISTLE TO THE GALATIANS.

Brief Greeting—Indignant Outburst—Vindication of his Apostolic Authority—Retrospect—Slight Intercourse with the Apostles—Co-ordinate Position—Kephas at Antioch—Second Outburst—Purpose of the Law—Its Relation to the Gospel—Boldness of his Arguments—Justification by Faith—Allegory of Sarah and Hagar—Bondage to the Law—Freedom in Christ—Lusts of the Flesh—Fruits of the Spirit—Practical Exhortations—Autograph Conclusion—Contemplates another Visit to Jerusalem, and a Letter to Rome 140

CHAPTER XXXVII.

THE EPISTLE TO THE ROMANS, AND THE THEOLOGY OF ST. PAUL.

The Jews at Rome—Numbers of the Christian Converts—Christianity Introduced into Rome—Not by St. Peter—Was the Church mainly Jewish or

CONTENTS.

Gentile?—Solution of Apparent Contradictions—Note on the Sixteenth Chapter—Probably Part of a Letter to Ephesus—Main Object of the Epistle—Written in a Peaceful Mood—Theory of Baur as to the Origin of the Epistle—Origin and Idea of the Epistle—Outlines of the Epistle . . 162

II.
GENERAL THESIS OF THE EPISTLE.

Salutation—Thanksgiving—Fundamental Theme—The Just shall live by Faith—Examination of the Meaning of the Phrase 184

III.
UNIVERSALITY OF SIN.

Guilt of the Gentiles—God's Manifestation of Himself to the Gentiles in His Works—Therefore their Sin inexcusable—Vices of Pagan Life—The Jew more inexcusable because more enlightened—Condemned in spite of their Circumcision and Legal Obedience 195

IV.
OBJECTIONS AND CONFIRMATIONS.

Has the Jew an Advantage?—Can God justly Punish?—Repudiation of False and Malignant Inferences—Jew and Gentile all under Sin—Quotations from the Psalms and Isaiah 205

V.
JUSTIFICATION BY FAITH.

"The Righteousness of God" explained—The Elements of Justification—Faith does not nullify the Law—Abraham's Faith—Peace and Hope the Blessed Consequences of Faith—Three Moments in the Religious History of Mankind—Adam and Christ—May we sin that Grace may abound?—The Conception of Life in Christ excludes the possibility of Wilful Sin—The Law cannot Justify—The Law Multiplies Transgressions—We are not under the Law, but under Grace—Apparent Contradictions—Faith and Works—Dead to the Law—The Soul's History—Deliverance—Hope—Triumph . 209

CHAPTER XXXVIII.
PREDESTINATION AND FREE WILL.

Rejection of the Jews—Foreknowledge of God—The Resistance of Evil—The Potter and the Clay—Man's Free Will—Fearlessness and Conciliatoriness of St. Paul's Controversial Method—Rejection of Israel—Not Total nor Final—Gleams of Hope—Christ the Stone of Offence to the Jews—Prophesies of a Future Restoration—The Heave-offering—The Oleaster and the Olive—The Universality of Redeeming Grace—Doxology . . . 240

CHAPTER XXXIX.

Fruits of Faith.

Break in the Letter—Practical Exhortation—Christian Graces—Obedience to Civil Powers—Value of Roman Law—Functions of Civil Governors—Payment of Civil Dues—Ebionitic Tendencies—Advice to "Strong" and "Weak"—Entreaty for the Prayers of the Church—Benediction—Reasons for concluding that the Sixteenth Chapter was addressed to the Ephesian Church—Concluding Doxology 257

CHAPTER XL.

The Last Journey to Jerusalem.

Preparing to Start for Jerusalem—Fury of the Jews—Plot to Murder St. Paul —How defeated—Companions of his Journey—He Remains at Philippi with St. Luke for the Passover—Troas—Eutychus—Walk from Troas to Assos—Sail among the Grecian Isles to Miletus—Farewell Address to the Elders of Ephesus—Sad Parting—Coos—Rhodes—Patara—Tyre—The Prayer on the Sea Shore—Cæsarea—Philip the Evangelist—The Prophet Agabus—Warnings of Danger—Fifth Visit to Jerusalem—Guest of Mnason the Cyprian—Assembly of the Elders—James the Lord's Brother—Presentation of the Contribution from the Churches—St. Paul's Account of his Work—Apparent Coldness of his Reception—An Humiliating Suggestion— Nazarite Vow—Elaborate Ceremonies—St. Paul Consents—His Motives and Justification—Political State of the Jews at this time—Quarrels with the Romans—Insolent Soldiers—Quarrel with Samaritans—Jonathan— Felix—Sicarii—St. Paul recognised in the Court of the Women—A Tumult —Lysias—Speech of St. Paul to the Mob—Preparation for Scourging— Civis Romanus sum—Trial by the Sanhedrin—Ananias the High Priest— "Thou Whited Wall"—Apology—St. Paul asserts himself a Pharisee—Was this Justifiable?—Is told in a Vision that he shall go to Rome—The Vow of the Forty Jews—Conspiracy revealed by a Nephew—St. Paul conducted to Cæsarea—Letter of Lysias to Felix—In Prison . . . 272

CHAPTER XLI.

Paul and Felix.

Trial before Felix—Speech of Tertullus—St. Paul's Defence—The Trial postponed—Discourse of St. Paul before Felix and Drusilla—Riot in Cæsarea— Felix recalled—Two Years in Prison 336

CHAPTER XLII.

Paul before Festus and Agrippa II.

Fresh Trial before Porcius Festus—His Energy and Fairness—St. Paul appeals to Cæsar—Visit of Agrippa II. and Berenice to Festus—A Grand Occasion —St. Paul's Address—Appeal to Agrippa II., and his Reply—Favourable Impression made by St. Paul 346

CONTENTS.

CHAPTER XLIII.
VOYAGE TO ROME AND SHIPWRECK.

Sent to Rome under charge of Julius—The Augustani—Prisoners chained to Soldiers—Plan of the Journey—Luke and Aristarchus—Day spent at Sidon—Voyage to Myra—The Alexandrian Wheatship—Sail to Crete—Windbound at Fair Havens—Advice of St. Paul—Rejected—Julius decides to try for Port Phœnix—The Typhoon—Euroaquilo—Great Danger—Clauda—Securing the Boat—Frapping the Vessel—Other measures to save the Ship—Misery caused by the continuous Gale—St. Paul's Vision—He encourages them—They near Land—Ras el Koura—Attempted Escape of the Sailors—The Crew take Food—Final Shipwreck—The Soldiers—Escape of the Crew 362

Book X.
ROME

CHAPTER XLIV.
PAUL AT ROME.

Received with Hospitality by the Natives of Melita—A Viper fastens on his Hand—Three Months at Malta—The Protos—The Father of Publius healed—Honour paid to St. Paul—Embarks on board the *Castor and Pollux*—Syracuse—Rhegium—Puteoli—Journey towards Rome—Met by Brethren at Appii Forum—Tres Tabernæ—The Appian Road—Enters Rome—Afranius Burrus—Observatio—Irksomeness of his Bondage—Summons the Elders of the Jews—Their cautious Reply—Its Consistency with the Epistle to the Romans—The Jews express a wish for further Information—A long Discussion—Stern Warning from the Apostle—Two Years a Prisoner in Rome—The Constancy of his Friends—Unmolestedly . . 383

CHAPTER XLV.
THE FIRST ROMAN IMPRISONMENT.

His hired Apartments—His general Position—His state of Mind—His Life and Teaching in Rome—Condition of various Classes in Rome—Improbability of his traditional Intercourse with Seneca—" Not many noble "—Few Converts among the Aristocracy of Rome—Condition of Slaves—Settlement of the Jews in Rome—First encouraged by Julius Cæsar—Their Life and Condition among the Roman Population—The Character and Government of Nero—The Downfall of Seneca—Fenius Rufus and Tigellinus, Prætorian Prefects 398

CHAPTER XLVI.
THE EPISTLES OF THE CAPTIVITY.

The History of St. Paul's Imprisonment derived from the Epistles of the Captivity—The four Groups into which the Epistles may be divided—The

Characteristics of those Groups—Key-note of each Epistle—The Order of the Epistles—Arguments in favour of the Epistle to the Philippians being the earliest of the Epistles of the Captivity—Parallels in the Epistle to the Philippians to the Epistle to the Romans—St. Paul's Controversy with Judaism almost at an end—Happier Incidents brighten his Captivity—Visit of Epaphroditus—His Illness and Recovery—The Purity of the Philippian Church—"Rejoice" the leading thought in the Epistle 410

CHAPTER XLVII.

THE EPISTLE TO THE PHILIPPIANS.

Greeting—Implied Exhortation to Unity—Words of Encouragement—Even Opposition overruled for good—Earnest Entreaty to follow the Example of Christ—His hopes of liberation—Epaphroditus—Sudden break—Vehement Outburst against the Jews—Pressing forward—Euodia and Syntyche —Syzygus—Farewell and Rejoice—Future of Philippian Church . . 424

CHAPTER XLVIII.

THE CHURCHES OF THE LYCUS VALLEY.

Colossians, "Ephesians," Philemon—Attacks on their Genuineness—Epaphras—Laodicea, Hierapolis, Colossæ—The Lycus Valley—Onesimus—Sad News brought by Epaphras—A new form of Error—An Essene Teacher—St. Paul develops the Counter-truth—Christ alone—Oriental Theosophy the germ of Gnosticism—The Christology of these Epistles—Universality and Antiquity of Gnostic Speculations—Variations in the Style of St. Paul . 438

CHAPTER XLIX.

EPISTLE TO THE COLOSSIANS.

Greeting—Christ the Eternal Son—Grandeur of the Ministry of the Gospel—The Pleroma—Warnings against False Teaching—Practical Consequences —A Cancelled Bond—A needless Asceticism—The true Remedy against Sin—Practical Exhortations—Personal Messages—Asserted Reaction against Pauline Teaching in Asia—Papias—Colossæ 455

CHAPTER L.

ST. PAUL AND ONESIMUS.

Private Letters—Onesimus—Degradation of Slaves—A Phrygian Runaway—Christianity and Slavery—Letter of Pliny to Sabinianus—A "Burning Question"—Contrast between the tone of Pliny and that of St. Paul. . 468

CHAPTER LI.

THE EPISTLE TO PHILEMON.

Paraphrase of the Epistle—Comparison with Pliny's appeal to Sabinianus—Did St. Paul visit Colossæ again? 478

CONTENTS.

CHAPTER LII.
THE EPISTLE TO THE "EPHESIANS."

Genuineness of the Epistle—Testimonies to its Grandeur—Resemblances and Contrasts between "Ephesians" and Colossians—Style of St. Paul—Christology of the later Epistles—Doctrinal and Practical—Grandeur of the Mystery—Recurrence of Leading Words—Greeting—"To the praise of His glory"—Christ in the Church—Resultant Duties—Unity in Christ—The New Life—Christian Submissiveness—The Christian Armour—End of the Acts of the Apostles—St. Paul's Expectations—The Neronian Persecution 482

CHAPTER LIII.
THE FIRST EPISTLE TO TIMOTHY.

Did St. Paul visit Spain?—Character of the First Epistle to Timothy—Peculiarities of the Greeting—False Teachers—Function of the Law—Digressions—Regulations for Public Worship—Qualifications for Office in the Church—Deacons—Deaconesses—The Mystery of Godliness—Dualistic Apostasy—Pastoral Advice to Timothy—Bearing towards Presbyters—Personal Advice—Duties of Slaves—Solemn Adjuration—Last Appeal . 515

CHAPTER LIV.
THE EPISTLE TO TITUS.

Probable Movements of St. Paul—Christianity in Crete—Missions of Titus—Greeting—Character of the Cretans—Sobermindedness—Pastoral Duties, and Exhortations to various classes—Warnings against False Teachers—Personal Messages—"Ours also"—Titus 529

CHAPTER LV.
THE CLOSING DAYS.

Genuineness of the Pastoral Epistles—The Second Epistle to Timothy—State of the Church in the last year of St. Paul—His possible Movements—Arrest at Troas—Trial and Imprisonment at Ephesus—Parting with Timothy—Companions of his last Voyage to Rome—Closeness and Misery of the Second Imprisonment—Danger of visiting him—Defection of his Friends—Loneliness—Onesiphorus—The Prima actio—St. Paul deserted—"Out of the mouth of the Lion"—The Trial—Paul before Nero—Contrast between the two—St. Paul remanded 539

CHAPTER LVI.
ST. PAUL'S LAST LETTER.

The Greeting—Digressions—Christian Energy—Warnings against False Teachers—Solemn Pastoral Appeals—Personal Entreaties and Messages—Pudens and Claudia—The Cloke—The Papyrus Books—The Vellum Rolls—Parallel with Tyndale—Triumph over Melancholy and Disappointment—Tone of Courage and Hope 561

CHAPTER LVII.

THE END.

The Last Trial—The Martyrdom—Earthly Failure and Eternal Success—Unequalled Greatness of St. Paul—"God Buries His Workmen, but carries on their Work" 576

APPENDIX.

Excursus I.—The Man of Sin 583

Excursus II.—Chief Uncial Manuscripts of the Acts and the Epistles . . 588

Excursus III.—Theology and Antinomies of St. Paul 590

Excursus IV.—Distinctive Words and Key-notes of the Epistle . . . 592

Excursus V.—Letter of Pliny to Sabinianus 593

Excursus VI.—The Herods in the Acts 594

Excursus VII.—Phraseology and Doctrine of the Epistle to the Ephesians . 601

Excursus VIII.—Evidence as to the Liberation of St. Paul . . . 604

Excursus IX.—The Genuineness of the Pastoral Epistles . . . 607

Excursus X.—Chronology of the Life and Epistles of St. Paul . . 623

Excursus XI.—Traditional Accounts of St. Paul's Personal Appearance . 629

THE LIFE AND WORK OF ST. PAUL.

Book II.

EPHESUS.

CHAPTER XXXI.

PAUL AT EPHESUS.

> "They say this town is full of cozenage;
> As, nimbling jugglers that deceive the eye,
> Disguised cheaters, prating mountebanks,
> And many such-like liberties of sin."
> — SHAKSP. *Comedy of Errors.*

> "Diana Ephesia; cujus nomen unicum . . . . totus veneratur orbis."
> — APPUL. *Metam.*

THE justice of Gallio had secured for St. Paul an unmolested residence in Corinth, such as had been promised by the vision which had encouraged him amid his earlier difficulties. He availed himself of this pause in the storm of opposition by preaching for many days—perhaps for some months—and then determined to revisit Jerusalem, from which he had now been absent for nearly three years. It may be that he had collected something for the poor; but in any case he felt the importance of maintaining amicable relations with the other Apostles and with the mother church. He wished also to be present at the approaching feast—in all probability the Pentecost

—and thereby to show that, in spite of his active work in heathen cities, and the freedom which he claimed for Gentile converts, in spite, too, of that deadly opposition of many synagogues which had already cost him so dear, he was still at heart a loyal although a liberal Jew. Accordingly, he bade farewell to the friends whom he had converted, and, accompanied by Priscilla and Aquila, set out for Cenchreæ. At that busy seaport, where a little church had been already formed, of which Phœbe was a deaconess, he gave yet another proof of his allegiance to the Mosaic law. In thanksgiving for some deliverance[1]—perhaps from an attack of sickness, perhaps from the Jewish riot—he had taken upon him the vow of the temporary Nazarite. In accordance with this, he abstained from wine, and let his hair grow long. At the legal purification which formed the termination of the vow, the head could only be shaved at Jerusalem; but as it was often impossible for a foreign Jew to reach the Holy City at the exact time when the period of his vow concluded, it seems to have been permitted to the Nazarite to cut his hair,[2] provided that he kept the shorn locks until he offered the burnt-offering, the sin-offering, and the peace-offering in the Temple, at which time his head was shaved, and all the hair burnt in the fire under the sacrifice of the peace-offerings. Accordingly, Paul cut his hair at Cenchreæ, and set sail for Ephesus. The mention of the fact is not by any means trivial or otiose. The

---

[1] See Jos. *B. J.* ii. 15, § 1, and the Mishna treatise *Nasir*, ii. 3. Spencer (*De Leg. Hebr.* iii. 6, § 1) thinks, most improbably, that it was done to obtain a fair voyage. Cf. Juv. *Sat.* xii. 81.

[2] The word used is κειράμενος, "polling," not ξυρησάμενος, "shaving," or as in E. V. "having shaved" (see 1 Cor. xi. 14; St. Paul dislikes long hair). The notion that it was Aquila and not Paul who made the vow may be finally dismissed; it merely arose from the fact that Aquila is mentioned after his wife; but this, as we have seen, is also the case in 2 Tim. iv. 19; Rom. xvi. 3, and is an undesigned coincidence, probably due to her greater zeal.

vow which St. Paul undertook is highly significant as a proof of his *personal* allegiance to the Levitic institutions, and his desire to adopt a policy of conciliation towards the Jewish Christians of the Holy City.[1]

A few days' sail, if the weather was ordinarily propitious, would enable his vessel to anchor in the famous haven of Panormus, which was then a forest of masts at the centre of all the Mediterranean trade, but is now a reedy swamp in a region of desolation. His arrival coincided either with the eve of a Sabbath, or of one of the three weekly meetings of the synagogue, and at once, with his usual ardour and self-forgetfulness, he presented himself among the Ephesian Jews. They were a numerous and important body, actively engaged in the commerce of the city, and had obtained some special privileges from the Roman Emperors.[2] Not only was their religion authorised, but their youth were exempted from military service. One of their number, the "Chaldean" or "astrologer" Balbillus, had at this period availed himself of the deepening superstition which always accompanies a decadent belief, and had managed to insinuate himself into the upper circles of Roman society until he ultimately became the confidant of Nero.[3] Accustomed in that seething metropolis to meet with opinions of every description, the Jews at first offered no opposition to the argu-

---

[1] "He that makes a vow builds, as it were, a private altar, and if he keeps it, offers, as it were, a sacrifice upon it" (*Yebhamoth*, f. 109, 2; *Nedarím*, f. 59, 1). The views of the Rabbis about vows may be found in *Erubhín*, f. 64, 2; *Chagigah*, f. 10, 1; *Rosh Hashanah*, f. 10, 1; *Nedarím*, f. 2, 1; f. 30, 2, &c. They have been collected by Mr. P. J. Hershon in his Hebrew commentary on Genesis exclusively drawn from the Talmud, in the synoptical note on Gen. xxviii. 20. They throw very little light on St. Paul's vow. The rule is that all votive terms, whether *corban, conem, cones,* or *conech*, are equally binding (*Nedarím*, f. 2, 1). Perhaps Paul liked the *temporary* ascetic element in the vow (1 Cor. ix. 25; Jos. *B. J.* ii. 15, § 1).

[2] Jos. *Antt.* xiv. 10.

[3] Suet. *Nero*, 40; Dio. 66, 9.

ments of the wandering Rabbi who preached a crucified Messiah. Nay, they even begged him to stay longer with them. His desire to reach Jerusalem and pay his vow rendered this impossible; but in bidding them farewell he promised that, God willing,[1] he would soon return. Once more, therefore, he weighed anchor, and sailed to Cæsarea. From thence he hastened to Jerusalem, which he was now visiting for the fourth time after his conversion. He had entered it once a changed man;[2] he had entered it a second time with a timely contribution from the Church of Antioch to the famine-stricken poor;[3] a third time he had come to obtain a decision of the loud disputes between the Judaic and the liberal Christians which threatened, even thus early, to rend asunder the seamless robe of Christ.[4] Four years had now elapsed, and he came once more, a weak and persecuted missionary, to seek the sympathy of the early converts,[5] to confirm his faithful spirit of unity with them, to tell them the momentous tidings of churches founded during this his second journey, not only in Asia, but for the first time in Europe also, and even at places so important as Philippi, Thessalonica, and Corinth. Had James, and the circle of which he was the centre, only understood how vast for the future of Christianity would be the issues of these perilous and toilsome journeys—had they but seen how insignificant, compared with the labours of St. Paul, would be the part which they themselves were playing in furthering the universality of the Church of Christ—with what affection and admiration would they have welcomed him! How would they have striven, by every form of kindness, of encouragement, of honour, of heartfelt prayer, to arm and strengthen him, and to fire into yet brighter lustre his

[1] James iv. 15.   [2] A.D. 44.   [5] About A.D. 54.
[3] About A.D. 37.   [4] About A.D. 50.

grand enthusiasm, so as to prepare him in the future for sacrifices yet more heroic, for efforts yet more immense! Had anything of the kind occurred, St. Luke, in the interests of his great Christian Eirenicon—St. Paul himself, in his account to the Galatians of his relations to the twelve —could hardly have failed to tell us about it. So far from this, St. Luke hurries over the brief visit in the three words that "he saluted the church,"[1] not even pausing to inform us that he fulfilled his vow, or whether any favourable impression as to his Judaic orthodoxy was created by the fact that he had undertaken it. There is too much reason to fear that his reception was cold and ungracious; that even if James received him with courtesy, the Judaic Christians who surrounded "the Lord's brother" did not; and even that a jealous dislike of that free position towards the Law which he established amongst his Gentile converts, led to that determination on the part of some of them to follow in his track and to undermine his influence, which, to the intense embitterment of his latter days, was so fatally successful. It must have been with a sad heart, with something even of indignation at this unsympathetic coldness, that St. Paul hurriedly terminated his visit. But none of these things moved him. He did but share them with his Lord, whom the Pharisees had hated and the Sadducees had slain. He did but share them with every great prophet and every true thinker before and since. Not holding even his life dear unto himself, it is not likely that the peevishness of unprogressive tradition, or the non-appreciation of suspicious narrowness, should make him swerve from his divinely appointed course. God had counted him worthy of being entrusted with a sacred cause. He had a work to do; he had a

---

[1] St. Luke does not so much as mention the word Jerusalem, but the word ἀναβὰς disproves the fancy that Paul went no further than Cæsarea.

Gospel to preach. If in obeying this call of God he met with human sympathy and kindness, well; if not, it was no great matter. Life might be bitter, but life was short, and the light affliction which was but for a moment was nothing to the exceeding and eternal weight of glory. Once more he set forth for a new, and, as it turned out, for the most brilliantly energetic, for the most eternally fruitful, for the most overwhelmingly afflictive period of his life of toil.

From Jerusalem he went to Antioch, where we can well imagine that a warmer and kindlier greeting awaited him. In that more cordial environment he rested for some little time; and thence, amid many a day of weariness and struggle, but cheered in all probability by the companionship of Timothy and Titus, and perhaps also of Gaius Aristarchus and Erastus, he passed once more through the famous Cilician gates of Taurus,[1] and travelled overland through the eastern region of Asia Minor,[2] confirming on his way the Churches of Galatia and Phrygia. In Galatia he ordered collections to be made for the poor at Jerusalem by a weekly offertory every Sunday.[3] He also found it necessary to give them some very serious warnings; and although, as yet, there had been no direct apostasy from the doctrines which he had taught, he could trace a perceptible diminution of the affectionate fervour with which he had been at first received by that bright but fickle population.[4] Having thus endeavoured to secure the foundations which he had laid in the past, he descended from the Phrygian uplands, and caught a fresh glimpse of

---

[1] From Antioch to the Cilician gates, through Tarsus, is 412 miles.
[2] ἀνωτερικὰ is practically equivalent to ἀνατολικά.
[3] 1 Cor. xvi. 1, 2. But the collection does not seem to have been sent with that of the Grecian churches (Rom. xv. 25, 26). Perhaps the Judaic emissaries got hold of it.
[4] Gal. iv. 16; v. 21.

EPHESUS.

the Marseilles of the Ægean, the hostelry and emporium of east and west,[1] the great capital of Proconsular Asia. Very memorable were the results of his visit. Ephesus was the third capital and starting-point of Christianity. At Jerusalem, Christianity was born in the cradle of Judaism; Antioch had been the starting-point of the Church of the Gentiles; Ephesus was to witness its full development, and the final amalgamation of its unconsolidated elements in the work of John, the Apostle of Love. It lay one mile from the Icarian Sea, in the fair Asian meadow where myriads of swans and other waterfowl disported themselves amid the windings of Cayster.[2] Its buildings were clustered under the protecting shadows of Coressus and Prion, and in the delightful neighbourhood of the Ortygian Groves. Its haven, which had once been among the most sheltered and commodious in the Mediterranean, had been partly silted up by a mistake in engineering, but was still thronged with vessels from every part of the civilised world. It lay at the meeting-point of great roads, which led northwards to Sardis and Troas, southwards to Magnesia and Antioch, and thus commanded easy access to the great river-valleys of the Hermus and Mæander, and the whole interior continent. Its seas and rivers were rich with fish; its air was salubrious; its position unrivalled; its population multifarious and immense. Its markets, glittering with the produce of the world's art, were the Vanity Fair of Asia. They furnished to the exile of Patmos the local colouring of those pages of the Apocalypse in which he speaks of "the merchandise of gold, and silver, and precious stones, and of pearls, and fine linen, and purple, and silk, and scarlet, and all thyine wood, and all manner vessels of

---
[1] Renan, p. 337.
[2] Now the Kutschuk Mendere, or Little Mæander.

ivory, and all manner vessels of most precious wood, and of brass, and iron, and marble, and cinnamon, and odours, and ointment and frankincense, and wine, and oil, and fine flour, and wheat, and beasts, and sheep, and horses, and chariots, and slaves, *and souls of men*."[1]

And Ephesus was no less famous than it was vast and wealthy. Perhaps no region of the world has been the scene of so many memorable events in ancient history as the shores of Asia Minor. The whole coast was in all respects the home of the best Hellenic culture, and Herodotus declares that it was the finest site for cities in the world of his day.[2] It was from Lesbos, and Smyrna, and Ephesus, and Halicarnassus that lyric poetry, and epic poetry, and philosophy, and history took their rise, nor was any name more splendidly emblazoned in the annals of human culture than that of the great capital of Ionia.[3] It was here that Anacreon had sung the light songs which so thoroughly suited the soft temperament of the Greek colonists in that luxurious air; here that Mimnermos had written his elegies; here that Thales had given the first impulse to philosophy; here that Anaximander and Anaximenes had learnt to interest themselves in those cosmogonic theories which shocked the simple beliefs of the Athenian burghers; here that the deepest of all Greek thinkers, "Heracleitus the Dark," had meditated on those truths which he uttered in language of such incomparable force; here that his friend Hermodorus had paid the penalty of virtue by being exiled from a city which felt that its vices were rebuked by his mere silent presence;[4] here that Hipponax had infused into his satire

[1] Rev. xviii. 12, 13.
[2] *Hist.* i. 142. For full accounts of Ephesus see Guhl's *Ephesiaca* (Berl. 1843).
[3] See Hausrath, p. 339, *seqq.*
[4] See Strabo, xiv., p. 642.

such deadly venom;[1] here that Parrhasius and Apelles had studied their immortal art. And it was still essentially a Greek city. It was true that since Attalus, King of Pergamos, nearly two hundred years before, had made the Romans heirs to his kingdom, their power had gradually extended itself in every direction, until they were absolute masters of Phrygia, Mysia, Caria, Lydia,[2] and all the adjacent isles of Greece, and that now the splendour of Ephesus was materially increased by its being the residence of the Roman Proconsul. But while the presence of a few noble Romans and their suites added to the gaiety and power of the city, it did not affect the prevailing Hellenic cast of its civilisation, which was far more deeply imbued with Oriental than with Western influences. The Ephesians crawled at the feet of the Emperors, flattered them with abject servility, built temples to their crime or their feebleness, deified them on their inscriptions and coins.[3] Even the poor simulacrum of the Senate came in for a share of their fulsomeness, and received its apotheosis from their complaisance.[4] The Romans, seeing that they had nothing to fear from these degenerate Ionians, helped them with subsidies when they had suffered from earthquakes, flung them titles of honour, which were in themselves a degradation, left them a nominal autonomy, and let them live without interference the bacchanalian lives which passed in a round of Panionic, Ephesian, Artemisian, and Lucullian games. Such then was the city in which St. Paul found a sphere of work unlike any in which he had hitherto laboured. It was more Hellenic than

---

[1] Cic. *ad Fam.* vii. 24.
[2] Cic. *pro Flacco*, 27; Plin. *H. N.* v. 28; *ap.* Hausrath, *l.c.*
[3] See the *Corpus Inscr. Gr.* 2957, 2961, &c. (Renan, p. 338, who also quotes Plut. *Vit. Anton.* 24). Chandler, *Travels*, i. 25; Falkener, *Ephesus*, p. 111; φιλοσέβαστος and φιλόκαισαρ are common in Ephesian inscriptions.
[4] Θεὸς or ἱερὰ Σύγκλητος on coins, &c. (Renan, p. 352).

Antioch, more Oriental than Corinth, more populous than Athens, more wealthy and more refined than Thessalonica, more sceptical and more superstitious than Ancyra or Pessinus. It was, with the single exception of Rome, by far the most important scene of all his toils, and was destined, in after-years, to become not only the first of the Seven Churches of Asia, but the seat of one of those great Œcumenical Councils which defined the faith of the Christian world.

The character of the Ephesians was then in very bad repute. Ephesus was the head-quarters of many defunct superstitions, which owed their maintenance to the self-interest of various priestly bodies. South of the city, and brightened by the waters of the Cenchrius, was the olive and cypress grove of Leto,[1] where the ancient olive-tree was still shown to which the goddess had clung when she brought forth her glorious "twin-born progeny."[2] Here was the hill on which Hermes had proclaimed their birth; here the Curetes, with clashing spears and shields, had protected their infancy from wild beasts; here Apollo himself had taken refuge from the wrath of Zeus after he had slain the Cyclopes; here Bacchus had conquered and spared the Amazons during his progress through the East. Such were the arguments which the Ephesian ambassadors had urged before the Roman Senate in arrest of a determination to limit their rights of asylum. That right was mainly attached to the great world-renowned Temple of Artemis, of which Ephesus gloried in calling herself the sacristan.[3] Nor did they see that it was a right which was ruinous to the morals and well-being of the city. Just as the mediæval sanctuaries attracted all the scum

---

[1] Strabo, xiv., p. 947. [2] Tac. *Ann.* iii. 61.
[3] Acts xix. 35, νεωκόρος.

and villainy, all the cheats and debtors and murderers of the country round, and inevitably pauperised and degraded the entire vicinity[1]—just as the squalor of the lower purlieus of Westminster to this day is accounted for by its direct affiliation to the crime and wretchedness which sheltered itself from punishment or persecution under the shadow of the Abbey—so the vicinity of the great Temple at Ephesus reeked with the congregated pollutions of Asia. Legend told how, when the temple was finished, Mithridates stood on its summit and declared that the right of asylum should extend in a circle round it as far as he could shoot an arrow, and the arrow miraculously flew a furlong's distance. The consequence was that Ephesus, vitiated by the influences which affect all great sea-side commercial cities, had within herself a special source of danger and contagion.[2] Ionia had been the corruptress of Greece,[3] Ephesus was the corruptress of Ionia—the favourite scene of her most voluptuous love-tales, the lighted theatre of her most ostentatious sins.

The temple, which was the chief glory of the city and one of the wonders of the world,[4] stood in full view of the crowded haven. Ephesus was the most magnificent of what Ovid calls "the magnificent cities of Asia,"[5] and the temple was its most splendid ornament. The *ancient*

---

[1] I have already pointed out this fact in speaking of Daphne and Paphos, *supra*, vol. i., pp. 294, 349. This was why Tiberius tried to abolish all "asyla" (Suet. *Tib.* 37).

[2] This is pointed out by Philostratus in the person of Apollonius. He praises them for their banquets and ritual, and adds μεμπτοὶ δὲ σύνοικοι τῇ θεῷ νύκτας τε καὶ ἡμέρας ἢ οὐκ ἂν ὁ κλέπτης τε καὶ λῃστὴς καὶ ἀνδραποδιστὴς καὶ πᾶς εἴ τις ἄδικος ἢ ἱερόσυλος ἦν ὁρμώμενος αὐτόθεν. τὸ γὰρ τῶν ἀποστερούντων τεῖχός ἐστιν. See, too, Strabo, xiv. 1, 23.

[3] Hence the proverb "Ionian effeminacy." On their gorgeous apparel, see Athen. p. 525. "Taught by the soft Ionians" (Dyer, *Ruins of Rome*).

[4] Philo, Byzant. *De Sept. orbis miraculis*, 7, μόνος ἐστὶ θεῶν οἶκος. Falkener's *Ephesus*, pp. 210—346.

[5] Ov. *Pont.* II. x. 21.

temple had been burnt down by Herostratus—an Ephesian fanatic who wished his name to be recorded in history—on the night of the birth of Alexander the Great. It had been rebuilt with ungrudging magnificence out of contributions furnished by all Asia—the very women contributing to it their jewels, as the Jewish women had done of old for the Tabernacle of the Wilderness. To avoid the danger of earthquakes, its foundations were built at vast cost on artificial foundations of skin and charcoal laid over the marsh.[1] It gleamed far off with a star-like radiance.[2] Its peristyle consisted of one hundred and twenty pillars of the Ionic order hewn out of Parian marble. Its doors of carved cypress-wood were surmounted by transoms so vast and solid that the aid of miracles was invoked to account for their elevation. The staircase which led to the roof was said to have been cut out of a single vine of Cyprus. Some of the pillars were carved with designs of exquisite beauty.[3] Within were the masterpieces of Praxiteles and Phidias, and Scopas and Polycletus. Paintings by the greatest of Greek artists, of which one—the likeness of Alexander the Great by Apelles—had been bought for a sum said to be equal in value to £5,000, of modern money, adorned the inner walls. The roof of the temple itself was of cedar-wood, supported by columns of jasper on bases of Parian marble.[4] On these pillars hung gifts of priceless value, the votive offerings of grateful

---

[1] See Plin. *H. N.* xxxvi. 21; Diog. *Laert.* ii. 8; Aug. *De Civ. Dei*, xxi. 4. Old London Bridge was built, not "on woolsacks," but out of the proceeds of a tax on wool. The anecdote of the discovery of the white marble by Pixidorus is given in Vitruv. x. 7.

[2] μετεωροφανὲς.

[3] One splendid example of the drum of one of these "columnae caelatae" (Plin.) is now in the British Museum. For a complete and admirable account of the temple and its excavation, see Wood's *Ephesus*, p. 267, *seq.*

[4] Now in the mosque of St. Sophia.

superstition. At the end of it stood the great altar adorned by the bas-relief of Praxiteles, behind which fell the vast folds of a purple curtain. Behind this curtain was the dark and awful adytum in which stood the most sacred idol of classic heathendom; and again, behind the adytum was the room which, inviolable under divine protection, was regarded as the wealthiest and securest bank in the ancient world.

The image for which had been reared this incomparable shrine was so ancient that it shared withthe Athene of the Acropolis, the Artemis of Tauris, the Demeter of Sicily, the Aphrodite of Paphos, and the Cybele of Pessinus, the honour of being regarded as a Διοπετὲς Ἄγαλμα —" an image that fell from heaven."[1] The very substance of which it was made was a matter of dispute; some said it was of vine-wood, some of ebony, some of cedar, and some of stone.[2] It was not a shapeless meteorite like the Kaaba at Mecca, or the Hercules of Hyettus,[3] or the blackstone of Pessinus; nor a phallic cone like the Phœnician Aphrodite of Paphos;[4] nor a mere lump of wood like the Cadmean Bacchus;[5] but neither must we be misled by the name Artemis to suppose that it in any way resembled the quivered " huntress chaste and fair " of Greek and Roman mythology. It was freely idealised in many of the current representations,[6] but was in reality a hideous fetish,

---

[1] Pliny (*H. N.* xvi. 79) and Athenagoras (*Pro Christ.* 14) say it was made by Endaeus, the pupil of Daedalus.

[2] Vitruv. ii. 9; Callim. *Hymn. Dian.* 239.

[3] Pausan. ix. 24.

[4] *V. supra*, p. 349.

[5] Pausan. ix. 12. See Guhl, *Ephesiaca*, p. 185; Falkener, *Ephesus*, 287. The Chaeronean Zeus was a sceptre (Pausan. ix. 40); the Cimmerian Mars, a scimitar (Hdt. iv. 62).

[6] *E.g.*, in the statue preserved in the Museo Borbonico at Naples, which, if we may judge from coins, is a very unreal representative of the venerable ugliness of the actual statue.

originally meant for a symbol of fertility and the productive power of nature. She was represented on coins—which, as they bear the heads of Claudius and Agrippina, must have been current at this very time, and may have easily passed through the hands of Paul—as a figure swathed like a mummy, covered with monstrous breasts,[1] and holding in one hand a trident and in the other a club. The very ugliness and uncouthness of the idol added to the superstitious awe which it inspired, and just as the miraculous Madonnas and images of Romanism are never the masterpieces of Raphael or Bernardino Luini, but for the most part blackened Byzantine paintings, or hideous dolls like the Bambino, so the statue of the Ephesian Artemis was regarded as far more awful than the Athene of Phidias or the Jupiter of the Capitol. The Jewish feelings of St. Paul—though he abstained from "blaspheming" the goddess[2]—would have made him regard it as pollution to enter her temple; but many a time on coins, and paintings, and in direct copies, he must have seen the strange image of the great Artemis of the Ephesians, whose worship, like that of so many fairer and more human idols, his preaching would doom to swift oblivion.[3]

Though the Greeks had vied with the Persians in lavish contributions for the re-erection of the temple, the

---

[1] πολύμαστος, multimamma; "omnium bestiarum et viventium nutrix" (Jer. Proem. in Ep. ad Eph.).

[2] Acts xix. 37, οὔτε βλασφημοῦντας τὴν θεὰν ὑμῶν.

[3] "What is become of the Temple of Diana? Can a wonder of the earth be vanished like a phantom, without leaving a trace behind? We now seek the temple in vain; the city is prostrate and the goddess gone" (Chandler; see *Sibyll. Orac.* v. 293—305). The wonder is deepened after seeing the massiveness of the superb fragments in the British Museum. That the Turkish name Aïa Solouk is a corruption of Ἁγία Θεολόγου, and therefore a reminiscence of St. John, is proved by the discovery of coins bearing this inscription, and struck at Ayasaluk (Wood, p. 183). Perhaps St. John originally received the name by way of contrast with the *Theologi* of the Temple.

worship of this venerable relic was essentially Oriental. The priests were amply supported by the proceeds of wide domains and valuable fisheries, and these priests, or Megabyzi, as well as the "Essen,"[1] who was at the head of them, were the miserable Persian or Phrygian eunuchs who, with the Melissae, or virgin-priestesses, and crowds of idle slaves, were alone suffered to conduct the worship of the Mother of the Gods. Many a time, in the open spaces and environs of Ephesus, must Paul have seen with sorrow and indignation the bloated and beardless hideousness of these coryphaei of iniquity.[2] Many a time must he have heard from the Jewish quarter the piercing shrillness of their flutes, and the harsh jangling of their timbrels; many a time have caught glimpses of their detestable dances and corybantic processions, as with streaming hair, and wild cries, and shaken torches of pine, they strove to madden the multitudes into sympathy with that orgiastic worship, which was but too closely connected with the vilest debaucheries.[3] Even the Greeks, little as they were liable to be swept away by these bursts of religious frenzy, seem to have caught the tone of these disgraceful fanatics. At no other city would they have assembled in the theatre in their thousands to yell the same cry over and over again for "about the space of two hours," as though they had

---

[1] The resemblance of the word and character to the "Essenes" is accidental. It means "a king (queen) bee."

[2] Quint. v. 12. What sort of wretches these were may be seen in Juv. vi. 512; Prop. ii. 18, 15; Appuleius, *Metamorph.*

[3] Apollonius, in his first address to the Ephesians, delivered from the platform of the temple, urged them to abandon their idleness, folly, and feasting, and turn to the study of philosophy. He speaks of these dances, and says αὐλῶν μὲν πάντα μεστὰ ἦν, μεστὰ δὲ ἀνδρογύνων, μεστὰ δὲ κτύπων, κ.τ.λ. (Philostr. *Vit. Apoll.* iv. 2, p. 141). He praises them, however, for their philosophic interests, &c. (viii. 8, p. 339). Incense-burners, flute-players, and trumpeters are mentioned in an inscription found by Chandler (*Inscr. Ant.*, p. 11).

been so many Persian dervishes or Indian yogis. This senseless reiteration was an echo of the screaming *ululatus* which was one of the characteristics of the cult of Dindymene and Pessinus.[1]

We are not surprised to find that under the shadow of such a worship superstition was rampant. Ephesus differed from other cities which Paul had visited mainly in this respect, that it was pre-eminently the city of astrology, sorcery, incantations, amulets, exorcisms, and every form of magical imposture. On the statue of the goddess, or rather, perhaps, on the inverted pyramid which formed the basis for her swathed and shapeless feet, were inscribed certain mystic formulæ to which was assigned a magic efficacy. This led to the manufacture and the celebrity of those "Ephesian writings," which were eagerly supplied by greedy imposture to gaping credulity. Among them were the words *askion, kataskion, lix, tetras, damnameneus,* and *aisia*,[2] which for sense and efficiency were about on a par with the *daries, derdaries, astataries,* or *ista, pista, sista,* which Cato the elder held to be a sovereign remedy for a sprain,[3] or the *shavriri, vriri, iriri, riri, iri, ri,* accompanied with knockings on the lid of a jug, which the Rabbis taught as an efficacious expulsion of the demon of blindness.[4]

Stories, which elsewhere would have been received with ridicule, at Ephesus found ready credence. About the very time of St. Paul's visit it is probable that the city was visited by Apollonius of Tyana; and it is here that his biographer Philostratus places the scene of some of his exploits. One of these is all the more inte-

---

[1] Hausrath, p. 342.
[2] Clem. Alex. *Strom.* v. 46.
[3] Cato, *De Re Rustica Fr.* 160 (see Donaldson, *Varron.*, p. 234).
[4] *Abhoda Zara,* f. 12, 2.

resting because it is said to have taken place in that very theatre into which St. Paul, though in imminent peril of being torn to pieces, could scarcely be persuaded not to enter. During his visit to Ephesus, the thaumaturge of Tyana found the plague raging there, and in consequence invited the population to meet him in the theatre. When they were assembled, he rose and pointed out to them a miserable and tattered old man as the cause of the prevailing pestilence. Instantly the multitude seized stones and, in spite of the old man's remonstrances, stoned him to death. When the heaped stones were removed, they found the carcase of a Molossian hound, into which the demon had transformed himself;[1] and on this spot they reared a statue of Herakles Apotropaios! Philostratus did not write his romance till A.D. 218, and his hero Apollonius has been put forth by modern infidels as a sort of Pagan rival to the Jesus of the Gospels. Let any one read this wretched production, and judge! The Pagan sophist, with all his vaunted culture and irritating euphuism, abounds in anecdotes which would have been regarded as pitiably foolish if they had been narrated by the unlettered fishermen of Galilee, strangers as they were to all cultivation, and writing as they did a century and a half before.

Another and a far darker glimpse of the Ephesus of this day may be obtained from the letter of the pseudo-Heraclitus. Some cultivated and able Jew,[2] adopting the pseudonym of the great ancient philosopher, wrote some letters in which he is supposed to explain the reason

[1] *Vit. Apoll.* iv. 10, p. 147. Alexander of Abonoteichos, a much more objectionable impostor than Apollonius, lived till old age on the wealth got out of his dupes, and seriously persuaded the world that the mother of his daughter was the goddess of the moon!

[2] The theory of Bernays is that the letters were written by a Pagan, but interpolated by a Jew.

why he was called "the weeping philosopher," and why he was never seen to laugh. In these he fully justifies his traditional remark that the whole Ephesian population deserved to be throttled man by man. He here asks how it is that their state flourishes in spite of its wickedness; and, in the inmost spirit of the Old Testament, he sees in that prosperity the irony and the curse of Heaven. For Artemis and her worship he has no scorn too intense. The dim twilight of her adytum is symbolical of a vileness that hateth the light. He supposes that her image is "stonen" in the contemptuous sense in which the word is used by Homer—*i.e.*, idiotic and brutish. He ridicules the inverted pyramid on which she stands. He says that the morals which flourish under her protection are worse than those of beasts, seeing that even hounds do not mutilate each other, as her Megabyzus has to be mutilated, because she is too modest to be served by a man. But instead of extolling her modesty, her priests ought rather to curse her for lewdness, which rendered it unsafe otherwise to approach her, and which had cost them so dear. As for the orgies, and the torch festivals, and the antique rituals, he has nothing to say of them, except that they are the cloak for every abomination. These things had rendered him a lonely man. This was the reason why he could not laugh. How could he laugh when he heard the noises of these infamous vagabond priests, and was a witness of all the nameless iniquities which flourished so rankly in consequence of their malpractices—the murder, and waste, and lust, and gluttony, and drunkenness? And then he proceeds to moral and religious exhortations, which show that we are reading the work of some Jewish and unconverted Apollos, who is yet an earnest and eloquent proclaimer of the one God and the Noachian law.

In this city St. Paul saw that "a great door and effectual was open to him," though there were "many adversaries."¹ During his absence an event had happened which was to be of deep significance for the future. Among the myriads whom business or pleasure, or what is commonly called accident, had brought to Ephesus, was a Jew of Alexandria named Apollonius,² or Apollos, who not only shared the culture for which the Jews of that city were famous in the age of Philo, but who had a profound knowledge of Scripture, and a special gift of fervid eloquence.³ He was only so far a Christian that he knew and had accepted the baptism of John; but though thus imperfectly acquainted with the doctrines of Christianity, he yet spoke and argued in the synagogue with a power and courage which attracted the attention of the Jewish tent-makers Priscilla and Aquila. They invited him to their house, and showed him the purely initial character of John's teaching. It may have been the accounts of the Corinthian Church which he had heard from them that made him desirous to visit Achaia, and perceiving how useful such a ministry as his might be among the subtle and intellectual Greeks, they not only encouraged his wish,⁴ but wrote for him "letters of commendation"⁵ to the Corinthian elders. At Corinth his eloquence produced a great sensation, and he became a pillar of strength to the brethren. He had so thoroughly profited by that reflection of St. Paul's teaching which he had caught from Priscilla and Aquila, that in his public disputations with the hostile Jews he proved from their own Scriptures, with an irresistible

---
¹ 1 Cor. xvi. 9.
² So in D.
³ Acts xviii. 25, ζέων τῷ πνεύματι (cf. Rom. xii. 11).
⁴ προτρεψάμενοι, sc. αὐτόν (Acts xviii. 27).
⁵ συστατικὴ ἐπιστολή (2 Cor. iii. 1).

cogency, the Messiahship of Christ, and thus was as acceptable to the Christians as he was formidable to the Jews. He watered what Paul had planted.[1]

By the time of St. Paul's arrival, Apollos had already started for Corinth. He had, however, returned to Ephesus before St. Paul's departure, and the Apostle must have gazed with curiosity and interest on this fervid and gifted convert. A meaner soul might have been jealous of his gifts, and all the more so because, while less valuable, they were more immediately dazzling and impressive than his own. St. Paul was of too noble a spirit to leave room for the slightest trace of a feeling so common, yet so ignoble. Apollos had unwittingly stolen from him the allegiance of some of his Corinthian converts; his name had become, in that disorderly church, a watchword of faction. Yet St. Paul never speaks of him without warm sympathy and admiration,[2] and evidently appreciated the high-minded delicacy which made him refuse to revisit Corinth,[3] in spite of pressing invitations, from the obvious desire to give no encouragement to the admiring partisans who had elevated him into unworthy rivalry with one so much greater than himself.

Ephesus, amid its vast population, contained specimens of every form of belief, and Apollos was not the only convert to an imperfect and half-developed form of Christianity. Paul found there, on his arrival, a strange backwater of religious opinion in the persons of some twelve

---

[1] 1 Cor. iii 6. There can be little reasonable doubt that Apollos was the author of the Epistle to the Hebrews. In reading that Epistle (which cannot be dealt with in these volumes) it is easy to see that, essentially Pauline as is much of its phraseology, the main method is original, and would probably be more pleasing and convincing to *Jews* than any which St. Paul was led to adopt. Some have seen a distinction between his pupils and St. Paul's in Titus iii. 14, οἱ ἡμέτεροι, but see *infra, ad loc.*

[2] Tit. iii. 13.

[3] 1 Cor. xvi. 12.

men who, like Apollos, and being perhaps in some way connected with him, were still disciples of the Baptist. Although there were some in our Lord's time who stayed with their old teacher till his execution, and though the early fame of his preaching had won him many followers, of whom some continued to linger on in obscure sects,[1] it was impossible for any reasonable man to stop short at this position except through ignorance. St. Paul accordingly questioned them, and upon finding that they knew little or nothing of the final phase of John's teaching, or of the revelation of Christ, and were even ignorant of the very name of the Holy Spirit, he gave them further instruction until they were fitted to receive baptism, and exhibited those gifts of the Spirit—the speaking with tongues and prophecy—which were the accepted proofs of full and faithful initiation into the Church of Christ.[2]

For three months, in accordance with his usual plan, he was a constant visitor at the synagogue, and used every effort of persuasion and argument to ripen into conviction the favourable impressions he had at first created. St. Luke passes briefly over the circumstances, but there must have been many an anxious hour, many a bitter struggle, many an exciting debate before the Jews finally adopted a tone not only of decided rejection, but even of so fierce an opposition, that St. Paul was forced once more, as at Corinth, openly to secede from their communion. We do not sufficiently estimate the pain which such circumstances must have caused to him. His life was so beset with trials, that each trial, however heavy in itself, is passed

---

[1] Sabaeans, Mendaeans, &c. (Neander, *Ch. Hist.* ii. 57). We find from the Clementine Recognitions that there were some of John's disciples who continued to preach him as the Messiah.
[2] Cf. Heb. vi. 4—6.

over amid a multitude that were still more grievous. But we must remember that St. Paul, though a Christian, still regarded himself as a true Israelite, and he must have felt, at least as severely as a Luther or a Whitefield, this involuntary alienation from the religious communion of his childhood. We must conjecture, too, that it was amid these early struggles that he once more voluntarily submitted to the recognised authority of synagogues, and endured some of those five beatings by the Jews, any one of which would have been regarded as a terrible episode in an ordinary life.

As long as opposition confined itself to legitimate methods, St. Paul was glad to be a worshipper in the synagogue, and to deliver the customary Midrash; but when the Jews not only rejected and reviled him, but even endeavoured to thwart all chance of his usefulness amid their Gentile neighbours, he saw that it was time to withdraw his disciples from among them;[1] and, as their number was now considerable, he hired the school of Tyrannus—some heathen sophist of that not very uncommon name.[2] It was one of those schools of rhetoric and philosophy which were common in a city like Ephesus, where there were many who prided themselves on intellectual pursuits. This new place of worship gave him the advantage of being able to meet the brethren daily, whereas in the synagogue this was only possible three times a week. His labours and his preaching were not unblessed. For two full years longer he continued to make Ephesus the centre of his missionary activity, and,

[1] Epænetus (Rom. xvi. 5, *leg.* Ασίας) was his first convert.
[2] Jos. *B. J.* i. 26, § 3; 2 Macc. iv. 40. It is very unlikely that this was a Beth Midrash (Meyer), as it was St. Paul's object to withdraw from the Jews. There was a Sophist Tyrannus mentioned by Suidas. The τινος is spurious (אּ, A, B), which shows that this Tyrannus was known in Ephesus (see Heinsen, *Paulus*, 218).

as the fame of his Gospel began to spread, there can be little doubt that he himself took short journeys to various neighbouring places, until, in the strong expression of St. Luke, "all they that dwelt in Asia heard the word of the Lord Jesus, both Jews and Greeks."[1] In Ephesus itself his reputation reached an extraordinary height, in consequence of the unusual works of power which God wrought by his hands.[2] On this subject he is himself silent even by way of allusion, and though he speaks to the Ephesian elders[3] of his tears, and trials, and dangers, he does not say a word as to the signs and wonders which in writing to the Corinthians he distinctly claims. Although St. Paul believed that God, for the furtherance of the Gospel, did allow him to work "powers" beyond the range of human experience, and in which he humbly recognised the work of the Spirit granted to faith and prayer, yet he by no means frequently exercised these gifts, and never for his own relief or during the sickness of his dearest friends. But it was a common thing in Ephesus to use all kinds of magic remedies and curious arts. We are not, therefore, surprised to hear that articles of dress which had belonged to Paul, handkerchiefs which he had used, and aprons with which he had been girded in the pursuit of his trade,[4] were assumed by the Ephesians to have caught a magic efficacy, and were carried about to sick

---

[1] Hence forty years later, in Bithynia, Pliny (*Ep.* 96) writes, "Neque enim civitates tantum, sed vicos etiam atque agros superstitionis istius contagio pervagata est."

[2] Acts xix. 11, δυνάμεις οὐ τὰς τυχούσας.

[3] The "Epistle to the Ephesians," being a circular letter, naturally contains but few specific allusions—which, if intelligible to one Christian community, would not have been so to another. We should have expected such allusions in his speech; but "omittit Doctor gentium narrare miracula, narrat labores, narrat aerumnas, narrat tribulationes quae Paulo Paulique imitatoribus ipsis miraculis sunt clariores" (Novarinus).

[4] σουδάρια, *sudaria*; ἡμικίνθια, *semicincta*.

people and demoniacs. St. Luke was not with the Apostle at Ephesus, and enters into no details; but it is clear that his informant, whoever he was, had abstained from saying that this was done by St. Paul's sanction. But since Ephesus was the head-quarters of diabolism and sorcery, the use of St. Paul's handkerchiefs or aprons, whether authorised by him or not, was so far overruled to beneficial results of healing as to prove the superiority of the Christian faith in the acropolis of Paganism, and to prepare the way for holy worship in the stronghold of Eastern fanaticism and Grecian vice. He who "followed not Jesus," and yet was enabled to cast out devils in His name, could hardly fail to be the prototype of others who, though they acted without sanction, were yet for good purposes, and in that unsearched borderland which lies between the natural and the supernatural, enabled by God's providence to achieve results which tended to the furtherance of truth.

But lest any sanction should be given to false and superstitious notions, we can hardly fail to see in the next anecdote which St. Luke has preserved for us a direct rebuke of mechanical thaumaturgy. Exorcism was a practice which had long been prevalent among the Jews, and it was often connected with the grossest credulity and the most flagrant imposture.[1] Now there was a Jewish priest of some distinction of the name of Sceva,[2] whose seven sons wandered about from place to place professing to eject demons; and on learning the reputation of St. Paul, and hearing doubtless of the cures effected by the

---

[1] Jos. *Antt.* viii. 2, § 5. For this ridiculous jugglery, which seems to have deceived Vespasian, see my *Life of Christ*, i. 237. The prevalence of Jewish exorcists is attested by Justin Martyr, *Dial.* 85.

[2] Acts xix. 14, ἀρχιερέως—a general expression; perhaps a head of one of the twenty-four courses.

application of his handkerchiefs, they thought that by combining his name with that of Jesus, they could effect cures in the most virulent cases, which defeated even the ring and root of Solomon.[1] Encouraged possibly by some apparent initial success—so at least the story seems to imply—two of these seven itinerant impostors[2] visited a man who was evidently a raving maniac, but who had those sufficiently lucid perceptions of certain subjects which many madmen still retain. Addressing the evil demon, they exclaimed, " We exorcise you by Jesus, whom Paul preacheth." In this instance, however, the adjuration proved to be a humiliating failure. The maniac astutely replied, " Jesus I recognise, and Paul I know;[3] but who are you?" and then leaping upon them with the superhuman strength of madness, he tore their clothes off their backs, and inflicted upon them such violent injuries that they were glad to escape out of the house stripped and wounded.

So remarkable a story could not remain unknown. It spread like wildfire among the gossiping Ephesians, and produced a remarkable feeling of dread and astonishment. One result of it was most beneficial. We have had repeated occasion to observe that the early Christians who had been redeemed from heathendom, either in the

---

[1] Jos. *Antt. l.c.* We find many traces of this kind of superstition in the Talmudic writings: *e.g.*, the belief that the *Minim* could cure the bites of serpents by the name of Jesus (*v. supra*, i., p. 112). In the *Toldôth Jeshu*, the miracles of our Lord are explained by an unutterably silly story as to the means by which He possessed himself of the *Shemhamephoresh* or sacred name. Witchcraft had in all ages been prevalent among the Jews (Ex. xxii. 18; 1 Sam. xxviii. 3, 9; Mic. v. 12); it continued to be so at the Christian era, and it was necessary even to warn converts against any addiction to it (Gal. v. 20; 2 Tim. iii. 13, γόητες).

[2] In verse 16 the reading ἀμφοτέρων of א, A, B, D, is almost certainly correct. They were actuated by exactly the same motives as Simon Magus, but had shown less cunning in trying to carry them out.

[3] Acts xix. 15, Τὸν Ἰησοῦν γιγνώσκω καὶ τὸν Παῦλον ἐπίσταμαι; Vulg., " Jesum novi et Paulum scio."

coarsenesses of slave-life or in the refined abominations of the higher classes, required a terrible struggle to deliver themselves by the aid of God's Holy Spirit from the thraldom of past corruption. The sternly solemn emphasis of St. Paul's repeated warnings—the actual facts which occurred in the history of the early churches— show conclusively that the early converts required to be treated with extreme forbearance, while, at the same time, they were watched over by their spiritual rulers with incessant vigilance. The stir produced by the discomfiture of the Benî Sceva revealed the startling fact that some of the brethren in embracing Christianity had not abandoned magic. Stricken in conscience, these secret dealers in the superstitious trumpery of "curious arts" now came forward in the midst of the community and confessed their secret malpractices. Nor was it only the dupes who acknowledged the error. Even the deceivers came forward, and gave the most decisive proof of their sincerity by rendering impossible any future chicanery. They brought the cabalistic and expensive books[1] which had been the instruments of their trade, and publicly burned them. It was like the *Monte della Pietà* reared

---

[1] On these Ἐφέσια γράμματα see the illustrations adduced by Wetstein. Some of them were copies of the mystic words and names engraved in enigmatic formulæ (αἰνιγματώδως—Eustath. in *Od.* xiv., p. 1864) on the crown, girdle, and feet of the statue of Artemis. Whole treatises were written in explanation of them, which resemble certain Chinese treatises. An addiction to magic, therefore, assumed almost necessarily a secret belief in idolatry. One of the titles of Artemis was *Magos*. Balbillus (Suet. *Ner.* 36) and Maximus (Gibbon, ii. 291, ed. Milman) were both Ephesian astrologers. Eustathius (*l.c.*—cf. Philostr. *Vit. Apol.* vii. 39) tells us that Crœsus was saved by reciting them on the pyre, and that in a wrestling bout a Milesian, who could not throw an Ephesian, found that he had Ephesian incantations engraved on a die. When this was taken from him the Milesian threw him thirty times in succession. Hence the Ἐφέσια γράμματα were sometimes engraved on seals (Athen. xii. 584). Renan says (p. 345) that the names of the "seven sleepers of Ephesus" are still a common incantation in the East.

by the repentant Florentines at the bidding of Savonarola; and so extensive had been this secret evil-doing, that the value of the books destroyed by the culprits in this fit of penitence was no less than fifty thousand drachms of silver, or, in our reckoning, about £2,030.[1] This bonfire, which must have lasted some time,[2] was so striking a protest against the prevalent credulity, that it was doubtless one of the circumstances which gave to St. Paul's preaching so wide a celebrity throughout all Asia.

This little handful of incidents is all that St. Luke was enabled to preserve for us of this great Ephesian visit, which Paul himself tells us occupied a period of three years.[3] Had we nothing else to go by, we might suppose that until the final outbreak it was a period of almost unbroken success and prosperity. Such, however, as we find from the Epistles[4] and from the Apostle's speech to the Ephesian elders,[5] was very far from being the case. It was indeed an earnest, incessant, laborious, house-to-house ministry, which carried its exhortations to each individual member of the church. But it was a ministry of many tears; and though greatly blessed, it was a time of such overwhelming trial, sickness, persecution, and misery, that it probably surpassed in sorrow any other period of St. Paul's life. We must suppose that during its course happened not a few of those perils which he recounts with such passionate brevity of allusion in his Second Epistle

---

[1] On the almost certain supposition that the "pieces of silver" were Attic drachms of the value of about 9¾d. If they were Roman denarii the value would be £1,770. Classic parallels to this public abjuration of magic are quoted from Liv. xl. 29; Suet. *Aug.* 31; Tac. *Ann.* xiii. 50; *Agric.* 2.

[2] κατέκαιον, impf.

[3] Acts xx. 31; but owing to the Jewish method of reckoning any *part* of time to the whole, the period did not *necessarily* much exceed two years.

[4] Chiefly those to the Corinthians. On the Epistle to "the Ephesians" see *infra*.

[5] Acts xx. 18—35.

to the Corinthians. Neither from Jews, nor from Pagans, nor from nominal Christians was he safe. He had suffered alike at the hands of lawless banditti and stately magistrates; he had been stoned by the simple provincials of Lystra, beaten by the Roman colonists of Philippi, hunted by the Greek mob at Ephesus, seized by the furious Jews at Corinth, maligned and thwarted by the Pharisaic professors of Jerusalem. Robbers he may well have encountered in the environs,[1] as tradition tells us that St. John the Evangelist did in later days, as well as in the interior, when he travelled to lay the foundation of various churches.[2] Perils among his own countrymen we know befell him there, for he reminds the elders of Ephesus of what he had suffered from the ambuscades of the Jews.[3] To perils by the heathen and in the city he must have often been liable in the narrow streets. Of his perils among false brethren, like Phygellus, and Hermogenes, and Alexander, we may see a specimen in the slanders against his person, and the internecine opposition to his doctrine, of which we shall meet with future proofs. Perils in the wilderness and in the sea were the inevitable lot of one who travelled over vast districts in those days, when navigation was so imperfect and intercourse so unprotected It was very shortly after his departure from Ephesus that he wrote of all these dangers, and if, as is possible, he took more than one voyage from the haven of Ephesus to various places on the shores of the Levant, it may have been at this time that he suffered that specially perilous

---

[1] 2 Cor. xi. 26.

[2] He had not, however, visited Laodicea or Colossæ, where churches were founded by Philemon and Epaphras (Col. i. 7; iv. 12—16). But he may well have made journeys to Smyrna, Pergamos, Thyatira, Sardis, Philadelphia, &c. (See 1 Cor. xvi. 19.)

[3] Acts xx. 19; which again shows the fragmentary nature of the narrative as regards all particulars of personal suffering.

shipwreck, in the escape from which he floated a day and a night upon the stormy waves.[1] And all this time, with a heart that trembled with sympathy or burned with indignation,[2] he was carrying out the duties of a laborious and pastoral ministry,[3] and bearing the anxious burden of all the churches, of which some, like the churches of Corinth and Galatia, caused him the most acute distress. Nor were physical cares and burdens wanting. True to his principle of refusing to eat the bread of dependence,[4] he had toiled incessantly at Ephesus to support, not himself only, but even Aristarchus and the others who were with him; and not even all his weariness, and painfulness, and sleepless nights of mingled toil and danger,[5] had saved him from cold, and nakedness, and the constant pangs of hunger during compulsory or voluntary fasts.[6] And while he was taking his place like a general on a battle-field, with his eye on every weak or endangered point; while his heart was constantly rent by news of the defection of those for whom he would gladly have laid down his life; while a new, powerful, and organised opposition was working against him in the very churches which he had founded with such peril and toil;[7] while he was being

---

[1] Whether a brief and unsatisfactory visit to Corinth was among these journeys is a disputed point, which depends on the interpretation given to 2 Cor. i. 15, 16; xiii. 1, and which will never be finally settled. A multitude of authorities may be quoted on both sides, and fortunately the question is not one of great importance.

[2] 2 Cor. xi. 29.

[3] Acts xx. 20, 31.

[4] Acts xx. 34.

[5] 2 Cor. xi. 27.

[6] And that, too, although the tents made at Ephesus had a special reputation, and were therefore probably in some demand (Plut. *Alcib.* 12; Athen. xii. 47).

[7] Perhaps the Judaic Christians were more content to leave him alone while he was working in Europe, and were only aroused to opposition by his resumption of work in Asia (Krenkel, *Paulus*, p. 183).

constantly scourged, and mobbed, and maltreated, and at the same time suffering from repeated attacks of sickness and depression; while he was at once fighting a hand-to-hand battle and directing the entire campaign;—he yet found time to travel for the foundation or confirming of other churches, and to write, as with his very heart's blood, the letters which should rivet the attention of thousands of the foremost intellects, eighteen centuries after he himself had been laid in his nameless grave. In these we find that at the very hour of apparent success he was in the midst of foolishness, weakness, shame—" pilloried," as it were, " on infamy's high stage," the sentence of death hanging ever over his head, cast down, perplexed, persecuted, troubled on every side, homeless, buffeted, ill-provided with food and clothes, abused, persecuted, slandered, made as it were the dung and filth of all the world.[1] Nay, more, he was in jeopardy not only every day, but every hour; humanly speaking, he had fought with wild beasts in the great voluptuous Ionic city; he was living every day a living death. He tells us that he was branded like some guilty slave with the stigmata of the Lord Jesus;[2] that he was being "killed all the day long;"[3] that he was "in deaths oft;"[4] that he was constantly carrying about with him the deadness of the crucified Christ;[5] his life an endless mortification, his story an inscription on a cross. What wonder if, amid these afflictions, there were times when the heroic soul gave way? What wonder if he speaks of tears, and trembling, and desolation of heart, and utter restlessness; of being pressed out of measure, above strength, despairing of life itself,[6] tried almost beyond the extreme of human endurance—without fight-

---

[1] 1 Cor. iv. 8—13; 2 Cor. iv. 8, 9.
[2] Gal. vi. 17.
[3] Rom. viii. 36.
[4] 2 Cor. xi. 23.
[5] 2 Cor. iv. 10.
[6] 2 Cor. i. 8.

ings, within fears? What wonder if he is driven to declare that if *this* is all the life belonging to our hope in Christ, he would be of all men the most miserable?[1] And yet, in the strength of the Saviour, how triumphantly he stemmed the overwhelming tide of these afflictions; in the panoply of God how dauntlessly he continued to fling himself into the never-ending battle of a warfare which had no discharge.[2] Indomitable spirit! flung down to earth, chained like a captive to the chariot-wheels of his Lord's triumph,[3] haled as it were from city to city, amid bonds and afflictions,[4] as a deplorable spectacle, amid the incense which breathed through the streets in token of the victor's might—he yet thanks God that he is thus a captive, and glories in his many infirmities. Incomparable and heroic soul! many saints of God have toiled, and suffered, and travelled, and preached, and been execrated, and tortured, and imprisoned, and martyred, in the cause of Christ. Singly they tower above the vulgar herd of selfish and comfortable men; but yet the collective labours of some of their greatest would not equal, nor would their collective sufferings furnish a parallel to those of Paul, and very few of them have been what he was—a great original thinker, as well as a devoted practical worker for his Lord.

But of this period we learn from the Acts only one closing scene,[5] and it is doubtful whether even this is painted for us in colours half so terrible as the reality. Certain it is that some of the allusions which we have been noticing must bear reference to this crowning peril,

[1] 1 Cor. xv. 19.
[2] See Greg. Naz. *Orat.* ii. 38—40.
[3] 2 Cor. ii. 14—16.
[4] Acts xx. 23.
[5] There are further hints in the farewell speech to the Ephesian elders (Acts xx. 18—35).

and that, accustomed though he was to the daily aspect of danger in its worst forms, this particular danger and the circumstances attending it, which are rather hinted at than detailed, had made a most intense impression upon the Apostle's mind.

At the close of about two years, his restless fervour made him feel that he could stay no longer in the school of Tyrannus. He formed the plan of starting after Pentecost, and visiting once more the churches of Macedonia and Achaia, which he had founded in his second journey, and of sailing from Corinth to pay a fifth visit to Jerusalem, after which he hoped to see Rome, the great capital of the civilisation of the world.[1] In furtherance of this purpose he had already despatched two of his little band of fellow-workers, Timothy and Erastus, to Macedonia with orders that they were to rejoin him at Corinth. Erastus[2]—if this be the chamberlain of the city—was a person of influence, and would have been well suited both to provide for the Apostle's reception and to superintend the management of the weekly offertory, about which St. Paul was at present greatly interested. The visit to Jerusalem was rendered necessary by the contribution for the distressed Christians of that city, which he had been collecting from the Gentile churches, and which he naturally desired to present in person, as the best possible token of forgiveness and brotherhood, to the pillars of the unfriendly community. This had not been his original plan.[3] He had originally intended, and indeed had announced his intention, in a letter no longer extant,[4] to sail straight from Ephesus to Corinth, make his way thence by land

---

[1] Cf. Rom. i. 15; xv. 23—28; Acts xix. 21.
[2] Rom. xvi. 23; 2 Tim. iv. 20, but there is no certainty in the matter. The name was common.
[3] 2 Cor. i. 16—23.
[4] *V. infra*, p. 58.

to the churches of Macedonia, sail back from thence to
Corinth, and so sail once more from Corinth to Jerusalem.
Weighty reasons, which we shall see hereafter, had compelled the abandonment of this design. The ill news
respecting the condition of the Corinthian churches which
he had received from the slaves of Chloe compelled him to
write his first extant letter to the Corinthians, in which
he tacitly abandons his original intention, but sends
Titus, and with him " the brother," to regulate to the best
of their power the gross disorders that had arisen.[1] Probably
at the same time he sent a message to Timothy—uncertain,
however, whether it would reach him in time—not to go
to Corinth, but either to return to him or to wait for him
in Macedonia. The first Epistle to the Corinthians was
written about the time of the Passover in April, and probably in the very next month an event occurred which, at
the last moment, endangered his stay and precipitated his
departure.

It was now the month of May, and nothing seemed
likely to interfere with the peaceful close of a troubled
ministry. But this month was specially dedicated to the
goddess of Ephesus, and was called from her the Artemisian.[2] During the month was held the great fair—
called Ephesia—which attracted an immense concourse of
people from all parts of Asia, and was kept with all possible splendour and revelry. The proceedings resembled
the Christmas festivities of the middle ages, with their
boy bishops and abbots of misrule. The gods were personated by chosen representatives, who received throughout the month a sort of mock adoration. There was an

---

[1] 1 Cor. xvi. 5—7.
[2] The decree dedicating the entire month to Artemis has been found by Chandler on a slab of white marble near the aqueduct, and is given by Boeck, *Corp. Inscr.* 2954. It is nearly contemporary with the time of St. Paul.

Alytarch, who represented Zeus; a Grammateus, who played the part of Apollo; an Amphithales, who personated Hermes; and in the numberless processions and litanies, and sacrifices, they paced the streets, and were elevated in public places, arrayed in robes of pure white or of tissued gold, and wearing crowns which were set with carbuncles and pearls. The theatre and stadium were densely crowded by festive throngs to listen to the musical contests, to watch the horse-races, and the athletic exhibitions, or to look on with thrills of fiercer emotion at the horrible combats of men and beasts. The vast expense of these prolonged festivities and superb spectacles was entirely borne by the College of the ten Asiarchs, who thus fulfilled the same functions as those of the Curule Ædiles at Rome. They were men of high distinction, chosen annually from the wealthiest citizens of the chief cities of Asia, and it was their duty to preside over the games, and to keep order in the theatre. The heavy pecuniary burden of the office was repaid in honorary privileges and social distinctions. Their names were recorded on coins and in public inscriptions, and the garlands and purple robes which distinguished them during the continuance of the feast were the external marks of the popular gratitude.[1]

During the sacred month the city rang with every sort of joyous sounds; gay processions were constantly sweeping to the famous temple; drunkenness and debauchery were rife; even through the soft night of spring the Agora hummed with the busy throngs of idlers and revellers.[2] It was inevitable that at such a time there should be a recrudescence of fanaticism, and it is far from improbable that the worthless and frivolous mob, incited by the Eunuch priests and Hierodules of Artemis, may have

[1] These particulars are mainly derived from the account of Malalas.
[2] Achill. Tat. 5.

marked out for insult the little congregation which met in the school of Tyrannus, and their well-known teacher. This year there was a perceptible diminution in the fast and furious mirth of the Artemisian season, and the cause of this falling off was perfectly notorious.[1] Not only in Ephesus, but in all the chief cities of Proconsular Asia, deep interest had been excited by the preaching of a certain Paulus, who, in the very metropolis of idolatry, was known to be quietly preaching that they were no gods which were made with hands. Many people had been persuaded to adopt his views; many more had so far at least been influenced by them as to feel a growing indifference for mummeries and incantations, and even for temples and idols. Consequently there arose in Ephesus "no small stir about that way." Paul and his preaching, the brethren and their assemblages, were in all men's mouths, and many a muttered curse was aimed at them by Megabyzos and Melissae, and the hundreds of hangers-on which gather around every great institution. At last this ill-concealed exasperation came to a head. The chief sufferer from the diminished interest in the goddess and her Hieromenia, had been a certain silversmith, named Demetrius, who sold to the pilgrims little silver shrines and images in memorial of their visits to Ephesus[2] and her

[1] No one will be astonished at this who reads Pliny's account of the utter neglect into which heathen institutions had fallen half a century after this time, in the neighbouring province of Bithynia, as a direct consequence of Christian teaching, and that though the Christians were a persecuted sect. There, also, complaints came from the priests, the purveyors of the sacrifices, and other people pecuniarily interested. They had the sagacity to see that their peril from Christianity lay in its universality.

[2] Called ἀμφιδρύματα ναίδια, aediculae. Chrysostom says ἴσως ὡς κιβώρια μικρά. Similar images and shrines are mentioned in Ar. Nub. 598; Dio. Sic. i. 15; xv. 49; Dio. Cass. xxxix. 20; Dion. Hal. ii. 22; Amm. Marcell. xxii. 13; Petron. 29. The custom is an extremely ancient one. "The tabernacle of Moloch, and the star of your god Remphan," which the Israelites took up in the wilderness, were of the same description. Little images of Pallas (παλλάδια

temple. They were analogous to the little copies in alabaster or silver of the shrine of Loretto, and other famous buildings of Italy; nor was it only at Ephesus, but at every celebrated centre of Pagan worship, that the demand for such memorials created the supply. Demetrius found that his trade was beginning to be paralysed, and since the emasculate throng of sacred slaves and musicians dared not strike a blow for the worship which fed their lazy vice, he determined, as far as he could, to stop the mischief. Calling together a trades-union meeting of all the skilled artisans and ordinary workmen who were employed in this craft,[1] he made them a speech, in which he first stirred up their passions by warning them of the impending ruin of their interests,[2] and then appealed to their latent fanaticism to avenge the despised greatness of their temple, and the waning magnificence of the goddess whom all Asia and the world worshipped.[3] The speech was like a spark on inflammable materials. Their interests were suffering,[4] and their superstition was being endangered; and the rage which might have been despised if it had only sprung from greed, looked more respectable when it assumed the cloak of fanaticism. The answer to the speech of Deme-

---

περιαυτόφορα) Demeter, &c., were in special request, and an interesting earthenware aedicula of Cybele found at Athens is engraved in Lewin, i. 414. Appuleius (*Metam.* xi.) says that at the end of the festival small silver images of Artemis were placed on the temple steps for people to kiss.

[1] We learn from numerous inscriptions that guilds and trades-unions (συνεργασίαι, συμβιώσεις) were common in Ionia (see Renan, p. 355). "τεχνῖται, artifices nobiliores, ἐργάται, *operarii*" (Bengel).

[2] Cf. Acts xvi. 19.

[3] "Diana Ephesia, cujus nomen unicum, multiformi specie, ritu vario, nomine multijugo, *totus veneratur orbis*" (Appul. *Metam.* ii.) Pliny calls the temple "orbis terrarum miraculum" (*N. H.* xxxvi. 14); and the image and temple are found on the coins of many neighbouring cities.

[4] Compare the case of the Philippians (Acts xvi. 19). They were, as Calvin says, fighting for their "hearths" quite as much as their "altars," "ut scilicet *culinam* habeant bene calentem."

trius was a unanimous shout of the watchword of Ephesus,
"Great is Artemis of the Ephesians!" So large a meeting
of the workmen created much excitement. Crowds came
flocking from every portico, and agora, and gymnasium,
and street. The whole city was thrown into a state of
riot, and a rush was made for the Jewish quarter and the
shop of Aquila. What took place we are not exactly told,
except that the life of the Apostle was in extremest danger.
The mob was, however, balked of its intended prey. Paul,
as in the similar peril at Thessalonica, was either not in
the house at the time, or had been successfully concealed
by Priscilla and her husband, who themselves ran great
risk of being killed in their efforts to protect him.[1] Since,
however, the rioters could not find the chief object of
their search, they seized two of his companions—Gaius
of Macedonia,[2] and the faithful Aristarchus.[3] With these
two men in their custody, the crowd rushed wildly into
the vast space of the theatre,[4] which stood ever open, and
of which the still visible ruins—"a wreck of immense
grandeur"—show that it was one of the largest in the
world, and could easily have accommodated 30,000 spectators.[5] Paul, wherever he lay hidden, was within reach
of communication from the disciples. Full of anxiety
for the unknown fate of his two companions, he eagerly
desired to make his way into the theatre and there address
the rioters. There is, perhaps, no courage greater than
that which is required from one who, in imminent danger of

[1] Rom. xvi. 4.
[2] Not Gaius of Derbe (xx. 4) or "mine host" (Rom. xvi. 23).
[3] Aristarchus of Thessalonica is mentioned in xx. 4; xxvii. 2; Col. iv. 10; Philem. 24.
[4] Cf. Acts xii. 21; Tac. *H.* ii. 80; Cic. *ad Fam.* viii. 2; Corn. Nep. *Timol.* iv. 2; Jos. *B. J.* vii. 3, § 3. The theatre was the ordinary scene of such gatherings.
[5] Fellowes, *Asia Minor*, p. 274. Wood says 25,000 (*Ephes.* p. 68).

being torn to pieces, dares to face the furious insults and raging passions of an exasperated crowd. But the powers and the spirit of the Apostle always rose to a great occasion, and though he was so sensitive that he could not write a severe letter without floods of tears, and so nervous that he could scarcely endure to be left for even a few days alone, he was quite capable of this act of supreme heroism. He always wished to be in the forefront of battle for his Master's cause. But his friends better appreciated the magnitude of the danger. Gaius and Aristarchus were too subordinate to be made scapegoats for the vengeance of the crowd; but they were sure that the mere appearance of that bent figure and worn and wasted face, which had become so familiar to many of the cities of Asia, would be the instant signal for a terrible outbreak. Their opposition was confirmed by a friendly message from some of the Asiarchs,[1] who rightly conjectured the chivalrous impulse which would lead the Apostle to confront the storm. Anxious to prevent bloodshed, and save the life of one whose gifts and greatness they had learnt to admire, and well aware of the excitability of an Ephesian mob, they sent Paul an express warning not to trust himself into the theatre.

The riot, therefore, spent itself in idle noise. The workmen had, indeed, got hold of Gaius and Aristarchus; but as the crowd did not require these poor Greeks, whose aspect did not necessarily connect them with what was generally regarded as a mere Jewish sect, they did not know what to do with them. The majority of that promiscuous assemblage, unable to make anything of the discordant shouts which were rising on every side, could only guess why they were there at all. There was,

[1] It was the Asiarch Philip at Smyrna, who resisted the cry of the mob, ἵνα ἀναφῇ Πολυκάρπῳ λέοντα (Euseb. *H. E.* iv. 15).

perhaps, a dim impression that some one or other was going to be thrown to the wild beasts, and doubtless among those varying clamours voices were not wanting like those with which the theatre of Smyrna rang not many years afterwards—at the martyrdom of Polycarp— of "Paul to the lions!" "The Christians to the lions!"[1] One thing, however, was generally known, which was, that the people whose proceedings were the cause for the tumult were of Jewish extraction, and a Greek mob was never behindhand in expressing its detestation for the Jewish race. The Jews, on the other hand, felt it hard that they, who had long been living side by side with the Ephesians in the amicable relations of commerce, should share the unpopularity of a sect which they hated quite as much as the Greeks could do. They were anxious to explain to the Greeks and Romans a lesson which they could not get them to learn—namely, that the Jews were not Christians, though the Christians might be Jews. Accordingly they urged Alexander to speak for them, and explain how matters really stood. This man was perhaps the coppersmith who, afterwards also, did Paul much evil, and who would be likely to gain the hearing of Demetrius and his workmen from similarity of trade. This attempt to shift the odium on the shoulders of the Christians entirely failed. Alexander succeeded in struggling somewhere to the front, and stood before the mob with

---

[1] See 1 Cor. iv. 9; 1 Cor. xv. 32; Act. Mart. Polycarp, 12. The stadium where the Bestiarii fought was near the theatre, and the Temple of Artemis was in full view of it. It is, however, very unlikely that St. Paul actually fought with wild beasts. The expression was recognised as a metaphorical one (2 Tim. iv. 17), ἀπὸ Συρίας μέχρι Ῥώμης θηριομαχῶ (Ignat. *Rom.* c. 5); οἵοις θηρίοις μαχόμεθα (Appian, *Bell. Civ.* p. 273). A legend naturally attached itself to the expression (Niceph, *H. E.* ii. 25). The pseudo-Heraclitus (Ep. vii.), writing about this time, says of the Ephesians, ἐξ ἀνθρώπων θηρία γεγονότες. Moreover, St. Paul uses the expression in a letter written *before* this wild scene at Ephesus had taken place.

outstretched hand in the attempt to win an audience for his oration. But no sooner had the mob recognised the well-known traits of Jewish physiognomy than they vented their hate in a shout of "Great is Artemis of the Ephesians!"[1] which was caught up from lip to lip until it was reverberated on every side by the rocks of Prion and Coressus, and drowned all others in its one familiar and unanimous roar.

For two hours, as though they had been howling dervishes, did this mongrel Greek crowd continue incessantly their senseless yell.[2] By that time they were sufficiently exhausted to render it possible to get a hearing. Hitherto the authorities, afraid that these proceedings might end in awakening Roman jealousy to a serious curtailment of their privileges, had vainly endeavoured to stem the torrent of excitement; but now, availing himself of a momentary lull, the Recorder of the city—either the mock officer of that name, who was chosen by the Senate and people for the Artemisia, or more probably the permanent city official—succeeded in restoring order.[3] It may have been all the more easy for

---

[1] I preserve the Greek name because their Asian idol, who was really Cybele, had still less to do with Diana than with Artemis.

[2] They probably were so far corrupted by the contact with Oriental worship as to regard their "vain repetitions in the light of a religious function" (see 1 Kings xviii. 26; Matt. vi. 7). Moreover, they distinctly believed that the glory, happiness, and perpetuity of Ephesus was connected with the maintenance of a splendid ritual. On the discovered inscription of the decree which dedicated the entire month of May to the Artemisian Paneguris, are these concluding words:—οὕτω γὰρ ἐπὶ τὸ ἄμεινον τῆς θρησκείας γινομένης ἡ πόλις ἡμῶν ἐνδοξοτέρα τε καὶ εὐδαίμων εἰς τὸν πάντα διαμενεῖ χρόνον (Boeckh, 2,954). It is probable that St. Paul may have read this very inscription, which seems to be of the age of Tiberius.

[3] The Proconsul of Asia was practically autocratic, being only restrained by the dread of being ultimately brought to law. Subject to his authority the chief towns of Asia were autonomous, managing their domestic affairs by the decisions of a Boulé and Ekklesia. The Recorder acted as Speaker, and held a very important position. The historic accuracy of St. Luke cannot be

him, because one who was capable of making so admirably skilful and sensible a speech could hardly fail to have won a permanent respect, which enhanced the dignity of his position. "Ephesians!" he exclaimed, "what human being is there who is unaware that the city of the Ephesians is a sacristan[1] of the great Artemis, and the Heaven-fallen? Since, then, this is quite indisputable, your duty is to maintain your usual calm, and not to act in the precipitate way in which you have acted,[2] by dragging here these men, who are neither temple-robbers,[3] nor blasphemers of your goddess.[4] If Demetrius and his fellow-artisans have any complaint to lodge against any one, the sessions are going on,[5] and there are proconsuls;[6] let them settle the

more strikingly illustrated than it is by one of the Ephesian inscriptions in Boeckh, No. 2,960, which records how the "*Augustus-loving*" (φιλοσέβαστος) senate of the Ephesians, and its *temple-adorning* (νεωκόρος) Demos consecrated a building in the *Proconsulship* (ἐπὶ ἀνθυπάτου) of Peducæus Priscinus, and by the decree of Tiberius Claudius Italicus, the "*Recorder*" (γραμματεὺς) of the Demos.

[1] νεωκόρον, "temple-sweeper." It was an honorary title granted by the Emperor to various cities in Asia, and often recorded on coins.

[2] Acts xix. 36, κατεσταλμένους ὑπάρχειν καὶ μηδὲν προπετὲς ποιεῖν. Cicero (*pro Flacco*, vii., viii.) gives a striking picture of the rash and unjust legislation of Asiatic cities, " quum in theatro imperiti homines rerum omnium rudes ignarique considerant " (cf. Tac. *H.* ii. 80).

[3] Wood, p. 14. This, strange to say, was a common charge against Jews (see on Rom. ii. 22).

[4] Another striking indication that St. Paul's method as a missionary was not to shock the prejudices of idolaters. Chrysostom most unjustly accuses the Recorder of here making a false and claptrap statement.

[5] ἀγόραιοι ἄγονται, "Conventûs peraguntur"—not as in E.V., "the law is open." Every province was divided into districts (διοικήσεις, conventûs), which met at some assize town. "Ephesum vero, alterum lumen Asiæ, remotiores conveniunt " (Plin. *H. N.*, v. 31).

[6] There was under ordinary circumstances only one Proconsul in any province. The plural may be generic, or may mean the Proconsul and his assessors (*consiliarii*), as ἡγεμόνες means "the Procurator or his assessors" in Jos. *B. J.* ii. 16, 1. But Basnage has ingeniously conjectured that the allusion may be to the joint authority of the Imperial Procurators, the knight P. Celer, and the freedman Helius. In the first year of Nero, A.D. 54, they had, at the instigation of Agrippina, poisoned Junius Silanus, Proconsul of Asia, whose

matter between them at law. But if you are making any further inquisition about any other matter, it shall be disposed of in the regular meeting of the Assembly.[1] For, indeed, this business renders us liable to a charge of sedition, since we shall be entirely unable to give any reasonable account of this mass meeting."

The effect of this speech was instantaneous.

> "He called
> Across the tumult, and the tumult fell."

The sensible appeal of the "*vir pietate gravis*" made the crowd repent of their unreasoning uproar, and afraid of its possible consequences, as the Recorder alternately flattered, intimidated, argued, and soothed. It reminded them very forcibly that, since Asia was a senatorial, not an imperial province, and was therefore governed by a Proconsul with a few officials, not by a Proprætor with a legion, they were responsible for good order, and would most certainly be held accountable for any breach of the peace. A day of disorder might forfeit the privileges of years. The Recorder's speech, it has been said, is the model of a popular harangue. Such excitement on the part of the Ephesians was *undignified*, as the grandeur of their worship was unimpeached; it was *unjustifiable*, as they could prove nothing against the men; it was *unnecessary*, as other means of redress were open; and, finally, if neither pride nor justice availed anything, fear

---

gentle nature did not preserve him from the peril of his royal blood (Tac. *Ann.* xiii. 1). As P. Celer at any rate did not return to Rome till the year A.D. 57, it is conjectured that he and Helius may have been allowed to be Vice-Proconsuls till this period by way of rewarding them for their crimes (Lewin, *Fasti Sacri*, 1806, 1838; Biscoe on the Acts, pp. 282—285).

[1] There were three regular meetings of the Assembly (ἔννομοι ἐκκλησίαι) every month (and see Wood, p. 50).

of the Roman power[1] should restrain them. They felt thoroughly ashamed, and the Recorder was now able to dismiss them from the theatre.

It is not, however, likely that the danger to St. Paul's person ceased, in a month of which he had spoiled the festivity, and in a city which was thronged, as this was, with aggrieved interests and outraged superstitions. Whether he was thrown into prison, or what were the dangers to which he alludes, or in what way God delivered him "from so great a death,"[2] we cannot tell. At any rate, it became impossible for him to carry out his design of staying at Ephesus till Pentecost.[3] All that we are further told is that, when the hubbub had ceased, he called the disciples together, and, after comforting them,[4] bade the Church farewell—certainly for many years, perhaps for ever.[5] He set out, whether by sea or by land we do not know, on his way to Macedonia. From Silas he had finally parted at Jerusalem. Timothy, Titus, Luke, Erastus, were all elsewhere; but Gaius and Aristarchus, saved from their perilous position in the theatre, were still with him, and he was now joined by the two Ephesians, Tychicus and Trophimus, who remained faithful to him till the very close of his career.

The Church which he had founded became the eminent

[1] Hackett, p. 246. There was nothing on which the Romans looked with such jealousy as a tumultuous meeting, "Qui coetum et concentum fecerit *capitale sit*" (Sen. *Controv.* iii. 8). The hint would not be likely to be lost on Demetrius.

[2] 2 Cor. i. 10.

[3] The period of his stay at Ephesus was τριετίαν ὅλην (Acts xx. 31). The ruin called "the prison of St. Paul" may point to a true tradition that he was for a time confined, and those who see in Rom. xvi. 3—20, the fragment of a letter to Ephesus, suppose that his imprisonment was shared by his kinsmen Andronicus and Junias, who were "of note among the Apostles," and earlier converts than himself.

[4] Acts xx. 1, παρακαλέσας (A, B, D, E).

It was only the elders whom he saw at Miletus.

Christian metropolis of a line of Bishops, and there, four centuries afterwards, was held the great Œcumenical Council which deposed Nestorius, the heretical Patriarch of Constantinople.[1] But "its candlestick" has been for centuries "removed out of his place;"[2] the squalid Mohammedan village which is nearest to its site does not count one Christian in its insignificant population;[3] its temple is a mass of shapeless ruins; its harbour is a reedy pool; the bittern booms amid its pestilent and stagnant marshes; and malaria and oblivion reign supreme over the place where the wealth of ancient civilisation gathered around the scenes of its grossest superstitions and its most degraded sins. "A noisy flight of crows," says a modern traveller, "seemed to insult its silence; we heard the partridge call in the area of the theatre and the Stadium."[4]

[1] A.D. 431.
[2] Rev. ii. 5.
[3] V. *supra*, p. 14. See, for the present condition of Ephesus, Arundell, *Seven Churches of Asia*, p. 27; Fellowes, *Asia Minor*, p. 274; Falkener, *Ephesus and the Temple of Diana*; and especially Mr. J. T. Wood's *Discoveries at Ephesus*. The site of the temple has first been established with certainty by Mr. Wood's excavations.
[4] See Chandler, pp. 109—137.

CHAPTER XXXII.

CONDITION OF THE CHURCH OF CORINTH.

> "Hopes have precarious life;
> They are oft blighted, withered, snapt sheer off;—
> But faithfulness can feed on suffering,
> And knows no disappointment."—*Spanish Gipsy*.

No one can realise the trials and anxieties which beset the life of the great Apostle during his stay at Ephesus, without bearing in mind how grave were the causes of concern from which he was suffering, in consequence of the aberrations of other converts. The First Epistle to the Corinthians was written during the latter part of his three years' residence at the Ionian metropolis;[1] and it reveals to us a state of things which must have rent his heart in twain. Any one who has been privileged to feel a deep personal responsibility for some great and beloved institution, will best appreciate how wave after wave of affliction must have swept across his sea of troubles as he heard from time to time those dark rumours from Galatia and Corinth, which showed how densely the tares of the enemy had sprung up amid the good wheat which he had sown.

Apollos, on his return to Ephesus, must have told him some very unfavourable particulars. St. Paul had now been absent from the Corinthians for nearly three years, and they may well have longed—as we see that they did long —for his presence with an earnestness which even made

[1] Probably about April, A.D. 57.

them unjust towards him. The little band of converts—mostly of low position, and some of them of despicable antecedents—not a few of them slaves, and some of them slaves of the most degraded rank—were left in the midst of a heathendom which presented itself at Corinth under the gayest and most alluring aspects. It is not in a day that the habits of a life can be thrown aside. Even those among them whose conversion was most sincere had yet a terrible battle to fight against two temptations: the temptation to dishonesty, which had mingled with their means of gaining a livelihood; and the temptation to sensuality, which was interwoven with the very fibres of their being. With Christianity awoke conscience. Sins to which they had once lightly yielded as matters of perfect indifference, now required an intense effort to resist and overcome, and every failure, so far from being at the worst a venial weakness, involved the agonies of remorse and shame. And when they remembered the superficially brighter and easier lives which they had spent while they were yet pagans;[1] when they daily witnessed how much sin there might be with so little apparent sorrow; when they felt the burdens of their life doubled, and those earthly pleasures which they had once regarded as its only alleviations rendered impossible or wrong—while as yet they were unable to realise the exquisite consolation of Christian joy and Christian hope—they were tempted either to relapse altogether, or to listen with avidity to any teacher whose doctrines, if logically developed, might help to relax the stringency of their sacred obligations. While Paul was with them

---

[1] "In the young pagan world
Men deified the beautiful, the glad,
The strong, the boastful, and it came to nought;
We have raised pain and sorrow into heaven" (Athelwold).

they were comparatively safe. The noble tyranny of his personal influence acted on them like a spell; and with his presence to elevate, his words to inspire, his example to encourage them, they felt it more easy to fling away all that was lower and viler, because they could realise their right to what was higher and holier. But when he had been so long away — when they were daily living in the great wicked streets, among the cunning, crowded merchants, in sight and hearing of everything which could quench spiritual aspirations and kindle carnal desires; when the gay, common life went on around them, and the chariot-wheels of the Lord were still afar— it was hardly wonderful if the splendid vision began to fade. The lustral water of Baptism had been sprinkled on their foreheads; they fed on the Sacrament of the Body and Blood of Christ; but alas! Corinth was not heaven, and the prose of daily life followed on the poetry of their first enthusiasm, and it was difficult to realise that, for them, those living streets might be daily brightened with manna dews. Their condition was like the pause and sigh of Lot's wife, as, amid the sulphurous storm, she gazed back on the voluptuous ease of the City of the Plain. Might they no longer taste of the plentiful *Syssitia* on some festive day? Might they not walk at twilight in the laughing bridal procession, and listen to the mirthful jest? Might they not watch the Hieroduli dance at some lovely festival in the Temples of Acrocorinth? Was all life to be hedged in for them with thorny scruples? Were they to gaze henceforth in dreaming phantasy, not upon bright faces of youthful deities, garlanded with rose and hyacinth, but on the marred visage of One who was crowned with thorns? Oh, it was hard to choose the kingdom of God; hard to remember that now they were delivered out of the land of Egypt; hard for their enervation to breathe the eager and difficult air of the pure wilderness. It was hard to give up the coarse and near for the immaterial and the far; hard not to lust after the reeking fleshpots, and not to loathe the light angel food; hard to give up the purple wine in the brimming goblet for the cold water from the spiritual rock; hard to curb and crucify passions which once they had consecrated under guise of religion; hard not to think all these temptations irresistible, and to see the way of escape which God had appointed them for each; hard to be bidden to rejoice, and not to be suffered even to murmur at all these hardnesses of life. And the voice which had taught them the things of God had now for so long been silent; for three years they had not seen the hand which pointed them to Heaven. It was with some of them as with Israel, when Moses was on Sinai: they sat down to eat and to drink, and rose up to play. Many, very many —some in shame and secrecy, others openly justifying their relapse by the devil-doctrines of perverted truth— had plunged once more into the impurity, the drunkenness, and the selfishness, as though they had never heard the heavenly calling, or tasted the eternal gift.

So much even Apollos must have told the Apostle; and when he had occasion, in a letter now lost[1]—probably because it was merely a brief and businesslike memorandum—to write and inform them of his intended, but subsequently abandoned, plan of paying them a double visit, and to bid them contribute to the collection for the poor saints at Jerusalem, he had, in a message which required subsequent explanation, briefly but emphatically bidden them not to keep company with fornicators.[2]

---

[1] The spurious letter of the Corinthians to St. Paul, and his answer, preserved in Armenian, are perfectly valueless.

[2] See 1 Cor. x. 1—14.

And now a letter had come from Corinth. So far from dwelling on the ruinous disorders into which many members of the Church had fallen, it was entirely self-complacent in tone; and yet it proved the existence of much doctrinal perplexity, and, in asking advice about a number of practical subjects, had touched upon questions which betrayed some of the moral and intellectual errors which the Church, in writing the letter, had so disingenuously concealed.[1]

1. After greeting him, and answering him, in words which he quotes, that "they remembered him in all things, and kept the ordinances as he delivered them,"[2] they had asked him a whole series of questions about celibacy and marriage, which had evidently been warmly discussed in the Church, and decided in very different senses. Was married life in itself wrong, or if not wrong, yet undesirable? or, if not even undesirable, still a lower and less worthy condition than celibacy? When persons were already married, was it their duty, or, at any rate, would it be saintlier to live together as though they were unmarried? Might widows and widowers marry a second time? Were mixed marriages between Christians and heathens to be tolerated, or ought a Christian husband to repudiate a heathen wife, and a Christian wife to leave a heathen husband? and ought fathers to seek marriages for their daughters, or let them grow up as virgins?

2. Again, what were they to do about meats offered to idols? They had prefaced their inquiry on this subject with the conceited remark that "they all had knowledge,"[3] and had perhaps indicated their own opinion by

---

[1] The interchange of such letters (אגרות) on disputed points of doctrine between the synagogues was common.
[2] 1 Cor. xi. 2.
[3] 1 Cor. viii. 1.

the argument that an idol was nothing in the world, and that all things were lawful to their Christian freedom. Still, they wished to know whether they might ever attend any of the idol festivals? The question was an important one for the poor, to whom a *visceratio*[1] was no small help and indulgence. Was it lawful to buy meat in the open market, which, without their knowing it, might have been offered to idols? Might they go as guests to their heathen friends and relations, and run the risk of partaking of that which had been part of a sacrifice?[2]

3. Then, too, a dispute had risen among them about the rule to be observed in assemblies. Was it the duty of men to cover their heads? Might women appear with their heads uncovered? And might they speak and teach in public?

4. They had difficulties, also, about spiritual gifts. Which was the more important, speaking with tongues or preaching? When two or three began at the same time to preach or to speak with tongues, what were they to do?

5. Further, some among them had been perplexed by

---

[1] Public feasts at funerals or idol festivals, &c., Cic. *Off.* ii. 16; Liv. viii. 32, &c. They played a large part in the joy and plenty of ancient life. Arist. *Eth.* viii. 9, 5; Thuc. ii. 38.

[2] The Jews had strong feelings on this subject (cf. Num. xxv. 2; Ps. cvi. 28; Tob. i. 10—14); but it is monstrous to say that St. Paul here teaches the violation of such scruples, or that he is referred to in Rev. ii. 14. On the contrary, he says, "Even if you as Gentiles think nothing of it, still *do not do it*, for the sake of others; only the concession to the weak need not become a tormenting scrupulosity." It is doubtful whether even St. Peter and St. John would not have gone quite as far as this. So strict were Judaic notions on the subject that, in the case of wine, for instance, not only did a cask of it become undrinkable to a Jew if a single heathen libation had been poured from it, but "even a touch with the presumed intention of pouring away a little to the gods is enough to render it unlawful." This is called the law of נסך.

great doubts about the Resurrection. There were even some who maintained that by the Resurrection was meant something purely spiritual, and that it was past already. This view had arisen from the immense material difficulties which surrounded the whole subject of a resurrection of the body. Would Paul give them his solution of some of their difficulties?

6. He had asked them to make a collection for the poor in Judæa: they would be glad to hear something more about this. What plans would he recommend to them?

7. Lastly, they were very anxious to receive Apollos once more among them. They had enjoyed his eloquence, and profited by his knowledge. Would Paul try to induce him to come, as well as pay them his own promised visit?

Such, we gather from the First Epistle to the Corinthians, were the inquiries of a letter which had been brought to the Apostle at Ephesus by Stephanas, Fortunatus, and Achaicus. It was inevitable that St. Paul should talk to these worthy slaves about the Church of which they were the delegates. There was quite enough in the letter itself to create a certain misgiving in his mind, and some of its queries were sufficient to betray an excited state of opinion. But when he came to talk with these visitants from Chloe's household, and they told him the simple truth, he stood aghast with horror, and was at the same time overwhelmed with grief. Reluctantly, bit by bit, in answer to his questionings, they revealed a state of things which added darkness to the night of his distress.

8. First of all, he learnt from them that the Church which he had founded was split up into deplorable factions.

It was the result of visits from various teachers who

had followed in the wake of Paul, and built upon his foundations very dubious materials by way of superstructure. "Many teachers, much strife," had been one of the wise and pregnant sayings of the great Hillel, and it had been fully exemplified at Corinth, where, in the impatient expression of St. Paul, they had had "ten thousand pedagogues." The great end of edification had been lost sight of in the violences of faction, and all deep spirituality had been evaporated in disputatious talk. He heard sad rumours of "strifes, heartburnings, rages, dissensions, backbitings, whisperings, inflations, disorderliness."[1]

i. It became clear that even the visit and teaching of Apollos had done harm—harm which he certainly had not intended to do, and which, as a loyal friend and follower of Paul, he was the first to regret. Paul's own preaching to these Corinthians had been designedly simple, dealing with the great broad fact of a Redeemer crucified for sin, and couched in language which made no pretence to oratorical ornament. But Apollos, who had followed him, though an able man, was an inexperienced Christian, and not only by the natural charm of his impassioned oratory, but also by the way in which he had entered into the subtle refinements so familiar to the Alexandrian intellect, had unintentionally led them first of all to despise the unsophisticated simplicity of St. Paul's teaching, and next to give the rein to all the sceptical fancies with which their faith was overlaid. Both the manner and the matter of the fervid convert had so delighted them that, with entire opposition to his own wishes, they had elevated him into the head of a party, and had perverted his views into dangerous extravagances. These Apollonians were so puffed up with the

[1] 2 Cor. xii. 20.

conceit of knowledge, so filled with the importance of their own intellectual emancipation, that they had also begun to claim a fatal moral liberty. They had distracted the Sunday gatherings with the egotisms of rival oratory; had showed a contemptuous disregard for the scruples of weaker brethren; had encouraged women to harangue in the public assemblies as the equals of men; were guilty of conduct which laid them open to the charge of the grossest inconsistency; and even threw the cloak of sophistical excuse over one crime so heinous that the very heathen were ready to cry shame on the offender. In the accounts brought to him of this Apollos-party, St. Paul could not but see the most extravagant exaggeration of his own doctrines—the half-truths, which are ever the most dangerous of errors. If it was possible to wrest the truths which he himself had taught into the heretical notions which were afterwards promulgated by Marcion, his keen eye could detect in the perversions of the Alexandrian eloquence of Apollos the deadly germs of what would afterwards develop into Antinomian Gnosticism.

ii. But Apollos was not the only teacher who had visited Corinth. Some Judaic Christians had come, who had been as acceptable to the Jewish members of the Church as Apollos was to the Greeks.[1] Armed with commendatory letters from some of the twelve at Jerusalem, they claimed the authority of Peter, or, as they preferred to call him, of Kephas. They did not, indeed, teach the necessity of circumcision, as others of their party did in Galatia. There the local circumstances

---

[1] The circumstances of Corinth were very similar when Clement wrote them his first Epistle. He had still to complain of that "strange and alien, and, for the elect of God, detestable and unholy spirit of faction, which a few rash and self-willed persons (πρόσωπα) kindled to such a pitch of dementation, that their holy and famous reputation, so worthy of all men's love, was greatly blasphemed" (*Ep. ad Cor.* i.).

would give some chance of success to teaching which in Corinth would have been rejected with contempt; and perhaps these particular emissaries felt at least some respect for the compact at Jerusalem. But yet their influence had been very disastrous, and had caused the emergence of a Petrine party in the Church. This party —the ecclesiastical ancestors of those who subsequently vented their hatred of Paul in the Pseudo-Clementines—openly and secretly disclaimed his authority, and insinuated disparagement of his doctrines. Kephas, they said, was the real head of the Apostles, and therefore of the Christians. Into his hands had Christ entrusted the keys of the kingdom; on the rock of his confession was the Church of the Messiah to be built. Paul was a presumptuous interloper, whose conduct to Kephas at Antioch had been most unbecoming. For who was Paul? not an Apostle at all, but an unauthorised innovator. He had been a persecuting Sanhedrist, and he was an apostate Jew. What had he been at Corinth? A preaching tent-maker, nothing more. Kephas, and other Apostles, and the brethren of the Lord, when they travelled about, were accompanied by their wives or by ministering women, and claimed the honour and support to which they were entitled. Why had not Paul done the same? Obviously because he felt the insecurity of his own position. And as for his coming again, a weak, vacillating, unaccredited pretender, such as he was, would take care not to come again. And these preachings of his were heretical, especially in their pronounced indifference to the Levitic law. Was he not breaking down that hedge about the law, the thickening of which had been the life-long task of centuries of eminent Rabbis? Very different had been the scene after Peter's preaching at Pentecost! It was the speaking with tongues—not mere dubious doctrinal exhortation—which was the true sign of spirituality. We are more than sure that the strong, and tender, and noble nature of St. Peter would as little have sanctioned this subterranean counter-working against the Apostle of the Gentiles, as Apollos discountenanced the impious audacities which sheltered themselves under his name.

iii. And then had come another set of Judaisers—one man in particular—to whom the name of even Kephas was unsatisfactory. He apparently was—or, what is a very different thing, he professed to be—an adherent of James,[1] and to him even Peter was not altogether sound. He called himself a follower of Christ, and disdained any other name. Perhaps he was one of the Desposyni. At any rate, he prided himself on having seen Christ, and known Christ in the flesh. Now the Lord Jesus had not married, and James, the Bishop of Jerusalem, was unmarried; and this teacher evidently shared the Essene abhorrence of marriage. He it was who had started all the subtle refinements of questions respecting celibacy and the married life. He it was who gathered around him a few Jews of Ebionite proclivities, who degraded into a party watchword even the sacred name of Christ.[2]

9. Thus, as St. Paul now learnt fully for the first time, the Church of Corinth was a scene of quarrels, disputes, partisanships, which, in rending asunder its unity, ruined

---

[1] We cannot for a moment believe that Peter and James really approved of the methods of these men, because to do so would have been a flagrant breach of their own compact (Gal. ii. 9). But it is matter of daily experience that the rank and file of parties are infinitely less wise and noble than their leaders.

[2] About the Christ party there have been three main views:—(1) That they were adherents of James (Storr, &c.); (2) that they were neutrals, who held aloof from all parties (Eichhorn, &c.); (3) that they were a very slight modification of the Peter-party (Baur, *Paul.* i. 272—292). It is remarkable that to this day there is in England and America a sect, which, professing to disdain human authority, usurps the exclusive name of "Christians" (see Schaff. *Apost. Ch.* i. 339).

its strength. On all these subjects the Corinthians, in their self-satisfied letter, had maintained a prudent but hardly creditable silence. Nor was this all that they had concealed. They had asked questions about spiritual gifts; but it was left for the household of Chloe to break to St. Paul the disquieting news that the assemblies of the Church had degenerated into scenes so noisy, so wild, so disorderly, that there were times when any heathen who dropped in could only say that they were all mad. Sometimes half a dozen enthusiasts were on their legs at once, all pouring forth wild series of sounds which no human being present could understand, except that sometimes, amid these unseemly—and might they not at times, with some of these Syrian emissaries, be these half-simulated—ecstasies, there were heard words that made the blood run cold with shuddering horror.[1] At other times, two or three preachers would interrupt each other in the attempt to gain the ear of the congregation all at the same moment. Women rose to give their opinions, and that without a veil on their heads, as though they were not ashamed to be mistaken for the Hetairæ, who alone assumed such an unblushing privilege. So far from being a scene of peace, the Sunday services had become stormy, heated, egotistic, meaningless, unprofitable.

10. And there was worse behind. It might at least have been supposed that the Agapæ would bear some faint traditional resemblance to their name, and be means of reunion and blessedness worthy of their connexion with the Eucharistic feast! Far from it! The deadly leaven of selfishness—displaying itself in its two forms of sensuality and pride—had insinuated itself even into these once simple and charitable gatherings. The kiss of peace could

---

[1] 1 Cor. xii. 3 (cf. 1 John ii. 22; iv. 1—3); ᾿Ανάθεμα ᾿Ιησοῦν.

hardly be other than a hypocritical form between brethren, who at the very moment might be impleading one another at law before the tribunal of a heathen Praetor about some matter of common honesty. The rich brought their luxurious provisions, and greedily devoured them, without waiting for any one; while the poor, hungry-eyed Lazaruses—half-starved slaves, who had no contributions of their own to bring—watched them with hate and envy as they sat famishing and unrelieved by their full-fed brethren. Greediness and egotism had thus thrust themselves into the most sacred unions; and the besetting Corinthian sin of intoxication had been so little restrained that men had been seen to stretch drunken hands to the very chalice of the Lord!

11. Last and worst, not only had uncleanness found its open defenders, so that Christians were not ashamed to be seen sitting at meat amid the lascivious surroundings of heathen temples, but one prominent member of the Church was living in notorious crime with his own step-mother during the lifetime of his father; and, though the very Pagans execrated this atrocity, yet he had not been expelled from the Christian communion, not even made to do penance in it, but had found brethren ready, not merely to palliate his offence, but actually to plume themselves upon leaving it unpunished. This man seems to have been a person of distinction and influence, whom it was advantageous to a Church largely composed of slaves and women to count among them. Doubtless this had facilitated his condonation, which may have been founded on some antinomian plea of Christian liberty; or on some Rabbinic notion that old ties were rendered non-existent by the new conditions of a proselyte; or by peculiarities of circumstance unknown to us. But though this person was the most notorious, he was by no means the only offender, and there were Corinthian Christians—even

many of them—who were impenitently guilty of uncleanness, fornication, and lasciviousness.[1] In none of his writings are the Apostle's warnings against this sin—the besetting sin of Corinth—more numerous, more solemn, or more emphatic.[2]

Truly, as he heard this catalogue of iniquities—while he listened to the dark tale of the shipwreck of all his fond hopes which he had learnt to entertain during the missionary labour of eighteen months—the heart of St. Paul must have sunk within him. He might well have folded his hands in utter despair. He might well have pronounced his life and his preaching a melancholy failure. He might well have fled like Elijah into utter solitude, and prayed, "Now, O Lord, take away my life, for I am not better than my fathers." But it was not thus that the news affected this indomitable man. His heart, indeed, throbbed with anguish, his eyes were streaming with tears, as, having heard to the bitter end all that the slaves of Chloe had to tell him, he proceeded to make his plans. First, of course, his intended brief immediate visit to Corinth must be given up. Neither he nor they were yet in a mood in which their meeting could be otherwise than infinitely painful. He must at once despatch Titus to Corinth to inform them of his change of plan, to arrange about the collection, and to do what little he could, before rejoining him at Troas. He must also despatch a messenger to Timothy to tell him not to proceed to Corinth at present. And then he *might* have written an apocalyptic letter, full of burning denunciation and fulminated anathemas; he might have blighted these conceited, and lascivious, and quarrelsome disgracers of the name of Christian with withering invectives, and

---

[1] 2 Cor. xii. 21.   [2] 1 Cor. v. 11; vi. 15–18; x. 8; xv. 33, 34.

rolled over their trembling consciences thunders as loud as those of Sinai. Not such, however, was the tone he adopted, or the spirit in which he wrote. In deep agitation, which he yet managed almost entirely to suppress, summoning all the courage of his nature, forgetting all the dangers and trials which surrounded him at Ephesus, asking God for the wisdom and guidance which he so sorely needed, crushing down deep within him all personal indignations, every possible feeling of resentment or egotism at the humiliations to which he had personally been subjected, he called Sosthenes to his side, and flinging his whole heart into the task immediately before him, began to dictate to him one of the most astonishing and eloquent of all his letters, the first extant Epistle to the Corinthians. Varied as are the topics with which it deals, profound as were the difficulties which had been suggested to him, novel as were the questions which he had to face, alienated as were many of the converts to whom he had to appeal, we see at once that the Epistle was no laborious or long-polished composition. Enlightened by the Spirit of God, St. Paul was in possession of that insight which sees at once into the heart of every moral difficulty. He was as capable of dealing with Greek culture and Greek sensuality as with Judaic narrowness and Judaic Pharisaism. He shows himself as great a master when he is applying the principles of Christianity to the concrete and complicated realities of life, as when he is moving in the sphere of dogmatic theology. The phase of Jewish opposition with which he has here to deal has been modified by contact with Hellenism, but it still rests on grounds of externalism, and must be equally met by spiritual truths. Problems however dark, details however intricate, become lucid and orderly at once in the light of eternal distinctions. In teaching his converts St. Paul had no need to burn **the** midnight oil in long studies. Even his most elaborate Epistles were in reality not elaborate. They leapt like vivid sparks from a heart in which the fire of love to God burnt until death with an ever brighter and brighter flame.

1. His very greeting shows the fulness of his heart. As his authority had been impugned, he calls himself "an Apostle of Jesus Christ by the will of God," and addresses them as a Church, as sanctified in Christ Jesus, and called to be saints, uniting with them in the prayer for grace and peace all who, whatever their differing shades of opinion or their place of abode, call upon the name of our Lord Jesus Christ, both theirs and ours.[1] Thus, in his very address to them, he strikes the key-note of his own claim to authority, and of the unity and holiness which they so deeply needed. "Observe, too," says St. Chrysostom, "how he ever nails them down to the name of Christ, not mentioning any man—either Apostle or teacher—but continually mentioning Him for whom they yearn, as men preparing to awaken those who are drowsy after a debauch. For nowhere in any other Epistle is the name of Christ so continuously introduced; here, however, it is introduced frequently, and by means of it he weaves together almost his whole exordium."[2]

2. Although he has united Sosthenes[3] with him in the superscription, he continues at once in the first person to tell them that he thanks God always for the grace given them in Christ Jesus, for the eloquence and knowledge with which they were enriched in Him, so that in waiting for the Apocalypse of Christ, they were behindhand in no spiritual gift; and as the testimony of Christ was confirmed among them, so should Christ confirm them to be blameless unto the end, since God was faithful,

---

[1] "Est enim haec periculosa tentatio nullam Ecclesiam putare ubi non appareat perfecta puritas" (Calvin). The absence of fixed ecclesiastical organisation is clear, as he addresses the entire community, and holds no "bishops" responsible for the disorders, and for carrying out the excommunication.

[2] 1 Cor. i. 1—8. The name of Christ occurs no less than nine times in the first nine verses.

[3] Whether the Sosthenes of Acts xviii. 17, who may have been subsequently converted (Wetst. ii. 576), or an unknown brother, we do not know. He may have been one of the bearers of the Corinthian letter to Ephesus; "one of the seventy, and afterwards Bishop of Colophon" (Euseb. *H. E.* i. 12)

who had called them unto the communion of His Son Jesus Christ our Lord.[1]

3. That communion leads him at once to one of the subjects of which his heart is full. He has heard on indisputable authority, and not from one person only, of schisms and strifes among them, and he implores them by the name of Christ to strive after greater unity in thought and action.[2] They were saying, "I am of Paul, and I of Apollos, and I of Kephas, and I of Christ." What! has Christ been parcelled into fragments?[3] Some of them called themselves *his* party; but had *he* been crucified for them? had they been baptised into *his* name? It may be that Apollos, fresh from his discipleship to John's baptism, had dwelt very prominently on the importance of that initial rite; but so liable were men to attach importance to the mere human minister, that Paul, like his Master, had purposely abstained from administering it, and except Crispus and Gaius—and, as he afterwards recalls, Stephanas and his household—he cannot remember that he has baptised any of them. Christ had sent him not to baptise, but to preach; and that not in wisdom of utterance, that Christ's cross might not be rendered void. The mention of preaching brings him to the aberrations of the Apollonian party. They had attached immense importance to eloquence, logic, something which they called and exalted as wisdom. He shows them that they were on a wholly mistaken track. Such human wisdom, such ear-flattering eloquence, such superficial and plausible enticements, he had deliberately rejected. Of human wisdom he thought little. It lay under the ban of revelation.[4] It had not led the world to the knowledge of God. It had not saved the world from the crucifixion of Christ. And, therefore, he had not preached to them about the Logos, or about Æons, or in Philonian allegories, or with philosophical refine-

---

[1] i. 4—9. Observe the perfect sincerity of the Apostle. He desires, as always, to thank God on behalf of his converts; here, however, he has no *moral* praise to imply. The Corinthians have received rich spiritual blessings and endowments, but he cannot speak of them as he does of the Thessalonians or Philippians.

[2] Ver. 10, ναῦ καὶ . . . γνώμῃ, "intus in credendis, et sententiâ prolatâ in agendis" (Bengel).

[3] It is deeply instructive to observe that St. Paul here refuses to enter into the differences of view from which the parties sprang. He does not care to decide which section of wrangling "theologians" or "churchmen" is right and which is wrong. He denounces the *spirit* of party as a sin and a shame where unity between Christians is the first of duties and the greatest of advantages.

[4] i. 20, τοῦ συζητητὴς κ. τ. λ., but in Isa. xxxiii. 18 (cf. Ps. xlviii. 12), "*where is he who counteth the towers?*"

ments. He had offered neither a sign to the Jews, nor wisdom to the Greeks. What he had to preach was regarded by the world as abject foolishness—it was the Cross—it was the doctrine of a crucified Messiah, which was to the Jews revolting; of a crucified Saviour, which was to the Greeks ridiculous; but it pleased God to save believers by the foolishness (in the world's view) of the thing preached,[1] and it was to those who were in the way of salvation the wisdom and the power of God. They were not the wise, and the mighty, and the noble of the world, but, as a rule, the foolish, and the weak, and the despised.[2] It was not with the world's power, but with its impotences; not with its strength, but with its feebleness; not with its knowledge, but with its ignorance; not with its rank, but its ignobleness; not with kings and philosophers, but with slaves and women, that its divine forces were allied; and with them did God so purpose to reveal His power that no glory could accrue to man, save from the utter abasement of *human* glory. That was why Paul had come to them, not with rhetoric, but with the simple doctrine of Christ crucified;[3] not with oratoric dignity, but in weakness, fear, and trembling; not with winning elocution, but with spiritual demonstration and spiritual power—so that man might be utterly lost in God, and they might feel the origin of their faith to be not human but divine.[4]

4. Yet they must not be misled by his impassioned paradox into the notion that the matter and method of his teaching was really folly. On the contrary, it was wisdom of the deepest and loftiest kind—only it was a wisdom of God hidden from the wise of the world; a wisdom of insight into things which eye hath not seen nor ear heard, and which had never set foot on human heart,[5] but which were revealed to him by that Spirit which alone searcheth the depths of God,[6] and which he had

---

[1] i. 21, διὰ τῆς μωρίας τοῦ κηρύγματος, not "the foolishness of preaching" (κηρύξεως). In 23, 24 " cross," " stumblingblock," " folly," " power" would be respectively *seccel*, *miscol*, *mashcal*, *secel*, and some see in it a sign that St. Paul had in his thoughts a Syriac paronomasia (Winer, *N. T. Gramm.*, E. T., p. 658).

[2] A needful warning to " Corinthios non minus lasciviâ, quam *opulentiâ*, et *philosophiae* studio insignes " (Cic. *De Leg. Agr.* ii. 32.)

[3] All the more remarkable because "a Corinthian style" meant "a polished style " (Wetst. *ad loc.*).

[4] i. 19; ii. 5; cf. Jer. ix. 23, 24; Isa. xxxiii. 18, is freely cited from the LXX.

[5] Possibly a vague echo of Isa. lxiv. 4 (cf. lii. 15, and lxv. 17); or from some lost book (Chrys.) like the " Revelation of Elias," ἐπὶ καρδίαν ἀνέβη, עָלָה עַל לֵב. *Both* explanations are possible, for the lost book may have echoed Isaiah. A modern theory regards the words as liturgical.

[6] Ver. 10. The attempt to make Rev. ii. 24 an ironical reference to this is most baseless.

taught in words not learnt from wisdom, but from that same Spirit of God, combining spirituals with spirituals.[1] And this spiritual wisdom was, to the natural man,[2] folly, because it could be only discerned by a spiritual faculty of which the natural man was absolutely devoid. It was to him what painting is to the blind, or music to the deaf.[3] But the spiritual man possesses the requisite discernment, and, sharing the mind of Christ, is thereby elevated above the reach of all merely natural judgment.

5. And then, with wholesome irony, he adds that this divine condition, which was earthly folly, he could only teach them in its merest elements; in its perfection it was only for the perfect, but they, who thought themselves so wise and learned, were in spiritual wisdom fleshen babes, needing milk such as he had given them, not meat, which they—being fleshly—were still too feeble to digest.[4] These might seem hard words, but while there were envy, and strife, and divisions among them, how could they be regarded as anything but fleshly and unspiritual? Paul and Apollos! who were Paul and Apollos but mere human ministers? Paul planting, Apollos watering—neither of them anything in himself, but each of them one in their ministry, and each responsible for his own share in it. God only gave the harvest. "God's fellow-workers are we; God's acre, God's building are ye." Paul, as a wise master-builder, had laid the foundation; others were building on it all sorts of superstructures. But the foundation was and could be only one—namely, Christ—and the gold, silver, precious marbles, logs, hay, stubble, built on it should be made manifest in its true quality in God's ever-revealing fire,[5] and if worthless, should be destroyed, however sincere the builder might be. If his superstructure was sound, he would be rewarded; if

---

[1] Ver. 13, πνευματικοῖς πνευματικὰ συγκρίνοντες, others render it "explaining spiritual things to spiritual men" (Gen. xl. 8; Dan. v. 12; LXX.) or "in spiritual words."

[2] Ver. 14, ψυχικὸς, "homines solius animae et carnis" (Tert. *De jejun.* 17).

[3] ii. 6—16. He refutes the Alexandrian teaching by accepting its very terms and principle—"mystery," "initiated," "spiritual man," &c., but showing that it is an eternal universal reality, not some apprehension of particular men (see Maurice, *Unity*, p. 408).

[4] iii. 2, σαρκινοί; 4, σαρκικοῖς. A severe blow at Alexandrian conceit. He has to treat them not as adepts but as novices, not as hierophants but as uninitiated, not as "theologians," but as catechumens, *for the very reason* that they thought so much of themselves (cf. the exactly analogous language of our Lord in John ix. 41).

[5] iii. 13, ἀποκαλύπτεται. By calling this a *praesens futurascens*, and not recognising the normal, unceasing operation of the moral laws of God, commentators have missed a great truth (cf. Matt. iii. 10; Col. iii. 6; Eph. v. 6).

perishable, it would be burnt in the consuming flame, and he should suffer loss, though he himself, since he had built on the true foundation, would be saved as by fire.[1] Did they not know then that they were a temple, a holy temple for the spirit of God? If any man destroy God's temple, God shall destroy him. And human wisdom might destroy it, for before God human wisdom was folly. The mere human wisdom of this or that favourite teacher has nothing to do with the real building. If a man wanted Divine wisdom, let him gain it by the humble paths of what was regarded as human folly. How unworthy, then, to be boasting about mere human teachers—how unworthy was it of their own immense privilege and hope—when all things were theirs —Paul, Apollos, Kephas, the universe, life, death, the immediate present, the far future—all theirs, and they Christ's, and Christ God's. Their party leaders were but poor weak creatures at the best, of whom was required one thing only—faithfulness. As for himself he regarded it as a matter utterly trivial whether he were judged by their tentative opinions or by man's insignificant feeble transient day;[2] nay, he even judged not himself. He was conscious indeed of no sin as regards his ministry;[3] but even on that he did not rely as his justification, depending only on the judgment of the Lord. "So then be not ye judging anything before the due time until the Lord come, who shall both illuminate the crypts of darkness and reveal the counsels of the heart." Then, and not till then, shall the praise which he deserves, and no other praise, accrue to each from God.[4]

6. He had, with generous delicacy, designedly put into prominence his own name and that of Apollos (instead of those of Kephas or the Jerusalem emissary) as unwilling leaders of factions which they utterly deprecated, that the Corinthians might learn in their case not to estimate them above the warrant of their actual words,[5] and might see that he was actuated by no mere jealousy of others, when he denounced their inflated exasperation amongst themselves in the rival display of what after all, even

---

[1] St. Paul does not care to make his metaphor "run on all fours." The general application is sufficient for him. (See Reuss, *Les Epîtres,* i. 169).

[2] Ver. iv. 3, ἀνακριθῶ. An *anakrisis* was an examination preliminary to trial. ἡμέρας, this forcible expression has been explained as a Hebraism (Jer. xvii. 16), a *Cilicism* (Jer. *ad Algas.* 10), and a Latinism (*diem dicere,* &c., Grot.).

[3] Ver. 4, οὐδὲν ... ἐμαυτῷ σύνοιδα, "I am conscious of no guilt" ("Nil conscire sibi," Hor. *Ep.* i. 1, 16). "I know nothing by myself," in this sense is old English. "I am sorry that each fault can be proved by the queen" (Cranmer, *Letter to Henry VIII.*).

[4] iv. 1—4.

[5] iv. 6. The word φρονεῖν is omitted by the chief Uncials. I take μὴ ὑπὲρ ἃ γέγραπται to be a sort of proverb, like "keep to your written evidence."

when they existed, were not intrinsic merits, but gifts of God.¹ And what swelling self-appreciation they showed in all this party spirit! For them the hunger, and the poverty, and the struggle, are all over. What plenitude and satiety of satisfaction you have gained; how rich you are; what thrones you sit on; and all without us. Ah, would it were really so, that we might at least share your royal elevation! For the position of us poor Apostles is very different. "God, I think, displayed us last as condemned criminals,² a theatric spectacle to the universe, both angels and men. We are fools for Christ's sake, but ye are wise in Christ; we weak, but ye strong; ye glorious, but we dishonoured. Up to this very hour we both hunger and thirst, and are ill-clad,³ and are buffeted, and are hustled from place to place, and toil, working with our own hands; being abused, we bless; being persecuted, we endure; being reviled, we entreat; as refuse of the universe⁴ are we become, the offscouring of all things till now." These are bitter and ironical words of contrast between you and us, I know; but I write not as shaming you. I am only warning you as my beloved children. For, after all, you *are* my children. Plenty of teachers, I know, have followed me; but (and here comes one of his characteristic impetuosities of expression) even if you have a myriad pedagogues⁵ in Christ—however numerous, or stern, or authoritative—you have not many fathers. It was I who begot you through the Gospel in Christ Jesus, and I therefore entreat you to follow my example; and on this account I sent you my beloved and faithful son Timothy, to remind you of my invariable practice and teaching.⁶ Do not think, however, that I am afraid to

---

Throughout this section St. Paul's mind is full of the word "inflation" (φυσιοῦσθε; ver. 18, ἐφυσιώθησαν; 19, πεφυσιωμένων; v. 2, πεφυσιωμένοι; viii. 1, ἡ γνῶσις φυσιοῖ; xiii. 4, ἡ ἀγάπη οὐ φυσιοῦται). This is because when St. Paul comes to them, he is afraid of finding this vice of a conceited theology. 2 Cor. xii. 20, φυσιώσεις. Elsewhere the word only occurs in Col. ii. 18.

¹ iv. 7, τίς γάρ σε διακρίνει;
² iv. 9, ὡς ἐπιθανατίους, "veluti *bestiarios*" (Tert. *De Pudic.* 14).
³ Cf. 2 Cor. xi. 27.
⁴ περικαθάρματα, purgamenta, "things vile, and worthless, and to be flung away," not "piacular offerings," περίψημα. The Scholiast on Ar. *Plut.* 456, says, that in famines and plagues it was an ancient Greek and Roman custom to *wipe off* guilt by throwing wretches into the sea, with the words "*Become our peripsema.*" The reference here is probably less specific, but cf. Prov. xi. 18; חפר (LXX.), Tob. v. 18. ἐγὼ περίψημά σου became (from this view) a common Christian expression (Wordsworth, *ad loc.*).
⁵ iv. 15, παιδαγωγούς.
⁶ St. Paul had already sent him, before the necessity had arisen for the more immediate despatch of Titus; but he seems to have countermanded the order,

confront in person the inflated opposition of some who say that *I do* not really mean to come myself. Come I will, and that soon, if the Lord will; and will ascertain not what these inflated critics *say*, but what they *are;* not their power of talk, but of action. "But what will ye? Am I to come to you with a rod, or in love and the spirit of gentleness?"[1]

7. One thing at least needs the rod. A case of incest—of a son taking his father's wife—so gross, that it does not exist even among the heathen,[2] is absolutely notorious among you, and instead of expelling the offender with mourning and shame, you—oh! strange mystery of the invariable connexion between sensuality and pride—have been inflated with sophistical excuses about the matter.[3] "I, at any rate, absent in body, but present in spirit, have already judged as though actually present the man who acted thus in this thing, in the name of our Lord Jesus Christ—you being assembled together, and my spirit which is present with you, though my body is absent—with the power of our Lord Jesus Christ, to hand over such a man to Satan, for destruction of the flesh, that the spirit may be saved in the day of the Lord Jesus Christ."[4] If any passage of the letter was written with sobs, which are echoed in his very words, as Sosthenes wrote them down from his lips, it is this. He summons up the scene and sentence of excommunication. He is absent, yet he is there; and there, with the power of Christ, he pronounces the awful sentence which hands over the offender to Satan in terrible mercy, that by destruction of his flesh he may be saved in the spirit. And then he adds, "The subject of your self-glorification is hideous.[5] Know ye not that a little leaven leaveneth the whole lump? Purge out then at once the old leaven, that ye may be a new lump, as

uncertain, however, whether the messenger would reach him in time, and rather expecting that Timothy would arrive among them before himself ("*if* Timotheus come," xvi. 10). In any case the Corinthians would have heard that Timothy had been sent to come to them through Macedonia, and Paul's enemies drew very unfavourable inferences from this.

[1] iv. 6—21.
[2] The ὀνομάζεται, "is named," of our text is spurious, being omitted in ℵ, A, B, C, D, E, F, G. As to the fact illustrated by the almost local tragedy of Hippolytus, see Cic. *pro Cluent.* 5, "O mulieris scelus incredibile et praeter hanc unam in omni vitâ inauditum" (Wetst. *ad loc.*).
[3] This might seem inconceivable; but v. *supra*, p. 57.
[4] It was the last awful, reluctant declaration, "that a man who has wilfully chosen an evil master, shall feel the bondage that he may loathe it, and so turn to his true Lord" (Maurice, *Unity*, p. 414). On the comparative leniency of excommunication see Hooker, *Eccl. Pol.* iii. 1—13.
[5] v. 8, οὐ καλὸν (litotes), τὸ καύχημα ὑμῶν (not καύχησις).

ye are (ideally) unleavened.¹ For indeed our Passover is slain²—Christ. Let us, then, keep the feast, not with the old leaven, neither with leaven of vice and wickedness, but with unleavenedness of sincerity and truth."³

And here he pauses to explain a clause in his last Epistle which had excited surprise. In it he had forbidden them to associate with fornicators. This had led them to ask the astonished question⁴ whether it was really their duty to go out of the world altogether? His meaning was, as he now tells them, that if any *Christian* were notoriously guilty, either of fornication or any other deadly sin,⁵ with such they were not to associate,—not even to sit at table with them. They really need not have mistaken his meaning on this point. What had he, what had they, to do with judging the outer world? This passage reads like a marginal addition, and he adds the brief, uncompromising order, "Put away at once that wicked man from among yourselves." ⁶

8. The allusion to judging naturally leads him to another point. Dare they, the destined judges of the world and of angels, go to law about mere earthly trifles, and that before the heathen? Why did they not rather set up the very humblest members of the Church to act as judges in such matters? Shame on them! So wise and yet no one of them wise enough to be umpire in mere trade disputes? Better by far have no quarrels among themselves, but suffer wrong and loss; but, alas! instead of this some of them inflicted wrong and loss, and that on their own brethren. Then follows a stern warning—the unjust should not inherit the kingdom of God—"Be not deceived"—the formula by which he always introduces his most solemn passages—neither sensual sinners in all their hideous varieties, nor thieves, nor over-reachers, nor drunkards, nor revilers, nor extortioners, shall inherit the kingdom of God. "And these abject things some of you were;⁷ but ye washed yourselves, but ye were sanctified, but ye were justified in the name of the Lord Jesus, and the Spirit of our God." It is evident that some of them were *liable* to be deceived; that they liked to be deceived on this

---

¹ St. Paul was writing near the time of the Passover; but the allusions are spiritual.

² v. 7, ἐτύθη, "slain" (Matt. xxii. 4; Acts x. 13). The "for us," ὑπὲρ ἡμῶν is a doctrinal gloss not found in A, B, C, D, E, F, G.

³ v. 1—9.

⁴ v. 10, ἐπεὶ ὀφείλετε ἄρα, κ. τ. λ.

⁵ Ver. 11, "or an idolater." Evidently as in x. 7; Col. iii. 5; otherwise how could he be a Christian? Unless he is thinking of some hybrid Christian of the type of Constantine, who "bowed in the house of Rimmon."

⁶ v. 9—13, Ἐξάρατε. The καὶ (omitted in ℵ, A, B, C, F, G) is spurious, and spoils the characteristic abruptness.

⁷ vi. 11, ταῦτά τινες ἦτε.

point, and they seem to have boldly said that the Christian is free, that "all things are lawful" to him because he is no longer under the law, but under grace. "All things are lawful to me." Yes, says St. Paul, but all things are not expedient. "All things are lawful to me"; yes, but I will not become the slave of the fatal tyranny of anything. The case of meats, which perhaps they adduced to show that they might do as they liked, irrespective of the Mosaic law, was not a case in point. They were ἀδιάφορα—matters of indifference about which each man might do as he liked; they, and the belly which assimilated them, were transient things, destined to be done away with. Not so the body; *that* was not created for fornication, but for the Lord, and as God had raised Christ so should He raise the bodies of Christ's saints. And then—thus casually as it were in this mere passing reference—he lays down for all time the eternal principles which underlie the sacred duty of chastity. He tells them that their bodies, their members, are not their own, but Christ's;—that the union with Christ is destroyed by unions of uncleanness;—that sensuality is a sin against a man's own body;—that a Christian's body is not his own, but a temple of the indwelling spirit, and that he is not his own, but bought with a price. "Therefore," he says, feeling that he had now laid down truths which should be impregnable against all scepticism, "glorify God in your body."[1]

9. This paragraph, touching as it has done on the three topics of chastity, meats offered to idols, and the resurrection, introduces very naturally his answers to their inquiries on these subjects, and nobly wise they are in their charity, their wisdom, their large-heartedness. He is not speaking of marriage in the abstract, but of marriage regarded with reference to the near advent of Christ, and relating to the circumstances and conditions of the most corrupt city of ancient Greece. The Corinthian letter seems to have been written by those members of the Church who, partly it may be in indignant revolt against the views of the small faction which had adopted Antinomian opinions, seem to have regarded celibacy as the only perfect form of life. In the abstract, somewhat hesitatingly, and with the confession that here he is not sure of his ground, and is therefore offering no authoritative decision, St. Paul on the whole agrees with them.[2] "He quotes, with something of

---

[1] vi. 1—20. The words which follow in our version, καὶ ἐν τῷ πνεύματι ὑμῶν, ἅτινά ἐστι τοῦ Θεοῦ, are omitted in א, A, B, C, D, E, F, G.

[2] "If we compare the letter of Gregory the Great to Augustine (in Bede), in answer to inquiries not altogether dissimilar, respecting the Anglo-Saxon converts, we see at once how immeasurably more decisive and minute the Pope is than the Apostle" (Maurice, *Unity*, p. 423). The chapter is the best

approval, their dictum that the maiden life is the best,[1] and utters the wish that all had the same spiritual grace[2]—the *charisma* of continence —as he himself. But since this was not the case, as a permitted remedy against the universal prevalence of unchastity, he recommended (but not by way of distinct injunction) that Christians should live together, and with no long ascetic separations, in the married state.[3] As regards widowers[4] and widows their celibacy for the rest of their lives would be an honourable state, but immediate marriage would be better than long-continued desires.[5] Divorce had been discouraged by Christ himself, and on that analogy he pronounced against any voluntary dissolution of unions already existing between Pagans and Christians, since the children of such unions were holy, and therefore the unions holy, and since the believing wife or husband might win to the faith the unbelieving partner. The general rule which he wished all Christians to observe was that they should abide in the state in which they were called, whether circumcised or uncircumcised, since "circumcision is nothing, and uncircumcision is nothing, but keeping of the commandments of God."[6] Even if a Christian were a slave and might obtain his

manual for the *ductor dubitantium*, because it teaches him "that he must not give himself airs of certainty on points where certainty is not to be had" (*id.* 429). See Kuenen, *Profeten*, ii. 67 *sq.*, and Lord Lyttelton in *Contemp. Rev.* xxi. p. 917.

[1] vii. 1, καλὸν ἀνθρώπῳ γυναικὸς μὴ ἅπτεσθαι. St. Jerome's characteristic comment is that "if it is good for a man not to touch a woman, it must be bad to do so, and therefore marriage is, to say the least, inferior to celibacy." St. Paul's own distinct permission, and in some cases injunction, to marry, might have shown him how false and dangerous are the results which spring from the undue pressure of incidental words (Eph. v. 24; 1 Tim. ii. 15, &c.) St. Paul does not say "good" (ἀγαθόν), but "fair" (which he afterwards limits by the present need, ver. 26), as we might say, "there is in holy celibacy a certain moral beauty." Hence Jerome's "Suspecta est mihi bonitas rei quam magnitudo alterius mali malum cogit esse inferius" (*adv. Jovin.* i. 9) is a mistake. Celibacy is καλόν, but there are *some* for whom marriage is even κάλλιον. See for the use of καλός Matt. xviii. 8, xxvi. 24; 1 Tim. i. 8. It is curious to see the ascetic tendency at work in vii. 3 (ὀφειλομένην εὔνοιαν, and 5, τῇ νηστείᾳ καὶ, and σχολάσητε and συνέρχησθε for ἦτε). The true readings are found in א, A, B, C, D, F, though not followed in our version.

[2] vii. 7, θέλω, but in later years his deliberate decision (βούλομαι) was that younger widows should marry (1 Tim. v. 14).

[3] vii. 1—7.

[4] τοῖς ἀγάμοις, v. *supra*, i. pp. 79—82.

[5] Ver. 9, γαμῆσαι (aor.), ἢ πυροῦσθαι (pres.).

[6] 1 Cor. vii. 18, 19. The μὴ ἐπισπάσθω refers to a method of obliterating the sign of the covenant adopted by apostate Jews in times of persecution (1 Macc. i. 15; Jos. *Antt.* xii. 5, § 1), and which a Christian might be tempted

freedom, it would be better for him to brook slavery,[1] seeing that earthly relations were utterly insignificant when regarded from the spiritual standpoint.[2] As to virgins he could only give his opinion that, considering the present distress, and the nearness of the end, and the affliction which marriage at such a period brought inevitably in its train, it was better for them not to marry. Marriage, indeed, he told them distinctly, was no sin, but he wished to spare them the tribulation it involved; he did not wish them, now that the time was contracted,[3] and the fleeting show of the world was passing away, to bear the distracting burden of transient earthly and human cares, or to use the world to the full,[4] but to let their sole care be fixed on God.[5] If

to adopt to save him from that ridicule which the manners of ancient life brought upon Jews (Mart. xvii. 29). The Rabbis decided that one who had done this must be re-circumcised. R. Jehudah denied this, because of the danger; but the wise men replied that it had been frequently done with no injurious results in the days of Bar-Coziba (*Yebhamôth*, f. 72, 1; Buxtorf, *Lex. Chald.*, s. v. משוכים, *meshookím* = *recutiti*).

[1] 1 Cor. vii. 21, ἀλλ' εἰ καὶ δύνασαι ἐλεύθερος γενέσθαι, μᾶλλον χρῆσαι. I have taken δουλείᾳ as the word to be understood with Chrysostom, Theodoret, Luther, Bengel, De Wette, Meyer, &c.; cf. 1 Tim. vi. 2. I take this view—i. Because the whole argument turns on the desirability of *staying in the present condition*, whatever it is, with a view to the nearness of the day of the Lord. ii. Because this was the view arrived at also by the lofty Stoic moralists who, like Epictetus, knew that even a slave could live a noble life (Epictet. *Dissert.* iii. 26; Ench. x., xxxii.). Earthly conditions were but a χρῆσις φαντασιῶν; cf. Col. iii. 22. iii. Because St. Paul may have been thinking at the moment of the Christian slaves of Christian masters who would be treated as brothers. iv. Because χρῆσθαι rather implies the continuance of an existing than the acceptance of a new condition. Otherwise we can hardly imagine his giving such advice, since "a man is to abide in his calling if it be not hurtful to faith and morals" (Aug. *ad Gal.* ii. 11); but that could hardly be said of slavery. "Impudicitia . . . in servo necessitas" (Sen. *Controv.* iv., *Praef.*). "Enfants, ils grandissaient en désordre; vieillards, ils mouraient souvent dans la misère" (Wallon, *De l'Esclavage*, i. 332).

[2] vii. 10—24. Verses 17—24 are a little digression on the general principle that it is best to remain contentedly in our present lot. In ver. 23 he says, with a fine play on words, "You *are* slaves in one sense; do not *become* so in another."

[3] Ver. 29, συνεσταλμένος.

[4] Ver. 31, καταχρώμενοι; cf. ix. 12, 18. μεριμνᾷ, εὐπάρεδρον, ἀπερισπάστως; cf. Luke x. 41.

[5] Alone of nations the Jews implied the sanctity of marriage by every name that they gave it. *Kiddushin* from *kadosh*, "to sanctify;" *mekadesh*, "a bridegroom," &c. The phrase *Hare ath mekoodesheth lî*, "Behold thou art sanctified for me," is still addressed by the bridegroom to the bride (Rabbinowicz, *Legislat. Criminelle du Talmud*, p. 227).

then a father determined not to give his maiden daughter in marriage, he did well; but if a lover sought her hand, and circumstances pointed that way, he was not doing wrong in letting them marry.[1] Widows might re-marry if they liked, but in accordance with the principles which he had been laying down, he thought they would be happier if they did not. It was but his wish and advice; he asserted no Divine authority for it; yet in giving it he thought that he too had—as other teachers had claimed to have—the spirit of God.[2]

10. As to the pressing question—a question which bore on their daily life[3]—about meats offered to idols, he quotes, but only by way of refutation, their self-satisfied remark that they "all had knowledge"—knowledge at the best was a much smaller thing than charity, and the very claim to possess it was a proof of spiritual pride and ignorance. If they knew that an idol was nothing in the world, and their conscience as to this matter was quite clear and strong, it was no sin for them personally to eat of these sacrifices; but if others, whose consciences were weak, saw them feasting in idol temples, and were led by this ostentatious display of absence of scruple[4] to do by way of imitation what they themselves thought wrong, then this knowledge and liberty of theirs became a stumbling-block, an edification of ruin,[5] a source of death to the

---

[1] vii. 25. On the rights of Jewish fathers over their unmarried daughters see *Ketubhoth*, f. 46, 2. They were so absolute that he might even *sell* his daughter (*Kiddushin*, 3 b; *Ketubhoth*, 46 b). When however she reached the "flower of her age," she might refuse any husband given her before she was really *nubile*. Her refusal was technically called *miôn*, מיאון (*Yebhamoth*, 107 b). She *might* even be married while yet a *ketanal*—i.e., not yet twelve. When she reached that age she was called *naarah* (נערה), and six months later was held to have reached her full maturity, and become a *bagroth*, בגרות. See the Talmudic authorities in Rabbinowicz, *Trad. des Traités Synhedrin, &c., Legislation Criminelle du Talmud*, p. 214; Weill, *La Femme Juive*, pp. 11—14. On the care for widows, *id.* p. 72.

[2] vii. 1—40.

[3] To this day the Jewish slaughterer, who must pass a course of study, practically decides what is clean (*tahôr*) and unclean (*tâmê*). When he has discovered that an animal has no legal blemish he attaches to it a leaden seal with the word "lawful" (*kâshár*) on it; (Disraeli, *Genius of Judaism*, 156; *Dict. Bibl.* s. v. *Pharisees*; McCaul, *Old Paths*, 380—386, 396—402; v. *supra.* i. p. 434).

[4] Ver. 10. Such feasts were often in temples:—

"Hoc illis curia templum,
Hae sacris sedes epulis; hic ariete caeso
Perpetuis soliti Patres considere mensis." (*Æn.* vii. 174.)

Cf. Hdt. i. 31; Judg. ix. 27; 2 Kings xix. 37.

[5] Tert. *De Praescr. Haer.* 8.

conscience of a brother; and since thus to smite the sick conscience of a brother was a sin against Christ, he for one would never touch flesh again while the world lasted rather than be guilty of putting a fatal difficulty in a brother's path."[1]

11. And at this point begins a remarkable digression, which, though a digression, indirectly supported the position which some of his adversaries had impugned, and though personal in its details, is, in Paul's invariable manner, made subservient to eternal truths. They might object that by what he had said he was curtailing their liberty, and making the conscience of the weak a fetter upon the intelligence of the strong. Well, without putting their objection in so many words, he would show them that he practised what he taught. He, too, was free, and an Apostle, *their* Apostle at any rate, and had every right to do as the other Apostles did—the Desposyni, and Kephas himself—in expecting Churches to support them and their wives.[2] That right he even defends at some length, both by earthly analogies of the soldier, husbandman, and shepherd,[3] and by a happy Rabbinic midrash on the non-muzzling of the ox that treadeth out the corn;[4] and by the ordinary rules of gratitude for benefits received;[5] and by the ordinance of the Jewish Temple,[6] and the rule of Christ;[7] yet plain as the right was, and strenuously as he maintained it, he had never availed himself of it, and, whatever his enemies might say, he never would. He *must* preach the Gospel; he could not help himself; his one reward would be the power to boast that he had not claimed his rights to the full, but had made the Gospel free, and so removed a possible source of hindrance. Free, then, as he was, he had made himself a slave (as in one small particular he was asking them to do) for the sake of others; a slave to all, that he might gain the more; putting himself in their place, meeting

---

[1] viii. 1—13. Here as usual St. Paul shows himself transcendently superior to the Rabbis. In *Abhoda Zara*, f. 8, 1, R. Ishmael lays down the rule that if Israelites "outside the land" are asked to a Gentile funeral they "eat of the sacrifices of the dead," even if they take with them their own food and are waited on by their own servants. In confirmation of which hard and bigoted decision he refers to Ex. xxxiv. 15, from which he inferred that the acceptance of the invitation was equivalent to eating the sacrifice. R. Joehanan the Choronite would not eat *moist* olives, even in a time of famine, if handled by an *am haarets*, because they might have absorbed water, and so become unclean (*Yebhamoth*, f. 15, 2).

[2] I have here endeavoured to make clear the by no means obvious connection of thought which runs through these chapters. Possibly there may have been some accidental transposition. Those who consider 2 Cor. vi. 14—vii. 1, to be misplaced, find an apt space for it here.

[3] ix. 7.   [4] ix. 8—10.   [5] 11, 12.   [6] 13.   [7] 14.

their sympathies, and even their prejudices, half way ; becoming a Jew to the Jews, a legalist to legalists, without law to those without law (never, however, forgetting his real allegiance to the law of Christ),[1] weak to the weak, all things to all men in order by all means to save some. And if he thus denied himself, should not they also deny themselves?[2] In their Isthmian games each strove to gain the crown, and what toil and temperance they endured to win that fading wreath of pine! Paul did the same. He ran straight to the goal. He aimed straight blows, and not in feint, at the enemy;[3] nay, he even blackened his body with blows, and led it about as a slave,[4] lest in any way after acting as herald to others he himself should be rejected from the lists.[5]

If *he* had to strive so hard, could *they* afford to take things so easily? The Israelites had not found it so in the wilderness; they, too, were in a sense baptised unto Moses in the cloudy pillar and the Red Sea waves;[6] they, too, in a sense partook of the Eucharist in eating the heavenly manna, and drinking of the symbolic following rock;[7] yet how many[8] of them fell because of gluttony, and idolatry, and lust, and rebellion, and murmuring, and were awful warnings against overweening self-confidence! Yes, the path of duty was difficult, but not impossible, and no temptation was beyond human power to resist, because with the temptation God provided also *the* escape. Let them beware, then, of all

---

[1] He describes the concessions (συγκατάβασις) of love. "Paulus non fuit anomus, nedum antinomus" (Bengel). "The Lawless" is the name by which he is covertly calumniated in the spurious letter of Peter to James (Clementines, ch. ii.).

[2] In these paragraphs exhortations to the general duty of self-denial are closely mingled with the arguments in favour of the particular self-denial— concession to the weak—which he is urging throughout this section. "In the one party faith was not strong enough to beget a liberalising knowledge, not strong enough in the other to produce a brotherly love" (Kling).

[3] His was no sham fight (σκιαμαχία); he struck anything rather than the air (ὡς οὐκ ἀέρα δέρων). The E.V. renders as though it were οὐχ ὡς ἀέρα δέρων. Cf. Æn. v. 446, and Wetst. *ad loc.*

[4] ὑπωπιάζω; lit., "blacken with blows under the eyes, as in a fight."

[5] *Lividum facio corpus meum et in servitutem redigo*" (Iren. iv. 7.).

[6] ix. 1—27; κηρύξας, the Christian herald of the laws of the contest, is also a candidate in it.

[7] Fiduciâ verbi Mosis commiserant se aquis (Melancthon).

[8] x. 1—xi. 1. The division of chapters here stops a verse too short. On St. Paul's spiritualisation and practical application of Old Testament history, see *supra*, i. pp. 47—58. For other instances see v. 7; Gal. iv. 22; Heb. vii. &c.).

[9] x. 8. "Twenty-*three* thousand." Perhaps a σφάλμα μνημονικὸν for 24,000 (Num. xxv. 9).

this scornful indifference about idolatry. As the Eucharist united them in closest communion with Christ, and with one another, so that by all partaking of the one bread they became one body and one bread, so the partaking of Gentile sacrifices was a communion with demons.[1] The idol was nothing, as they had urged, but it *represented* an evil spirit;[2] and fellowship with demons was a frightful admixture with their fellowship in Christ, a dangerous trifling with their allegiance to God. He repeats once more that what is lawful is not always either expedient or edifying. Let sympathy, not selfishness, be their guiding principle. Over-scrupulosity was not required of them. They might buy in the market, they might eat, at the private tables of the heathen, what they would, and ask no questions; but if their attention was prominently drawn to the fact that any dish was part of an idol-offering, then—though they might urge that "the earth was the Lord's, and the fulness thereof," and that it was hard for them to be judged, or their liberty abridged in a purely indifferent act, which they might even perform in a religious spirit—still let them imitate Paul's own example, which he had just fully explained to them, which was, indeed, Christ's example, and consisted in being absolutely unselfish, and giving no wilful offence either to Jews or Gentiles, or the Church of God.

In this noble section of the Epistle, so remarkable for its tender consideration and its robust good sense, it is quite clear that the whole sympathies of St. Paul are theoretically with the strong, though he seems to feel a sort of *practical* leaning to the ascetic side. He does not,

---

[1] Cf. 2 Cor. vi. 14 *sq*. Evil spirits occupied a large part of the thoughts and teaching of Jewish Rabbis; *e.g.*, Lilith, Adam's first wife, was by him the mother of all demons (*Psachim*, f. 112, 2). As the Lord's Supper puts the Christian in mystical union with Christ, so partaking of idol feasts puts the partaker into symbolic allegiance to devils. Pfleiderer compares the Greek legend that by eating a fruit of the nether world a man is given over to it (*Paulinism*, i. 239).

[2] The heathen gods as idols were εἴδωλα, *Elilim*, supposititious, unreal, imaginary; but in another aspect they were demons. The Rabbis, in the same way, regard idols from two points of view—viz., as dead material things, and as demons. "Callest thou an idol a dog?" said "a philosopher" to Rabban Gamaliel. "An idol is really something." "What is it?" asked Gamaliel. "There was once a conflagration in our town," said the philosopher, "and the temple of the idol remained intact when every house was burnt down." At this remark the Rabban is silent (*Abhoda Zara*, f. 54, 2). Almost in the very words of St. Paul, Zonan once said to R. Akibha, "Both thou and I know that an idol hath nothing in it;" but he proceeds to ask how it is that miracles of healing are undoubtedly wrought at idol shrines? Akibha makes the healing a mere accidental coincidence with the time when the chastisements would naturally have been withdrawn (*Abhoda Zara*, f. 55, 1).

indeed, approve, under any circumstances, of an ostentatious, defiant, insulting liberalism. To a certain extent the prejudices—even the absurd and bigoted prejudices—of the weak ought to be respected, and it was selfish and wrong needlessly to wound them. It was above all wrong to lead them by example to do violence to their own conscientious scruples. But when these scruples, and this bigotry of the weak, became in their turn aggressive, then St. Paul quite sees that they must be discouraged and suppressed, lest weakness should lay down the law for strength. To tolerate the weak was one thing; to let them tyrannise was quite another. Their ignorance was not to be a limit to real knowledge; their purblind gaze was not to bar up the horizon against true insight; their slavish superstition was not to fetter the freedom of Christ. In matters where a little considerateness and self-denial would save offence, there the strong should give up, and do less than they might; but in matters which affected every day of every year, like the purchase of meat in the open market, or the acceptance of ordinary invitations, then the weak must not attempt to be obtrusive or to domineer. Some, doubtless, would use hard words about these concessions. They might charge St. Paul, as they had charged St. Peter, with violating the awful and fiery law. They might call him "the lawless one," or any other ugly nickname they liked; he was not a man to be "feared with bugs," or to give up a clear and certain principle to avoid an impertinent and senseless clamour. Had he been charged with controverting the wise and generous but local and temporary agreement which has been exalted into "the decree of the Council of Jerusalem," he would have quietly answered that that was but a recommendation addressed to a few predominantly Jewish Churches; that it did not profess to have any universal or permanent authority; and that he was now arguing the case on its own merits, and laying down principles applicable to every Church in which, as at Corinth, the Gentiles formed the most numerous element.

12. A minor point next claimed his attention. Some men, it appears, had sat with covered heads at their assemblies, and some women with uncovered heads, and they had asked his opinion on the matter. Thanking them for their kind expressions of respect for his rules and wishes, he at once decides the question on the highest principles. As to men it might well have seemed perplexing, since the Jewish and the Roman custom was to pray with covered, and the Greek custom to pray with uncovered, heads. St. Paul decides for the Greek custom. Christ is the head of the man, and man might therefore stand with unveiled head before God, and if he veiled his head he did it needless dishonour, because he abnegated the high glory which had been bestowed on him by Christ's incarnation. Not so with the woman. The head of the

woman is the man, and therefore in holy worship, in the presence of the Lord of her lord, she ought to appear with veiled head.[1] Nature itself taught that this was the right decision, giving to the woman her veil of hair, and teaching the instinctive lesson that a shorn head was a disgrace to a woman, as long hair, the sign of effeminacy, was a disgrace to a man. The unveiled head of the man was also the sign of his primeval superiority, and the woman having been the first to sin, and being liable to be seduced to sin, ought to wear "power on her head because of the angels."[2] Man and woman were indeed one in Christ, but for that very reason these distinctions of apparel should be observed. At any rate, St. Paul did not mean to enter into any dispute on the subject. If nature did not teach them that he had decided rightly, he could only refer them to the authority of custom, and that ought to be decisive, except to those who loved contentiousness.[3]

13. Then follows a stern rebuke—all the sterner for the self-restraint of its twice-repeated "I praise you not"—for the shameful selfishness and disorder which they had allowed to creep into the love-feasts which accompanied the Supper of the Lord—especially the gluttony, drunkenness, and ostentation of the wealthier members of the community, and the contemptuous indifference which they displayed to the needs and sensibilities of their poorer neighbours. The simple narrative of the institution and objects of the Supper of the Lord, which he had received from the Lord and delivered unto them, and the solemn warning of the danger which attended its profanation, and which was already exhibited in the sickness, feebleness, and deaths of many among them, is meant

---

[1] For *exousian*, see Stanley, Corinth. *ad loc.* The attempts to read *exiousa*, &c., are absurd. The word may be a mere colloquialism, and if so we may go far astray in trying to discover the explanation of it. If St. Paul invented it, it may be a Hebraism, or be meant to imply her own true power, which rests in accepting the sign of her husband's power over her. Chardin says that in Persia a veil is the sign that married women "are under subjection." Compare Milton's—

> "She as a veil down to the slender waist
> Her unadornèd golden tresses wore . . .
> As the vine waves its tendrils, which *implied*
> *Subjection*, but required with gentle sway,
> And by her yielded, by him best received."

See Tert. *De Vel. Virg.* 7, 17; and in illustration of Chrysostom's view there alluded to, see Tob. xii. 12; Ps. cxxxviii. 1 (LXX.); Eph. iii. 10.

[2] For the explanation of this allusion v. *supra*, i., Excursus IV.

[3] xi. 1—17. The last phrase—interesting as showing St. Paul's dislike to needless and disturbing innovations—is like the Rabbinic phrase, "Our Halacha is otherwise;" your custom is a *Thekanah*, or novelty, a חדש (*Babha Metsia*, f. 112).

to serve as a remedy against their gross disorders. He tells them that the absence of a discrimination (διάκρισις) in their own hearts had rendered necessary a judgment (κρίμα) which was mercifully meant as a training (παιδευόμεθα) to save them from final condemnation (κατάκριμα).[1] All minor matters about which they may have asked him, though they kept back the confession of this their shame, are left by the Apostle to be regulated by himself personally on his arrival.[2]

14. The next three chapters—of which the thirteenth, containing the description of charity, is the most glorious gem, even in the writings of St. Paul—are occupied with the answer to their inquiries about spiritual gifts. Amid the wild disorders which we have been witnessing we are hardly surprised to find that the Glossolalia had been terribly abused. Some, we gather—either because they had given the reins to the most uncontrollable excitement, and were therefore the impotent victims of any blasphemous thought which happened for the moment to sweep across the troubled horizon of their souls; or from some darkening philosophical confusion, which endeavoured to distinguish between the Logos and Him that was crucified, between the Man Jesus and the Lord Christ; or perhaps again from some yet unsolved Jewish difficulty about the verse "Cursed is he that hangeth on a tree;"[3]—amid their unintelligible utterances, had been heard to exclaim, *Anathema Iesous*, "Jesus is accursed;" and, having as yet very vague notions as to the true nature of the "gift of tongues," the Corinthians had asked Paul in great perplexity what they were to think of this? His direct answer is emphatic. When they were the ignorant worshippers of dumb idols they may have been accustomed to the false inspiration of the Pythia, or the Sibyl—the possessing mastery by a spiritual influence which expressed itself in the broken utterance, and streaming hair, and foaming lip, and which they might take to be the spirit of Python, or Trophonius, or Dis. But now he lays down the great principles of that "discernment of spirits," which should enable them to distinguish the rapt utterance of divine emotion from the mechanical and self-induced frenzy of feminine feebleness or hypocritical superstition. Whatever might be the external phenomena, the utterances

---

[1] These distinctions, so essential to the right understanding of the passage, are hopelessly obliterated in the E.V., which also swerves from its usual rectitude by rendering ἢ "*and*" instead of "*or*" in ver. 27, that it might not seem to sanction "communion in one kind." The "unworthily" in ver. 29 is perhaps a gloss, though a correct one. The κλώμενον, "broken," of ver. 24 seems to have been tampered with from dogmatic reasons. It is omitted in א, A, B, C, and D reads θρυπτόμενον, perhaps because of John xix. 36.

[2] xi. 17—34.

[3] Deut. xxi. 23.

of the Spirit were one in import. No man truly inspired by Him could say, "Anathema is Jesus;"[1] or uninspired by Him could say from the heart, "Jesus is the Lord." The *charismata*, or gifts, were different; the "administrations" of them, or channels of their working, were different; the operations, energies, or effects of them were different; but the source of them was One—one Holy Ghost, from whom they are all derived; one Lord, by whom all true ministries of them are authorised; one God, who worketh all their issues in all who possess them.[2] And this diverse manifestation of one Spirit, whether practical wisdom or scientific knowledge; whether the heroism of faith with its resultant gifts of healing, or energies of power, or impassioned utterance, or the ability to distinguish between true and false spiritual manifestations; or, again, kinds of tongues, or the interpretation of tongues,[3] were all subordinated to one sole end—edification. And, therefore, to indulge in any conflict between gifts, any rivalry in their display, was to rend asunder the unity which reigned supreme through this rich multiplicity; to throw doubt on the unity of their origin, to ruin the unity of their action. The gifts, whether healings, helps, governments, or tongues, occurred separately in different individuals; but each of these—whether Apostle, or prophet, or teacher—was but a baptised member of the one body of Christ; and by a fresh application of the old classic fable of Menenius Agrippa, he once more illustrates the fatal results which must ever spring from any strife between the body and its members.[4] Let them covet the better gifts—and tongues, in which they gloried most, he has studiously set last—and yet he is now about to point out to them a path more transcendent than any gifts. And then, rising on the wings

---

[1] Perhaps a gross and fearful abuse of the *principle* involved in 2 Cor. v. 16, as though people of spiritual intuitions were emancipated from the mere acknowledgment of Jesus. One could easily expect this from what we know of the "everlasting Gospel" in the thirteenth century, and of similar movements in different times of the Church (Maurice, *Unity*, 445). How startling to these *illuminati* to be told that the *highest* operation of the Spirit was to acknowledge Jesus!

[2] James i. 17.

[3] xii. 8—10. I have indicated, without dwelling on, the possible classification hinted at by the ἑτέρῳ (9, 10), as contrasted with the ᾧ μὲν and ἄλλῳ. " Knowledge (γνῶσις) as distinguished from "wisdom," deals with "mysteries" (xiii. 2; xv. 51; viii. *passim*).

[4] xii. 1—31. See a noble passage in Maurice, *Unity*, 469, sq., contrasting this conception with the *artificial* view of society in Hobbes' *Leviathan*. The absolute unity of Jews and Gentiles (ver. 13) exhibited in baptism and the Lord's Supper,—whence it resulted that the Jews would henceforth be but "a dwindling majority in the Messianic kingdom,"—was, with the Cross, the chief stumbling-block to the Jews.

of inspired utterance, he pours forth, as from the sunlit mountain heights, his glorious hymn to CHRISTIAN LOVE. Without it a man may speak with human, aye, and even angelic tongues, and yet have become but as booming gong or clanging cymbal.[1] Without it, whatever be his unction, or insight, or knowledge, or mountain-moving faith, a man is nothing. Without it he may dole away all his possessions, and give his body to be burned, yet is profited nothing. Then follows that description of love, which should be written in letters of gold on every Christian's heart—its patience, its kindliness; its freedom from envy, vaunting self-assertion,[2] inflated arrogance, vulgar indecorum; its superiority to self-seeking; its calm control of temper; its oblivion of wrong;[3] its absence of joy at the wrongs of others; its sympathy with the truth; its gracious tolerance; its trustfulness; its hope; its endurance.[4] Preaching, and tongues, and knowledge, are but partial, and shall be done away when the perfect has come; but love is a flower whose petals never fall off.[5] Those are but as the lispings, and emotions, and reasonings of a child; but this belongs to the perfect manhood, when we shall see God, not as in the dim reflection of a mirror, but face to face, and know him, not in part, but fully, even as now we are fully known. Faith, and hope, and love, are all three, not transient gifts, but abiding graces; but the greatest of these—the greatest because it is the root of the other two; the greatest because they are for ourselves, but love is for others; the greatest because neither in faith nor in hope is the entire and present fruition of heaven, but only in the transcendent and illimitable blessedness of "faith working by love;" the greatest because faith and hope are human, but love is essentially divine—the greatest of these is love.[6]

15. On such a basis, so divine, so permanent, it was easy to build the decision about the inter-relation of spiritual gifts; easy to see that preaching was superior to glossolaly; because the one was an intro-

---

[1] "Ephyreïa aera" (Virg. *Georg.* ii. 264); Corinthian brass (Plin. *H. N.* 34, 2, 3).

[2] Ver. 4, οὐ περπερεύεται. *Perperus*, "a braggart." "Heavens! how I *showed off* (ἐνεπερπερευσάμην) before my new auditor, Pompeius!" (Cic. *ad Att.* i. 14).

[3] xiii. 5, "does not reckon the wrong." The opposite of "all his faults observed, *set in a note-book.*"

[4] Ver. 7, στέγει means "bears," "endures." Its classic meaning is "holds water;" and this is also true of love with its gracious reticences and suppressions, οὐδὲν βάναυσον ἐν ἀγάπῃ (Clem. *Rom.*).

[5] Ver. 8, οὐδέποτε ἐκπίπτει. So we may understand the metaphor, as in James i. 11, ἐξέπεσε (Isa. xxviii. 4); others prefer the classic sense, "is never hissed off the stage;" has its part to play on the stage of eternity.

[6] xii. 31—xiii. 13.

spective and mostly unintelligible exercise, the other a source of general advantage. The speaker with tongues, unless he could also interpret, or unless another could interpret for him his inarticulate ecstacies, did but utter indistinct sounds, like the uncertain blaring of a trumpet or the confused discordances of a harp or flute. Apart from interpretation "tongues" were a mere talking into air. They were as valueless, as completely without significance, as the jargon of a barbarian. Since they were so proud of these displays, let them pray for ability to interpret their rhapsodies. The prayer, the song of the spirit, should be accompanied by the assent of the understanding, otherwise the "tongue" was useless to any ordinary worshipper, nor could they claim a share in what was said by adding their Amen[1] to the voice of Eucharist. Paul, too—and he thanked God that he was capable of this deep spiritual emotion—was more liable to the impulse of glossolaly than any of them;[2] yet so little did he value it—we may even say so completely did he disparage it as a part of public worship—that after telling them that he had rather speak five intelligible words to teach others than ten thousand words in "a tongue,"[3] he bids them not to be little children in intelligence, but to be babes in vice, and quotes to them, in accordance with that style of adaptation with which his Jewish converts would have been familiar, a passage of Isaiah,[4] in which Jehovah threatens the drunken priests of Jerusalem that since they would not listen to the simple preaching of the prophet, he would teach them— and that, too, ineffectually—by conquerors who spoke a tongue which they did not understand. From this he argues that "tongues" are not meant for the Church at all, but are a sign to unbelievers; and that, if exercised in the promiscuous way which was coming into vogue at Corinth, would only awaken, even in unbelievers, the contemptuous remark that they were a set of insane fanatics, whereas the effect of preaching might be intense conviction, prostrate worship, and an acknowledgment of the presence of God among them.[5]

---

[1] xiv. 16, τῷ σῷ ἐρεῖ τὸ 'Αμήν. "He who says Amen is greater than he who blesses" (*Berachôth*, viii. 8).

[2] Why does he thank God for a gift which he is rating so low as an element of worship? Because the highest value of it was *subjective*. He who was capable of it was, at any rate, not dead; his heart was not petrified; he was not past feeling; he could feel the direct influence of the Spirit of God upon *his* spirit.

[3] "Rather half of ten of the edifying sort than a thousand times ten of the other" (Besser).

[4] xiv. 21, ἐν τῷ νόμῳ. So Ps. lxxxii. 6 is quoted as "the Law" in John x. 34. On this passage v. *supra*, i. p. 52.

[5] xiv. 1—26.

16. The disorders, then, in the Corinthian Church had sprung from the selfish struggle of each to show off his own special gift, whether tongue, or psalm, or teaching, or revelation. If they would bear in mind that edification was the object of worship, such scenes would not occur. Only a few at a time, therefore, were to speak with tongues, and only in case some one could interpret, otherwise they were to suppress the impulse. Nor were two people ever to be preaching at the same time. If the rivalry of unmeaning sounds among the glossolalists had been fostered by some Syrian enthusiast, the less intolerable but still highly objectionable disorder of rival preachers absorbed in the "egotism of oratory" was an abuse introduced by the admirers of Apollos. In order to remedy this, he lays down the rule that if one preacher was speaking, and another felt irresistibly impelled to say something, the first was to cease. It was idle to plead that they could not control themselves. The spirits which inspire the true prophet are under the prophet's due control, and God is the author, not of confusion but of peace. Women were not to speak in church at all; and if they wanted any explanations they must ask their husbands at home. This was the rule of all Churches, and who were they that they should alter these wise and good regulations? Were they the earliest Church? Were they the only Church? A true preacher, a man truly spiritual, would at once recognise that these were the commands of the Lord; and to invincible bigotry and obstinate ignorance Paul has no more to say. The special conclusion is that preaching is to be encouraged, and glossolaly not forbidden, provided that it did not interfere with the general rule that everything is to be done in decency and order. It is, however, extremely probable that the almost contemptuous language of the Apostle towards "the tongues"—a manifestation at first both sacred and impressive, but liable to easy simulation and grave abuse, and no longer adapted to serve any useful function—tended to suppress the display of emotion which he thus disparaged. Certain it is that from this time forward we hear little or nothing of "the gift of tongues." It—or something which on a lower level closely resembled it—has re-appeared again and again at different places and epochs in the history of the Christian Church. It seems, indeed, to be a natural consequence of fresh and overpowering religious emotion. But it can be so easily imitated by the symptoms of hysteria, and it leads to consequences so disorderly and deplorable, that except as a rare and isolated phenomenon it has been generally discountenanced by that sense of the necessity for decency and order which the Apostle here lays down, and which has been thoroughly recognised by the calm wisdom of the Christian Church. The control and suppression of the impassioned emotion which expressed itself in glossolaly is practically

its extinction, though this in no way involves the necessary extinction of the inspiring convictions from which it sprang.[1]

17. Then follows the immortal chapter in which he confirms their faith in the resurrection, and removes their difficulties respecting it. If they would not nullify their acceptance of the Gospel in which they stood, and by which they were saved, they must hold fast the truths which he again declares to them, that Christ died for our sins, was buried, and had been raised the third day. He enumerates His appearances to Kephas, to the Twelve, to more than five hundred at once of whom the majority were yet living, to James, to all the Apostles; last, as though to the abortive-born, even to himself.[2] "For I am the least of the Apostles, who am not adequate to be called an Apostle, because I persecuted the Church of God. Yet by the grace of God I am what I am, and His grace towards me has not proved in vain, but more abundantly than all of them I laboured—yet not I, but the grace of God which was with me; whether, then, it be I or they, so we preach, and so ye believed."[3]

If, then, Christ had risen, whence came the monstrous doctrine of some of them that there was no resurrection of the dead? The two truths stood or fell together. If Christ had not risen, their faith was after all a chimera, their sins were unforgiven, their dead had perished; and if their hope in Christ only was a hope undestined to fruition, they were the most pitiable of men. But since Christ had risen, we also shall rise, and as all men share the death brought in by Adam, so all shall be quickened unto life in Christ.[4] But each in his own rank. The firstfruits Christ; then His redeemed at His appearing, when even death, the last enemy, shall be reduced to impotence; then the end, when Christ shall give up His mediatorial kingdom, and God shall be all in all. And if there were no resurrection, what became of their

---

[1] xiv. 26—40.
[2] xv. 8, τῷ ἐκτρώματι (cf. Num. xii. 12, LXX.; see also Ps. lviii. 8).
[3] xv. 1—12 (cf. Epict. Diss. iii. 1, 36).
[4] "Even so *in Christ* shall *all* be made alive." Here is one of the antinomies which St. Paul leaves side by side. On the one hand, "life in Christ" is co-extensive with "death in Adam;" on the other, only those who are "in Christ" shall be made alive. Life here can hardly mean less than salvation. But it is asserted of all universally, and Adam and Christ are contrasted as death and life. Certainly in this and other places the Apostle's language suggests the natural conclusion that "the principle which has come to actuality in Christ is of sufficient energy to quicken all men for the resurrection to the blessed life" (Baur, *Paul.* ii. 219). But if we desire to arrive at a rigid eschatological doctrine we must compare one passage with another. See Excursus II., "Antinomies in St. Paul's Writings."

practice of getting themselves baptised for the dead?[1] And why did the Apostles brave the hourly peril of death? By his boast of them in Christ he asseverates that his life is a daily dying. And if, humanly speaking, he fought beasts at Ephesus,[2] what would be the gain to him if the dead rise not? The Epicureans would then have some excuse for their base sad maxim, "Let us eat and drink, for to-morrow we die." Was it intercourse with the heathen that produced their dangerous unbelief? Oh, let them not be deceived! let them beware of this dangerous leaven! "Base associations destroy excellent characters." Let them awake at once to righteousness out of their drunken dream of disbelief, and break off the sinful habits which it engendered! Its very existence among them was an ignorance of God, for which they ought to blush.[3]

And as for material difficulties, Paul does not merely fling them aside with a "Senseless one!" but says that the body dies as the seed dies, and our resurrection bodies shall differ as the grain differs with the nature of the sown seed, or as one star differs from another in glory. The corruption, the indignity, the strengthlessness of the mortal body, into which at birth the soul is sown, shall be replaced by the incorruption, glory, power of the risen body. The spiritual shall follow the natural; the heavenly image of Christ's quickening spirit replace the earthly image of Adam, the mere living soul.[4] Thus in a few simple words does St. Paul sweep away the errors of Christians about the physical identity of the resurrection-body with the actual corpse, which have given rise to so many scornful materialist objections. St. Paul does not say with Prudentius—

"Me nec dente, nec ungue
Fraudatum redimet patefacti fossa sepulcri;"

but that "flesh and blood" cannot enter into the kingdom of God;

---

[1] Perhaps this is only a passing *argumentum ad hominem*; if so it shows St. Paul's large tolerance that he does not here pause to rebuke so superstitious a practice. It needs no proof that "baptism for the dead" *means* "baptism for the dead," and not the meanings which commentators put into it, who go to Scripture to support tradition, not to seek for truth.

[2] Of course metaphorically, or he would have mentioned it in 2 Cor. xi. His three points in 29—34 are—if there be no resurrection (1) why do some of you get yourselves baptised to benefit your relatives who have died unbaptised? (2) Why do we live in such self-sacrifice? (3) What possibility would there be of resisting Epicurean views of life among men in general?

[3] xv. 12—35.

[4] xv. 35—50. In this chapter there is the nearest approach to *natural* (as apart from *architectural* and *agonistic*) metaphors. Dean Howson (*Charact. of St. P.* 6) points out that there is more imagery from natural phenomena in the single Epistle of St. James than in all St. Paul's Epistles put together.

that at Christ's coming the body of the living Christian will pass by transition, that of the dead Christian by resurrection, into a heavenly, spiritual, and glorious body.[1]

The body, then, was not the same, but a spiritual body; so that all coarse material difficulties were idle and beside the point. In one moment, whether quick or dead, at the sounding of the last trumpet, we should be changed from the corruptible to incorruption, from the mortal to immortality. "Then shall be fulfilled the promise that is written, Death is swallowed up into victory. Where, O death, is thy sting? where, O death, thy victory?"[2] The sting of death is sin, the power of sin is the law. But thanks be to God, who is giving us the victory through our Lord Jesus Christ. Therefore, my brethren beloved, prove yourselves steadfast, immovable, abounding in the work of the Lord always, knowing that your toil is not fruitless in the Lord."[3]

---

[1] Ver. 52. "The *dead* shall be raised, *we* (the living) shall be changed." Into the question of the intermediate state St. Paul, expecting a near coming of Christ, scarcely enters. Death was κοιμᾶσθαι, resurrection was συνδοξασθῆναι. Did he hold that there was an intermediate provisional building of God's which awaited us in heaven after the stripping off of our earthly tent? The nearest allusion to the question may be found in 2 Cor. v. 1—4 (Pfleiderer, i. 261).

[2] θάνατε (not ᾅδη), א, A, B, C, D, E, F, G.

[3] xv. 50—58. "It is very evident that the Apostle here regards the whole history of the world and men as the scene of the conflict of two principles, one of which has sway at first, but is then attacked and conquered, and finally destroyed by the other. The first of these principles is death; the history of the world begins with this, and comes to a close when death, and with death the dualism of which history is the development, has entirely disappeared from it" (Baur, *Paul.* ii. 225). In this chapter the only resurrection definitely spoken of is a resurrection "in Christ." On the *final* destiny of those who are now perishing (ἀπολλύμενοι) St. Paul never touches with any definiteness. But he speaks of the final conquest of death, the last enemy—where "death" seems to be used in its deeper spiritual and scriptural sense; he says (Rom. viii. 19—23) that "the whole creation (πᾶσα ἡ κτίσις) shall be delivered from the bondage of corruption into the glorious liberty of the children of God;" he contrasts the universality of man's disobedience with the universality of God's mercy; he says where sin abounded there grace did *much more* abound (Rom. v. 20); he speaks of God's *will* to bestow universal favour commensurate with universal sin (Rom. xi. 32); he dwells on the solution of dualism in unity and the tending of all things into God (εἰς αὐτὸν τὰ πάντα, Rom. xi. 30—36); his whole splendid philosophy of history consists in showing (Rom. Gal. *passim*) that each lower and sadder stage and moment of man's condition is a necessary means of achieving the higher; and he says that God, at last, "shall be all in all." Whatever antinomies may be left unsolved, let Christians duly weigh these truths.

So ends this glorious chapter—the hope of millions of the living, the consolation for the loss of millions of the dead. And if, as we have seen, Paul was the most tried, in this life the most to be pitied of men, yet what a glorious privilege to him in his trouble, what a glorious reward to him for all his labours and sufferings, that he should have been so gifted and enlightened by the Holy Spirit as to be enabled thus, incidentally as it were, to pour forth words which rise to a region far above all difficulties and objections, and which teach us to recognise in death, not the curse, but the coronation, not the defeat, but the victory, not the venomous serpent, but the veiled angel, not the worst enemy, but the greatest birthright of mankind. Not by denunciation of unorthodoxy, not by impatient crushing of discussion, not by the stunning blows of indignant authority, does he meet an unbelief even so strange, and so closely affecting the very fundamental truths of Christianity, as a denial of the resurrection; but by personal appeals, by helpful analogies, by calm and lofty reasoning, by fervent exhortations, by the glowing eloquence of inspired convictions. Anathema would have been worse than useless; at excommunication he does not so much as hint; but the refutation of perilous error by the presentation of ennobling truth has won, in the confirmation of the faith, in the brightening of the hope of centuries, its high and permanent reward.

Let us also observe that St. Paul's inspired conviction of the Resurrection rests, like all his theology, on the thought that the life of the Christian is a life "in Christ." On Plato's fancies about our reminiscence of a previous state of being he does not touch; but for the unfulfilled ideas on which Plato builds he offers the fulfilled ideal of Christ. He founds no arguments, as Kant does, on the failure of mankind to obey the "categorical imperative" of duty; but he points to the Sinless Man. He does not follow the ancients in dwelling on false analogies like the butterfly; nor is he misled like his very ablest contemporaries and successors by the then prevalent fable of the Phœnix. He does not argue from the law of continuity, or the indestructibility of atoms, or the permanence of force, or the general belief of mankind. But his main thought, his main argument is—Ye are Christ's, and Christ is risen; if ye died with him to sin, ye shall also live with him to righteousness here, and therefore to glory hereafter. The life ye now live is lived in the faith of the Son of God, and being eternal in its very nature, contains in itself the pledge of its own inextinguishable vitality. He teaches us alike in the phenomena of human sin and of human sanctity to see the truth of the Resurrection. For the forgiveness of sin Christ died; for the reward and the hope and the support of holiness he lives at the right hand of God. He does not so much *argue in favour of* the Resurrection as *represent* it, and make us feel its force. The Christian's resurrection from the death of sin to the life of righteousness transcends and involves the lesser miracle of his resurrection from the sleep of death to the life of heaven.

18. The Epistle closes with practical directions and salutations. He establishes a weekly offertory, as he had done in Galatia, for the saints at Jerusalem. He tells them that he will either—should it be worth while—take it himself to Jerusalem, or entrust it with commendatory letters from them, to any delegates whom they might approve. He announces without comment his altered intention of not taking them *en route* as he went to Macedonia, as well as on his return, and so giving them a double visit, but tells them that he should come to them by way of Macedonia, and probably spend the winter with them, that they might help him on his further journey; and that he means to remain in Ephesus till Pentecost, because a great door is open to him, and there are many adversaries.

Timothy will perhaps come to them. If so they are not to despise his youth, or alarm his timidity by opposition, but to aid his holy work, and to help him peacefully on his way to the Apostle with those who accompanied him. They had asked that Apollos might visit them. St. Paul had done his best to second their wishes, but Apollos—though holding out hopes of a future visit—declined to come at present, actuated in all probability by a generous feeling that, under present circumstances, his visit would do more harm than good.[1]

Then a brief vivid exhortation. "Watch! stand in the faith! be men! be strong! let all your affairs be in love."

Then a few words of kindly eulogy of Stephanas, Fortunatus, and Achaicus—of whom Stephanas had been the earliest Achaian convert—who devoted themselves to ministry to the saints, and by their visit had consoled *him* for his absence from them, and *them* by eliciting this Epistle. He urges them to pay due regard and deference to all such true labourers. It is not impossible that these few words may have been added by an afterthought, lest the Corinthians should suppose that it was from these—especially if they were of Chloe's household—that St. Paul had heard such distressing accounts of the Church, and so should be inclined to receive them badly on their return. Then the final autograph salutation :—

"The salutation of me, Paul, with my own hand;" but before he can pen the final benediction, there is one more outburst of strong and indignant feeling. "If any one loveth not the Lord, let him be

---

[1] xvi. 12, θέλημα does not mean "Apollos' will," but (probably) "God's will."

Anathema;[1] Maranatha, the Lord is near. The grace of our Lord Jesus Christ be with you." That would have been the natural ending, but he had had so much to reprobate, so many severe things to say, that to show how unabated, in spite of all, was his affection for them, he makes the unusual addition, " My love be with you all in Christ Jesus. Amen."[2] So ends the longest and, in some respects, the grandest and most characteristic of his Epistles. He had suppressed indeed all signs of the deep emotion with which it had been written; but when it was despatched he dreaded the results it might produce—dreaded whether he should have said too much; dreaded the possible alienation, by any over-severity, of those whom he had only desired to win. His own soul was all quivering with its half-stifled thunder, and he was afraid lest the flash which he had sent forth should scathe too deeply the souls at which it had been hurled. He would even have given much to recall it,[3] and awaited with trembling anxiety the earliest tidings of the manner in which it would be received. But God overruled all for good; and, indeed, the very writings which spring most naturally and spontaneously from a noble and sincere emotion, are often those that produce the deepest impression upon the world, and are less likely to be resented—at any rate, are more likely to be useful—than the tutored and polished utterances which are carefully tamed down into the limits of correct conventionality. Not only the Church of Corinth, but the whole world, has gained from the intensity of the Apostle's feelings, and the impetuous spontaneity of the language in which they were expressed.

[1] I cannot pretend to understand what St. Paul exactly meant by this. Commentators call it an "imprecation;" but such an "imprecation" does not seem to me like St. Paul. Anathema is the Hebrew *cherem* of Lev. xxvii. 29; Num. xxi. 2, 3 (*Hormah*); Josh. vi. 17. But the later Jews used it for "excommunication," whether of the temporary sort (*nidui*) or the severe. The severest form was called *Shematha*. The Fathers mostly take it to mean "excommunication" here, and in Gal. i. 8, 9, and some see in *Maranatha* an allusion to *Shem atha* (the name cometh). But probably these are after-thoughts. It is a sudden expression of deep feeling; and that it is less terrible than it sounds we may hope from 1 Cor. v. 5; 1 Tim. i. 20, where the object is amendment, not wrath. For "anathematise" see Matt. xxvi. 74; Acts xxiii. 12.

[2] The subscription is, as usual, spurious. It arose from a mistaken inference from xvi. 5. The letter itself shows that it was written in Ephesus (xvi. 8), and though Stephanas, Fortunatus, and Achaicus may have been its bearers, Timotheus could not have been.

[3] 2 Cor. vii. 8.

CHAPTER XXXIII.

SECOND EPISTLE TO THE CORINTHIANS.

"There are three crowns: the crown of the Law, the crown of the Priesthood, and the crown of Royalty: but the crown of a good name mounts above them all."—Pirke Abhôth, iv. 19.

WHEN St. Paul left Ephesus he went straight to Troas, with the same high motive by which he was always actuated—that of preaching the Gospel of Christ.[1] He had visited the town before, but his stay there had been shortened by the imploring vision of the man of Macedon, which had decided his great intention to carry the Gospel into Europe. But though his preaching was now successful, and "a door was opened for him in the Lord,"[2] he could not stay there from extreme anxiety. "He had no rest for his spirit, because he found not Titus his brother." Titus had been told to rejoin him at Troas; but perhaps the precipitation of St. Paul's departure from Ephesus had brought him to that town earlier than Titus had expected, and, in the uncertain navigation of those days, delays may easily have occurred. At any rate, he did not come, and Paul grew more and more uneasy, until in that intolerable oppression of spirit he felt that he could no longer continue his work, and left Troas for Macedonia. There, at last, he met Titus, who relieved his painful tension of mind by intelligence from Corinth, which, although chequered, was yet on the main point favourable. From Titus he learnt that

---

[1] 2 Cor. ii. 12, 13.

[2] The use of this expression by St. Luke is one of the many interesting traces of his personal intercourse with St. Paul. (See 1 Cor. xvi. 9.)

his change of plan about the visit had given ground for unfavourable criticism,[1] and that many injurious remarks on his character and mode of action had been industriously disseminated, especially by one Jewish teacher.[2] Still, the effect of the first Epistle had been satisfactory. It had caused grief, but the grief had been salutary, and had issued in an outburst of yearning affection, lamentation, and zeal.[3] Titus himself had been received cordially, yet with fear and trembling.[4] The offender denounced in his letter had been promptly and even severely dealt with,[5] and all that St. Paul had said to Titus in praise of the Church had been justified by what he saw.[6] Accordingly, he again sent Titus to them,[7] to finish the good work which he had begun, and with him he sent the tried and faithful brother " whose praise is in the Gospel through all the Churches;"[8] and this time Titus was not only ready but even anxious to go.[9]

In what town of Macedonia St. Paul had met with Titus, and also with Timothy, we do not know. Great uncertainty hangs over the details of their movements, and indeed all the events of this part of the journey are left in obscurity: we can only conjecture that during it St. Paul had even travelled as far as Illyricum.[10] At some point in the journey, but probably not at Philippi, as the subscription to the Epistle says—because, as is evident from the Epistle itself, he had visited most of the Churches of Macedonia,[11]—

---

[1] 2 Cor. i. 17.
[2] iii. 1; v. 11; vii. 2, 3; x. 10; xi. 18—20.
[3] vii. 6—11.
[4] vii. 13, 15.
[5] ii. 5—10.
[6] vii. 14.
[7] viii. 6.
[8] viii. 18, 23.
[9] viii. 17. That there was a slight unwillingness the first time seems to be shown by the way in which St. Paul felt himself obliged to encourage him in his mission.
[10] Rom. xv. 19.

2 Cor. viii. 1; ix. 2. Philippi, on the other hand, would be the first city which he would reach.

he wrote his Second Epistle to the Corinthians. From it we learn that, whatever may have been in this region the special nature of his affliction—whether grievous sickness, or external persecutions, or inward anxieties, or apparently all of these combined—his stay in Macedonia had suffered from the same overwhelming distress which had marked the close of his residence in Ephesus, and which had driven him out of Troas.[1] The Churches were themselves in a state of affliction, which Paul had naturally to share,[2] and he describes his condition as one of mental and physical prostration: "Our flesh had no rest, but we are troubled on every side; from without fightings, from within fears."[3] And this helps to explain to us the actual phenomena of the letter written amid such circumstances. If HOPE is the key-note of the Epistle to the Thessalonians, JOY of that to the Philippians, FAITH of that to the Romans, and HEAVENLY THINGS of that to the Ephesians, AFFLICTION is the one predominant word in the Second Epistle to the Corinthians.[4] The Epistles to the Thessalonians contain his views on the Second Advent; the Epistle to the Galatians is his trumpet-note of indignant defiance to retrograding Judaisers; the Epistle to the Romans is the systematic and, so to speak, scientific statement of his views on what may be called, in modern language, the scheme of salvation; the Epistle to the Philippians is his outpouring of tender and gladdened affection to his most beloved converts; the First Epistle to the Corinthians shows us how he applied the principles of Christianity to daily life in dealing with the flagrant aberrations of a most unsatisfactory Church; his Second Epistle to the Corinthians opens a window into the very emotions of his heart, and is the agitated self-defence of a

---

[1] viii. 2. [2] iv. 8—12. [3] vii. 5.
[4] θλίψις, θλίβομαι (2 Cor. i. 4, 6, 8; ii. 4; iv. 8; viii. 13).

wounded and loving spirit to ungrateful and erring, yet not wholly lost or wholly incorrigible souls."[1]

And this self-defence was not unnecessary. In this Epistle we find St. Paul for the first time openly confronting the Judaising reaction which assumed such formidable dimensions, and threatened to obliterate every distinctive feature of the Gospel which he preached. It is clear that in some of the Churches which he had founded there sprang up a Judaic party, whose hands were strengthened by commendatory letters from Jerusalem, and who not only combated his opinions, but also grossly abused his character and motives. By dim allusions and oblique intimations we trace their insidious action, and in this Epistle we find ourselves face to face with them and their unscrupulous opposition. It differs greatly from the one that preceded it. St. Paul is no longer combating the folly of fancied wisdom, or the abuse of true liberty. He is no longer occupied with the rectification of practical disorders and theoretical heresies. He is contrasting his own claims with those of his opponents, and maintaining an authority which had been most rudely and openly impugned.

It is not impossible that the attack had been suggested by St. Paul's sentence on the incestuous offender.[2] His

---

[1] "The Apostle pours out his heart to them, and beseeches them, in return, not for a cold, dry, critical appreciation of his eloquence, or a comparison of his with other doctrines, but the sympathy of churchmen, if not the affection of children." Parts of the Epistle, taken alone, might seem to be "almost painfully personal," and we "might have thought that the man had got the better of the ambassador. But when we learn how essentially the man and the ambassador are inseparable, then the 'folly,' the boasting, the shame, are not mere revelations of character, but revelations of the close bonds by which one man is related to another" (Maurice, *Unity*, 488).

[2] The theory that the offender of the second Epistle is an entirely different person, alluded to in some lost intermediate letter, seems to me untenable, in spite of the consensus of eminent critics (De Wette, Bleek, Credner, Olshausen, Neander, Ewald, &c.), who, in some form or other, adopt such a hypothesis. I see nothing inconsistent with the older view either in the tone of 1 Cor., or

case seems to have originated a quarrel among the Corinthian Christians, of whom some sided with him and some with his father. It is clear upon the face of things that we do not know all the circumstances of the case, since it is all but inconceivable that, had there been no extenuating fact, he should have found defenders for a crime which excited the horror of the very heathen. Even those who placed sensuality on the same level as eating meats offered to idols, and therefore regarded it as a matter of indifference—whose view St. Paul so nobly refutes in his first Epistle—could not have sided with this person if there were no palliating element in his offence. And, indeed, if this had not been the case, he would scarcely have ventured to continue in Church membership, and to be, with his injured father, a frequenter of their love-feasts and partaker in their sacraments. It may be quite true, and indeed the allusions to him in the Second Epistle show, that he was weak rather than wicked. But even this would have been no protection to him in a wrong on which Gallio himself would have passed a sentence of death or banishment, and which the Mosaic law had punished with excision from the congregation.[1] There must therefore have been something which could be urged against the heinousness of his transgression, and St. Paul has distinctly to tell the Corinthians that there was no personal feeling mixed up with his decision.[2] His words had evidently implied that the Church was to be assembled, and there, with his spirit present with them, to hand him over to Satan, so that judgment might come on his body

---

the effect it produced, or in St. Paul's excitement, or in the movements of Titus, or in the language about the offence. But I have not space to enter more fully into the controversy.

[1] Lev. xvii. 8; xx. 11; Deut. xxvii. 20.
[2] 2 Cor. vii. 11, 12.

for the salvation of his soul. That is what he practically tells the Church to do. Did they do it? It seems to be at least doubtful. That they withdrew from his communion is certain; and the very threat of excommunication which hung over him—accompanied, as he and the Church thought that it would be, with supernatural judgments—was sufficient to plunge him into the depths of misery and penitence. Sickness and death were at this time very prevalent among the Corinthian converts, and St. Paul told them that this was a direct punishment of their profanation of the Lord's Supper. It is clear that the offender was not contumacious, and in his Second Epistle St. Paul openly forgives him, and remits his sentence, apparently on the ground that the Corinthians had already done so. In fact, since the desired end of the man's repentance, and the purging of the Church from all complicity with or immoral acquiescence in his crime had been attained without resorting to extreme measures, St. Paul even exhorts the Corinthians to console and forgive the man, and, in fact, restore him to full Church membership. Still, it does seem as if they had not exactly followed the Apostle's advice, and as if the party opposed to him had, so to speak, turned upon him and repudiated his authority. They said that he had not come, and he would not come. It was all very well to write stern and threatening letters, but it was not by letters, but by the exercise of miraculous power, that Kephas had avenged the wrongs of the Church and of the Spirit on Ananias and Sapphira, and on Simon Magus. Paul could not do this. How could it be expected of a man so mean of aspect, so vacillating in purpose, so inefficient in speech? It was not Paul who had been chosen as the twelfth Apostle, nor was he an Apostle at all. As the abuses among his followers showed that his teaching was dangerous, so his inability to rectify them was a proof that his authority was a delusion. The very fact that he had claimed no support from his converts only marked how insecure he felt his position to be. What the Church really wanted was the old stringency of the Mosaic Law; some one from Jerusalem; some true Apostle, with his wife, who would rule them with a real supremacy, or at least some emissary from James and the brethren of the Lord, to preach "another Gospel," more accordant with the will of Jesus Himself.[1] Paul, they implied, had never known Jesus, and misrepresented Him altogether;[2] for He had said that no jot or tittle of the law should pass, and that the children's bread should not be cast to dogs. Paul preached himself,[3] and indeed seemed to be hardly responsible for what he did preach. He was half demented; and yet there was some method in his madness, which showed itself partly in self-importance and partly in avarice, both of which were very injurious to the interests of his followers.[4] What, for instance, could be more guileful and crafty than his entire conduct about this collection which he was so suspiciously eager to set on foot?[5] He had ordered them to get up a subscription in his first letter;[6] had, in answer to their inquiries,[7] directed that it should be gathered, as in the Galatian Churches, by a weekly offertory, and had, since this, sent Titus to stimulate zeal in the matter. Now certainly a better emissary could not possibly have been chosen, for

[1] See Hausrath, p. 420.
[2] 2 Cor. xi. 4.
[3] 2 Cor. xii. 5.
[4] v. 13, εἴτε γὰρ ἐξέστημεν xi. 1, ὄφελον ἠνείχεσθέ μου μικρόν τι τῆς ἀφροσύνης· 16, μή τίς με δόξῃ ἄφρονα εἶναι (cf. xii. 6).
[5] xii. 16, ὑπάρχων πανοῦργος δόλῳ ὑμᾶς ἔλαβον. Evidently the quotation of a slander, which he proceeds to refute.
[6] The one no longer extant.
[7] 1 Cor. xvi. 1—4.

Titus was himself a Greek, and therefore well fitted to manage matters among Greeks; and yet had visited Jerusalem, so that he could speak from ocular testimony of the distress which was prevalent among the poorer brethren; and had further been present at the great meeting in Jerusalem at which Paul and Barnabas had received the special request to be mindful of the poor. Yet even this admirably judicious appointment, and the transparent independence and delicacy of mind which had made Paul —with an insight into their character which, as events showed, was but too prescient—entirely to refuse all support from them, was unable to protect him from the coarse insinuation that this was only a cunning device to hide his real intentions, and give him a securer grasp over their money. Such were the base and miserable innuendoes against which even a Paul had deliberately to defend himself! Slander, like some vile adder, has rustled in the dry leaves of fallen and withered hearts since the world began. Even the good are not always wholly free from it, and the early Christian Church, so far from being the pure ideal bride of the Lord Jesus which we often imagine her to be, was (as is proved by all the Epistles) in many respects as little and in some respects even less pure than ours. The chrisom-robe of baptism was not preserved immaculate either in that or in any other age. The Church to which St. Paul was writing was, we must remember, a community of men and women of whom the majority had been familiar from the cradle with the meanness and the vice of the poorest ranks of heathenism in the corruptest city of heathendom. Their ignorance and weakness, their past training and their present poverty, made them naturally suspicious; and though we cannot doubt that they were morally the best of the class to which they belonged, though there may have been among them many a voiceless Epictetus—a slave, but dear to the immortals—and though their very reception of Christianity proved an aspiring heart, a tender conscience, an enduring spirit, yet many of them had not got beyond the inveteracy of lifelong habits, and it was easy for any pagan or Judaic sophister to lime their "wild hearts and feeble wings." But God's mercy overrules evil for good, and we owe to the worthless malice of obscure Judaic calumniators the lessons which we may learn from most of St. Paul's Epistles.[1] A trivial characteristic will often show better than anything else the general drift of any work, and as we have already pointed out the prominence in this Epistle of the thought of "tribulation," so we may now notice that, though "boasting" was of all things the most alien to St. Paul's genuine modesty, the most repugnant to his sensitive humility, yet the boasts of his unscrupulous opponents so completely drove him into the attitude of self-defence, that the word "boasting" occurs no less than twenty-nine times in these few chapters, while it is only found twenty-six times in all the rest of St. Paul's writings.[2]

The Second Epistle to the Corinthians, and those to the Galatians and Romans, represent the three chief phases of his controversy with Judaism. In the Epistle to the Galatians he overthrew for ever the repellent demand that the Gentiles should be circumcised; in the Epistle to the Romans he established for ever the thesis that Jews and Gentiles were equally guilty, and could be

---

[1] The authenticity of the letter has never been questioned. The three main divisions are : i.—vii. Hortatory and retrospective, with an under-current of apology. viii., ix. Directions about the contribution. x.—xiii. Defence of his Apostolic position. The more minute analysis will be seen as we proceed. But it is the least systematic, as the First is the most systematic of all his writings.

[2] Especially in 2 Cor. x., xi., xii. This finds its illustration in the prominence of "*inflation*" in 1 Cor. *passim*; but only elsewhere in Col. ii. 18.

justified only by faith, and not by works. In both these Epistles he establishes, from different points of view, the secondary and purely disciplinary functions of the law as a preparatory stage for the dispensation of free grace. In both Epistles he shows conclusively that instead of the false assertion that "it is in vain to be a Christian without being a Jew," should be substituted the very opposite statement, that it is in vain to be a Christian if, as a Christian, one relies on being a Jew as well. But, however irresistible his arguments might be, they would be useless if the Judaists succeeded in impugning his Apostolic authority, and proving that he had no right to be regarded as a teacher. The defence of his claims was, therefore, very far from being a mere personal matter; it involved nothing less than a defence of the truth of his Gospel. Yet this defence against an attack so deeply wounding, and so injurious to his cause, was a matter of insuperable difficulty. His opponents could produce their "commendatory letters," and, at least, claimed to possess the delegated authority of the Apostles who had lived with Jesus (2 Cor. iii. 1—18). This was a thing which Paul could not and would not do. He had *not* derived his authority from the Twelve. His intercourse with them had been but slight. His Apostolate was conferred on him, not mediately by them, but immediately by Christ. He had, indeed, "seen the Lord" (1 Cor. ix. 1), but on this he would not dwell, partly because his direct intercourse with Christ had been incomparably smaller than that of a Peter or a James; and partly because he clearly saw, and wished his converts to see, that spiritual union was a thing far closer and more important than personal companionship. To two things only could he appeal: to the visions and revelations wnich he had received from the Lord, above all, his miraculous conversion; and to the success, the activity, the spiritual power, which set a seal of supernatural approval to his unparalleled ministry.[1] But the first of these claims was deliberately set aside as subjective, both in his own lifetime and a century afterwards.[2] The difficulty of convincing his opponents on this subject reflects itself in his passion, a passion which rose in part because it forced upon him the odious semblance of self-assertion. His sole irresistible weapon was "the sword of the Spirit, which is the word of God."

I will now proceed to give an outline of this remarkable letter, which, from the extreme tension of mind with which it was written, and the constant struggle between the emotions of thankfulness and indignation,[3] is more difficult in its expressions and in its causal connections than any other. The labouring style,—the interchange of bitter irony with pathetic sincerity,—the manner in which word after word—now "tribulation," now "consolation," now "boasting," now "weakness,"—now "simplicity," now "manifestation," takes possession of the Apostle's mind —serve only to throw into relief the frequent bursts of impassioned eloquence. The depth of tenderness which is here revealed towards all who were noble and true, may serve as a measure for the insolence and wrong which provoked

---

[1] 2 Cor. ii. 14; iii. 2; x. 20—23; 1 Cor. ix. 1; xv. 10, &c.

[2] Pr. Clement. *Hom.* xvii. 13, *seq.* πῶς δέ σοι καὶ πιστεύσομεν αὐτό . . . ; πῶς δέ σοι καὶ ὤφθη ὁπότε αὐτοῦ τὰ ἐνάντια τῇ διδασκαλίᾳ φρονεῖς ;

[3] But, as Dean Stanley observes (*Cor.*, p. 348), "the thankfulness of the first part is darkened by the indignation of the third, and even the directions about the business of the contribution are coloured by the reflections both of his joy and of his grief. And in all those portions, though in themselves strictly personal, the Apostle is borne away into the higher region in which he habitually lived, so that this Epistle becomes the most striking instance of what is the case more or less with all his writings, a new philosophy of life poured forth not through systematic treatises, but through occasional bursts of human feeling."

in the concluding chapters so stern an indignation. Of all the Epistles it is the one which enables us to look deepest into the Apostle's heart.

Another characteristic of the letter has been observed by the quick insight of Bengel. "The whole letter," he says, "reminds us of an itinerary, but interwoven with the noblest precepts." "The very stages of his journey are impressed upon it," says Dean Stanley; "the troubles at Ephesus, the anxiety of Troas, the consolations of Macedonia, the prospect of moving to Corinth."[1]

After the greeting, in which he associates Timothy—who was probably his amanuensis—with himself, and with brief emphasis styles himself an "Apostle of Jesus Christ by the will of God," he begins the usual expression of thankfulness, in which the words "tribulation" and "consolation" are inextricably intertwined, and in which he claims for the Corinthians a union with him in both.

"Blessed be the God and Father of our Lord Jesus Christ, the Father of mercies, and God of all consolation, who consoleth us in all our tribulation, that we may be able to console those in all tribulation, by the consolation wherewith we are ourselves consoled by God. For as the sufferings of Christ abound towards us, so by Christ aboundeth also our consolation. But whether we are troubled, it is for your consolation and salvation which worketh in the endurance of the same sufferings which we also suffer, and our hope is sure on your behalf;[2] or whether we are consoled, it is for your consolation and salvation, knowing that as ye are partakers of the sufferings, so also of the consolation."[3]

He then alludes to the fearful tribulation, excessive and beyond his strength, whether caused by outward enemies or by sickness, through which he has just passed in Asia, which has brought him to the verge of despair and of the grave, in order that he may trust solely in Him who raiseth the dead. "Who from such a death rescued us, and will

---

[1] The thread of the Epistle is historical, but it is interwoven with digressions. The broken threads of narrative will be found in i. 8, 15; ii. 1, 12 13; vii. 5; viii. 1; ix. 2; xiii. 1.

[2] Verse 6. This is the position of these words in most uncials.

[3] "Communio sanctorum," Phil. ii. 26 (Bengel).

rescue, on whom we have hoped that even yet will He rescue." And as it was the supplication of many which had won for him this great charism, he asks that their thanksgivings may be added to those of many, and that their prayers may still be continued in his behalf.[1]

For however vile might be the insinuations against him, he is proudly conscious of the simplicity[2] and sincerity of his relations to all men, and especially to them, "not in carnal wisdom, but in the grace of God." Some had suspected him of writing private letters and secret messages, of intriguing in fact with individual members of his congregation; but he tells them that he wrote nothing except what they are now reading, and fully recognise, as he hopes they will continue to recognise, and even more fully than heretofore, even as some of them[3] already recognised, that they and he are a mutual subject of boasting in the day of the Lord. *This* was the reason why he had originally intended to pay them two visits instead of one. Had he then been guilty of the levity, the fickleness, the caprice with which he had been charged in changing his plan? Did the "Yes, yes" of his purposes mean much the same thing as "No, no," like the mere shifting feebleness of an aimless man?[4] Well, if they chose to say this of him *as a man*, at any rate, there was *one* emphatic "Yes," one unalterable fixity and affirmation about him, and that was his preaching of Christ. Jesus Christ, the Son of God, preached by him and Silvanus and Timotheus, had proved Himself to be not "Yes" and "No;" but in Him was God's infinite "Yes," and therefore also the Christian's everlasting Amen to all God's promises.[5] He who

---

[1] i. 1—11; i. 8, ὥστε ἐξαπορηθῆναι, though generally he was ἀπορούμενος οὐκ ἐξαπορούμενος, iv. 8. ἀπόκριμα τοῦ θανάτου to the question, "How will it all end?" the only answer seemed to be "Death." καθ᾽ ὑπερβολὴν, iv. 17; Rom. vii. 13; 1 Cor. xii. 31; Gal. i. 13.

[2] i. 12. ἁπλότης, in answer to the charge of duplicity, is a characteristic word of this Epistle (viii. 2; ix. 11, 13; xi. 3); but here, א A, B, C, K, read ἁγιότητι.

[3] i. 14, ἀπὸ μέρους.

[4] I have never been even approximately satisfied with any explanation of this passage. St. Chrysostom makes it mean, "Did I show levity, or do I plan after the flesh that the yea with me must be always yea, and the nay always nay, as it is with a man of the world who makes his plans independently of God's over-ruling of them?" As there are no emphatic affirmations in the case, Matt. v. 37, James v. 12, throw no light on the passage, unless some such words had been quoted against him in the perverted sense that when once you have said a thing you must at all costs do it, however completely circumstances have changed.

[5] Compare the Ἀμὴν ἀμὴν ("Verily, verily") of which the Gospels are so full. I read διὸ καὶ δι᾽ αὐτοῦ, with א, A, B, C, D, F, G.

confirmed all of them alike into the Anointed (εἰς χριστον), and anointed them (χρίσας), was God, who also set His seal on them, and gave them in their hearts the earnest of His Spirit.[1] He called God to witness upon his own soul that it was with a desire to spare them that he no longer came[2] to Corinth. And then, conscious that jealous eyes would dwell on every phrase of his letter, and if possible twist its meaning against him, he tells them that by using the expression "sparing them," he does not imply any claim to lord it over their *faith*, for faith is free and by it they stand; but that he is speaking as a fellow-worker of their joy, and therefore he had decided that his second visit to them should not be in grief.[3] Was it natural that he should like to grieve those who caused him joy, or be grieved by those from whom he ought to receive joy? His joy, he felt sure, was theirs also, and therefore he had written to them instead of coming; and that previous letter—sad as were its contents—had not been written to grieve them, but had been written in much tribulation and compression of heart and many tears, that they might recognise how more abundantly he loved them. Grief, indeed, there had been, and it had fallen on him, but it had not come on him only, but partly on them, and he did not wish to press heavily on them all.[4] And the sinner who had caused that common grief had been

---

[1] ἀρραβὼν, earnest-money, part-payment, προκαταβολή; an ancient (עֵרָבוֹן, Gen. xxxviii. 17, 18; *arrhabo*—Plaut. *Rud. Prol.* 46) and modern word (Fr. *arrhes*) made current by Semitic commerce. (Cf. ἀπαρχή, Rom. viii. 23.)

[2] i. 23. Here, and as, I believe, in ii. 1 and xiii. 1, he speaks of his *intended* visit as a real one. The E. V. mistakes οὐκέτι, "no longer," for οὔπω, "not yet;" but the expression really illustrates the much-disputed verses to which I have referred, and inclines me to the opinion that St. Paul had not visited Corinth more than once when this letter was written. But the question is one of very small importance, though so much has been written on it.

[3] Lit., " not again to come to you in grief," as he would be doing *if* he had visited them once in grief, and were then obliged to come a second time in the same spirit. No doubt the words literally imply that he had *already once* visited them in grief, and that expression would hardly be correct for his *first* visit; but he merely uses it in his vivid way as though his *intended* visit— which, had he carried it out, *would* have been in grief—had been a real visit. The πάλιν is even omitted in D, E, F, G. Theodoret, who ought to know what Greek means, takes πάλιν ἐλθεῖν merely in the sense of "re-visit," separating it from ἐν λύπῃ altogether.

[4] This is another of those ambiguous expressions—due to the emotion of the writer and the delicacy of the subjects of which he is treating, and his desire to be kind and just though there was so much to blame—about which it is impossible to feel any certainty of the exact explanation. I have partly followed the view of St. Chrysostom.

sufficiently censured by the reprobation of the majority of them;[1] so that now, on the contrary, they should forgive and comfort him, that a person such as he was—guilty, disgraced, but now sincerely penitent— may not be swallowed up by his excessive grief. Let them now assure him of their love. The object of the former letter had been fulfilled in testing their obedience. If *they* forgave (as they had partially done already, in not strictly carrying out his decision), so did he; "and what I have forgiven, if I have forgiven anything,[2] is for your sakes, in the presence[3] of Christ, that we may not be over-reached by Satan, for we are not ignorant of his devices."[4]

Well, he did *not* come to them, and he *did* write, and what was the consequence? His anxiety to know the effect produced by his letter and change of plan was so intense, that it almost killed him. Successful as was the opening which he found for the Gospel of Christ at Troas, he abandoned his work there, because he could not endure the disappointment and anguish of heart which the non-arrival of Titus caused him. He therefore went to Macedonia. There at last he met Titus, but he omits to say so in his eagerness to thank God, who thus drags him in triumph in the service of Christ. Everywhere the incense of that triumph was burnt; to some it was a sweet savour that told of life, to others a sign of imminent death. St. Paul is so possessed by the metaphor that he does not even pause to disentangle it. He is at once the conquered enemy dragged in triumph, and the incense burned in sign of the victor's glory. The burning incense is a sign to some of life ever-renewed in fresh exultation; to others of defeat ever deepening into death. To himself, at once the captive and the sharer in the triumph, it is a sign of death, and of daily death, and yet the pledge of a life

---

[1] *Some* had evidently been recalcitrant. In ii. 6 the word for "punishment" is ἐπιτιμία, not κόλασις or τιμωρία; but the general meaning is that of punishment (Wisd. iii. 10). Philo, περὶ ἄθλων καὶ ἐπιτιμιῶν, " on rewards and punishments."

[2] ii. 10. The best reading seems to be ὃ κεχάρισμαι, εἴ τι κεχάρισμαι, א, A, B, C, F, G. Evidently we are here in the dark about many circumstances; but we infer that St. Paul's sentence of excommunication, as ordered in his former letter, had *not* been carried out, partly because some opposed it, but also in part because the man repented in consequence of his exclusion from the communion of the majority of the Church. St. Paul might have been angry that his plain order had been disobeyed by the Church as such; but, on the contrary, he is satisfied with their partial obedience, and withdraws his order, which timely repentance had rendered needless.

[3] Cf. Prov. viii. 30, LXX.

[4] i. 12—ii. 11.

beyond life itself.¹ And who is sufficient for such ministry? For he is not like the majority²—the hucksters, the adulterators, the fraudulent retailers of the Word of God,—but as of sincerity, but as of God—in the presence of God he speaks in union with Christ.³

Is this self-commendation to them? Does he need letters of introduction to them?⁴ And here, again, follows one of the strangely mingled yet powerful metaphors so peculiar to the greatest and most sensitive imaginations. "Ye are our Epistle," says St. Paul, "written on our hearts, recognised and read by all men, being manifestly an Epistle of Christ, ministered by us, written not with ink, but with the Spirit of the living God; not on stonen tablets, but on fleshen tablets —hearts."⁵ He does not need a commendatory letter to them; they are themselves his commendatory letter to all men; it is a letter of Christ, of which he is only the writer and carrier;⁶ and it is not engraved on granite like the Laws of Moses, but on their hearts. Thus they are at once the commendatory letter written on Paul's heart, and they have a letter of Christ written on their own hearts by the Spirit, and of that letter Paul has been the human agent.⁷

It was a bold expression, but one which sprang from a confidence which Christ inspired, and had reference to a work for God. That work was the ministry of the New Covenant—not of the slaying letter but of the vivifying spirit,⁸ for which God gave the sufficiency. And what a glorious ministry! If the ministry of the Law—tending

¹ On this metaphor, v. supra, i., Excursus III. The last great triumph at Rome had been that of Claudius, when Caradoc was among the captives.

² ii. 17. οἱ πολλοί is a strong expression, but οἱ λοιποί, "the rest," the reading of D, E, F, G, J, is still more impassioned. It is possible that this may have been softened into the other reading, just as οἱ πολλοί has been softened into πολλοί. We must remember how many and diverse were the elements of error at Corinth—conceit, faction, Pharisaism, licence, self-assertion; and St. Paul (Rom. v.) seems to use οἱ πολλοί peculiarly.

³ ii. 12—17 (cf. Isa. i. 22, LXX.).

⁴ iii. 1. It is astonishing to find Ebionite hatred still burning against St. Paul in the second century, and covertly slandering him because he had no ἐπιστολαὶ συστατικαί from James. All who came without such letters were to be regarded as false prophets, false apostles, &c. (Cf. 2 Cor. xi. 13; Gal. ii. 12.) (Ps. Clem. *Recogn.* iv. 34; *Hom.* xi. 35.)

⁵ Read καρδίαις, א, A, B, C, D, E, G. For the metaphor compare Prov. iii. 3; vii. 3; Ezek. xi. 19; Ex. xviii. 31.

⁶ Compare the identification of the seed sown and the hearts that receive it in Mark iv. 16.

⁷ iii. 1—3.

⁸ iii. 6, ἀποκτείνει; Rom. iv. 15; vii. 6, 7, 10, 11; Gal. iii. 10; John vi. 63 (ζωοποιεῖ, Rom. vi. 4, 11; viii. 2, 10; Gal. v. 2.

in itself to death, written in earthly letters, graven on granite slabs,—yet displayed itself in such glory that the children of Israel could not gaze on the face of Moses because of the glory of his countenance, which was rapidly fading away,[1] how much more glorious was the Ministry of Life, of Righteousness, of the Spirit, which by comparison outdazzles that other glory into mere darkness,[2] and is not transitory (διὰ δόξης) but permanent (ἐν δόξῃ). It was the sense of being entrusted with that ministry which gave him confidence. Moses used to put a veil over his face that the children of Israel might not see the evanescence of the transient; and the veil which *he* wore on his bright countenance when he spoke to them reminds him of the veil which *they* yet wore on their hardened understandings when his Law was read to them, which should only begin to be removed the moment they turned from Moses to Christ,[3] from the letter to the spirit, from slavery to freedom. But he and all the ministers of Christ gazed with no veil upon their faces upon *His* glory reflected in the mirror of His Gospel; and in their turn seeing that image as in a mirror,[4] caught that ever-brightening glory as from the Lord, the Spirit. How could one entrusted with such a ministry grow faint-hearted? How could he—as Paul's enemies charged him with doing—descend into "the crypts of shame?" Utterly false[5] were such insinuations. He walked not in craftiness; he did not adulterate the pure Word of God; but his commendatory letter, the only one he needed, was to manifest the truth to all consciences in God's sight. There was no veil over the truths he preached; if veil there was, it was only in the darkened understandings of the perishing, so darkened into unbelief by the god of the present world,[6] that the brightness of the gospel of the glory of Christ could not illuminate them. He it is—Christ Jesus the Lord, the image of God—He it is, and not ourselves, whom Paul and all true Apostles preached. He had been accused of self-seeking and self-assertion. Such sins were *impossible* to one who estimated as he did the glory of His message. All that he could preach of himself was that

---

[1] iii. 7. The word "*till*" in the E.V. of Ex. xxxiv. 33 seems to be a mistake for "when." He put on the veil, not to dim the splendour while he spoke, but (so St. Paul here implies) to veil the evanescence when he had ended his words—καταργοῦμαι (1 Cor. i. 28; ii. 6; vi. 13; xiii. 8, 11; xv. 24—twenty-two times in this group of Epistles).

[2] iii. 10, 11, οὐ δεδόξασται τὸ δεδοξασμένον ἐν τούτῳ τῷ μέρει.

[3] iii. 16, ἐπιστρέψῃ . . . περιαιρεῖται.

[4] iii. 18, κατοπτριζόμενοι. Chrysostom, &c., make it mean "reflecting," but there seems to be no instance of that sense.

[5] iv. 2. Cf. 1 Cor. iv. 5. Hence the prominence of the word φανερόω in this Epistle (ii. 14; iii. 3; iv. 10; v. 10, 11; vii. 12; xi. 6).

[6] Cf. John xiv. 30; Eph. ii. 2. "Grandis sed horribilis descriptio Satanae" (Bengel).

Christ was Lord, and that he was their slave for Christ's sake. For God had shone in the hearts of His ministers only in order that the bright knowledge which they had caught from gazing, with no intervening veil, on the glory of Christ, might glow for the illumination of the world.[1]

A glorious ministry; but what weak ministers! Like the torches hid in Gideon's pitchers, their treasure of light was in earthen vessels,[2] that the glory of their victory over the world and the world's idolatries might be God's, not theirs. This was why they were at once weak and strong—weak in themselves, strong in God—"in everything being troubled, yet not crushed; perplexed, but not in despair; persecuted, but not forsaken; flung down, but not destroyed; always carrying about in our body the putting to death of the Lord Jesus Christ, in order that also the life of Jesus may be manifested in our body. For we, living as we are, are ever being handed over to death for Jesus' sake, in order that the life of Jesus also may be manifested in our mortal flesh. So that death is working in us—seeing that for Christ's sake and for your sakes we die daily—but life in you. The trials are mainly ours; the blessings yours. Yet we know that this daily death of ours shall be followed by a resurrection. He who raised Christ shall also raise us from the daily death of our afflicted lives[3] and from the death in which they end, and shall present us, with you, to God's glory, by the increase of grace and more abundant increase of thanksgiving. For this reason we do not play the coward, but even if our outward man is being destroyed, yet the inward man is being renewed day by day. For the lightness of our immediate affliction is working out for us, in increasing excess, an eternal weight of glory, since our eyes are fixed not on the visible, but on the invisible; for the things visible are transient, but the things invisible are eternal.[4] The tents of our earthly bodies shall be done away, but then we shall have an eternal building. We groan, we are burdened in this tent of flesh,[5] we long to put on over it, as a robe, our house from heaven—if, as I assume, we shall not indeed be found bodiless[6]—that the mortal may be swallowed up by life.[7] And God,

---

[1] iii. 4—iv. 6.

[2] He was a σκεῦος ἐκλογῆς (Acts ix. 15), but the σκεῦος was itself ὀστράκινον. "Lo vas d'elezione" (Dante, *Inf.* ii. 28).

[3] "God exhibits death in the living, life in the dying" (Alford).

[4] Cf. Plat. *Phaedo*, 79.

[5] Wisd. ix. 15, "the earthly tabernacle (γεῶδες σκῆνος) weigheth down the mind."

[6] v. 3. So I understand this difficult clause. It seems to imply some condition which is *not* that of disembodied spirits, between the death of the mortal and the reception of the resurrection body (cf. Hdt. v. 92; Thuc. iii. 58).

[7] Again, notice the strange confusion of metaphors. It is only the very greatest writers who can venture to write thus; only those whose thoughts

who wrought us for this end, has given us the earnest of His Spirit that it shall be so. Hence, since we walk by faith, death itself has for us lost all terrors; it will be but an admission into the nearer presence of our Lord. To please Him is our sole ambition, because we shall each stand before His tribunal to receive the things done by the body;—to be paid in kind for our good and evil, not by arbitrary infliction, but by natural result.[1] This is our awful belief, and we strive to make it yours.[2] To God our sincerity is manifest already, and we hope that it will be to your consciences, since we tell you all this not by way of commending ourselves, but that you may have something of which to boast about us against those whose boasts are but of superficial things. They call us mad [3]—well, if so, it is for God; or if we be sober-minded, it is for you.[4] Our one constraining motive is Christ's love. Since He died for all, all in His death died to sin, and therefore the reason of His death was that we may not live to ourselves, but to Him who died and rose again for us. From henceforth, then, we recognise no relation to Him which is not purely spiritual. Your Jerusalem emissaries boast that they knew the living Christ; and in consequence maintain their superiority to us. If we ever recognised any such claim—if we ever relied on having seen the living Christ—we renounce all such views from this moment.[5] 'He who is in Christ is a new creation; the old

are like a flame, that cracks the enclosing lamp of language that it may emit more heat and light.

[1] It is not easy to see the exact correlation between the judicial process of result according to good and evil conduct—even as regards saints—and that free absolute justification by faith in Christ, that complete forgiveness of sins, and tearing up of the bond which is against us, on which St. Paul dwells in v. 19, 21; Rom. iii. 25; Col. ii. 14. But faith is as little troubled by unsolved antinomies in the kingdom of grace as in that of nature (see *infra*, Excursus II.).

[2] v. 11. So Chrysostom, &c., but it is one of the many verses in this Epistle about which no absolute certainty is attainable. It *may* mean "knowing that the fear of God (*timorem Domini*, Vulg.) is the principle of my own life, I try to persuade you of this truth;—that it *is* so God knows already."

[3] Cf. Acts xxvi. 24.

[4] "My revelations, ecstacies, glossolaly, are phases of intercourse of my soul with God; my practical sense and tact are for you."

[5] 2 Cor. v. 16, ἀπὸ τοῦ νῦν. In Gal. i. 15, 16, St. Paul has said that "it pleased God to reveal His Son in him," and in his view "the entire, absolute importance of Christianity resided in the person of Christ. God had disclosed to him as the Son of God that Jesus whom he had opposed as a false Messiah. But the resurrection had elevated the historic Christ far above a Jewish Messiah (1 Cor. xv. 8). The death of Christ had severed His

things are passed away; lo! all things have become new.' It is the spiritual Christ, the glorified Christ—whom God made to be sin for us—in whom God reconciled the world unto Himself, not imputing their trespasses unto them—whom we preach; and our ministry is the Ministry of Reconciliation which God entrusted to us, and in virtue of which we, as ambassadors on Christ's behalf, entreat you to be reconciled to God. 'Him who knew not sin He made sin on our behalf, that we may become the righteousness of God in Him.'[1] As His fellow-workers we entreat you, then, not to render null the acceptance of His grace in this the day of salvation, and that this our ministry may not be blamed, we give no legitimate cause of offence in anything, but in everything commend ourselves[2] as ministers of God "in much endurance, in tribulations, in necessities, in pressure of circumstance, in blows, in prisons, in tumults, in toils, in spells of sleeplessness, in fastings, in pureness, in knowledge, in long-suffering, in kindness, in the Holy Spirit, in love unfeigned, in the word of truth, in the power of God, by the arms of righteousness on the right and left, by glory and dishonour, by ill report and good report; as deceivers and yet true, as being ignored and yet recognised, as dying and behold we live, as being chastened yet not being slain, as being grieved and yet rejoicing, as paupers yet enriching many, as having nothing yet as having all things in full possession."[3]

He may well appeal to this outburst of impassioned eloquence as a proof that his mouth is open and his heart enlarged towards them, and

connection with mere national elements, and He was then manifested in the universal and spiritual sphere in which all absolute importance of Judaism was obliterated. St. Paul here says that since he began to live for Christ, who died and rose, Jesus is no longer for him a Messiah after the flesh. *That conception of Him is now purged of all sensuous, Judaic, personal limitations, and Christ becomes not only one who lived and died in Judæa, but who lives and reigns in the heart of every Christian on the absolute principle of the spiritual life.*" (Baur, *Paul.* ii. 126.) When Paul had once shaken himself free, first from his unconverted Pharisaism, then from the Judæo-Christian stage of his earlier convictions, he grasped the truth that the risen and ascended Lord of all dwarfed and shamed the notion of all mere local, and family, and national restrictions.

[1] The meaning of this verse will be brought out *infra*, p. 209, *sq.*
[2] The reader will observe how much the mention of the συστατικαὶ ἐπιστολαὶ has dominated throughout this majestic self-defence. The statement of the nature and method of His ministry is the only commendatory letter which to them, at least, Paul will deign to use. Yet in making a self-defence so utterly distasteful to him, observe how noble and eternal are the thoughts on which he dwells, and the principles upon which he insists.
[3] iv. 7—vi. 10.

as the ground of entreaty that, instead of their narrow jealousies and suspicions, they would, as sons, love him with the same large-heartedness, and so repay him in kind, and separate themselves from their incongruous yoke-fellowship with unbelief [1]—the unnatural participations, symphonies, agreements of righteousness and light with lawlessness and darkness, of Christ with worthlessness,[2] of God's temple with idols, which forfeited the glorious promises of God.[3] Let them cleanse themselves from these corruptions from within and from without. And then to clench all that he has said, and for the present to conclude the subject, he cries, 'Receive us! we wronged nobody, ruined nobody, defrauded nobody—such charges against us are simply false. I do not allude to them to condemn you. I have said already that you are in my heart to die together and live together. I speak thus boldly because of the consolation and superabundant joy—in the midst of all the tribulations—which came on me in Macedonia with overwhelming intensity—without, battles; within, fears. But God, who consoleth the humble,[4] consoled us by the coming of Titus, and the good news about your reception of my letter, and the yearning for me, and the lamentation, and the zeal which it awoke on my behalf. At one time I regretted that I had written it, but, though it pained you, I regret it no longer, because the pain was a holy and a healing pain, which awoke earnestness in you—self-defence and indignation against wrong, and a fear and yearning towards me, and zeal for God, and punishment of the offender. It was not to take either one side or the other in the quarrel that I wrote to you, but that your allegiance and love to me might be manifested to yourselves[5] before God. I did not care for those people—their offence and quarrel. I cared only for you. And you stood the test. You justified all that I had boasted to Titus about you, and the respect and submission with which you received him have inspired me with deep joy on his account, and him with a deep affection

---

[1] An allusion to the "diverse kinds," and ox and ass ploughing together (Lev. xix. 19; Deut. xxii. 10). I am unable to see so strongly as others the digressive and parenthetic character of vi. 14—vii. 1.

[2] vi. 15, βελίαρ. Belial is not originally a proper name (Prov. vi. 12, "a naughty person" is Adam belial); and this is why there was no worship of Belial.

[3] These are given (vi. 18) in "a mosaic of citations" from 2 Sam. vii. 14, 8; Is. xliii. 6 (Plumptre); perhaps, however, St. Paul had in his mind also Jer. xxxi. 3—33; Ezek. xxxvi. 28.

[4] Cf. x. 1. He touchingly accepts the term applied to him.

[5] vii. 12. The reading seems to be τὴν σπουδὴν ὑμῶν τὴν ὑπὲρ ἡμῶν πρὸς ὑμᾶς. (C, E, J, K.)

for you. I rejoice, then, that in everything I am in good heart about you."[1]

He proceeds to give them a proof of it. The churches of Macedonia, he tells them, poor as they are,[2] afflicted as they are, yet with a spontaneous liberality, absolute self-devotion, and affectionate enthusiasm for his wishes, giving themselves first to God beyond his hopes, had not only subscribed largely to the collection for the saints, but had entreated him to take part in its management. Encouraged by this, he had asked Titus to finish the arrangement of this matter with the rest of his good work among them. As they abounded in so many gifts and graces, let them abound in this. He did not want to order them, he only told them what others had done, and asked (not on his own behalf) a proof of their love, even as Christ had set them the example of enriching others by His own poverty. They had begun the collection first, but Macedonia had finished it first. They need not give more than they could afford, for God looked not to the gift, but to the spirit of the giver. Nor did he wish to pauperise them in order to set others at ease, but only to establish between Jewish and Gentile churches a reciprocity of aid in time of need. Titus had gladly accepted the commission, and with him he sent the brother, whose praise in the Gospel is known in all the churches, and who has been specially elected by the churches to this office; since so great was Paul's determination to give not the slightest handle to mean insinuations, that he would have nothing to do with the money himself.[3] With Titus and this brother he sent a third, whose earnestness had been often tested in many circumstances, and who was now specially stimulated by his confidence in the Corinthians. If they wanted to know anything about these three visitors, Titus was his partner and fellow-worker towards them; the other two brethren were delegates of the churches,[4] the glory of Christ. Let the Corinthians give a proof of their love, and a justification to all churches of his boasting about them. As to the general desirability of the collection he surely need say nothing. He had been boasting of their

---

[1] vi. 11—vii. 16.

[2] Dean Stanley refers to Arnold, *Rom. Commonwealth*, ii. 382.

[3] viii. 20 (cf. Prov. iii. 3, LXX.), ἀδρότης, *lit.* "ripeness." These *hapax legomena* occur freely in Paul's unquestioned Epistles. He readily took up new words. He may, for instance, have picked up the word ἐπιχορηγῶν (first used in ix. 10, and then in Gal. iii. 5; Col. ii. 19; Eph. iv. 16) at Athens. It is unknown to the LXX. of the Old Testament, and only found in Ecclus xxv. 22.

[4] Lit. "apostles," but here in its untechnical sense of "authorised delegates." Who these two brethren were is quite uncertain;—perhaps Luke and Trophimus.

zeal, and had told the Macedonian churches that the Achaians had been ready a year ago. In this there was some reason to fear that he had been in error, having mistaken their ready professions for actual accomplishment. He had therefore sent on these brethren, lest, if Macedonians came with him on his arrival, and found them unprepared, he— to say nothing of them—should be ashamed of a boast which would turn out to be false. He exhorts them, therefore, to willing liberality, trusting that God would reward them. Let them give beneficently, not grudgingly. "But (notice) this—He who soweth sparingly, sparingly also shall reap, and he who soweth with blessings, with blessings."[1] "And God is able to make all grace abound towards you, that in everything, always, having all sufficiency, ye may abound to every good work." And this collection was not only for the aid of the saints, but also for the glory of God by the thanksgiving to Him, and prayer for them which it called forth. The recipients would glorify God for it as a sign of genuine religion, and would yearn towards them in love, because of the grace of God abounding in them. "Thanks," he says, identifying himself with the feelings of the grateful recipients—"thanks to God for His unspeakable gift."[2]

At this point the whole tone of the Epistle changes— changes so completely that, in this section of it (x. i.— xiii. 10), many have not only seen an entirely separate letter, but have even with much plausibility identified it with that stern missive alluded to in vii. 8—12, which caused the Corinthians so much pain, and stirred them up to such vigorous exertion, which is usually identified with the first extant Epistle.[3] It is difficult to accept any such hypothesis in the teeth of the evidence of all manuscripts; and when we remember the perpetual interchange of news between different Churches, it is a much simpler and more natural supposition that, as the first part of the letter had been written while he was in anxiety about them, and the

---

[1] ix. 6, ἐν' εὐλογίαις, i.e., in a large, gracious, liberal spirit (Prov. xi. 24; xxii. 9).

[2] viii. 1—ix. 15.

[3] If such a supposition were at all probable, we should rather infer from xii. 18 that this section was an Epistle written *after* the mission of Titus and the brother alluded to in viii. 18. But the suggestion in the text seems to me to meet most of the difficulties.

second after his mind had been relieved by the arrival of Titus, so this third part of the letter was written after the arrival of some other messenger, who bore the disastrous tidings that some teacher had come from Jerusalem whose opposition to St. Paul had been more marked and more unscrupulous than any with which he had yet been obliged to deal. However that may be, certain it is that these chapters are written in a very different mood from the former.[1] There is in them none of the tender effusiveness and earnest praise which we have been hearing, but a tone of suppressed indignation, in which tenderness, struggling with bitter irony, in some places renders the language laboured and obscure,[2] like the words of one who with difficulty restrains himself from saying all that his emotion might suggest. Yet it is deeply interesting to observe that "the meekness and gentleness of Christ" reigns throughout all this irony, and he utters no word of malediction like those of the Psalmists. And there is also a tone of commanding authority, which the writer is driven to assume as a last resource, since all forbearance has been so grievously misunderstood. Some among them—one person in particular[3]—had been passing their censures and criticisms on St. Paul very freely, saying that his person was mean;[4] that he was untutored in speech;[5] that he was only bold in letters, and at a distance; that he

---

[1] A change of tone of an analogous character—from a more distant and respectful to a more stern and authoritative style—is observable in Rom. xiv., xv. (*v. infra*, p. 170). So there is a wide difference between the apologetic and the aggressive part of Demosthenes, *De Coronâ* (Hug.). Semler was the first to suggest that this Epistle was an amalgamation of three, which is also the view of Weisse. The Αὐτὸς δὲ ἐγὼ Παῦλος of x. 1 (cf. Gal. v. 2; Eph. iii. 1; Philem. 19) at once marks the change.

[2] Theodoret says of x. 12—18 that St. Paul wrote it obscurely (ἀσαφῶς) from a desire not to expose the offenders too plainly.

[3] x. 2, τινας; 7, εἴ τις πέποιθεν ἑαυτῷ; 10, φησι, "says he;" 11, ὁ τοιοῦτος; 12, τισι; 18, ὁ ἑαυτὸν συνιστῶν; xi. 4, ὁ ἐρχόμενος.

[4] x. 1, 10.   [5] xi. 6.

walked "according to the flesh;"[1] that he was certainly a weakling, and probably a madman.[2] They had been urging their own near connexion with Christ as a subject of self-commendation;[3] had been preaching another Jesus, and a different Gospel, and imparting a different spirit;[4] had been boasting immeasurably of their superiority, though they were thrusting themselves into spheres of work in which they had not laboured;[5] and by whispered seductions had been beguiling the Corinthians from the simplicity of their original faith.[6] In contrast to the self-supporting toils and forbearance of St. Paul, these men and their coryphaeus had maintained their claim to Apostolic authority by an insolence, rapacity, and violence,[7] which made Paul ironically remark that his weakness in having any consideration for his converts, instead of lording it over them, had been a disgrace to him. And, strange to say, the ministry and doctrine of this person and his clique had awakened a distinct echo in the hearts of the unstable Corinthians. They had taken them at their own estimate; had been dazzled by their outrageous pretensions; benumbed by the "torpedo-touch" of their avarice; and confirmed in a bold disregard for the wishes and regulations of their true Teacher.[8]

It is at these intruders that St. Paul hurls his indignant, ironical, unanswerable apology. "Mean as he was of aspect,"[9] he entreats them

---

[1] x. 2, κατὰ σάρκα, i.e., with mere earthly motives; that he was timid, complaisant, inconsistent, self-seeking.
[2] xi. 16, 17, 19. Compare the blunt "Thou art mad, Paul!" of Festus.
[3] x. 7.
[4] xi. 4, ἄλλον Ἰησοῦν ... ἕτερον πνεῦμα ... εὐαγγέλιον ἕτερον.
[5] x. 15.
[6] xi. 3.
[7] xi. 20, 21.
[8] x. 18; xi. 8, 20; xii. 13, 14.
[9] Many of these expressions, as St. Chrysostom saw, are quotations of the sneers of his opponents—κατ' εἰρωνείαν φησὶ τὰ ἐκείνων φθεγγόμενος. For traces of similar irony, see 1 Cor. iv. 8—11; vi. 3—8; ix. 1—16; xv. 6.

by the gentleness and mildness of Christ that when he came he might
not be forced to show that if "he walked after the flesh," at any rate the
weapons he wielded were not after the flesh, but strong enough to
humble insolence, and punish disobedience, and rase the strongholds of
opposition, and take captive every thought into the obedience of Christ.
Did they judge by outward appearance? They should find that he was
as near to Christ as any member of the party that used His name.
They should find that his personal action, founded on a power of which he
well might boast, but which God had given him for their edification, not
for destruction, could be as weighty and powerful, as calculated to terrify
them, as his letters.[1] He would not, indeed, venture to enter with them
into the mean arena of personal comparisons,[2] which proved the unwisdom
of his opponents; nor would he imitate them in stretching his boasts to
an illimitable extent. He would confine these boasts to the range of
the measuring-line which God had given him, and which was quite large
enough without any over-straining to reach to them, even as His Gospel
had first reached them; for, unlike his opponents, he was not exercising
these boasts in spheres of labour not his own, but had hope that, as their
faith enlarged, he would be still more highly esteemed, and the limit of
his work extended to yet wider and untried regions. Let the boaster
then boast in the Lord, since the test of a right to boast was not in self-
commendation, but in the commendation of the Lord.[3]

He entreats them to bear with him, just a little, in this folly—nay,
he is sure they do so.[4] He feels for them a godly jealousy, desiring to
present them as a chaste virgin to Christ, but fearful lest they should be
seduced from their simplicity as the serpent beguiled Eve. It would
have been easy for them (it appears) to tolerate this new preacher[5] if

---

[1] x. 1—11. This comparison of his letters and his personal conduct (ver. 10)
is quoted from the Jerusalem emissary (φησιν, "he says;" 7, τις; 11, τοιοῦτος).

[2] x. 12, ἐγκρῖναι ἢ συγκρῖναι, an untranslatable paronomasia.

[3] x. 12—18. The haunting word is, as in so many parts of the Epistle,
"boast" and "commendation" (iii. 1; iv. 2; v. 12; x. 12, 16, 17, 18; xi. 10,
12, 18, 30; xii. 1, 5, 6, 11), with especial reference to the commendatory letters.
It was an easy thing, he hints, for these Judaisers to come comfortably
with "letters" from Jerusalem to Corinth, and there be supported by admiring
adherents whom *his* toils had converted; a very different thing to traverse
the world as a friendless missionary, and sow the seed of the Gospel in
virgin soil.

[4] xi. 1, μικρόν τι . . . ἀλλὰ καί. This Epistle is characterised by haunting
words, and the key-words of this chapter are ἀνέχομαι (1, 4, 19, 20) and
ἄφρων (1, 16, 17, 19, 21; xii. 6, 11). Dr. Plumptre sees in this the echo of
some taunt which Titus had reported—"His folly is becoming intolerable."

[5] xi. 4, ὁ ἐρχόμενος.

he is preaching another Jesus, a different spirit, a different gospel; but he professes to preach the *same*, and such being the case he had no more authority than Paul, who claimed that he had in no respect fallen short of the most super-apostolic Apostles.[1] A mere laic in eloquence he might be, but there was at any rate no defect in his knowledge; and the proof of this as regards *them* was obvious in everything among all men,[2] unless, indeed, he had transgressed by humiliating himself for their exaltation by preaching to them gratuitously. Other Churches he plundered, preaching to the Corinthian, and being paid his wages by others. And though he was in positive want while among them, he did not benumb them with his exactions, as though he were some gymnotus, but was helped by Macedonians, and kept and would keep himself from laying any burden whatever on them. That boast no one should obstruct,[3] not (God knows) because he did not love them, but because he would cut off the handle from those who wanted a handle, and that, in this topic of boasting, he and his opponents might be on equal grounds. The last remark is a keen sarcasm, since, if they charged Paul with taking money, they charged him with the very thing which he did *not* do, and which they *did*.[4] "For such," he adds with passionate severity, "are false Apostles, deceitful workers, transforming themselves into Apostles of Christ; nor is this to be wondered at, for Satan himself transforms himself into an angel of light.[5] It is no great thing then, if also His ministers transform themselves as ministers of righteousness, whose end shall be according to their works. Again I say, Let no one think me a fool; or, if you do, receive me even as you would receive a fool, that I too, as well as they, may boast a little." He claims nothing lofty or sacred or spiritual for this determined

[1] xi. 5, τῶν ὑπερλίαν 'Αποστόλων, literally "the extra-super Apostles." There is undoubtedly a sense of indignation in the use, twice over, of this strange colloquialism; but it is aimed, not at the Twelve, with whom St. Paul's relations were always courteous and respectful, but at the extravagant and purely human claims (mere superiority, κατὰ σάρκα) asserted for them by these emissaries. He compares himself with them in knowledge (xi. 5), in self-denial about support (xi. 6—21), in privileges of birth (22), in labours and perils (23—33), in the fact that his weakness resulted from pre-eminent revelations (xii. 1—10), and in the supernatural signs of Apostleship (xii. 11, 12).

[2] xi. 6. If φανερώσαντες (א, B, F, G) be the right reading, it means "manifesting it (*i.e.*, *knowledge*) to you in everything among all."

[3] xi. 10, *leg.* φραγήσεται.

[4] How long this vile calumny continued may be seen in the identification of him with Simon Magus in the Clementines.

[5] This incidentally alludes to a Hagadah respecting Job i. 6, or the angel who wrestled with Jacob (Eisenmenger, *Entd. Judenth.* i. 845).

boasting. It was a folly, but not one of his own choosing. Since many adopted this worldly style of boasting, he would meet them with their own weapons; and the Corinthians, since they were so wise, would, he was sure, gladly tolerate mere harmless fools, seeing that they tolerated people much more objectionable—people who enslaved, devoured,[1] took them in—people who assumed the most arrogant pretensions—people who smote them in the face.[2] "Of course all this is to my discredit, it shows how weak I was in not adopting a similar line of conduct. Yet, speaking in this foolish way, I possess every qualification which inspires them with this audacity. I, like them, am a Hebrew, an Israelite, of the seed of Abraham;[3] I am not only, as they claim to be, a minister of Christ, but (I am speaking in downright madness) something more." And then follows the most marvellous fragment ever written of any biography; a fragment beside which the most imperilled lives of the most suffering saints shrink into insignificance, and which shows us how fractional at the best is our knowledge of the details of St. Paul's life—"in toils more abundantly, in stripes above measure, in prisons more abundantly, in deaths oft; of the Jews five times received I forty stripes save one; thrice was I beaten with rods; once was I stoned; thrice I suffered shipwreck; a night and day have I spent in the deep;[4] in journeyings often; in perils of rivers, in perils of robbers, in perils from my own race, in perils from Gentiles, in perils in the city, in perils in the wilderness, in perils in the sea, in perils among false brethren; in toil and weariness, in sleeplessness often, in hunger and thirst, in fastings often; besides the things additional to all these, the care which daily besets me,[5] my anxiety for all the Churches. Who is weak, and I share not his weakness? who is made to stumble, and I do not burn with indignation? If I *must* boast, I will boast of this, the weakness to which I alluded. The God and Father of our Lord Jesus Christ, who is blessed for evermore, knoweth that I am not lying. In Damascus the ethnarch of Aretas the king was guarding the

---

[1] It is very probable that the Claudian famine had made many needy Jewish Christians from Jerusalem go the round of the Churches, *demanding* and receiving the *Chaluka*.

[2] Cf. 1 Kings xxii. 24; Matt. v. 39; Luke xxii. 64; Acts xxiii. 2. Even teachers could act thus. 1 Tim. iii. 3; Titus i. 7.

[3] We can hardly imagine that the Ebionite lie that St. Paul was a Gentile, who had got himself circumcised in order to marry the High Priest's daughter, had as yet been invented; yet the Tarsian birth and Roman franchise may have led to whispered insinuations.

[4] Ex. xv. 5 (LXX.). Theophylact makes it mean "in Bythos," a place near Lystra, after the stoning.

[5] xi. 28, ἐπίστασις (א, B, D, E, F, G).

city of the Damascenes, wishing to seize me; and through a window in a large basket, I was let down through the wall, and escaped his hands."[1]

Such had been his "preparation of feebleness," without which he could neither have been what he was, nor have done what he did. Such is one glimpse of a life never since equalled in self-devotion, as it was also "previously without precedent in the history of the world." Here he breaks off that part of the subject. Did he intend similarly to detail a series of other hair-breadth escapes? or glancing retrospectively at his perils, does he end with the earliest and most ignominious? Or was it never his intention to enter into such a narrative, and did he merely mention the instance of ignominious escape at Damascus, so revolting to the natural dignity of an Oriental and a Rabbi, as a climax of the disgraces he had borne? We cannot tell. At that point, either because he was interrupted, or because his mood changed, or because it occurred to him that he had already shown his ample superiority in the "weakness" of voluntary humiliation to even the most "super-apostolic Apostles," he here stops short, and so deprives us of a tale inestimably precious, which the whole world might have read with breathless interest, and from which it might have learnt invaluable lessons. However that may be, he suddenly exclaims, "Of course it is not expedient for me to boast.[2] I will come to visions and revelations of the Lord." I know a man in Christ fourteen years ago (whether in the body or out of the body[3] I know not, God knows) snatched such an one as far as the third heaven.[4] And I know such a man (whether in the body or apart from the body I know not, God knows) that he was snatched into Paradise, and heard unspeakable utterances which it is not lawful for man to speak. Of such an one I will boast—but of myself I will not boast except in these weaknesses; for even should I wish to boast I shall not be a fool; for I will speak the truth. But I forbear lest any one should

---

[1] xi. 1—33. On the escape from Damascus, see *supra*, Excursus VIII.

[2] δή is the most forcible and natural reading, and here the MSS. variations δὲ (א, D) and δεῖ (B, E, F, G) are probably due to itacism or misapprehension. The δή implies, "You will see from the humiliating escape to which I have just so solemnly testified that in my case boasting is not expedient." If the following "for" (D) be correct, it is due to counter-currents of feeling; but it is omitted in א, B, G.

[3] xii. 3. *leg.* χωρίς, B, D, E. The physical condition was probably identical with that to which Hindu psychologists give the name of *Túrga*,—a fourth state, besides those of waking, dreaming, and slumber. The Hindu yogis call it *Vidéha sthiti*, and dwell rapturously on it in their mystic writings and songs.

[4] The "third heaven" occurs here only. For paradise, see Luke xxiii. 43.

estimate about me above what he sees me to be, or hears at all from me. And to prevent my over-exaltation by the excess of the revelation, there was given me a stake in the flesh,[1] a messenger of Satan to buffet me, that I may not be over-exalted. About this I thrice besought the Lord that it (or he) may stand off from me. And He has said to me, 'My grace sufficeth thee; for my power is perfected in weakness.' Most gladly then will I rather boast in my weaknesses that the power of Christ may spread a tent over me.[2] *That* is why I boast in weaknesses, insults, necessities, persecutions, distresses, for Christ's sake. For when I am weak, then I am mighty. I have become a fool in boasting. You compelled me. For I ought to be 'commended' by *you*. For in no respect was I behind the 'out and out' Apostles,[3] even though I am nothing. Certainly the signs of an Apostle were wrought among you in all patience, by signs, and portents, and powers. The single fact that I did not benumb you with exactions is your sole point of inferiority to other Churches. Forgive me this *injustice!* See a third time I am ready to come to you, and I will not benumb you, for I seek not yours but you. Children ought to treasure up for their parents, but so far from receiving from you, I will very gladly spend and be utterly spent for your souls, even though the more exceedingly I love you, the less I am loved. But stop! though I did not burden you, yet 'being a cunning person I caught you by guile.' Under the pretext of a collection I got money out of you by my confederates! I ask you, is that a fact? Did Titus or the brother whom I have sent with him over-reach you in any respect? Did not they behave exactly as I have done? You have long been fancying that all this is by way of self-defence to you.[4] Do not think it! *You* are no judges of mine. My appeal is being made in the presence of God in Christ; yet, beloved, it has all been for your edification. It was not said to defend myself, but to save us from a miserable meeting, lest we mutually find each other what we should not wish; lest I find you buzzing with quarrels, party spirit, outbreaks of rage, self-seekings, slanders, whisperings, inflations, turbulences; and lest, on my return to you, my God humble me in my relation to you, and I shall mourn over many of those who have sinned before and not repented for the uncleanness, fornication, and wantonness which they practised. It is the third time that I am intending to visit you;[5] it

[1] On this "stake in the flesh," *v. supra*, Excursus X. κολαφίζῃ, lit. "should slap in the face."
[2] xii. 9, ἐπισκηνώσῃ ἐπ' ἐμέ.
[3] xii. 1—11. The colloquialism closely reproduces that of St. Paul.
[4] πάλαι (א, A, B, F, G, Vulg.).
[5] xii. 14. He has been at Corinth once; is now going a second time (πάλιν); and had once intended to go. This is like a thing attested by two or three

will be like the confirming evidence of two or three witnesses. **I have forewarned, and I now warn these persons once more that, if I come, I will not spare.** Since you want a proof that Christ speaks in me, ye shall have it. He was crucified in weakness; we share His death and His weakness, but we shall also share His life and power. Prove *yourselves, test yourselves.* Is Christ in you, or are you spurious Christians, unable to abide the test? You will, I hope, be forced to recognise that *I* am not spurious; but my prayer is that *you* may do no evil, not that *my* genuineness may be manifested; that *you* may do what is noble, even if therewith *we* be regarded as spurious. Against the truth, against genuine faithfulness, I have no power, but only *for* it. Be true to the Gospel, and I shall be powerless; and you will be mighty, and I shall rejoice at the result. I ever pray for this, for your perfection. That is why I write while still absent, in order that when present I may have no need to exercise against you with abrupt severity[1] the power which the Lord gave me, and gave me for building up, not for rasing to the ground."[2]

He would not end with words in which such uncompromising sternness mingled with his immense and self-sacrificing forbearance. He adds, therefore, in his own hand—"Finally, brethren, farewell; be perfect, be comforted, be united, be at peace; then shall the God of love and peace be with you. Salute one another with a holy kiss. All the saints salute you." And then follows the fullest of his Apostolic benedictions, "thence adopted by the Church in all ages as the final blessing of her services"—"The grace of our Lord Jesus Christ, and the love of God, and the fellowship of the Holy Ghost be with you all."[3]

witnesses, and will certainly be fulfilled. I agree with Baur in saying, " Let us give up the fiction of a *journey* for which we can find no reasonable grounds " (*Paul.* ii. 320).

[1] ἀποτόμως only in Titus i. 13, not in LXX. The metaphor is either "by way of amputation" or "precipitately," as in Wisd. v. 23; ἀποτομία (Rom. xi. 22).

[2] xii. 13—xiii. 10.

[3] xiii. 11—13. As these are the last extant words of St. Paul to the Corinthians, it is interesting to see what was the condition of the Church when St. Clement of Rome wrote to them thirty-five years later. We find that they were still somewhat turbulent, somewhat disunited, somewhat sceptical, and St. Clement has to recall to them the examples of St. Peter and St. Paul. On the whole, however, we can see that the appeals and arguments of the Apostle in these two letters have not been in vain. About A.D. 135 the Church was visited by Hegesippus (Euseb. *H. E.* iv. 22), who spoke favourably of their obedience and liberality. Their Bishop Dionysius was exercising a widespread influence. In speaking of the Resurrection, St. Clement alludes to the Phœnix (*ad* Rom. i. 24, 25), which in that age excited much interest (Tac. *Ann.* vi. 28; Plin. *H. N.* x. 2). Can any one fail to see a "grace of superintendency" in the absence of such illustrations from the page of the Apostles?

CHAPTER XXXIV.

THE SECOND VISIT TO CORINTH.

Διδακτικὸν, ἀνεξίκακον.—2 Tim. ii. 24.

St. Luke passes over with the extremest brevity the second sojourn of St. Paul in Macedonia. The reason for his silence may have been that the period was not marked by any special events sufficiently prominent to find room in his pages. It was no part of his plan to dwell on the sources of inward sorrow which weighed so heavily upon the mind of St. Paul, or to detail the afflictions which formed the very groundwork of his ordinary life. It was the experience of St. Paul, more perhaps than that of any man who has ever lived—even if we select those who have made their lives a sacrifice to some great cause of God—that life was a tissue of minor trials, diversified by greater and heavier ones. But St. Luke—not to speak of the special purposes which seem to have guided his sketch—only gives us full accounts of the events which he personally witnessed,[1] or of those which he regarded of capital importance, and about which he could obtain information which he knew to be trustworthy. It is one of the many indications of the scantiness of his biography that he does not even once mention a partner and fellow-worker of St. Paul so dear to him, so able, so energetic, and so deeply trusted as the Greek Titus, of whose activity and enthusiasm the Apostle made so much use in furthering

---

[1] So the Muratorian Canon: "acta antē omniũ apostolorum sub uno libro scribta sunt lucas optime theofile comprindit quia sub praesentia ejus singula gerebantur."

the Offertory, and in the yet more delicate task of dealing with the Christian Corinthians at this most unsatisfactory crisis of their troubled history.

St. Luke accordingly, passing over the distress of mind and the outward persecution which St. Paul tells us he had at this time encountered, says nothing about the many agitations of which we are able from the Epistles to supply the outline. All that he tells us is that Paul passed through these regions, and encouraged them with much exhortation. He does not even mention the interesting circumstance that having preached during his second journey at Philippi, Thessalonica, and Berœa, the capitals respectively of Macedonia Prima, Secunda, and Tertia, he now utilised the intentional postponement of his visit to Corinth by going through Macedonia Quarta as far as Illyricum. Whether he only went to the borders of Illyricum, or whether he entered it and reached as far as Dyrrachium, and even as Nicopolis, and whether by Illyricum is meant the Greek district or the Roman province[1] that went by that name, we cannot tell; but at any rate St. Paul mentions this country as marking the circumference of the outermost circle of those missionary journeys of which Jerusalem was the centre.

That the Offertory greatly occupied his time and thoughts is clear from his own repeated allusions, and the prominence which he gives to this subject in the Epistles to the Corinthians. It must have been one of his trials to be perpetually pleading for pecuniary contributions, among little bodies of converts of whom the majority were not only plunged in poverty, but who had already made the most conspicuous sacrifices on behalf of their Christian faith. It was clear to him that this fact would be unscrupulously used as a handle against him. How-

[1] Titus unto Dalmatia, 2 Tim. iv. 10.

ever careful and businesslike his arrangements might be —however strongly he might insist on having no personal share in the distribution, or even the treasurership of these funds—persons would not be wanting to whisper the base insinuation that Paul found his own account in them by means of accomplices, and that even the laborious diligence with which he worked day and night at his trade, and failed even thus to ward off the pains of want, was only the cloak for a deep-laid scheme of avarice and self-aggrandisement. It was still worse when these charges came from the emissaries of the very Church for the sake of whose poor he was facing this disagreeable work of begging.[1] But never was there any man in this world—however innocent, however saintly—who has escaped malice and slander; indeed, the virulence of this malice and the persistency of this slander are often proportionate to the courage wherewith he confronts the baseness of the world. St. Paul did not profess to be indifferent to these stings of hatred and calumny; he made no secret of the agony which they caused him. He was, on the contrary, acutely sensible of their gross injustice, and of the hindrance which they caused to the great work of his life; and the irony and passion with which, on fitting occasions, he rebuts them is a measure of the suffering which they caused. But, as a rule, he left them unnoticed, and forgave those by whom they were perpetrated :—

> "Assailed by slander and the tongue of strife,
> His only answer was a blameless life ;
> And he that forged and he that flung the dart,
> Had each a brother's interest in his heart."

[1] To this day the Chaluka and Kadima at Jerusalem are the source of endless heart-burnings and jealousies, and cause no particle of gratitude, but are accepted by the Jews as a testimonial to the high desert of living in the Holy City.

For he was not the man to neglect a duty because it was disagreeable, or because his motives in undertaking it might be misinterpreted. And the motives by which he was actuated in this matter were peculiarly sacred. In the first place, the leading Apostles at Jerusalem had bound him by a special promise to take care of their poor, almost as a part of the hard-wrung compact by which their Church had consented to waive, in the case of Gentile converts, the full acceptance of legal obligations. In the second place, the need really existed, and was even urgent; and it was entirely in consonance with St. Paul's own feelings to give them practical proof of that brotherly love which he regarded as the loftiest of Christian virtues. Then, further, in his early days, his ignorant zeal had inflicted on the Church of Jerusalem a deadly injury, and he would fain show the sincerity and agony of his repentance by doing all he could, again and again, to repair it. Lastly, he had a hope—sometimes strong and sometimes weak—that so striking a proof of disinterested generosity on the part of the Gentile Churches which he had founded would surely touch the hearts of the Pharisaic section of the mother Church, and if it could not cement the differences between the Christians of Judæa and Heathendom, would at least prevent the needless widening of the rift which separated them. At moments of deeper discouragement, writing from Corinth to Rome,[1] while he recognises the ideal fitness of an effort on the part of Gentile Christians to show, by help in temporal matters, their sense of obligation for the spiritual blessings which had radiated to them from the Holy City, and while he looks on the contribution as a harvest gathering to prove to Jewish Christians the genuineness

---

[1] Rom. xv. 25—32.

of the seed sown among the heathen, he yet has obvious
misgivings about the spirit in which even this offering
may be accepted, and most earnestly entreats the Romans
not only to agonise with him in their prayers to God that
he may be delivered from Jewish violence in Judæa, but
also that the bounty of which he was the chief minister
might be graciously received. It may be that by that time
experiences of conflict with the Judaisers in Corinth may
have somewhat damped the fervour of his hopes; for *before*
his arrival there,[1] he gives expression to glowing anticipations that their charitable gifts would not only relieve
undeserved distress, but would be a proof of sincere
allegiance to the Gospel of Christ, and would call forth deep
thankfulness to God.[2] Alas! those glowing anticipations
were doomed—there is too much reason to fear—to utter
disappointment.

Having finished his work in the whole of Macedonia,
and finding no more opportunity for usefulness in those
parts,[3] he at last set out on his way to Corinth. It
was probably towards the close of the year 57, but
whether Paul travelled by sea or land, and from
what point he started, we do not know. After his
journey into Macedonia Quarta, he perhaps returned to
Thessalonica, which was a convenient place of rendezvous
for the various brethren who now accompanied him.
The number of his associates makes it most probable
that he chose the less expensive, though, at that late
season of the year, more dangerous mode of transit, and
took ship from Thessalonica to Cenchreae. The care of
the money, and his own determination to have nothing
to do with it, rendered it necessary for the treasurers

---

[1] 2 Cor. viii. 24; ix. 12—15.
[2] 2 Cor. ix. 14.
[3] Rom. xv. 23, μηκέτι τόπον ἔχων ἐν τοῖς κλίμασι τούτοις.

appointed by the scattered communities to accompany his movements. The society of these fellow-travellers must have been a source of deep happiness to the over-tried and over-wearied Apostle, and the sympathy of such devoted friends must have fallen like dew upon his soul. There was the young and quiet Timothy, the beloved companion of his life; there was Tychicus, who had been won in the school of Tyrannus, and remained faithful to him to the very last;[1] there was Gaius of Derbe, a living memorial of the good work done in his earliest missionary journey. Thessalonica had contributed no less than three to the little band—Jason, his fellow-countryman, if not his kinsman, whose house at St. Paul's first visit had been assaulted by a raging mob, which, failing to find his guest, had dragged him before the Politarchs; Aristarchus, who had shared with him the perils of Ephesus, as he subsequently shared his voyage and shipwreck; and Secundus, of whom no particulars are known. Besides these Beroea had despatched Sopater, a Jewish convert, who is one of those who sends his greetings to the Roman Christians.[2] In Corinth itself he was again looking forward to a meeting with some of his dearest friends—with Titus, whose courage and good sense rendered him so invaluable; with Luke the beloved physician, who was in all probability the delegate of Philippi; with Trophimus, an Ephesian Greek, the fatal but innocent cause of St. Paul's arrest at Jerusalem, destined long afterwards to start with him on his voyage as a prisoner, but prevented from sharing his last sufferings by an illness with which he was seized at Miletus;[3] and with the many Corinthian Christians—Justus, Sosthenes, Erastus, Tertius, Quartus,

---

[1] 2 Tim. iv. 12.

[2] Rom. xvi. 21. The exact sense which St. Paul attributed to συγγενὴς is uncertain.

[3] 2 Tim. iv. 20.

Stephanas, Fortunatus, Achaicus, and lastly Gaius of Corinth, with whom St. Paul intended to stay, and whose open house and Christian hospitality were highly valued by the Church.

The gathering of so many Christian hearts could not fail to be a bright point in the cloudy calendar of the Apostle's life. What happy evenings they must have enjoyed, while the toil of his hands in no way impeded the outpouring of his soul! what gay and genial intercourse, such as is possible in its highest degree only to pure and holy souls! what interchange of thoughts and hopes on the deepest of all topics! what hours of mutual consolation amid deepening troubles; what delightful Agapæ; what blessed partaking of the Holy Sacrament; what outpourings of fervent prayer! For three months St. Paul stayed at Corinth, and during those three months he wrote, in all probability, the Epistle to the Galatians, and certainly the Epistle to the Romans—two of the most profound and memorable of all his writings.[1] And since it was but rarely that he was his

---

[1] The subtle indications that the Epistle to the Galatians was written nearly at the same time as the Second Epistle to the Corinthians consist of casual reflections of the same expression and pre-occupation with the same order of thought. The tone, feeling, style, and mode of argument show the greatest similarity. Compare, for instance—

2 CORINTHIANS.	GALATIANS.	2 CORINTHIANS.	GALATIANS.
i. 1	i. 1.	xi. 2	iv. 17.
xi. 4	i. 6.	xi. 20	v. 15.
v. 11	i. 10.	xii. 20, 21	v. 20, 21.
xii. 11	ii. 6.	ii. 7	vi. 1.
v. 15	ii. 20.	xiii. 5	vi. 4.
viii. 6	iii. 3.	ix. 6	vi. 8.
v. 21	iii. 13.	v. 17	vi. 15.

These are but specimens of coincidence in thought and expression, which might be almost indefinitely multiplied. To dwell on the close resemblance between Galatians and Romans is needless. It was noticed a thousand years ago. The Epistle to the Galatians is the rough sketch, that to the Romans the finished picture. The former is an impassioned controversial personal statement of

own amanuensis—since it is his custom to associate one or more and sometimes the whole body of his fellow-travellers with himself in the superscriptions of his letters, as well as to send greetings from them—may we not regard it as certain that those letters were read aloud to the little knot of friends, and formed fruitful topics of long and earnest discussion? Did even St. Paul anticipate that those few rolls of papyrus would be regarded to the latest ages of the world as a priceless treasure?

But what was the state of things which the Apostle found when he stepped out of the house of Gaius into the house of Justus? It was St. Luke's object to show the fundamental unity which existed among Christians, and not to dwell upon the temporary differences which unhappily divided them. He does not, indeed, conceal the existence of discordant elements, but his wish seems to have been to indicate the essential harmony which these discords might disturb, but not destroy. He has not, therefore, told us a single detail of St. Paul's encounter with the false Apostles, the deceitful workers who had huckstered and adulterated the Word of God, or with that one insolent and overbearing emissary, who with his stately presence, trained utterance, and immense pretensions, backed with credentials from Jerusalem and possibly with the prestige of a direct knowledge of Christ, had denied St. Paul's Apostleship, and omitted no opportunity of blackening his character. Did this man face St. Paul? Did his followers abide by the defiance which they had expressed towards him? Was there a crisis in which it

---

the relation of Gentile Christians mainly to one legal obligation—circumcision; the latter is a calm, systematic, general treatise on the relations of the Gospel to the Law. An instructive comparison of Gal. iii. 6—29 with Rom. iv., &c., will be found in Lightfoot's *Galatians*, pp. 44—46.

was decisively tested on which side the true power lay? Did he after all come with a rod, or in the spirit of meekness? was the proof of his Apostleship given by the exercise of discipline, and the utterance of excommunications which struck terror into flagrant apostates, or did the returning allegiance of the erring flock, and the increase of holiness among them, render it unnecessary to resort to stringent measures? To all these questions we can return no certain answer. We may imagine the hush of awful expectation with which the little community gathered in the room of Justus would receive the first entrance and the first utterances of one whose love they had so terribly tried, and against whose person they had levelled such unworthy sarcasms. Personal questions would, however, weigh least with him. They knew well that it was not for party opposition but for moral contumacy that his thunders would be reserved. Since many of them were heinous offenders, since many had not even repented after serious warnings, how must they have shuddered with dread, how must their guilty consciences have made cowards of them all, when at last, after more than three years, they stood face to face with one who could hand them too over to Satan with all the fearful consequences which that sentence entailed! Over all these scenes the veil of oblivion has fallen. The one pen that might have recorded them has written nothing, nor do we hear a single rumour from any other source. But that for the time the Apostle triumphed—that whether in consequence of an actual exertion of power, or of a genuine repentance on the part of his opponents, his authority was once more firmly established—we may infer from his hint that until the Corinthian difficulties were removed he could take no other task in hand, and that in the Epistles which he wrote during these three months of his residence at the Achaian capital he contemplates yet wider missions and freely yields himself to new activities.[1]

Yet, amid our ignorance of facts, we do possess the means of reading the inmost thoughts which were passing through the soul of St. Paul. The two Epistles which he despatched during those three months were in many respects the most important that he ever wrote, and it inspires us with the highest estimate of his intellectual power to know that, within a period so short and so much occupied with other duties and agitations, he yet found time to dictate the Letter to the Galatians, which marks an epoch in the history of the Church, and the Letter to the Romans, which may well be regarded as the most important of all contributions to the system of its theology.

[1] Rom. i. 13; xv. 24, 32.

CHAPTER XXXV.

IMPORTANCE OF THE EPISTLE TO THE GALATIANS.

"In Ex. xxxii. 16, for *charuth*, 'graven,' read *cheruth*, 'freedom,' for thou wilt find no freeman but him who is engaged in the Thorah."—R. MEIR (*Perek.* 2).

"He is a freeman whom THE TRUTH makes free,
And all are slaves beside."

. . . παρακύψας εἰς νόμον τέλειον τὸν τῆς ἐλευθερίας . . . (JAMES i. 25).

WE have already seen that in his brief second visit to the Churches of Galatia, on his road to Ephesus, St. Paul seems to have missed the bright enthusiasm which welcomed his first preaching. His keen eye marked the germs of coming danger, and the warnings which he uttered weakened the warmth of his earlier relationship towards them. But he could hardly have expected the painful tidings that converts once so dear and so loving had relapsed from everything which was distinctive in his teaching into the shallowest ceremonialism of his Judaising opponents. Already, whoever sanctioned them, these men had spoilt his best work, and troubled his happy disciples at Antioch and at Corinth, and they had their eye also on Ephesus. Thus to intrude themselves into other men's labours—thus to let him bear the brunt of all dangers and labours while they tried to monopolise the result—to watch indifferently and unsympathetically while the sower bore forth his good seed, weeping, and then securely to thrust their blunt and greedy sickles into the ripening grain—to dog the footsteps of the bold, self-sacrificing missionary with easy, well-to-do men-pleasers, who, with no personal risk, stole in his absence into the folds which he had constructed, in order to worry with privy paws his defenceless sheep—to trouble with their petty formalisms and artificial orthodoxies the crystal water of Christian simplicity and Christian happiness—to endanger thus the whole future of Christianity by trying to turn it from the freedom of a universal Gospel into the bondage of a Judaic law—to construct a hedge which, except at the cost of a cutting in the flesh, should exclude the noblest of the Gentiles while it admitted the vilest of the Jews—all this, to the clear vision of St. Paul, seemed bad enough. But thus to thrust themselves among the little communities of his Galatian converts — to take advantage of their warm affections and weak intellects— to play on the vacillating frivolity of purpose which made them such easy victims, especially to those who offered them an external cult far more easy than spiritual religion, and bearing a fascinating resemblance to their old ceremonial paganism—this to St. Paul seemed intolerably base.

Vexed at this Galatian fickleness, and stung with righteous indignation at those who had taken advantage of it, he seized his pen to express in the most unmistakable language his opinion of the falsity and worthlessness of the limits into which these Christian Pharisees wished to compress the principles of Christianity—the worn-out and burst condition of the old bottles in which they strove to store the rich, fresh, fermenting wine. It was no time to pause for nice inquiries into motives, or careful balancing of elements, or vague compromise, or polished deference to real or assumed authority. It was true that this class of men came from Jerusalem, and that they belonged to the very Church of Jerusalem for whose poorer members he was making such large exertions. It was true that, in one flagrant instance at any rate, they had, or professed to have, the authority of James. Could it be that James, in the bigotry of lifelong habit, had so wholly failed to add understanding and knowledge to his scrupulous holiness, that he was lending the sanction of his name to a work which St. Paul saw to be utterly ruinous to the wider hopes of Christianity? If so, it could not be helped. James was but a man—a holy man indeed, and a man inspired with the knowledge of great and ennobling truths—but no more faultless or infallible than Peter or than Paul himself. If Peter, more than once, had memorably wavered, James also might waver; and if so, James in this instance was indubitably in the wrong. But St. Paul, at least, never says so; nor does he use a word of disrespect to "the Lord's brother." The Church of Jerusalem had, on a previous occasion, *expressly repudiated* others who professed to speak in their name; nor is there any proof that they had ever sanctioned this sort of counter-mission of espionage, which was subversive of all progress, of all liberty, and even of all morals. For, whoever may have been these Judaic teachers, vanity, party spirit, sensuality, had followed in their wake. They must be tested by their fruits, and those fruits were bitter and poisonous. Some of them, at least, were bad men, anxious to stand well with everybody, and to substitute an outward observance for a true religion. Greed, self-importance, externalism, were everything to them; the Cross was nothing. If they had not been bad men they would not have been so grossly inconsistent as to manipulate and evade the Law to which they professed allegiance. If they had not been bad men they would not have made the free use they did of the vilest of controversial weapons—surreptitious sneers and personal slanders. Yet by such base means as these they had persistently tried to undermine the influence of their great opponent. They systematically disparaged his authority. He was, they said, no Apostle whatever; he was certainly not one of the Twelve; he had never seen Jesus except in a vision, and therefore lacked one essential of the Apostolate; all that he knew of Christianity he had learnt at Jerusalem, and that he had wilfully perverted; his Gospel was not the real Gospel; such authority as he had was simply derived from the heads of the Church at Jerusalem, to whom his doctrines must be referred. Many of his present developments of teaching were all but blasphemous. They were a daring apostasy from the oral and even from the written Law; a revolt against the traditions of the fathers, and even against Moses himself. Was not his preaching a denial of all inspiration? Could they not marshal against him an array of innumerable texts? Was not well-nigh every line of the five books of Moses against him? Who was this Paul, this renegade from the Rabbis, who, for motives best known to himself, had become a nominal Christian from a savage persecutor? Who was he that he should set himself against the Great Lawgiver?[1] If he argued that the Law was abrogated, how could he prove it? Christ had never said so. On the contrary, He had said that not a fraction of a letter of the Law should pass till all was fulfilled. To that the Twelve could bear witness. They kept the Law. They

---

[1] The elements of the above paragraph are drawn partly from the "Galatians," partly from the "Corinthians." For the Ebionite slanders against St. Paul, see Iren. *Adv. Haer.* i. 28; Euseb. *H. E.* iii. 27; Epiphan. *Haer.* xxx. 25; Ps. Clem. *Hom.* ii. 17—19. "Totius mundi odio me oneravi," says Luther, "qui olim eram tutissimus. Ministerium Ecclesiae omnibus periculis expositum est, Diaboli insultationibus, mundi ingratitudini, sectarum blasphemiis" (*Colloq.* i. 13).

were living at peace with their Jewish brethren who yet did not recognise Jesus as the Messiah. Must not Paul's opinions be antagonistic to theirs, if he was the only Christian who could not show his face at Jerusalem without exciting the danger of a tumult? Besides, he was really not to be trusted. He was always shifting about, now saying one thing and now another, with the obvious intention of pleasing men. What could be more inconsistent than his teaching and conduct with regard to circumcision? He had told the Galatians that they need not be circumcised, and yet he himself had once preached circumcision—aye, and more than preached it, he had practised it! Would he answer these two significant questions — Who circumcised Timothy? Who circumcised Titus?

St. Paul saw that it was time to speak out, and he did speak out. The matter at issue was one of vital importance. The very essence of the Gospel—the very liberty which Christ had given—the very redemption for which He had died—was at stake. The fate of the battle hung apparently upon his single arm. He alone was the Apostle of the Gentiles. To him alone had it been granted to see the full bearings of this question. A new faith must not be choked at its birth by the past prejudices of its nominal adherents. Its grave-clothes must not thus be made out of its swaddling-bands. The hour had come when concession was impossible, and there must be no facing both ways in the character of his conciliatoriness. Accordingly he flung all reticence and all compromise to the winds. Hot with righteous anger, he wrote the Epistle to the Galatians. It was his gage of battle to the incompetence of traditional authority—his trumpet-note of defiance to all the Pharisees of Christianity, and it gave no uncertain sound.[1]

Happily, he could give distinctness to his argument by bringing it to bear on one definite point. In recovering the lost outwork of Galatia he would carry the war into the camp of Jerusalem. The new teachers asserted, as at Antioch, the necessity of circumcision for Gentile Christians. If Paul could storm that bastion of Judaising Christianity, he knew that the whole citadel must fall. Circumcision was the very badge of Jewish nationality—the very nucleus of Jewish ceremonialism; the earliest, the most peculiar, the most ineffaceable of Jewish rites. Adam, Noah, Jacob, Joseph, Moses, Balaam, had all been born circumcised.[2] So completely was it the seal of the Covenant, that it had been given not even to Moses, but to Abraham. Joseph had seen that it was duly performed in Egypt. Moses had insisted upon it at all risks in Midian. Joshua had renewed it in Canaan; and so sacred was it deemed to be that the stone knives with which it had been performed were buried in his grave at Timnath Serah. Was there a king or prophet who had not been circumcised? Had not Jesus Himself submitted to circumcision? Was not Elias supposed to be always present, though unseen, to witness its due performance? Was not the mechanical effacement of it regarded as the most despicable of Hellenising apostasies? It was true that in the temporary and local letter which the Apostles had sanctioned they had said that it was not *indispensable* for Gentile converts; but a thing might not

---

[1] "It was necessary that the particularisms of Judaism, which opposed to the heathen world so repellent a demeanour and such offensive claims, should be uprooted, and the baselessness of its prejudices and pretensions fully exposed to the world's eye. This was the service which the Apostle achieved for mankind by his magnificent dialectic" (Baur, *First Three Centuries*, i. 73).

[2] *Abhoth* of Rabbi Nathan, ch. ii.

be indispensable, and yet might be pre-eminently *desirable*. Let them judge for themselves. Did they not hear the Law read? Was not the Law inspired? If so, how could they arbitrarily set it aside?[1]

It was ever thus that Judaism worked, beginning with the Psalms and pure Monotheism, and then proceeding to the knife of circumcision, and the yoke of the Levitic Law, in which they entangled and crushed their slaves.[2] It was ever thus that they compassed sea and land to make one proselyte, and when they had got him, made him ten times more the child of Gehenna than themselves. There was nothing at which the Jew gloried so much as thus leaving his mark on the very body of the despised and hated heathen—hardly less despised and hated, almost even more so, if he had hoped to equal them and their privileges by consenting to become a Jew. It was thus that they had got into their net the royal family of Adiabene. Helena, the amiable queen who fed the paupers of Jerusalem with dried figs and grapes in the famine of Claudius, and who now lies interred with some of her children in the Tombs of the Kings, had taken upon her the vow of the Nazarite for seven years. Just before the completion of the vow at Jerusalem, she had—was it accidentally, or by some trickery?—touched a corpse, and therefore had to continue the vow for seven

---

[1] "But for circumcision, heaven and earth could not exist; for it is said, 'Save for (the sign of) my covenant, I should not have made day and night the ordinances of heaven and earth'" (*Nedarim*, f. 32, col. 1, referring to Jerem. xxxiii. 25). The same remark is made about the whole Law. Rabbi (Jada Hakkadosh) says how great is circumcision, since it is equivalent to all the commandments of the Law, for it is said, "Behold the *blood* of the covenant which the Lord hath made with you, concerning all (Heb., *above* all) these words" (Ex. xxiv. 8).—*Nedarim*, f. 32, 1. Angels so detest an uncircumcised person that, when God spoke to Abraham before circumcision, He spoke in Aramaic, which, it appears, the angels do not understand (*Yalkuth Chadash*, f. 117, 3).

[2] See Hausrath, p. 263.

years more. Once more at the conclusion of this term she had again incurred some trivial pollution, and had again to renew it for yet seven years more. Ananias, a Jewish merchant, in pursuance of his avocations, had got access to the seraglio of King Abennerig, and there had made a proselyte of the queen, and, through her influence, of her two sons, Izates and Monobazus. But he had had the good sense and large-heartedness to tell them that the essence of the Law was love to God and love to man. He was probably a Hagadist, who valued chiefly the great broad truths of which the outward observances of Mosaism were but the temporary casket; and he had the insight to know that for the sake of an outward rite, which could not affect the heart, it was not worth while to disturb a people and imperil a dynasty. His advice must not be confused with the cynical and immoral indifference which made Henri IV. observe that "Paris was well worth a mass." It was, on the contrary, an enlightenment which would not confound the shadow with the substance.[1] It was the conviction that the inscription on the *Chêl* should be obliterated, and the *Chêl* itself broken down.[2] But on the steps of the enlightened Ananias came a narrow bigot, the Rabbi Eliezer of Galilee, and he employed to the facile weakness of the young princes the very argument which the Judaising teacher, whoever he was, employed to the Galatians: "My king, you are sinning against the Law, and therefore against God. It is not enough to read the Law; you must do the

---

[1] Josephus had the good sense to take the same line when "two great men" came to him from Trachonitis; but though for the time he succeeded in persuading the Jews not to force circumcision upon them, yet afterwards these fugitives were nearly massacred by a fanatical mob, and could only secure their lives by a hasty flight. See the very instructive passage in *Vit. Jos.* 23, 31.

[2] Eph. ii. 14.

Law. Read for yourself what it says about circumcision, and you will see how wrong you are."[1] Prince Izates was so much struck with this "uncompromising orthodoxy" that he secretly withdrew into another chamber, and there had the rite performed by his physician. Not long after he and his brother were reading the Pentateuch, and came to the passage about circumcision in Ex. xii. 48. Monobazus looked up at his brother, and said, "I am sorry for you, my brother," and Izates made the same remark to him. This led to a conversation, and the brothers confessed, first to each other and then to Queen Helena, that they had both been secretly circumcised. The queen was naturally alarmed and anxious, and dangerous consequences ensued. But these were nothing to the Jewish fanatic. They would only be a fresh source of publicity, and therefore of glorifying in the flesh of his proselyte. Again, we read in the Talmud that Rabbi[2] was a great friend of "the Emperor Antoninus." On one occasion the Emperor asked him, "Wilt thou give me a piece of Leviathan in the world to come?"—since the flesh of Leviathan and of the bird Barjuchneh are to be the banquet of the blessed hereafter. "Yes," answered Rabbi. "But why dost thou not allow me to partake of the Paschal Lamb?" "How can I," answered Rabbi, "when it is written that

---

[1] Jos. *Antt.* xx. 2, § 2. This interesting royal family had a house in Jerusalem (Jos. *B. J.* v. 6, § 1; vi. 6, § 3).

[2] Rabbi Juda Hakkadosh is thus called κατ' ἐξοχήν. The anecdote is from *Jer. Megillah*, cap. 1. For another wild story about their intercourse, see *Abhoda Zara*, f. 10, 2. The Talmud being the most utterly unhistorical and unchronological of books, it is difficult to say which Emperor is the one alluded to in this and a multitude of similar fables about his supposed intercourse with Rabbi. It cannot be Antoninus Pius, who never left Rome; nor M. Aurelius, who was unfavourable both to Jews and Christians. Possibly the worthless Caracalla may be alluded to, since he once visited Palestine. Heliogabalus appears to be alluded to in some passages of the Talmud as "the younger Antoninus," and he, too, is said to have accepted circumcision.

'no uncircumcised person shall eat thereof'?" Upon hearing this, Antoninus submitted to the rite of circumcision, and embraced Judaism. The imagination of Rabbis and Pharisees was flattered by the thought that even emperors were not too great to accept their *Halachoth*. What would be their feelings towards one who offered the utmost blessings of the Chosen People without a single Judaic observance to the meanest slave?

Self-interest was an additional and a powerful inducement with these retrogressive intruders. Although Christian, they, like the Twelve, like even Paul himself, were still Jews. At Jerusalem they continued regularly to attend the services of the Temple and the gatherings of their synagogue. To be excommunicated from the synagogue in little Jewish communities like those that were congregated in Ancyra and Pessinus was a very serious matter indeed. It was infinitely more pleasant for them to be on good terms with the Jews, by making proselytes of righteousness out of St. Paul's converts. Thus circumcision was only the thin end of the wedge.[1] It obviated the painful liability to persecution. It would naturally lead to the adoption of all the observances, which the converts would constantly hear read to them in the Jewish service. But, if not, it did not much matter. It was not really necessary for them to keep the whole Law. A sort of decent external conformity was enough. So long as they made "a fair show in the flesh," they might in reality do pretty much as they liked. It was against all this hypocrisy, this retrogression, this cowardice, this mummery of the outward, this reliance on the mechanical, that Paul used words which were half battles. There should be no further

---

[1] Gal. v. 3, 6, 12—14.

doubt as to what he really meant and taught. He would leap ashore among his enemies, and burn his ships behind him. He would draw the sword against this false gospel, and fling away the scabbard. What Luther did when he nailed his Theses to the door of the Cathedral of Wittenberg, that St. Paul did when he wrote the Epistle to the Galatians. It was the manifesto of emancipation. It marked an epoch in history. It was for the early days of Christianity what would have been for Protestantism the Confession of Augsburg and the Protest of Spires combined; but it was these "expressed in dithyrambs, and written in jets of flame;" and it was these largely intermingled with an intense personality and impassioned polemics. It was a De Corona, a Westminster Confession, and an Apologia in one. If we wish to find its nearest parallel in vehemence, effectiveness, and depth of conviction, we must look forward for sixteen centuries, and read Luther's famous treatise, *De Captivitate Babylonica*, in which he realised his saying " that there ought to be set aside for this Popish battle a tongue of which every word is a thunderbolt."[1] To the Churches of Galatia he never came again; but the words scrawled on those few sheets of papyrus, whether they failed or not of their immediate effect, were to wake echoes which should "roll from soul to soul, and live for ever and for ever."

[1] Luther, *Tisch-Reden*, 249. But though Luther constantly defends his polemical ferocity by the example of St. Paul, St. Paul never (not even in Gal. v. 12) shows the violence and coarseness which deface the style of Luther.

CHAPTER XXXVI.

THE EPISTLE TO THE GALATIANS.

"The Epistle to the Galatians is my Epistle; I have betrothed myself to it; it is my wife."—LUTHER.

"Principalis adversus Judaismum Epistola."—TERT. *adv. Marc.* v. 2.

"Discrimen Legis et Evangelii est depictum in hoc dicto 'posteriora mea videbitis, faciem meam non videbitis.'

$$\text{Lex} \begin{cases} \text{Dorsum} \\ \text{Ira} \\ \text{Peccatum} \\ \text{Infirmitas} \end{cases} \text{Evangelium} \begin{cases} \text{Facies} \\ \text{Gratia} \\ \text{Donum} \\ \text{Perfectio.} \end{cases}$$

LUTHER, *Colloq.* i., p. 20, ed. 1571.

"Judaism was the narrowest (*i.e.* the most special) of religions, Christianity the most human and comprehensive. In a few years the latter was evolved out of the former, taking all its intensity and durability without resort to any of its limitations. . . . In St. Paul's Epistles we see the general direction in which thought and events must have advanced; otherwise the change would seem as violent and inconceivable as a convulsion which should mingle the Jordan and the Tiber."—MARTINEAU, *Studies of Christianity*, p. 420.

IN the very first line of the Apostle's greeting a part of his object—the vindication of his Apostolic authority—becomes manifest.[1] In the Epistles to the Thessalonians he

[1] The general outline of the Epistle is as follows:—It falls into three divisions—1. Personal (an element which recurs throughout); 2. Dogmatic; 3. Practical. In the first part (i., ii.) he vindicates his personal independence (a) *negatively*, by showing that he was an Apostle before any intercourse with the Twelve (i. 17, 18); and (β) *positively*, since he had secured from the Apostles the triumphant recognition of his own special principles on three occasions, viz., (i.) in an association on perfectly equal terms with Peter (18, 19); (ii.) when they were compelled by facts to recognise his equal mission (ii. 9, 10); and (iii.) when he convinced Peter at Antioch that he was thoroughly in the wrong (ii. 11—21). 2. Passing naturally to the dogmatic defence of justification by faith, he proves it (a) by the Christian consciousness (iii. 1—5), and (β) from the Old Testament (iii. 6—18). This leads him to the question as to the true position of the Law, which he shows to be entirely secondary, (a) *objectively*, by the very nature of

had adopted no title of authority; but, since those Epistles had been written, the Judaists had developed a tendency to limit the term Apostle almost exclusively to the Twelve, and overshadow all others with their immense authority. The word had two technical senses. In the lower sense it merely meant a messenger or worker in the cause of the Gospel, and, as an equivalent to the common Jewish title of *Sheliach*, was freely bestowed on comparatively unknown Christians, like Andronicus and Junias.[1] Now Paul claimed the title in the highest sense, not from vanity or self-assertion, but because it was necessary for the good of his converts. He had the primary qualification of an Apostle, in that he had seen Christ, though for reasons which he explained in the last Epistle he declined to press it. He had the yet further qualification that his Apostolate and that of Barnabas had been publicly recognised by the Church of Jerusalem. But this claim also he wished to waive as unreal and even misleading; for his Apostolate was derived from no merely human authority. Writing to the Corinthians, some of whom had impugned his rights, he had intentionally designated himself as "a called Apostle of Jesus Christ by the will of God." Writing to these weak and apostatising Galatians it was necessary to be still more explicit, and consequently he addresses them with his fullest greeting, in which he speaks both of his own authority and of the work of

---

Christianity (iii. 19—29); and (β) *subjectively*, by the free spiritual life of Christians (iv. 1—11). After affectionate warnings to them about those who had led them away (iv. 11—30), he passes to—3. The practical exhortation to Christian freedom (v. 1—12), and warnings, both general (13—18) and special (v. 16—vi. 10), against its misuse. Then follows the closing summary and blessing (vi. 11—18).

[1] Rom. xvi. 7; cf. Phil. ii. 25; 2 Cor. viii. 23. Similarly the title Imperator was used by Cicero and other Romans down to Junius Blæsus, long after its special sense had been isolated to connote the absolute head of the state.

Christ. By impugning the first they were setting temporary relations above spiritual insight; by errors respecting the latter they were nullifying the doctrine of the Cross.

> "Paul, an Apostle, not from men, nor by the instrumentality of any man, but by Jesus Christ and God our Father, who raised Him from the dead, and all the brethren with me,[1] to the Churches of Galatia. Grace to you and Peace from God the Father and our Lord Jesus Christ, who gave Himself for our sins that He may deliver us from this present evil state of the world, according to the will of our God and Father, to whom is His due glory[2] for ever and ever. Amen."[3]

This greeting is remarkable, not only for the emphatic assertion of his independent Apostleship, and for the skill with which he combines with this subject of his Epistle the great theologic truth of our free deliverance[4] by the death of Christ, but also for the stern brevity of the terms with which he greets those to whom he is writing. A sense of wrong breathes through the fulness of his personal designation, and the scantiness of the address to his converts. He had addressed the Thessalonians as "the Church of the Thessalonians in God our Father and the Lord Jesus Christ." He had written "to the Church of God which is in Corinth, to the sanctified in Christ Jesus, called to be saints." About this very time he wrote to the Romans as "beloved of God, called to be saints." To the Philippians, Ephesians, Colossians, he adds the words "saints in Christ Jesus," and "saints and faithful brethren;" but to these Galatians alone, in his impetuous desire to deal at once with their errors, he

---

[1] At this time he was accompanied by a larger number of brethren than at any other. This is one of the minute circumstances which support the all-but-certain inference that the Epistle was written at this particular period, during St. Paul's three months' stay at Corinth, towards the close of A.D. 57.

[2] ἡ δόξα, sub. ἐστιν. Matt. vi. 13; 1 Pet. iv. 11.

[3] i. 1—5.

[4] i. 4, ἐξέληται. "*Deliver* strikes the keynote of the Epistle" (Lightfoot). ἐνεστῶτος, "present," Rom. viii. 38.

uses only the brief, plain address, "To the Churches of Galatia."

And then without one word of that thanksgiving for their holiness, or their gifts, or the grace of God bestowed on them, which is found in every one of his other general Epistles, he bursts at once into the subject of which his mind is so indignantly full.

"I am amazed that you are so quickly shifting from him who called you in the grace of Christ into a *different* Gospel, which is not merely *another*,[1] only there are some who are troubling you, and wanting to reverse the Gospel of Christ. But even though we, or an angel from heaven, should preach contrary to what we preached to you, *let him be accursed.*[2] As we have said before, so now again I say deliberately, If any one is preaching to you anything contrary to what ye received, LET HIM BE ACCURSED.[3] Well, am I NOW trying to be plausible to men, or to conciliate God Himself? Had I still been trying to be a man-pleaser, I should not have been what I am—a slave of Christ."[4]

Such was the startling abruptness, such the passionate plainness with which he showed them that the time for conciliation was past. Their Jewish teachers said that Paul was shifty and complaisant, and that he did not preach the real Gospel. He tells them that it is they who are perverters of the Gospel, and that if they, or any one of them, or any one else, even an angel, preaches contrary to what he has preached, let the ban—the cherem—fall on him. He has said this before, and to show them that it is not a mere angry phrase, he repeats it

---

[1] If μετατίθεσθε is really a mental pun (as Jerome thought) on *Galatae* and 'ה, we might almost render it *galatising*. For ἕτερον, "different," and ἄλλο, "another," see 2 Cor. xi. 4. Hence ἕτερος came to mean "bad;" θάτερον is the opposite to "good."

[2] i. 8, ἀνάθεμα; the meaning "excommunicated" is later, and would not suit ἄγγελος.

[3] There is a sort of *syllepsis* in this, and the τὸν Θεὸν is more emphatic than the ἀνθρώπους. Probably Paul had been accused of emancipating the Gentiles from Judaism out of mere complaisance.

[4] i. 1—10, ἔτι, "after all I have endured;" v. 11; vi. 17; 1 Cor. xv. 30—32.

more emphatically now, and appeals to it as a triumphant proof that whatever they could charge him with having done and said before, now, at any rate, his language should be unmistakably plain.

"Now I declare to you, brethren, as to the Gospel preached by me that it is not a mere human Gospel. For neither did I myself receive it from man, nor was I taught it, but by revelation from Jesus Christ. For you heard my manner of life formerly in Judaism, that I extravagantly[1] persecuted the Church of God, and ravaged it, and was making advance in Judaism above many my equals in age in my own race, being to an unusual degree a zealot for the traditions of my fathers. But when He who set me apart even from my mother's womb and called me by His grace thought good to reveal His Son in me that I should preach Him among the Gentiles, immediately I did not confer with mere human teachers, nor did I go away to Jerusalem to those who were Apostles before me, but I went away into Arabia, and again returned to Damascus.

"Next, after three years, I went up to Jerusalem to visit Kephas, and I stayed at his house fifteen days; but not a single other Apostle did I see, except James, the Lord's brother.[2] Now in what I am writing to you, see, before God, I am not lying.[3]

"Next I came into the regions of Syria and Cilicia; and was quite unknown by person to the Churches of Judæa which were in Christ, only they were constantly being told that our former persecutor is now a preacher of the faith which once he ravaged. And they glorified God in me.[4]

"Next, after fourteen years, I again went up to Jerusalem with Barnabas, taking with me Titus also.[5] And I went up by revelation, and referred to them the Gospel which I preach among the Gentiles,[6] privately however to those of repute, lest perchance I might be running,

---

[1] i. 13, καθ' ὑπερβολήν, à outrance.

[2] Who in one sense was, and in another was not, an Apostle, not being one of the Twelve.

[3] *V. supra*, i., pp. 232—239. As I have already examined many of the details of this Epistle for biographical purposes, I content myself with referring to the passages. The strong appeal in i. 20 shows that Paul's truthfulness had been questioned. (Cf. 1 Thess. v. 27.)

[4] i. 11—24.

[5] *V. supra*, i., pp. 412—420. Paul's purpose here is not the tedious pedantry of chronological exactitude.

[6] ii. 2, ἀνεθέμην, not to submit to their decision, but with the strong belief he could win their concurrence. (Cf. Acts xxv. 14.)

or even ran, to no purpose.¹ But not even Titus, who was with me, being a Greek, was *compelled* to be circumcised—but because of the false brethren secretly introduced, who slank in to spy out our liberty which we have in Christ Jesus that they might utterly enslave us—[to whom not even (?)] for an hour we yielded *by way of the subjection they wanted*, in order that the truth of the Gospel may permanently remain with you.² From those, however, who are reputed to be something—whatever they once were, makes no matter to me, God cares for no man's person³—for to me those in repute contributed nothing, but, on the contrary, seeing that I have been entrusted with the Gospel of the uncircumcision, as Peter of the circumcision—for He who worked for Peter for the Apostolate of the circumcision, worked also for me towards the Gentiles—and recognising the grace granted to me, James, and Kephas, and John, who are in repute as pillars, gave right hands of fellowship to me and Barnabas, that we to the Gentiles, and they to the circumcision—only that we should bear in mind the poor, which very thing I was of my own accord even eager to do.⁴

"But when Kephas came to Antioch I withstood him to the face, because he was a condemned man.⁵ For before the arrival of certain from James⁶ he used to eat with the Gentiles; but on their arrival⁷ he began to withdraw and separate himself, being afraid of these Jewish

---

¹ Phil. ii. 16. I have already explained the probable meaning of this—"that I might feel *quite* sure of the truth and *practicability* of my views." Even Luther admits, "Sathan saepe mihi dixit, quid si falsum esset dogma tuum?" (*Colloq.* ii. 12.)

² *V. supra*, i., p. 415.

³ ii. 6, Θεὸς ἀνθρώπου. The position is emphatic. This seems to glance at the absurdity of founding *spiritual* authority on mere *family* or *external* claims. (See Martineau, *Studies in Christianity*, p. 428.)

⁴ ii. 1 — 10. It was, as Tertullian says, a *distributio officii*, not a *separatio evangelii* (*De Praescr. Haer.* 28). He had already shown his care for the poor (Acts xi. 30).

⁵ ii. 11, κατεγν. Manifestly and flagrantly in the wrong. Cf. Rom. xiv. 23. To make κατὰ πρόσωπον mean " by way of mask," and treat the scene as one got up (κατὰ σχῆμα) between the Apostles—as Origen and Chrysostom do—or to assume that Kephas does not mean Peter—as Clemens of Alexandria does—is a deplorable specimen of the power of dogmatic prejudice to blind men to obvious fact. St. Peter's weakness bore other bitter fruit. It was one ultimate cause of Ebionite attacks on St. Paul, and of Gnostic attacks on Judaism, and of Porphyry's slanders of the Apostles, and of Jerome's quarrel with Augustine. (See Lightfoot, pp. 123—126.)

⁶ Cf. Acts xv. 24.

⁷ ii. 12, ἦλθεν (κ, B, D, F, G), if St. Paul really wrote it, could only mean "when *James* came;" and so Origen understood it (*c. Cels.* ii. 1).

k

converts. And the rest of the Jews joined in this hypocrisy, so that even Barnabas was swept away by their hypocrisy.[1] But when I perceived that they were not walking in the straight truth of the Gospel, I said to Kephas, before them all, If you, a born Jew, are living Gentile-wise and not Judaically, how can you try to compel the Gentiles to Judaise? We, Jews by birth and not 'sinners' of the Gentiles,[2] but well aware that no man is justified as a result of the works of the Law, but only by means of faith in Jesus Christ—even *we* believed on Jesus Christ that we may be justified as a result of faith in Christ, and not of the works of Law; for from works of Law 'no flesh shall be justified.'[3] But (you will object) if, while seeking to be justified in Christ, we turn out to be even ourselves 'sinners' (men no better than the Gentiles), is then Christ a minister of sin?[4] Away with the thought! For if I rebuild the very things I destroyed, *then* I prove myself to be not only a 'sinner,' but a transgressor." The very rebuilding (he means) would prove that the previous destruction was guilty; "but it was not so," he continues to argue, "for it was by Law that I died to Law;" in other words, it was the Law itself which led me to see its own nullity, and thereby caused my death to it that I might live to God.[5] "I have been crucified with Christ;" my old sins are nailed to His cross, no less than my old Jewish obligations; yet this death is life—not mine, however, but the life of Christ in me; and so

---

[1] We can scarcely even imagine the deadly offence caused by this boldness, an offence felt a century afterwards (Iren. *Haer.* i. 26; Euseb. *H. E.* iii. 27; Epiphan. *Haer.* xxx. 16; Baur, *Ch. Hist.* 89, 98). Even when the Pseudo-Clementine Homilies were written the Jewish Christians had not forgiven the word κατεγνωσμένος. Εἰ κατεγνωσμένον με λέγεις θεοῦ ἀποκαλύψαντός μοι τὸν Χριστὸν κατηγορεῖς (Clem. Hom. xvii. 19). And yet, however bitter against unscrupulous Judaism, St. Paul is always courteous and respectful when he speaks of the Twelve. The *Praedicatio Petri* (in Cyprian, *De Rebapt.*) says that Peter and Paul remained unreconciled till death.

[2] Cf. Rom. ix. 30, ἔθνη τὰ μὴ διώκοντα δικαιοσύνην; Luke vi. 32, 33; Matt. v. 47; ix. 10, 11.

[3] Ps. cxliii. 2. St. Paul's *addition* ἔργοις νόμου is an obvious inference. The accentuation of meaning on *ritual* or *moral* observance must depend on the context. Here the latter is *mainly* in question (Neander, *Planting*, i. 211).

[4] It is impossible to say how much of this argument was actually addressed to Peter. μὴ γένοιτο, חָלִילָה; cf. Gen. xliv. 7, 17.

[5] The Latin fathers and Luther understand it "by the law (of Christ) I am dead to the law (of Moses)." The best commentary is Rom. vii. 1—11. Expressions like this led to the charge of antinomianism, which St. Paul sets aside in 1 Cor. ix. 21. Celsus taunts the Apostles with the use of such language while yet they could denounce each other (*ap.* Orig. v. 64). But they did not profess to have attained their own *ideal* (Phil. iii. 13).

far as I now live in the flesh, I live in faith on the Son of God who loved me, and gave Himself up for me. I am not, therefore, setting at nought the grace of God by proclaiming my freedom from the Levitical Law; *you* are doing that, not I; "for had righteousness been at all possible by Law, then it seems Christ's death was superfluous."[1]

He has now sufficiently vindicated his independent Apostleship, and since this nullification of the death of Christ was the practical issue of the Galatian retrogression into Jewish ritualism, he passes naturally to the doctrinal truth on which he had also touched in his greeting, and he does so with a second burst of surprise and indignation :—

"Dull Galatians![2] who bewitched you with his evil eye,—you before whose eyes Jesus Christ crucified was conspicuously painted?[3] This is the only thing I want to learn of you;—received ye the Spirit as a result of works of Law, or of faithful hearing? Are ye so utterly dull? After beginning the sacred rite spiritually, will ye complete it carnally? Did ye go through so many experiences in vain?[4] if it be indeed in vain. He then that abundantly supplieth to you the Spirit, and worketh powers in you, does he do so as a result of works of Law or of faithful hearing? Of faith surely—just as 'Abraham believed God and it was accounted to him for righteousness.' Recognise then that they who start from faith, *they* are sons of Abraham. And the Scripture foreseeing[5] that God justifies the Gentiles as a result of faith,[6] preached

---

[1] ii. 11—21. For an examination of this paragraph, v. *supra*, i. 442—444.

[2] iii. 1, ἀνόητοι, as in Luke xxiv. 25. So far from being dull in things not spiritual, Themistius calls them ὀξεῖς καὶ ἀγχίνοι καὶ εὐμαθέστεροι τῶν ἄγαν Ἑλλήνων (*Plat.* 23).

[3] If προγράφω has here the same sense as in Rom. xv. 4, Eph. iii. 3, Jude 4, it must mean "prophesied of;" but this gives a far weaker turn to the clause.

[4] iii. 4, ἐπάθετε seems here to have its more general sense, as in Mark v. 26; if the common sense "suffered" be retained, it must allude to troubles caused by Judaisers.

[5] A Hebraic personification. "What saw the Scripture?" is a Rabbinic formula (Schöttg. *ad loc.*). The passages on which the argument is founded are Gen. xv. 6; xii. 3; Deut. xxvii. 26; xxi. 23; Lev. xviii. 5; Hab. ii. 4. The reasoning will be better understood from 2 Cor. v. 15—21; Rom. vi. 3—23.

[6] ἐκ πίστεως, "*from* faith" as a cause; or διὰ τῆς πίστεως, *per fidem*, "by means of faith as an instrument;" never διὰ πίστιν, *propter fidem*, "on account of faith" as a merit.

to Abraham as an anticipation of the Gospel, 'In thee shall all the Gentiles be blessed.' So they who start from faith are blessed with the faithful Abraham. For as many as start from works of law are under a curse. For it stands written, 'Cursed is every one who does not abide by all the things written in the book of the Law to do them.' But that by law no man is justified with God is clear because 'The just shall live by faith.' But the Law is not of faith, but (of works, for its formula is) he that *doth* these things shall live by them. Christ ransomed us from the curse of the Law,—becoming on our behalf a curse, since it is written, 'Cursed is every one who hangeth on a tree'[1]—that the blessing of Abraham may by Christ Jesus accrue to the Gentiles, that we may receive the promise of the Spirit by means of faith."[2]

Then came some of the famous arguments by which he establishes these weighty doctrines—arguments incomparably adapted to convince those to whom he wrote, because they were deduced from their own principles, and grounded on their own methods, however startling was the originality of the conclusions to which they lead. Merely to translate them without brief explanatory comment would add very little to the reader's advantage. I will endeavour, therefore, to throw them into a form which shall supply what is necessary to render them intelligible.

"Brethren," he says, "I will give you an every-day illustration.[3] No one annuls, or vitiates by additions, even a mere human covenant when it has been once ratified. Now the Promises were uttered to Abraham 'and to his seed.' The word employed is neither plural in form nor in significance. A plural word might have been used had *many* been referred to; the reason for the use of a collective term is because *one* person is pre-eminently indicated, and that one person is Christ.[4] What I mean is this: God made and ratified a covenant with Abraham; and the Law which came four hundred and thirty years

---

[1] The original reference is to the exposure of the body on a stake after death (Deut. xxi. 23; Josh. x. 26). St. Paul omits the words "of God" after "cursed," which would have required long explanation, for the notion that it meant "a curse, or insult, against God" is a later gloss. Hence the Talmud speaks of Christ as "the hung" (תלוי).

[2] iii. 1—14.

[3] iii. 15, κατὰ ἄνθρωπον, i.e., ἐξ ἀνθρωπίνων παραδειγμάτων (Chrys.).

[4] V. supra, i., pp. 53, 54.

afterwards[1] cannot possibly nullify the covenant or abrogate the promise. Now God has bestowed the gift on Abraham by promise, and therefore clearly it was not bestowed as a result of obedience to a law.[2]

"Why, then, was the Law? you ask; of what use was it?" Very briefly St. Paul gives them the answer, which in the Epistle to the Romans he elaborates with so much more fulness.

Practically, the answer may be summed up by saying that the Law was damnatory, temporary, mediate, educational.[3] It was added to create in the soul the sense of sin, and so to lead to the Saviour, who in due time should come to render it no more necessary;[4] and it was given by the ministry of angels[5] and a human mediator. It was not, therefore, a promise, but a contract; and a promise direct from God is far superior to a contract made by the agency of a human mediator between God and man.[6] The Law, therefore, was but "supplementary, paren-

---

[1] In Gen. xv. 13, Acts vii. 6, &c., the period in Egypt seems to count from Abraham's visit.

[2] iii. 15—18.

[3] iii. 15, ἐπιδιατάσσεται; 19, προσετέθη; Rom. v. 20, παρεισῆλθεν. The Law was (1) τῶν παραβάσεων χάριν, restricted and conditioned; (2) ἄχρις οὗ, κ.τ.λ., temporary and provisional; (3) διαταγείς, κ.τ.λ., mediately (but not immediately) given by God; (4) ἐν χειρὶ μεσ., mediately (not immediately) received from God (Bp. Ellicott, ad loc.). The Law is a harsh, imperious incident in a necessary divine training.

[4] iii. 19, παραβάσεων χάριν means "to bring transgression to a head." See Rom. v. 20; 1 Cor. xv. 56. The fact is here stated in all its harshness, but in Rom. vii. 7, 13, the Apostle shows by a masterly psychological analysis in what way this was true—namely, because (i.) law actually tends to provoke disobedience, and (ii.) it gives the sting to the disobedience by making us fully conscious of its heinousness. The Law thus brought the disease of sin to a head, that it might then be cured. We might not be able to follow these pregnant allusions of the Epistle if we did not possess the Epistle to the Romans as a commentary upon it. The Galatians could only have understood it by the reminiscences of Paul's oral teaching.

[5] Jos. Antt. xv. 5, § 3; Acts vii. 53; Deut. xxxiii. 2. These angels at Sinai are often alluded to in the Talmud. R. Joshua ben Levi rendered Psalm lxviii. 12, "The Angels (מלאכי) of hosts kept moving" the Children of Israel nearer to Sinai when they retired from it (Shabbath, f. 88, 2).

[6] iii. 19, 20. A "mediator" in Jewish language meant one who stands in the middle position between two parties.

> "The voice of God
> To mortal ear is dreadful. They beseech
> That Moses might repeat to them His will,
> And terror cease." (Milton, P. L. xii. 235.)

Moses receives the Law direct from God (ἐν χειρὶ), and hands it to man (Ex. xx. 19). He therefore was not one of the contracting parties; but God is

thetical, provisional, manuductory." How startling would such arguments be to those who had, from their earliest childhood, been taught to regard the Law as the one divine, inspired, perfect, and eternal thing on earth; the one thing which alone it was worth the labour of long lives to study, and the labour of long generations to interpret and to defend! And how splendid the originality which could thus burst the bonds of immemorial prejudice, and the courage which could thus face the wrath of outraged conviction! It was the enlightenment and inspiration of the Holy Spirit of God; yes, but the Spirit works by the human instruments that are fitted to receive His indwelling power; and, in the admirable saying of the Chinese philosopher, "The light of heaven cannot shine into an inverted bowl." To many a thoughtful and candid Jew it must have come like a flash of new insight into the history of his nation, and of mankind, that he had elevated the Law to too exclusive a position; that the promise to Abraham was an event of far deeper significance than the legislation of Sinai; that the Promise, not the Law, was the *primary* and *original* element of Judaism; and that therefore to fall back from Christianity to Judaism was to fall back from the spirit to the letter—an unnatural reversion of what God had ordained.

But he proceeds, "Is there any opposition between the Law and the Promise? Away with the thought! In God's œconomy of salvation both are united, and the Law is a *relative* purpose of God which is taken up into His *absolute* purpose as a means.[1] For had a Law been given such as could give life, righteousness would in reality have been a result of law; but the Scripture shut up all things under sin, that the promise which springs from faith in Jesus Christ may be given to all who believe.

---

one, *i.e.*, He is no mediator, but one of the parties to the covenant (διαθήκη). It is only under a *different* aspect that Christ is a mediator (1 Tim. ii. 5). The passage has no reference to the eternal unity of God, which is not at all in question, but to the fact that He stands by Himself as one of the contracting parties. The "Law," then, has the same subordinate position as the "Mediator" Moses. The Promise stands above it as a "covenant," in which God stands alone—"is one"—and in which no mediator is concerned. Such seems to be the clear and simple meaning of this endlessly-disputed passage. (See Baur, *Paul*, ii. 198.) Obviously, (1) the Promise had a wider and nobler scope than the Law; (2) the Law was provisional, the Promise permanent; (3) the Law was given directly by angels, the Promise directly by God; but, while he leaves these three points of contrast to be inferred, he adds the fourth and most important, that (4) the Promise was given, without any mediating human agency, from God to man. On the sources of the (perfectly needless) "three hundred explanations" of a passage by no means unintelligible, see Reuss, *Les Epîtres*, i. 109.

[1] iii. 19, 20. Holsten, *Inhalt des Briefs an die Galater*, p. 30.

EPISTLE TO THE GALATIANS. 151

For before the faith came we were under watch and ward of Law, till the faith which was to be revealed. So the Law became our tutor unto Christ, the stern slave guiding us from boyish immaturity to perfect Christian manhood,[1] in order that we may be justified as a result of faith. But when the faith came we are no longer under a tutor. For by the faith ye are all sons of God in Jesus Christ. For as many of you as were baptised into Christ, put on Christ. There is no room for Jew or Greek, no room for slave or free, no room for male and female; for ye are all one man in Christ Jesus;[2] and if ye are of Christ then it seems ye are Abraham's seed, heirs according to promise.[3]

"Now, what I mean is, that so long as the heir is an infant he differs in no respect from a slave, though he is lord of all, but is under tutors and stewards till the term fixed by his father. So we, too, when we were infants, were enslaved under elements of material teaching; but when the fulness of time came God sent forth His Son—born of a woman, that we may receive the adoption of sons;[4] born under Law, that He may ransom those under Law. But because ye are sons, God sent forth the Spirit of His Son into our hearts crying, Abba, our Father! So thou art no longer a slave, but a son, and if a son, an heir also by God's means. Well, in past time not knowing God ye were slaves to those who by nature are not gods, but now after recognising God—nay, rather being recognised by God—how can ye turn back again to the weak and beggarly rudiments,[5] to which again from the

---

[1] iii. 24, παιδαγωγὸς εἰς Χριστόν. The παιδαγωγὸς was often the most valueless of the slaves. Perikles appointed the aged Zopyrus as the παιδαγωγὸς of Alkibiades. This fact can, however, hardly have entered into St. Paul's meaning. The world, until Christ came, was in its pupilage, and the Law was given to hold it under discipline, till a new period of spiritual freedom dawned. The more inward relation between Law and sin, and its power to bring sin more to our conscience, and so bring about the possibility of its removal, are, as we shall see, worked out in the Epistle to the Romans.

[2] Contrast this with the Jewish morning prayer, in which in three benedictions a man blesses God who has not made him a Gentile, a slave, or a woman.

[3] iii. 21—29.

[4] iv. 4, 5. Notice the chiasmus of the original which would not suit the English idiom. Notice, too, the importance of the passage as showing that men did not *begin* to be sons of God, when they were *declared* sons of God, just as the Roman act of emancipation did not *cause* sons to be sons, but merely put them in possession of their rights (Maurice, *Unity*, p. 504).

[5] iv. 3, στοιχεῖα τοῦ κόσμου; 9, ἀσθενῆ καὶ πτωχὰ στοιχεῖα, physical elements of religion, symbols, ceremonies (cf. Col. ii. 8), &c., which invest the natural with religious significance. Both in Judaism and heathenism religion was so much bound up with the material and the sensuous as to place men in bondage

beginning ye want to be slaves? Ye are anxiously keeping days and months and seasons and years. I fear for you that I have perhaps toiled for you in vain."[1]

In this clause the boldness of thought and utterance is even more striking. He not only urges the superiority of the Christian covenant, but speaks of the Jewish as mere legal infancy and actual serfdom; nay, more, he speaks of the ceremonial observances of the Levitical Law as "weak and beggarly rudiments;" and, worse than all, he incidentally compares them to the ritualisms of heathendom, implying that there is no essential difference between observing the full moon in the synagogue and observing it in the Temple of Mên; between living in leafy booths in autumn, or striking up the wail for Altis in spring; nay, even between circumcision and the yet ghastlier mutilations of the priests of Cybele.[2] Eighteen hundred years have passed since this brief letter was written, and it has so permeated all the veins of Christian thought that in these days we accept its principles as a matter of course; yet it needs no very violent effort of the imagination to conceive how savage would be the wrath which would be kindled in the minds of the Jews—aye, and even of the Jewish Christians—by words which not only spoke with scorn of the little distinctive observances which were to them as the very breath of their nostrils, but wounded to the quick their natural pride, by placing their cherished formalities, and even the antique and highly-valued badge of their nationality, on a level with the pagan customs which they had ever regarded with hatred and contempt. Yet it was with no desire to

In neither was God recognised as a Spirit (Baur, *New Test. Theol.*, p. 171). Or the notion may be that ritualism is only the elementary teaching, the A B C of religion.

[1] iv. 1—11. Cf. Col. ii. 16.
[2] Hausrath, p. 268.

waken infuriated prejudice that St. Paul thus wrote. The ritualisms of heathen worship, so far as they enshrined or kept alive any spark of genuine devotion, were not objectionable—had a useful function; in this respect they stood on a level with those of Judaism. The infinite superiority of the Judaic ritual arose from its being the shadow of good things to come. It had fulfilled its task, and ought now to be suffered to drop away. It is not for the sake of the calyx, but for the sake of the corolla, that we cultivate the flower, and the calyx may drop away when the flower is fully blown. To cling to the shadow when it had been superseded by the substance was to reverse the order of God.

Then comes a strong and tender appeal.

"Become as I, because I too became as you, brethren, I beseech you.[1] It is not I whom you wronged at all, by your aberrations. Nay, to me you were always kind. You know that the former time it was in consequence of a sickness that I preached to you; and though my personal condition might well have been a trial to you, ye despised me not, nor loathed me,[2] but as an angel of God ye received me, as Christ Jesus. What, then, has become of your self-felicitation? for I bear you witness that, if possible, ye dug out your very eyes and gave them me. So, have I become your enemy by speaking the truth to you?[3]

"Mere alien teachers are paying court to you assiduously, but not honourably; nay, they want to wall you up from every one else, that you may pay court to them.[4] Now, to have court paid to you is honourable in an honourable cause always, and not only when I am with you,[5] my little children whom again I travail with, until Christ be

---

[1] *i.e.*, free from the bondage of Judaism.

[2] iv. 14, ἐξεπτύσατε—lit., "spat out," Krenkel (*v. supra*, i., Excursus X.) explains this of the "spitting" to avert epilepsy. "Despuimus comitiales morbos" (Plin. xxviii. 4, 7; Plaut. *Capt.* iii. 4, 18, 21).

[3] iv. 12—16. On this passage, *v. supra*, i., Excursus X.

[4] iv. 17, ἵνα—ζηλοῦτε (ind.), but probably *meant* for a subjunctive; the apparent solecism is probably due to the difficulty of remembering the inflexions of the contract verb; cf. 1 Cor. iv. 6.

[5] He seems to mean, "I do not blame zealous attachment, provided it be (as mine to you was) from noble motives, and provided it be not terminated (as yours to me was) by a temporary separation."

formed in you. But I could have wished to be with you now, and to change my voice to you,[1] for I am quite at a loss about you."[2]

Then, returning as it were to the attack, he addresses to them the curious allegory of the two wives of Abraham, Sarah and Hagar, and their sons Ishmael and Isaac.[3]

These are types of the two covenants—Hagar represents Sinai, corresponds to, or is under the same head with bondage, with the Law, with the Old Covenant, and therefore with the earthly Jerusalem, which is in bondage under the Law; but Sarah corresponds to freedom, and the promise, and therefore to the New Covenant, and to the New Jerusalem which is the free mother of us all. There must be antagonism between the two, as there was between the brother-sons of the slave and the freewoman; but this ended in the son of the slave-woman being cast out. So it is now; the unbelieving Jews, the natural descendants of the real Sarah, are the spiritual descendants of Hagar, the ejected bondwoman of the Sinaitic wilderness, and they persecute the Gentiles, who are the prophesied descendants of the spiritual Sarah. The spiritual descendants of Sarah shall inherit the blessing of which those Jews who are descended physically from her should have no share. Isaac, the supernatural child of promise, represents the spiritual seed of Abraham,—that is Christ, and all who, whether Jew or Gentile, are in Him. "Therefore, brethren, we," he adds—identifying himself far more entirely with Gentiles than with Jews, "are not children of a slave-woman, but of the free. In the freedom wherewith Christ freed us, stand then, and be not again enyoked with the yoke of slavery."

Again, how strange and how enraging to the Jews would be such an allegory! It was Philonian, Rabbinic; but it was more admirable than any allegory in Philo, because it did not simply merge the historical in the metaphorical; and more full of ability and insight than any in the Rabbis.[4] This was, indeed, "to steal a feather from the spicy nest of the Phœnix" in order to wing the shaft which should pierce her breast. The Jews, the descendants of Sarah, by the irresistible logic of their own most cherished

---

[1] *i.e.*, to speak to you in gentler tones.
[2] iv. 17—20.
[3] On this allegory see *supra*, vol. i., p. 57.
[4] It was no mere pretty application of a story. It was the detection in one particular case of a divine law, which might be traced through every fact of the divine history" (Maurice, *Unity*, 508). How different from Philo's allegory, in which Charran is the senses; Abraham, the soul; Sarah, divine wisdom; Isaac, human wisdom; Ishmael, sophistry; &c.

method, here find themselves identified with the descendants of the despised and hated Hagar, just as before they had heard the proof that not they but the converted Gentiles were truly Abraham's seed![1]

And the Galatians must be under no mistake; they cannot serve two masters; they cannot combine the Law and the Gospel. Nor must they fancy that they could escape persecution by getting circumcised and stop at that point. "See," he says, "I, Paul—who, as they tell you, once preached circumcision—I, Paul, tell you that, if you hanker after reliance on circumcision, Christ shall profit you nothing. Nay, I protest again to every person who gets himself circumcised, that he is a debtor to keep the whole Law. Ye are nullified from Christ, ye who seek justification in Law, ye are banished from His grace; for we spiritually, as a consequence of faith, earnestly await the hope of righteousness. For in Christ neither circumcision availeth anything, nor uncircumcision, but faith working by means of love."[2] "In these," as Bengel says, "stands all Christianity."

"Ye were running bravely. Who broke up your path to prevent your obeying truth? This persuasion is not from Him who calleth you. It is an alien intrusion—it comes only from one or two—yet beware of it. A little leaven leaveneth the whole lump. *I* feel confident with respect to you[3] in the Lord that you will adopt my views; and he who troubles you shall bear the burden of his judgment, be he who he may. And as for me, if I am still preaching circumcision, why am I still an object of persecution? The stumbling-block of the cross has been done away with, it appears! *They* are not persecuted,—just because they preach circumcision; why then should *I* be, if as they say I preach it too? Would that these turners of you upside down would go a little further than circumcision, and make themselves like the priests of Cybele!"[4]

"I cannot help this strong language; for *ye* were called for freedom, brethren; only, not freedom for a handle to the flesh, but by love be slaves to one another.[5] For the whole Law is absolutely fulfilled[6] in one

---

[1] iv. 21—31. [2] v. 1—6.
[3] v. 10, ἐγὼ πέποιθα εἰς ὑμᾶς.
[4] v. 7—12, ἀποκόψονται; cf. ἀποκεκομμένοι, Deut. xxiii. 1. I have given the only admissible meaning. Reuss calls it "une phrase affreuse, qui révolte notre sentiment." This is to judge a writer by the standard of two millenniums later. Accustomed to Paul's manner and temperament it would have been read as a touch of rough humour, yet with a deep meaning in it—viz., that circumcision to Gentiles was mere *concision* (Phil. iii. 2, 3), and if as such it had any virtue in it, there was something to be said for the priests at Pessinus.
[5] 1 Peter ii. 16.
[6] v. 14, πεπλήρωται, has been fulfilled; Matt. xxii. 40; Rom. xiii. 8 (Lev. xix. 18).

word in the 'Thou shalt love thy neighbour as thyself.' But if ye are biting and devouring one another, take heed that ye be not consumed by one another.[1]

"I mean then, walk spiritually, and there is no fear of your fulfilling the lusts of the flesh. The flesh and the spirit are mutually opposing principles, and their opposition prevents your fulfilling your highest will. But if ye are led by the spirit ye are not under Law. Now the deeds of the flesh are manifest; such are fornication, uncleanness, wantonness, idolatry, witchcrafts,[2]—enmities, discord, rivalry, wraths, cabals, party-factions, envies, murders,[3]—drunkenness, revellings,[4] and things like these; as to which I warn you now, as I warned you before, that all who do such things shall not inherit the kingdom of God. But the fruit of the Spirit[5] is love, joy, peace, longsuffering, kindness, beneficence, faith, gentleness, self-control. Against such things as these there is no law. But they that are of Christ Jesus crucified the flesh with its passions and desires. If we are living spiritually, spiritually also let us walk. Let us not become vainglorious, provoking one another, envying one another."[6]

At this point there is a break. It may be that some circumstance at Corinth had powerfully affected him. Another lapse into immorality may have taken place in that unstable church, or something may have strongly reminded St. Paul of the overwhelming effect which had been produced by the sentence on the particular offender whom he had decided to hand over to Satan. However this may be, he says with peculiar solemnity:—

---

[1] v. 13—15. To a great extent the Apostle's warning was fulfilled. Julian, *Ep.* 52, speaks of their internecine dissensions. Galatia became not only the stronghold of Montanism, but the headquarters of Ophites, Manichees, Passalorynchites, Ascodrogites, Artotyrites, Borborites, and other

"Gorgons and hydras, and chimæras dire;"

and St. Jerome speaks of Ancyra as *Schismatibus dilacerata, dogmatum varietatibus constuprata* (Lightfoot, *Gal.*, p. 31).

[2] Sins *with others* against God.
[3] Sins against our neighbour.
[4] Personal sins (Bengel).
[5] *Deeds* of the flesh, because they spring from ourselves; *fruit* of the spirit, because they need the help of God's grace (Chrys.).
[6] v. 16—26.

"Brethren, even though a man be surprised in a transgression, ye the spiritual restore such an one in a spirit of meekness, considering thyself lest even thou shouldst be tempted. Bear ye the burdens of one another's cares,[1] and so shall ye fulfil the law of Christ. But if any man believes himself to be something when he is nothing, he is deceiving himself. But let each man test his own work, and then he shall have his ground of boasting with reference to himself, and not to his neighbour. For each one shall bear his own appointed load.[2]

"Let then him who is taught the word communicate with the teacher in all good things.[3] Be not deceived, God is not mocked. Whatsoever a man soweth, that also he shall reap. For he that soweth to his flesh, from his flesh shall reap corruption; but he that soweth to the Spirit, from the Spirit shall reap life eternal. [That is the general principle; apply it to the special instance of the contribution for which I have asked you.] Let us not lose heart in doing right, for at the due time we shall reap if we faint not. Well, then, as we have opportunity, let us do good to all men, but especially to those who are of the family of the faith.[4]

"Look ye with what large letters I write to you with my own hand.[5] As many as want to make fair show in the flesh, want to compel you to get yourselves circumcised, only that they may not be persecuted for the cross of Christ. For not even the circumcision party themselves keep the law, yet they want to get you circumcised that they may boast in your flesh. But far be it from me to boast except in the cross of our Lord Jesus Christ, by whom the world has been crucified to me, and I to the world. For neither circumcision is anything nor uncircumcision, but a new creation.[6] And as many as shall walk by this rule, peace on them and mercy, and on the Israel of God." And then, as though by a sudden after-thought, we have the "Henceforth let no

---

[1] vi. 2, $\beta\alpha\rho\eta$, weaknesses, sufferings, even sins.

[2] vi. 1—5. vi. 5, $\phi o \rho \tau i o \nu$ of responsibility and moral consequence.

[3] 1 Cor. ix.; Rom. xii. 13; 1 Thess. v. 12.

[4] vi. 6—10.

[5] Theodore of Mopsuestia, believing that only the conclusion of the letter was autograph, makes the size of the letters a sort of sign that the Apostle does not blush for anything he has said. But the style of the letter seems to show that it was not dictated to an amanuensis.

[6] It will be seen that in those two clauses he has resumed both the polemical (12, 13) and the dogmatic theses (14, 16) of the letter; and that the personal (17) as well as the doctrinal truth (18) on which he has been dwelling recur in the two last verses. Thus, from first to last, the Epistle is characterised by remarkable unity.

man trouble me, for I bear in triumph on my body the brands of Jesus."[1]

"The grace of our Lord Jesus Christ be with your spirit, brethren. Amen."[2]

Such was the Epistle to the Galatians; nor can we without some knowledge of what Judaism then was, and what it was daily becoming, form any adequate conception of the daring courage, the splendid originality—let us rather say the inspired and inspiring faith—which enabled the Apostle thus to throw off the yoke of immemorial traditions, and to defy the hatred of those among whom he had been trained as a Hebrew and a Pharisee. We must remember that at this very time the schools of Rabbinism were fencing the Law with a jealous exclusiveness which yearly increased in its intensity; and that while St. Paul was freely flinging open all, and more than all, of the most cherished hopes and exalted privileges of Judaism, without one of its burdens, the Rabbis and Rabbans were on the high road to the conclusion that any Gentile who dared to get beyond the seven Noachian precepts—any Gentile, for instance, who had the audacity to keep the Sabbath as a day of rest—without becoming a proselyte of righteousness, and so accepting the entire yoke of Levitism, "neither adding to it nor diminishing from it," deserved to be beaten and punished, and to be

---

[1] Hence, as one marked with the brands of his master, in his next Epistle (Rom. i. 1) he for the first time calls himself "a slave of Jesus Christ." Stigmata were usually a punishment, so that in classic Greek, *stigmatias* is "a rascal." Whether St. Paul's metaphor turns on his having been a deserter from Christ's service before his conversion, or on his being a Hierodoulos (Hdt. ii. 113), is doubtful. There seem, too, to be traces of the branding of *recruits* (Rönsch. *Das N. T. Tertullian's*, p. 700). The use of "stigmata" for the "five wounds" has had an effect analogous to the notion of "unknown" tongues.

[2] vi. 11—18. The one unusual last word, "brethren," beautifully tempers the general severity of tone.

informed that he thereby legally incurred the penalty of death.[1] What was the effect of the Epistle on the Churches of Galatia we cannot tell; but for the Church of Christ the work was done. By this letter Gentiles were freed for ever from the peril of having their Christianity subjected to impossible and carnal conditions. In the Epistle to the Romans circumcision does not occur as a practical question. Judaism continued, indeed, for some time to exercise over Christianity a powerful influence, but in the Epistle of Barnabas circumcision is treated with contempt, and even attributed to the deception of an evil angel;[2] in the Epistle of Ignatius, St. Paul's distinction of the true and false circumcision is absolutely accepted;[3] and even in the Clementine Homilies, Judaistic as they are, not a word is said of the necessity of circumcision, but he who desires to be un-Hellenised must be so by baptism and the new birth.[4]

The Epistle to the Galatians was quickly followed by that to the Romans, which was at once singularly like and singularly unlike its immediate predecessor. No violent external opposition, no deep inward sorrow was at that particular moment absorbing the Apostle's soul. It was a little pause in his troubled life. The period of his winter stay at Corinth was drawing to a close. He was already contemplating a yet wider circle for his next missionary tour. The tide of his thoughts was turning wholly towards the West. He wished to see Rome, and, without making any prolonged visit, to confirm the Gospel in the capital of the world. He did not contemplate a long stay

[1] See Sanhedrin, f. 58, c. 2; and Maimonides Yad Hachezakah (Hilchoth Melachim, § 10, Hal. 9).
[2] Ep. Ps. Barnab. ix.
[3] Ep. ad Philad. 6, ὁ τῆς κάτω περιτομῆς ψευδοιουδαῖος.
[4] ἀφελληνισθῆναι (Ps.-Clem. Hom. iii. 9).

among the Roman Christians, because it was his invariable principle not to build on other men's foundations. But he wished to be helped by them—with facilities which a great capital alone can offer—on his journey to Spain, where as yet the Gospel had been unpreached. His heart was yearning towards the shores whose vessels he saw in the ports of Lechæum and Cenchreæ, and whose swarthy sailors he may have often met in the crowded streets.

But before he could come to them he determined to carry out his long-planned visit to Jerusalem. Whether the members of that church loved or whether they hated him—whether they would give to his converts the right hand of fellowship or hold them at arm's-length—he at least would repay evil with good; he would effectually aid their mass of struggling pauperism; he would accompany the delegates who carried to them a proof of Gentile love and generosity, and would himself hand over to the Apostles the sums—which must by this time have reached a considerable amount—which had been collected solely by his incessant endeavours. How earnestly and even solemnly had he brought this duty before the Galatians, both orally and by letter! how carefully had he recommended the Corinthians to prevent all uncertainty in the contributions by presenting them in the form of a weekly offering! how had he stimulated the Macedonians by the forwardness of the Achaians, and the Achaians by the liberality of the Macedonians. And after all this trouble, forethought, and persistence, and all the gross insinuations which he had braved to bring it to a successful issue, it was but natural that one so warm-hearted should wish to reap some small earthly reward for his exertions by witnessing the pleasure which the subscription afforded to the mother church, and the relief which it furnished to its humbler members. But he did not conceal from himself that this visit to Jerusalem would be accompanied by great dangers. He was thrusting his head into the lion's den of Judaism, and from all his past experience it was but too clear that in such a place, and amid the deepened fanaticism of one of the yearly feasts, perils among his own countrymen and perils among false brethren, would beset every step of his path. Whether he would escape those perils was known to God alone. Paul was a man who cherished no illusions. He had studied too deeply the books of Scripture and the book of experience to be ignorant of the manner in which God deals with His saints. He knew how Elijah, how Isaiah, how Jeremiah, how Ezekiel, how Daniel, how John the Baptist, how the Lord Jesus Himself, had lived and died. He knew that devotion to God's work involved no protection from earthly miseries and trials, and he quoted without a murmur the sad words of the Psalmist, "For Thy sake are we killed all the day long; we are accounted as sheep appointed to be slain."[1] But whether it was God's will that he should escape or not, at any rate it would be well to write to the Roman Christians, and answer all objections, and remove all doubts respecting the real nature of his teaching, by a systematic statement of his beliefs as to the true relations between Jews and Gentiles, between the Law and the Gospel, as viewed in the light of the great Christian revelation that we are justified through faith in Christ. This, if anything, might save him from those Judaic counter-efforts on the part of nominal Christians, which had undone half his work, and threatened to render of no effect the cross of Christ. He therefore availed himself of the earliest opportunity to write and to despatch the greatest of all his Epistles—one of the greatest and deepest and most memorably influential of all compositions ever written by human pen—the Epistle to the Romans.

[1] Rom. viii. 36.

CHAPTER XXXVII.

THE EPISTLE TO THE ROMANS, AND THE THEOLOGY OF ST. PAUL.

Πῶς γὰρ ἔσται βροτὸς δίκαιος ἔναντι κυρίου;—JOB xxv. 4 (LXX.).

> But to the cross He nails thy enemies,
> The Law that is against thee, and the sins
> Of all mankind; with Him these are crucified,
> Never to hurt them more who rightly trust
> In this His satisfaction.
> MILTON, *Par. Lost*, xii.

Παῦλος ὁ μέγας τῆς ἀληθείας κῆρυξ, τὸ καύχημα τῆς ἐκκλησίας, ὁ ἐν οὐρανοῖς ἄνθρωπος.—PS. CHRYS. *Orat. Encom.*

I.—INTRODUCTORY.

BEFORE we enter on the examination of the Epistle to the Romans, it will be necessary to understand, as far as we can, the special objects which the Apostle had in view, and the conditions of the Church to which it was addressed.

The first conqueror who had introduced the Jews in any numbers into Rome was the great Pompeius, who treated the nation with extreme indignity.[1] In the capital of the world they showed that strong self-reliance by which they have ever been distinguished. From the peculiarities of their religious conviction, they were useless and troublesome as ordinary slaves, but they displayed in every direction the adaptability to external conditions, which, together with their amazing patience, have secured them an ever-strengthening position throughout the world. They soon, therefore, won their emancipation, and began to multiply and flourish. The close relations of friend-

---

[1] Jos. *Antt.* xiv. 4, 1—5; *B. J.* i. 7; Florus. iii. 5; Tac. *H.* v. 9; Cic. *pro Flac.* xxvii., &c.

ship which existed between Augustus and Herod the Great improved their condition; and at the dawn of the Christian era, they were so completely recognised as an integral section of the population, with rights and a religion of their own, that the politic Emperor assigned to them that quarter beyond the Tiber which they have occupied for ages since.[1] From these dim purlieus, where they sold sulphur matches, and old clothes, and broken glass, and went to beg and tell fortunes on the Cestian or Fabrician bridge,[2] 8,000 of them swarmed forth to escort fifty deputies who came from Jerusalem with a petition to Augustus.[3] It was doubtless the danger caused by their growing numbers which led to that fierce attempt of Sejanus to get rid of them which Tacitus records, not only without one touch of pity, but even with concentrated scorn.[4] The subsequent, but less atrocious decree of Claudius,[5] brought about St. Paul's friendship with Aquila and Priscilla, and is probably identical with the measure alluded to by Suetonius in the famous passage about the *"Impulsor Chrestus."*[6] If so, it is almost certain that Christians must have been confounded with Jews in the common misfortune caused by their Messianic differences.[7] But, as Tacitus confesses in speaking of the attempt to expel astrologers from Italy, these measures

---

[1] I have described this quarter of Rome in *Seekers after God*, p. 168.

[2] Mart. *Ep.* i. 42, 109; vi. 93; x. 3, 5; xii. 57; Juv. xiv. 134, 186, 201; Stat. *Silv.* i., vi. 72. They continued here for many centuries, but were also to be found in other parts of Rome. On their mendicancy see Juv. iii. 14, 296; vi. 542. On their *faithfulness to the Law*, see Hor. *Sat.* i., ix. 69; Suet. *Aug.* 76; Juv. xiv. 96; Pers. v. 184; &c.

[3] Jos. *Antt.* xvii. 1.

[4] Tac. *Ann.* ii. 85; Sueton. *Tib.* 36; Jos. *Antt.* xviii. 3, 5.

[5] Acts xviii. 2.

[6] *V. supra*, i., pp. 57, 493. Since *Christus* would be meaningless to classic ears, the word was *surfrappé* (see my *Families of Speech*, p. 119). *Chrestianus* is common in inscriptions; Renan, *St. Paul*, 101.

[7] And perhaps by the commencing troubles in Judæa, early in A.D. 52.

were usually as futile as they were severe.[1] We find that those Jews who had left Rome under immediate pressure began soon to return.[2] Their subterranean proselytism[3] as far back as the days of Nero, acquired proportions so formidable that Seneca,[4] while he characterised the Jews as a nation steeped in wickedness (*gens sceleratissima*) testifies to their immense diffusion. It is therefore certain that when St. Paul first arrived in Rome (A.D. 61), and even at the time when he wrote this letter (A.D. 58), the Jews, in spite of the unrepealed decree of Claudius, which had been passed only six years before, formed a large community, sufficiently powerful to be an object of alarm and jealousy to the Imperial Government.

Of this Jewish community we can form no conjecture how many were Christians; nor have we a single *datum* to guide us in forming an estimate of the numbers of the Christian Church in Rome, except the vague assertion of Tacitus, that a "vast multitude" of its innocent members were butchered by Nero in the persecution by which he strove to hide his guilty share in the conflagration of July 19, A.D. 64.[5] Even the salutations which crowd the last chapter of the Epistle to the Romans do not help us. Twenty-six people are greeted by name, besides "the Church in the house" of Aquila and Priscilla, some of

---

[1] Tac. *Ann.* xii. 52, "atrox et irritum." It is not impossible that these may be one and the same decree, for the Mathematici, and impostors closely akin to them, were frequently Jews.

[2] Dion Cass. (lx. 6) who is probably alluding to this decree, says that the Jews were not expelled, but only forbidden to meet in public assemblies. Aquila, however, as a leading Christian, would be naturally one of those who was compelled to leave.

[3] Hor. *Sat.* i. 9, 70; Pers. *Sat.* v. 180; Ovid. A. A. i. 76; Juv. vi. 542; Suet. *Aug.* 76; Merivale, vi. 257, *seq.*, &c.

[4] Ap. Aug. *De Civ. Dei.*, vi. 11; *v. supra*, Excursus XIV.

[5] Tac. *Ann.* xv. 40, 41; Suet. *Nero*, 38.

the "households" of Aristobulus and Narcissus,[1] the "brethren," with Asyncritus and others, and the "saints" with Olympas and others.[2] All that we could gather from these notices, if we could be sure that the sixteenth chapter was really addressed to Rome, is that the Roman Christians possessed as yet no common place of meeting, but were separated into at least three communities grouped around different centres, assembling in different places of worship, and with no perceptible trace of ecclesiastical organisation. But there is nothing whatever to show whether these communities were large or small, and we shall see that the sixteenth chapter, though unquestionably Pauline, was probably addressed to the Ephesian and not to the Roman Church.

Assuming, however, that the Christians were numerous, as Tacitus expressly informs us, two questions remain, of which both are involved in deep obscurity. The one is, "When and how was Christianity introduced into Rome?" The other is, "Was the Roman Church predominantly Jewish or predominantly Gentile?"

1. Tradition answers the first question by telling us that St. Peter was the founder of Latin Christianity, and this answer is almost demonstrably false. It is first

---

[1] The mention of these two names has been regarded as an argument that the sixteenth chapter really belongs to the Roman letter, since Aristobulus, the son of Herod, and other Herodian princes of that time, had been educated in Rome, whose slaves and freedmen these might be. Again, although Narcissus, the celebrated freedman of Claudius, had been put to death in A.D. 54 (Tac. *Ann.* xiii. 1), four years before the date of this letter, "they of the household of Narcissus" may have been some of his slaves. On the other hand, neither of these names was uncommon, and it is less intrinsically improbable that there should have been a Narcissus and an Aristobulus at Ephesus, than that there should have been so many Asiatic intimates and Jewish kinsmen of St. Paul at Rome. Muratori (No. 1328) and Orelli (No. 720) give an inscription found at Ferrara from a tablet erected by *Tib. Claud. Narcissus*, to the *manes* of his wife, *Dicæosune* (Righteousness). See an interesting note on this in Plumptre, *Bibl. Stud.*, p. 428.

[2] Rom. xvi. 5, 14, 15.

found in a work, at once malignant and spurious, written late in the second century, to support a particular party. That work is the forged Clementines,[1] in which we are told that Peter was the first Bishop of Rome. Tradition, gathering fresh particulars as it proceeds, gradually began to assert, with more or less confidence, that he came to Rome in the second year of Claudius (A.D. 42); that he met and confounded Simon Magus; that he continued Bishop of Rome for twenty-five years; that he was ultimately martyred by being crucified, head downwards at his own humble desire; and that this took place on June 29th, the same day as the execution of St. Paul. In attestation of their martyrdom, Gaius refers to their "trophies" near the city.[2] The lateness of these details, the errors with which they are mingled, and the obvious party reasons for their invention, forbid our attaching to them any historic value. It is not at all probable that St. Peter arrived at the city till the year of his death. This at least is certain—that, in the New Testament, the sole asserted trace of his presence in Rome is to be found in the highly disputable allusion, "They of Babylon salute you."[3] He may have died in Rome; he may even

[1] *Recognit.* i. 6.
[2] Euseb. *H. E.* ii. 14, 25 (quoting Dionysius of Corinth); Id. *Dem. Ev.* iii. 3; Origen (*ap. Euseb.* iii. 1); Justin Martyr, *Apolog.* ii. 26; Tert. *De praescr. Haer.* 36; *c. Marc.* iv. 5; Gaius *ap. Euseb.* ii. 25. Justin, and perhaps others, were misled by the inscription to the Sabine deity Semo Sancus, which they read *Simoni Sancto*. Peter is also associated with Paul in the founding of Christianity at Rome by Clemens, *Ep. ad Cor.* 5; by the Κήρυγμα Πέτρου; by Lactant. *Instt. Div.* iv. 21; by Iren. *Haer.* iii. 3; by Epiphan. *Haer.* i. 27; Oros. vii. 7; *Constt. Apost.* vii. 46; &c. &c.
[3] The Acts prove that St. Peter was at Jerusalem about A.D. 49 (Acts xv.); and in Antioch about A.D. 53 (Gal. ii. 11); and the Epistles with the Acts prove all but conclusively that he was not at Rome during the first or second imprisonment of St. Paul. If "Babylon," in 1 Pet. v. 13, means Babylon and not Rome—a question which cannot be *positively* decided—then St. Peter was in Babylon ten years later than this. (See Baur, *Paul.* ii. 291 *seqq.*) Spanheim, in his celebrated *Dissertatio* (1679) dwells much on Gal. ii. 9 as a

have preached in Rome; he may even have been accepted by the Jewish section of Roman Christians as their nominal "Bishop;" but that he was not, and could not have been, in any true sense the *original founder* of the Roman Church is freely admitted even by Roman Catholics themselves.

At what time the chance seeds of Christianity had been wafted to the shores of Italy[1] we are utterly unable to say. That this took place in our Lord's lifetime is improbable, nor is it worth while to do more than allude to the fiction which ascribes to the Emperor Tiberius a favourable opinion respecting the divinity of Christ.[2] All that we can safely assert is the likelihood that the good tidings may first have been conveyed by some of those Jews and proselytes from Rome who heard the speech of St. Peter at Pentecost;[3] or by others who, like St. Paul himself, received their first impressions from the close reasoning and fiery eloquence of St. Stephen as they sat among chance visitors in the synagogue of the Libertini.[4]

2. If this conjecture be correct, we see that, from the first, the Church of Rome must have contained both Jewish and Gentile elements. The mere probabilities of the case will not enable us to decide which of the two elements preponderated, and if we turn to the Epistle we are met by indications so dubious that critics have arrived at the most opposite conclusions.[5] Baur cannot even

---

strong argument against the likelihood of Peter's visiting Rome. Ellendorf (a Roman Catholic writer) admits that it cannot be *proved*; but even Neander and Gieseler admit it to be probable.

[1] Acts xxviii. 14.
[2] Tert. *Apolog.* 5, 21 (Just. Mart. *Apolog.* i. 35, 48).
[3] Acts ii. 9.
[4] Acts vi. 9.
[5] Neander, Meyer, De Wette, Olshausen, Tholuck, Reuss, &c., are confident that it was mainly intended for Gentiles; Baur, Schwegler, Thiersch, Davidson, Wordsworth, &c., for Jews.

imagine how it is possible for any one to avoid the conclusion that the Apostle has Jewish Christians in view throughout. Olshausen, on the other hand, pronounces with equal confidence on the prominence of Gentiles. Each can refer to distinct appeals to both classes. If, at the very outset of the Epistle, St. Paul seems to address the whole Church as Gentiles, and in xi. 13 says, " I speak unto you Gentiles," and in xv. 15, 16, writes in the exclusive character of Apostle of the Gentiles,[1] and in x. 1 speaks of the Jews in the third person;[2] yet, on the other hand, in iv. 1 he speaks of " Abraham *our* father," and says that he is writing to those who " know the Law," and have once been under its servitude. If, again, the multitude of quotations from the Jewish scriptures[3] might be supposed to have most weight with Jews (though we find the same phenomenon in the Epistle to the Galatians), yet, on the other hand, in the apologetic section (ix.—xi.) the argument is rather *about* the Jews than addressed *to* them,[4] and the moral precepts of the practical chapters seem to have in view the liberal Gentiles far more than the Ebionising Jews. The views of the latter are not directly combated, while the former are bidden to waive their personal liberty rather than cause any personal offence.

Of these apparent contradictions the solution most commonly accepted is that suggested by Professor Jowett,[5] that even the Gentile converts had been mainly drawn from the ranks of proselytes, who at Rome were par-

---

[1] i. 13. "Among you, as among other Gentiles" (cf. 5, 6).

[2] x. 1, "My heart's desire and prayer for them" (ὑπὲρ αὐτῶν—א, A, B, D, E, F, G—not ὑπὲρ τοῦ Ἰσραήλ).

[3] The phrase καθὼς γέγραπται occurs no less than *nineteen* times in this single Epistle, as it does on almost every page of the Talmud.

[4] ix. 1; x. 1; xi., *passim*.

[5] Jowett, *Romans*, vol. ii. 23.

ticularly numerous,[1] so that "the Roman Church appeared to be at once Jewish and Gentile—Jewish in feeling, Gentile in origin; Jewish, for the Apostle everywhere argues with them as Jews; Gentile, for he expressly addresses them as Gentiles." This, no doubt, was the condition of other Churches, and may have been that of the Church at Rome. But as this hypothesis by no means solves all the difficulties, it seems to me a preferable supposition that St. Paul is not so much addressing a special body as purposely arguing out a fundamental problem, and treating it in an ideal and dramatic manner. To the Roman Christians as a body he was avowedly a stranger, but he knew that Jews and Gentiles, each with their special difficulties and prejudices, existed side by side in every Church which he had visited, and he wished once for all to lay down, not only for the Roman Christians, but for all who might read his letter, the principles which were to guide their mutual relations. He is stating the truths which could alone secure the perfect unity of that Church of the future in which the distinctions between Jew and Greek were to be no more. It was natural that before he visited a strange Church, and one so important as the Church of Rome, he should desire plainly to state to them the Gospel

---

[1] Tac. *H.* v. 5; Cic. *pro Flacco*, 28, &c. We read of Jewish slaves in the noblest houses. There was an Acme in the household of Livia; a Samaritan named Thallus was a freedman of Tiberius; Aliturus was a favourite mime of Nero, &c. The Judaic faithfulness of these Jews is proved by the inscriptions on their graves; Garucci, *Cimitero*, 4; Grätz, iv. 123, 506; and by the allusions of classic writers. Suet. *Aug.* 57, 76, &c. It is remarkable that among Jewish proselytes are found such names as Fulvia, Flavia, Valeria, &c., while the Christians were mainly Tryphænas and Tryphosas, slave names ("Luxurious," "wanton") which no human being would voluntarily bear. It appears from inscriptions given by Gruter and Orelli that there were many Jewish synagogues in Rome, *e.g.*, *Synagoga Campi, Augusti, Agrippae, Suburrae, Oleae.* The titles φιλέντολος and φιλόλαος on their tombs significantly indicate their orthodoxy and patriotism. (See too Hor. *Sat.* ii. 3, 288.)

which he meant to preach. But surely it is hardly probable that he would wish the benefits of this consummate effort to be confined to a single Church. The hypothesis that several copies of the letter were made, and that, with appropriate conclusions, it was sent in whole or in part to other Churches beside that of Rome, is not only intrinsically reasonable, but also accounts for some of the peculiar phenomena presented by the manuscripts, and especially by the structure of the concluding chapters.[1]

---

[1] (i.) The mission of Phœbe to Ephesus is more probable than a mission to Rome, which was nearly three times more distant; nor could Paul well have addressed a *strange* Church in language of such urgent request on the subject of her visit (Rom. xvi. 1, 2). (ii.) It is strange that St. Paul should salute twenty-six people at a Church which he had never visited, and address them in terms of peculiar intimacy and affection, when he only salutes one or two, or none at all, in Churches which he had founded. (iii.) Aquila and Priscilla were at Ephesus when St. Paul wrote 1 Cor. xvi. 19, and again at Ephesus when he wrote 2 Tim. iv. 19. It is strange to find them settled at Rome with a Church in their house between these two dates. ("Quoi! toute l'Eglise d'Ephèse s'était donc donné rendezvous in Rome?" Renan, *St. Paul*, lxviii.) (iv.) How is it that there are *no* salutations to Eubulus, Pudens, Linus, Claudia (2 Tim. iv. 21)? (v.) How comes it that "Epænetus, the firstfruits of Asia," is at Rome? and that so many others are there who have—*in other places*, of which, from the nature of the case, Ephesus is the one which most prominently suggests itself—toiled so much, and suffered so much for Paul, and even shared his frequent prisons (xvi. 7, 9, 12, 13)? (vi.) If so many were at Rome who deserve to be specially signalised as "beloved," and "approved," and "elect," and "kinsmen," and "toilers," how is it that they all deserted him at the hour of need (2 Tim. iv. 16)? Was the Church at Rome so mere a sand-cloud that all these had been scattered from Rome? or had they all been put to death in the persecution of A.D. 64? How is it that not one of these exemplary twenty-six are among the three Jewish friends who are alone faithful to him, even before the Neronian persecutions began, and only a few years after this letter was despatched (Col. iv. 10, 11)? (vii.) Again, how comes it that the severe yet fraternal reproachfulness of xvi. 17—20 is so unlike the apologetic and distant politeness of xv. 15—20? (viii.) How came Timothy and St. Paul's other friends, whose salutations to Thessalonica or to Ephesus would be natural, to send them so freely to distant and unvisited Rome? (ix.) Even if these considerations were unimportant, how is it that they are so well supported by the apparently different terminations of the Epistle at xv. 33, and xvi. 20 and 24, as well as xvi. 27? Why is the concluding doxology missing in F, G, and some MSS. mentioned by Jerome? Why is it placed after xiv. 23 in L in most cursives, in Greek Lectionaries, in

3. We come, then, to the question, What is the main object of the Epistle to the Romans? And here we must not be surprised if we meet with different answers. The highest works of genius, in all writings, whether sacred or secular, are essentially many-sided. Who will pretend to give in a few words the central conception of the Prometheus Vinctus or of Hamlet? Who will profess to unite all suffrages in describing the main purpose of Ecclesiastes or of Job? Yet, although the purpose of the Epistle has been differently interpreted, from our ignorance of its

Chrysostom, Theodoret, &c.? Why is it found twice in Codex A (xiv. 24 and xvi. 25)? Why did Marcion, with no apparent dogmatic reason, omit the two last chapters altogether? Why, lastly, does so important a manuscript as G, founded as it is on a very ancient manuscript, omit the words ἐν Ῥώμῃ in i. 7, 15? No fair critic will, I think, assert that these difficulties are collectively unimportant; and they find a perfectly simple and adequate solution if, without accepting the entire details of Renan's theory, we suppose with him (*St. Paul*, lxiii.—lxxv.) that the main body of the Epistle was sent not only to Rome, but also to Ephesus, Thessalonica, and possibly some other Church, *with differing conclusions*, which are all preserved in the present form of the Epistle. On the other side may be set the remark of Strabo (xiv. 5), that many Tarsians were at Rome, and that Rome swarmed with Asiatics (Friedländer, *Sittengesch. Roms.* i. 59); the certainty that even in the days of Scipio, and much more in each succeeding generation, the majority of the inhabitants of Rome —the *faex populi*—were but "stepsons of Italy" (Sen. *ad Helv., Cons.* 6, "Non possum ferre Quirites *Graecam* urbam," Juv. *Sat.* iii. 61, 73, *seq.*, "St.! tacete quibus nec pater nec mater est") and predominantly Greek (see Lightfoot, *Philippians*, p. 20); and that the names of Amplias, Urbanus, Stachys, Apelles, Nereus, Hermes, Hermas, are all found, as Dr. Lightfoot has shown (*ib.* 172—175), in the inscriptions of the *Columbaria* among the slaves in the households of various Cæsarian families; and not only these, but the rarer names Tryphæna, Tryphosa, Patrobas, and even Philologus and Julia *in connexion*, which is at least a curious coincidence. But when we remember the many hundreds of slaves in each great Roman household; and the extreme commonness of the names by which they were mostly called; and the fact that Garucci found that Latin names were twice as numerous as the Greek in the old Jewish cemetery at Rome,—we must still consider it more likely that chap. xvi., in whole or in part, was addressed to Ephesus as a personal termination to the copy of the Roman Epistle, which could hardly fail to be sent to so important a Church. (See Schulz, *Stud. u. Krit.* 1829; Ewald, *Sendschr.* 428; Reuss, *Les Epîtres*, ii. 19.) Of all theories, that of Baur, that the chapter was forged to show how intimate were the relations of Paul with the Roman Church, seems to me the most wanton and arbitrary.

origin, and of the exact condition of the Church to which it was written, it is impossible so to state it as not to express one or other of its essential meanings.

The first question which meets us affects the general character of the Epistle. Is it didactic or polemical? Is it general or special? The divergent views of commentators may here be easily reconciled. It is only indirectly and secondarily polemical; the treatment is general even if the immediate motive was special. Its tone has nothing of the passionate intensity which the Apostle always betrays when engaged in controversy with direct antagonists. It has been supposed by some that he desired to vindicate to the Roman Church his Apostolic authority. Undoubtedly such a vindication is implicitly involved in the masterly arguments of the Epistle; yet how different is his style from the vehemence with which he speaks in the Epistles to the Corinthians! Bishop Wordsworth says that it is " an apology for the Gospel against Judaism;" but where is the burning invective and indignant eloquence of the Epistle to the Galatians? We have no trace here of the ultra-liberalism of Corinth, or the dreamy asceticisms of Colossæ, or the servile Pharisaisms of Galatia. Clearly he is not here dealing with any *special* dissensions, heresies, or attacks on his authority.[1] The very value of the Epistle, as a systematic exposition of "the Gospel of Protestantism," depends on the calmness and lucidity with which the Apostle appeals to an ideal public to follow him in the discussion of abstract truths. We seem already to be indefinitely removed from the narrow fanaticism of those who insisted on the impossibility of salvation apart from circumcision. The Hellenistic Judaism of a great city, however ignorant and however stereotyped,

---

[1] Reuss, *Les Epîtres*, ii. 11.

was incapable of so gross an absurdity, and in the wider and deeper questions which were naturally arising between the Jew and the Gentile Christian, there was as yet nothing sufficiently definite to exasperate the Apostle with a sense of ruinous antagonism. The day indeed was not far distant when, in the very city to which he was writing, some would preach Christ even of contention, hoping to add affliction to his bonds.[1] But this lay as yet in the unknown future. He wrote during one of those little interspaces of repose and hope which occur in even the most persecuted lives. The troubles at Corinth had been temporarily appeased, and his authority established. He was looking forward with the deepest interest to fresh missions, and although he could not deliberately preach at Rome, because he had made it a rule not to build on another man's foundation, he hoped to have his heart cheered by a kindly welcome in the imperial city before he started to plant the Cross on the virgin soil of Spain. And the Church of Rome stood high in general estimation. It was composed of Jews and Gentiles, of whom, not long afterwards, the former seem to have ranged themselves in uncompromising hostility to the Gospel; but he could as little foresee this as he could be aware that, in the second century, the Ebionism of this section of the Church would lead to a malignant attack on his character. At this time there do not seem to have been any open divisions or bitter animosities.[2] Differences of opinion there were between "the weak," who attached importance to distinctions of meats and drinks, and "the strong," who somewhat scornfully discarded them; but it seems a

---

[1] Phil. i. 16. These were evidently Judaisers (iii. 2; Col. iv. 11).
[2] The only trace of these is in xvi. 17—20; τὰς διχοστασίας, τὰ σκάνδαλα. But this furnishes one of the arguments against that chapter as part of the Epistle to the Romans.

though, on the whole, the Jews were forbearing and the Gentiles moderate. Perhaps the two parties owed their immunity from dissensions to the passage of the Gentiles into the Church through the portals of the synagogue; or perhaps still more to the plasticity of ecclesiastical organisation which enabled the foreign and Græco-Roman converts to worship undisturbed in their own little congregations which met under the roof of an Aquila or an Olympas. If the Jewish and Gentile communities were separated by a marked division, collisions between the two sections would have been less likely to occur.

Be this as it may, it is evident that it was in a peaceful mood that the Apostle dictated to Tertius the great truths which he had never before so thoroughly contemplated as a logical whole.[1] The broad didactic character of the Epistle, its freedom from those outbursts of emotion which we find in others of his writings, is perfectly consistent with its having originated in historic circumstances; in other words, with its having been called forth, as was every one of the other Epistles, by passing events. St. Paul was on his way to Jerusalem, and his misgivings as to the results of the visit were tempered by the hope that the alms which he had collected would smooth the way for his favourable reception. Rome was the next place of importance which he intended to visit. How would he be received by the Christians of the great city? Would they have heard rumours from the Pharisees of Jerusalem that he was a godless and dangerous apostate, who defied all authority and abandoned all truth? It was at any rate probable that, even if he had not been represented to them

---

[1] See the much more tender tone towards the Jews, and also towards the Law, in Rom. iv. 16, xi. 26, &c., compared with Gal. iv. 3, 2 Cor. iii. 6, &c. In the "not only—but also" of iv. 16 is reflected the whole conciliatory character of the Epistle to the Romans (Pfleiderer, ii. 45).

in the most unfavourable light, he would have been spoken of as one who was prepared to abandon not only the peculiarities, but even the exclusive hopes and promises of Judaism. To a great extent this was true; and, if true, how serious, nay, how startling, were the consequences which such a belief entailed! They were views so contrary to centuries of past conviction, that they at least deserved the most careful statement, the most impregnable defence, the most ample justification, from the ancient scriptures. Such a defence, after deep meditation on the truths which God's Spirit had revealed to his inmost soul, he was prepared to offer in language the most conciliatory, the most tender—in language which betrayed how little the unalterable fixity of his conviction had quenched the fire of his patriotism, or deadened the quickness of his sensibility.[1] He expresses an inextinguishable love for his countrymen, and a deep sense of their glorious privileges, at the very moment that he is explaining why those countrymen have been temporarily rejected, and showing that those privileges have been inexorably annulled.[2] He declares his readiness to be even "anathema from Christ" for the sake of Israel, in the very verses in which he is showing, to the horrified indignation of his Jewish readers, that not the physical, but the spiritual seed of Abraham, are alone the true Israel of God.[3]

[1] "We see," says Dr. Davidson, "a constant conflict between his convictions and feelings; the former too deep to be changed, the latter too strong to be repressed, too ardent to be quenched by opposition of the persons he loved" (*Introdn.* i. 127).

[2] We can judge what the Jewish estimate of these privileges was by such passages of the Talmud as *Yebhamoth*, f. 47, 2; *supra*, i., p. 403.

[3] There can be no more striking contrast to the whole argument of the Epistle to the Romans than the following very remarkable passage in the *Abhoda Zara* (f. 3, col. 1—3), which will serve to show to what infinite heights above the ordinary Rabbinism of his nation St. Paul had soared. I appeal to any candid and learned Jew which is noblest, truest, divinest, manliest

If the current feelings of the Jews towards the Gentiles were much embittered—if they habitually regarded them in the spirit of hostile arrogance—it is very possible that the section respecting the relative position of the Jews and Gentiles (ix.—xi.) may be, as Baur argues, the kernel of the whole Epistle, in the sense that these were the first thoughts which had suggested themselves to the

—the tone and the reasoning of the Epistle to the Romans, or the bigotry and frivolity of the following passage:—

"In the days of the Messiah, the Holy One, blessed be He, holding the roll of the Law in His bosom, will call upon those who have studied it to come forward and receive their reward. Instantly the idolatrous nations will appear in a body (Isa. xliii. 9), but will be told to present themselves separately with their Scribes at their head, that they may understand the answers severally addressed to them. The Romans, as the most renowned of all, will enter first. 'What has been your occupation?' will be demanded of them. They will point to their baths and forums, and the gold and silver with which they enriched the world, adding, 'All this we *have done that Israel may have leisure for the study of the Law.*' 'Fools!' will be the stern answer: 'have you not done all this for your own pleasure, the market-places, and the baths alike, to pamper your own self-indulgence? and as for the gold and silver it is Mine (Hagg. ii. 8). Who among you can declare this Law?' (Isa. xliii. 9.)

"The Romans retire crestfallen, and then the Persians enter. They too will urge that they built bridges, took cities, waged wars to give Israel leisure to study the Law; but receiving the same rebuke as the Romans, they too will retire in dejection.

"Similarly all other nations, in the order of their rank, will come in to hear their doom; the wonder is that they will not be deterred by the failure of the others, but will still cling to their vain plea. But then the Persians will argue that they built the Temple, whereas the Romans destroyed it; and the other nations will think that since they, unlike the Romans and Persians, never oppressed the Jews, they may expect more lenience.

"The nations will then argue, 'When has the Law been offered to us, and we refused it?' In answer it is inferred from Deut. xxxiii. 2 and Hab. iii. 3 that the Law had been offered to each in turn, but that they would not have it. Then they will ask, 'Why didst Thou not place us also underneath the mount (Ex. xix. 17) as Thou didst Israel, bidding us accept the Law, or be crushed by the mountain?' To whom Jehovah will reply, 'Let us hear the first things (Isa. xliii. 9). Have you kept the Noachic precepts?' They answer, 'Have the Jews kept the Law though they received it?' God answers, 'Yes; I Myself bear them witness that they have.' 'But is not Israel thy firstborn, and is it fair to admit the testimony of a Father?' 'The heaven and earth shall bear them witness.' 'But are not they interested

mind of the Apostle. Yet it is not correct to say that "the whole dogmatic treatment of the Epistle can be considered as nothing but the most radical and thorough-going refutation of Judaism and Jewish Christianity."[1] In his reaction against the purely dogmatic view which regards the Epistle as "a compendium of Pauline dogma in the form of an apostolic letter,"[2] Baur was led into a view too purely historical; and in his unwillingness to regard the central section as a mere *corollary* from the doctrines enunciated in the first eight chapters, he goes too far in calling them the heart and pith of the whole, to which everything else is only an addition. These chapters may have been first in the order of thought, without being first in the order of importance; they may have formed the original motive of the Epistle, and yet

---

witnesses?'* 'Well, then, you yourselves shall testify;' and accordingly Nimrod has to testify for Abraham, Laban for Jacob, Potiphar's wife for Joseph, Nebuchadnezzar for the three children, Darius for Daniel, Job's friends for Job. Then the nations entreat, 'Give us *now* the Law, and we will keep it.' 'Fools! do ye want to enjoy the Sabbath without having prepared for it? However, I will give you one easy precept—keep the Feast of Tabernacles' (Zech. xiv. 16). Then they will all hurry off to make booths on the roofs of their houses. But the Holy One, blessed be He, will make the sun blaze with midsummer heat, and they will desert the booths with the scornful exclamation, 'Let us break His bands asunder, and fling away His cords from us' (Ps. ii. 3). Then the Lord, sitting in the heavens, shall laugh at them. The only occasion on which He laughs *at* His creatures," though He does so *with* His creatures, notably with Leviathan, every day.

[1] Baur, *Paul.* i. 349; Olshausen, *Romans,* Introd. § 5. Philippi calls it "a connected doctrinal statement of the specifically Pauline Gospel."

[2] In any case this statement would be far too broad. If the Epistle to the Romans be a complete statement of what may be called the Apostle's "Soteriology," it contains little or none of the Eschatology which distinguishes these Epistles to the Thessalonians, or the Christology of the Epistle to the Colossians, or the Ecclesiology of the Epistle to the Ephesians. It is hardly worth while to notice the opinions that it is a mere defence of his Apostolate (Mangold), or a description and vindication of the Pauline system of missionary labours (Schott.). See Lange's *Romans,* p. 38, E. T.

* Because they only exist for the sake of the Law (*Nedarim,* f. 32, col. 1).

may have been completely thrown into subordination by the grandeur of the conceptions to which they led.

May we not well suppose that the Epistle originated as follows? The Apostle, intending to start for Jerusalem, and afterwards to open a new mission in the West, thought that he would utilise an interval of calm by writing to the Roman Church, in which, though not founded by himself, he could not but feel the deepest interest. He knows that, whatever might be the number of the Gentile Christians, the nucleus of the Church had been composed of Jews and proselytes who would find it very hard to accept the lesson that God was no respecter of persons. Yet this was the truth which he was commissioned to teach; and if the Jews could not receive it without a shock—if even the most thoughtful among them could not but find it hard to admit that their promised Messiah—the Messiah for whom they had yearned through afflicted centuries—was after all to be even more the Messiah of the Gentiles than of the Jews—then it was pre-eminently necessary for him to set this truth so clearly, and yet so sympathetically, before them, as to soften the inevitable blow to their deepest prejudices. It was all the more necessary because, in writing to the more liberal Judaisers, he had not to deal with the ignorant malignity of those who had seduced his simple Galatians. In writing to the Churches of Galatia, and smiting down with one shattering blow their serpent-head of Pharisaism, he had freed his soul from the storm of passion by which it had been shaken. He could now write with perfect composure on the larger questions of the position of the Christian in reference to the Law, and of the relations of Judaism to Heathenism, and of both to Christianity. That the Gentiles were in no respect inferior to the Jews in spiritual privileges—nay, more, that the Gentiles were

actually superseding the Jews by pressing with more
eagerness into the Church of Christ[1]—was a fact which
no Jewish Christian could overlook. Was God, then,
rejecting Israel? The central section of the Epistle
(ix.—xi.) deals with this grave scruple; and the Apostle
there strives to show that (1) spiritual sonship does not
depend on natural descent, since the only justification
possible to man—namely, justification by faith—was
equally open to Jews and Gentiles (ix.); that (2), so far
as the Jews are losing their precedence in the divine
favour, this is due to their own rejection of a free offer
which it was perfectly open to them to have embraced
(x.); and that (3) this apparent rejection is softened by
the double consideration that (a) it is partial, not absolute,
since there was "a remnant of the true Israelites according to the election of grace"; and (β) it is temporary,
not final, since, when the full blessing of the Gentiles has
been secured, there still remains the glorious hope that
all Israel would at last be saved.[2]

But was it not inevitable that from this point his
thoughts should work backwards, and that the truths to
which now, for the first time, he gave full and formal
expression should assume an importance which left but
subordinate interest to the minor problem? From the
relative his thoughts had been led on to the absolute. From
the question as to the extinction of the exclusive privileges of the Jews, he had ascended to the question of God's
appointed plan for the salvation of mankind—its nature,
its world-wide freedom, its necessity. That plan the
Apostle sums up in the one formula, JUSTIFICATION BY
FAITH, and in order to establish and explain it he had to

---

[1] Just as in the days of Christ the publicans and harlots were admitted before the Pharisees into the kingdom of God (Matt. xxi. 31, 32).

[2] See Baur, *Paul.* ii. 328.

prove the universality of human sin; the inability alike of Jew and Gentile to attain salvation by any law of works; the consequent "subordinate, relative, negative" significance of the Law; the utter and final evanescence of all difference between circumcision and uncircumcision in the light of a dispensation now first revealed. And thus the real basis of this, as of every other Epistle, is "Christ as the common foundation on which Jew and Gentile could stand, the bond of human society, the root of human righteousness."[1] It may be quite true that throughout all these high reasonings, and the many questions to which they give rise, there runs an undertone of controversy, and that the Apostle never lost sight of the fact that he was endeavouring to prove for the Roman Christians, and through them to the entire Church, the new and startling doctrine that, since the annihilation of sin was rendered possible by faith, and faith alone, all claims founded on Jewish particularism were reduced to nothingness. This is the main point; but even the practical questions which receive a brief decision at the close of the Epistle, are handled in strict accordance with the great principles which he has thus established of the Universality of Sin and the Universality of Grace.[2]

Such seems to me to be the origin and the idea of the Epistle to the Romans, of which Luther says that "it is the masterpiece of the New Testament, and the purest gospel, which can never be too much read or studied, and the more it is handled the more precious it

---

[1] Maurice, *Unity*, p. 477.
[2] If we were to choose one phrase as expressing most of the idea of the Epistle, it would be, "As in Adam all die, even so in Christ shall all be made alive" (1 Cor. xv. 22). "Its precepts naturally arise from its doctrinal assertions, that (1) all are guilty before God; that (2) all need a Saviour; that (3) Christ died for all; that (4) we are all one body in Him" (Bp. Wordsworth's *Epistles*, p. 200).

becomes;" on which Melancthon founded the doctrinal system of the Reformed Church; which Coleridge called "the most profound work in existence;" in which Tholuck, who wrote the first really important and original commentary upon it in recent times, saw "a Christian philosophy of universal history." Its general outline may be given as follows:—After a full and solemn greeting, he passes, in the simplest and most natural manner, to state his fundamental thesis of justification by faith,[1] which he illustrates and supports by quoting the Septuagint version of Hab. ii. 4. The necessity for this mode of salvation rests in the universality of sin—a fact taught, indeed, by human experience, but too apt to be overlooked, and therefore needing to be argumentatively enforced. Thus Jews and Gentiles are reduced to the same level, and the exceptional privileges of the Jew do but add to his condemnation (i. 16—iii. 20). Consequently by the works of the Law—whether the natural or the Mosaic Law—no flesh can be justified, and justification can only be obtained by the faith of man accepting the redemption of Christ, so that all alike are dependent on the free will of God (iii. 21—30).[2] Aware of the extreme novelty of these conclusions, he illustrates them by Scripture (iii. 31—iv. 25), and then dwells on the blessed consequences of this justification (v. 1—11). These consequences are foreshadowed in the whole moral and religious history of mankind as summed up in the two periods represented by Adam and by Christ (v. 12—21). Having thus completed the statement of his great doctrine, he meets the objections which may be urged against it. So far from

---

[1] ὁ δὲ δίκαιος ἐκ πίστεώς [μου] ζήσεται. The μου is omitted by St. Paul, and, indeed, by many MSS. of the LXX. (see *supra* on Gal. iii. 11).

[2] This passage contains the very quintessence of Pauline theology. See it admirably explained and developed by Reuss, *Théol. Chrét.* ii. 18—107.

diminishing the heinousness, or tending to the multiplication of sin, he shows that it involves the radical annihilation of sin (vi.). If any were startled at the close juxtaposition of the Law and sin, he points out that while the Law in itself is holy, just, and good, on the other hand what he has said of it, relatively to mankind, is demonstrated by its psychological effects, and that in point of fact the Law is, for the changed nature of the believer, superseded by a new principle of life—by the Spirit of God quickening the heart of man (vii. 1—viii. 11). This naturally leads him to a serious appeal to his readers to live worthily of this changed nature, and to a magnificent outburst of thanksgiving which rises at last into a climax of impassioned eloquence (viii. 12—39).

At this point he finds himself face to face with the question from which his thoughts probably started—the relations of Judaism to Heathenism, and of Christianity to both. In an episode of immense importance, especially to the age in which he wrote, he shows that God's promises to Israel, when rightly understood, both *had* been, and *should* be, fulfilled, and that—so far as they seemed for the moment to have been made void—the failure was due to the obstinate hardness of the chosen people (ix.—xi.). The remainder of the Epistle is more practical and popular. He urges the duties of holiness, humility, unity, the faithful use of opportunities, hope, and above all love, on which he dwells earnestly and at length (xii.). Then, perhaps with special reference to the theocratic prejudices of Jewish Christians, he enforces the duty of obedience to civil authority, and reverts once more to love as the chief of Christian graces; enforcing these practical exhortations by the thought that the night of sin and ignorance was now far spent, and the day was near (xiii.). He then points out the necessity for mutual forbearance and mutual charity between the strong and the weak—that is, between those who considered themselves bound by legal prescriptions, and those who realised that from such elements they were emancipated by the glorious liberty of the children of God; mingling with these exhortations some reference to the views which he had already expressed about the mutual relation of Jews and Christians (xiv.—xv. 13). The remainder of the Epistle is chiefly personal. He first offers an earnest and graceful apology for having thus ventured to address a strange Church—an apology based on his apostolic mission (xv. 14—21)—and then sketches the outline of his future plans, specially entreating their prayers for the good success of his approaching visit to Jerusalem. In the last chapter, which I have given reasons for believing to have been addressed, at any rate in part, not to Romans, but to Ephesians, he recommends Phœbe to the kindly care of the Church (1, 2); sends affectionate salutations to six-and-twenty of the brethren (3—16); gives a severe warning against those who fostered divisions, which concludes with a promise and a benediction (17—20); repeats the benediction after a few salutations from the friends who were with him (21—24); and ends with an elaborate and comprehensive doxology, in which some have seen "a liturgical antiphony in conformity with the fundamental thought of the Epistle."[1]

[1] v. Lange, ad loc.

II.

GENERAL THESIS OF THE EPISTLE.

Ὦ τοῦ ἰδιώτου τὸ θαῦμα, ὦ τοῦ ἀγραμμάτου ἡ σοφία.—Ps. Chrys. *Orat. Encom.* (Opp. viii. 10).

"Such we are in the sight of God the Father, as is the very Son of God Himself. Let it be counted folly, or frenzy, or fury, or whatsoever. It is our wisdom and our comfort; we care for no knowledge in the world but this, that man hath sinned, and God hath suffered; that God hath made Himself the Son of men, and men are made the righteousness of God."—Hooker, *Serm.* ii. 6.

"It breaketh the window that it may let in the light; it breaketh the shell that we may eat the kernel; it putteth aside the curtain that we may enter into the most Holy Place: it removeth the cover of the well that we may come by the water."—*Pref. to Authorised Version.*

WE must now look more closely at this great outline of one of the most essential factors of Christian theology; and I must ask my readers, Bible in hand, to follow step by step its solemn truths as they gradually expand themselves before our view.

The Salutation, which occupies the first seven verses, is remarkable as being the longest and most solemnly emphatic of those found in any of his Epistles. Had he adopted the ordinary method of his day, he would have simply headed his letter with the words, "Paul, an Apostle of Jesus Christ, to the Roman Christians, greeting."[1] But he had discovered an original method of giving to his first salutation a more significant and less conventional turn, and of making it the vehicle for truths to which he desired from

---

[1] This is the earliest letter which he addresses to "the saints." His former letters were all addressed "to the Church" or "Churches" (1, 2 Thess., 1, 2 Cor., Gal.). It is also the first in which he calls himself "a slave of Jesus Christ."

the first to arrest attention. Thus, in one grand single sentence, of which the unity is not lost in spite of digressions, amplifications, and parentheses, he tells the Roman Christians of his solemn setting apart,[1] by grace, to the Apostolate; of the object and universality of that Apostolate; of the truth that the Gospel is no daring novelty, but the preordained fulfilment of a dispensation prophesied in Scripture;[2] of Christ's descent from David, according to the flesh, and of his establishment with power as the Son of God according to the spirit of holiness[3] by the resurrection of the dead.[4]

We ask, as we read the sentence, whether any one has ever compressed more thoughts into fewer words, and whether any letter was ever written which swept so vast an horizon in its few opening lines?[5]

He passes on to his customary thanksgiving "by Jesus Christ" for the widely-rumoured faith of the Christians at Rome;[6] and solemnly assures them how, in his unceasing prayers on their behalf, he supplicates God that he may be enabled to visit them, because he yearns to see them, and impart to them, for their stability, some spiritual gift.[7]

---

[1] ἀφωρισμένος. Cf. Acts xiii. 2, ἀφορίσατε.

[2] γραφαὶ ἅγιαι, not "sacred writings," but like ἱερὰ γράμματα, a proper name for the Scriptures, and therefore anarthrous.

[3] The form of expression is of course antithetical, but it seems to me that Dr. Forbes, in his *Analytical Commentary*, pushes this antithesis to most extravagant lengths.

[4] 1—7. In ver. 4, ἀνάστασις νεκρῶν, is not "from" (ἐκ), but "of" the dead, regarded as accomplished in Christ. The notions of χάρις and εἰρήνη are united in Num. vi. 25, 26.

[5] "Epistola tota sic methodica est, ut ipsum quoque exordium ad rationem artis compositum sit" (Calvin).

[6] The ἐν ὅλῳ τῷ κόσμῳ of course only means among the humble and scattered Christian communities, and therefore furnishes no argument against the truth of Acts xxviii. 21, 22.

[7] The expressions in these verses (ἐπιποθῶ, 11; συμπαρακληθῆναι, 12; προεθέμην, ἐκωλύθην, καρπόν, 13; ὀφειλέτης, 14) are closely analogous to those in xv. (ἐνεκοπτόμην, 22; ἐπιποθίαν, 23; ὀφειλέται, 27; συναναπαύσωμαι, 32).

Then, with infinite delicacy, correcting an expression which, to strangers, might seem to savour of assumed authority, he explains that what he longs for is an *interchange* between them of mutual encouragement;[1] for he wishes them to know[2] that, though hindered hitherto, he has often planned to come to them, that he might reap among them, as among all other Gentiles, some of the fruit of his ministry. The Gospel has been entrusted to him, and he regards it as something due from him, a debt which he has to pay to all Gentiles alike, whether Greeks or non-Greeks, whether civilised or uncivilised. He is therefore eager, so far as it depends on him, to preach the Gospel even in the world's capital, even in imperial Rome.[3]

This leads him to the fundamental theme, which he intends to treat. Many are ashamed of that Gospel; he is not;[4] *"for it is the power of God unto salvation to every one that believeth, to the Jew first,[5] and also to the Greek. For in it God's righteousness is being revealed from faith to faith, even as it is written, 'But the just shall live by faith.'"*[6]

How easy are these words to read! Yet they require the whole Epistle for their adequate explanation, and many volumes have been written to elucidate their meaning. Rome is the very centre of human culture, the seat of the widest, haughtiest despotism which the world has ever seen, and he is well aware that to the world's culture the Cross is foolishness, and feebleness to the world's power.

---

[1] Cf. xv. 24. Erasmus goes too far in calling this a "*sancta adulatio.*"
[2] οὐ θέλω δὲ ὑμᾶς ἀγνοεῖν, xi. 25; 1 Thess. iv. 13; 1 Cor. x. 1, xii. 1; 2 Cor. i. 8.
[3] i. 8—15.
[4] What cause he might have had to be tempted to shame by the feelings of the lordlier and more cultivated Gentiles may be seen in the remark of Tacitus (*Ann.* xv. 44), who classes Christianity among the "cuncta atrocia aut pudenda" which flow together into the vortex of Roman life.
[5] πρῶτον, precedence, genetic and historical (John iv. 22; Acts i. 8).
[6] i. 16, 17.

Yet he is not ashamed of the Gospel of that Cross, for to all who will believe it, whether the Jew to whom it was first offered or the Greek to whom it is now proclaimed, it is the display of God's power in order to secure their salvation. Even those few words "to the Jew first, and *also to the Greek*" are the sign that a new aeon has dawned upon the world; and having thus indicated in two lines the source (God's power), the effect (salvation), and the universality of the Gospel (to Jew and Gentile), he proceeds to sum up its essence. "In it," he says, "God's righteousness is being revealed from faith to faith."

We repeat the familiar words, but what meaning should we attach to them? It would take a lifetime to read all that has been written about them in interminable pages of dreary exegesis, drearier metaphysics, and dreariest controversy. Traducianist and Pelagian, Calvinist and Arminian, Sublapsarian and Supralapsarian, Solifidian and Gospeller, Legalist and Antinomian, Methodist and Baptist, have wrangled about them for centuries, and strewn the field of polemical theology with the scattered and cumbering *débris* of technicalities and anathemas. From St. Augustine to St. Thomas of Aquinum, and from St. Thomas to Whitefield, men have—

> "Reasoned high
> Of providence, foreknowledge, will, and fate,
> Fixed fate, free-will, foreknowledge absolute,
> And found no end in wandering mazes lost;"

and their controversies have mainly turned on these words. Does it not seem presumptuous to endeavour to express in one simple sentence what they appear to state?[1] Not if

---

[1] It will be observed that the true explanation of the *meaning of the words* is one thing, and one which may be regarded as approximately certain; the adequate explanation of the *doctrine* is quite another thing, and all attempt to do it lands us at once in the region of insoluble mysteries. "We cannot measure the arm of God with the finger of man."

we distinguish between "ideas of the head" and "feelings of the heart." Not if we bear in mind that these controversies arise mainly from "the afterthoughts of theology." We can only understand St. Paul's views in the light of his own repeated elucidations, comments, and varied modes of expression; yet with this guidance we should sum up the results of endless discussions, prolonged for a thousand years, by interpreting his words to mean that *In the Gospel is being made known*[1] *to the world that inherent righteousness of God, which, by a judgment of acquittal pronounced once for all in the expiatory death of Christ, He imputes to guilty man, and which beginning for each individual, with his trustful acceptance of this reconciliation of himself to God in Christ, ends in that mystical union with Christ whereby Christ becomes to each man a new nature, a quickening spirit.*

It is impossible, I think, in fewer words to give the full interpretation of this pregnant thesis. The end and aim of the Gospel of God is the salvation of man. Man is sinful, and cannot by any power of his own attain to holiness. Yet without holiness no man can see the Lord. Therefore, without holiness no man can be saved. How, then, is holiness to be attained? The Gospel is the answer to that question, and this Epistle is the fullest and most consecutive exposition of this divine dispensation. The essence of the answer is summed up in the one phrase "JUSTIFICATION BY FAITH." In this verse it is expressed as "the righteousness and justice of God" which "is being revealed in the Gospel from faith to faith." The word for "righteousness" is also rendered "justification." But neither of this word, nor of the word

---

[1] ἀποκαλύπτεται—"progressive revelation," but ἐφανερώθη, it has been once for all manifested; or rather πεφανέρωται (iii. 21) has been manifested *now and for ever.*

"faith," has St. Paul ever given a formal definition. It is only from his constantly-varied phrases, and from the reasonings by which he supports, and the quotations by which he illustrates them, that we can ascertain his meaning. Many writers have maintained that this meaning is vague and general, incapable of being reduced to rigid and logical expression, impossible to tesselate into any formal scheme of salvation. We must not overlook the one element of truth which underlies these assertions. Undoubtedly there is a vast gulf between the large impassioned utterances of mystic fervour and the cold analytic reasonings of technical theology; between emotional expressions and elaborate systems; between Orientalism and scholasticism; between St. Paul and St. Thomas of Aquinum. Speculative metaphysics, *doctrines* of sin, *theories* of imputation, transcendental ontology—these in the course of time were inevitable; but these are not the foundation, not the essence, not the really important element of Christianity. This has been too much forgotten. Yet there is all the difference in the world between understanding what Paul meant to express, and pretending to have fathomed to their utmost depths the Eternal Truths which lie behind his doctrine; and it is perfectly possible for us to comprehend God's scheme, so far as it affects our actions and our hopes, without attempting to arrange in the pigeon-holes of our logical formulæ the incomprehensible mysteries encircling that part of it which has alone been opened for our learning.

1. We may, then, pronounce with reasonable certainty that in this memorable thesis of the Epistle, "*God's righteousness*," which, in the first instance, means a quality of God, is an expression which St. Paul uses to express the imputation of this righteousness by free bestowal upon man, so that man can regard it as a thing

given to himself—a righteousness which proceeds from God and constitutes a new relation of man towards Him—a justification of man, a declaration of man's innocence—an acquittal from guilt through Christ given by free grace—the principle, ordained by God himself, which determines the religious character of the race, and by which the religious consciousness of the individual is conditioned.[1]

2. And when St. Paul says that this "righteousness of God" springs "*from faith*," he does not mean that faith is in any way the meritorious *cause* of it, for he shows that man is justified by free grace, and that this justification has its *ground* in the spontaneous favour of God, and its *cause* in the redemptive work of Christ;[2] but what he means is that faith is the receptive instrument[3] of it—the personal appropriation of the reconciling love of God, which has once for all been carried into effect for the race by the death of Christ.

3. Lastly, when he says that this righteousness of God

[1] Pfleiderer, *Paulinism*, i. 178. "The acceptance wherewith God receives us into His favour as if we were righteous—it consists in the forgiveness of sins and the imputation of the righteousness of Christ" (Calvin). "Faith taketh hold of Christ, and hath Him enclosed, as the ring doth the precious stone. And whosoever shall be found having this confidence in Christ apprehended in the heart, him will God accept for righteous," (Luther). [See, too, the twelve ancient authorities quoted in the Homily on the salvation of mankind.] "The righteousness wherewith we shall be clothed in the world to come is both perfect and inherent; that whereby here we are justified is perfect, but not inherent—that whereby we are sanctified, inherent, but not perfect" (Hooker). "The righteousness which God gives and which he approves" (Hodges). "The very righteousness of God Himself . . . imputed and imparted to men in Jesus Christ (Jer. xxiii. 6; xxxiii. 16) . . . who . . . is made righteousness to us (1 Cor. i. 30) . . . so that we may be not only acquitted by God, but may become the righteous of God in Him (2 Cor. v. 21)" (Bishop Wordsworth).

[2] The Tridentine decree speaks of God's glory and eternal life as the *final*, of God as the *efficient*, of Christ as the *meritorious*, of baptism as the *instrumental*, and of God's righteousness as the *formal* cause of justification.

[3] ὄργανον ληπτικόν. We are justified *per*, not *propter* fidem (Acts x. 1, 2).

is being revealed in the Gospel "from faith *to faith*," he implies the truth, which finds frequent illustration in his writings, that there are ascensive degrees and qualities of Christian faith.[1] Leaving out of sight the dead faith (*fides informis*) of the schoolmen, its lowest stage (i.) is the being theoretically persuaded of God's favour to us in Christ on higher grounds than those of sensuous perception and ordinary experience, namely, because we have confidence in God (*assensus fiducia*). In a higher stage (ii.) it has touched the inmost emotions of the heart, and has become a trustful acceptance of the gift of favour offered by God, "a *self-surrender of the heart* to the favourable will of God as it presents itself to us in the word of reconciliation." But it has a higher stage (iii.) even than this, in which it attains a mystical depth, and becomes a mystical *incorporation with Christ* (*unio mystica*) in a unity of love and life—a practical acquaintance with Christ, which completes itself by personal appropriation of His life and death. In its final and richest development (iv.) it has risen from the passive attitude of receptivity into a spontaneous active force—"*a living impulse and power of good in every phase of personal life.*"[2] In this last stage it becomes so closely allied to *spirit*, that what is said of the one may be said of the other, and that which regarded

---

[1] "From faith to faith," *i.e.*, "which begins in faith and ends in faith, of which faith is the beginning, middle, and end" (Baur, who compares ὀσμὴ ζωῆς εἰς ζωήν, 2 Cor. ii. 16). In the first stage the *Glaube* passes into *Treue*.

[2] For these ascensive uses of the word faith see (i.) Rom. iv. 18, Heb. xi. 1; (ii.) Rom. x. 9, Phil. iii. 7; (iii.) Phil. i. 21, Gal. ii. 20; (iv.) 1 Cor. vi. 17. (Baur, *N. Test. Theol.* 176.) It should be observed that in his earlier Epistles St. Paul does not use the word at all in the modern sense of "a body of doctrine," though this meaning of the word begins to appear in the Pastoral Epistles. From the lowest stage of the word, in which it merely means "belief" and "faithfulness," he rises at once to the deeper sense of "fast attachment to an unseen power of goodness," and then gradually mounts to that meaning of the word in which it is peculiar to himself, namely, mystic union, absolute incorporation, with Christ.

from without is "faith," regarded from within is "spirit." Faith, in this full range of its Pauline meaning, is both a single act and a progressive principle. As a *single act*, it is the self-surrender of the soul to God, the laying hold of Christ, the sole means whereby we appropriate this reconciling love, in which point of view it may be regarded as the root of the new relation of man to God in justification and adoption. As a *progressive principle* it is the renewal of the personal life in sanctification[1]—a preservation of the "righteousness of God" *objectively*

---

[1] Rom. xii. 3; 2 Cor. x. 15. "Faith," says Luther (*Preface to Romans*), "is a divine work in us, which changes us, and creates us anew in God." " Oh es ist ein lebendig, geschäftig, thätig, mächtig Ding um den Glauben, dass es unmöchtig ist dass er nicht ohne Unterlass, sollte Gutes wirken. Er fragt auch nicht ob gute Werke zu thun sind, sondern ehe man fragt hat er sie gethan, und ist immer im Thun. . . . Also dass unmöglich ist Werke vom Glauben zu scheiden: ja so unmöglich als brennen und leuchten vom Feuer mag geschieden werden." Coming from hearing (ἀκοὴ πίστεως, Gal. iii. 2), it is primarily a belief of the Gospel (π. τοῦ εὐαγγελίῳ). As Christ is the essence of the Gospel, it becomes π. τοῦ Χριστοῦ (Gal. ii. 16, iii. 26), the faith which has its principle in Christ. It is further defined as "faith in His blood" (Rom. iii. 24, 25), and thus is narrowed stage by stage in proportion as it grows more intense and inward, passing from theoretical assent to certainty of conviction (Baur, *Paul.* ii. 149). The antithesis of faith and works is only one of abstract thought; it is at once reconciled in the simple moral truth of such passages as 1 Cor. iii. 13, ix. 17, Gal. vi. 7, &c. I cannot here enter on the supposed contradiction between St. Paul and St. James. It will be sufficient to remark that they were dealing with entirely different provinces of religious life, and were using every one of the three words, "faith," "works," and "justification," in wholly different senses. By "faith" St. James (who knew nothing of its Pauline meaning), only meant outward profession of dead Jewish religiosity. By "works" Paul meant Levitism. and even moral actions regarded as external; whereas James meant the *reality* of a moral and religious life. Their meeting-point may be clearly seen in 2 Cor. v. 10; Rom. ii.; 1 Cor. xiii. 1. And in the superficial contrast lies a real coincidence. "The regal law of St. James (i. 25, ii. 8) is the law of liberty in the Epistle to the Galatians. Both are confuting Jewish vanity and Pharisaism. Only the work of St. James was to confute the Pharisee by showing what was the true service of God, and that of St. Paul to show what foundation had been laid for a spiritual and universal economy after the Jewish ceremonial had crumbled" (Maurice, *Unity*, 511). See Wordsworth, *Epistles*, p. 205; Hooker, *Eccl. Pol.*, 1, xi. 6.

bestowed upon us, in the inward and ever-deepening righteousness of our own life; it is, in fact, a new and spiritual life, lived in the faith of the Son of God, who loved us, and gave Himself for us.[1] And hence will be seen at once the absurdity of any radical antithesis between Christian faith and Christian works, since they can no more exist apart from each other than the tree which is severed from the root, or, to use the illustration of Luther, than fire can exist apart from light and heat. "Justification and sanctification," says Calvin, "cohere, but they are not one and the same. It is faith alone which justifies, and yet the faith which justifies is not alone; just as it is the heat alone of the sun which warms the earth, and yet in the sun it is not alone, because it is always conjoined with light."

In accordance with his usual manner when he is enunciating a new truth, St. Paul seeks to support it by the Old Testament Scriptures, and reads the deeper meaning which he has now developed into the words, "The just shall live by faith," which Habakkuk had used in the far simpler sense of "the just shall be delivered by his fidelity." But St. Paul reads these simple words by the light of his own spiritual illumination, which, like the fabled splendour on the graven gems of the Urim, makes them flash into yet diviner oracles. Into the words "faith" and "life" he infuses a significance which he had learnt from revelation, and, as has been truly said, where

[1] See the two very valuable sections on Faith and Justification in Pfleiderer's *Paulinismum*, § v. Other explanations of "from faith to faith" are—1, "from the Old to the New Testament" (Origen, Chrys., &c.); 2, "Ex fide legis in fidem evangelii" (Tert.); 3, "from faith *to the believer*" (iii. 22; Olshausen, &c.); 4, "from weak to strong faith" (cf. 2 Cor. iii. 18; Ps. lxxxiv. 7; Luther, &c.); 5, "An intensive expression = *mera fides*; faith the *prora et puppis* (Bengel, &c.); 6, From Divine faithfulness to human faith (Ewald). Cf. Heb. xii. 2, "the *author* and *finisher* of our faith" (Lange, *ad. loc.*).

Habakkuk ends, Paul begins. And, in fact, his very phrase, "justification by faith," marks the meeting-point of two dispensations. The conception of "justification" has its roots in Judaism; the conception of "faith" is peculiarly Christian. The latter word so completely dominates over the former, that δικαιοσύνη from its first meaning of "righteousness," a quality of God, comes to mean subjectively "justification" as a condition of man—the adequate relation in which man has to stand towards God. Man's appropriation of God's reconciling love in Christ has issued in a change in man's personal life: justification has become sanctification, which is the earnest of future glory

III.

UNIVERSALITY OF SIN.

"Ruit in vetitum, damni secura, libido."—CLAUD.

HAVING thus endeavoured to render clear the one subject which underlies the entire system of St. Paul's theology, we can proceed more rapidly in trying to catch his line of thought through the remainder of the Epistle.

i. Now, since the Apostle had already dwelt on the universality of the Gospel, it was necessary to show that it applied equally to Jews and Pagans; that the universality of free grace was necessitated by the universality of wilful sin. Righteousness and sin, soteriology and hamartiology, are the fundamental thoughts in St. Paul's theological system. The first is a theoretic consequence of our conception of God's nature; the second an historic fact deducible from experience and conscience.

As there is a righteousness of God which is being revealed in the Gospel, so, too, there is a wrath of God against sin which is ever being revealed from heaven, by the inevitable working of God's own appointed laws, against all godlessness and unrighteousness of those who in their unrighteousness suppress the truth.[1] And since the world is mainly Gentile, he speaks of the Gentiles first. Some might imagine that their ignorance of God made them excusable. Not so. The facts which render them inexcusable[2] are (i.) that God did in reality manifest Himself to them, and the invisibilities of His eternal power and God-

---

[1] κατεχόντων (τὴν ἀλήθειαν), i. 18. In 19, τὸ γνωστὸν is "that which *is* known," not "which *may be* known." Ἀποκαλύπτεται, is being revealed. "The modes of the New Testament converge towards the present moment" (Jowett).

[2] In verse 20, obviously εἰς τὸ εἶναι, κ. τ. λ., expresses rather a *consequence* than a *purpose*.

head were clearly visible in His works;[a] and (ii.) that though they knew God, yet by denying Him the due glory and gratitude, they suffered themselves to plunge into the penal darkness of ignorant speculation, and the penal folly of self-asserted wisdom, and the self-convicted boast of a degraded culture, until they sank to such depths of spiritual imbecility as to end even in the idolatry of reptiles;[1] and (iii.) because mental infatuation, both as its natural result and as its fearful punishment, issued in moral crime. Their sin was inexcusable, because it was the outcome and the retribution, and the natural child, of sin. Because they guiltily abandoned God, God abandoned them to their own guiltiness.[2] The conscious lie of idolatry became the conscious infamy of uncleanness. Those "passions of dishonour" to which God abandoned them rotted the heart of manhood with their retributive corruption, and affected even women with their execrable stain.[3] Pagan society, in its hideous disintegration, became one foul disease of unnatural depravity. The cancer of it ate into the heart; the miasma of it tainted the air. Even the moralists of Paganism were infected with its vileness.[4] God scourged their moral ignorance by suffering it to become a deeper ignorance. He punished their contempt by letting them make themselves utterly contemptible. The mere consequence of this abandonment of them was a natural Nemesis, a justice in kind, beginning even in this life, whereby their unwillingness to discern *Him* became an *incapacity* to discern[5] the most elementary distinctions between nobleness and shame. Therefore, their hearts became surcharged with every element of vileness;—with impurity in its most abysmal degradations,

[1] ἀόρατα καθορᾶται, "*Invisibilia videntur*" an admirable oxymoron. "Deum non vides, tamen Deum agnoscis ex ejus operibus" (Cic. *Q. T.* i. 29. Cf. *De Div.* ii. 72). The world was to the Gentiles a θεογνωσίας παιδευτήριον (Basil). On this point see Humboldt, *Cosmos*, ii. 16.

[2] As in Egypt. Egyptian worship was now spreading in Italy:—

"Nos in templa tuam Romana recepimus Isim
Semideosque canes" (Luc. *Phars.* viii. 83).

[3] Verse 24, παρέδωκε, "non *permissivè*, nec ἐκβατικῶς sed δικαστικῶς"—i.e., not as a mere result, but as a judgment in kind.

[4] This is the period of which Seneca says that women counted their years by the number of their divorced husbands (*De Benef.* iii. 15).

[5] There are only too awful and only too exhaustive proofs of all this, and (if possible), worse than all this, in Döllinger, *Heidenthum und Judenthum*, 684. But "Ostendi debent *scelera* dum puniuntur *abscondi flagitia.*"

[6] i. 28, καθὼς οὐκ ἐδοκίμασαν . . . παρέδωκεν . . . εἰς ἀδόκιμον νοῦν, "As they *refused* . . . God gave them to a *refuse* mind" (Vaughan, *ad loc.*). St. Paul was deeply impressed (24, 26, 28) with the ethic retributive law of the punishment of sin with sin. It was recognised both by Jews and Gentiles (*Pirke Abhôth*, iv. 2; Sen. *Ep.* 16).

with hatred alike in its meanest and its most virulent developments, with insolence culminating in the deliberate search for fresh forms of evil,[1] with cruelty and falsity in their most repulsive features. And the last worst crime of all—beyond which crime itself could go no further—was the awfully *defiant* attitude of moral evil, which led them—while they were fully aware of God's sentence of death,[2] pronounced on willing guilt—not only to incur it themselves, but, with a devilish delight in human depravity and human ruin, to take a positive pleasure in those who practise the same. Sin, as has been truly said, reaches its climax in wicked *maxims* and wicked *principles*. It is no longer Vice the result of moral weakness, or the outcome of an evil education, but Vice deliberately accepted with all its consequences, Vice assuming the airs of self-justification, Vice in act becoming Vice in elaborate theory—the unblushing shamelessness of Sodom in horrible aggravation of its polluting sin.[3]

Thus did Paul brand the insolent brow of Pagan life. It is well for the world—it is above all well for the world in those ages of transition and decay, when there is ever an undercurrent of tendency towards Pagan ideals—to know what Paganism was, and ever tended to become. It is well for the world that it should have been made to see, once for all, what features lurked under the smiling mask, what a heart of agony, rank

---

[1] i. 30, ἐφευρετὰς κακῶν (2 Macc. vii. 31). Pliny (*H. N.* xv. 5) applies this very expression to the Greeks. *Some* of these words occur in speaking of corruptions *within* the Church (2 Tim. iii. 2); "of so little avail is *nominal* Christianity" (Vaughan); εὑρετὴς ἀγαθῶν (Prov. xvi. 20).

[2] i. 32, τὸ δικαίωμα, "the just decree;" ποιοῦσιν, "single acts;" πράσσουσιν, "habitual condition." Possibly an οὐκ has dropped out before ἐπιγνόντες ("they did *not fully* know "), of which some readings show a trace.

[3] i. 16—32. The Apostle is fond of these accumulative lists (συναθροισμὸς) of good and evil (2 Cor. xii. 20; Gal. v. 19; Eph. v. 3, 4; 1 Tim. i. 9; 2 Tim. iii. 2). No satisfactory classification of the order can be made. Bengel says, "Per membra *novem*, in affectibus; *duo* in sermone; *tria* respectu Dei et sui, et proximi; *duo* in rebus gerendis; *sex* respectu necessitudinum." On verses 27, 28, the best comment is to be found in Aristophanes, Juvenal, and Suetonius; on 29—31, in Thuc. iii. 82—84. See the contemporary testimony of Sen. *De Irâ.* ii. 8, " Omnia sceleribus ac vitiis plena sunt . . . nec furtiva jam scelera sunt." The special horror of the age is reflected in Tac. *H.* i. 2, and *passim*. " Le premier siècle de notre ère a un cachet infernal qui n'appartient qu'à lui; le siècle des Borgia peut seul lui être comparé en fait de scélératesse " (Renan, *Mélanges*, p. 167).

with hatred, charred with self-indulgence,[1] lay throbbing under the purple robe. And in St. Paul's description not one accusation is too terrible, not one colour is too dark. He does but make known to us what heathen writers unblushingly reveal in those passages in which, like waves of a troubled sea, they foam out their own mire and dirt.[2] It is false to say that Christianity has added to the gloom of the world. It is false that it has weakened its literature, or cramped its art. It has been wilfully perverted; it has been ignorantly misunderstood. Rightly interpreted it does not sanction a single doctrine, or utter a single precept, which is meant to extinguish one happy impulse, or dim one innocent delight. What it does is to warn us against seeking and following the lowest and most short-lived pleasures as a final end. This was the fatal error of the popular Hedonism. St. Paul's sketch of its moral dissolution and the misery and shame which it inevitably involved, is but another illustration of the truth that

> "Who follows pleasure, pleasure slays,
>   God's wrath upon himself he wreaks;
> But all delights attend his days
>   Who takes with thanks but never seeks."

ii. Having thus accomplished his task of proving the guilt of the Gentiles, he turns to the Jews. But he does so with consummate tact. He does not at once startle them into antagonism, by shocking all their prejudices, but begins with the perfectly general statement, "Therefore[3] thou art inexcusable, O man—*every one* who judgest." The "therefore" impetuously anticipates the reason why he who judges others is, in this instance, inexcusable—

---

[1] i. 27, ἐξεκαύθησαν.
[2] Jud. 13; Isa. lvii. 20.
[3] This Διό of ii. 1 is clearly *proleptic*.

namely, because he does the same things himself. He does not at once say, as he might have done, "You who are Jews are as inexcusable as the Gentiles, because in judging them you are condemning yourselves, and though you habitually call them 'sinners' you are no less sinners yourselves."[1] This is the conclusion at which he points, but he wishes the Jew to be led step by step into self-condemnation, less hollow than vague generalities.[2] He is of course speaking alike of Jews and of Pagans *generically*, and not implying that there were no exceptions. But he has to introduce the argument against the Jews carefully and gradually, because, blinded by their own privileges, they were apt to take a very different view of their own character. But they were less excusable because more enlightened. He therefore begins, "O man," and not "O Jew," and asks the imaginary person to whom he is appealing whether he thinks that God will in his case make an individual exception to His own inflexible decrees? or whether he intends to despise the riches of God's endurance, by ignoring[3] that its sole intention is to lead him to repentance—and so to heap up against himself a horrible treasury of final ruin? God's law is rigid, universal, absolute. It is that God will repay every man all to his works.[4] This law is illustrated by a twofold ampli-

[1] Gal. ii. 15, ἡμεῖς φύσει Ἰουδαῖοι, καὶ οὐκ ἐξ ἐθνῶν ἁμαρτωλοί. Meyer truly says this judging of the Gentiles (which they little dreamt would be pointed out to them as self-condemnation, by one of themselves) was a characteristic of the Jews.

[2] Thus the High-priest said over the scapegoat, "Thy people have failed, sinned, and transgressed before Thee" (*Yoma*, 66 a).

[3] Ver. 4, ἀγνοῶν. "Ἄγει, "Deus ducit *volentem* duci . . . non cogit necessitate" (Bengel).

[4] The apparent contradiction to the fundamental theme of the Epistle is due to his speaking here of ordinary morality. "The Divine valuation placed on men apart from redemption" (Tholuck). Fritzsche's comment that "the Apostle is here inconsistent, and opens a *semita per honestatem* near the *via regia* of justification" is very off-hand and valueless.

fication, which, beginning and ending with the reward of goodness, and inserting twice over in the middle clause the punishment of sin,[1] expresses the thought that this rule applies to *all*, by twice repeating that it applies to the Jew first and also to the Greek; but to the Jew *first*, only because of his fuller knowledge and, therefore, deeper responsibility. And having thus introduced the name of the Jew, he lays down with a firm hand the eternal principle—so infinitely blessed, yet so startlingly new to the prejudices of a nation which for more than a thousand years had been intoxicating itself with the incense of spiritual pride—that *there is no respect of persons with God.* Each section of humanity shall be judged in accordance with its condition.

"As many as sinned without the Law, shall also without the Law perish; and as many as sinned in the Law, shall be condemned by the Law." Righteousness before God depends, not on *possession* of the Law, but on *obedience* to it. Gentiles as well as Jews had a law; Jews the Mosaic law, Gentiles a natural law written on their hearts, and sufficiently clear to secure, at the day of judgment,[2] their acquittal or condemnation before the prophetic session of their own consciences, in accordance with the decision of Christ the Judge.[3] Jew, then, and Gentile stand before God equally guilty, because equally condemned of failure to fulfil the moral law which God had laid down to guide their

[1] The figure of speech is called *Chiasmus*, or introverse parallelism. "Glory and honour, and immortality—precious pearls; eternal life—the goodly pearl, Matt. xiii. 46" (Lange).

[2] ii. 16, leg. κρίνει "is judging," not κρινεῖ "shall judge."

[3] ii. 1—16. St. Paul adds κατὰ τὸ εὐαγγέλιόν μου. "Suum appellat ratione ministerii" (Calv.). It means, of course, the Gospel of free grace which he preached to Gentiles (Gal. ii. 7). In verse 14, "Do by nature the things of the law," St. Paul (who is not here speaking with theologic precision, but dealing with general external facts) recognises even in heathens the existence of the nobler nature and its better impulses. See the remarkable expression of Aristotle, ὁ ἐλεύθερος οὕτως ἕξει οἷον νόμος ὢν ἑαυτῷ (*Eth. Nic.* iv. 14). It is strange to see so great a commentator as Bengel joining φύσει with τὰ μὴ νόμον ἔχοντα and interpreting it to mean "do the same things that the Law does," *i.e.*, commanding, condemning, punishing, &c.! Nothing would have been more amazing to St. Paul than the notion that he discouraged good works. The phrase occurs no less than fourteen times in his three last short Epistles.

CONDEMNATION OF THE JEW. 201

lives. The word "*ALL*," as has been truly observed, is the governing word of the entire Epistle. *All*—for whatever may be the modifications which may be thought necessary, St. Paul does not himself make them—*all* are equally guilty, *all* are equally redeemed. All have been temporarily rejected, all shall be ultimately received. All shall be finally brought into living harmony with that God who is above all, and through all, and in all,—by whom, and from whom, and unto whom, all things are, and all things tend.[1]

And then Paul turns upon the self-satisfied Jew, who has been thus insensibly entrapped (as it were) into the mental admission of his own culpability, and after painting in a few touches his self-satisfied pretensions to spiritual, moral, and intellectual superiority, and then leaving his sentence unfinished, bursts into a question of indignant eloquence, in which there is no longer any masked sarcasm, but terribly serious denunciation of undeniable sins. He does not use one word of open raillery, or give offence by painting in too glaring colours the weaknesses, follies, and hypocrisies of the Pharisee, yet the picture which stands out from phrases in themselves perfectly polished, and even apparently complimentary, is the picture of the full-blown religionist in all his assumed infallibility, and the very air of the "Stand aside, for I am holier than thou."

"But if"[2] (so we may draw out the splendid rhetoric), "if thou vauntest the proud name of Jew,[3] and makest the Law the pillow of thy confidence,[4] and boastest thy monopoly in God, and art the only one who canst recognise His will, and discriminatest the transcendent[5] in

---

[1] See Rom. v. 15—20; x. 12; 1 Cor. xv. 28; Col. iii. 11; 2 Cor. v. 15; Heb. ii. 8, &c.

[2] ii. 17, εἰ δέ, and not ἴδε, is almost unquestionably the true reading, א, A, B, D, K, "oratio vehemens et splendida" (Est.).

[3] ἐπονομάζῃ.

[4] verse 17, ἐπαναπαύῃ.

[5] verse 18, δοκιμάζεις τὰ διαφέροντα. See Heb. v. 14. The διαστολὴ ἁγίων καὶ βεβήλων (Philo) was the very function of a Rabbi; and the Pharisee was a Separatist, because of his scrupulosity in these distinctions.

niceties of moral excellence, being trained in the Law from infancy,—if thou art quite convinced that thou art a Leader of the blind, a Light of those in darkness, one who can train the foolishness, and instruct the infancy of all the world besides, possessing as thou dost the very form and body of knowledge and of truth in the Law—*thou then that teachest another, dost thou not teach thyself ?* thou that preachest against theft, art thou a thief? thou that forbiddest adultery, art thou an adulterer ?[1] loather of idols, dost thou rob temples ?[2] boaster in the Law, by violation of the Law dost thou dishonour God ? For "—and here he drops the interrogative to pronounce upon them the categorical condemnation which was as true then as in the days of the Prophet—" for on your account the name of God is being blasphemed among the Gentiles."[3] They had relied on sacrifices and offerings, on tithes and phylacteries, on ablutions and *mezuzoth*,—but "*omnia vanitas praeter amare Deum et illi soli servire*,"—"all things are emptiness save to love God, and serve Him only,"—and this weightier matter of the Law they had utterly neglected in scrupulous attention to its most insignificant minutiæ. In fact, the difference between Heathenism and Judaism before God was the difference between Vice and Sin. The Jews were guilty of the sin of violating express commands; the heathens sank into an actual degradation of nature. The heathens had been punished for an unnatural transposition of the true order of the universe by being suffered to pervert all natural relations, and so to sink into moral self-debasement; but the Jews had been "admitted into a holier sanctuary," and so were "guilty of a deeper sacrilege."[4]

[1] verse 21, on the morality of the Pharisees and Rabbis, see Surenhusius, *Mishna*, ii. 290—293, and cf. Jas. iv. 4—13; v. 1—6; Matt. xix. 8; xxiii. 13—25. Josephus calls his own generation the most ungodly of all, and says that earthquake and lightning must have destroyed them if the Romans had not come. *B. J.* iv. 3—3; v. 9, 4, 10, 5, 13, 6. Take the single fact that the "ordeal of jealousy" had been abolished, because of the prevalence of adultery, by R. Johanan ben Zaccai quoting Hos. iv. 14 (*Sotah*, f. 47, 1).

[2] verse 22, ὁ βδελυσσόμενος. They called idols נדָּוִה, βδελύγματα, 2 Kings xxiii. 13, &c. LXX. ἱεροσυλεῖς. The reference is not clear, but see Deut. vii. 25; Acts xix. 36—37; Jos. *Antt.* iv. 8, 10; xx. 9, 2. Or does it refer to defrauding their own Temple? (Mal. i. 8; iii. 8—10.) σπηλαιον ληστῶν (Matt. xxi. 13). Josephus quotes a Greek historian, Lysimachus, who said that from the conduct of the Jews in robbing the Temples of their charms that city was called *Hierosyla* (*Temple-plunder*) and afterwards changed to Hierosolyma; a story which he angrily rejects (*c. Ap.* i. 34).

[3] ii. 17—24. In verse 24 the *words* of Isa. lii. 5 are curiously combined with the *sense* of Ezek. xxxvi. 21—23.

[4] The needfulness of this demonstration may be seen from the fact that some of the Talmudists regarded perfection as possible. They denied the

THE TRUE CIRCUMCISION.

From this impassioned strain he descends—in a manner very characteristic of his style—into a calmer tone. "But"—some Jew might urge, in accordance with the stubborn prejudices of theological assumption, which by dint of assertion, has passed into invincible belief—"but *we* are *circumcised!* Surely you would not put *us* on a level with the uncircumcised—the dogs and sinners of the Gentiles?" To such an implied objection, touching as it does on a point wholly secondary, however primary might be the importance which the Jew attached to it, St. Paul can now give a very decisive answer, because with wonderful power he has already stripped them of all genuine precedence and involved them in a common condemnation. He therefore replies in words which, however calm and grave, would have sounded to a Jerusalem Pharisee like stinging paradox.

"Circumcision is indeed an advantage if thou keepest the Law; but if thou art—as I have generically shown that thou art—a violator of the Law, then *thy circumcision has become uncircumcision.*[1] If, then, the circumcision of the disobedient Jew is really uncircumcision, is it not conversely plain that the 'uncircumcision of the obedient Gentile is virtually circumcision,'[2] and is even in a position to pass judgment upon

---

sinfulness of *evil thoughts* by interpreting Ps. lxvi. 18 to mean—"If I contemplate iniquity in my heart, the *Lord does not notice* it" (*Kiddushin*, f. 40, 1). R. Jehoshua Ben Levi, admitted to Paradise without dying, is asked if the rainbow has appeared in his days, and answers "Yes." "Then," said they, "thou art not the son of Levi, for the rainbow never appears when there is one perfectly righteous man in the world." "The fact was that no rainbow had appeared, but he was too modest to say so"! (*Kiddushin*, f. 40, 1).

[1] This is reluctantly admitted even in the Talmud. The Rabbis hold generally that "no circumcised man can see hell" (*Midr. Tillin*, 7, 2); but they get over the moral danger of the doctrine by saying that when a guilty Jew comes to Gehenna, an angel makes his περιτομή into ἀκροβυστία (*Shem. Rabbah*, 138, 13; cf. 1 Macc. i. 15; Jos. *Antt.* xii. 6, 2) and they even entered into minute particulars to show how it was done.

[2] Ford quotes an imitation from Tillotson,—if we walk contrary to the Gospel "our *baptism is no baptism*, and *our Christianity is heathenism*" (Sermon on 2 Tim. ii. 19).

Jewish circumcision? God (strange and heretical as you may think it) loves the man who does his duty more than the man who bears a cutting in his flesh. You praise literal circumcision; God praises the unseen circumcision of the heart. Offensive as the antithesis may sound to you, the faithless Jew is but a Gentile; the faithful Gentile is, in God's sight, an honoured Jew! Though none may have told you this truth before—though you denounce it as blasphemous, and dangerous, and contrary to Scripture—yet, for all that, the mere national Judaism is a spiritual nonentity; the Judaism of moral faithfulness alone is dear to God."[1]

[1] ii. 25—29.

IV.

OBJECTIONS AND CONFIRMATIONS.

> "The stars of morn shall see Him rise
> Out of His grave, fresh as the dawning light;
> Thy ransom paid, which man from death redeems,
> His death for man, as many as offered life
> Neglect not, and the benefit embrace
> Of faith, not void of works."—MILTON, *Par. Lost*, xii.

So far then, both by fact and by theory, he has shown that Jews and Gentiles are equal before God; equally guilty, equally redeemed. But here a Jew might exclaim in horror, "Has the Jew then no superiority? Is circumcision wholly without advantage?" Here St. Paul makes a willing concession, and replies, "Much advantage every way. First, because they were entrusted with the oracles of God." The result of that advantage was that the Jew stood at a higher stage of religious consciousness than the Gentile. Judaism was the religion of revelation, and therefore the religion of the promise; and therefore the religion which typically and symbolically contained the elements of Christianity; and the religion of the idea which in Christianity was realised. Christianity was, indeed, *spiritualised* Judaism, an advance from servitude to freedom, from nonage to majority, from childhood to maturity, from the flesh to the spirit; yet even in this view Judaism had been, by virtue of its treasure of revelation, preparatory to the absolute religion.[1] This was its

---

[1] iii. 2. "In vetere Testamento Novum latet, in Novo Testamento vetus patet."

first advantage. What he might have added as his secondly and thirdly, we may conjecture from a subsequent allusion,[1] but at this point he is led into a digression by his eagerness to show that his previous arguments involved no abandonment on God's part of His own promises. This might be urged as an objection to what he has been saying. He answers it in one word:—

Some of the Jews had been unfaithful; shall their unfaithfulness nullify God's faith? Away with the thought![2] Alike Scripture and reason insist on God's truthfulness, though every man were thereby proved a liar. The horror with which he rejects the notion that God has proved false, interferes with the clearness of his actual reply. It lies in the word "*some.*" God's promises were true; true to the nation as a nation; for *some* they had been nullified by the moral disobedience which has its root in unbelief, but for all true Jews the promises were true.[3]

A still bolder objection might be urged—"All men, you say, are guilty. In their guilt lies the Divine necessity for God's scheme of justification. Must not God, then, be unjust in inflicting wrath?" In the very middle of the objection the Apostle stops short—first to apologise for even formulating a thought so blasphemous—"I am speaking as men speak;"[4] "these thoughts are not my own;"—then to repudiate it with horror, "Away with the thought!"—lastly, to refute it by anticipation, "If it were so, how shall God judge the world?"[5] Thus fortified, as it were, by the *reductio ad absurdum*, and purified by the moral justification, he follows this impious logic to its conclusion—"God's truth, it seems, abounded in my falseness; why, then, am I still being judged as a sinner? and why"—"such [he pauses to remark] is the blasphemous language attributed to *me!*"—"why may we not do evil that good may come?" To this monstrous perversion of his teaching he deigns no further immediate reply. There are in

---

[1] ix. 4, 5.
[2] *Ten* times in this Epistle (iii. 4, 6, 31; vi. 2, 15; vii. 7, 13; ix. 14; xi. 1, 11), and in 1 Cor. vi. 15; Gal. ii. 17; iii. 21.
[3] iii. 1—4.
[4] iii. 5. There is an interesting reading, κατὰ ἀνθρώπων. "Is God unjust who inflicts His anger against men?" (MSS. mentioned by Rufinus). τί ἐροῦμεν; cf. vi. 1; vii. 7; ix. 14, 30. It is found in no other Epistle.
[5] For similar instances of entangled objection and reply, Tholuck refers to vii. and Gal. iii. See, too, Excursus II., on the Antinomies of St. Paul.

theology, as in nature, admitted antinomies. The relative truth of doctrines, their truth as regards mankind, is not affected by pushing them into the regions of the absolute, and showing that they involve contradictions if thrown into syllogisms. We may not push the truths of the finite and the temporal into the regions of the infinite and the eternal. Syllogistically stated, the existence of evil might be held to *demonstrate* either the weakness or the cruelty of God; but such syllogisms, without the faintest attempt to answer them, are flung aside as valueless and irrelevant by the faith and conscience of mankind. The mere *statement* of some objections is their most effective refutation. It shows that they involve an absurdity easily recognisable. However logically correct, they are so morally repulsive, so spiritually false, that silence is the only answer of which they are worthy. Such an objection is the one which Paul has just stated. It is sufficient to toss it away with the sense of shuddering repulsion—the *horror naturalis*—involved in a μὴ γένοιτο. It is enough to bid it avaunt, as we might avert with a formula an evil omen. People say that Paul has taught the hideous lie that we may sin to get experience—or sin to add to Christ's redeeming glory—or that the end justifies the means—or that we may do evil that good may come. "*They say——What say they? Let them say!*" All that Paul has to say to them is merely that "their judgment is just."[1]

What further, then, can the Jew allege?[2] Absolutely nothing! In spite of every objection, Jew and Gentile are all proved to be under sin. Here this section of the proof might close, and on a demonstrated fact of human history Paul might have based his Gospel theology. But neither to himself nor to his readers would the proof have seemed complete without Old Testament sanction. He therefore proceeds to quote a number of fragmentary passages from the fifth, tenth, fourteenth, and hundred-and-fortieth Psalms, and from the fifty-ninth of Isaiah, the validity of which, in this connexion, he rests upon their use of the word "all," which implies Jews as well as Gentiles. The Law (which here means the Old Testament generally) must *include* the Jews, because it is specially *addressed* to Jews. The intention, then, of the Law "is that *every* mouth may be stopped, and *all the world* be recognised as guilty

---

[1] iii. 5—8.
[2] iii. 9. προεχόμεθα properly means "use as a pretext;" the reading προκατέχομεν περισσόν of D, G, Syr. is a gloss to give the meaning of προέχομεν, "do we excel?" which suits the sense far better. Wetstein renders it " are we (the Jews) surpassed by the Gentiles?" But as the Greek fathers made it mean "have we the advantage?" (Vulg. *praecellimus*), perhaps the sense is admissible here.

before God;" guilty because[1] by the works of the Law[2]—seeing that, as a fact, neither Jew nor Gentile has obeyed it—no flesh shall be justified before God. Half, then, of his task is done. For before he could prove the thesis of i. 17, that in the Gospel was being revealed a justification by faith—it was necessary for him to demonstrate that *by no other means* could justification be attained. "For"—and here he introduces an anticipative thought, which later on in his epistle he will have seriously to prove—"by the Law is the full knowledge of sin."[3]

[1] iii. 19. λέγει speaks, λαλεῖ utters, cf. John viii. 43, λαλίαν, λόγον. This is the only place in the New Testament where our translators have rendered διότι by "therefore," though it occurs twenty-two times. Everywhere else they render it "for" or "because." It may mean "therefore" in classical Greek, but διὸ is the usual New Testament word in this sense. If rendered "because," a comma only should be placed after Θεό.

[2] ἔργα νόμου, the works of *any* law, whether ritual, Mosaic, or general, and whether as to the works *prescribed* by it, or those *produced* by it.

[3] iii. 9—20.—ἐπίγνωσις ἁμαρτίας, and therefore the Law cannot justify, since, as Calvin says, "Ex eadem scatebrâ non prodeunt vita et mors."

V.

JUSTIFICATION BY FAITH.

"1. ⎧ Paedagogica (Caerimoniae) ⎫ illae sunt necessariae sed non justi-
Justitia 2. ⎨ Civilis (Decalogus) ⎬ ficant.
3. ⎩ Dei et fidei, coram Deo justificat."
LUTHER, *Colloqu.* i. 30.

iii. "But now," he says, and this introduces one of the fullest and weightiest passages in all his writings, "without the Law"—which all have failed to keep—"the righteousness of God," both in itself and as an objective gift of justification to man, "has been manifested, being witnessed to by the Law and the Prophets." The nature of that witness he will show later on; at present he pauses to give a fuller, and indeed an exhaustive, definition of what he means by "the righteousness of God." "I mean the righteousness of God accepted by means of faith in Jesus Christ, coming to and upon *all* believers—*all*, for there is no difference. For all sinned, and are failing to attain the glory of God, being justified freely by His grace, by means of the redemption which is in Christ Jesus, whom God set forth as a propitiation,[1] by

---

[1] Ver. 25. This verse is "the Acropolis of the Christian faith" (Olshausen). Ἀπολύτρωσις (not in LXX.) implies i., bondage; ii., ransom; iii., deliverance (Eph. i. 7). Many most eminent theologians (Origen, Theodoret, Theophylact, Augustine, Erasmus, Luther, Calvin, Grotius, Calovius, Olshausen, Tholuck, &c.) make ἱλαστήριον mean "mercy-seat," since ἱλαστήριον is the *invariable* word for the *capporeth* in the LXX. (Ex. xxv., *passim*, &c.) which *never* uses it for an expiatory sacrifice (θῦμα). Philo also (*Vit. Mos.*, p. 668; cf. Jos. *Antt.* iii. 6, 5) calls the mercy-seat a symbol, ἵλεω δυνάμεως. It is, therefore, difficult to suppose how Hellenist readers of this Epistle could attach any other meaning to it. The *capporeth* between the Shekinah and the Tables of the Law, sprinkled with atoning blood by the High Priest as he stood behind the rising incense, is a striking image of Christ (Heb. ix. 25). I quite agree with Lange in calling Fritzsche's remark, "Valeat *absurda explicatio*," an "ignorantly contemptuous one;" but as Christ is *nowhere else* in the New Testament compared to the mercy-seat, and the comparison would here be confined to the *single word*, I cannot help thinking that the word, though ambiguous, must here bear an analogous meaning to ἱλασμός, also rendered "a propitiation" in 1 John iv. 10.

means of faith in His blood, for the manifestation of His own righteousness"—which righteousness might otherwise have been doubted or misunderstood—"because of the prætermission of past sins in God's forbearance; with a view (I say) to the manifestation of this righteousness at this present epoch, that He might, by a divine paradox, and by a new and divinely predestined righteousness, be just and the justifier of him whose life springs from faith in Jesus."[1]

Let us pause to enumerate the separate elements of this great statement. It brings before us in one view—

1. *Justification*,—the new relation of reconcilement between man and God.

2. *Faith*,—man's trustful acceptance of God's gift, rising to absolute self-surrender, culminating in personal union with Christ, working within him as a spirit of new life.

3. The *universality* of this justification by faith,—a possibility offered to, because needed by, all.

4. This means of salvation *given*, not earned, nor to be earned; a free gift due to the free favour or grace of God.

5. The object of this faith, the source of this possibility of salvation, *the life and death of Christ*, as being (i.) a redemption—that is, a ransom of mankind from the triple bondage of the law, of sin, and of punishment; (ii.) a propitiatory victim,[2]—not (except by a rude, imperfect, and most misleading anthropomorphism) *as regards God*, but from the finite and imperfect standpoint of man; and

---

[1] iii. 22—27. Bengel points out the grandeur of this evangelic paradox. In the Law God is just and condemns; in the Gospel He is just and forgives. God's judicial righteousness both condemns and pardons. On God's "prætermission" of past sins (iii. 25, πάρεσις, *praetermissio*, not ἄφεσις, *remissio*) compare Ps. lxxxi. 12; Acts xiv. 16; xvii. 30; Lev. xvi. 10. Tholuck calls the Atonement "the divine theodicy for the past history of the world."

[2] "Here is a foundation for the Anselmic theory of satisfaction, but not for its grossly anthropopathic execution." Schaff. *ad loc.* (Lange's *Romans*, 2—7). And this is only the *external* aspect of the death of Christ, the merely judicial aspect pertaining to the sphere of Law. The inward motive—the element in which God's essential nature is revealed, is the grace of God (Rom. iii. 24).

therefore the Apostle adds that Christ becomes such *to us* by means of faith is His blood.

6. The *reason* for this,—the manifestation of God's righteousness, which might otherwise have been called in question, because of the prætermission of past sins.

7. The *end* to be attained,—that, in perfect consistency with justice, God might justify all whose new life had its root in faith.

Boasting then is impossible, since merit is non-existent. By *works* it is unattainable; by the very conception of *faith* it is excluded. This holds true alike for Jew and Pagan, and Justification is God's free gift to man as man,[1] because He is One, and the God alike of Jews and Gentiles. To the Jew faith is the source, to the Gentile the instrument of this justification.[2]

But here another objection has to be combated. The Jew might say, "By this faith of yours you are nullifying the Law"—meaning by the Law the whole Mosaic dispensation, and generally the Old Testament as containing the history of the covenant people. On the contrary, St. Paul replies, I am establishing it on a firmer basis;[3] for I

---

[1] Ver. 28, "Therefore [but γὰρ, ͅ A] we reckon that a man is justified by faith without the works of the Law." This is the verse in which Luther interpolated the word "alone" — "Vox SOLA tot clamoribus lapidata" (Erasm.). Hence the name Solifidian. It was a legitimate *inference*, and was already existing in the Nuremberg Bible (1483) and the Genoese (1476), but was an unfortunate apparent contradiction of οὐκ ἐκ πίστεως μόνον (James ii. 24). But Luther's famous preface shows sufficiently that he recognised the necessity of works in the same sense as St. James (see Art. xi., xii.). Luther was not guilty of the foolish error which identifies faith with mere belief; and yet, perhaps, his mode of dealing with this verse led to his rash remark as to the impossibility of reconciling the two Apostles (*Colloqu.* ii. 203).

[2] iii. 27—30, περιτομὴν ἐκ πίστεως . . . ἀκροβυστίαν διὰ τῆς πίστεως seems to imply some real difference in the Apostle's view, though Meyer (usually such a purist) here denies it. Calvin sees a shade of irony in it—"*This* is the grand difference: the Jew is saved *ex* fide, the Gentile *per* fidem!" Bengel is probably right when he says that it implies the priority of the Jews, and the acceptance of the Gospel from them by the Gentiles;—the Jews as an outgrowth of faith, the Gentiles by the means of *the* faith" (see Gal. iii. 22—26).

[3] iii. 31. See chap. vi.; viii. 4; xiii. 10.

am exhibiting it in its true position, manifesting it in its true relations; showing it to be the divinely-necessary part of a greater system; adding to the depth of its spirituality, rendering possible the cheerful obedience to its requirements; indicating its divine fulfilment. I am showing that the consciousness of sin which came by the Law is the indispensable preparation for the reception of grace. Let us begin at the very beginning. Let us go back from Moses even to Abraham. What did he, our father, gain by works?[1] By his works he gained nothing before God, as St. Paul proves by the verse that "He *believed* God, and it was *imputed* to him for righteousness."[2] That word "*imputed*" repeated eleven times in the chapter, is the keynote of the entire passage, and is one of very primary importance in the argument with the Jews, who held that Abraham obeyed the Law before it was given.[3] To us, perhaps, it is of secondary importance, since the Apostle did not *derive* his views from these considerations, but discovered the truths revealed to him in passages which, until he thus applied them, would not have been seen to involve this deeper significance. It required, as De Wette says, no small penetration thus to unite the *climax* of religious development with the historic point at which the series of religious developments began. To a worker, he argues, the pay is not "*imputed*" as a favour, but *paid* as a debt; but Abraham's faith was "*imputed*" to him for righteousness, just as it is to all who believe on Him who justifies the ungodly. This truth David also indicates when he speaks of the blessedness of the man to whom God *imputeth* righteousness, or, which comes to the same thing, "does not impute sin." Now this imputation can have nothing to do with circumcision, because the phrase is used at a time before Abraham was circumcised, and circumcision was only a *sign*[4] of the righteousness imputed to him because of

---

[1] iv. 1. If we do not omit εὑρηκέναι (with B), κατὰ σάρκα must go with εὑρηκέναι, not as in A. V. with πατέρα. It means, "What did he obtain by purely human efforts?" *e.g.*, by circumcision (Baur); *propriis viribus* (Grot.); *Nach rein menschlicher Weise* (De Wette). St. Paul here attacks a position which afterwards became a stronghold of Talmudists.

[2] St. Paul here follows the LXX., which changes the active into the passive. The faith of Abraham was a common subject of discussion in Jewish schools. See some remarkable parallels in 1 Macc. ii. 52; Philo's eulogy of faith, *De Abrahamo*, ii. 39; *De Mut. Nom.* i. 586. Nay, since the plural "laws" is used in Gen. xxvi. 5, Rabh held that he kept both the written and the oral law (*Yoma*, f. 28, 2).

[3] *Kiddushin*, f. 82, 1.

[4] iv. 11. The word "seal" (אות) occurs in the formula of circumcision (*Berachoth*, xiii. 1). A circumcised child was called "an espoused of blood" &c., to God (Ex. iv. 26).

THE FAITH OF ABRAHAM.

his faith, that he might be regarded as "the father of the faithful," whether they be circumcised or uncircumcised. Had the great promise to Abraham, on which all Jews relied, come to him by the Law? Not so, for two reasons. First, because the promise was long prior to the Law, and would have been nullified if it were made to depend on a subsequent law; and, secondly, because the Law causes the sense of wrongdoing,[1] and so works wrath not promise. Hence, it was the strength of Abraham's faith looking to God's promise in spite of his own and Sarah's age,[2] which won him the imputed righteousness; and this was recorded for us because the faith, and the promise, and the paternity, are no mere historic circumstances, but have all of them a spiritual significance, full of blessedness for all who "believe on Him who raised Jesus our Lord from the dead, who was delivered up for our sins, and raised for our justification."[3]

This, then, is the proof that the doctrine of Justification is not contrary to Scripture, and does not vilipend, but really establish the Law; and into the last verse are skilfully introduced the new conceptions of Christ's death for our sin, and His resurrection to procure our imputed righteousness, which are further developed in the subsequent chapters.

But first, having proved his point, he dwells on its blessed consequences, which may be summed up in the two words Peace and Hope.

These are treated together. We have Peace,[4] because through Christ we have our access into the free favour of God, and can exult not only in the hope of the future, but even in the afflictions of the present, which

---

[1] See vii. 7, seqq.

[2] In iv. 19 the οὐ should be omitted (א, A, B, C, Syr., &c.). He *did* perceive and consider the weakness of his own body, but *yet* had faith. In fact, "not considering his own body" contradicts Gen. xvii. 17.

[3] iv. 1—25. In verse 25 the first διὰ is retrospective, the second is prospective; διὰ τὰ παραπτώματα, "on account of our transgressions;" διὰ τὴν δικαίωσιν, "to secure our being justified." Luther calls this verse "a little covenant, in which all Christianity is comprehended."

[4] v. 1, ἔχωμεν is the better supported reading (א, A, B, C, D, K, L); but ἔχομεν gives by far the better sense, and the other reading may be due to the Pietistic tendency of the Lectionaries to make sentences hortative,—which apparently began to work very early. For a defence of ἔχομεν, I may refer to the Rev. J. A. Beet's able commentary on the Epistle, which reached me too late for use.

tend to hope because first they work endurance, then approved firmness.[1] The certainty of our Hope is due to the love of God poured into our hearts by His Holy Spirit, and unmistakable to us, since, by a stretch of self-sacrifice unknown to humanity,[2] Christ died for us, not because of any justice much less any goodness of ours, but while we were yet sinners and enemies. And since we have been reconciled to God by His death, much more shall we be saved by His life, so that our hope —founded on this reconciliation to God—may even acquire a tinge of exultation.[3] Our Peace, then, is an immediate sentiment which requires no external proof; and our Hope is founded on the love of God assured to us in three ways—namely, by Christ's death for us while we were yet enemies to God; on the strength to endure afflictions and see their blessed issue; and above all on union with Christ in death and life.[4]

And this universality of Sin, and universality of Justification, leads Paul to one of his great sketches of the religious history of humanity. To him that history was summed up in three great moments connected with the lives of Adam, Moses, and Christ, of which the mission of Moses was the least important. Those three names corresponded to three stages in the world's religious history—Promise, Law, and Faith—of which the third is the realisation of the first. Adam was a type of Christ, and each stood as it were at the head of long lines of representatives. Each represents the principle of a whole æon. Adam's first sin developed a *principle* from which none of his posterity could be free; and Christ introduced the possibility of a new and saving principle, the necessity for which had been made manifest by the dispensation of Moses. Here, how-

[1] Matt. v. 10—12; Acts v. 41; 1 Pet. iv. 13, 14; 2 Cor. xii. 10, 11.
[2] v. 7, Chrysostom, Theodoret, Erasmus, Calvin, Meyer, &c., make no difference between ἀγαθός, "good," and δίκαιος, "just," as though St. Paul meant "one would scarcely die for a good man, though possibly one *might*." It is, however, more probable that St. Paul meant "one would not die merely for a man of ordinary integrity, but for a *truly good* man one might even dare to die" (cf. Cic. *De Off*. iii. 15).
[3] v. 11, ἀλλὰ καὶ καυχώμενοι.
[4] Verses 1—12.

ever, as so often, the logical statement is incomplete and entangled, owing to the rush of the Apostle's thoughts.[1]

"So then, *as* by one man sin entered into the world, and by sin death, and so death extended to all men on the ground that all sinned,"[2] he probably meant to add as the second half of the parallel, "*so, too*, by one man came justification, and so life was offered to all." The conclusion of the sentence was, however, displaced by the desire to meet a difficulty. He had said, "all sinned," but some one might object, "How so ? you have already told us that where there is no law there is no transgression; how, then, could men sin between Adam and Moses ?" The answer is far from clear to understand. St. Paul might perhaps have referred to the law of nature, the transgression of which involved sin; but what he says is that "till the law, sin was in the world, but sin is not imputed when there is no law." If he had said, "sin is not brought into prominent self-consciousness," his meaning would have been both clear and consistent, but the verb used (ἐλλογεῖται) does not admit of this sense. Perhaps we may take the word popularly to imply that "it is not *so fully* reckoned or imputed," a view which may find its illustration in our Lord's remark that the sin of Sodom and Gomorrah was less unpardonable than that of Chorazin and Bethsaida.

[1] 1 Cor. xv. 45. The difference between Adam and Eve (1 Tim. ii. 14) was a smaller matter, and one which had little or no bearing on the destiny of the human being, whether male or female.

[2] Pages and almost volumes of controversy have been written on verse 12. ἐφ' ᾧ πάντες ἥμαρτον. Many make the ᾧ masc., and, referring it to Adam, render it "in whom" (Aug.), or, "by whose means" (Grot.), or, "on whose account" (Chrys.). There can, however, be no doubt that ᾧ is neuter (cf. 2 Cor. v. 4; Phil. iii. 12, iv. 10), and that it means neither "unto which (death)," as a *final cause*, nor any variation on this meaning, but "inasmuch as." Since, however, the argument of St. Paul seems simply to be that sin was universal, and that the universality of death was *a proof of this*, it certainly seems admissible to understand ἐφ' ᾧ in the universal sense of "in accordance with the fact that." It is here used in a larger and looser causal connection than usual. Sin and death are universal, and are inseparably linked together; it might be supposed that where there was no law there was no sin; it is true that sin is not *fully imputed* where there is no law; but death entered the world through sin, and so death passed upon all men, "which shows that—which involves the presupposition that—all sinned." This is Baur's view, and if it be tenable, the discussions about "original sin,' "inherent total depravity," &c., are irrelevant to this passage (Baur, *Paul* ii. 183—186). Let us, at any rate, imitate St. Paul in dwelling rather on the positive than the negative side, rather on Christ than Adam, rather on the superabundance of grace than the origin of sin.

It seems as if he meant to imply a distinction between "*sin*" in general, and the "*transgression*" of some special law or laws in particular.¹ "Every sin," as St. Thomas Aquinas says, "may be called a transgression in so far as it transgresses a natural law ; but it is a more serious thing to transgress a law both natural and written. And so, when the law was given, transgression increased and deserved greater anger." But the only proof which St. Paul offers that there *was* sin during this period is that, throughout it, death also reigned.² When, however, he passes from this somewhat obscure reply (13, 14), to show how Adam was a type of Christ, his meaning again becomes clear. He dwells first on the points of difference (15—18), and then on those of resemblance (18, 19). The differences between the results caused by Adam and Christ are differences both qualitative and quantitative—both in degree and kind.

i. By Adam's one transgression the many died, but the free grace of Christ abounded to the many in a far greater degree.³

¹ So most of the commentators. "*Sine ego potest esse quis iniquus sed non praevaricator*" (Augustine). Luther explains ἐλλογεῖται, "sin is not minded"—"*man achtet ihrer nicht.*"

² Ver. 14, "Even over those who had not sinned after the similitude of Adam's transgression"—*i.e.*, who had broken no positive direct command—whose ἁμαρτία was not a definite παράβασις. Dr. Schaff (Lange's *Romans*, p. 191, E.T.) gives a useful sketch of the theories about original sin and imputation. 1. The PANTHEISTIC and Necessitarian makes sin inherent in our finite constitution, the necessary result of matter. 2. The PELAGIAN treats Adam's sin as a mere *bad example*. 3. The PRÆ-ADAMIC explains sin by antenatal existence, metempsychosis, &c. 4. The AUGUSTINIAN—all men sinned in Adam (cf. Heb. vii. 9, 10). "*Persona corrumpit naturam, natura corrumpit personam*"—*i.e.*, Adam's sin caused a sinful nature, and sinful nature causes individual sin. This has many subdivisions according as the imputation of Adam's sin was regarded as (α) Immediate ; (β) Mediate ; or (γ) Antecedent. 5. The FEDERAL—vicarious representation of mankind in Adam, in virtue of a one-sided (μονόπλευρον) contract of God with man (*foedus operum*, or *naturae*) ; with subdivisions of (α) The Augustino-federal; (β) The purely federal or forensic. 6. The NEW ENGLAND CALVINISTS, who deny imputation and distinguish between *natural ability* and *moral inability* to keep innocence. 7. The ARMINIAN, which regards hereditary corruption not as sin or guilt, but as infirmity, a maladive condition, &c. I ask, would Paul have been willing to enter into all these questions? Have they in any way helped the cause of Christianity or deepened vital religion? Can they be of primary importance, since the traces of them in Scripture are so slight that scarcely any two theologians entirely agree about them? Do they tend to humility and charity and edification, or to " vain word-battlings " ?

³ The contrast is between *plurality* and *unity* ; the phrase "*the many*" (not "many," as in Luther and the E.V.) does not for a moment imply any exception (*e.g.*, Enoch, or Elijah). It is merely due to the fact that " all "

ADAM AND CHRIST.

ii. The condemnation of the race to death sprang from the *single* transgression of one; the sentence of acquittal was freely passed in spite of *many* transgressions.

iii. By the transgression of Adam began the reign of *death*; far more shall all who are receiving the superabundance of grace of the gift of righteousness reign in life by the One, Jesus Christ. But with these differences there is also a parallel of deeper resemblance. One transgression (Adam's sin), and one sentence of condemnation on all; one act of righteousness (Christ's death), and one justification which gives life to all;—by the disobedience of the one,[1] the many were made sinners;[2] by the obedience of the one, the many shall be made righteous.[3] Thus St. Paul states the origin of sin in this passage; but however he might have solved the antinomy of its *generic* necessity and *individual* origin, which he leaves unsolved, he would certainly have been ready to say with Pseudo-Baruch that "every one of us is the Adam to his own soul."

But here once more the question recurs, What then of the Law? Is that divine revelation to go for nothing?

may sometimes be "a few" (Aug.). "Adamus et Christus," says Bengel, "secundum rationes contrarias, conveniunt in positivo, differunt in comparativo." See Bentley, Sermon upon Popery. *Opp.* iii. 244. Observe the parallel between the κρῖμα, κατάκριμα, χάρισμα, δικαίωμα, of verse 16 and the παράπτωμα, κατάκριμα, δικαίωμα, and δικαίωσις of verse 18. The distinction between these words seems to be as follows:—1. δικαίωμα, *actio justificativa, Rechtsfertigungsthat*, the act which declares us just. 2. δικαίωσις, the process of justification. 3. δικαιοσύνη, the condition of being justified. Rothe quotes Arist., *Eth. Nic.*, v. 10, where δικαίωμα is defined as τὸ πανόρθωμα τοῦ ἀδικήματος. In verse 16, D, E, F, G, read ἁμαρτήματος.

[1] Adam, says Luther, stuck his tooth, not into an *apple*, but into a *stachel*, namely, the Divine command. Pelagius, in his commentary on Romans (preserved in Augustine's works), renders δι' ἑνὸς ἀνθρώπου, "*per unum hominem, Evam!*" Philo's views about the Fall may be seen in his *Legg. Alleg.* ii. 73—106. He regards gluttony and lust as the source of all evil, and considers that all men are born in sin, *i.e.*, under the dominion of sensuality (*De Mundi Opif.* 37; *Vit. Mos.* iii. 675). "God made not death, but ungodly men with their works called it to them" (Wisd. i. 13—16).

[2] *In what way* they were made sinners St. Paul nowhere defines. There is no distinctive Pelagianism, or Traducianism, here. To say with Meyer, "men were placed in the category of sinners because they sinned in and with Adam's fall," is, as Lange remarks, not exegesis, but Augustinian dogmatics. St. Paul simply accepted the universal fact of death as a proof of the universal fact of sin, and regards death and sin as beginning with Adam. Beza, Bengel, Reuss, &c., understand κατεστάθησαν and κατασταθήσονται in an imputative sense—"*regarded* as sinners"—which is a defensible translation, and makes the parallel more complete.   [3] Vs. 12—20.

To that question St. Paul has already given one answer in the Epistle to the Galatians; he now gives another, which, till explained, might well have caused a shock. To the Galatians he had explained that the ante-Messianic period was the *tirocinium* of the world, and that during this period the Law was necessary as a pædagogic discipline. To the Romans he presents a new point of view, and shows that the Law was not merely a corrective system thrust in between the promise and its fulfilment, but an essential factor in the religious development of the world. It appears in the new aspect of a "power of sin," in order that by creating the knowledge of sin it may mediate between sin and grace. The Law, he says, came in (the word he uses has an almost disparaging sound,[1] which probably, however, he did not intend) "that transgression might multiply." A terrible purpose indeed, and one which he subsequently explained (chap. vii.); but even here he at once hastens to add that where sin multiplied, grace superabounded, that as sin reigned in death, so also grace might reign through righteousness into life eternal, by Jesus Christ our Lord.[2]

---

[1] v. 20, παρεισῆλθεν, Vulg. *Subintravit*, "supervened," "came in besides," cf. προσετέθη, Gal. iii. 19. In Gal. ii. 4 the surreptitious notion of πάρα is derived from the context. The notion of "between," "*medio tempore* subingressa est," is not in the word itself.

[2] v. 20, 21. The old Protestant divines thus stated the uses of the Law:— 1. *Usus primus*, civil or political—to govern states. 2. *Usus secundus*, convictive or pædagogic—to convince us of sin. 3. *Usus tertius*, didactic or formative—to guide the life of a believer (*Formula Concordiae*, p. 594). Dr. Schaff, in his useful additions to the translation of Lange's *Romans*, points out that these three correspond to the German sentence that the Law is a *Zügel* (1, a restraint); a *Spiegel* (2, a mirror); and a *Riegel* (3, a rod). The Law multiplies transgressions because—i. "Nitimur in vetitum semper, cupimus que negata." "Ignoti nulla cupido." ii. "Because desires suppressed forcibly from without increase in virulence" (St. Thomas). iii. "Because suppressive rules kindle anger against God" (Luther). But the real end of the Law was not the multiplication of transgressions *per se*, but that the precipitation of sin might lead to its expulsion; that the culmination of sin

The next chapter (vi.) is of vast importance as stating an objection which might well be regarded as deadly, and as showing us how best to deal with an apparent paradox. If grace superabounds over sin, why should we not continue in sin? After first throwing from him the hateful inference with a "Perish the thought!" he proceeds in this chapter to prove, first in a mystic (vi. 1—15), and then in a more popular exposition (15—23), the moral consequences of his doctrine. In the first half of this chapter he uses the metaphor of death, in the latter the metaphor of *emancipation*, to illustrate the utter severance between the Christian and sin.

Ideally, theoretically, it should be needless to tell the Christian not to sin; he is *dead* to sin; the very name of "elect" or "saint" excludes the entire conception of sin, because the Christian is "IN CHRIST." Those two words express the very quintessence of all that is most distinctive in St. Paul's theology, and yet they are identical with the leading conception of St. John, who (we are asked to believe) rails at him in the Apocalypse as Balaam and Jezebel, a sham Jew, and a false apostle! That the two words "in Christ" sum up the distinctive secret, the revealed mystery of the Christian life, especially as taught by St. Paul and by St. John, will be obvious to any thoughtful reader. If this mystic union, to which both Apostles again and again recur, is expressed by St. Paul in the metaphors of stones in a temple of which Christ is the foundation,[1] of members of a body of which Christ is the head,[2] St. John records, and St. Paul alludes to, the metaphor of the branches and the vine,[3] and both Apostles without any image again and again declare that the Christian life is a spiritual life, a supernatural life, and one which we can only live by faith in, by union with, by partaking of the life of the Son of God.[4] With both Apostles Christ is our life,

---

might be the introduction of grace. "Non crudeliter hoc fecit Deus sed ratione medicinae—augebatur morbus, crescit malitia, quaeritur medicus, et totum sanatur" (Aug. in Ps. cii.).

[1] Eph. ii. 19—22 (1 Pet. ii. 5; Isa. xxviii. 16).
[2] Rom. xii. 5; Eph. iv. 16; 1 Cor. xii. 12, 13, 27; Col. i. 18.
[3] John xv. 5; Rom. vi. 5; Phil. i. 11.
[4] 2 Cor. v. 17; Rom. vi. 8; Gal. ii. 20; Eph. iii. 6; Col. iii. 3; John x. 28; xiv. 19; xv. 4—10; 1 John v. 20; ii. 24, &c.

and apart from Him we have no true life.[1] St. Paul, again, is fond of the metaphor of wearing Christ as a garment, putting on Christ, putting on the new man,[2] reflecting Him with ever-brightening splendour.[3] In fact, the words "in Christ" and "with Christ" are his most constantly recurrent phrases. We work for Him, we live in Him, we die in Him, we rise with Him, we are justified by Him. We are His sheep, His scholars, His soldiers, His servants.

The life of the Christian being hid with Christ in God, his death with Christ is a death to sin, his resurrection with Christ is a resurrection to life. The dipping under the waters of baptism is his union with Christ's death; his rising out of the waters of baptism is a resurrection with Christ, and the birth to a new life. "What baptism is for the individual," it has been said "Christ's death is for the race." If the Christian has become *coalescent* with Christ in His death, he shall also in His resurrection.[4] The old sin-enslaved humanity is crucified with Christ, and the new man has been justified from sin, because he is dead to it, and lives in Christ. This is the ideal. Live up to it. Dethrone the sin that would rule over your frail nature. "Be not ever presenting your members as weapons of unrighteousness, but present yourselves once for all[5] to God as alive from the dead, and your members as instruments of righteousness to God. For sin shall not lord it over you; for ye are not under the Law, but under grace."[6] Die to sin, die to lust, die to your old vulgar, enslaved, corrupted self, die to the impulses of animal passion, and the self-assertion of worldly desire; for Christ too died, and you are one with Him in death, that you may be one in life. But these words, again, raise the ghost of the old objection. "Shall we then *sin*, since we are not under the Law, but under grace?" and this objection St. Paul again refutes by the same argument, clothed in a more obvious and less mystic illustration, in which he amplifies the proverb of Jesus, "Ye cannot serve two masters." A man must either be a slave of sin unto death, or of obedience unto righteousness.[7]

---

[1] John iii. 27; v. 24; xi. 25; xiv. 20; Gal. ii. 20; Col. iii. 4; 1 John i. 1; v. 12, &c.

[2] Gal. iii. 27; Rom. xiii. 14; Eph. iv. 24; Col. iii. 10.

[3] 2 Cor. iii. 18.

[4] vi. 5, σύμφυτοι. The Vulg. "*complantati*" is too strong. It is from φύω, not φυτεύω.

[5] vi. 13, παριστάνετε . . . παραστήσατε. In the New Testament ὅπλα is always "weapons." Cf. Rom. xiii. 12; 2 Cor. vi. 7.

[6] vi. 1—15.

vi. 16. The phrase "a slave of obedience" is strange. Perhaps he used ὑπακοῆς, instead of δικαιοσύνης, because of the two senses of the word, "righteousness" and "justification."

Thank God from that old past slavery of sin you were freed, when you submitted to the form of doctrine to which you were handed over by God's providence; and then—if in condescension to your human weakness I may use an imperfect expression—you were enslaved to righteousness.[1] The fruit of that former slavery was shame and misery; its end was death. This new enslavement to God is perfect freedom; its fruit is sanctification, its end eternal life. "For the wages of sin is death; but the free gift of God is eternal life in Christ Jesus our Lord."[2]

iv. At this point of his argument the Apostle felt it imperative to define more clearly, and establish more decisively, his view as to the position of the Law in the scheme of salvation. Apart from his discussion of this question in the Epistle to the Galatians, he has already, in this Epistle, made three incidental remarks on the subject, which might well horrify those Jews and Jewish Christians who were unfamiliar with his views. He has said—

1. That "by the works of the Law shall no flesh be justified before God: for by the Law is the full knowledge of sin" (iii. 20).

2. That "the Law came in as an addition that transgression might abound" (v 20).

3. That the Christian "is not under the Law, but under grace," and that *therefore* sin is not to lord it over him (vi. 14).

Such statements as these, if left unsupported and unexplained, might well turn every Jewish reader from respectful inquiry into incredulous disgust; and he therefore proceeds to the difficult task of justifying his views.

The task was difficult because he has to prove scripturally and dialectically the truths at which he had

---

[1] vi. 18, Ἐδουλώθητε. "Deo servire vera libertas est" (Aug.). "Whose service is perfect freedom." Ἀνθρώπινον λέγω—Calvin, following Origen and Chrysostom, renders this clause, "I require nothing which your fleshly weakness could not do."

[2] vi. 15—23.

arrived by a wholly different method. The central point of his own conviction was that which runs through the Epistle to the Galatians,[1] that if salvation was to be earned by "*doing*"—if the Law was sufficient for justification—then Christ's death was needless and vain. If he were right in his absolute conviction that only by faith in the blood of Christ are we accounted righteous before God, then clearly the Law stood condemned of incapacity to produce this result. Now by the Law St. Paul meant the *whole* Mosaic Law, and there is not in him a single trace of any distinction between the degree of sacredness in the ceremonial and the moral portion of it. If there had been, he might perhaps have adopted the luminous principle of the author of the Epistle to the Hebrews, and shown that the Law was only abrogated by the completeness of its fulfilment; that its inefficiency only proves its typical character; and that the type disappeared in the fulness of the antitype, as a star is lost in the brightness of the sun. This method of allegory was by no means unfamiliar to St. Paul; he not only adopts it freely,[2] but must have learnt it as no small element of his Rabbinic training in the school of Gamaliel. But, on the one hand, this attribution of a spiritual depth and mystery to every part of the ceremonial Law would have only tended to its glorification in the minds of Judaisers who had not yet learnt its abrogation; and on the other hand, it was not in this way that the relation of the Law to the Gospel had specially presented itself to the mind of Paul. The typical relation of the one to the other was real, and to dwell upon it would, no doubt, have made St. Paul's arguments "less abrupt and less oppressive to the con-

---

[1] Gal. ii. 21; iii. 21.

[2] The muzzled ox, 1 Cor. ix. 9; Sarah and Hagar, Gal. iv. 24; the evanescence of the light on the face of Moses, 2 Cor. iii. 7—13; the following rock, 1 Cor. x. 4; the cloud and sea, 1 Cor. x. 1, 2.

sciousness of the Jews;"[1] but it would also have made
them less effective for the emancipation of the Church
and the world. The Law must be deposed, as it were,
from its long primacy in the minds of the Jews, into
that negative, supplementary, secondary, inefficient position which alone belonged to it, before it could with any
prudence be reinstalled into a position of reflected honour.
It had only a subordinate, provisional importance; it was
only introduced *per accidens*. Its object was pædagogic,
not final. St. Paul's reasoning might inflict pain, but
the pain which he inflicted was necessary and healing;
and it was well for the Jews and for the world that,
while he strove to make his arguments acceptable by
stating them in a tone as conciliatory as possible, he did
not strive to break the shock of them by any unfaithful
weakening of their intrinsic force.

i. His first statement had been that the Law could
not justify.[2] That it could not justify he saw at once,
because had it been adequate to do so, then the death of
Christ would have been superfluous. But *why* was it that
the Law was thus inefficacious? St. Paul rather indicates
than clearly states the reason in the next chapter (viii.).
It is because the Law, as regards its form, is external;
it is a command from without; it is a letter which denounces sentence of death on its violators;[3] it has no
sympathy wherewith to touch the heart; it has no power
whereby to sway the will. "Spiritual" in one sense it
is, because it is "holy, just, and good;" but it is in no
sense a "quickening spirit," and therefore can impart
no life. And why? Simply because it is met, opposed,
defeated by a strong counter-principle of man's being—the

---

[1] Pfleiderer, *Paulinismus*, i. 73, E. T.
[2] Rom. iii. 20.
[3] 2 Cor. iii. 6.

dominion of sin in the flesh. It was "weak through the flesh"—that is, through the sensuous principle which dominates the whole man in body and soul.[1] In the human *spirit*, Paul perceived a moral spontaneity to good; in the *flesh*, a moral spontaneity to evil; and from these different elements results "the dualism of antagonistic moral principles."[2] Man's natural self-will resists the Divine determination; the subjective will is too strong for the objective command. Even if man could obey a part of the Law he could not be justified, because the Law laid a curse on him who did not meet *all* its requirements, which the moral consciousness knew that it could not do.[3]

ii. But St. Paul's second proposition—that the Law multiplied transgressions[4]—sounded almost terribly offensive. "The Law," he had already said in the Galatians, was added until the coming of the promised seed, *"for the sake of transgressions."*[5] To interpret this as meaning ": a *safeguard* against transgressions"—though from another point of view, and in another order of relations, this might be true[6]—is in this place an absurdity, because St. Paul is proving the inability of the Law to perform this function at all effectually. It would, moreover, entirely contradict what he says—namely, that the object

---

[1] The σάρξ is not only the material body, but an active inherent principle, which influences not only the ψυχὴ or natural life, but even the νοῦς or *human* spirit (Baur, *Paul.* ii. 140).

[2] Gal. v. 17; Pfleiderer, i. 54. To this writer I am much indebted, as well as to Baur and Reuss, among many others, for my views of Pauline theology. I must content myself with this large general acknowledgment, because they write from a standpoint widely different from my own, and because I find in the pages of all three writers very much with which I entirely disagree.

[3] Gal. iii. 10; James ii. 10.   [4] Rom. v. 20.

[5] Gal. iii. 19, χάριν παραβάσεων προσετέθη.

[6] *The usus primus* or *politicus* of the Law—*v. supra*, p. 218. It is a safeguard against acts which, when the law is uttered, become transgressions.

of the Law was the *multiplication* of transgressions. Apart from the Law, there may indeed be "sin" (ἁμαρτία), although, not being brought into the light of self-consciousness, man is not aware of it (Rom. v. 13; vii. 7); but he has already told us that there is not "transgression" (iv. 15), and there is not "imputation" (v. 13), and man lives in a state of relative innocence, little pained by the existence of objective evil.[1] It was, therefore, St. Paul's painful and difficult task to sever the Law finally from all *direct* connexion with salvation, by showing that, theologically considered—and this was the point which to the Jew would sound so paradoxical and so wounding—God had expressly designed it, not for the prevention of sin, and the effecting of righteousness, but for the *increase of sin*, and the *working of wrath*.[2] It *multiplied sin*, because, by a psychological fact, which we cannot explain, but which St. Paul here exhibits with marvellous insight into human nature, the very existence of a commandment acts as an incitement to its violation ("Permissum fit vile nefas"); and it *worked wrath* by forcing all sin into prominent self-consciousness,[3] and thus making it the source of acute misery; by bringing home to the conscience that

---

[1] To be "naked and not ashamed" is, in the first instance, the prerogative of innocence; but it becomes ultimately the culmination of guilt.

[2] Pfleiderer, i. 81. "Whoever separates himself from the words of the Law is consumed by fire" (*Babha Bathra*, f. 79, 1).

[3] "The strength of sin is the Law" (1 Cor. xv. 56), because it is what it is essentially through man's consciousness of it. It strengthens the perception of sin, and weakens the consciousness of any power in the will to resist it.

> "And therefore Law was given them to *evince*
> *Their natural pravity*, by stirring up
> Sin against Law to fight; that when they see
> Law can discover sin, but not remove,
> Save by those shadowy expiations weak,
> The blood of bulls and goats, they may conclude
> Some blood more precious must be paid for man."
>   Milton, *P. L.* xii. 286.

The last three lines express the argument in the Epistle to the Hebrews.

sense of guilt which is the feeling of disharmony with God; by darkening life with the shadows of dread and self-contempt; by creating the sense of moral death, and by giving to physical death its deadliest sting.[1]

iii. The third proposition—that "we are not under the Law, but under grace"[2]—has been already sufficiently illustrated; and it must be borne in mind that the object of St. Paul throughout has been to show that the true theological position of the Law—its true position, that is, in the Divine œconomy of salvation—is to come in between sin and grace, to be an impulse in the process of salvation. He has already shown this, historically and exegetically, in the fifth chapter, as also in Gal. iii., by insisting on the fact that the Law, as a supplementary ordinance,[3] cannot disannul a free promise which was prior to it by 430 years, and which had been sanctioned by an oath. The Law, then, shows (1) the impossibility of any *other* way of obtaining the fulfilment of the promise, except that of free favour; and (2) the impossibility of regarding this promise as a *debt* (ὀφείλημα) when it was a free gift. In this point of view the Law fulfils the function of driving man to seek that justification which is possible by faith alone. *Objectively* and historically, therefore, the history of man may be regarded in four phases—Sin, Promise, Law, Grace—Adam, Abraham, Moses, Christ; *subjectively* and individually, also in four phases—relative innocence, awakened consciousness, imputable transgression, free justification. The one is the Divine, the other is the human side of one and the same process; and both find their illustration, though each independently of the other, in the theology of St. Paul.[4]

And if it be asserted, by way of modern objection to

[1] Rom. iv. 15; vii. 10—13.　[2] Gal. iii.
[3] Rom. vi. 14.　[4] Rom. v., vii., xi.; Gal. iii., iv.

this theology, and to St. Paul's methods of argument and exegesis, that they suggest multitudes of difficulties; that they pour new wine into old wine-skins, which burst under its fermentation; that they involve a mysticising idealisation of 1,500 years of history and of the plain literal intention of large portions of the Old and New Testament Scriptures; that Moses would have been as horrified to be told by St. Paul that the object of his Law was only to multiply transgression, and intensify the felt heinousness of sin, as he is said to have been when in vision he saw Rabbi Akhibha imputing to him a thousand rules which he had never sanctioned; that the Law was obviously given with the intention that it should be obeyed, not with the intention that it should be broken; that St. Paul himself has spoken in this very Epistle of "doers of the Law being justified," and of "works of the Law," and of "working good," and of a recompense for it,[1] and of "reaping what we have sown;"[2] that he has in every one of his Epistles urged the necessity of moral duties, not as an *inevitable result* of that union with Christ which is the Christian's life, but as things after which Christians should *strive*, and for the fulfilment of which they should train themselves with severe effort;[3] and that in his Pastoral Epistles these moral considerations, as in the Epistles of St. Peter and St. James, seem to have come into the foreground,[4] while the high theological verities seem to have melted farther into the distance—if these objections be urged, as they often have been urged, the answers to them are likewise manifold. We have not the smallest temptation to ignore the diffi-

[1] Rom. ii. 6—13; iv. 4.
[2] Gal. vi. 7; 2 Thess. iii. 13; 1 Cor. xv. 58.
[3] 1 Cor. ix. 25—27; Phil. iii. 14.
[4] Mic. vi. 12; 1 Tim. iv. 7, 8; ii. 3; Tit. iii. 8; ii. 14; 2 Pet. i. 10, 11 James ii. 17, 24.

culties, though it would be easy by separate examination to show that to state them thus is to shift their true perspective. As regards St. Paul's style of argument, those who see in it a falsification of Scripture, a treacherous dealing with the Word of God, which St. Paul expressly repudiates,[1] should consider whether they too may not be intellectually darkened by suspicious narrowness and ignorant prepossessions.[2] St. Paul regarded the Scripture as the irrefragable Word of God, and yet, even when he seems to be attaching to mere words and sounds a "talismanic value," he never allows the letter of Scripture to becloud the illumination ($\phi\omega\tau\iota\sigma\mu\grave{o}\varsigma$) of spiritual enlightenment.[3] Even when he seemed to have the whole Pentateuch against him, he never suffered the outward expression to enthral the emancipated idea. He knew well that one word of God cannot contradict another, and his allegorising and spiritualising methods—(which, in one form or other, are absolutely essential, since the Law speaks in the tongue of the sons of men, and human language is at the best but an asymptote to thought)—are not made the vehicle of mechanical inference or individual caprice, but are used in support of formative truths, of fruitful ideas, of spiritual convictions, of direct revelations, which are as the Eternal Temple, built within the temporary scaffolding of abrogated dispensations. In this way of dealing with Scripture he was indeed regarded as a blasphemer by a Pharisaism which was at once unenlightened and unloving; but he was a direct successor of the Prophets, who dealt in a spirit of sacred independence with earlier revelations,[4] and with their

---

[1] 2 Cor. ii. 17, οὐ καπηλεύοντες; 2 Cor. iv. 2, μηδὲ δολοῦντες.
[2] 2 Cor. iv. 1—7.
[3] 2 Cor. iv. 4.
[4] Jer. xxxi. 29. Ezek. xviii. 2; xx. 25, "Wherefore I gave them also statutes that were not good, and judgments whereby they should not live."

mantle he had caught a double portion of their spirit. He felt that the truths his opponents characterised as "temerities" and "blasphemies" were as holy as the Trisagion of the Seraphim; that his "apostasy from Moses"[1] was due to a reverence for him far deeper than that of his upholders, and that there was an immemorial, nay, even an eternal validity, in the most extreme of his asserted innovations.

And as for apparent contradictions, St. Paul, like all great thinkers, was very careless of them. It is even doubtful whether they were distinctly present to his mind. He knew that the predestinations of the Infinite cannot be thrust away—as though they were ponderable dust inurned in the Columbaria—in the systems of the finite. He knew that in Divine as well as in human truths there are certain *antinomies*, irreconcilable by the mere understanding, and yet perfectly capable of being fused into unity by the divinely enlightened reason, or, as he would have phrased it, by the spirit of man which has been mystically united with the Spirit of Christ. As a scheme, as a system, as a theory of salvation—abstractly considered, ideally treated—he knew that his line of argument was true, and that his exposition of the Divine purpose was irrefragable, because he knew that he had received it neither from man, nor by any man,[2] but by the will of God. But there is a difference between the ideal and the actual—between the same truths regarded in their theological bearing as parts of one vast philosophy of the plan of

---

Hos. vi. 6, "I desired mercy and not sacrifice; and the knowledge of God more than burnt offering." Jer. vii. 22, 23, "I spake not unto your fathers concerning burnt offerings or sacrifices, but this thing commanded I them, saying, Obey my voice."

[1] Acts xxi. 21, "They have been indoctrinated with the view that you teach apostasy from Moses."

[2] Gal. i. 1, οὐκ ἀπ' ἀνθρώπων, οὐδὲ δι' ἀνθρώπου.

salvation, and stated in everyday language in their immediate bearing upon the common facts of life. In the language of strict and accurate theology, to talk of the "merit" of works, and the "reward" of works, or even the possibility of "good" works, was erroneous; but yet—without any of such Protestant after-thoughts as that these works are the fruits of unconscious faith, or that without this faith they cannot in any sense be good, and without dreaming of any collision with what he says elsewhere, and untroubled by any attempt to reconcile his statements with the doctrine of original sin—he could and did talk quite freely about "Gentiles doing *by nature* the things of the Law," and says that "the doer of the Law shall be justified," and that God will render to every man *according to his works*.[1] St. Paul would probably have treated with contempt, as a mere carping criticism, which allowed no room for common sense in dealing with the truths of revelation, any attempt to show that in such passages—both on this and on other subjects—he appears to contradict himself.[2] He would very briefly, and with profound indifference, have contented himself with saying that his remarks in these passages are not *in pari materiâ*.[3] He is not there speaking or thinking at all of the doctrine of redemption. He is there talking about "the justification of the Law," which is a very different thing from "the justification by faith." He is there using general language, altogether irrespective of the

[1] Rom. ii. 13, 14; xiv. 10. See, too, 2 Cor. v. 10; Gal. vi. 7; Eph. vi. 8; Col. iii. 24, 25.

[2] For these antinomies, which exist in theology as they exist in nature, and are complementary truths of which the harmony is to be found in the Infinite, see Excursus II.

[3] "Haec descriptio justitiae legis, quae nihil impedit alia dicta de justitia fidei" (Melancthon in Rom. ii. 13). He is here "laying down those general principles of justice, according to which, irrespective of the Gospel, all men are to be judged" (Hodge on Rom. ii. 6).

Gospel. Protestant commentators with all their elaborate and varying theories—that in these works faith is included as the highest work;[1] that they are perfected in faith;[2] that "works will be adduced in the day of judgment, not as meriting salvation, but as proofs and results of faith;"[3] that "the imperfect works of the sanctified will be rewarded, not on the ground of the Law, but on the ground of grace;"[4] that he was mentally referring to a "prevenient grace" over the Gentile world, and so on—are doubtless dogmatically right, but they are far more anxious to save St. Paul's orthodoxy and consistency than he would have been himself. It is at least doubtful whether such considerations were consciously present to his mind. He would have held it enough to reply that, in these passages, he was only applying the current language of morality to the concrete relations of actual life;[5] and that "the doctrine of justification cannot conflict with the doctrine of God's righteousness by virtue of which He will reward every man according to his works."[6] When St. Paul was using the language of accurate theology, he would have shown the nullity of righteousness by works. But, in any case, he would have thought far more highly of the possibility of such righteousness than of the righteousness of dogmatic orthodoxy, or the righteousness of the letter; the righteousness of the jealous heresy-hunter, or the righteousness of the religious partisan.[7]

Lastly, it will be seen how little St. Paul is troubled by the apparent paradoxes which result from the doctrines which he enforces. By those who manipulated truth to

[1] Limborch.   [2] Luthardt.   [3] Gerhard.   [4] Stuart.
[5] Baur, *N. Test. Theol.* 181; Pfleiderer, i. 78.
[6] Lange on Rom. ii. 6—10.
[7] Lehrgerechtigkeit; Buchstabende Echtigkeit, Negationsgerechtigkeit, Parteigerechtigkeit (Lange, *ubi supra*).

suit their own parties and purposes; by those who hucksisted the Word of Life; by those who pushed truths into extravagant inferences, and then condemned them on the ground of their possible misapplication—his doctrines were denounced as "dangerous;" and we know as a fact that, even in his own lifetime, what he taught was made a handle for evil doctrine,[1] and was subjected to perilous perversions.[2] When such arguments as these were urged against him, St. Paul treated them with entire disdain. Truth may be wrested, truth may be distorted, truth may be made an instrument of self-destruction—but truth is truth, and can take care of itself, and needs no "lying for God" to serve as its buttress.[3] The doctrine of free grace might be, and was, quoted in the cause of antinomianism, and degraded into a justification of sensuality. The predominance of grace over sin was twisted into a reason for doing evil that good might come. The hope of future forgiveness was pleaded as a ground for continuing in sin. Well, let it be so. The ocean of truth did not cease to be an ocean because here and there a muddy river of error flowed stealthily in its tides. In answer to the moral perversity which abused truth into an occasion of wickedness, St. Paul thought it sufficient to appeal to the right feeling of mankind. If a man chooses to pervert a Divine and gracious doctrine into a "dangerous downfall," he does so at his own peril. Evil inferences St. Paul merely repudiates with a "God forbid!"[4]—of malignant misinterpreters he thought it enough to say that "their condemnation was just!"[5]

[1] Rom. iii. 8.
[2] 2 Pet. iii. 16, στρεβλοῦσιν . . . πρὸς τὴν ἰδίαν αὐτῶν ἀπώλειαν.
[3] Job xiii. 7, 8.
[4] Rom. iii. 4, 6, 31; vi. 2, 15; vii. 7, &c.; Gal. ii. 17; iii. 21; vi. 14; 1 Cor. vi. 15.
[5] Rom. iii. 8.

DEAD TO THE LAW.

After these preliminary considerations we are in a position to proceed uninterruptedly with our sketch of the Epistle, since we are now in possession of its main conceptions. Proceeding then to a further expansion of his views respecting the Law, and speaking (chap. vii.) to those who know it, the Apostle further enforces the metaphor that the Christian is dead to his past moral condition, and has arisen to a new one. A woman whose husband is dead is free to marry again; we are dead to the Law, and are therefore free to be united to Christ. Obviously the mere passing illustration must not be pressed, because if used as *more* than an illustration it is doubly incomplete— incomplete because the word "dead" is here used in two quite different senses; and because, to make the analogy at all perfect, the Law ought to have died to us, and not we to the Law. But St. Paul merely makes a cursory use of the illustration to indicate that the new life of the Christian involves totally new relationships;[1] that death naturally ends all legal obligations; and that our connexion with the risen Christ is so close that it may be compared to a conjugal union. Hence our whole past condition, alike in its character and its results, is changed, and a new Law has risen from the dead with our new life—a Law which we must serve in the newness of the spirit, not in the oldness of the letter. He who is dead to sin is dead to the Law, because the Law can only reign so long as sin reigns, and because Christ in His crucified body has destroyed the body of sin.[2]

But St. Paul is conscious that in more than one pas-

---

[1] 2 Cor. xi. 2; Eph. v. 25.

[2] vii. 1—6. The very harshness of the construction ἀποθανόντες ἐν ᾧ ("by dying to that in which we were held fast") seems to make it more probable than the τοῦ θανάτου of D, E, F, G. The E.V. renders ἀποθανόντος, the unsupported conjecture of Beza, or Erasmus.

sage he has placed the Law and Sin in a juxtaposition which would well cause the very deepest offence. To show his meaning he enters on a psychological study, of which the extreme value has always been recognised entirely apart from its place in the scheme of theology. Here he writes as it were with his very heart's blood; he dips his pen in his inmost experience. He is not here dealing with the ideal or with the abstract, but with the sternest facts of actual daily life. There have been endless discussions as to whether he is speaking of himself or of others; whether he has in view the regenerate or the unregenerate man. Let even good men look into their own hearts and answer. Ideally, the Christian is absolutely one with Christ, and dead to sin; in reality, as again and again St. Paul implies even of himself, his life is a warfare in which there is no discharge. There is an Adam and a Christ in each of us. "The angel has us by the hand, and the serpent by the heart." The old Adam is too strong for young Melancthon.[1] Here, then, he explains, from a knowledge of his own heart, confirmed by the knowledge of *every* heart, that the Law, though not the *cause* of sin, is yet the *occasion* of it; and that there are in every human being *two* laws—that is, two opposing tendencies—which sway him from time to time, and in greater or less degree in opposite directions. And in this way he wrote an epitome of the soul's progress. When we have once realised that the "I" of the passage is used in different senses—sometimes of the flesh, the lower nature, in the contemplation of which St. Paul could speak of himself as the chief of sinners; sometimes of the

[1] " Our little lives are kept in equipoise
By struggles of two opposite desires:
The struggle of the instinct that enjoys,
And the more noble instinct that aspires."

higher nature, which can rise to those full heights of spiritual life which he has been recently contemplating; sometimes generically of himself as a member of the human race—it is then easy to follow his history of the soul.

The Law is not sin—Heaven forbid!—but it provokes disobedience,[1] and it creates the *consciousness* of sin. Without it there is sin indeed, but it is dead; in other words, it is latent and unrecognised. That is the age of fancied innocence, of animal irreflective life, of a nakedness which is not ashamed. But it is a condition of "immoral tranquillity" which cannot be permanent; of misplaced confidence which causes many an aberration from duty. When the blind tendency of wrong becomes conscious of itself by collision with a direct command, then sin acquires fresh life at the expense of that misery and shame which is spiritual death.[2] Thus sin, like Satan, disguises itself under the form of an angel of light, and seizes the opportunity furnished by the command which in itself is holy, just, and good,[3] to utterly deceive and to slay me.[4]

"What?" one may ask, "did that which is *good* become *death* to me?" Nay, but sin *by means of* that which was good effected my death, because by means of the commandment sin's exceeding sinfulness was dragged into recognition. How came this? It came out of the struggle of the higher and the lower elements of our being; out of the contest between my fleshen and servile nature[5] and the Law's spirituality of origin,—the result of which is that I am two men in one, and live two lives in one, not doing what I desire, and doing what I detest. In me—that is, in my flesh—dwelleth no good thing; but I am not my flesh. I

---

[1] Of this thought there are many interesting classical parallels. Liv. xxxiv. 4: "Parricidae cum lege coeperunt, et illis facinus poena monstravit." Sen. *De Clem.* i. 23 : "Gens humana ruit per vetitum et nefas." Hor. i. 3: "Quod licet ingratum est, quod non licet acrius urit." Ov. *Amor.* ii. 19, &c.: "The Law produces reflection on the forbidden object, curiosity, doubt, distrust, imagination, lust, susceptibility of the seed of temptation and of seduction, and finally rebellion—the παράβασις" (Lange).

[2] "Mors peccati vita est hominis; vita peccati mors hominis" (Calvin). "By the *jetser ha-râ*" (the evil impulse), says Rabbi Simeon Ben Lakish, "is meant the angel of death" (Tholuck).

[3] Holy in its origin, just in its requirements, good in its purpose.

[4] vii. 7—12.

[5] vii. 14. σαρκινὸς, "fleshen," *carneus*; σαρκικὸς, "fleshly," *carnalis*. The former is here the true reading, and involves (of course) less subjection to the flesh than the latter.

identify my own individuality with that higher nature which *wills* what is noble, but is too often defeated by the indwelling impulses of sin.[1] My true self, my inward man,[2] delights in the law of God; but my spirit, my intellect and my reason are in constant warfare with another law— a sensual impulse of my fleshy nature—which often reduces me into the bondage of its prison-house. Wretched duality of condition which makes my life a constant inconsistency! Wretched enchainment of a healthy, living organism to a decaying corpse! Who shall rescue me from these struggles of a disintegrated individuality?

"Thanks to God through Jesus Christ our Lord!" It is a sign of the intensity of feeling with which he is writing that he characteristically omits to mention the very thing for which he thanks God. But the words "through Jesus Christ our Lord" sufficiently show that his gratitude is kindled by the conviction that the deliverance is possible —that the deliverance has been achieved.[3] I, my very self—the human being within me[4]—serve with my mind the law of God. Through my weakness, my inconsistency, my imperfect faith, my imperfect union with Christ, I still serve with my flesh the law of sin;[5]

---

[1] The most commonly-quoted of the classic parallels is Ovid's "Video meliora proboque, Deteriora sequor" (*Met.* vii. 19). The nearest is ὁ μὲν θέλει (ὁ ἁμαρτάνων) οὐ ποιεῖ καὶ ὁ μὴ θέλει ποιεῖ. Δύο γὰρ σαφῶς ἔχω ψυχάς (Xen. *Cyr.* vi. 1). Chrysostom calls ver. 21 ἀσαφὲς εἰρημένον, but the obscurity is only caused by the trajection of ὅτι, which involves the repetition of ἐμοί. It means "I find, then, the law that evil is close at hand to me when my will is to do good."

[2] Cf. 1 Pet. iii. 4. ὁ κρυπτὸς τῆς καρδίας ἄνθρωπος. German writers speak of the "pseudo-plasmatic man" with his νοῦς τῆς σαρκός, φρόνημα τῆς σαρκός, σῶμα τῆς ἁμαρτίας, νόμος ἐν τοῖς μέλεσι, σάρξ, &c. Schuh. *Pathologie und Therapie des Pseudo-plasmen*, 18. "This double personality is a dethronement of the ἐγώ in favour of the ἁμαρτία."

[3] Instead of "I thank God" (εὐχαριστῶ), the easier, and therefore less probable reading, of D, E, F, G is ἡ χάρις τοῦ Θεοῦ, or Κυρίου. More probable is the χάρις τῷ Θεῷ of B and the Sahidic.

[4] vii. 25, αὐτὸς ἐγώ. I believe this to be the true meaning, though many reject it. St. Paul is speaking in his own person, not by μετασχηματισμός (see 1 Cor. iv. 6). An "infection of nature" remains even in the regenerate (Art. ix.).

[5] There is a determining power in the "flesh" which Paul calls "a law in the members," and which by its predominance becomes "a law of sin." This is opposed by the rational principle, the νοῦς or human πνεῦμα—the ἔσω ἄνθρωπος— the higher spiritual consciousness, which can however never, by itself, invade and conquer the flesh. Its power is rather potential than actual. Reason is the *better* principle in man, but the flesh is the stronger. It is not the Divine πνεῦμα. Nothing but union with Christ can secure to the νοῦς the victory over the σάρξ (Baur, *Paul.* ii. 146).

but that servitude is largely weakened, is practically broken. There is no condemnation for those who by personal union with Christ[1] live in accordance with the Spirit. Sin is slavery and death; the Spirit is freedom and life. The Law was rendered impotent by the flesh, but God, by sending His own Son in the form of sinful flesh[2] and as a sin-offering,[3] condemned to death[4] the victorious power of sin in the flesh, and so enabled us, by a spiritual life, to meet the otherwise impossible requirements of the Law. Our life is no longer under the dominion of the flesh, which obeys the law of sin, but of the spirit.[5] The death of Christ has, so to speak, shifted the centre of gravity of our will. If Christ be in us, the body indeed is still liable to death because of sin, but the spirit,—our own spiritual life—(he does not say merely '*contains* the elements of life,' but in his forcible manner)—*is* life, because of the righteousness implanted by the sanctifying Spirit of God. If that Spirit which raised Jesus from the dead dwell in us, He who raised Christ from the dead will also quicken us to full life, partially but progressively here, but triumphantly and finally beyond the grave.[6] And even here, in a measure, we attain to the "life of the spirit." Never, indeed, can we fulfil the *whole* Law (Gal. iii. 10); but for the quantitative is substituted a qualitative fulfilment, and the "totality of the disposition contains in itself the totality of the Law." In that stage life becomes life indeed. The "law of the spirit" is the "*law of the spirit of life in Christ Jesus.*"

This, then, shows us the true law, and the final issue of our lives. If we are led by the Spirit of God we are the sons of God, and the spirit of fear becomes the spirit of sonship, and the cry of slavery the cry of confident appeal to a Father in heaven. Thus we become joint-heirs with Christ; and, therefore, to share His glory we must share His sufferings. The full glory of that sonship is to be ours beyond the grave, and in comparison with it the sufferings of this life are nothing. The life of

---

[1] viii. 1. "Christus in homine, ubi fides in corde" (Aug.). The true reading is "There is, then, *now* no condemnation to those in Christ Jesus." The rest of the verse is a gloss.

[2] *Lit.*, "in a flesh-likeness of sin."

[3] περὶ ἁμαρτίας "as a sin-offering" חטאת, *chattath*. Lev. xvi. 5: λήψεται δύο χιμάρους περὶ ἁμαρτίας. Ps. xl. 7: περὶ ἁμαρτίας οὐκ ᾔτησας (Heb. x. 5). Lev. iv. 25: ἀπὸ τοῦ αἵματος τοῦ τῆς ἁμαρτίας.

[4] κατέκρινεν, "condemned to execution" (Matt. xxvii. 13).

[5] Verse 6. On the φρόνημα τῆς σαρκός, see Art. ix. Philo also dwells strongly on the impotence of man apart from Divine grace (*Legg. Alleg.* i. 48, 55, 101).

[6] vii. 13—viii. 11. The change from τοῦ ἐγείραντος Ἰησοῦν to ὁ ἐγείρας τὸν Χριστὸν is remarkable. "Appellatio Jesu spectat ad ipsum, Christi refertur ad nos" (Bengel, viii. 1) partly resumes the subject of v. 11 after the separate points handled in v. 12—21; vi. 1—23; vii. 1—6, 7—25.

all creation is now in anguish, in bondage, in corruption, yearning for a freedom which shall be revealed when we too have entered on the full glory of our inheritance as the children of God. We, though we have the first-fruits of the spirit, share in the groaning misery of nature, as it too shares in inarticulate sympathy with our impatient aspirations. We live, we are saved BY HOPE, and the very idea of Hope is the antithesis of present realisation.[1]

Hope is not possession, is not reality; it can but imply *future* fruition; it is Faith in Christ directed to the future. But we have something more and better than Hope. We have the help in weakness, the intercession even in prayer that can find no utterance, of the Holy Spirit Himself. We know, too, that *all things* work together for good to all them that love God and are called according to His purpose. He ends the Divine work that He begins. Election—predestination to conformity and brotherhood with Christ—vocation—justification—these four steps all follow, all must inevitably follow each other, and must end in glorification. So certain is this glorification, this entrance into the final fulness of sonship and salvation, that St. Paul—with one of those splendid flashes of rhetoric which, like all true rhetoric, come directly from the intensities of emotion, and have nothing to do with the technicalities of art—speaks of it in the same past tense which he has employed for every other stage in the process. Those whom He foreknew,[2] predestined, called, justified—them He also *glorified*.[3]

"What shall we then say to these things?" What, but that magnificent burst of confidence and rapture[4] which we will not degrade by the name of peroration, because in St. Paul no such mere artificiality of construction is conceivable, but which fitly closes this long and intricate discussion, in which he has enunciated truths never formulated since the origin of the world, but never to be forgotten till its final conflagration. The subtleties of dialectic, the difficulties of polemical argument, the novelties of spiritualising exegesis, are concluded; and, firm in his own revealed conviction, he has urged upon the conviction of

---

[1] viii. 18—25.

[2] There are four explanations of "foreknew," and each is claimed alike by Calvinists and Arminians! (Tholuck). But, "in the interpretation of Scripture, if we would feel as St. Paul felt, or think as he thought, we must go back to that age in which the water of life was still a running stream."

[3] viii. 26—30.

[4] Compare the outburst in 1 Cor. xv. 54. "In fact, as verses 19—23 may be called a sacred elegy, so we may term 31—39 a sacred ode; that is as tender and fervent as this is bold and exalted—that, an amplification of "we do groan being burdened" (2 Cor. v. 4); this, a commentary on "this is the victory that overcometh the world" (1 John v. 4). Philippi, *ad loc.*

BURST OF EXULTATION.

the world, and fixed in the conviction of Christians for ever, the deepest truths of the Gospel entrusted to his charge. What remains but to give full utterance to his sense of exultation in spite of earthly sufferings, and "to reduce doubt to absurdity" by a series of rapid, eager, triumphant questions, which force on the minds of his hearers but one irresistible answer? In spite of all the anguish that persecution can inflict, in spite of all the struggles which the rebellious flesh may cause, "we are more than conquerors through Him that loved us. For I am convinced that neither death nor life, nor angels nor principalities, nor things present, nor things to come, nor height nor depth, nor any other created thing, shall be able to separate us for a moment[1] from God's love manifested towards us in Christ Jesus our Lord." In spite of failure, in spite of imperfection, our life is united with the life of Christ, our spirit quickened by the Spirit of Christ, and what have we to fear if all time, and all space, and all nature, and all the angels of heaven, and all the demons of hell, are utterly powerless to do us harm?[2]

[1] viii. 39, χωρίσαι.
[2] Compare this rapture of faith and hope with the aching despair of materialism. "To modern philosophical unbelief the beginning of the world, as well as its end, is sunk in mist and night, because to it the centre of the world—the historical Christ—is sunk in mist and night" (Lange). The time was ripe for the recognition of a deliverer. Plato and Seneca had clearly realised and distinctly stated that man was powerless to help himself from his own misery and sin. (Sen. *Ep.* 53. Cf. Tac. *Ann.* iii. 18; Cic. *De Off.* i. 4, 18.)

CHAPTER XXXVIII.

PREDESTINATION AND FREE WILL.

"Everything is foreseen, and free will is given. And the world is judged by grace, and everything is according to work."—R. AKHIBHA in *Pirke Abôth*, iii. 24.

'Ορᾷς ὅτι οὐ φύσεως οὐδὲ ὑλικῆς ἀνάγκης ἐστὶ τὸ εἶναι χρυσοῦν ἢ ὀστράκινον, ἀλλὰ τῆς ἡμετέρας προαιρέσεως.—CHRYS. *ad* 2 Tim. ii. 21.

"Reasoned high
Of Providence, foreknowledge, will and fate,
Fixed fate, free will, foreknowledge absolute,
And found no end in wandering mazes lost."
MILTON, *Paradise Lost*, ii.

"Soll ich dir die Gegend Zeigen
Musst du erst das Dach besteigen."—GÖTHE.

WE now come to the three memorable chapters (ix., x., xi.) in which St. Paul faces the question which had, perhaps, led him to state to the Jews and Gentiles of Rome the very essence of his theology. He has told them "his Gospel"—that revealed message which he had to preach, and by virtue of which he was the Apostle of the Gentiles. He has shown that Jews and Gentiles were equally guilty, equally redeemed. The Redemption was achieved; but only by faith, in that sense of the word which he has so fully explained, could its blessings be appropriated. Alas! it was but too plain that while the Gentiles were accepting this great salvation, and pressing into the Kingdom of Heaven, the Jews were proudly holding aloof, and fatally relying on a system now abrogated, on privileges no longer exclusive. Their national hopes, their individual hopes, were alike based on a false foundation, which it has been the Apostle's duty inexorably to overthrow. Their natural exclusiveness he meets by the unflinching principle that there is no favouritism with our Heavenly Father; he meets their attempts after a legal righteousness by proving to them that they, like the Gentiles, are sinners, that they cannot attain a legal righteousness, and that no such endeavour can make them just before God. Obviously he was thus brought face to face with a tragic fact and a terrible problem. The *fact* was that the Jews were being rejected, that the Gentiles were being received. Even thus early in the history of Christianity it had become but too plain that the Church of the future would be mainly a Church of Gentiles, that the Jewish element within it would become more and more insignificant, and could only exist by losing its Judaic distinctiveness. The *problem* was, how could this be, in the face of those immemorial promises, in the light of that splendid history? Was God breaking His promises? Was God forgetting that they were "the seed of Abraham His servant, the children of Jacob whom He had chosen?"[1] To this grave question there was (1) a theologic answer, and (2) an historic answer. (1) The theologic answer was—that acceptance and rejection are God's absolute will, and in accordance with His predestined election to grace or wrath. (2) The historic answer was—that the rejection of the Jews was the natural result of their own obstinacy and hardness. The two answers might seem mutually irreconcilable; but St. Paul, strong in faith, in inspiration, in sincerity, never shrinks from the seeming oppositions of an eternal para

---

[1] "Who hath not known passion, cross, and travail of death, cannot treat of foreknowledge without injury and inward enmity towards God. Wherefore, take heed that thou drink not wine while thou art yet a sucking babe" (Luther). He also said, "The *ninth* chapter of the Epistle to the Romans *is* the ninth. Learn first the eight chapters which precede it."

dox. He often gives statements of truth regarded from different aspects, without any attempt to show that they are, to a higher reason than that of man, complementary, not (as they appear) contradictory, of each other. Predestination is a certain truth of reason and of revelation; free will is a certain truth of revelation and of experience. They are both true, yet they seem mutually exclusive, mutually contradictory. The differences between Supralapsarians and Sublapsarians do not really touch the question; God's foreknowledge is always recognised, but in no way does it solve the difficulty of the absolute decree. If we say that St. Paul is here mainly arguing about great masses of men, about men in nations, and the difference between Jews and Gentiles, that is partially true; but he most definitely recognises the case of individuals also, and God is the God not only of nations, but of individuals. In any case, this sacrifice of the individual to the interests of the mass would be but a thrusting of the difficulty a little further back. The thought that many, though Edomites, will be saved, and many, though of Israel, will be lost, may make the antenatal predilection for Israel and detestation of Esau less startling to us, and it is quite legitimate exegetically to soften, by the known peculiarities of Semitic idiom, the painful harshness of the latter term. But even then we are confronted with the predestined hardening of Pharaoh's heart. St. Paul recognises—all Scripture recognises—the naturalness of the cry of the human soul; but the remorseless logic of a theology which is forced to reason at all about the Divine prescience can only smite down the pride of finite arguments with the iron rod of revealed mysteries. Man is but clay in the potter's hands. God is omnipotent; God is omniscient; yet evil exists, and there is sin, and there is death, and after death the judgment; and sin is freely forgiven, and yet we shall receive the things done in the body, and be judged according to our works. All things end in a mystery, and all mysteries resolve themselves into one—the existence of evil. But, happily, this mystery need in no way oppress us, for it is lost in the Plenitude of God. The explanation of it has practically nothing to do with us. It lies in a region wholly apart from the facts of common life. When St. Paul tells us "that it is not of him that willeth, nor of him that runneth," he is dealing with one order of transcendental ideas; but when he comes to the common facts of Christian life, he bids us will, and he bids us run, and he bids us work out our own salvation with fear and trembling; exactly as he tells us that justification is of faith alone, and not of works, and yet constantly urges us to good works, and tells us that God will reward every man according to his works.[1] Beyond this we cannot get. "Decretum horribile fateor," said Calvin, "at tamen verum." Theology must illustrate by crushing analogies its irreversible decrees, but it cannot touch the sphere of practical experience, or weaken the exhortations of Christian morality. God predestines; man is free. How this is we cannot say; but *so* it is. St. Paul makes no attempt to reconcile the two positions. "Neither here nor anywhere else does he feel called upon to deal with speculative extremes. And in whatever way the question be speculatively adjusted, absolute dependence and moral self-determination are *both* involved in the immediate Christian self-consciousness."[2] The finite cannot reduce the infinite to conditions, or express by syllogisms the mutual relations of the two. The truths must be stated, when there is need to state them,

---

[1] ἀποδιδόναι (Rom. ii. 6; 2 Tim. iv. 8); ἀνταπόδοσις (Col. iii. 24); μισθὸς (1 Cor. iii. 8; ix. 17), &c.
[2] Baur, *Paul.* ii. 259.

although each of them belongs to separate orders of ideas. Since they cannot be reconciled, they must be left side by side. It is an inevitable necessity, implied throughout all Scripture, that, as regards such questions, the sphere of dogma and the sphere of homily should often be regarded as though they were practically separate from each other, though in reality they intersect each other. And the reason of this is that both are enclosed in the circumference of a sphere by far more vast—that sphere of the Divine, of which for us the centre is everywhere, and the circumference, not indeed "nowhere," but immeasurably beyond our ken.[1] This is one comfort. And again, just as St. Paul refuses to find the substantial essence of morality anywhere but in the inmost disposition, so he does away with the *individual ego* by raising it to the *universal ego*—to that humanity which is present, and is identified with itself, in every separate individual.[2] It is unquestionable that he *categorically asserts*, and that without limitations, the redemption of the universe and of the race.[3] In that thought, and in the thought of God's infinite love, lies the gleam of light in the saddest destinies or the most perplexed enigmas of the individual. The logical conclusions of an exaggerated dogmatism are rectified by the unchangeable certainties of moral conviction, and the inspired hopes of a child-like love.

"Ah, truly," says Reuss,[4] "if the last word of the Christian revelation is contained in the image of the

---

[1] The Rabbis, to avoid even the most distant semblance of irreverent anthropomorphism, often spoke of God as *Ha-Makôm*, "the place;" and it is one of their grand sayings that "the Universe is not the place of God, but God is the Place of the Universe."

[2] Baur, *Three Centuries*, p. 32.

[3] See Rom. viii. 19—24; xi. 32; 1 Tim. ii. 3—6 (Acts iii. 21; Rev. xxi. 4; xxii. 3).

[4] *Théol. Chrét.* ii. 115.

potter and the clay, it is a bitter derision of all the deep needs and legitimate desires of a soul aspiring towards its God. This would be at once a satire of reason upon herself, and the suicide of revelation." But it is neither the *last* word, nor the *only* word; nor has it any immediate observable bearing on the concrete development of our lives. It is not the *only* word, because in nine-tenths of Scripture it is as wholly excluded from the sphere of revelation as though it had been never revealed at all; and it is not the *last* word, because throughout the whole of Scripture, and nowhere more than in the writings of the very Apostle who has faced this problem with the most heroic inflexibility, we see bright glimpses of something beyond. How little we were intended to draw logical conclusions from the metaphor, is shown by the fact that we are living souls, not dead clay; and St. Paul elsewhere recognised a power, both within and without our beings, by which, as by an omnipotent alchemy, mean vessels can become precious, and vessels of earthenware be transmuted into vessels of gold.[1] Vessels fitted for destruction may be borne with much long-suffering. Apparent loss is made the immediate instrument of wider gain. Partial rejection is to pave the way for universal acceptance. God wills the salvation of all.[2] Where sin abounds, there grace superabounds.[3] God giveth freely to all, and freely calleth all, and His gifts and calling are without repentance. Israel is rejected, Israel in part is hardened, yet "all Israel shall be saved."[4] "God shut up all into disobedience, that He might pity all."[5] The duality of election resolves itself into the higher unity of an all-embracing counsel of favour; and the sin

---

[1] 2 Tim. ii. 21.
[2] 1 Tim. ii. 4; Tit. ii. 11; 2 Pet. iii. 9.
[3] Rom. v. 20, 21.
[4] Rom. xi. 26.
[5] Rom. xi. 32.

of man, even through the long Divine œconomy of the *æons*, is seen to be but a moment in the process towards that absolute end of salvation, which is described as the time when God shall be "all things in all things," and therefore in all men; and when the whole groaning and travailing creation shall be emancipated into "the freedom of the glory of the children of God."[1] If disobedience has been universal, so too is mercy; and Divine mercy is stronger and wider, and more infinite and more eternal, than human sin. Here, too, there is an antinomy. St. Paul recognises such a thing as "perdition;" there are beings who are called "the perishing."[2] There are warnings of terrible significance in Scripture and in experience. But may we not follow the example of St. Paul, who quite incontestably dwells by preference upon the wide prospect of infinite felicity; who seems always lost in the contemplation of the final triumph of all good? However awful may be the future retribution of sinful lives, we still cannot set aside—what true Christian would wish to set aside?—the Scriptures, which say that "as in Adam all die, even so in Christ shall all be made alive;" that all things tend "unto God," as all things are from Him and by Him;[3] that Christ shall reign until He hath put all enemies under His feet, and that the last which shall be destroyed is death.[4]

Let us, then, see more in detail how the Apostle deals with a fact so shocking to every Jew as the deliberate rejection of Israel from every shadow of special privilege

---

[1] 1 Cor. xv. 22; Rom. xi. 15—36; viii. 19—23. See Baur, *First Three Centuries*, p. 72; Pfleiderer, ii. 256, 272—275; Reuss, *Théol. Chrét.* ii. 23, *seqq.*

[2] Ἀπολλύμενοι. This word does not mean "the lost," a phrase which does not exist in Scripture, but "the perishing."

[3] Rom. xi. 36; 1 Cor. viii. 6; Col. i. 16, 17.

[4] 1 Cor. xv. 25—28; Eph. i. 20—22; 2 Tim. i. 10 (Matt. xi. 27; Heb. ii. 8, 14).

in the kingdom of God; let us see how he proves a
doctrine against which, at first sight, it might well have
seemed that the greater part of the Old Testament and
1,500 years of history were alike arrayed.

It should be observed that in his most impassioned
polemic he always unites a perfect conciliatoriness of tone
with an absolute rigidity of statement. If he must give
offence, he is ready to give offence to any extent, so
far as the offence must inevitably spring from the truth
which it is his sacred duty to proclaim. Doubtless,
too, much that he said might be perverted to evil
results; be it so. There are some who abuse to evil
purposes God's own sunlight, and who turn the doctrine
of forgiveness into a curse. Are we to quench His
sunlight? are we to say that He does not forgive?
Some Jews were, doubtless, dangerously shaken in all their
convictions by the proclamation of the Gospel, as some
Romanists were by the truths of the Reformation. Is
error to be immortal because its eradication is painful?
Is the mandrake to grow, because its roots shriek when
they are torn out of the ground? Or is it not better, as
St. Gregory the Great said, that a scandal should be
created than that truth should be suppressed? There
is no style of objection to the proclamation of a new or
a forgotten truth which is so false, so faithless, and so
futile, as the plea that it is "dangerous." But one duty
is incumbent on all who teach what they believe to be
the truths of God. It is that they should state them
with all possible candour, courtesy, forbearance, considerateness. The controversial method of St. Paul
furnishes the most striking contrast to that of religious
controversy in almost every age. It is as different as
anything can be from the reckless invective of a Jerome
or of a Luther. It bears no relation at all to the

unscrupulousness of a worldly ecclesiasticism. It is removed by the very utmost extreme of distance from the malice of a party criticism, and the Pharisaism of a loveless creed.

Thus, though he knows that what he has to enforce will be most unpalatable to the Jews, and though he knows how virulently they hate him, how continuously they have thwarted his teaching and persecuted his life, he begins with an expression of love to them so tender and so intense, that theologians little accustomed to an illimitable unselfishness felt it incumbent upon them to explain it away.

"I say the truth in Christ, I lie not, my conscience bearing me witness in the Holy Spirit, that I have great grief and incessant anguish in my heart;" and then, in the intensity of his emotion, he omits to state the cause of his grief, because it is sufficiently explained by what follows and what has gone before. It is grief at the thought that Israel should be hardening their hearts against the Gospel. "For I could have wished my own self to be anathema from Christ[1] on behalf of my brethren, my kinsmen according to the flesh, seeing that they are Israelites, whose is the adoption,[2] and the Shechinah,[3] and the covenants, and the legislation, and the ritual, and the promises, whose are the fathers, and of whom is Christ, according to the flesh, who is over all—God blessed for ever. Amen."[4] On his solemn appeal to the fact of his

---

[1] חרם, Deut. vii. 46; Zech. xiv. 11; Gal. i. 8, 9; 1 Cor. xii. 3; xvi. 22. Strong natures have ever been capable of braving even the utmost loss for a great end. "If not, blot me, I pray thee, out of the book which Thou hast written" (Ex. xxxii. 32). "Que mon nom soit flétri," said Danton, "pourvu que la France soit libre." "Let the name of George Whitefield perish if God be glorified."

[2] 2 Cor. vi. 18.

[3] Ex. xvi. 10; 1 Sam. iv. 22, &c. (LXX.)

[4] Rom. ix. 1—5. On the punctuation of this last verse a great controversy has arisen. Many editors since the days of Erasmus (and among them Lachmann, Tischendorf, Rückert, Meyer, Fritzsche) put the stop at "flesh;" others at "all" (Locke, Baumgarten, Crusius); and regard the concluding words as a doxology to God for the grandest of the privileges of Israel. In favour of this punctuation is the fact that Paul, even in his grandest Christological passages, yet nowhere calls Christ "*God over all*," nor ever applies to Him

readiness even to abandon all hopes of salvation if thereby he could save his brethren, I think it only necessary to say that the very form in which it is expressed shows his sense that such a wish is by the very nature of things impossible. Further explanation is superfluous to those who feel how natural, how possible, is the desire for even this vast self-sacrifice to the great heart of a Moses or a Paul.

"Not, however, as though the Word of God has failed."[1] This is the point which St. Paul has to prove, and he does it by showing that God's gifts are matters of such free choice that the Jew cannot put forward any exclusive claim to their monopoly.

In fact, all who are Jews naturally are not Jews spiritually—are not, therefore, in any true sense heirs of the promise. To be of the seed of Abraham is nothing in itself. Abraham had many sons, but only one of them, the son of Sarah, was recognised in the promise.[2]

Not only so, but even of the two sons of the son of promise one was utterly rejected; and so completely was this a matter of choice, and so entirely was it independent of merit, that before there could be any question of merit, even in the womb, the elder was rejected to servitude, the younger chosen for dominion. And this is stated in the strongest way by the prophet Malachi—" Jacob I loved, but Esau I hated."[3]

the word εὐλογητός. (See i. 25; 1 Cor. iii. 23; viii. 6; 2 Cor. i. 3; xi. 31; Eph. i. 17; iv. 6; 1 Tim. ii. 5, &c.) But, on the other hand, a doctrinal ἅπαξ λεγόμενον may, as Lange says, mark a culminating point; and having regard (i.) to the language which Paul uses (Phil. ii. 6; Col. i. 15; ii. 9; 1 Cor. viii. 6; 2 Cor. iv. 4), and (ii.) to the grammatical structure of the sentence, and (iii.) to the *position* of εὐλογητός (which in doxologies in the New Testament stands always first), and (iv.) to the unanimity of all ancient commentators, and (v.) to the fact that the clause probably alludes to Ps. lxvii. 19 (LXX.), and in Eph. iv. 8, St. Paul quotes the *previous* verse of this Psalm, and applies it to Christ,—the punctuation of our received text can hardly be rejected. Yet there is weight in Baur's remark that κατὰ σάρκα is added to show that it is as only "after the flesh" that the Jews could claim the birth of the Messiah, and that the "God over all blessed for ever" would have been allowing too much to Jewish particularism. (Cf. Gal. iv. 4, γενόμενος ἐκ γυναικός.) For a full examination of the question, I may refer to my papers on the text in the *Expositor*, 1879.

[1] ἐκπέπτωκεν, "fallen like a flower," Job xiv. 2; but see 1 Cor. xiii. 8; James i. 11.

[2] ix. 6—9; comp. *Nedarim*, f. 31, 1. "Is not Ishmael an alien, and yet of the seed of Abraham?" It is written, "In *Isaac* shall thy seed be called." "But is not Esau an alien, and yet of the seed of Isaac?" "No. 'In Isaac,' but *not all Isaac*."

[3] Mal. i. 2, 3. Hated = "loved less" (Gen. xxix. 31; Matt. vi. 24; x. 37, compared with Luke xiv. 26); and the next verse shows that *temporal* position is alluded to.

"Is God unjust then?" To a natural logic the question might seem very excusable, but St. Paul simply puts it aside as irrelevant and impossible, while he re-states the fact which suggests it by quoting as decisive two passages of Scripture.[1] God has an absolute right to *love* whom He will; for He says to Moses, "Whomsoever I pity, him I will pity; and whomsoever I compassionate, him I will compassionate;" so that pity is independent of human will or effort. And God has an absolute right to *hate* whom He will; for Scripture says to Pharaoh, "For this very purpose I raised thee up, to display in thee my power, and that my name may be proclaimed in all the earth."[2]

So then God pities, and God hardens, whom He will.

Again, the natural question presents itself—"Why does He then blame? If wickedness be the result of Divine Will, what becomes of moral responsibility?"

In the first place, Paul implies that the question is absurd. Who are you, that you can call God to account? No matter what becomes of moral responsibility, it does not at any rate affect God's decree. Man is but passive clay in the Potter's hands; He can mould it as He will.[3]

But Paul would not thus *merely* smite down the timid questioning of sinners by the arbitrary irresponsibility of

---

[1] "These arguments of the Apostle are founded on two assumptions. The first is that the Scriptures are the word of God; and the second, that what God actually does cannot be unrighteous" (Hodge). At the same time it is most necessary, as Bishop Wordsworth says, "not to allow the mind to dwell exclusively or mainly on single expressions occurring here or there, but to consider their relation to the context, to the whole scope of the Epistle, to the other Epistles of St. Paul, and to the general teachings of Holy Writ" *Epistles*, p. 201).

[2] ix. 14—18. "Satis habet," says Calvin, "Scripturae testimoniis *impuros latratus* compescere;" but the "impure barkings" (a phrase which St. Paul would never have used) shows the difference between the Apostle of the Gentiles and the Genevan Reformer. Σκληρύνει, however, in ver. 18, cannot mean "treats hardly." Calovius says that God does not harden ἐνεργητικῶς, "by direct action," but συγχωρητικῶς (permissively), ἀφορμητικῶς (by the course of events), ἐγκαταλειπτικῶς (by abandonment), and παραδοτικῶς (by handing men over to their worse selves). It may be said that this chapter contradicts the next, and Fritzsche goes so far as to say that "Paul would have better agreed with himself if he had been the pupil of Aristotle, not of Gamaliel;" but the contradiction, or rather the antinomy, is not in any of St. Paul's arguments, but in the very nature of things.

[3] ix. 19—22. It was a common metaphor (Jer. xviii. 6; Isa. xlv. 9; Wisd. xv. 7; Sirach xxxiii. 13).

Infinite Power. He gives a gleam of hope; he sheds over the ultimate Divine purposes a flash of insight. He asks a question which implies a large and glorious answer, and the very form of the question shows how little he desires to dwell on the unpractical insoluble mysteries of Divine reprobation.[1]

What if God, willing to display His wrath, and to make known His power—(he will not say, "created vessels of wrath," or "prepared them for destruction," but, swerving from a conclusion too terrible for the wisest)—"*endured in much long-suffering* vessels of wrath fitted for destruction . . . ? And what if He did this that He might also make known the riches of His glory towards the vessels of mercy which He before prepared for glory . . . ?" What if even those decrees which seemed the harshest were but steps towards an ultimate good? . . . By that blessed purpose *we* profit, whom God called both out of the Jews and out of the Gentiles. This calling is illustrated by the language of two passages of Hosea,[2] in which the prophet calls his son and daughter Lo-ammi and Lo-ruhamah (Not-my-people and Not-pitied) because of the rejection of Israel, but at the same time prophesies the day when they shall again be His people, and He their God:—and by two passages of Isaiah[3] in which he at once prophesies the rejection of the mass of Israel and the preservation of a remnant.[4]

Having thus established the fact on Scriptural authority, what is the conclusion? Must it not be that—so entirely is election a matter of God's free grace—the Gentiles, though they did not pursue righteousness, yet laid hold of justification by faith; and that the Jews, though

---

[1] When we read such passages as Rom. viii. 22—24; Acts iii. 19, 21, we think that St. Paul would have seen a phase of truth in the lines—

> "Safe in the hands of one disposing power,
> Or in the natal or the mortal hour;
> All Nature is but Art, unknown to thee;
> All Chance, Direction which thou canst not see;
> All Discord, Harmony not understood;
> All partial evil, universal good."

[2] Hos. i. 9, 10; ii. 23.
[3] Isa. x. 22; i. 9.
[4] ix. 22—30. Ver. 28 is an exegetical translation which St. Paul adopts from the LXX. As the form of quotation has only an indirect bearing on he argument, the reader must refer to special commentaries for its elucidation.

they did pursue a legal righteousness, have not attained to justification?
How can such a strange anomaly be explained? Whatever may be
the working of Divine election, humanly speaking, their rejection is the
fault of the Jews. They chose to aim at an impossible justification by
works, and rejected the justification by faith. Again St. Paul refers
to Isaiah in support of his views.¹ They stumbled at Christ. To them,
as to all believers, He might have been a firm rock of foundation;
they made Him a stone of offence.² The desire of his heart, his prayer
to God, is for their salvation. But their religious zeal has taken an
ignorant direction. They are aiming at justification by works, and
therefore will not accept God's method, which is justification by faith.³

In the path of works they cannot succeed, for the Law finds its sole
end, and aim, and fulfilment in Christ,⁴ and through Him alone is justification possible. Even these truths the Apostle finds in Scripture, or
illustrates by Scriptural quotations. He contrasts the statement of Moses,
that he who obeyed the ordinances of the Law should live by them,⁵
with those other words which he puts into the mouth of Justification
personified, " Say not in thine heart who shall ascend into heaven, or
who shall descend into the abyss, but the word is very nigh thee in thy
mouth and in thy heart," which (being used originally of the Law) he
explains of the nearness and accessibility of the Gospel which was now
being preached, and which was summed up in the confession and belief
in Him as a risen Saviour. This is again supported by two quotations in
almost the same words—one from Isaiah (xxviii. 16), "Every one that
believeth on Him shall not be ashamed;" and one from Joel (ii. 32),
"Every one that calleth on the name of the Lord shall be saved"—and
the "every one" of course includes the Gentile no less than the Jew.⁶

But had the Jews enjoyed a real opportunity of hearing the Gospel?
In a series of questions, subordinated to each other with great rhetorical
beauty, St. Paul shows that each necessary step has been fulfilled—the
hearing, the preachers, the mission of those whose feet were beautiful
upon the mountains, and who preach the glad tidings of peace; but,

¹ Isa. viii. 14; xxviii. 16.

² In ix. 33, the " be ashamed " of the LXX., followed by St. Paul, is an exegetical translation of " make haste " or " flee hastily."

³ ix. 30—x. 4.

⁴ x. 4, τέλος—i.e., the righteousness at which the Law aims is accomplished in Christ, and the Law leads to Him; He is its fulfilment and its termination. Its glory is done away, but He remains, because His eternal brightness is the τέλος τοῦ καταργουμένου (Gal.).

⁵ א, A, B, ἐν αὐτῇ.

⁶ x. 4—12. It is remarkable that in verse 11 the important word πᾶς is found neither in the Hebrew nor in the LXX. Cf. ix. 33.

alas! the *faith* had been wanting, and, therefore, also the calling upon God. For all had not hearkened to the Gospel. It was not for want of hearing, for in accordance with prophecy (Ps. xix. 4) the words of the preachers had gone out to all the world; but it was for want of faith, and this, too, had been prophesied, since Isaiah said, "Who believed our preaching?" Nor, again, was it for want of warning. Moses (Deut. xxxii. 21) had told them ages ago that God would stir up their jealousy and kindle their anger by means of those Gentiles whom in their exclusive arrogance they despised as "no nation;" and Isaiah (lxv. 1, 2) says with daring energy, "I was found by such as sought me not, I became manifest to such as inquire not after me," whereas to Israel he saith, "The whole day long I outspread my hands to a disobedient and antagonistic people."[1]

Thus, with quotation after quotation—there are nine in this chapter alone, drawn chiefly from Deuteronomy, Isaiah, and the Psalms—does St. Paul state his conviction as to the present rejection of the Gospel by his own nation; while he tries to soften the bitter rage which it was calculated to arouse both against himself and against his doctrine, by stating it in words which would add tenfold authority to the dialectical arguments into which they are enwoven. But having thus established two very painful, and at first sight opposing truths—namely, that the Jews were being deprived of all exclusive privileges by the decree of God (ix.), and that this forfeiture was due to their own culpable disbelief (x.)—he now enters on the gladder and nobler task of explaining how these sad truths are robbed of their worst sting, when we recognise that they are but the partial and transient phenomena incidental to the evolution of a blessed, universal, and eternal scheme.

"I ask, then, did God reject His people? Away with the thought! for at worst the rejection is but partial." Of this he offers himself as a proof, being as he is "an Israelite, of the seed of Abraham, of the

[1] x. 14—21.

tribe of Benjamin;" and he then quotes the analogy of the 7,000 whom God "reserved for Himself," who in the days of Elijah had not bowed the knee to Baal. On this he pauses to remark that the very phrase, "I reserved for myself," implies that this remnant was saved by faith, and not by works. But how came it that the majority had missed the end for which they sought? Because, he answers, they were hardened; God (as Isaiah prophesied) had sent them a spirit of stupor which finds its illustration in the phrase, "let their eyes be darkened," amid David's prayer for the humiliation and bewilderment of his enemies.[1]

But then another awful question occurs: is this hardening, this spiritual blindness, to be final? "Did they stumble that they may utterly fall?" Again Paul exclaims, Perish the thought! Their very fall was meant for salvation to the Gentiles, and to stimulate their own hearts to better things. And here his readers could not but feel that he was explaining facts which were taking place under their very eyes. In every instance the Gospel had been offered first to the Jew; in every instance the Jew had rejected it; and it was through this very obstinacy that it had now been offered everywhere to the Gentile. The Messiah rejected by the Jew was daily being glorified as the Redeemer of the Gentile. The Church of the Christ was now securely founded, but even already Antioch, and Rome, and Ephesus, and Thessalonica were far more its capitals than the Holy City. But this fact revealed a glorious anticipation. If their *deficiency* was thus the wealth of the Gentiles, how much more would their replenishment! It was his grand mission to preach this to the Gentiles, and thereby, if possible, to stir the Jews to emulation, for if their rejection be the world's reconciliation, what will be their acceptance but life from the dead?

And that there will be this restoration of Israel he illustrates by a double metaphor.

i. When the heave-offering was offered, the whole lump of dough acquired sacredness from the fact that a portion of it was sanctified to the Lord. So with Israel. Their first-fruits—Abraham and their patriarchal fathers—were holy, and their holiness was ideally attributable to all the race.

ii. The second metaphor has a wider applicability. The root of the olive-tree is the source of its fruitfulness; but if some of its branches lose their fruitfulness and become withered, they are lopped off and are replaced by grafts of the wild olive, which then shares the richness of

[1] xi. 1—11.

the tree. Such withered branches were the present unbelieving majority of Israel. That they should be lopped off is a part of God's just and necessary severity. To explain this truth—to bring it home to the pained and angry consciousness of his people—has been one of his objects in this great Epistle; and he has carried it out, at whatever cost, with a most unflinching sincerity. But meanwhile, if the Gentiles in their turn were tempted to assume the airs of particularism with which the Jews had so long gloried over them, what a warning should be conveyed to them by the state of things here shadowed forth! And how much consolation might the Jew find in this metaphor to revive the fainting hopes of his patriotism, and to alleviate his wounded pride of nationality by gentler and holier thoughts! For Christ, after all, was a rod of the stem of Jesse, and a branch out of his roots. The Gentiles were admitted into the Church through the vestibule of the Temple. With the Jews had remained till this moment the oracles of God. In Judaism—its privileges, its promises, its prophecies—were the germs of Christianity. The new rich fruitfulness of the Gentiles was drawn from the tree into which they had been grafted. Little cause had they to boast against the natural branches. Deep cause had they to take warning by the fate which those branches had undergone. They, in their turn, might be lopped off, and—though here the metaphor as such breaks down—the old branches might be grafted into their proper place once more.[1] Let them remember that faith was the source of their new privileges, as the want of it had caused the ruin of those whom they replaced; let them not be high-minded, but fear.[2]

The concluding words of this section of the Epistle open a glorious perspective of ultimate hope for all whose hearts are sufficiently large and loving to accept it. He calls on the brethren not to ignore the mystery that the partial hardening of Israel should only last till the fulness of the Gentiles should come in; and he appeals to Scripture (Isa. lix. 20) to support his prophecy that "all Israel shall be saved," beloved as they are for the sake of their fathers as regards the election of grace, though now alienated for the blessing of the Gentiles as regards the Gospel.

[1] This of course was, physically, an impossible method of ἐγκεντρισμός; the other, if adopted at all, was most rare. (*V. supra*, i., p. 21.)
[2] xi. 16—24.

For God's gifts and calling admit of no revocation; once given, they are given for ever.[1] Once themselves disobedient, the Gentiles were now pitied in consequence of the disobedience of the Jews; so the Jews were now disobedient, but when the pity shown to the Gentiles had achieved their full redemption, the Jews in turn should share in it.[2] "For"—such is the grand conclusion of this sustained exposition of the Divine purposes—"God shut up all into disobedience,[3] that He might show mercy unto all."—Many are anxious, in accordance with their theological views, to weaken or explain away the meaning of these words; to show that "all" does not really mean "all" in the glad, though it does in the gloomy clause; or to show that "having mercy upon all" is quite consistent with the final ruin of the vast majority. Be that as it may, the Apostle, as he contemplates the universality of free redeeming grace, bursts into a pæan of praise and prophecy: "O the depth of the riches, and wisdom, and knowledge of God! how unsearchable are His judgments, and untrackable His ways! For who ever fathomed the mind of the Lord, or who ever became His counsellor? Or who gave Him first, and it shall be repaid to him? For from Him, and through Him, and unto Him are all things. To Him be glory for ever. Amen."

[1] Hos. xiii. 14, "I will redeem them from death . . . repentance shall be hid from mine eyes."

[2] xi. 31. If, as in this explanation, the comma is placed after ἠπείθησαν, the connexion of τῷ ὑμετέρῳ ἐλέει is very awkward, and almost unparalleled. On the other hand, the antithesis is spoiled if we place the comma after ἐλέει, and render it, "So they too now disbelieved (or disobeyed) the pity shown to you."

[3] In the declaratory sense.

CHAPTER XXXIX.

FRUITS OF FAITH.

"La foi justifie quand il opère, mais il n'opère que par la charité" (Quesnel).

"Not that God doth require nothing unto happiness at the hands of man save only a naked belief (for hope and charity we may not exclude), but that without belief all other things are as nothing; and it is the ground of those other divine virtues" (Hooker, *Eccl. Pol.* I. xi. 6).

"Faith doth not shut out repentance, hope, love, dread, and the fear of God, to be joined with faith in every man that is justified; but it shutteth them out from the office of justifying" (*Homily of Salvation*, pt. ii.).

[It is needless to point out that the sense of the word "faith" in these passages is by no means the Pauline sense of the word."]

AT this point there is a marked break in the letter, and we feel that the writer has now accomplished the main object for which he wrote. But to this, as to all his letters, he adds those noble practical exhortations, which are thus made to rest, not on their own force and beauty, but on the securer basis of the principles which he lays down in the doctrinal portion. No one felt more deeply than St. Paul that it requires great principles to secure our faithfulness to little duties, and that every duty, however apparently insignificant, acquires a real grandeur when it is regarded in the light of those principles from which its fulfilment springs. Since, then, the mercy and pity of God, as being the source of His free grace, have been dwelt upon throughout the Epistle, St. Paul begins the practical part of it—"I exhort you therefore, brethren, by the compassions of God"—for these, and not the difficult doctrines of election and reprobation, are prominent in his mind—"to present your bodies," not like the dead offerings of Heathenism or Judaism, but "a *living* sacrifice, holy, well-pleasing to God—your reasonable service, and not to be conformed to this world, but to be transformed[1] in the renewing of your mind, that ye may discriminate what is the will of God, good and acceptable to Him, and perfect."

This general exhortation is then carried into details, unsystematically indeed, and even unsyntactically, but with an evident rush and glow of feeling which gives to the language a perfection transcending that of conscious art.[2] The prevalent thought is the duty of love:—to the brethren, love without dissimulation; to the Church, love without struggling self-assertion; to the civil power, love without fear; to the world, love without despising its rights or mingling with its immoralities.[3] First, by the grace given to him, he urges them "not to be high-minded above what they ought to be minded, but to mind to be sober-minded,[4] each in proportion to their God-apportioned receptivity of faith;" and he illustrates and enforces this duty of modest simplicity in the fulfilment of their mutual ministries,[5] by touching once more on the apologue of the body and the members,[6] which he

---

[1] Ver. 2, συσχηματίζεσθε, "*fashioned* in accordance;" μεταμορφοῦσθε, "*transformed.*" Σχῆμα, as in Phil. ii. 8, is the outward, transitory fashion; μορφή, the abiding and substantial form.

[2] Ver. 3, μὴ ὑπερφρονεῖν παρ' ὃ δεῖ φρονεῖν, ἀλλὰ φρονεῖν εἰς τὸ σωφρονεῖν.

[3] Lange *ad loc.*

[4] xii. 3.

[5] In ver. 6 the "prophecy [*i.e.*, high Christian teaching] according to the proportion of faith" (κατὰ τὴν ἀναλογίαν τῆς πίστεως) means that the Christian teacher is to keep within the limits of his gift assigned him by his individuality (Tholuck), *i.e.*, not to push his χάρισμα as a preacher into disproportionate prominence (Deut. xviii. 18). The objective sense of πίστις as a body of doctrines is later. Hence the common rule of explaining Scripture, "according to the analogy of faith," though most true and necessary, is a misapplication of the original meaning of the phrase.

[6] 1 Cor. xii. 12—27.

has already applied in his Letter to the Corinthians. The moral of the metaphor is that "Diversity without unity is disorder; unity without diversity is death."[1] Then with a free interchange of participles, infinitives, and imperatives, and with a mixture of general and special exhortations, he urges them to love, kindliness, zeal, hope, patience, prayer, generosity, forgiveness, sympathy, mutual esteem, self-restraint, the steady love of God, the steady loathing of evil, the deliberate victory of virtue over vice. It is clear that the dangers which he most apprehended among the Roman Christians were those exacerbations which spring from an unloving and over-bearing self-confidence; but he gives a general form to all his precepts, and the chapter stands unrivalled as a spontaneous sketch of the fairest graces which can adorn the Christian life.[2]

The first part of the thirteenth chapter has a more

[1] Lange. The conception of Christian fellowship involves both unity and variety. "The Spirit resolves the variety into unity, introduces variety into the unity, and reconciles unity to itself through variety" (Baur).

[2] xii. 1—21. As regards special expressions in this chapter, we may notice—ver. 9, ἀποστυγοῦντες "loathing;" κολλώμενοι, "bridal intimacy with." Ver. 10, τῇ φιλαδελφίᾳ φιλόστοργοι, "love your brethren in the faith as though they were brethren in blood;" προηγούμενοι, Vulg. "*invicem praevenientes*," "anticipating one another, and going before one another as guides in giving honour" (ver. 11). The evidence between the readings καιρῷ, "serving the opportunity," and Κυρίῳ, "the Lord," is very nicely balanced, but probably rose from the abbreviation κρῳ. The other clause is, "In zealous work not slothful; boiling in spirit" (cf. the נבא, "a prophet"). In ver. 13, μνείαις, "memories," can hardly be the true reading. In ver. 14, the διώκοντες, "pursuing hospitality," may have suggested the thought of διώκοντας, "persecutors;" ver. 16, τοῖς ταπεινοῖς συναπαγόμενοι is either "modestissimorum exempla sectantes" (Grot.), "letting the lowly lead you with them by the hand" (*masc.*), or "humilibus rebus obsecundantes," "going along with lowly things" (*neut.*). Ver. 19, δότε τόπον τῇ ὀργῇ, either (1) "Give place for the divine wrath to work" (Chrys., Aug., &c.); or (2), "Give room to your own anger"—i.e., defer its outbreak—this, however, would be a Latinism, "irae spatiumd are (cf. Virg. Æn. iv. 433); or (3) "Give place to, yield before, the wrath of your enemy." The first is right. Ver. 20, "coals of fire" (Prov. xxv. 21, 22) to melt him to penitence and beneficent shame. The chapter is full of beautiful trilogies of expression.

obviously special bearing. It is occupied by a very earnest exhortation to obedience towards the civil power, based on the repeated statements that it is ordained of God; that its aim is the necessary suppression of evil; that it was not, under ordinary circumstances, any source of terror to a blameless life; and that it should be obeyed and respected, not of unwilling compulsion, but as a matter of right and conscience.[1] This was, indeed, the reason why they paid taxes,[2] and why the payment of them should be regarded as a duty to God.[3]

The warmth with which St. Paul speaks thus of the functions of civil governors may, at first sight, seem surprising, when we remember that a Helius was in the Præfecture, a Tigellinus in the Prætorium, a Gessius Florus in the provinces, and a Nero on the throne. On the other hand, it must be borne in mind that the Neronian persecution had not yet broken out; and that the iniquities of individual emperors and individual governors, while it had free rein in every question which affected their greed, their ambition, or their lust, had not as yet by any means destroyed the magnificent ideal of Roman Law. If there were bad rulers, there were also good ones. A Cicero as well as a Verres had once been provincial governors; a Barea Soranus as well as a Felix. The Roman government, corrupt as it often was in special instances, was yet

---

[1] xiii. 5, ἀνάγκῃ (7, 8, Aug.) ὑποτάσσεσθε (D, E, F, G, Vulg. Luther), "Yield to necessity." "Pray for the established Government," said Rabbi Chaneena, "for without it men would eat one another" (*Abhoda Zara*, f. 4, 1). Josephus calls Judas the Gaulonite "the author of the fourth sect of Jewish philosophy," who have "an inviolable attachment to liberty," and say that God is to be the only Ruler (*Antt.* xxiii. 1, § 6).

[2] xiii. 6, τελεῖτε is the indicative; not, as in the A.V., an imperative (Matt. xxii. 21). In ver. 4 the μάχαιρα refers to the *jus gladii*. A provincial governor on starting was presented with a dagger by the Emperor. Trajan, in giving it, used the words—"*Pro* me; si merear, *in me.*"

[3] xiii. 1—7.

the one grand power which held in check the anarchic forces which but for its control were "nursing the impatient earthquake." If now and then it broke down in minor matters, and more rarely on a large scale, yet the total area of legal prescriptions was kept unravaged by mischievous injustice. St. Paul had himself suffered from local tyranny at Philippi, but on the whole, up to this time, he had some reason to be grateful to the impartiality of Roman law. At Corinth he had been protected by the disdainful justice of Gallio, at Ephesus by the sensible appeal of the public secretary; and not long afterwards he owed his life to the soldier-like energy of a Lysias, and the impartial protection of a Festus, and even of a Felix. Nay, even at his first trial his undefended innocence prevailed not only over all the public authority which could be arrayed against him by Sadducean priests and a hostile Sanhedrin, but even over the secret influence of an Aliturus and a Poppæa. Nor had the Jews any reason to be fretful and insubordinate. If the ferocity of Sejanus and the alarm of Claudius had caused them much suffering at Rome, yet, on the other hand, they had been protected by a Julius and an Augustus, and they were in possession of legal immunities which gave to their religion the recognised dignity of a *religio licita*. It may safely be said that, in many a great city, it was to the inviolable strength and grandeur of Roman law that they owed their very existence; because, had it not been for the protection thus afforded to them, they might have been liable to perish by the exterminating fury of Pagan populations by whom they were at once envied and disliked.[1]

No doubt the force of these considerations would be fully felt by those Jews who had profited by Hellenistic

[1] Thus the later Rabbis found it necessary to say, with Shemuel, "The law of the Gentile kingdom is valid" (*Babha Kama*, f. 113, 1).

culture. It is obvious, however, that St. Paul is here dealing with religious rather than with political or even theocratic prejudices. The early Church was deeply affected by Essene and Ebionitic elements, and St. Paul's enforcement of the truth that the civil power derives its authority from God, points to the antithesis that it was *not* the mere vassalage of the devil. It was not likely that at Rome there should be any of that zealot fanaticism which held it unlawful for a Jew to recognise any other earthly ruler besides God, and looked on the payment of tribute as a sort of apostasy.[1] It is far more likely that the Apostle is striving to counteract the restless insubordination which might spring from the prevalence of chiliastic notions such as those which we find in the Clementine Homilies, that "the present world with all its earthly powers is the kingdom of the devil," and that so far from regarding the civil governor as "the minister of God for good," the child of the future could only look upon him as the embodied representative of a spiritual enemy. This unpractical and dualistic view might even claim on its side certain phrases alluding to the moral wickedness of the world, which had a wholly different application;[2] and therefore Paul, with his usual firmness, lays down in unmistakable terms the rule which, humanly speaking, could alone save the rising Church from utter extinction—the rule, namely, of holding aloof from political disturbances. On the whole, both Jews and Christians had learnt the lesson well, and it was, therefore, the more necessary that the good effects of that faithful fulfilment of the duties of citizenship, to which both Jewish historians and Christian fathers constantly appeal, should not be

---

[1] Matt. xxii. 17.
[2] John xii. 31, ὁ ἄρχων τοῦ κόσμου τούτου; Eph. ii. 2, τὸν ἄρχοντα τῆς ἐξουσίας τοῦ ἀέρος.

obliterated by the fanatical theories of incipient Manichees.

The question as to the payment of civil dues leads St. Paul naturally to speak of the payment of other dues. The one debt which the Christian owes to all men is the debt of love—that love which prevents us from all wrong-doing, and is therefore the fulfilment of the law. To this love he invites them in a powerful appeal, founded on the depth of the night and the nearness of the dawn, so that it was high time to put away the works of darkness and put on the arms of light[1]—nay, more, to put on, as a close-fitting robe, by close spiritual communion, the Lord Jesus Christ Himself.[2]

The fourteenth chapter again reveals the existence of Ebionitic elements in the Roman Church. In a strange city, and especially if he were not free, a scrupulous Jew, uninfluenced by Hellenism, would find it so impossible to fulfil the requirements of the Law respecting clean and unclean meats, and still more the many minute additions which Rabbinic Pharisaism had made to those requirements, that he would be forced either to sacrifice his convictions, or to reduce his diet to the simplest elements. As St. Paul does not allude to the Law, it is probable that he is here dealing with scruples even more deeply seated. His object is to reconcile the antagonistic feelings of two classes of Christians, whom he calls respectively the "strong" and the "weak." The "strong" regarded all days as equally sacred, or, as the "weak" would have said, as equally profane; whereas the "weak" surrounded the Sabbath and the Jewish festivals with regulations intended to secure their rigid observance.[3] Again, the "strong" ate food of every

---

[1] xiii. 12, or "the deeds of light" (ἔργα, A, D, E).

[2] Cf. Gal. iii. 27, Χριστὸν ἐνδύσασθε.

[3] Rom. xiv. 6. The words, "and he who regardeth not the day, to the Lord he doth not regard it," are omitted by ℵ, A, B, C, D, E, F, G, Vet., It., Vulg.,

description without the smallest scruple, whereas the "weak" looked on all animal food with such disgust and suspicion that they would eat nothing but herbs.[1] It is obvious that in adopting so severe a course they went far beyond the requirements of Levitism, and when we find the very same views and practices existing in Rome during the next century,[2] it is hardly possible to avoid the suspicion that the Judaic Christianity of these "weak" brethren was tinged with those Essene, Phrygian, or Pythagorean elements which led them to look on the material and the sensuous as something intrinsically dangerous, if not as positively evil. Epiphanius says that Ebion visited Rome;[3] and although it is more than doubtful whether there ever was such a person, yet the statement shows the prevalence of such views. Now one of the Ebionitic principles was that all meat is impure,[4] and in the Clementine Homilies the eating of meat is attributed to impure demons and blood-thirsty giants; and the Apostle Peter is made to say to Clement that "he makes use only of bread and olives and (sparingly) of other vegetables"[5]—a tradition which we also find attached by Clemens of Alexandria to the names of St. Matthew and James the Lord's brother, and the latter we are told drank no wine or strong drink.[6]

Copt. On the other hand, the Syriac has it, and the omission may be due to the *homœoteleuton* of φρονεῖ, or to doctrinal prejudices, which regarded the clause as dangerous. The clause is far too liberal to have been inserted by a second century scribe; but even if it be omitted, the principle which it involves is clearly implied in the first half of the verse, and in the previous verse.

[1] Seneca tells us that in his youth he had adopted from his Pythagorean teacher Sotion the practice of vegetarianism, but his father made him give it up because it rendered him liable to the suspicion of foreign superstitions (probably Judaism). See *Seekers after God*, p. 15.

[2] The Ebionites regarded the Sabbath as the holiest command of the Jewish religion.

[3] *Haer.* xxx. 18.
[4] Epiphan. *Haer.* xxx. 15.
[5] *Hom.* xii. 6.
[6] *Paedag.* ii. 1; Euseb. *H. E.* ii. 2, 3; Baur, *Paul.* i. 358.

It is very possible that St. Paul did not see the necessity of formally warning the Roman Christians against the tendency to dualism. This might be the subterranean origin of wrong notions long before it had risen into clear consciousness. What St. Paul *did* see was the danger that if "the weak" prevailed, Christianity might be frittered away into a troublesome and censorius externalism; or that the "strong" might treat their weaker brethren with a rough and self-exalting contempt which would either put force on tender consciences, or create a permanent disruption between the different members of the Church.[1]

He treats the difficulty in the same masterly manner—broad yet sympathetic, inflexible in convictions yet considerate towards prejudices—which he had already displayed in dealing with a similar question in his Epistle to the Corinthians. But the difference between the tone adopted in this chapter and that in the Epistle to the Galatians is very remarkable, and shows the admirable tact and versatility of the Apostle. He is there establishing the rights of Christian freedom against the encroachments of Pharisaism, so that the assertion of the liberty of the Gentiles was a matter of essential importance. He therefore speaks, as it was a duty to speak, with an almost rough contempt of attaching any vital importance to "beggarly elements." Here his tone is altogether different, because his object is altogether different, as also were his readers. The *right* to enjoy our liberty he can here in the most absolute manner assume. As to the merit of the particular scrupulosities which were in vogue among the weak, he has no occasion to do more than imply his own indifference. What is here necessary is to warn the "strong" not to be arrogant in their condemnations, and the "weak" not to be super-

[1] Gal. iii.; v. 1—9; vi. 12, 13.

cilious in their self-esteem. He has shown the universality of guilt, and the universality of grace, and he has now to show the sacred duty of unanimity among those thus universally called, defending this unanimity against censoriousness on the one hand, and against disdain on the other.

He does not attempt to conceal the bent of his own sympathies; he declares himself quite unambiguously on the side of the " strong." The life of the Christian is a life in Christ, and rises transcendantly above the minutiæ of ritual, or the self-torments of asceticism. "The kingdom of God"—such is the great axiom which he lays down for the decision of all such questions—" is not meat and drink; but righteousness, and peace, and joy in the Holy Ghost." The "strong," therefore, in St. Paul's judgment, were in the right. But, for this very reason, it was necessary to warn them against the contemptuous assertion of their superior wisdom.

i. Let each party follow their own course if they believe it to be the best, but let each abstain from the guilt and folly of condemning the other. God, not man, is the judge, by whose judgment each man stands or falls. Nay, he shall stand, for God is able to make him stand. Conceited illuminism is as deep an offence against charity as saintly self-satisfaction. The first counsel, then, on which he strongly insists is mutual forbearance, the careful avoidance of arguments and discussions about disputed points. Let there be no intolerant scrupulosity, and no uncharitable disdain, but an avoidance of dispute and a reciprocal recognition of honest convictions. These differences are not about essentials, and it is not for any man to adopt a violently dogmatic or uncharitably contemptuous tone towards those who differ from himself respecting them. The party-spirit of religious bodies too often finds the fuel for its burning questions in mere weeds and straw.[1]

ii. The second counsel is the cultivation of careful consideration which shall not shock tender consciences; it is, in short, condescendence

---

[1] xiv. 1—12, προσλαμβάνεσθε, "take by the hand;" μὴ εἰς διακρίσεις διαλογισμῶν, "not by way of criticising for them their scrupulous niceties" (Tholuck).

towards the weakness of others, a willingness to take less than our due, and a readiness to waive our own rights,[1] and enjoy as a private possession between ourselves and God the confidence of our faith. His own positive and sacred conviction is that these rules about food are unessential; that no food is intrinsically unclean. But if by acting on this conviction we lead others to do the same, in spite of the protest of their consciences, then for a paltry self-gratification we are undoing God's work, and slaying a soul for which Christ died.[2] Rather than do this, rather than place a needless stumbling-block in any Christian's path, it were well neither to eat meat nor to drink wine, because Christian love is a thing more precious than even Christian liberty.[3]

iii. His third counsel is the obedience to clear convictions.[4] Happy the man who has no scruples as to things intrinsically harmless. But if another cannot emancipate himself from these scruples, however needless, and exhibits in his own conduct the same freedom in defiance of his scruples, then he stands self-condemned. Why? Because in that case he is acting falsely to that faith which is the ruling principle of his Christian life, and whatsoever is not of faith,—whatsoever involves the life of self, and not the life of Christ—is sin.[5]

The true principle, then, is that we ought not to please ourselves, even as Christ pleased not Himself, but to bear the infirmities of the

---

[1] Συγκατάβασις (see Rom. xv. 1), ἱλασσοῦσθαι (John iii. 30), ὑστερεῖσθαι (Phil. iv. 12; 1 Cor. vi. 7); three great Christian conceptions which have in the practice of "religious" parties become perilously obsolete.

[2] 1 Cor. viii. 13.

[3] xiv. 13—21.

[4] Augustine's "Omnis infidelium vita, peccatum est" is an instance of the many extravagant inferences which are the curse of theology, and which arise from recklessly tearing words from the context, and pushing them beyond their legitimate significance. We have no right to apply the text apart from the circumstances to which it immediately refers. As a universal principle it is only applicable to the party of which the Apostle is speaking. When applied analogically, "faith" can here only be taken to mean "the moral conviction of the rectitude of a mode of action" (Chrys., De Wette, Meyer, &c.). To pervert the meaning of texts, as is done so universally, is to make a bad play upon words. Our Art. XIII. does not in the least exclude the possibility of *gratia praeveniens* even in heathens (see Rom. ii. 6—15). If Augustine meant that even the morality and virtue of pagans, heretics, &c., is sin, his axiom is not only morose and repellent, Pharisaical and anti-scriptural, but historically, spiritually, and morally false.

[5] xiv. 22, 23. It is at this point that some MSS. place the doxology of xvi. 25—27; but this would be a most awkward break between the fourteenth and fifteenth chapters, and the reasons for regarding the fifteenth chapter as spurious seem to me to be wholly inconclusive.

weak, and aim at mutual edification. This is the lesson of Scripture, and he prays that the God of that patience and comfort which it is the object of Scripture to inspire, may give them mutual unanimity in Jesus Christ. And addressing alike the "weak" Judaizers and the "strong" Gentiles, he concludes his advice with the same general precept with which he began, "Wherefore take one another by the hand, as Christ also took us by the hand for the glory of God."[1]

And Christ had thus set His example of love and help to both the great divisions of the Church. He had become the minister of the circumcision on behalf of God's truth, to fulfil the promise made to the fathers; and to the Gentiles out of compassion. Christ therefore had shown kindness to both, and that the Gentiles were indeed embraced in this kindness—which perhaps, in their pride of liberty they did not always feel inclined to extend to their weaker brethren—he further proves by an appeal to Deuteronomy, Isaiah, and the Psalms.[2] The last citation ends with the words "shall hope," and he closes this section with yet another prayer that the God of hope would fill them with all joy and peace in believing, that they might abound in hope in the power of the Holy Ghost.

But once more he takes up the pen to assure them of his confidence in them, and to apologise for the boldness of his letter. His plea is that he wished to fulfil to the utmost that ministry to the Gentiles which he here calls a priestly ministry, because he is as it were instrumental in presenting the Gentiles as an acceptable offering to God.[3] Of this Apostolate (giving all the glory to God)—of the signs by which it had been accompanied—of the width of its range, from Jerusalem to Illyricum—he may make a humble boast.

And he is still ambitious to preach in regions where Christ has not been named. He will not stay with them, because he has seen enough of the evil caused by those who built on a foundation which they had not laid; but he has often felt a strong desire to visit them on his way

---

[1] xv. 1—8.
[2] Deut. xxxii. 43; Ps. xviii. 49; cxvii. 1; Isa. xi. 10.
[3] xv. 16, Ἱερουργοῦντα. It is a ἅπ. λεγόμενον not due to any sacrificial conception of the Christian ministry (of which there is not in St. Paul so much as a single trace), but to the particular illustration which he here adopts.

to Spain,[1] and after a partial enjoyment of their society,[2] to be furthered on his journey by their assistance. He has hitherto been prevented from taking that journey, but now—since for the present his duties in the East are over—he hopes to carry it out, and to gratify his earnest desire to see them. At present, however, he is about to start for Jerusalem, to accompany the deputies who are to convey to the poor saints there that temporal gift from the Christians of Macedonia and Achaia which is after all but a small recognition of the spiritual gifts which the Gentiles have received from them. When this task is over he will turn his face towards Spain, and visit them on his way, and he is confident that he shall come in the fulness of the blessing of the Gospel of Jesus Christ. He, therefore, earnestly entreats their prayers that he may be rescued from the perils which he knows await him from the Jews in Jerusalem, and that the contribution due to his exertions may be favourably received by the saints, that so by God's will he may come to them in joy, and that they may mutually refresh each other.[3] "And the God of peace be with you all. Amen."[4]

There in all probability ended the Epistle to the Romans. I have already given abundant reason in support of the ingenious conjecture[5] that the greater part of the sixteenth chapter was addressed to the Ephesian Church.[6] Even a

---

[1] xv. 24 omit ἐλεύσομαι πρὸς ὑμᾶς with all the best MSS. "Having a desire for many years past to come to you whenever I journey into Spain."

[2] ἀπὸ μέρους "non quantum vellem sed quantum liceret" (Grot.).

[3] xv. 32, καὶ συναναπαύσωμαι ὑμῖν is omitted by B.

[4] xv. 9—33.

[5] First made by Schulz.

[6] We may be very thankful for its preservation, as it has a deep personal interest. On deaconesses see Bingham i. 334—366. Phœbe was probably a widow. Verse 4, ὑπέθηκαν, "laid their own necks under the axe," a probable allusion to some risk at Corinth (Acts xviii. 12; xix. 32). In verse 5 the true reading is Ἀσίας. Verse 7, συναιχμαλώτους—probably at Ephesus, ἐπίσημοι ἐν τοῖς ἀποστόλοις, "illustrious among the missionaries of the truth" (2 Cor. viii. 23; Acts xiv. 4), in the less restricted sense of the word. It is hardly conceivable that St. Paul would make it a merit that the Apostles knew them and thought highly of them (Gal. i. ii.)—verse 13. Rufus, perhaps one of the sons of Simon of Cyrene (Mark xv. 22)—verse 14. Hermas, not the author of *The Shepherd*, who could hardly have been born at this time. Verse 16, φίλημα ἅγιον, 1 Thess. v. 26; 1 Pet. v. 14; Luke vii. 45. The attempted identification of Tertius with Silas, because the Hebrew for Tertius (שְׁלִישִׁי) sounds like Silas, is one of the imbecilities of fanciful exegesis.

careless reader could scarcely help observing what we should not at all have conjectured from the earlier part of the Epistle that there were schisms and scandals (17—20) in the Roman Church, and teachers who deliberately fomented them, slaves of their own belly, and by their plausibility and flattery deceiving the hearts of the simple.[1] Nor, again, can any one miss the fact that the position of the Apostle towards his correspondents in verse 19 is far more severe, paternal, and authoritative than in the other chapters. If—as is surely an extremely reasonable supposition—St. Paul desired other Churches besides the stranger Church of Rome to reap the benefit of his ripest thoughts, and to read the maturest statement of the Gospel which he preached, then several copies of the main part of the Epistle must have been made by the amanuenses, of whom Tertius was one, and whose services the Apostle was at that moment so easily able to procure. In that case nothing is more likely than that the terminations of the various copies should have varied with the circumstances of the Churches, and nothing more possible than that in some one copy the various terminations should have been carefully preserved. We have at any rate in this hypothesis a simple explanation of the three final benedictions (20, 24, 27) which occur in this chapter alone.

The fullest of the Apostle's letters concludes with the most elaborate of his doxologies.[2]

On such names as Tryphæna and Tryphosa, voluptuous in sound and base in meaning, which may have suggested to St. Paul the κοπιάσας ἐν Κυρίῳ as a sort of noble *paronomasia*, see Merivale, *Hist.* vi. 260, and Wordsworth, *ad loc.*

[1] Phil. iii. 2, 18; 2 Cor. xi. 20.

[2] "Whether the Epistle proceeded in two forms from the Apostle's hands, the one closing with chapter xiv. and the doxology, the other extended by the addition of the two last chapters, or whether any other more satisfactory explanation can be offered of the phenomenon of omission, repetition, transposition, authenticity, must be left for further investigation." Westcott (Vaughan's *Romans*, p. xxv.). One theory is that xii.—xiv. were substituted later for xv. xvi., and then both were accumulated in one copy with some modifications.

FINAL DOXOLOGY.

"Now to Him who is able to establish you according to my Gospel, and the preaching of Jesus Christ, according to the revelation of the mystery, buried in silence in eternal ages, but manifested now and made known by the prophetic Scriptures, according to the command of the Eternal God unto obedience to the faith to all nations:—To the only wise God, through Jesus Christ—to whom be the glory for ever. Amen."

[1] Cf. Eph. iii. 20, 21. The text, as it stands, involves an anacoluthon, since the ᾧ should properly be ἐκείνῳ. Tholuck, &c., think that the Apostle was led by the parenthesis from a doxology to God to a doxology to Christ. It may be that he meant to insert the word χάρις, but lost sight of it in the length of the sentence. Here, as in Hab. iii. 6, the word αἰώνιος is used in two consecutive clauses, where in the first clause all are agreed that it *cannot* mean "endless" since it speaks of things which have already come to an end.

CHAPTER XL.

THE LAST JOURNEY TO JERUSALEM.

"Show me some one person formed according to the principles he professes. Show me one who is sick and happy; in danger and happy; dying and happy; exiled and happy; disgraced and happy."—EPICTETUS.

IT was now about the month of February, A.D. 58, and the work which St. Paul had set before him at Corinth was satisfactorily concluded. Having been nine months in Europe,[1] he was anxious to get to Jerusalem by the Passover, and intended to sail straight from Corinth to one of the ports of Palestine. Every preparation was made; it almost seems that he had got on board ship; when he was informed of a sudden[2] plot on the part of the Jews to murder him. As to all the details we are left in the dark. We know that the previous plot of the Jews, nearly five years earlier,[3] had been foiled by the contemptuous good sense of Gallio; but even if their revenge were otherwise likely to be laid aside, we cannot doubt that ample fuel had since been heaped upon the smouldering fire of their hatred. From every seaport of the Ægean, from the highlands of Asia Minor, from its populous shores, from Troas under the shadows of Mount Ida, to Athens under the shadow of Mount

---

[1] He left Ephesus before the Pentecost of A.D. 57.
[2] Acts xx. 3, μέλλοντι ἀνάγεσθαι, γενομένης.
[3] A.D. 53.

Pentelicus, they would hear rumours of that daring creed which seemed to trample on all their convictions, and fling to the Gentiles their most cherished hopes. The Jewish teachers who tried to hound the Judaising Christians against St. Paul would stand on perfectly good terms with them, and these Judaisers would take a pleasure in disseminating the deadliest misrepresentations of Paul's doctrine and career. But apart from all misrepresentation, his undeniable arguments were quite enough to madden them to frenzy. We may be sure that St. Paul taught as he wrote, and since we have noticed it as a characteristic of his intellect that he is haunted by *words* and expressions,[1] we might infer, *à priori*, even if it were not abundantly evident in his writings, that he is still more powerfully possessed and absorbed by any *thoughts* which might have been forced into immediate prominence. We may regard it as psychologically certain that his discourses at Corinth were the echo of the arguments which fill the two Epistles which he wrote at Corinth; and to the Jews the conclusions which they were meant to establish would be regarded as maddening blasphemies. "There is neither Jew nor Gentile"—where, then, is the covenant to Abraham and to his seed? "There is neither circumcision nor uncircumcision"—where, then, is Moses and all the splendour of Sinai? "Weak and beggarly elements"—are these the terms to apply to the inspired, sacred, eternal Thorah, in which God himself meditates, which is the glory of the world? We are not surprised that the Jews should get up a plot. Paul, under the ægis of Roman authority, might be safe in the city, but they would avenge themselves on him as soon as his ship had left the shore. The wealthy Jewish merchants of Corinth

---

[1] *V. supra*, I. pp. 481, 633; II. 65, 98; *infra*, 281.

would find no difficulty in hearing of sailors and captains of country vessels who were sufficiently dependent on them to do any deed of violence for a small consideration.

How was the plot discovered? We do not know. Scenes of tumult, and hairbreadth escapes, and dangerous adventures, were so common in St. Paul's life, that neither he, nor any one else, has cared to record their details. We only know that, after sudden discussion, it was decided, that Paul, with an escort of the delegates, quite sufficiently numerous to protect him from ordinary dangers, should go round by Macedonia. The hope of reaching Jerusalem by the Passover had, of course, to be abandoned; the only chance left was to get there by Pentecost. It was doubtless overruled for good that it should be so, for if St. Paul had been in the Holy City at the Passover he would have been mixed up by his enemies with the riot and massacre which about that time marked the insane rising of the Egyptian impostor who called himself the Messiah.[1]

Of the seven converts[2] who accompanied St. Paul—Sosipater son of Pyrrhus,[3] a Beroean, Aristarchus and Secundus of Thessalonica, Gaius of Derbe, Timotheus of Lystra, Tychicus and Trophimus of Ephesus, and Luke—all except the latter left him apparently at Philippi, and went on to Troas to await him there.[4] St. Luke was

---

[1] Verse 3, ἐγένετο γνώμη.

[2] In verse 4 the reading, ἀχρὶ τῆς Ἀσίας, is not quite certain, since it is omitted in ℵ, B, Coptic (both versions), and the Æthiopic. Some, at any rate, of the converts—Luke, Aristarchus, and Trophimus, if not others—accompanied him all the way to Jerusalem—xxi. 29, xxvii. 2, 1 Cor. xvi. 3, 4. How is it that there were no Corinthian delegates? Had the large promises of Corinth ended, after all, in words? or did they entrust their contributions to some of the other deputies?

[3] The Πύρρου was, perhaps, added to distinguish him from the Sosipater of Rom. xvi. 21, ℵ, A, B, D, E.

[4] Verse 5. If προσελθόντες (ℵ, A, B, E,) be the right reading, Tychicus and Trophimus must have met Paul at Troas.

closely connected with Philippi, where St. Paul had left him on his first visit,[1] and the two stayed at the Roman colony to keep the Passover. Very happy, we may be sure, was that quiet time spent by St. Paul in the bosom of the Church which he loved best of all—amid the most blameless and the most warm-hearted of all his converts. Years must have elapsed before he again spent a Passover in circumstances so peaceful and happy.[2]

The eight days of the feast ended in that year on Monday, April 3, and on the next day they set sail. Detained by calms, or contrary winds, they took five days[3] to sail to Troas, and there they again stayed seven days.[4] The delay was singular, considering the haste with which the Apostle was pressing forward to make sure of being at Jerusalem by Pentecost. It was now about the 10th of April, and as the Pentecost of that year fell on May 17, St. Paul, dependent as he was on the extreme uncertainties of ancient navigation, had not a single day to spare. We may be quite sure that it was neither the splendour of the town, with its granite temples and massive gymnasium, that detained him, nor all the archaic and poetic associations of its neighbourhood, nor yet the loveliness of the groves and mountains and gleams of blue sea. Although his former visits had been twice cut short—once by the Macedonian vision, and once by his anxiety to meet Titus—it is even doubtful whether he would have been kept there by the interest which he must have necessarily felt in the young and

---

[1] The first person plural is resumed in the narrative at xx. 5, having been abandoned at xvi. 17. It is now continued to the end of the Acts, and Luke seems to have remained with St. Paul to the last (2 Tim. iv. 11).

[2] Lewin, *Fasti Sacri*, § 1857.

[3] It had only taken them two days to sail from Troas to Neapolis, the port of Philippi, on a former occasion, xvi. 11.

[4] Compare xx. 6, xxi. 4, xxviii. 14.

flourishing Church of a town which was one of the very few in which he had not been subjected to persecution. The delay was therefore probably due to the difficulty of finding or chartering a vessel such as they required.[1]

Be that as it may, his week's sojourn was marked by a scene which is peculiarly interesting, as one of the few glimpses of ancient Christian worship which the New Testament affords. The wild disorders of vanity, fanaticism, and greed, which produced so strange a spectacle in the Church of Corinth, would give us, if we did not regard them as wholly exceptional, a most unfavourable conception of these Sunday assemblies. Very different, happily, is the scene to which we are presented on this April Sunday at Alexandria Troas, A.D. 58.[2]

It was an evening meeting. Whether at this period the Christians had already begun the custom of meeting twice,—early in the morning, before dawn, to sing and pray, and late in the evening to partake of the Love Feast and the Lord's Supper, as they did some fifty years after this time in the neighbouring province of Bithynia,[3]—we are not told. Great obscurity hangs over the observance of the Lord's day in the first century. The Jewish Christians doubtless continued to keep the Sabbath, but St. Paul reprobates the adoption of any such custom among the Gentiles; and, indeed, his language seems to show that he did not regard with favour any observance of times or seasons which savoured at all of Sabbatical scrupulosity.[4] All that we know is, that from the Resurrection onwards,

---

[1] 2 Cor. ii. 13.
[2] It was early called Sunday, even by Christians. τῇ τοῦ Ἡλίου λεγομένῃ ἡμέρᾳ (Just. Mart. *Apol.* ii. 228).
[3] Plin. *Ep.* x. 96. Quod essent soliti stato die *ante lucem* convenire . . . quibus peractis morem sibi discedendi fuisse rursusque coeundi ad capiendum cibum, promiscuum tamen et innoxium.
[4] Rom. xiv. 5; Gal. iv. 10; Col. ii. 16.

the first day of the week was signalised by special Christian gatherings for religious purposes, and that on this particular Sunday evening the members of the Church of Troas were assembled, in accordance with their usual custom, to partake of the Love Feast, and to commemorate the death of Christ in the Holy Communion.[1]

The congregation may have been all the more numerous because it was known that on the next day the Apostle and his little company would leave the place. They were gathered in one of those upper rooms on the third storey, which are the coolest and pleasantest part of an Eastern house. The labours of the day were over, and the sun had set, and as three weeks had now elapsed since the full moon of the Passover, there was but a pale crescent to dispel the darkness. But the upper room was full of lamps,[2] and in the earnestness of his overflowing heart, Paul, knowing by many a mysterious intimation the dangers which were awaiting him, continued discoursing to them till midnight. On the broad sill of one of the open windows, of which the lattice or enclosing shutter had been flung wide open to catch the cool sea breeze, sat a boy named Eutychus.[3] The hour was very late, the discourse unusually long, the topics with which it dealt probably beyond his comprehension. Though he was sitting in the pleasantest place in the room, where he would enjoy all the air there was, yet the heat of a crowded meeting, and the glare of the many lamps, and

---

[1] This is implied by the expression συνηγμένων ἡμῶν κλάσαι ἄρτον. Cf. the word ἐπισυναγωγή, Heb. x. 25, and σύναξις.

[2] This is with St. Luke the casual incident mentioned by an eye-witness, on whose mind the scene was vividly impressed. The lamps are sufficiently accounted for by the darkness, but the mention of them is valuable, as showing how little of secrecy or disorder attended these late meetings. They had not as yet become subjects of suspicion, but it was not long before they did.

[3] It is a common slave name, but nothing more is known of him.

the unbroken stream of the speaker's utterance,[1] sent the lad fast asleep. The graphic description of St. Luke might almost make us believe that he had been watching him, not liking, and perhaps not near enough to awaken him, and yet not wholly insensible of his danger, as first of all he began to nod, then his head gradually sank down on his breast, and, at last, he fell with a rush and cry from the third storey into the courtyard beneath.[2] We can imagine the alarm and excitement by which the voice of the speaker was suddenly interrupted, as some of the congregation ran down the outside staircase[3] to see what had happened. It was dark,[4] and the poor lad lay senseless, and "was taken up dead."[5] A cry of horror and wailing rose from the bystanders; but Paul, going down-stairs, fell on him, and clasping his arms round him,[6] said, "Do not be alarmed, for his life is in him." After he had calmed the excitement by this remark, he left the lad to the effects of rest and quiet, and the kindly care, perhaps, of the deaconesses and other women who were present; for the narrative simply adds that the Apostle went up-stairs again, and after "breaking the bread,"[7]—words descriptive probably of the eucharistic consecration—and making a meal, which describes the subsequent Agapê, he continued in friendly intercourse with the congregation till the dawn of day, and then went

---

[1] Ver. 9, διαλεγομένου τοῦ Παύλου ἐπὶ πλεῖον.

[2] Vs. 9. καταφερόμενος ὕπνῳ βαθεῖ . . . κατενεχθεὶς ἀπὸ τοῦ ὕπνου ἔπεσεν. καταφέρεσθαι is a vox solemnis de hâc re. Aristot. de Insomniis, iii. &c.

[3] ἀναβαθμοί.

[4] Being now late at night, the crescent moon must have set.

[5] De Wette, Olshausen, Meyer, Ewald, and many others, take νεκρὸς to mean "as dead," "apparently dead," "in a dead swoon," interpreting this word by St. Paul's μὴ θορυβεῖσθε . . γάρ, but the ἤγαγον . . . ζῶντα of vs. 12 seems to show St. Luke's meaning.

[6] ἐπιπεσὼν . . . συμπεριλαβὼν, 1 Kings xvii. 21; 2 Kings iv. 34.

[7] Vs. 11. κλάσας τὸν ἄρτον, καὶ γευσάμενος.

out. By that time Eutychus had fully recovered. "They led the boy alive"—apparently into the upper chamber—"and were not a little comforted."

Next day the delegates—these "first Christian pilgrims to the Holy Land"—went down to their vessel to sail round Cape Lectum, while Paul went by land[1] across the base of the promontory to rejoin them at Assos. Whether he had friends to visit on the way, or whether he wished to walk those twenty miles through the pleasant oak-groves along the good Roman roads in silent commune with his own spirit, we do not know. Natures like his, however strong may be their yearning for sympathy, yet often feel an imperious necessity for solitude. If he had heard the witty application by Stratonicus, of Homer's line,

Ἆσσον ἴθ᾽ ὥς κεν θᾶσσον ὀλέθρου τέρμαθ᾽ ἵκηαι,

he might, while smiling at the gay jest directed against the precipitous descent from the town to the harbour, have thought that for him too—on his way to bonds and imprisonment, and perhaps to death itself—there was a melancholy meaning in the line.[2] Passing between the vast sarcophagi in the street of tombs, and through the ancient gate which still stands in ruin, he made his way down the steep descent to the port, and there found the vessel awaiting him. St. Luke, who was one of those on board, here gives a page of his diary, as the ship winged her way among the isles of Greece. The voyage seems to have been entirely prosperous. The north-west wind which prevails at that season would daily swell the great main-sail, and waft the vessel merrily through blue

---

[1] πεζεύειν—possibly, but not necessarily, on foot.
[2] *Il.* vi. 143. The pun may be freely rendered "Go to Assos, if you want to meet your fate." The Vulgate, too, confuses the name Assos and the adverb *asson* ("near") in xxvii. 13.

seas under the shadow of old poetic mountains, by famous cities, along the vernal shores. That same evening they arrived at Mitylene, the bright capital of Lesbos, the home of Sappho and Alcæus, and the cradle of lyric song. Here they anchored because the moonless night rendered it unsafe to thread their course among the many intricacies of that sinuous coast. Next day they anchored off rocky Chios, whose green fields were the fabled birthplace of Homer.[1] Next day they touched for a short time at Samos, and then sailed across the narrow channel to anchor for the night in the island-harbour of Trogyllium, under the ridge of Mycale, so famous for Conon's victory. Next day, sailing past the entrance of the harbour of Ephesus, they came to anchor at Miletus. St. Paul would gladly have visited Ephesus if time had permitted, but he was so anxious to do all in his power to reach Jerusalem by Pentecost, and therefore to avoid all delays, whether voluntary or accidental, that he resisted the temptation. At Miletus, however, the vessel had to stop, and Paul determined to utilise the brief delay. He had probably arrived about noon, and at once sent a messenger to the elders of the Church of Ephesus to come and see him.[2] It was but a distance of from thirty to forty miles along a well-kept road, and the elders[3] might easily be with him by the next day, which, reckoning from his departure at Troas, was probably a Sunday. He spent the day in their company, and before parting delivered them an address which

---

[1] τυφλὸς ἀνὴρ οἰκεῖ δὲ Χίῳ ἐνὶ παιπαλοέσσῃ (ap. Thuc. iii. 104).

[2] It is impossible to determine whether the vessel had been chartered by Paul and his companions, or whether they were dependent on its movements. Verse 16 is not decisive.

[3] It is of course known that the words "presbyter" and "bishop" are used interchangeably in the New Testament (see ver. 28, where the E.V. has "overseers" for "bishops.") Ἐπισκόπους τοὺς πρεσβυτέρους καλεῖ ἀμφότερα γὰρ εἶχεν κατ' ἐκεῖνον τὸν καιρὸν τὰ ὀνόματα (Theodor. ad Phil. i. 1).

abounds in his peculiar forms of expression, and gives a deeply interesting sketch of his work at Ephesus.

"Ye know," he said, "how from the first day on which I set foot in Asia I bore myself with you, serving the Lord with all lowly-mindedness, and tears, and trials that happened to me in the plots of the Jews;[1] how I reserved nothing that was profitable,[2] but preached to you, and taught you publicly, and from house to house, testifying both to Jews and Greeks repentance towards God and faith towards our Lord Jesus Christ. And now behold I, bound in the spirit,[3] am on my way to Jerusalem, not knowing what may happen to me there, save that in every city the Holy Spirit testifies to me, saying that bonds and tribulations await me. But I regard it as of no moment, nor do I hold my soul so precious to myself[4] as to finish my course,[5] and the ministry which I received from the Lord Jesus to testify[6] the Gospel of the grace of God. And now behold I know

---

[1] These are not mentioned in the narrative. This is one of the many casual indications that St. Luke knew many more particulars than it entered into his plan to detail.

[2] Vs. 20, ὑπεστειλάμην (lit. "reefed up"). The nautical word (cf. πληροφορία, Col. ii. 2, iv. 12; στελλόμενοι, 2 Thess. iii. 6; 2 Cor. viii. 20), so natural in a speaker who must have heard the word every day in his voyage, is very characteristic of St. Paul, who constantly draws his metaphors from the sights and circumstances immediately around him. He uses it again in vs. 27. These little peculiarities of style are quite inimitable, and, as Ewald says, "to doubt the genuineness of this speech is folly itself." Besides many other indications of authenticity, it contains at least a dozen phrases and constructions which are more or less exclusively Pauline.

[3] Vs. 22. Though the true order is δεδεμένος ἐγὼ, ℵ, A, B, C, E, the emphasis is best brought out in English, by putting "I" first.

[4] In the extreme varieties of the MSS. in this clause I follow ℵ, οὐδενὸς λόγου —οὐδὲ ἔχω. This is the very spirit of Luther on his way to Worms.

[5] Omit μετὰ χαρᾶς with ℵ, A, B, D. It is interpolated from Phil. i. 4; Col. i. 11; cf. 2 Tim. iv. 7.

[6] The third time that this verb has occurred in these few verses. It is quite true of St. Paul that "un mot l'obsède." This is an interesting sign of the genuineness of the speech.

that ye shall never see my face again, all you among whom I passed proclaiming the kingdom.[1] Therefore, I call you to witness this very day that I am pure from the blood of all. For I reserved nothing, but preached to you the whole counsel of God. Take heed, then, to yourselves, and to all the flock over which the Holy Ghost appointed you bishops to feed the Church of the Lord[2] which He made His own by His own blood. I know that

---

[1] St. Paul speaks partly with a view to the dangers he is about to face, partly with reference to his intention to go to the far west. His οἶδα was not necessarily infallible (compare Phil. i. 25 with ii. 24), and in point of fact it is probable that he *did* visit Ephesus again (1 Tim. i. 3, iii. 14, iv. 12—20). But that was long afterwards, and it is quite certain that as a body (πάντες ὑμεῖς) the elders never saw him again.

[2] I accept the reading Κυρίου here with A, C, D, E, the Coptic, Sahidic, Armenian versions, Irenæus, Didymus, Cyril, Jerome, Augustine, &c., rather than Θεοῦ, the remarkable reading of א, B, the Vulgate, Syriac, Chrysostom, Basil, Ambrose, &c., because "the blood of God" is an expression which, though adopted—perhaps from the variation of this very text—by some of the Fathers (Tert. *ad Uxor.* ii. 3), the Church has always avoided. Athanasius, indeed, distinctly says, οὐδαμοῦ δὲ αἷμα Θεοῦ δίχα σαρκὸς παραδεδώκασιν αἱ γραφαί. That St. Paul held in the most absolute sense the Divinity of the Eternal Son is certain; but he would never have said, and never has said, anything like "the blood of God," and I cannot but think it much more probable that he would have used the uncommon but perfectly natural expression "*Church of the Lord*," than seem to sanction the very startling "blood of God." I cannot attach much, if any, importance to the fact that "Church of the Lord" is a less usual combination than "Church of God;" for just in the same way St. Paul, in the Epistle to the Philippians, abandons his favourite expression of "the day of the Lord," and uses instead "day of Christ" (Phil. i. 10, ii. 16). If he had written Θεοῦ, it seems to me very improbable that the reading would have been early tampered with. Such a phrase would rank with terms like *Adelphotheos* and *Theotokos*, which are at once unscriptural and ecclesiastical, whereas, if St. Paul said Κυρίου, the *marginal* Θεοῦ of some pragmatic scribe might easily have obtruded itself into the text. Indeed, the very fact that "Church of the Lord" is not Paul's normal phrase may have suggested the gloss. If, however, Θεοῦ be the right reading, the nominative to περιεποιήσατο may simply have been suppressed by a grammatical inadvertency of the Apostle or his amanuensis. (See further, Scrivener, *Introd.* 540.) The mysterious doctrine of the περιχώρησις is one which the Apostle always treats with deepest reverence, and such a collocation as αἷμα Θεοῦ would have given at least *primâ facie* countenance to all kinds of Sabellian, Eutychian, and Patripassian heresies. (I have made some further remarks on this reading in the *Expositor*, May, 1879.)

there shall come after my departure grievous wolves among you, not sparing the flock; and from your own selves[1] shall arise men speaking perverse things, so as to drag away disciples after them. Therefore be watchful, remembering that for three years, night and day,[2] I ceased not with tears[3] to admonish each one. And now I commend you to God, and to the word of His grace, who is able to build you up, and give you an inheritance among all the sanctified. No man's silver or gold or raiment did I covet. Yourselves know that to my needs, and to those with me, these hands"—and there he held up those thin, toilworn hands before them all—"these hands ministered. In all things I set you the example, that, thus labouring, you ought to support the weak, and to remember the words of the Lord Jesus, how He said, 'It is blessed rather to give than to receive.'"[4]

After these words, which so well describe the unwearied thoroughness, the deep humility, the perfect tenderness, of his Apostolic ministry, he knelt down with them all, and prayed. They were overpowered with the touching solemnity of the scene. He ended his prayer amidst a burst of weeping, and as they bade him farewell—anxious for his future, anxious for their own—they each laid their heads on his neck,[5] and passionately kissed him,[6] pained above all at his remark that never again should they gaze,

---

[1] This sad prediction was but too soon fulfilled (1 Tim. i. 20; Rev. ii. 6; 1 John ii. 19).

[2] Undoubtedly this expression—though not meant to be taken *au pied de la lettre*—tells against the theory of a visit to Corinth during this period.

[3] Tears are thrice mentioned in this short passage—tears of suffering (19); of pastoral solicitude (31); and of personal affection (37). Monod, *Cinq Discours* (*Les Larmes de St. Paul*).

[4] The only "unwritten saying" (ἄγραφον δόγμα) of our Lord in the New Testament not preserved for us in the Gospels.

[5] cf. Gen. xlv. 14, xlvi. 29.

[6] κατεφίλουν, deosculabantur (cf. Matt. xxvi. 49).

as they had gazed so often,[1] on the dear face of the teacher who had borne so much for their sakes, and whom they loved so well. If Paul inspired intense hatreds, yet, with all disadvantages of person, he also inspired intense affection. He had—to use the strong expression[2] of St. Luke —to tear himself from them. Sadly, and with many forebodings, they went down with him to the vessel, which was by this time awaiting him ; and we may be very sure that Paul was weeping bitterly as he stepped on board, and that sounds of weeping were long heard upon the shore, until the sails became a white speck on the horizon, and with heavy hearts the Elders of Ephesus turned away to face once more, with no hope of help from their spiritual father, the trials that awaited them in the city of Artemis.

The wind blew full in favour of the voyagers, and before the evening they had run with a straight course to Cos. Neither the wines, nor the purple, nor the perfumes of Cos, would have much interest for the little band ;[3] but, if opportunity offered, we may be sure that "the beloved physician" would not miss the opportunity of seeing all that he could of the scientific memorials of the Asclepiadæ—the great medical school of the ancient world. Next day the little vessel rounded the promontory of Cnidus, and sped on for Rhodes, where, as they entered the harbour, they would admire the proverbial fertility of the sunny island of roses, and gaze with curiosity on the prostrate mass of its vast Colossus, of which two legs still stood on their pedestal,[4] though the huge mass of bronze had been hurled down by an earthquake, there to stay till,

---

[1] Vs. 38, θεωρεῖν. He had only said ὄψεσθε (cf. John xx. 5, 6). The word implies the feeling here alluded to.
[2] xxi. 1, ἀποσπασθέντας ἀπ' αὐτῶν (cf. Luke xxii. 41).
[3] Strab. xiv. 2; Hor. Od. iv. 13, 13; Athen. x. 688 (Alf.).
[4] Plin. H. N., xxxiv. 18; Strab. xiv. 2.

thirteen centuries later, they were broken up, and carried away on 900 camels, to be the ignoble spoil of a Jew.[1] The monstrous image—one of the wonders of the world—was a figure of the sun; and, with whatever lingering artistic sympathy it might have been regarded by the Gentile converts, St. Paul would perhaps think with a smile of Dagon, "when he fell flat, and shamed his worshippers," or point to it as a symbol of the coming day when all idols should be abolished at the returning dawn of the Sun of Righteousness. The empire of the sea, which this huge statue had been reared to commemorate, had not passed away more completely than the worship of Apollo should pass away; and to St. Paul the work of Chares of Lindos, spite of all its grace and beauty, was but a larger idol, to be regarded with pity, whereas the temple reared to that idol by the apostate Idumean usurper who had called himself king of the Jews could only be looked upon with righteous scorn.[2]

Next day, passing the seven capes which terminate the mountain ridge of "verdant Cragus," and the mouth of the yellow river which gave its name of Xanthus to the capital of Lycia, and so catching a far-off glimpse of temples rich with the marbles which now adorn our British Museum, the vessel which bore so much of the fortune of the future, turned her course eastward to Patara. Beneath the hill which towered over its amphitheatre rose also amid its palm-trees, the temple and oracle of Apollo Patareus. A single column, and a pit,—used possibly for some of the trickeries of superstition,—alone remain as a monument of its past splendour;[3] and it was due in no small measure to the life's work of the

---

[1] Cedrenus, *Hist.* p. 431.
[2] The Pythium.
[3] Sprat and Forbes, i. 30; ap. C. and H. ii. 232.

poor Jewish Apostle who now looked up at the vast world-famed shrine, that Christian poets would tell in later days how

> "The oracles are dumb,
>   No voice nor hideous hum
> Runs through the arched roof in words deceiving;
>   Apollo from his shrine
>   Can no more divine,
> With hollow shriek the steep of Delphos leaving;
>   No nightly trance or breathed spell
> Inspires the pale-eyed priest from the prophetic cell."

They could now no longer avail themselves of the vessel in which so far they had accomplished a prosperous, and, in spite of all misgivings, a happy voyage. Either its course ended there, or it would continue to coast along the shores of Pamphylia and Cilicia. But here they were fortunate enough to find another vessel bound straight for Phœnicia, and they at once went on board, and weighed anchor. Once more they were favoured by wind and wave. Sailing with unimpeded course—through sunlight and moonlight—at the rate of a hundred miles a day, they caught sight[1] at dawn of the snowy peaks of Cyprus, and passing by Paphos—where Paul would be reminded of Sergius Paulus and Elymas—in some four days, they put in at Tyre, where their ship was to unload its cargo. The Apostle must have ceased to feel anxiety about being at Jerusalem by Pentecost, since, owing to providential circumstances, he had now a full fortnight to spare. There were some disciples at Tyre, and St. Paul may have seen them on previous occasions;[2] but in so populous and

---

[1] xxi. 3, ἀναφάναντες, cf. aperire (see Ps. Lucian, *Ver. Hist.* § 33, p. 687); the opposite technical term is, ἀποκρύπτειν, abscondere (Thuc. v. 65; Virg. *Æn.* iii. 275, 291).

[2] Acts xxvi. 20; Gal. i. 21.

busy a town it required a little effort to find them.[1] With them Paul stayed his usual period of seven days, and they by the Spirit told him not to go to Jerusalem. He knew, however, all that they could tell him of impending danger, and he too was under the guidance of the same Spirit which urged him along—a fettered but willing captive. When the week was over[2] St. Paul left them; and so deeply in that brief period had he won their affections, that all the members of the little community, with their wives and children, started with him to conduct him on his way. Before they reached the vessel they knelt down side by side, men and women and little ones, somewhere on the surf-beat rocks[3] near which the vessel was moored, to pray together—he for them, and they for him—before they returned to their homes; and he went once more on board for the last stage of his voyage from Tyre to Ptolemais, the modern Acre. There they finally left their vessel, and went to greet the disciples, with whom they stayed for a single day, and then journeyed by land across the plain of Sharon—bright at that time with a thousand flowers of spring—the forty-four miles which separate

---

[1] xxi. 4, ἀνευρόντες τοὺς μαθητάς, "Seeking out the disciples," not as in E. V. "finding disciples."

[2] xxi. 5. ἐξαρτίσαι usually means "to refit," but here with ἡμέρας it seems to mean "complete." Hesychius makes it equivalent to τελειῶσαι, and so Theophylact and Œcumenius understood it. Meyer is probably mistaken in giving the word its first meaning here.

[3] Ver. 5, αἰγιαλόν. Cf. xxvii. 39. There is, indeed, a long range of sandy shore between Tyre and Sidon, but near the city there are also rocky places. Dr. Hackett, ad loc., quotes a strikingly parallel experience of an American missionary, Mr. Schneider, at Anîtab, near Tarsus :—" More than a hundred converts accompanied us out of the city; and there, near the spot where one of our number had once been stoned, we halted, and a prayer was offered, amid tears. Between thirty and forty escorted us two hours farther . . Then another prayer was offered, and with saddened countenances and with weeping they forcibly broke away from us. (Cf. ἀποσπασθέντας, ver. 1.) It really seemed as though they could not turn back."

Acre from Cæsarea. Here St. Paul lingered till the very eve of the feast. Ready to face danger when duty called, he had no desire to extend the period of it, or increase its certainty. At Cæsarea, therefore, he stayed with his companions for several days, and they were the last happy days of freedom which for a long time he was destined to spend. God graciously refreshed his spirit by this brief interval of delightful intercourse and rest. For at Cæsarea they were the guests of one who must have been bound to Paul by many ties of the deepest sympathy—Philip the Evangelist. A Hellenist like himself, and a liberal Hellenist, Philip, as Paul would have been most glad to recognise, had been the first to show the large sympathy and clear insight, without which Paul's own work would have been impossible. It was Philip who had evangelised the hated Samaritans; it was Philip who had had the courage to baptise the Ethiopian eunuch. The lots of these two noble workers had been closely intertwined. It was the furious persecution of Saul the Pharisee which had scattered the Church of Jerusalem, and thus rendered useless the organisation of the seven deacons. It was in flight from that persecution that the career of Philip had been changed. On the other hand, that new career had initiated the very line of conduct which was to occupy the life of Paul the Apostle. As Paul and Philip talked together in those few precious hours, there must have flourished up in their minds many a touching reminiscence of the days when the light of heaven, which had once shone on the face of Stephen upturned to heaven in the agony of martyrdom, had also flashed in burning apocalypse on the face of a young man whose name was Saul. And besides a community of thoughts and memories, the house of Philip was hallowed by the gentle ministries of four daughters who, looking for the coming of

Christ, had devoted to the service of the Gospel their virgin lives.[1]

To this happy little band of believers came down from Judæa the Prophet Agabus, who, in the early days of St. Paul's work at Antioch, had warned the Church of the impending famine. Adopting the symbolic manner of the ancient prophets,[2] he came up to Paul, unbound the girdle which fastened his *cetôneth*, and tying with it his own feet and hands said, "Thus saith the Holy Spirit, Thus shall the Jews in Jerusalem bind the man whose girdle this is, and shall deliver him into the hands of the Gentiles." They had long been aware of the peril of the intended visit, but no intimation had been given them so definite as this, nor had they yet foreseen that a Jewish assault would necessarily end in a Roman imprisonment. On hearing it, St. Paul's companions earnestly entreated him to stay where he was, while they went to Jerusalem to convey the Gentile contribution; and the members of the Cæsarean Church joined their own tears and entreaties to those of his beloved companions. Why should he face a certain peril? Why should he endanger an invaluable life? Since the Spirit had given him so many warnings, might there not be even something of presumption in thus exposing himself in the very stronghold of his most embittered enemies? St. Paul was not insensible to their loving entreaties and arguments; there might have been an excuse, and something more than an excuse, for him had he decided that it was most unwise to persist in his intentions; but it was not so to be. His purpose was inflexible. No voices of even prophets should turn him aside from obedience to a call which he felt to be from God. A captive bound to Christ's triumphant chariot-wheel, what could he do?

[1] Cf. Plin. *Ep.* x. 96.
[2] Cf. 1 Kings xxii. 11; Isa. xx. 2; Jer. xiii. 1, &c.

What could he do but thank God even if the Gospel, which was to some an aroma of life, became to him an aroma of earthly death? When the finger of God has pointed out the path to a noble soul, it will not swerve either to the right hand or the left. "What are ye doing, weeping and breaking my heart?" he said. "I am willing not only to go to Jerusalem to be bound, but even to die, for the name of the Lord Jesus." They saw that further importunity would be painful and useless—

> "He saw a hand they could not see
> Which beckoned him away,
> He heard a voice they could not hear
> Which would not let him stay."

They desisted and wiped away their tears, saying, "The Lord's will be done."

Too soon the happy days of rest and loving intercourse came to an end. It was seventy-five miles, an ordinary three days' journey, from Cæsarea to Jerusalem. That year the feast began at sunset on Wednesday, May 17.[1] The last day at Cæsarea was a Sunday. Next day they packed up their baggage[2]—and it was precious, for it contained the *chaluka*—and, accompanied by some of the Cæsarean converts, who, with multitudes of other Jews, were streaming up to Jerusalem on that last day before the feast began,[3] they started for the Holy City, with hearts on which rested an ever-deepening shadow. The crowd at these gatherings was so immense that the ordinary stranger might well fail to find accommodation, and be driven to some

---

[1] *Fasti Sacri*, No. 1857.

[2] Verse 15. Leg. ἐπισκευασάμενοι, א, A, B, E, G, and a mass of cursives. In the E. V. "carriages" means "baggage:" cf. Judges xviii. 21; 1 Sam. xvii. 22; Isa. x. 28. "We trussed up our fardeles," Genev. Vers.

[3] That St. Paul had only arrived on the very eve of the feast may be at once inferred from Acts xxiv. 11.

temporary booth outside the walls. But the brethren had taken care to secure for Paul and his delegates a shelter in the house of Mnason, a Cyprian, and one of the original disciples. St. Paul seems to have had a sister living at Jerusalem, but we do not know that she was a Christian, and in any case her house—which might be well known to many Tarsian Jews—would be an uncertain resting-place for an endangered man. And so for the fifth time since his conversion Paul re-entered Jerusalem. He had rarely entered it without some cause for anxiety, and there could have been scarcely one reminiscence which it awoke that was not infinitely painful. The school of Gamaliel, the Synagogue of the Libertines, the house where the High Priest had given him his commission to Damascus, the spot where the reddened grass had drunk the blood of Stephen must all have stirred painful memories. But never had he trod the streets of the Holy City with so deep a sadness as now that he entered it, avoiding notice as much as possible, in the little caravan of Cæsarean pilgrims and Gentile converts. He was going into a city where friends were few, and where well-nigh every one of the myriads among whom he moved was an actual or potential enemy, to whom the mere mention of his name might be enough to make the dagger flash from its scabbard, or to startle a cry of hatred which would be the signal for a furious outbreak. But he was the bearer of help, which was a tangible proof of his allegiance to the mother church, and the brethren whom he saw that evening at the house of Mnason gave him a joyous welcome. It may have cheered his heart for a moment, but it did not remove the deep sense that he was in that city which was the murderess of the Prophets. He knew too well the burning animosity which he kindled, because he remembered too well what had been his own, and that of his party, against the Christian Hellenists of old. The wrath which he had then felt was now a furnace heated sevenfold against himself.

The next day till sunset was marked by the ceremonies of the feast, and the greater part of it was spent by St. Paul and his little company in an assembly of the elders, who met to receive him under the presidency of James.[1] The elders were already assembled when the visitors came in, and we may imagine that it was with something more than a thrill of curiosity—that it must have been with an almost painful shyness—that "timid provincial neophytes" like Timothy and Trophimus (the latter especially, an uncircumcised Gentile, whom his teacher had encouraged to regard himself as entirely emancipated from the Jewish law)—found themselves in the awful presence of James, the Lord's brother—James, the stern, white-robed, mysterious prophet, and the conclave of his but half-conciliated Judaic presbyters. No misgiving could assail them in their own free Asiatic or Hellenic homes; but here in Jerusalem, in "the Holy, the Noble city," under the very shadow of the Temple, face to face with zealots and Pharisees, it required nothing less than the genius of a Paul to claim without shadow of misgiving that divine freedom which was arraigned in the name of a history rich in miracles, and a whole literature of inspired books. That free spirit was a lesson which the Jews themselves as a body could not learn. It required, indeed, the earthquake shock which laid their temple in ruins, and scattered their nationality to the four winds of heaven, effectively to teach them the futility of the convictions

[1] As none of the Twelve are mentioned, it is probable that none were present. The twelve years which, as tradition tells us, had been fixed by Christ for their stay in Jerusalem, had long elapsed, and they were scattered on their various missions to evangelise the world. St. Luke was aware of the contributions brought by St. Paul (xxiv. 17), though he does not mention them here.

to which they so passionately clung. They would have resisted without end the logic of argument had not God Himself in due time refuted their whole theology by the irresistible logic of facts. The destruction of Jerusalem did more to drive them from an immemorial "orthodoxy" than the Epistles of St. Paul himself.

As we read the narrative of the Acts in the light of the Epistles, it is difficult to resist the impression that the meeting between the Apostle and the Elders of Jerusalem was cold. It is, of course, certain that the first object of the meeting was the presentation of the contribution from which Paul had hoped so much. One by one he would call forward the beloved delegates, that they might with their own hands lay at the feet of James the sums of money which his Gentile Churches had contributed out of their deep poverty, and which in many and many a coin bore witness to weeks of generous self-denial. There lay all this money, a striking proof of the faithfulness with which Paul, at any rate, had carried out his share of the old compact at Jerusalem, when—almost by way of return for concessions which the Judaisers had done their best to render nugatory—the Three had begged him to be mindful of the poor. It must have been a far larger bounty than they had any reason to expect, and on this occasion, if ever, we might surely have looked for a little effusive sympathy, a little expansive warmth, on the part of the community which had received so tangible a proof of the Apostle's kindness. Yet we are not told about a word of thanks, and we see but too plainly that Paul's hardly disguised misgiving as to the manner in which his gift would be accepted[1] was confirmed. Never in any age have the recipients of alms at Jerusalem been remarkable

---

[1] Rom. xv. 31.

for gratitude.[1] Was the gratitude of the Zealots and Pharisees of the community extinguished in this instance by the fact that one of the bags of money was carried by the hands of an uncircumcised Gentile? Had it been otherwise, nothing would have lain more entirely in the scope of St. Luke's purpose to record. Though some at least of the brethren received Paul gladly, the Elders of the Church had not hurried on the previous evening to greet and welcome him, and subsequent events prove too clearly that his chief reward lay in the sense of having done and taught to his converts what was kind and right, and not in any softening of the heart of the Judaic Christians. Gratitude is not always won by considerateness. The collection for the saints occupies many a paragraph in St. Paul's Epistles, as it had occupied many a year of his thoughts. But there is little or no recorded recognition of his labour of love by the recipients of the bounty which but for him could never have been collected.

When the presentation was over, Paul narrated in full detail[2] the work he had done, and the Churches which he had confirmed or founded in that third journey, of which we have seen the outline. What love and exultation should such a narrative have excited! All that we are told is, that "they, on hearing it, glorified God, and said"— what? The repetition, the echo, of bitter and even deadly reproaches against St. Paul, coupled with a suggestion which, however necessary they may have deemed it, was none the less humiliating. "You observe, brother, how many myriads of the Jews there are that have embraced the faith, and they are all zealots of the Law." The expression is a startling one. Were there, indeed, at that

---

[1] Witness the treatment in recent days of Sir M. Montefiore and Dr. Frankl, after conferring on them the largest pecuniary benefits.
[2] xxi. 19, καθ' ἓν ἕκαστον.

early date "*many myriads*" of Jewish Christians, when we know how insignificant numerically were the Churches even at such places as Rome and Corinth, and when we learn how small was the body of Christians which, a decade later, took refuge at Pella from the impending ruin of Jerusalem? If we are to take the expression literally—if there were even as many as *two* myriads of Christians who were all zealous for the Law, it only shows how fatal was the risk that the Church would be absorbed into a mere slightly-differentiated synagogue. At any rate, the remark emphasised the extreme danger of the Apostle's position in that hotbed of raging fanaticism, especially when they added, "And they"—all these myriads who have embraced the faith and are zealots of the Law!—"have been studiously indoctrinated[1] with the belief about you, that you teach APOSTASY FROM MOSES, telling all THE JEWS of the dispersion not to circumcise their children, and not to walk in obedience to the customs. What then is the state of affairs? That a crowd will assemble is quite certain; for they will hear that you have come. At once then do what we tell you. We have four men who have a vow upon them. Take them, be purified with them, and pay their expenses that they may get their heads shaved. All will then recognise that there is nothing in all which has been so carefully inculcated into them about you, but that you yourself also walk in observance of the Law. But as regards the *Gentiles* that have embraced the faith, we enjoined their exemption from everything of this kind, deciding only that they should keep themselves from meat offered to idols, and blood, and strangled, and fornication."

What did this proposal mean? It meant that the emancipation from the vow of the Nazarite could only

---

[1] Ver. 21, κατηχήθησαν. Very much stronger than the E. V., "they are informed."

take place at Jerusalem, and in the Temple, and that it was accompanied by offerings so costly that they were for a poor man impossible. A custom had therefore sprung up by which rich men undertook to defray the necessary expenses, and this was regarded as an act of charity and piety. The Jews, indeed, looked so favourably on a species of liberality which rendered it possible for the poor no less than the rich to make vows at moments of trial and danger, that when Agrippa I. paid his first visit to Jerusalem, he had paid the expenses which enabled a large number of Nazarites to shave their heads,[1] not only because he wished to give an ostentatious proof of his respect for the Levitical law, but also because he knew that this would be a sure method of acquiring popularity with the Pharisaic party. The person who thus defrayed the expenses was supposed so far to share the vow, that he was required to stay with the Nazarites during the entire week, which, as we gather from St. Luke, was the period which must elapse between the announcement to the priest of the termination of the vow and his formal declaration that it had been legally completed.[2] For a week then, St. Paul, if he accepted the advice of James and the presbyters, would have to live with four paupers in the chamber of the Temple which was set apart for this purpose; and then to pay for sixteen sacrificial animals and the accompanying meat offerings; and to stand among these Nazarites while the priest offered four he-lambs of the first year without blemish for burnt offerings, and four ewe-lambs of the first year without blemish for sin offerings, and four rams without

---

[1] Jos. *Antt.* xix. 6, § 1, εἰς Ἱεροσόλυμα ἐλθὼν χαριστηρίους ἐξεπλήρωσε θυσίας οὐδὲν τῶν κατὰ νόμον ἀπολιπών. διὸ καὶ Ναζιραίων ξυρᾶσθαι διέταξε μάλα συχνούς.

[2] Neither the Talmud nor the Pentateuch mentions this circumstance. Numb. vi. 9, 10 refers only to the cases of accidental pollution during the period of the vow. It may have been on the analogy of this rule that a week was fixed as the period of purification.

blemish for peace offerings; and then, to look on while the men's heads were being shaved and while they took their hair to burn it under the boiling caldron of the peace offerings, and while the priest took four sodden shoulders of rams and four unleavened cakes out of the four baskets, and four unleavened wafers anointed with oil, and put them on the hands of the Nazarites, and waved them for a wave-offering before the Lord—which, with the wave-breads and the heave-shoulders, the priest afterwards took as his own perquisites. And he was to do all this, not only to disprove what was undoubtedly a calumny if taken strictly—namely, that he had taught the Jews apostasy from Moses (as though his whole Gospel was this mere negation!)—but also to prove that there was no truth in the reports about him, but that he also was a regular observer of the Law.

That it was an expensive business was nothing. Paul, poor as he had now become, could not, of course, pay unless he had the money wherewith to pay it; and if there were any difficulty on this score, its removal rested with those who made the proposal. But *was* the charge against him false in spirit as well as in letter? Was it true that he valued, and—at any rate with anything approaching to scrupulosity—still observed the Law? Would there not be in such conduct on his part something which might be dangerously misrepresented as an abandonment of principle? If those Judaisers on whom he did not spare to heap such titles as "false apostles," "false brethren," "deceitful workers," "dogs," "emissaries of Satan," "the concision,"[1] had shaken the allegiance of his converts by charging him with inconsistency before, would they not have far more ground to do so

[1] 2 Cor. xi. 13; Gal. ii. 4; Phil. iii. 2; 2 Cor. xi. 13.

now? It is true that at the close of his second journey he had spontaneously taken on himself the vow of the Nazarite. But since that time circumstances had widely altered. At that time the animosity of those false brethren was in abeyance; they had not dogged his footsteps with slander; they had not beguiled his converts into legalism; they had not sent their adherents to undo his teaching and persuade his own churches to defy his authority. And if all these circumstances were changed, he too was changed since then. His faith had never been the stereotype of a shibboleth, or the benumbing repetition of a phrase. His life, like the life of every good and wise man, was a continual education. His views during the years in which he lived exclusively among Gentile churches and in great cities had been rendered clearer and more decided. Not to speak of the lucid principles which he had sketched in the Epistles to the Corinthians, he had written the Epistle to the Galatians, and had developed the arguments there enunciated in the Epistle to the Romans. It had been the very object of those Epistles to establish the nullity of the Law for all purposes of justification. The man who had written that the teaching of the Judaisers was a quite different gospel to his, and that any one who preached it was accursed [1]—who had openly charged Peter with tergiversation for living Judaically after having lived in Gentile fashion [2]—who had laid it down as his very thesis that "from works of Law no flesh shall be justified"[3]—who had said that to build again what he destroyed was to prove himself a positive transgressor [4]—who had talked of the Law as "a curse" from which Christ redeemed us, and declared that the Law could never bring righteous-

---

[1] Gal. i. 6—9.
[2] Id. ii. 14; supra, I., p. 442.
[3] Id. ii. 16.
[4] Id. ii. 18.

ness[1]—who had even characterised that Law as a slavery to "weak and beggarly elements" comparable to the rituals of Cybele worship and Moon worship, and spoken of circumcision as being in itself no better than a contemptible mutilation [2]—who had talked again and again of being dead to the Law, and openly claimed fellowship rather with the Gentiles, who were the spiritual, than with the rejected and penally blinded Jews, who were but the physical descendants of Abraham—was this the man who could without creating false impressions avoid danger of death, which he had braved so often, by doing something to show how perfectly orthodox he was in the impugned respects? A modern writer has said that he could not do this without untruth; and that to suppose the author of the Epistles to the Romans and Galatians standing seven days, oilcakes in hand, in the Temple vestibule, and submitting himself to all the manipulations with which Rabbinic pettiness had multiplied the Mosaic ceremonials which accompanied the completion of the Nazaritic vow—to suppose that, in the midst of unbelieving Priests and Levites, he should have patiently tolerated all the ritual nullities of the Temple service of that period, and so have brought the business to its tedious conclusion in the elaborate manner above described, "is just as credible as that Luther in his old age should have performed a pilgrimage to Einsiedeln with peas in his shoes, or that Calvin on his deathbed should have vowed a gold-embroidered gown to the Holy Mother of God."[3]

[1] Rom. iii. 20; Gal. ii. 16.
[2] Phil. iii. 2; Gal. v. 12.
[3] Hausrath (p. 453), who, however, erroneously imagines that Paul had himself on this occasion the vow of a Nazarite upon him. The person who paid the expense of the Nazarite had not, I imagine, to make offerings for himself—at least it is nowhere so stated—though we infer that he lived with the Nazarites during the period of their seclusion, and in some undefined way shared in their purification.

But the comparison is illusory. It may be true that the natural temperament of St. Paul—something also, it may be, in his Oriental character—inclined him to go much farther in the way of concession than either Luther or Calvin would have done; but apart from this his circumstances were widely different from theirs in almost every respect. We may well imagine that this unexpected proposal was distasteful to him in many ways; it is hardly possible that he should regard without a touch of impatience the tedious ceremonialisms of a system which he now knew to be in its last decadence, and doomed to speedy extinction. Still there were two great principles which he had thoroughly grasped, and on which he had consistently acted. One was acquiescence in things indifferent for the sake of charity, so that he gladly became as a Jew to Jews that he might save Jews; the other that, during the short time which remained, and under the stress of the present necessity, it was each man's duty to abide in the condition wherein he had been called. He was a Jew, and therefore to him the Jewish ceremonial was a part of national custom and established ordinance. For him it had, at the very lowest, a *civil* if not a religious validity. If the Jews misinterpreted his conduct into more than was meant, it would only be a misrepresentation like those which they gratuitously invented, and to which he was incessantly liable. Undoubtedly during his missionary journey he must again and again have broken the strict provisions of that Law to the honour and furtherance of which he had devoted his youth. But though he did not hold himself bound to do all that the Law and the Rabbis required, yet neither did he feel himself precluded from any observance which was not wrong. His objection to Levitism was not an objection to external conformity, but only to that substitution of externalism for faith to which conformity might lead. He did not so much object to ceremonies as to placing any *reliance* on them. He might have wished that things were otherwise, and that the course suggested to him involved a less painful sacrifice. He might have been gladder if the Elders had said to him, "Brother, you are detested here; at any moment the shout of a mob may rise against you, or the dagger of a Sicarius be plunged into your heart. We cannot under such circumstances be responsible for your life. You have given us this splendid proof of your own loyalty and of the Christian love of your converts. The feast is over.[1] Retire at once with safety, and with our prayers and our blessings continue your glorious work." Alas! such advice was only a "might have been." He accepted the suggestion they offered, and the very next day entered the Temple with these four Nazarites, went through whatever preliminary purification was deemed necessary by the Oral Law, and gave notice to the priests that from this time they must begin to count the seven days which must pass before the final offerings were brought and the vow concluded.[2]

If the Elders overrated the conciliatory effect of this act of conformity, they had certainly underrated the peril

---

[1] The Pentecost only lasted one day.

[2] In some such way I understand the obscure and disputed expressions of ver. 26; but even with the Talmudic treatise *Nasir* beside us, we know too little of the details to be sure of the exact process gone through, or of the exact meaning of the expressions used. Some take ἁγνισθείς and ἁγνισμός to mean that St. Paul took on him the Nazarite vow with them (cf. Numb. vi. 3, 5, LXX.). This seems to be impossible, because thirty days is the shortest period mentioned by the Mishna for a temporary vow. Mr. Lewin and others have conjectured that he was himself a Nazarite, having taken the vow after his peril at Ephesus, as on the previous occasion after his peril at Corinth; and that this was the reason why he was so anxious to get to Jerusalem. But if so, why did not St. Luke mention the circumstance as he had done before? And if so, why was it necessary to pay the expenses of these four Nazarites when the fulfilment of his own personal vow would have been a sufficient and more striking proof of willingness to conform to Mosaism in his personal conduct? Moreover, the proposal of the Elders evidently came to St. Paul unexpectedly.

to which it would expose the great missionary who, more than they all, had done his utmost to fulfil that last command of Christ that they should go into all the world and preach the Gospel to every creature. The city was full of strangers from every region of the world, and the place where of all others they would delight to congregate would be the courts of the Temple. Even, therefore, if St. Paul, now that the storms of years had scarred his countenance and bent his frame, was so fortunate as to remain unrecognised by any hostile priest who had known him in former days, it was hardly possible that every one of the thousands whom he had met in scores of foreign cities should fail to identify that well-known face and figure. It would have been far safer, if anything compelled him to linger in the Holy City, to live unnoticed in the lowly house of Mnason. He might keep as quiet as he possibly could in that chamber of the Nazarites; but even if, during those seven days of enforced idleness, he confined himself there to the utmost extent, and even if the other Nazarites abstained from divulging the secret of a name so famous, it was impossible that he should escape the eyes of the myriads who daily wandered through the Temple courts and took part in its multitudinous ceremonies.

For the Jews at that period were in a most inflammable state of mind, and the tremors of the earthquake were already felt which was soon to rend the earth under their feet, and shake their Temple and city into irretrievable ruin. On the death of Herod Agrippa I.,[1] Claudius, thinking that his son was too young to succeed to the government of so turbulent a people, kept him under his own eye at Rome, and appointed Cuspius Fadus to the Procuratorship of Judæa. To secure an additional hold upon the Jews,

A.D. 44.

he ordered that the crown of Agrippa, and, what was of
infinitely greater importance, the "golden robes" of the
High Priest, should be locked up under the care of the
Romans in the Tower of Antonia. So deep was the fury
of the Jews at the thought that these holy vestments
should be under the impure care of Gentiles, that the order
could only be enforced by securing the presence at Jerusalem of C. Cassius Longinus, the Præfect of Syria, with
an immense force. Claudius almost immediately afterwards cancelled the order, at the entreaty of a deputation
from Jerusalem, supported by the influence of the young
Agrippa. Claudius had owed to Agrippa's father his very
empire, and since the youth inherited all the beauty, talent,
and versatility of his family, he was a great favourite at
the Imperial Court. Fadus had been succeeded by Tiberius
Alexander, a nephew of Philo,[1] who was peculiarly hateful
to the Jews because he was a renegade from their religion.
He was superseded by Cumanus, and about the same
time Agrippa II. was invested with the little kingdom
of Chalcis, vacant by the death of his uncle Herod, and
also with the functions of guarding the Temple and the
Corban, and nominating to the High Priesthood.[2] The
Procuratorship of Cumanus marked the commencement of
terrible disturbances. At the very first Passover at which
he was present an event occurred which was a terrible
omen of the future. Just as at this day the Turkish
soldiers are always prepared to pour down from the house
of the Turkish Governor on the first occurrence of any
discord between the Greek and Latin Churches, so it was
the custom of the Roman commandant of the Tower of
Antonia to post detachments of soldiers along the roof of
the cloister which connected the fortress with the Temple

---

[1] Josephus calls him θαυμασιώτατος (c. Ap. i. 9).
[2] A.D. 49.

area—ready at any moment to rush down the stairs and plunge into the very midst of the crowded worshippers. What occurred on this occasion is singularly characteristic. While standing there at guard, one of the Roman soldiers, weary of having nothing to do, and disgusted with watching what he despised as the mummeries of these hateful Jews, expressed his contempt for them by a gesture of the most insulting indecency.[1] Instantly the Jews were plunged into a paroxysm of fury. They cursed the new Procurator, and began to pelt the soldiers with stones, which seem to have been always ready to hand among this excitable race. Fearing that the Antonia detachment would be too weak to cope with so savage an onslaught, Cumanus marched his entire forces round from the Prætorium. At the clash of their footsteps, and the gleam of their swords, the wretched unarmed mass of pilgrims was struck with panic, and made a rush to escape. The gates of the Temple were choked up, and a multitude, variously stated at ten and at twenty thousand, was trampled and crushed to death.

This frightful disaster was followed by another tragedy. An imperial messenger was robbed by bandits at Bethhoron, not far from Jerusalem. Furious at such an insult, Cumanus made the neighbouring villages responsible, and in sacking one of them a Roman soldier got hold of a copy of the Scriptures, and burnt it before the villagers with open blasphemies. The horror of the insult consisted in the fact that the sacred roll contained in many places the awful and incommunicable Name. As they had done when Pilate put up the gilt votive shields in Jerusalem, and when Caligula had issued the order that his image should be placed in the Temple, the Jews poured in

---

[1] Jos. *B. J.* ii. 12, § 1; *Antt.* xx. 5, § 3.

myriads to Cæsarea, and prostrated themselves before the tribunal of the Procurator. In this instance Cumanus thought it best to avert dangerous consequences by the cheap sacrifice of a common soldier, and the Jews were for the time appeased by the execution of the offender.

Then had followed a still more serious outbreak. The Samaritans, actuated by the old hatred to the Jews, had assassinated some Galilæan pilgrims to the Passover at En Gannim, the frontier village of Samaria which had repulsed our Lord.[1] Unable to obtain from Cumanus—whom the Samaritans had bribed—the punishment of the guilty village, the Jews, secretly countenanced by the High Priest Ananias, and his son Ananus, flew to arms, and, under the leadership of the bandit Eleazar, inflicted on the Samaritans a terrible vengeance. Cumanus, on hearing this, marched against them and routed them. A renewal of the contest was prevented by the entreaties of the chief men at Jerusalem, who, aware of the tremendous results at issue, hurried to the battle-field in sackcloth and ashes. Meanwhile the Præfect of Syria, Titus Ummidius Quadratus, appeared on the scene, and, after hearing both sides, found Cumanus and his tribune Celer guilty of having accepted a bribe, and sent them to Rome with Ananias and Ananus to be tried by the Emperor.[2] Jonathan, one of the very able ex-High Priests of the astute house of Annas, was sent to plead the cause of the Jews. At that time Agrippina was all-powerful with the Emperor, and the freedman Pallas all-powerful both with him and with Agrippina, who owed her elevation to his friendly offices. The supple Agrippa introduced Jonathan to Pallas, and it seems as if

---

[1] Luke ix. 53.

[2] The discrepancies in this story as told by Josephus in *B. J.* ii. 12, § 5, and *Antt.* xx. 6, § 2, are glaring, yet no one doubts either the honesty of Josephus or the general truth of the story. How scornfully would it have been rejected as a myth or an invention if it had occurred in the Gospels!

a little compact was struck between them, that Pallas should induce the Emperor to decide in favour of the Jews, and that Jonathan should petition him on behalf of the Jews to appoint to the lucrative Procuratorship his brother Felix. The plot succeeded. The Samaritans were condemned; their leaders executed; Cumanus banished; Celer sent to Jerusalem to be beheaded; Ananias and Ananus triumphantly acquitted; and A.D. 52, six years before St. Paul's last visit to Jerusalem, Felix—like his brother, an Arcadian slave—who had taken the name of Antonius in honour of his first mistress, and the name of Claudius in honour of his patron—became Procurator of Judæa.[1]

At first the new Procurator behaved with a little decent reserve, but it was not long before he began to show himself in his true colours, and with every sort of cruelty and licentiousness "to wield the power of a king with the temperament of a slave." After his emancipation he had been entrusted with a command in a troop of auxiliaries, and acting with the skill and promptitude of a soldier, he had performed a really useful task in extirpating the bandits. Yet even the Jews murmured at the shameless indifference with which this Borgia of the first century entrapped the chief bandit Eleazar into a friendly visit, on pretence of admiring his skill and valour, and instantly threw him into chains, and sent him as a prisoner to Rome. They were still more deeply scandalised by his intimacy with Simon Magus, who lived with him at Cæsarea as a guest, and by whose base devices this "husband or adulterer of three queens" succeeded in seducing Drusilla, the beautiful sister of Agrippa II.—who had now come as a king to Judæa—from her husband Aziz, King of Emesa. A crime of yet deeper and darker dye had taken place the

[1] A.D. 52.

very year before Paul's arrival. Jonathan, who was often bitterly reminded of his share in bringing upon his nation the affliction of a Procurator, who daily grew more infamous from his exactions and his savagery, thought that his high position and eminent services to Felix himself entitled him to expostulate. So far from taking warning, Felix so fiercely resented the interference that he bribed Doras, a friend of Jonathan's, to get rid of him. Doras hired the services of some bandits, who, armed with *sicae*, or short daggers, stabbed the priestly statesman at one of the yearly feasts. The success and the absolute impunity of the crime put a premium upon murder; assassinations became as frequent in Jerusalem as they were at Rome during the Papacy of Alexander VI. The very Temple was stained with blood. Any one who wanted to get rid of a public or private enemy found it a cheap and easy process to hire a murderer. It is now that the ominous term *sicarius* occurs for the first time in Jewish history.

This had happened in A.D. 57, and it was probably at the Passover of A.D. 58—only seven weeks before the time at which we have now arrived—that the Egyptian Pseudo-Messiah had succeeded in raising 30,000 followers, with no better pretensions than the promise that he would lead them to the Mount of Olives, and that the walls of Jerusalem should fall flat before him. Four thousand of these poor deluded wretches seem actually to have accompanied him to the Mount of Olives. There Felix fell upon them, routed them at the first onslaught, killed four hundred, took a multitude of prisoners, and brought the whole movement to an impotent conclusion. The Egyptian, however, had by some means or other made good his escape—was at this moment uncaptured—and, in fact, was never heard of any more. But the way in which followers had flocked in thousands to so poor an impostor showed the tension of men's minds.

Such was the condition of events—in so excited a state were the leaders and the multitude—at the very time that St. Paul was keeping himself as quiet as possible in the chambers of the Nazarites. Four days had already passed, and there seemed to be a hope that, as the number of pilgrims began to thin, he might be safe for three more days, after which there would be nothing to prevent him from carrying out his long-cherished wish to visit Rome, and from thence to preach the Gospel even as far as Spain. Alas! he was to visit Rome, but not as a free man.

For on the fifth day there were some Jews from Ephesus and other cities of Asia—perhaps Alexander the coppersmith was one of them—in the Court of the Women, and the glare of hatred suddenly shot into the eyes of one of these observers as he recognised the marked features of the hated Shaûl. He instantly attracted towards him the attention of some of the compatriots to whom Paul's teaching was so well known. The news ran in a moment through the passionate, restless, fanatical crowd. In one minute there arose one of those deadly cries which are the first beginnings of a sedition. These Asiatics sprang on Paul, and stirred up the vast throng of worshippers with the cry, "Israelites! help! This is the wretch who teaches all men everywhere against the people, and the Thorah, and the Temple. Ay, and besides that, he brought Greeks into the Temple, and hath polluted this holy place." Whether they really thought so or not we cannot tell, but they had no grounds for this mad charge beyond the fact that they had seen the Ephesian Trophimus walking about with Paul in the streets of Jerusalem, and supposed that Paul had taken him even into the holy precincts. To defile the Temple was what every enemy of the Jews tried to do. Antiochus, Heliodorus, Pompey, had profaned it; and very recently the Samaritans had been charged with deliberately polluting it by scattering dead men's bones over its precincts. Instantly the rumour flew from lip to lip that this was Shaûl, of whom they had heard—Paul, the *mesith*—Paul, one of the Galilæan *Minim*—one of the believers in "the Hung"—Paul, the renegade Rabbi, who taught and wrote that Gentiles were as good as Jews—the man who blasphemed the Thorah—the man whom the synagogues had scourged in vain—the man who went from place to place getting them into trouble with the Romans; and that he had been caught taking with him into the Temple a Gentile dog, an uncircumcised *ger*.[1] The punishment for that crime was death—death by the full permission of the Romans themselves; death even against a Roman who should dare to set foot beyond the *Chêl*. They were now in the Court of the Women, but they only had to go through the Corinthian gate, and down the fifteen steps outside of it, to come to the *Chêl*—the "middle-wall of partition," that low stone balustrade with obelisks, on each of which was engraved on stone tablets the inscription in Greek and Latin that "No alien must set foot within

---

[1] Had he done this he would have incurred the censure in Ezek. xliv. 7; cf. Eph. ii. 14. The following remarkable passage of the Talmud is a self-condemnation by the Jewish teachers:—"What," it is asked, "was the cause of the destruction of the first Temple? The prevalence of idolatry, adultery, and murder. . . . But what was the cause of the destruction of the second Temple, *seeing that the age was characterised by study of the Law*, observance of its precepts, and the practice of benevolence? *It was groundless hatred; and it shows that groundless hatred is equal in heinousness to idolatry, adultery, and murder combined*" (*Joma*, f. 9, 2). As specimens of the groundless and boundless hatred of the Talmudists to Christians, see *Abhôda Zarah*, f. 26, 1, 2 (Amsterdam edition); Maimonides, *Hilch. Accum*, § 9.

that enclosure on pain of certain death."[1] Here, then, was a splendid opportunity for most just vengeance on the apostate who taught apostasy. A rush was made upon him, and the cry "To the rescue!" echoed on all sides through the streets.[2] To defend himself was impossible. What voice could be heard amid the wild roar of that momentarily increasing hubbub? Was this to be the end? Was he to be torn to pieces then and there in the very Temple precincts? If he had been in the court below, that would have been his inevitable fate, but the sacredness of the spot saved him. They began dragging him, vainly trying to resist, vainly trying to speak a word, through the great "Beautiful" gate of Corinthian brass, and down the fifteen steps, while the Levites and the Captain of the Temple, anxious to save the sacred enclosure from one more stain of blood, exerted all their strength to shut the ponderous gate behind the throng which surged after their victim.[3] But meanwhile the Roman centurion stationed under arms with his soldiers on the roof of the western cloisters, was aware that a wild commotion had suddenly sprung up. The outburst of fury in these Oriental mobs is like the scream of mingled sounds in a forest which sometimes suddenly startles the deep stillness of a tropic night. The rumour had spread in a moment from the Temple to the city, and streams of men were thronging from every direction into the vast area of the Court of the Gentiles. In another moment it was

---

[1] The חיל. (Jos. *B. J.* v. 5, § 2; vi. 2, § 4; *Antt.* xv. 11, § 5.) The discovery of one of these inscriptions by M. Clermont Ganneau—an inscription on which the eyes of our Lord Himself and of all His disciples must have often fallen—is very interesting. He found it built into the walls of a small mosque in the Via Dolorosa (*Palestine Exploration Fund Report*, 1871, p. 132). Paul had not indeed *actually* brought any Gentile inside the *Chêl*; but to do so *ideally* and *spiritually* had been the very purpose of his life. *V. infra*, *ad* Eph. ii. 14.

[2] xxi. 30, ἐκινήθη ἡ πόλις ὅλη, καὶ ἐγένετο συνδρομή.

[3] Jos. *B. J.* vi. 5, § 3; *c. Ap.* ii. 9.

certain that those white pillars and that tessellated floor would be stained with blood. Without a moment's delay the centurion sent a message to Lysias, the commandant of Antonia, that the Jews had seized somebody in the Temple, and were trying to kill him. The Romans were accustomed to rapid movements, taught them by thousands of exigencies of their career in hostile countries, but nowhere more essential than in a city which Præfect after Præfect and Procurator after Procurator had learnt to detest as the head-quarters of burning, senseless, and incomprehensible fanaticism. A single word was enough to surround Lysias with a well-disciplined contingent of centurions and soldiers, and he instantly dashed along the cloister roof and down the stairs into the Court of the Gentiles. The well-known clang of Roman arms arrested the attention of the mob. They had had some terrible warnings very lately. The memory of that awful day, when they trampled each other to death by thousands to escape the cohort of Cumanus, was still fresh in their memory. They did not dare to resist the mailed soldiery of their conquerors.

Lysias and his soldiers forced their way straight through the throng to the place where Paul was standing, and rescued him from his enraged opponents. When he had seized him, and had his arms bound to two soldiers by two chains, he asked the question, "Who the man might be, and what he had done?"[1] Nothing was to be learnt from the confused cries that rose in answer, and, in despair of arriving at anything definite in such a scene, Lysias ordered him to be marched into the barracks.[2] But no sooner had he got on the stairs which led up to the top of the cloister, and so into

---

[1] xxi. 33, τίς ἂν εἴη, καὶ τί ἐστιν πεποιηκώς.   [2] παρεμβολή.

the fortress,[1] than the mob, afraid that they were going to be baulked of their vengeance, made another rush at him, with yells of "Kill him! kill him!"[2] and Paul, unable in his fettered condition to steady himself, was carried off his legs, and hurried along in the arms of the surrounding soldiers. He was saved from being torn to pieces chiefly by the fact that Lysias kept close by him; and, as the rescue-party was about to disappear into the barracks, Paul said to him in Greek, "May I speak a word to you?" "Can you speak Greek?" asked the commandant in surprise. "Are you not then really that Egyptian[3] who a little while ago made a disturbance,[4] and led out into the wilderness those 4,000 *sicarii?*"[5] "No," said Paul; "I am a Jew, a native of Tarsus, in Cilicia, a citizen of no undistinguished

---

[1] Fort Antonia was a four-square tower, at the N.W. angle of the Temple area, with a smaller tower fifty cubits high at each corner except the southern, where the tower was seventy cubits high, with the express object of overlooking everything that went on in the Temple courts. Stairs from these towers communicated with the roofs of two porticoes, on which at intervals (διιστάμενοι) stood armed Roman soldiers at the times of the great festivals, to prevent all seditious movements (Jos. *B. J.* v. 5, § 8; *Antt.* xx. 5, § 3).

[2] Cf. Luke xxiii. 18, and the cry of Pagan mobs, αἶρε τοὺς ἀθέους.

[3] Ver. 38, οὐκ ἄρα σὺ εἶ ὁ Αἰγύπτιος . . . ; One hardly sees why Lysias should have *inferred* that the Egyptian could not speak Greek, but he may have known that this was the fact. Since the Egyptian had only escaped a few months before, and the mass of the people—never favourable to him—would be exasperated at the detection of his imposture, the conjecture of Lysias was not surprising.

[4] ἀναστατώσας. Cf. xvii. 6; Gal. v. 12.

[5] Ver. 38, τοὺς τετρακισχιλίους ἄνδρας τῶν σικαρίων. Josephus (*Antt.* xx. 8, § 6) says that Felix, when he routed them, killed 400 and took 200 prisoners. In *B. J.* ii. 13, § 5, he says that he collected 30,000 followers, and led them to the Mount of Olives from the wilderness, and that the majority of them were massacred or taken prisoners. Most critics only attach importance to such discrepancies when they find or imagine them in the sacred writers. For the *sicarii,* see Jos. *B. J.* ii. 13, § 3. He says that they murdered people in broad day, and in the open streets, especially during the great feasts, and that they carried their daggers concealed under their robes.

REQUEST TO SPEAK.

city,[1] and, I entreat you, allow me to speak to the people."

It was an undaunted request to come from one whose life had just been rescued, and barely rescued, from that raging mob, and who was at that moment suffering from their rough treatment. Most men would have been in a state of such wild alarm as to desire nothing so much as to be hurried out of sight of the crowd. Not so with St. Paul. Snatched from his persecutors after imminent risk—barely delivered from that most terrifying of all forms of danger, the murderous fury of masses of his fellow-men—he asks leave not only to face, but even to turn round and address, the densely-thronging thousands, who were only kept from him by a little belt of Roman swords.[2]

Lysias gave him leave to speak, and apparently ordered one of his hands to be unfettered; and taking his stand on the stairs, Paul, with uplifted arm, made signals to the people that he wished to address them.[3] The mob became quiet, for in the East crowds are much more instantly swayed by their emotions than they are among us; and Paul, speaking in Syriac, the vernacular of Palestine, and noticing priests and Sanhedrists among the crowd, began—

"Brethren and Fathers,[4] listen to the defence I have now to make to you!"

The sound of their own language, showing that the

---

[1] οὐκ ἀσήμου πόλεως (Eur. *Ion.* 8). It was αὐτόνομος, and a μητρόπολις, and had a famous university.

[2] Knox, who thought that Paul did wrong to take the vow, says, "He was brought into the most desperate danger, God designing to show thereby that we must not do evil that good may come."

[3] Ver. 40, κατέσεισε τῇ χειρί. Cf. xii. 17; xix. 33; xxi. 40. Cf. Pers. iv. 5, "Calidus fecisse silentia turbae Majestate manûs."

[4] See St. Stephen's exordium (vii. 2).

speaker was at any rate no mere Hellenist, charmed their rage for the moment, and produced a still deeper silence. In that breathless hush Paul continued his speech. It was adapted to its object with that consummate skill which, even at the most exciting moments, seems never to have failed him. While he told them the truth, he yet omitted all facts which would be likely to irritate them, and which did not bear on his immediate object. That object was to show that he could entirely sympathise with them in this outburst of zeal, because he had once shared their state of mind, and that nothing short of divine revelations had altered the course of his religion and his life. He was, he told them, a Jew,[1] born indeed in Tarsus, yet trained from his earliest youth in Jerusalem, at the feet of no less a teacher than their great living Rabban Gamaliel; that he was not merely a Jew, but a Pharisee who had studied the inmost intricacy of the *Halacha*;[2] and was so like themselves in being a zealot for God, that he had persecuted "this way" to the very death, haling to prison not only men, but even women; in proof of which he appealed to the testimony of the ex-High Priest Theophilus,[3] and many still surviving members of the Sanhedrin who had given him letters to Damascus. What, then, had changed the whole spirit of his life? Nothing less than a divine vision of Jesus of Nazareth, which had stricken him blind to earth, and bidden him confer with Ananias.[4] He does not tell them that Ananias was a Christian, but

---

[1] xxii. 3, ἀνὴρ Ἰουδαῖος. To Lysias he had used the *general* expression ἄνθρωπος Ἰουδ. (xxi. 39).

[2] xxii. 3, κατὰ ἀκρίβειαν τοῦ πατρῴου νόμου. Cf. xxvi. 5; Jos. *B. J.* ii. 8, § 18. This "accuracy" corresponds to the Hebrew *tsedakah*, and the Talmudic *dikdukey* (דקדוקי).

[3] See Vol. I., p. 178.

[4] The narratives of St. Paul's conversion in ix., xxii., xxvi. are sufficiently considered and "harmonised"—not that they really need any harmonising—in Vol. I., pp. 190—199.

—which was no less true—that he was an orthodox observer of the Law, for whom all the Jews of Damascus felt respect. Ananias had healed his blindness, and told him that it was "the God of our fathers," who foreordained him to know His will and see "the Just One,"[1] and hear the message from His lips, that he might be for Him "a witness to all men" of what he had heard and seen. He then mentions his baptism and return to Jerusalem, and, hurrying over all needless details, comes to the point that, while he was worshipping—now twenty years ago—in that very Temple, he had fallen into a trance, and again seen the risen Jesus, who bade him hurry with all speed out of Jerusalem, because there they would not receive his testimony. But so far from wishing to go, he had even pleaded with the heavenly vision that surely the utter change from Saul the raging persecutor—Saul who had imprisoned and beaten the believers throughout the synagogues—Saul at whose feet had been laid the clothes of them that slew His witness[2] Stephen—the change from such a man to Saul the Christian and the preacher of the Gospel of Jesus Christ—could not fail to win credence to his testimony. But He who spake to him would not suffer him to plead for a longer opportunity of appealing to his fellow-countrymen. Briefly but decisively came the answer which had been the turning-point for all his subsequent career—"Go, for I will send thee far away TO THE GENTILES!"

That fatal word, which hitherto he had carefully avoided, but which it was impossible for him to avoid any longer, was enough. Up to this point they had continued listening to him with the deepest attention. Many of

---

[1] "The Just One." See the speech of Stephen (vii. 52).

[2] $\mu\alpha\rho\tau\grave{o}s$, not yet "martyr," as in Rev. xvii. 6. (Clem. *Ep.* 1 *Cor.* v.) But St. Paul would here have used the word *edh*, "witness."

them were not wholly unacquainted with the facts to which he appealed. His intense earnestness and mastery over the language which they loved charmed them all the more, because the soldiers who stood by could not understand a word of what he was saying, so that his speech bore the air of a confidential communication to Jews alone, to which the alien tyrants could only listen with vain curiosity and impatient suspicion. Who could tell but what some Messianic announcement might be hovering on his lips? Might not he who was thrilling them with the narrative of these visions and revelations have some new ecstasy to tell of, which should be the signal that now the supreme hour had come, and which should pour into their hearts a stream of fire so intense, so kindling, that in the heat of it the iron chains of the Romans should be as tow? But was *this* to be the climax? Was a trance to be pleaded in defence of the apostasy of the renegade? Was this evil soul to be allowed to produce holy witness for his most flagrant offences? Were they to be told, forsooth, that a vision from heaven had bidden him preach to "sinners of the Gentiles," and fling open, as he had been doing, the hallowed privileges of the Jews to those dogs of the uncircumcision? All that strange multitude was as one; the same hatred shot at the same instant through all their hearts. That word "GENTILES," confirming all their worst suspicions, fell like a spark on the inflammable mass of their fanaticism. No sooner was it uttered[1] than they raised a simultaneous yell of "Away with such a wretch from the earth; he ought never to have lived!"[2]

Then began one of the most odious and despicable spectacles which the world can witness, the spectacle of an

---

[1] xxii. 22, ἤκουον δὲ αὐτοῦ ἄχρι τούτου τοῦ λόγου, καὶ ἐπῆραν τὴν φωνὴν αὐτῶν λέγοντες, κ.τ.λ.

[2] Ver. 22, οὐ καθῆκεν. א, A, B, C, D, E, G.

AN ORIENTAL RIOT.

Oriental mob, hideous with impotent rage, howling, yelling, cursing, gnashing their teeth, flinging about their arms, waving and tossing their blue and red robes, casting dust into the air by handfuls, with all the furious gesticulations of an uncontrolled fanaticism.[1]

Happily Paul was out of the reach of their personal fury.[2] It might goad them to a courage sufficient to make them rend the air with their cries of frenzy, and make the court of the Temple look like the refuge for a throng of demoniacs; but it hardly prompted them to meet the points of those Roman broadswords. In great excitement, the commandant ordered the prisoner to be led into the barracks, and examined by scourging; for, being entirely ignorant of what Paul had been saying, he wanted to know what further he could have done to excite those furious yells. The soldiers at once tied his hands together, stripped his back bare, and bent him forward into the position for that horrid and often fatal examination by torture which, not far from that very spot, his Lord had undergone.[3] Thrice before, on that scarred back, had Paul felt the fasces of Roman lictors; five times the nine-and-thirty strokes of Jewish thongs; here was a new form of agony, the whip—the *horribile flagellum*—which the Romans employed to force by torture the confession of the truth.[4] But at this stage of the proceedings, Paul, self-

---

[1] xxii. 23. On the sudden excitability of Eastern mobs, and the sudden calm which often follows it, see *Palest. Explor. Fund* for April, 1879, p. 77.

[2] St. James had spoken of the "many myriads" (Acts xxi. 20) of Jews who, though zealots for the Law, had embraced the faith. How came it that not one of these "many myriads" lifted an arm or raised a voice to liberate St. Paul from the perils into which he had been brought by religious hatred greedily adopting a lying accusation?

[3] xxii. 25, προέτεινεν αὐτὸν τοῖς ἱμᾶσιν—"stretched him forward with the thongs" to prepare him for examination by being scourged with μάστιγες. The word ἱμάντες seems never to mean a scourge.

[4] See *Life of Christ*, I. 187; II. 380.

possessed even in extremes, interposed with a quiet question. It had been useless before, it might be useless now, but it was worth trying, since both the soldiers and their officers seem already to have been prepossessed by his noble calm and self-control in the midst of dangers so awful and so sudden. He therefore asked in a quiet voice, "Is it lawful for you to scourge a Roman who has not been tried?" The question was addressed to the centurion who was standing by to see that the torture was duly administered, and he was startled by the appeal. This was evidently no idle boaster; no man who would invent a privilege to escape pain or peril. Few under any circumstances would ever venture to invent the proud right of saying CIVIS ROMANUS SUM,[1] for the penalty of imposture was death;[2] and the centurion had seen enough to be quite sure that this prisoner, at any rate, was not the man to do so. He made the soldiers stop, went off to the commandant and said to him, with something of Roman bluntness, "What are you about?[3] This man is a Roman." This was important. If he was a Roman, the Chiliarch had already twice broken the law which entitled him to protection; for he had both bound him and, in contravention of an express decree of Augustus, had given orders to begin his examination by putting him to the torture. Moreover, as being one who himself placed the highest possible value on the *jus civitatis*, he respected the claim. Hurrying to him, he said—

"Tell me, are *you* a Roman?"

"Yes."

But Lysias, as he looked at him, could not help having his doubts. He was himself a Greek or Syrian, who had

---

[1] Cic. *in Verr.* v. 63.
[2] At any rate in certain cases. Suet. *Claud.* 25.
[3] Ver. 26, τί μέλλεις ποιεῖν. The ἄρα is omitted in ℵ, A, B, C, E.

bought the franchise, and thereupon assumed the prænomen Claudius, at a time when the privilege was very expensive.[1] Whether Paul was a Roman or not, he was clearly a Jew, and no less clearly a very poor one: how could *he* have got the franchise?

"*I* know how much it cost *me*[2] to get this citizenship," he remarked, in a dubious tone of voice.

"But I have been a citizen from my birth," was the calm answer to his unexpressed suspicion.

The claim could not be resisted. Paul was untied, and the soldiers dropped their scourges. But Lysias was not by any means free from anxiety as to the consequences of his illegal conduct.[3] Anxious to rid his hands of this awkward business in a city where the merest trifles were constantly leading to most terrible consequences, he told the chief priests to summon next day a meeting of the Sanhedrin in order to try the prisoner.

The Sanhedrin met in full numbers. They no longer sat in the *Lishcath Haggazzith*, the famous hall, with its tessellated pavement, which stood at the south side of the Court of the Priests.[4] Had they still been accustomed to meet there, Lysias and his soldiers would never

---

[1] Some ten years before this time it had, however, become much cheaper. Messalina, the infamous wife of Claudius, who was put to death A.D. 48, openly sold it, first, at very high terms, but subsequently so cheap that Dion Cassius (ix. 17) says it could be bought for one or two broken glasses.

[2] Ver. 28, Ἐγὼ οἶδα πόσου, D. Though unsupported by evidence, the colloquialism sounds very genuine. Perhaps Lysias had bribed one of Claudius's freedmen, who made money in this way.

[3] Ver. 29. There is a little uncertainty as to what is meant by ἐφοβήθη .. ὅτι ἦν αὐτὸν δεδεκώς. If it means the chaining him with two chains (xxi. 33), Lysias did not at any rate think it necessary to *undo* what he had once done, for it is clear that Paul remained chained (xxii. 30, ἔλυσεν αὐτόν). I therefore refer it to the binding with the thongs (ver. 25), by which Lysias seems to have broken two laws: (1) The Lex Porcia (Cic. *pro Rabirio*, 3; *in Verr.* v. 66); (2) "Non esse a tormentis incipiendum Div. Augustus constituit" (*Digest. Leg.* 48, tit. 18, c. 1).

[4] See Lightfoot, *Hor. Hebr.*, i. 1,105.

have been suffered to obtrude their profane feet into a chamber which lay within the middle wall of partition —beyond which even a Procurator dare not even have set a step on pain of death. But at this period the Sanhedrin had probably begun their meetings in the *Chanujôth*, or "booths," the very existence of which was a proof of the power and prosperity of "the Serpent House of Hanan."[1] To this place Lysias led his prisoner, and placed him before them. The *Nasi*, or President, was, as usual, the High Priest.[2] The preliminary questions were asked, and then Paul, fixing on the assembly his earnest gaze,[3] began his defence with the words, "Brethren, my public life has been spent in all good conscience towards God till this day."[4] Something in these words jarred particularly on the mind of the High Priest. He may have disliked the use of the term "brethren," an address which implied a certain amount of equality, instead of one of those numerous expressions of servility which it was only fitting that a man like this should use to the great assembly of the wise. But Paul was no *Am-ha-arets*, on the contrary, he was as much a Rabbi, as much a *Chakam*, as the best "remover of mountains" among them all, and it may have

---

[1] *V. supra*, I., pp. 153, 166; *Life of Christ*, I. 77; II. 337. Jost, *Gesch.* i. 145; Herzfeld, *Gesch.* i. 394. By this time, A.D. 58, the change had undoubtedly taken place.

[2] Endless mistakes have apparently arisen from confusing the President of the Sanhedrin with the President of the Schools. The subject is very obscure; but while undoubtedly the title of *Nasi*, or President of the Sanhedrin, was borne by great Rabbis like Hillel, Simeon, and Gamaliel, no less undoubtedly the High Priest—unless most flagrantly incompetent—presided as *Nasi* at the judicial meetings of the Sanhedrin, regarded as a governing body.

[3] xxiii. 1, ἀτενίσας. Cf. Luke iv. 20; Acts x. 4; xiii. 9.

[4] πεπολίτευμαι (Phil. i. 27; Jos. *Vit.* § 49; 2 Macc. vi. 1). Besides the general assertion of his innocence, he may mean that, whatever he had *taught* to the Gentiles, he had *lived* as a loyal Jew.

THE HIGH-PRIEST ANANIAS.

been that he designedly used the term "brethren" instead of "fathers" because he too had been once a Sanhedrist. The bold assertion of perfect innocence further irritated the presiding *Nasi*, and he may have felt, somewhat painfully, that his own public life had not by any means been in all good conscience either towards God or towards man. This High Priest, Ananias, the son of Nebedoeus,[1] who had been appointed by Herod of Chalcis, was one of the worst, if not the very worst specimen of the worldly Sadducees of an age in which the leading hierarchs resembled the loosest of the Avignon cardinals, or of the preferment-hunting bishops in the dullest and deadest period of Charles the Second or George the First.[2] History records the revengeful unwisdom of his conduct towards the Samaritans, and the far from noble means which he took to escape the consequences of his complicity in their massacre. The Talmud adds to our picture of him that he was a rapacious tyrant who, in his gluttony and greed, reduced the inferior priests almost to starvation by defrauding them of their tithes;[3] and that he was one of those who sent his creatures with bludgeons to the threshing-floors to seize the tithes by force.[4] He held the high-priesthood

---

[1] On this man see Jos. *Antt*. xx. 5, § 2; 6, §§ 2, 3; 8, § 8; 9, § 2; *B. J.* ii. 17, § 9.

[2] No wonder that in these days there lay upon the Jews an abiding sense of the wrath of God against their race. No wonder that the Talmud records the legends how at this time the sacred light, which was to burn all night on the candlestick (*ner ma'arabi*), was often quenched before the daybreak; how the red tongue of cloth round the neck of the scapegoat on the Day of Atonement was no longer miraculously turned to white; how the huge brazen Nikanor-gate of the Temple, which required twenty Levites to shut it every evening, opened of its own accord; and how Johanan Ben Zacchai exclaimed, on hearing the portent, "Why wilt thou terrify us, O Temple? We know that thou art doomed to ruin."

[3] The Talmud tells us that when this person was High Priest the sacrifices were always eaten up, so that no fragments of them were left for the poorer priests (*Pesachim*, 57, 1). (Grätz, iii. 279.)

[4] *Pesachim, ubi supra*. St. Paul might well have asked him, ὁ βδελυσσόμενος τὰ εἴδωλα, ἱεροσυλεῖς (Rom. ii. 22; *v. supra*.)

for a period which, in these bad days, was unusually long,[1] a term of office which had, however, been interrupted by his absence as a prisoner to answer for his misconduct at Rome. On this occasion, thanks to an actor and a concubine, he seems to have gained his cause,[2] but he was subsequently deposed to make room for Ishmael Ben Phabi, and few pitied him when he was dragged out of his hiding-place in a sewer to perish miserably by the daggers of the Sicarii, whom, in the days of his prosperity, he had not scrupled to sanction and employ.[3]

His conduct towards St. Paul gives us a specimen of his character. Scarcely had the Apostle uttered the first sentence of his defence when, with disgraceful illegality, Ananias ordered the officers of the court to smite him on the mouth.[4] Stung by an insult so flagrant, an outrage so undeserved, the naturally choleric temperament of Paul flamed into that sudden sense of anger which ought to be controlled, but which can hardly be wanting in a truly noble character. No character can be perfect which does not cherish in itself a deeply-seated, though perfectly generous and forbearing, indignation against intolerable wrong. Smarting from the blow, "God shall smite thee," he exclaimed, "thou white-washed wall![5] What! Dost thou sit there judging me according to the Law,

---

[1] From A.D. 48 to A.D. 59. The voyage as a prisoner to Rome was in A.D. 52.

[2] Wieseler, *Chron. d. Ap. Zeit.*, 76.

[3] Jos. *Antt.* xx. 9, § 2; *B. J.* ii. 17, § 9.

[4] To this style of argument the Jews seem to have been singularly prone (cf. Luke vi. 29; John xviii. 22; 2 Cor. xi. 20; 1 Tim. iii. 3; Tit. i. 7). This brutality illustrates the remark in *Joma*, 23, 1, *Sota*, 47, 2, that at that period no one cared for anything but externalism, and that Jews thought more of a pollution of the Temple than they did of assassination (Grätz, iii. 322).

[5] xxiii. 3, τοῖχε κεκονιαμένε. Cf. Matt. xxiii. 27, τάφοι κεκονιαμένοι. Dr. Plumptre compares Jeffreys' treatment of Baxter.

and in violation of law biddest me to be smitten?"[1]
The language has been censured as unbecoming in its
violence, and has been unfavourably compared with the
meekness of Christ before the tribunal of his enemies.
"Where," asks St. Jerome, "is that patience of the
Saviour, who—as a lamb led to the slaughter opens not
his mouth—so gently asks the smiter, 'If I have spoken
evil, bear witness to the evil; but if well, why smitest thou
me?' We are not detracting from the Apostle, but declaring the glory of God, who, suffering in the flesh, reigns
above the wrong and frailty of the flesh."[2] Yet we need
not remind the reader that not once or twice only did
Christ give the rein to righteous anger, and blight hypocrisy and insolence with a flash of holy wrath. The
bystanders seem to have been startled by the boldness
of St. Paul's rebuke, for they said to him, "Dost thou
revile the High Priest of God?" The Apostle's anger
had expended itself in that one outburst, and he instantly
apologised with exquisite urbanity and self-control. "I
did not know," he said, "brethren, that he is the High
Priest;" adding that, had he known this, he would not
have addressed to him the opprobrious name of "whited
wall," because he reverenced and acted upon the rule of
Scripture, "Thou shalt not speak ill of a ruler of thy
people."[3]

[1] For a Jew to order a Jew to be struck on the cheek was peculiarly offensive. "He that strikes the cheek of an Israelite strikes, as it were, the cheek of the Shechinah," for it is said (Prov. xx. 25), "He that strikes a man" (i.e., an Israelite who alone deserves the name; Rashi quotes *Babha Metsia*, f. 114, col. 2), strikes the Holy One. *Sanhedr*. f. 58, col. 2, דך = cheekbone, and וקד, "to strike," in Syriac (*collidere*, cf. Dan. v. 6; Buxtorf, *Lex. Chald*, *s. v*.), as well as to snare.

[2] *Adv. Pelag*. iii. 1.

[3] Ex. xxii. 28, LXX. (cf. 2 Pet. ii. 10). Under the good breeding of the answer we notice the admirable skill which enabled Paul thus to show at once his knowledge of and his obedience to the Law, for the supposed apostasy from which he was impugned.

It has been thought very astonishing that St. Paul should not know that Ananias was the High Priest, and all sorts of explanations have consequently been foisted into his very simple words. These words cannot, however, mean that he was unable to recognise the validity of Ananias's title;[1] or that he had spoken for the moment without considering his office;[2] or that he could not be supposed to acknowledge a high priest in one who behaved with such illegal insolence.[3] Considering the disrepute and insignificance into which the high-priesthood had fallen during the dominance of men who would only, as a rule, take it for a short time in order to "pass the chair;"[4] considering that one of these worldly intruders took to wearing silk gloves that he might not soil his hands with the sacrifices; considering, too, that the Romans and the Herods were constantly setting up one and putting down another at their own caprice, and that the people often regarded some one as the *real* high priest, who was no longer invested with the actual office; considering, too, that in such ways the pontificate of these truckling Sadducees had sunk into a mere simulacrum of what once it was, and that the real allegiance of the people had been completely transferred to the more illustrious Rabbis—it is perfectly conceivable that St. Paul, after his long absence from Jerusalem,[5] had not, during the few and much occupied days which had elapsed since his return, given himself the trouble to

---

[1] Lightfoot, Schoettgen, Kuinoel, Baumgarten.

[2] Bengel (non veniebat mihi in mentem), Wetstein, Bp. Sanderson (non noveram, non satis attente consideravi), Bp. Wordsworth, &c.

[3] Calvin.

[4] The Jews themselves take this view of them. Grätz (iii. 322) refers to *Pesachîm*, 57, 1, *Joma*, 23, 1, which speaks of their narrowness, envy, violence, love of precedence, &c.; Josephus (*Antt.* xx. 8, § 8, 9, § 4) speaks of their impudence and turbulence (see *Life of Christ*, II. 329—342).

[5] This is the view of Chrysostom.

inquire whether a Kamhit, or a Boethusian, or a Canthera was at that particular moment adorned with the empty title which he probably disgraced. He must, of course, have been aware that the high priest was the *Nasi* of the Sanhedrin, but in a crowded assembly he had not noticed who the speaker was. Owing to his weakened sight, all that he saw before him was a blurred white figure issuing a brutal order, and to this person, who in his external whiteness and inward worthlessness thus reminded him of the plastered wall of a sepulchre, he had addressed his indignant denunciation. That he should retract it on learning the hallowed position of the delinquent, was in accordance with that high breeding of the perfect gentleman which in all his demeanour he habitually displayed.

But while we can easily excuse any passing touch of human infirmity, if such there were, in his sudden vehemence, we cannot defend his subsequent conduct at that meeting. Surely it was more than pardonable if on that day he was a little unhinged, both morally and spiritually, by the wild and awful trials of the day before. In the discussion which was going on about his case, his knowledge of the Sanhedrin, of which he had been a member, enabled him easily to recognise that his judges were still mainly divided into two parties—the Sadducean priests and the Pharisaic elders and scribes. The latter were the more popular and numerous, the former were the more wealthy and powerful. Now St. Paul well knew that these two parties were separated from each other by an internecine enmity, which was only reconciled in the presence of common hatreds. He knew, too, that one main point of contention between them arose from questions about the Unseen World, and the life beyond the grave.[1] Seeing, therefore, that he would meet with neither justice nor

---

[1] Matt. xxii. 28; Jos. *B. J.* ii. 8, § 16; *Antt.* xviii. 1, § 4.

mercy from that tribunal, he decided to throw among them the apple of discord, and cried out amid the Babel of tongues, "Brethren, I am a Pharisee, a son of Pharisees. I am being judged about the hope and resurrection of the dead." The plan showed great knowledge of character, and the diversion thus caused was for the time eminently successful; but was it worthy of St. Paul? Undoubtedly there were points in common between him and the Pharisees. "They taught a resurrection of the dead: so did he. They taught the coming of the Kingdom of God: so did he. They taught the Advent of the Messiah: so did he. They taught an intercourse of God with men by the medium of angels, dreams, and visions: so did he. He shared with the Pharisees exactly those doctrines, on account of which he was regarded by the Sadducees as a seducer of the people." This is true; but, on the other hand, his belief in the risen Messiah was *not* the point on which he was mainly being called in question.[1] That belief, had it stood alone, would have been passed over by the Sanhedrin as, at the worst, a harmless delusion. Nay, some of the Pharisaic Sanhedrists may even have been nominally Christians.[2] But the fury against St. Paul was kindled by the far more burning questions which arose out of his doctrine of the nullity of the Law, and the admission of the Gentiles to equal privileges with the seed of Abraham. Did not, then, the words of the Apostle suggest a false issue? And had he any right to inflame an existing animosity?[3] And

[1] Reuss, whose *Actes des Apôtres* I had not read till these pages were written, takes a very similar view, p. 218. Yet it is, of course, possible that St. Paul's exclamation *may* have been justified by some circumstances of the discussion which have not been preserved in the narrative.

[2] Acts xv. 5.

[3] Those who, in the teeth of all Scripture, will not believe that an Apostle can make a mistake, have built disastrous conclusions on this action of St. Paul's, quoting it to sanction the Machiavellian policy of the Romans, "Divide

could he worthily say, "I am a Pharisee?" Was he not in reality at variance with the Pharisees in every fundamental particular of their system? Is not the Pharisaic spirit in its very essence the antithesis of the Christian?[1] Did not the two greatest Epistles which he had written prove their whole theology, as such, to be false in every line? Was it not the very work of his life to pull down the legal prescriptions around which it was their one object to rear a hedge? Had not they been occupied—as none knew better than himself—in riveting the iron fetters of that yoke of bondage, which he was striving to shatter link by link? Was there not the least little touch of a *suggestio falsi* in what he said? Let us make every possible deduction and allowance for a venial infirmity; for a sudden and momentary "œconomy," far less serious than that into which his great brother-Apostle had swerved at Antioch; and let us further admit that there is a certain nationality in the chivalry of rigidly minute and scrupulously inflexible straightforwardness, which is, among Northern nations, and among the English in particular, the hereditary result of centuries of training. Let us also acknowledge, not without a blush of shame, that certain slight *managements* and *accommodations* of truth have in later ages been reckoned among Christian virtues. Yet, after all these qualifications, we cannot in this matter wholly see how St. Paul could say without qualification, in such an assembly, "I am a Pharisee." If we think him very little to blame for his stern rebuke of the High Priest; if, referring his conduct to that final court of appeal, which consists in

et impera." Corn. à Lapide, on this passage, says, "Bellum haereticorum est pax ecclesiae,"—a maxim on which the Romish Church has sometimes acted (see Wordsworth, *ad loc.*). On the other hand, Luther says, with his robust good sense, "Non mihi placet studium illud sanctos nimis efferendi et excusandi si sacræ scripturæ vim negat."

[1] Matt. xxiii. 25, 27; John xii. 43; Rom. ii.

comparing it with the precepts and example of his Lord, we can quite conceive that He who called Herod "a fox" would also have called Ananias "a whited wall;" on the other hand, we cannot but think that this creating of a division among common enemies on the grounds of a very partial and limited agreement with certain other tenets held by some of them, was hardly worthy of St. Paul; and knowing, as we do know, what the Pharisees were, we cannot imagine his Divine Master ever saying, under any circumstances, "I am a Pharisee." Moreover, the device, besides being questionable, was not even politic. It added violence to a yet more infuriated reaction in men who felt that they had been the victims of a successful stratagem, and in the remark of St. Paul before the tribunal of Felix[1] I seem to see—though none have noticed it—a certain sense of compunction for the method in which he had extricated himself from a pressing danger.

But, as we have said, the stratagem was for the time almost magically successful. Paul's enemies were instantly at each other's throats. The High Priest, Ananias, was so singularly detested by the Pharisaic party that centuries afterwards the tradition still lingered of his violence and greed.[2] There rose a sudden uproar of angry voices, and the scribes, who sided with the Pharisees, started up in a body to declare that Paul was innocent. "We find the defendant not guilty; but if a spirit or angel spoke to him——?"[3] Again the Jews, even these

[1] Acts xxiv. 21, which I take to be a confession of his error on this occasion.

[2] Derenbourg, *Palest.*, § 31.

[3] The expression is an aposiopesis, or suppression of the apodosis, not uncommon after εἰ, as suggesting an alternative. See my *Brief Greek Syntax*, § 309. The μὴ θεομαχῶμεν of the Received Text (omitted in א, A, B, C, E, the Æthiopic, the Coptic, &c.) is a gloss from chap. v. 39. Chrysostom fills up the sentence with ποῖον ἔγκλημα, "What sort of charge is that?"

distinguished Hierarchs and Rabbis, showed their utter incapacity for self-control. Even in the august precincts of the Sanhedrin the clamour was succeeded by a tumult so violent that Paul was once more in danger of being actually torn to pieces, this time by learned and venerable hands. Claudius Lysias, more and more amazed at the impracticability of these Jews, who first unanimously set upon Paul in the Temple, and half of whom in the Sanhedrin appeared to be now fighting in his defence, determined that his fellow-citizen should not at any rate suffer so ignoble a fate, and once more ordered the detachment of soldiers to go down to snatch him from the midst of them, and lead him to the one spot in Jerusalem where the greatest living Jew could alone find security—the barracks of foreign conquerors.

St. Paul might well be exhausted and depressed by the recurrence, on two consecutive days, of such exciting scenes, and even a courage so dauntless as his could not face unshaken this continual risk of sudden death. The next day was again to bring a fresh peril; but before it came, God in His mercy, who had ever encouraged His faithful servant at the worst and darkest crises, sent him a vision which saved him from all alarm as to his actual life for many a long and trying day. As at Jerusalem on his first visit, and as at Corinth, and as afterwards on the stormy sea, the Lord stood by him and said, "Cheer thee, Paul; for as thou didst bear witness respecting me at Jerusalem, so must thou also bear witness at Rome."

The dawn of the next day sufficed to prove that his manœuvre in the Sanhedrin had only won a temporary success at the cost of a deeper exasperation. So unquenchable was the fury against him, and so inflamed was the feeling of disappointment that Lysias should have snatched him away from their revenge, that in the morning no less than forty Jews bound themselves with a terrible *cherem* not to eat or drink till they had killed him.[1] The Jews, like some Christians in the worst days of Christendom, believed in the divine right of assassination as the means of getting rid of a tyrant or an apostate.[2] Their penal blindness had deceived them into the sanctification of religious murder. How dark a picture does it present to us of the state of Jewish thought at this period that, just as Judas had bargained with the chief priests for the blood-money of his Lord, so these forty *sicarii* went, not only without a blush, but with an evident sense of merit, to the hostile section of the Sanhedrin, to suggest to them the concoction of a lie for the facilitation of a murder. "We are bound under a curse not to touch food till we slay Paul. Do you then, and the Sanhedrin, give notice to the commandant to bring him down to you, under pretext of a more accurate inquiry into his case. We, before he gets near you, are prepared to slay him." So far from rejecting the suggestion with execration, as many a heathen would have done, these degenerate Jews and worldly priests agreed to it with avidity. But a secret known to forty conspirators, and requiring the complicity of an indefinite number more, is no secret at all. There were sure to be dark hints, ominous gestures, words of ill-concealed triumph, and, indeed, so unanimous among the orthodox Jews, and even, we fear, among some nominal Jewish Christians, was the detestation of the man who taught "apostasy from Moses," that in most circles there was no need for any pretence of concealment. When St. Peter had been in prison, and in peril of execution, the Christian community of Jerusalem had been in a ferment

---

[1] For instances of a similar *cherem*, see 1 Sam. xiv. 24; Jos. *Antt.* 8, § 3, &c.
[2] *Sanhedr.* 9; Jos. *Antt.* xii. 6, § 2; Philo, *De Sacrif.*, p. 855.

of alarm and sorrow, and prayer had been made day and night without ceasing to God for him; but St. Peter, and especially the St. Peter of that early period, was regarded with feelings very different from those with which the Judaic believers looked on the bold genius whose dangerous independence treated Mosaism and its essential covenant as a thing of the past for converted Gentiles. We hear of no prayer from any one of the Elders or the "many myriads" on behalf of St. Paul. He owed to a relative, and not to the Church, the watchful sympathy which alone rescued him from murder. He had a married sister living in Jerusalem, who, whether she agreed or not with the views of her brother—and the fact that neither she nor her family are elsewhere mentioned, and that St. Paul never seems to have put up at her house, makes it at least very doubtful—had yet enough natural affection to try to defeat a plot for his assassination. Most gladly would we have known something further about the details. All that we are told is, that the son of this lady, apparently a mere boy, on hearing of the intended ambuscade, went at once to the barracks of Fort Antonia, and gaining ready access to his uncle, who, as an untried Roman citizen, was only kept in *custodia militaris*, revealed to him the plot. The Apostle acted with his usual good sense and promptitude. Sending for one of the ten centurions of the garrison, he said to him, "Lead this youth to the commandant, for he has something to tell him."[1] The centurion went immediately to Lysias, and said, "The prisoner Paul called me to him, and asked me to lead this youth to you, as he has something to say to you." There is a touch of very natural

[1] The minuteness of the narrative, perhaps, indicates that St. Luke, who sought for information from all sources, had received the story from the youth himself.

kindness in the way in which the Roman officer received the Jewish boy. Seeing, perhaps, that he was nervous and flustered, both from the peril to which he was subjecting himself by revealing this secret—since suspicion would naturally fall on him—and also by finding himself in the presence of the most powerful person in Jerusalem, the military delegate of the dreaded Procurator—Lysias took him by the hand, and walking with him to a place where they were out of earshot, began to ask him what his message was. The youth told him that he would immediately receive a request from the Sanhedrin to summon a meeting next day, and bring Paul once more before them to arrive at some more definite result; and that more than forty *sicarii* had agreed on time and place to murder his prisoner, so that the only way to defeat the plot was to refuse the request of the Sanhedrin. Lysias saw the importance of the secret, and instantly formed his plans. He told the youth not to mention to any one that he had given him information of the conspiracy, and, summoning two centurions, ordered them to equip two hundred legionaries, seventy cavalry soldiers, two hundred lancers,[1] with two spare horses, to be ready to escort Paul safely to Cæsarea that very evening at nine o'clock. He was extremely glad to get rid of a prisoner who created such excitement, and who was the object of an animosity so keen that it might at any moment lead to a riot. At that day, too, charges of bribery flew about in the most dangerous manner. Celer, a Roman knight of far higher rank than himself, had actually been dragged by Jews round the walls of Jerusalem, and finally be-

---

[1] δεξιολάβοι, Vulg. *lancearii*. The only passage to throw light on the word is one adduced by Meyer from Constantine the Porphyrogenete, which proves nothing. A reads δεξιόβολοι. One explanation is *gens du train*—men who held a second horse by the right hand.

headed, for receiving a bribe from the Samaritans.[1] Agrippa I. had been dismissed from Antioch; and no less a person than the Procurator Cumanus had been imprisoned and disgraced. So corrupt was the Roman administration in the hands of even the highest officials, that if Paul were murdered Lysias might easily have been charged with having accepted a bribe to induce him to connive at this nefarious conspiracy.[2] There was now sufficient pretext to send Paul away swiftly and secretly, and so get rid of an embarrassing responsibility. At nine that evening, when it was dark and when the streets would be deserted, the large escort of four hundred and seventy soldiers—an escort the necessity of which shows the dangerous condition of the country, and the extent of Lysias's alarm—stood ready at the gate of the barracks; and before the tramp of horse and foot began to startle the silent city, the commandant handed to the centurion in command a letter which, in its obvious genuineness, exhibits a very dexterous mixture of truth and falsehood, and by no means bears out the representation that Lysias was a stupid person. It was one of those abstracts of criminal charges called *elogia*, which it was the custom to write in submitting a prisoner to the cognisance of a superior judge; and it was ingeniously framed with a view to obviate beforehand any possible charge of illegal conduct towards a Roman citizen. The conduct of Lysias, though a little hasty at first, had however been, on the whole, both kind and honourable; and he would probably be assured by St. Paul that, so far as he was concerned, he might lay aside all anxiety as to any proceedings intended to vindicate the inalienable rights conferred by the citizenship.

---

[1] Jos. *Antt.* xx. 6, § 3; *B. J.* ii. 12, § 7.
[2] One of the cursives (137) actually adds ἐφοβήθη γὰρ μήποτε ἁρπάσαντες αὐτὸν οἱ Ἰουδαῖοι ἀποκτείνωσι καὶ αὐτὸς μεταξὺ ἔγκλημα ἔχῃ ὡς χρήματα εἰληφώς.

The letter ran as follows:—

"Claudius Lysias to his Excellency the Procurator Felix, greeting.

"The prisoner whom I send to you is one who was seized by the Jews, and was on the point of being killed by them when I came down upon them with my forces, and rescued him on being informed that he was a Roman. As I wanted to know further the reason why they accused him, I took him down into their Sanhedrin, and found that he was being accused of questions of their law, but had against him no charge which deserved death or chains. But on receiving secret intimation of a plot which was to be put in force against him, I immediately sent him to you, at the same time giving notice to his accusers also to say all they had to say about him in your presence. Farewell!"

Paul was mounted on one of the horses provided for him, and the escort rode rapidly through the disturbed country, in the vicinity of Jerusalem, with a sharp lookout against any ambuscade. After that, being too numerous and well-armed to have any dread of mere brigands, they went at their ease along a Roman road, the thirty-five miles to Antipatris.[1] Here they rested for the remainder of the night. Next day the four hundred legionaries and lancers marched back to Jerusalem, while the mounted soldiers rode forward on the remaining twenty-five miles to Cæsarea. St. Paul thus entered Cæsarea with a pomp of attendance very unlike the humble guise in which he had left it, amid the little caravan of his fellow-Christians. They entered the town in broad daylight, and so large a body passing

[1] Kefr Saba; Jos. *Antt.* vi. 5, § 2.

through the streets must have attracted many curious eyes. How must Philip and the other Christians of Cæsarea have been startled to recognise the rapid fulfilment of their forebodings as they saw the great teacher, from whom they had parted with so many tears, ride through the streets, with his right hand chained to the arm of a horseman, amid a throng of soldiers from the garrison of Antonia! That ride, in the midst of his Roman body-guard, was destined to be his last experience of air and exercise, till—after two years of imprisonment —his voyage to Rome began.

The centurion and his prisoner were at once introduced into the presence of Felix. Felix read the letter of Lysias, and after briefly inquiring to what province Paul belonged, and being told that he was a Cilician, he said, "I will hear out your case when your accusers have arrived."[1] He then handed Paul over to a soldier to be kept in one of the guard-rooms attached to the old Herodian palace which now formed the splendid residence of the procurators of Judæa.

[1] "Qui cum elogio mittuntur ex integro audiendi sunt."

CHAPTER XLI.

PAUL AND FELIX.

"Antonius Felix, per omnem saevitiam et libidinem, jus regium servili ingenio exercuit."—TAC. *Hist.* v. 9.

"Jam pridem Judaeae impositus . . . et cuncta malefacta sibi impune ratus."—*Ann.* xii. 54.

A ROMAN judge to whom a prisoner had been sent with an *elogium* was bound, if possible, to try him within three days. Felix, however, had to send a message to Jerusalem, and fix a time for the case to come on, in order that the accusers might be present; and as the journey took nearly two days, it was the fifth day after St. Paul's arrival at Cæsarea that he was brought to trial. The momentary diversion in his favour, of which by this time the Pharisees were probably ashamed, had settled into an unanimous hatred, and the elders, probably of both parties, hurried down to accuse their adversary. Ananias in person accompanied them, eager for revenge against the man who had compared him to a plastered sepulchre. It must have been intensely disagreeable to these dignified personages to be forced to hurry on a fatiguing journey of some seventy miles from the religious to the political capital of Judæa, in order to induce a Gentile dog to give up an apostate *mesîth* to their jurisdiction; but the Sanhedrists, smarting under defeat, would not be likely to leave any stone unturned which should bring the offender within reach of vengeance.

They wished to make sure of the extradition of their

victim, and being little able to plead either in Greek or
Latin, and more or less ignorant of the procedure in
Roman courts, they gave their brief to a provincial
barrister named Tertullus. Everything was done with
due formality. They first lodged their complaint, and
then the prisoner was confronted with them that he might
hear, and if possible refute, their accusations. Tertullus
was evidently a practised speaker, and St. Luke has faithfully preserved an outline of his voluble plausibility.
Speaking with politic complaisance as though he were
himself a Jew, he began by a fulsome compliment to Felix,
which served as the usual *captatio benevolentiae*. Alluding
to the early exertions of Felix against the banditti and the
recent suppression of the Egyptian false Messiah, he began
to assure his Excellency, with truly legal rotundity of
verbiage, of the quite universal and uninterrupted gratitude of the Jews for the peace which he had secured to
them, and for the many reforms [1] which had been initiated
by his prudential wisdom. The real fact was that Felix
was most peculiarly detested, and that though he had
certainly suppressed some brigands, yet he had from the
earliest times of his administration distinctly encouraged
more,[2] and was even accused of having shared their
spoils with Ventidius Cumanus when he had the separate
charge of Samaria.[3] He then apologised for intruding
ever so briefly on his Excellency's indulgent forbearance,
but it was necessary to trouble him with three counts of
indictment against the defendant—namely, that first, he
was a public pest, who lived by exciting factions among all
the Jews all over the world; secondly, that he was a ring-

---

[1] xxiv. 2, διορθωμάτων, κ, A, B, E. The other reading κατορθωμάτων is a more general expression.

[2] Jos. *Antt*. xx. 8, § 5; *B. J*. ii. 13, § 3; Euseb. *H. E.* ii. 20—22.

[3] Jos. *Antt*. xx. 8, § 9; Tac. *Ann*. xii. 54, "*quies provinciae reddita.*"

leader of the Nazarenes; and thirdly, that he had attempted to profane the Temple. They had accordingly seized him, and wanted to judge him in accordance with their own law; but Lysias had intervened with much violence and taken him from their hands, ordering his accusers to come before the Procurator. By reference to Lysias[1] his Excellency might further ascertain the substantial truth of these charges. When the oration was over, since there were no regular witnesses, the Jews one after another "made a dead set" against Paul,[2] asseverating the truth of all that Tertullus had stated.

Then the Procurator, already impatient with the conviction that this was, as Lysias had informed him, some Jewish squabble about Mosaic minutiæ, flung a haughty nod to the prisoner, in intimation that he might speak. St. Paul's *captatio benevolentiae* was very different from that of Tertullus. It consisted simply in the perfectly true remark that he could defend himself all the more cheerfully before Felix from the knowledge that he had now been Procurator for an unusual time,[3] and could therefore, from his familiarity with Jewish affairs, easily ascertain that it was but twelve days[4] since the Pentecost, to which feast he had come, not only with no seditious purpose, but actually to worship in Jeru-

---

[1] This entire clause (Acts xxiv. 6—8) is omitted from καὶ κατὰ down to 'ἐπὶ σέ in א, A, B, G, H, and in the Coptic, Sahidic, Latin, and other versions. If it be an interpolation, the παρ' οὗ must refer to Paul, but there are great difficulties either way, and verse 22 is in favour of their genuineness. On the other hand, if genuine, why should the passage have been omitted? D, which has so many additions, is here deficient.

[2] Ver. 9, συνεπέθεντο. א, A, B, E, G, H.

[3] xxiv. 10, ἐκ πολλῶν ἐτῶν, since A.D. 52, i.e., six years. "Non ignoravit Paulus artem rhetorum *movere laudando*.'" (Grot.)

[4] 1. Arrival. 2. Interview with James, &c. 3—7. Vow and arrest. 8. Sanhedrin. 9. Conspiracy. 10. Arrival at Cæsarea. 11, 12. In custody. 13. Trial.

salem; and that during that time he had discoursed with
no one, and had on no occasion attracted any crowd, or
caused any disturbance, either in the Temple or in the
Synagogues, or in any part of the city. He, therefore, met
the first and third counts of the indictment with a positive
contradiction, and challenged the Jews to produce any
witnesses in confirmation of them. As to the second count,
he was quite ready to admit that he belonged to what they
called a sect; but it was no more an illegal sect than those
to which they themselves belonged, since he worshipped
the God whom, as a Jew, he had been always taught to
worship—frankly accepted their entire Scriptures—and
believed, exactly as the majority of themselves did, in a
resurrection of the just and unjust. In this faith it had
always been his aim to have a conscience void of offence
towards God and towards man. He had now been five
years absent from Jerusalem, and on returning with alms
for the poor of his people, and offerings to the Temple, they
found him in the Temple, a quiet and legally purified worshipper. For the riot which had ensued he was not responsible. It had been stirred up by certain Asiatic Jews, who
ought to have been present as witnesses, and whose absence
was a proof of the weakness of the case against him. But
if their attendance could not be secured, he called upon his
accusers themselves to state the result of their trial of him
before the Sanhedrin, and whether they had a single fact
against him, unless it were his exclamation as he stood
before them, that he was being tried about a question of
the resurrection of the dead.

The case had evidently broken down. St. Paul's
statement of facts directly contradicted the only charge
brought against him. The differences of doctrine between
the Jews and himself were not in any way to the point,
since they affected questions which had not been touched

upon at all, and of which the Roman law could take no cognisance. It was no part of his duty to prove the doctrine of the Nazarenes, or justify himself for having embraced it, since at that time it had not been declared to be a *religio illicita*. Of this fact Felix was perfectly aware. He had a more accurate knowledge of "that way" than the Jews and their advocate supposed.[1] He was not going, therefore, to hand Paul over to the Sanhedrin, which might be dangerous, and would certainly be unjust; but at the same time he did not wish to offend these important personages. He therefore postponed the trial—*rem ampliavit*—on the ground of the absence of Lysias, who was a material witness, promising, however, to give a final decision whenever he came down to Cæsarea. Paul was remanded to the guard-room, but Felix gave particular instructions to the centurion[2] that his custody was not to be a severe one, and that his friends were to be permitted free access to his prison. St. Luke and Aristarchus certainly availed themselves of this permission, and doubtless the heavy hours were lightened by the visits of Philip the Evangelist, and other Christians of the little Cæsarean community to whom Paul was dear.[3]

[1] xxiv. 22, ἀκριβέστερον.

[2] Ver. 23, τῷ ἑκατοντάρχῃ—the centurion who was present at the trial not at all necessarily, or even probably, the centurion who had escorted him from Antipatris to Cæsarea.

[3] It seems to have been about this time that Felix used the machinations of Simon Magus to induce Drusilla, the younger sister of Agrippa II., to elope from her husband Aziz, and to become his wife. It was a strange thing, and one which must have required all the arts of Simon to effect, that this young and beautiful princess, who was at this time only twenty years old, should have abandoned all her Jewish prejudices, and risked the deadliest abhorrence of her race, by leaving a prince who loved her, and had even been induced to accept circumcision to gratify her national scruples, in order to form an adulterous connexion with a cruel and elderly profligate, who had been nothing better than a slave. Felix would never have dreamt for one moment of making for her sake the immense sacrifice which Aziz had accepted, and which her previous lover, the Prince of Commagene, had refused. Such,

On his return to Cæsarea with his wife Drusilla, and apparently in order to gratify her curiosity to see and hear a person whose strange history and marvellous powers were so widely known, Felix once more summoned Paul into his presence, and bade him discourse to them about his beliefs. Right nobly did Paul use his opportunity. Felix was a Gentile, and was moreover his judge, and it was no part of St. Paul's duty to judge those that are without. Had he assumed such a function, his life must have become one incessant and useless protest. And yet, with perfect urbanity and respect for the powers that be, he spoke of the faith in Christ which he was bidden to explain, in a way that enabled him to touch on those virtues which were most needed by the guilty pair who listened to his words. The licentious princess must have blushed as he discoursed of continence; the rapacious and unjust governor as he spoke of righteousness—both of them as he reasoned of the judgment to come. Whatever may have been the thoughts of Drusilla, she locked them up in her own bosom; but Felix, less accustomed to such truths, was deeply agitated by them. As he glanced back over the stained and guilty past, he was afraid. He had been a slave, in the vilest of all positions, at the vilest of all epochs, in the vilest of all cities. He had crept with his brother Pallas into the position of a courtier at the most morally degraded of all courts. He had been an officer of those auxiliaries who were the worst of all troops. What secrets of lust and blood lay hidden in his earlier life we do not

---

however, were the subtle arts of the Cyprian sorcerer, and such the Greek-like fascinations of the seducer, that he had gained his end, and had thus still further obliterated the memories of his servile origin by marrying a third princess. "Trium reginarum maritum aut adulterum" (Suet. *Claud.* 28). Another of his wives was also a Drusilla, daughter of Juba, King of Mauretania, and granddaughter of Antony and Cleopatra. The third is unknown.

know; but ample and indisputable testimony, Jewish and Pagan, sacred and secular, reveals to us what he had been—how greedy, how savage, how treacherous, how unjust, how steeped with the blood of private murder and public massacre—during the eight years which he had now spent in the government, first of Samaria, then of Palestine. There were footsteps behind him; he began to feel as though "the earth were made of glass." He could not bear the novel sensation of terror which crept over him, or the reproaches of the blushing, shamefaced spirit which began to mutiny even in such a breast as his. He cut short the interview. "Go," he said, "for the present; I will take some future opportunity to summon you to a hearing." Even his remorse was not purely disinterested. Paul had indeed acquired over him some of that ascendency which could hardly fail to be won by so lofty a personality; and Felix, struck by his bearing, his genius, his moral force, sent for him not unfrequently to converse with him respecting his beliefs. But this apparent interest in religious subjects was, in reality, akin to that vein of superstition which made him the ready dupe of Simon Magus, and it did not exclude a certain hankering after a bribe, which he felt sure that Paul, who had brought considerable sums of money to Jerusalem, could either procure or give. He took care to drop hints which should leave no doubt as to his intentions. But Paul was innocent, and neither would he adopt any illicit method to secure his liberty, nor in any case would he burden the affection of his converts to contribute the ransom which he was too poor to offer. He did not wish by dubious human methods to interfere with God's plan respecting him, nor to set a questionable example to the future *libellatici*. He therefore declined to take the hints of Felix, and two years glided away, and he was still in prison.

Towards the end of that time he must have been startled by a terrible clamour in the streets of Cæsarea. Disputes, indeed, were constantly occurring in a city composed half of Jews and half of Greeks, or Syrians, between whom there was a perpetual feud for precedence. All the splendour of the place—its amphitheatre, its temples, its palace—was due to the passion for building which animated the first Herod. The Jewish population was large and wealthy, and since their king had done so much for the town, they claimed it as their own. It was quite true that, but for Herod, Cæsarea would never have been heard of in history. Its sole utility consisted in the harbour which he had constructed for it at enormous cost of money and labour, and which was extremely needed on that inhospitable coast. But the Greeks maintained that it was *their* town, seeing that it had been founded by Strato, and called Strato's Tower until Herod had altered the name in his usual spirit of flattery towards the Imperial House. Towards the close of Paul's imprisonment, the Greeks and Jews came to an open quarrel in the market-place, and the Greeks were being worsted in the combat by their enraged adversaries, when Felix appeared with his cohorts and ordered the Jews to disperse. As his command was not instantly obeyed by the victorious party, Felix, who like all the Romans sided with the Gentile faction, let loose his soldiers upon them. The soldiers were probably not Romans, but provincials.[1] They were therefore delighted to fall on the Jews, many of whom were instantly put to the sword. Not content with this, Felix, whose dislike to the whole race only deepened every year, allowed them to plunder the houses of the

---

[1] There were no Jews among them, because no Jew could serve in the army without a constant necessity of breaking the rules of his religion, so that on this ground they were exempted from the liability to conscription.

wealthier Jews.[1] This crowning act of injustice could not pass unnoticed. Felix, indeed, as Tacitus tells us, had so long learnt to rely on the overwhelming influence of Pallas over Claudius, that he began to think that he might commit any crime he liked without being called to question. But Claudius had now been dismissed to his *apotheosis* by the poisoned mushrooms of Agrippina, and the influence both of Pallas and Agrippina were on the wane. The Jews laid a formal impeachment against Felix for his conduct at Cæsarea, and he was recalled to answer their complaints. Accompanied by Drusilla and Simon Magus, who had by this time assumed the position of his domestic sorcerer, he sailed to Italy, and his very last act was one of flagrant injustice. He had already abused the power of a provincial governor by delaying the trial of Paul for two years. It was a defect in Roman law that, though it ordered the immediate trial of a prisoner sent to a superior court with an *elogium*, it laid down no rule as to the necessary termination of his trial, and thus put into the hands of an unjust Præfect a formidable instrument of torture. Paul had now languished for two full years in the Herodian palace, and Felix had not decided his case. Philo mentions a similar instance in which Flaccus kept Lampo for two years in prison at Alexandria [2] on a charge of *laesa majestas*, in hopes of breaking his heart by a punishment worse than death. Felix had no such object, for he seems to have felt for Paul a sincere respect; but since Paul would not offer a bribe, Felix would not set him free, and—more the slave of self-interest than he had ever been the slave of Antonia—he finally left him bound in order to gratify the malice of the Jews whom he thus strove, but quite

---

[1] The scenes which took place on this occasion were analogous to those which happened at Alexandria under Flaccus.
[2] Philo *in Flacc.* xvi.

vainly, to propitiate. He thought that he could, perhaps, settle some awkward items of their account against him by sacrificing to their religious hatreds a small scruple on the score of justice. Perhaps this was the last drop in the overflowing cup of his iniquity. How he closed his bad career we do not know. It required the utmost stretch of the waning influence of his brother Pallas to save him from the punishment which his crimes had deserved; and, although he was not put to death or banished, he had to disgorge the greater portion of his ill-gotten wealth. Drusilla had one son by her marriage with him, and this son, whose name was Agrippa, perished in the eruption of Vesuvius nineteen years after these events.[1] Felix himself vanishes henceforth into obscurity and disgrace.

[1] A.D. 79. Jos. *Antt.* xx. 7, § 2.

CHAPTER XLII.

ST. PAUL BEFORE AGRIPPA II.

"When I consider this Apostle as appearing either before the witty Athenians, or before a Roman Court of Judicature, in the presence of their great men and ladies, I see how handsomely he accommodateth himself to the apprehension and temper of these politer people."—SHAFTESBURY, *Characteristics*, i. 30.

THE successor of Felix was Porcius Festus (A.D. 60),[1] who, though he too was probably of no higher rank than that of a freedman, was a far worthier and more honourable ruler. His Procuratorship was of very brief duration, and he inherited the government of a country in which the wildest anarchy was triumphant, and internecine quarrels were carried on in the bloodiest spirit of revenge. Had he been Procurator for a longer time, difficult as was the task to hold in the leash the furious hatreds of Jews and Gentiles, he might have accomplished more memorable results. The sacred narrative displays him in a not unfavourable light, and he at any rate contrasts most favourably with his immediate predecessor and successor, in the fact that he tried to administer real justice, and did not stain his hands with bribes.[2]

His first movements show an active and energetic spirit. He arrived in Palestine about the month of August, and three days after his arrival at Cæsarea went direct to Jerusalem. One of the first questions which he had to

---

[1] This furnishes one of the few certain *points de repère* for the precise chronology of the Acts. He died the next year.
[2] Jos. *Antt* xx. 8, § 9; 9, § 1; *B. J.* ii. 14, § 1.

face was the mode of dealing with St. Paul. Two years
of deferred hope, and obstructed purposes, and dreary imprisonment had not quenched the deadly antipathy of the
Jews to the man whose free offer of the Gospel to the Gentiles seemed to them one of the most fatal omens of their
impending ruin. The terrible fight in the market-place
between Jews and Syrian Greeks, which had caused the
disgrace of Felix, had left behind it an unappeased exasperation, and the Jews of Cæsarea were unanimous[1] in
demanding the immediate punishment of Paul. When
Festus reached Jerusalem the same cry[2] met him, and the
death of Paul was demanded, not only by the mob, but
by deputations of all the chief personages in Jerusalem,
headed by Ishmael Ben Phabi, the new High Priest.[3] We
have seen already that the Jews, with great insight into
human nature, eagerly seized the first opportunity of playing upon the inexperience of a newly-arrived official, and
moulding him, if possible, while he was likely to be most
plastic in his desire to create a favourable impression.
But Festus was not one of the base and feeble Procurators
who would commit a crime to win popularity. The Palestinian Jews soon found that they had to do with one who
more resembled a Gallio than a Felix. The people and
their priests begged him as an initial favour not to exempt
Paul's case from their cognisance, but to bring him to
Jerusalem, that he might once more be tried by the Sanhedrin, when they would take care that he should cause no
second fiasco by turning their theologic jealousies against
each other. Indeed, these sacerdotalists, who thought far
less of murder than of a ceremonial pollution,[4] had taken

---

[1] Acts xxv. 24, ἅπαν τὸ πλῆθος τῶν Ἰουδαίων . . . ἐνθάδε.
[2] Id., ἐπιβοῶντες.
[3] He had been appointed by Agrippa II., A.D. 59.
[4] See *Sota*, f. 47, 2; *Tosifta Sota*, c. 14; *Joma*, f. 23, 1; Jos. *B. J. passim*. (Grätz, iii. 321, *seqq.*)

care that if Festus once granted their petition, their hired
assassins should get rid of Paul on the road " or ever he
came near." Festus saw through them sufficiently to
thwart their design under the guise of a courteous offer
that, as Paul was now at Cæsarea, he would return thither
almost immediately, and give a full and fair audience to
their complaints. On their continued insistence, Festus
gave them the haughty and genuinely Roman reply that,
whatever their Oriental notions of justice might be, it was
not the custom of the Romans to grant any person's life
to his accusers by way of doing a favour, but to place the
accused and the accusers face to face, and to give the
accused a full opportunity for self-defence. The High
Priest and his fellow-conspirators, finding that they could
not play either on the timidity of Festus or his complaisance, had to content themselves once more with
organising a powerful deputation to carry out the accusation. Eight or ten days afterwards Festus returned to the
palace at Cæsarea, and the very next day took his seat on
the tribunal to hear the case. The Jews had not again
hired a practised barrister to help them, and the trial
degenerated into a scene of passionate clamour, in which
St. Paul simply met the many accusations against him
by calm denials. The Jews, tumultuously surrounding
the tribunal, reiterated their accusations of heresy, sacrilege, and treason; but as not a single witness was forth-
coming, Paul had no need to do more than to recount
the facts. This time the Jews seem to have defined the
old vague charge that Paul was a stirrer-up of sedition
throughout the Diaspora, by trying to frighten Festus, as
they had frightened Pilate, with the name of Cæsar;[1] but
Festus had too thorough a knowledge of the Roman law

---

[1] Acts xxv. 8.

not to see, through all this murky storm of rage, the two plain facts, that he was trying a false issue, since the inquiry really turned on matters which affected the arcana of Jewish theology; and that even if there was a grain of truth in the Jewish accusations, Paul had not been guilty of anything approaching to a capital crime. Wishing to put an end to the scene—for nothing was more odious to the dignity of a well-trained Roman than the scowling faces, and gleaming eyes, and screaming interpellations of despised Orientals—Festus asked Paul whether he was willing to go up to Jerusalem, and be tried before the Sanhedrin under his protection.[1] This was practically a proposal to transfer the question back from the Roman to the Jewish jurisdiction. But Paul knew very well that he had far more chance of justice at the hands of the Romans than at the hands of Jews, whose crimes were now dragging Jerusalem to her destruction. Jewish tribunals had invariably and even savagely condemned him; Gentile tribunals—Gallio, the Politarchs, the Asiarchs, Lysias, Felix, Festus, even the "Prætors," at Philippi, and at last even the monster Nero—always saw and proclaimed his innocence. But he was sick of these delays; sick of the fierce reiteration of calumnies which he had ten times refuted; sick of being made the bone of contention for mutual hatreds; sick of the arbitrary caprice of provincial governors. Terrible as the black dungeon of Machærus to the free soul of the Baptist, must have been the dreary barracks of Cæsarea to the ardent zeal of Paul. How he must have hated that palace, dripping with the blood of murdered Herods, and haunted

---

[1] This must be the meaning of ἐπ' ἐμοῦ, xxv. 9. There could be no conceivable object in taking Paul to Jerusalem, unless it were to have him once more tried by the Sanhedrin; but of course Festus could not preside at a meeting of the Sanhedrin, though he might be present (somewhat as Lysias was), and see that the accused received fair treatment.

by the worst memories of their crimes! How tired he must have been of the idleness and the ribaldries of provincial soldiers, and the tumultuous noises of collision between Jews and Gentiles which were constantly resounding in those ill-managed streets. Doubtless his imprisonment had been a period of deep inward calm and growth. He knew that his course was not yet over. He was awaiting the fulfilment of God's will. He saw that he had nothing more to hope for from High Priests or Procurators, and seized his opportunity. As a Roman citizen he had one special privilege—that right of appeal to Cæsar, which was still left as the venerable trophy of popular triumph in the struggles of centuries. He had only to pronounce the one word *Appello*, and every enemy would, for a time, be defeated, who was now thirsting for his blood.[1] He determined to exercise his privilege. The Procurator was but a shadow of the Cæsar. His offer sounded plausibly fair, but perhaps Paul saw through it. "I am standing," he said, "at Cæsar's tribunal. There, and not before the Sanhedrin, I ought to be judged. Even you, O Festus! know full well that I never in any respect wronged the Jews. If I am an offender, and have committed any capital crime, it is not against them, but against the Empire; and if I am found guilty, I do not refuse to die. But if all the accusations which these bring against me are nothing, *no one* can sacrifice me to them as a favour." And then he suddenly exclaimed, "Caesarem appello!"

The appeal was a surprise; even Festus, who meant well and kindly, though perhaps with a touch of natural complaisance towards his new subjects, was a little offended by it. It was not agreeable to have his jurisdiction super-

---

[1] By the Lex Julia *De Appellatione.* Cf. Plin. *Epp.* x. 97.

seded by an "appeal" to a superior on the very first occasion
that he took his seat on the tribunal. Paul had not yet
had time to learn his character. He might doubtless
have trusted him more, if he had known him better; but
matters had fallen into a hopeless imbroglio, and perhaps
Paul had some inward intimation that this, at last, was
God's appointed way in which he was to visit Italy, and
to bear witness at Rome.

The appeal at once put an end to all the proceedings
of the court. Festus held a very brief consultation with
his *consiliarii*—or council of his assessors—as to whether
the appeal was legally admissible or not. The case was
too clear to admit of much doubt under this head, and,
after a moment's delay, Festus exclaimed, in words which,
however brusquely spoken, must have thrilled the heart
of more than one person in that assembly, and most of
all the heart of the Apostle himself, " Caesarem appellasti;
ad Caesarem ibis." Perhaps Festus avenged his momentarily wounded vanity by the thought, "You little know
what an appeal to Cæsar means!"

Of course some days must elapse before an opportunity would occur to send Paul from Cæsarea to Italy.
A ship had to be provided, and other prisoners had to be
tried whom it might be necessary to remand to the
Emperor's decision. The delay was a providential one.
It furnished Paul with a happy opportunity of proclaiming the truths and the arguments of Christianity in the
presence of all the Jewish and Gentile magnates of the
capital and of the last scions of that Idumean house of
brilliant adventurers who had allied themselves with
the Asmonæan princes, and worn the title of Jewish
kings.

For only a day or two had elapsed after the appeal,
when Agrippa II., the last of the Herods, and his sister

Berenice came down to Cæsarea to pay their respects to the new Procurator. It was a compliment which they could never safely omit, and we find that they paid similar visits to each Procurator in succession. The regal power of Agrippa, such as it was, depended on no popular support, but simply and solely on the will of the Emperor. As a breath had made him first king of Chalcis (A.D. 48), then of the tetrarchy of Philip (A.D. 52), and finally of various other cities (A.D. 55), so on any day a breath might unmake him. He was not, like his father, "the king of the Jews," and therefore St. Luke, with his usual accuracy in these details, only calls him "the king;" but as he had succeeded his uncle Herod of Chalcis in the guardianship of the Temple, with its sacred robes, and the right of nominations to the High-priesthood, he practically became a mere gilded instrument to keep order for the Romans, and it was essential for him to remain on good terms with them.[1] They in their turn found it desirable to flatter the harmless vanities of a phantom royalty.

During the visit of Agrippa and Berenice to Festus, he took the opportunity of referring to the perplexing case of the prisoner Paul. He told Agrippa of the fury which seemed to inspire the whole Jewish people at the mention of his name, and of the futile results of the trial just concluded. However much the Jews might try to misrepresent the real questions at issue, it was clear that they turned on Mosaic technicalities,[2] and "on one Jesus who

[1] The Romans would have resented any neglect towards their representative, as much as we should resent the conduct of Scindiah or Holkar if they entered the district of one of our Indian Residents without paying their respects.

[2] xxv. 19. The use of the phrase, περὶ τῆς ἰδίας δεισιδαιμονίας, "about their own religious matters" (cf. xvii. 22), shows sufficiently that among Gentiles Agrippa was accustomed to speak of his religion quite in the tone of a man of the world.

was dead whom Paul alleged to be alive"[1]—matters about which Festus had no jurisdiction, and could not be supposed to know anything. The prisoner, however, had refused to be tried again by the Sanhedrin, and had appealed to the decision of the Augustus.

"I should have liked myself also to hear this person," said Agrippa.[2] Festus eagerly closed with the wish, and fixed the next day for the gratification of the king's fancy.

It was not, as is commonly represented, a new trial. That would have been, on all grounds, impossible. Agrippa was without judicial functions, and the authority of the Procurator had been cut short by the appeal. It was more of the nature of a private or drawing-room audience —a sort of show occasion designed for the amusement of these princely guests, and the idle aristocracy of Cæsarea, both Jewish and Gentile. Festus ordered the auditorium to be prepared for the occasion, and invited all the chief officers of the army, and the principal inhabitants of the town. The Herods were fond of show, and Festus gratified their humour by a grand processional display. He would doubtless appear in his scarlet paludament, with his full attendance of lictors and body-guard, who would stand at arms behind the gilded chairs which were placed for himself and his distinguished visitors. We are expressly told that Agrippa and Berenice went in state to the Prætorium, she, doubtless, blazing with all her jewels, and he in his purple robes, and both with the golden circlets of royalty around their foreheads, and attended by a suite of followers in the most gorgeous apparel of Eastern pomp.

---

[1] St. Luke and the early Christians were far too much in earnest in their belief to make them shrink in the least from recording the scorn with which it was spoken of.

[2] xxv. 22, 'Εβουλόμην καὶ αὐτὸς; cf. Gal. iv. 20. It might, however, mean, "I, too, was feeling a personal desire."

It was a compliment to the new governor to visit him with as much splendour as possible, and both he and his guests were not sorry to furnish a spectacle which would at once illustrate their importance and their mutual cordiality. Did Agrippa think of his great-grandfather Herod, and the massacre of the innocents? of his great-uncle Antipas, and the murder of John the Baptist? Of his father Agrippa I., and the execution of James the Elder? Did he recall the fact that they had each died or been disgraced, soon after, or in direct consequence of, those inflictions of martyrdom? Did he realise how closely, but unwittingly, the faith in that "one Jesus" had been linked with the destinies of his house? Did the pomp of to-day remind him of the pomp sixteen years earlier, when his much more powerful father had stood in the theatre, with the sunlight blazing on the tissued silver of his robe, and the people shouting that he was a god?[1] Did none of the dark memories of the place overshadow him as he entered that former palace of his race? It is very unlikely. Extreme vanity, gratified self-importance, far more probably absorbed the mind of this titular king, as, in all the pomp of phantom sovereignty, he swept along the large open hall, seated himself with his beautiful sister by the Procurator's side, and glanced with cold curiosity on the poor, worn, shackled prisoner—pale with sickness and long imprisonment—who was led in at his command.

Festus opened the proceedings in a short, complimentary speech, in which he found an excuse for the gathering, by saying that on the one hand the Jews were extremely infuriated against this man, and that on the other he was entirely innocent, so far as he could see,

[1] A.D. 44. It was now A.D. 60.

of any capital crime. Since, however, he was a Roman citizen, and had appealed to Cæsar, it was necessary to send to "the Lord"[1] some minute of the case, by way of *elogium*, and he was completely perplexed as to what he ought to say. He was, therefore, glad of the opportunity to bring the prisoner before this distinguished assembly, that they, and especially King Agrippa, might hear what he had to say for himself, and so, by forming some sort of preliminary judgment, relieve Festus from the ridiculous position of sending a prisoner without being able to state any definite crime with which he had been charged.

As no accusers were present, and this was not in any respect a judicial assembly, Agrippa, as the person for whom the whole scene was got up, told Paul that he was allowed to speak about himself. Had the Apostle been of a morose disposition he might have despised the hollowness of these mock proceedings. Had he been actuated by any motives lower than the highest, he might have seized the opportunity to flatter himself into favour in the absence of his enemies. But the predominant feature in his, as in the very greatest characters, was a continual seriousness and earnestness, and his only desire was to plead not his own cause, but that of his Master. Festus, with the Roman adulation, which in that age outran even the appetite of absolutism, had used that title of "the Lord," which the later Emperors seized with avidity, but which the earliest and ablest of them had contemptuously refused.[2] But Paul was neither imposed upon by these colossal titles of reverence, nor daunted by these pompous inanities of reflected power.

There is not a word of his address which does not prove how completely he was at his ease. The scarlet sagum of

---

[1] xxv. 26.   [2] Suet. *Oct.* 59; *Tiber.* 27; *Domit.* 13.

the Procurator, the fasces of the lictors, the swords of the legionaries, the gleaming armour of the Chiliarchs, did not for one moment daunt him,—they were a terror, not to good works but to the evil; and he felt that his was a service which was above all sway.

Stretching out his hand in the manner familiar to the orators whom he had often heard in Tarsus or in Antioch,[1] he began by the sincere remark that he was particularly happy to make his defence before King Agrippa, not—which would have been false—for any special worth of his, but because the prince had received from his father—whose anxiety to conform to the Law, both written and oral, was well known—an elaborate training in all matters of Jewish religion and casuistry which could not fail to interest him in a question of which he was so competent to judge. He begged, therefore, for a patient audience, and narrated once more the familiar story of his conversion from the standpoint of a rigid and bigoted Pharisee to a belief that the Messianic hopes of his nation had now been actually fulfilled in that Jesus of Nazareth, whose followers he had at first furiously persecuted, but who had won him, by a personal revelation of His glory, to the knowledge that He had risen from the dead. Why should that belief appear incredible to his hearers? It once had been so to himself; but how could he resist the eye-witness of a noonday vision? and how could he disobey the heavenly voice which sent him forth to open the eyes both of Jews and Gentiles that they might turn from darkness to light and the power of Satan unto God, that, by faith in Jesus, they might receive remission of sins and a lot among the sanctified? He had not been disobedient to it. In Damascus, in Jerusalem,

---

[1] Plut. *Caes.*, p. 729; Appul. *Metam.* ii., "porrigit dextram et ad instar oratorum conformat articulum."

throughout all Judæa, and subsequently among the Gentiles, he had been a preacher of repentance and conversion towards God, and a life consistent therewith. This was why the Jews had seized him in the Temple and tried to tear him to pieces; but in this and every danger God had helped him, and the testimony which he bore to small and great was no blasphemy, no apostasy, but simply a truth in direct accordance with the teachings of Moses and the Prophets, that the Messiah should be liable to suffering, and that from His resurrection from the dead a light should dawn to lighten both the Gentiles and His people.

Paul was now launched on the full tide of that sacred and impassioned oratory which was so powerful an agent in his mission work. He was delivering to kings and governors and chief captains that testimony which was the very object of his life. Whether on other topics his speech was as contemptible as his enemies chose to represent, we cannot say; but on this topic, at any rate, he spoke with the force of long familiarity, and the fire of intense conviction. He would probably have proceeded to develop the great thesis which he had just sketched in outline—but at this point he was stopped short. These facts and revelations were new to Festus. Though sufficiently familiar with true culture to recognise it even through these Oriental surroundings, he could only listen open-mouthed to this impassioned tale of visions, and revelations, and ancient prophecies, and of a Jewish Prophet who had been crucified, and yet had risen from the dead and was Divine, and who could forgive sins and lighten the darkness of Jews as well as of Gentiles. He had been getting more and more astonished, and the last remark was too much for him. He suddenly burst out with the loud and excited interruption, "You are mad, Paul;[1] those many writings are turning your brain." His startling ejaculation checked the majestic stream of the Apostle's eloquence, but did not otherwise ruffle his exquisite courtesy. "I am not mad," he exclaimed with calm modesty, giving to Festus his recognised title of "your Excellency;" "but I am uttering words of reality and soberness." But Festus was not the person whom he was mainly addressing, nor were these the reasonings which he would be likely to understand. It was different with Agrippa. He had read Moses and the Prophets, and had heard, from multitudes of witnesses, some at least of the facts to which Paul referred. To him, therefore, the Apostle appealed in proof of his perfect sanity. "The king," he said, "knows about these things, to whom it is even with confidence that I am addressing my remarks. I am sure that he is by no means unaware of any of these circumstances, for all that I say has not been done in a corner." And then, wishing to resume the thread of his argument at the point where it had been broken, and where it would be most striking to a Jew, he asked—

"King Agrippa, dost thou believe the Prophets? I know that thou believest."

But Agrippa did not choose to be entrapped into a discussion, still less into an assent. Not old in years, but accustomed from his boyhood to an atmosphere of cynicism and unbelief, he could only smile with the good-natured contempt of a man of the world at the enthusiastic earnestness which could even for a moment fancy that *he* would be converted to the heresy of the Nazarenes with their crucified Messiah! Yet he did not wish to be uncourteous. It was impossible not to admire the burning zeal which

---

[1] Wisd. v. 4; 2 Cor. v. 13. There is an iambic rhythm in Festus's interpellation which makes it sound like a quotation.

neither stripes nor prisons could quench—the clear-sighted faith which not even such a surrounding could for a moment dim.

"You are trying to persuade me offhand to be 'a Christian!'"[1] he said, with a half-suppressed smile; and this finished specimen of courtly *eutrapelia* was his bantering answer to St. Paul's appeal. Doubtless his polished remark on this compendious style of making converts sounded very witty to that distinguished company, and they would with difficulty suppress their laughter at the notion that Agrippa, favourite of Claudius, friend of Nero, King of Chalcis, Ituræa, Trachonitis, nominator of the High Priest, and supreme guardian of the Temple treasures, should succumb to the potency of this "short method with a Jew." That a Paul should make the king *a Christian* (!) would sound too ludicrous. But the laugh would be instantly suppressed in pity and admiration of the poor but noble prisoner, as with perfect dignity he took advantage of Agrippa's ambiguous expression, and said, with all the fervent sincerity of a loving heart, "I could pray to God that whether 'in little' or 'in much,'[2] not thou only, but even all who are listening to me to-day might become even such as I am—except," he added, as he raised his fettered hand—" except these bonds." They saw that

---

[1] ἐν ὀλίγῳ, "in brief," "in few words" (cf. προέγραψα ἐν ὀλίγῳ, Eph. iii. 3), "*tout d'un coup*." It cannot mean "almost," which would be παρ' ὀλίγον, or ὀλίγου δεῖ. On the *conatus* involved in the present πείθεις, see my *Brief Greek Syntax*, § 136. But it is very doubtful whether we have got Agrippa's real remark. A reads πείθῃ (Lachm.), and perhaps πείθεις may have come from an original πείθει, '*you are persuading yourself*' (cf. οὐ πείθομαι, ver. 26); for instead of γενέσθαι, the reading of א, A, B is ποιῆσαι, which with πείθεις is unintelligible. From the confusion of readings we might almost conjecture that Agrippa ironically said, με χριστιανὸν ποιήσεις—' you'll soon be making me —*a Christian !*'

[2] St. Chrysostom thinks that St. Paul mistook Agrippa's meaning, and, from ignorance of colloquial Greek (?), supposed him to mean "almost." But Eph. iii. 3 is enough to disprove this.

this was indeed no common prisoner; one who could argue as he had argued, and speak as he had spoken; one who was so filled with the exaltation of an inspiring idea, so enriched with the happiness of a firm faith and a peaceful conscience, that he could tell them how he prayed, that they all—all these princely and distinguished people—could be even such as he—and who yet in the spirit of entire forgiveness desired that the sharing in his faith might involve no share in his sorrows or misfortunes—must be such a one as they never yet had seen or known, either in the worlds of Jewry or of heathendom. But it was useless to prolong the scene. Curiosity was now sufficiently gratified, and it had become clearer than ever that though they might regard Paul the prisoner as an amiable enthusiast or an inspired fanatic, he was in no sense a legal criminal. The king, by rising from his seat, gave the signal for breaking up the meeting; Berenice and Festus, and their respective retinues, rose up at the same time, and as the distinguished assembly dispersed they were heard remarking on all sides that Paul was undeserving of death, or even of imprisonment. He had made, in fact, a deeply favourable impression. Agrippa's decision was given entirely for his acquittal. "This person," he said to Festus, "might have been permanently set at liberty, if he had not appealed to Cæsar." Agrippa was far too little of a Pharisee, and far too much of a man of the world, not to see that mere freedom of thought could not be, and ought not to be, suppressed by external violence. The proceedings of that day probably saved St. Paul's life full two years afterwards. Festus, since his own opinion, on grounds of Roman justice, was so entirely confirmed from the Jewish point of view by the Protector of the Temple, could hardly fail to send to Nero an *elogium* which freely exonerated the prisoner from every legal charge; and even if Jewish intrigues were put in play against him, Nero could not condemn to death a man whom Felix, and Lysias, and Festus, and Agrippa, and even the Jewish Sanhedrin, in the only trial of the case which they had held, had united in pronouncing innocent of any capital crime.

CHAPTER XLIII.

THE VOYAGE AND SHIPWRECK.

"Non vultus instantis tyranni
Mente quatit solida, nec Auster
Dux inquieti turbidus Adriae."—HOR. Od.

"The flattering wind that late with promised aid
From Candia's bay the unwilling ship betrayed,
No longer fawns, beneath the fair disguise,
But like a ruffian on his quarry flies."
FALCONER, *Shipwreck*, canto ii.

AT the earliest opportunity which offered, St. Paul, and such other prisoners [1] as were waiting the result of an appeal, were despatched to Italy under the charge of Julius, a centurion of an Augustan cohort. This Augustan cohort may either be some local troop of soldiers of that name stationed at Cæsarea, since the name "Augustan" was as common as "Royal" among us; or they may have belonged to the body of *Augustani*—veterans originally enrolled by Augustus as a body-guard;[2] or they may have been the Prætorian guards themselves, who occasionally, though not frequently, were sent out of Italy on imperial missions.[3] It is not, however, said that Julius was accompanied by his cohort, and it is not at all impossible that he may have been sent with a few of those chosen soldiers of the most distinguished Roman regiments

---

[1] xxvii. 1. ἑτέρους is not necessarily used with classical accuracy to denote "prisoners of a different class" (Luke viii. 3; Mark xv. 41).

[2] It certainly was not a cohort of "Sebasteni," *i.e.*, natives of Sebaste, the name which Herod had given to Samaria (Jos. *B. J.* ii. 12, § 5).

Pliny, *H. N.* vi. 35. (Lewin, ii. 183.)

to give *éclat* to the arrival of Festus in one of the wealthiest but most disaffected of imperial provinces.[1] If this were the case, Julius may very well have been that Julius Priscus who afterwards rose to the splendid position of one of the two Præfects of the Prætorians, and committed suicide on the disgraceful overthrow of his patron.[2] We see enough of him during this voyage to lead us to believe that he was a sensible, honourable, and kindly man.

Roman soldiers were responsible with their own lives for the security of their prisoners, and this had originated the custom—so painful to the prisoners, and all the more painful because so necessarily irritating to the legionaries— of keeping the prisoners safe by chaining them with a long light chain by the right wrist to the left wrist of soldiers, who relieved each other in turn. It may be imagined how frightfully trying it must have been to have no moment and no movement free, and to be fettered in such horrible proximity to a man who would certainly have been an uneducated specimen of the lowest classes, and who, surrounded from boyhood upwards by rough and demoralising companionships, might be a coarse and loose provincial, or a morose and brutal peasant from the dregs of the Italian population. It is tolerably certain that ashore prisoners were not allowed to go anywhere without this galling protection, but we may hope that they were not always subject to it in the narrow fetid cribs and hatchways of the huge, rolling, unwieldly merchantmen in which their compulsory voyages had to be performed.

Since Festus had arrived in Palestine towards the end of June, it must now have been late in August, and the time was rapidly drawing on in which ancient navigation

---

[1] More strictly Procuratorships. St. Luke, however, uses the general word ἐπαρχία.
[2] Tac. *Hist.* ii. 92; iv. 11. "Pudore magis quam necessitate."

was closed for the year. Every day made the weather more uncertain and the voyage more perilous, and since time was pressing, Julius, to whom the commission was entrusted, embarked his prisoners on board a coasting merchantman of the Mysian town of Adramyttium. As the vessel would touch at the chief ports on the west of Asia, there was every possibility of their finding a ship at Ephesus, or at some nearer port, in which they could perform the rest of their voyage; but if not, Julius might, as a last resource, march his soldiers and their prisoners from Adramyttium to Troas, and thence sail to Neapolis, whence he could proceed along the great Egnatian Road, already so familiar to St. Paul, through Philippi and Thessalonica to Dyrrhachium. Dyrrhachium and Brundusium were to the Romans what Calais and Dover are to the English; and after crossing the Ægean, Julius would march along the Appian Road—in a reverse order through the scenes described with such lively humour by Horace in his *Iter ad Brundusium*—till his journey ended at Rome. This was the route traversed by St. Ignatius and his "ten leopards" who conducted him to his martyrdom, and in his disagreeable connexion with whom he says that he fought with wild beasts all the way. It is, however, most unlikely that a land journey entered into the immediate plans of Julius. As he had several prisoners under his charge, each of whom would require ten soldiers to relieve guard, such a journey would be inexpressibly tedious and extremely expensive; and Julius might rely with tolerable certainty on finding some vessel which was bound from one of the great emporiums of Asia for the capital of the world.

St. Paul was spared one at least of the circumstances which would have weighed most heavily on his spirits— he was not alone. Luke and Aristarchus accompanied him, and, whether such had been their original intention or not, both were at any rate driven by stress of circumstances to remain with him during great part of his Roman imprisonment. They, no doubt, were passengers, not prisoners, and they must either have paid their own expenses,[1] or have been provided with money for that purpose by Christians, who knew how necessary was some attendance for one so stricken with personal infirmities as their illustrious Apostle.

The voyage began happily and prosperously. The leading westerly wind was so far favourable that the day after they started they had accomplished the sixty-seven miles which lay between them and the harbour of Sidon. There they touched, and Julius, who can hardly have been absent from the brilliant throng who had listened to Paul's address before Agrippa, was so indulgently disposed towards him that he gave him leave—perhaps merely on parole—to land and see his friends who formed the little Christian community of that place. This kindness was invaluable to St. Paul. The two years' imprisonment must have told unfavourably upon his health, and he must have been but scantily provided with the requisites for a long voyage. The expression used by St. Luke that Julius allowed him to go to his friend and "be cared for,"[2] seems to imply that even during that one day's voyage he had suffered either from sea-sickness or from general infirmity. The day at Sidon was the one happy interlude which was to prepare him for many anxious, miserable, and storm-tossed weeks.

For from that day forward the entire voyage became a succession of delays and accidents, which, after two months of storm and danger, culminated in hopeless

---

[1] Luke, as a physician, might easily have procured a free passage.
[2] xxvii. 3, ἐπιμελείας τυχεῖν.

shipwreck. No sooner had they left the harbour of Sidon than they encountered the baffling Etesian winds, which blow steadily from the north-west. This was an unlooked-for hindrance, because the Etesians usually cease to blow towards the end of August, and are succeeded by south winds, on which the captain of the merchantman had doubtless relied to waft him back to his port of Adramyttium. His natural course would have been to sail straight across from Sidon to Patara, leaving Cyprus on the starboard; but the very winds which sped St. Paul so blythely along this course to his Cæsarean imprisonment more than two years before, were now against his return, and the vessel had to sail towards Cape Pedalium, the south-eastern promontory of Cyprus, hugging the shore under the lee of the island as far as Cape Dinaretum.[1] On rounding this cape they could beat to windward by the aid of land-breezes and westward currents right across the sea which washes the coasts of Cilicia and Pamphylia, until they dropped anchor in the mouth of the river Andriacus, opposite to a hill crowned with the magnificent buildings of Myra, the former capital of Lycia.[2]

Here they were fortunate—or, as it turned out, unfortunate—enough to find a large Alexandrian wheat-ship,[3] which had undergone the common fate of being driven out of the direct course by the same winds which had baffled the Adramyttian vessel, and which now intended to follow the usual alternative of creeping across the

---

[1] ὑπεπλεύσαμεν, "we sailed under the lee of," i.e., in this instance, "we left Cyprus on the left." Observe that in this narrative alone there are no less than thirteen different expressions for "sailing."

[2] Cf. Thuc. viii. 35.

[3] The Emperor Titus (Suet. *Vit.* 5) did the same on his return from Palestine (cf. Jos. *B. J.* vii. 2; Tac. *H.* iv. 81). At this period that part of the Mediterranean is almost always stormy (Falconer *Dissert.*, p. 16).

Ægean from island to island, northward of Crete, and so to the south of Cythera, and across to Syracuse.[1] This vessel, built for the purposes of the trade which supplied to all Italy the staff of life, could easily provide room for the centurion with his soldiers and prisoners, and such passengers as chose to accompany them. They were, therefore, shifted into this vessel, and sailed for Cnidus, the last point at which they could hope for any help from the protection of the shore with its breezes and currents. The distance between the two spots is only one hundred and thirty miles, and under favourable circumstances they might have got to their destination in twenty-four hours. But the baffling Etesians still continued with unseasonable steadiness, and to reach even to Cnidus occupied many weary and uncomfortable days. And when they got off the beautiful and commodious harbour they were destined to a fresh and bitter disappointment, for they could not enter it. Had they been able to do so the season was by this time so far advanced, and the wind was so steadily adverse, that we can hardly doubt that, unless they continued their journey by land, they would either have waited there for a more favourable breeze, or decided to winter in a port where there was every pleasant requisite at hand for the convenience of so large a vessel, and its numerous crew. Since, however, the wind would neither suffer them to put in at Cnidus,[2] nor to continue their direct voyage, which would have passed north of Crete, the only alternative left them was

---

[1] It will, of course, be borne in mind that (1) they had no compass; and (2) could not work to windward. The Cilician land breeze, which had helped the Adramyttian vessel to Myra, was quite local. Compare Socr. *H. E.* ii. 24; Sozomen, vi. 25 (speaking of the voyage of Athanasius from Alexandria to Rome). Wetst.

[2] xxvii. 7, μὴ προσεῶντος τοῦ ἀνέμου. It is not said that they got to Cnidus, but only that they got "opposite to" or "off" it, and that with difficulty.

to make for Cape Salmone, at the eastern end of the
island, and there sail under its lee. To get to Salmone
was comparatively easy; but when they had rounded it
they had the utmost difficulty in creeping along the
weather shore until they came to a place called Fair
Havens, a little to the east of Cape Matala, and not
far from an obscure town of the name of Lasæa.
While the wind remained in its present quarter it
was useless to continue their voyage, for beyond Cape
Matala the shore trends sharply to the north, and
they would have been exposed to the whole force of the
Etesians, with a lee shore on which they would inevitably
have been dashed to pieces. At Fair Havens, therefore,
they were obliged to put in, and wait for a change of
wind. Time passed, and found them still windbound. It
was now getting towards the close of September. At Fair
Havens St. Paul and any Jewish Christians on board would
probably keep the *Kippor*, or great day of Atonement,[1] the
one fast in the Jewish calendar, which this year fell on
September 24. The autumnal equinox passed. The Feast
of Tabernacles passed, and perhaps some of the sailors regarded with superstitious terror the partial eclipse which
occurred on that evening. The Jewish season for navigation was now over,[2] but the Gentiles did not regard the
sea as closed until November 11.[3] Discussions took place
as to whether they should winter where they were or
choose the first favourable chance of pushing on round Cape
Matala to Port Phœnix, which lay only thirty-four miles
beyond it. St. Paul, whose remarkable ascendency had

[1] It was observed on the tenth of Tisri, which in this year (A.D. 60) fell at the autumnal equinox.
[2] Sept. 28. See Lewin, *Fasti Sacri*, § 1899; and *L'Art de vérifier les Dates*, iv., p. 51.
[3] See Schoettgen, *Hor. Hebr. ad loc.*; Plin. *H. N.* ii. 47; *Veget. De Re Milit.* v. 9.

already displayed itself, was allowed to give his opinion, and he gave it emphatically in favour of staying where they were. "Sirs," he said, "I perceive that this voyage will certainly result in violent weather, and much loss not only of the cargo and of the ship, but even of our lives." His opinion was entitled to great weight, because his many voyages had made him thoroughly familiar with the winds and dangers of a sea in which he had thrice been shipwrecked, and had once floated for a night and a day. The captain, however, and the owner of the vessel gave their opinion the other way; and it must be admitted that they had much to urge. Fair Havens afforded a shelter from the norwester which had so long been prevalent, but it was entirely unprotected against east winds, and indeed lay open to most points of the compass. It would, therefore, be a dangerous haven in which to pass the winter, and it was further unsuitable because the place itself was a poor one, not quite close even to the town of Lasæa, and offering no means of employment or amusement for the soldiers and sailors. It would have been a serious matter to spend three or four months in a place so dreary and desolate, and it seemed worth while, if possible, to get to Port Phœnix. That town, the modern Lutro, which they could reach in a few hours' sail, enjoyed the advantage of the only harbour on the south of Crete which is safe in all weathers, and which was therefore a familiar resort of Alexandrian corn-ships. Its harbour was closed and protected by a little island, and was described by those who advocated its claims as "looking towards Libs and towards Caurus," or, as we should say, towards the southwest and the north-west. It has greatly puzzled commentators to account for this expression, seeing that the entrance to the harbour of Lutro (which is undoubtedly the ancient Phœnix) looks towards the east, and its two openings at the extremities of its sheltering island look precisely in the opposite directions, namely, north-east and south-east. The explanation of this singular anomaly is not to be sought in grammatical illustrations, but in the subjectivity of the sailors, who simply regard the bearings of the harbour from the directions in which they sail into it, and might say, for instance, that a harbour "looked towards" the north, if they could only sail into it by turning their prow northward; just as farther on in the chapter they speak of "some land approaching them," when in reality they are approaching some land.[1] But besides the security of Port Phœnix, it was evidently a far more desirable place for nearly three hundred people to winter in than the comparatively obscure and lonely Fair Havens, and on both these grounds it seemed to be worth a slight risk to reach it. These arguments won the adhesion of the majority, and the centurion, with whom the decision rested, decided that this should be done. St. Paul claimed no inspiration for the solemn advice he gave,[2] and of course there was a fair chance of safely traversing so short a distance. Yet results proved that his advice was right. Fair Havens, though not a first-rate harbour, is yet partially protected by reefs and islets, and though it might not be wholly safe to winter there, yet the risk was much smaller than that which must be incurred by doubling Cape Matala, and so getting possibly seized in the grasp of one of the prevalent and sudden northerly gales, which would drive the ship into almost certain destruction. But there is a gambling element in human nature, and the centurion, at any rate, could hardly avoid following the opinion of the experts, whose interests were so deeply concerned, in preference to that of a prisoner, whose knowledge was not professional and who had so much less at stake.

[1] See further, Smith, p. 49.   [2] Ver. 10, θεωρῶ.

A TYPHOON.

It was not long before the wished-for opportunity occurred.[1] A soft south wind sprang up, and gladly weighing anchor, they hoisted the great mainsail, took their boat in tow, sailed close along the shore to the point of Cape Matala, and then gaily prepared for a delightful run of a few hours to the beautiful and hospitable harbour for which they were abandoning the dull, dreary Lasæa. Now at last a little gleam of prosperity seemed to have shone on their tedious and unfortunate voyage. Perhaps they had a good-natured laugh against Paul the prisoner for advice which would have made them throw away a golden chance. But, alas! the gentle breathing of the south wind in the sails and cordage was but a siren song which had lured them to their destruction. They had not long passed the cape, when a tempestuous typhoon[2]—such as often in those latitudes succeeds a brief spell of the south wind—burst down from the Cretan Ida, and smote with terrible fury on the hapless vessel. The ancient name of this "Levanter," as it is now called, was probably Euroaquilo, a name which exactly describes its direction, since we see from St. Luke's subsequent remarks that it must have been an east-north-easter, which, indeed, continued to blow during the remainder of their voyage.[3] From the first moment that this fatal blast rushed down from the hills and

---

[1] Ver. 13, ἄραντες ἆσσον παρελέγοντο τὴν Κρήτην. The E.V. misses the exact force of the aorist ὑποπνεύσαντος.

[2] The word τυφωνικὸς describes the circular whirling of the clouds caused by the meeting of the S. and the E.N.E. winds. See Plin. *H. N.* ii. 48, "praecipua navigantum pestis;" A. Gell. xix. 1. This change of wind is exactly what might have been expected (Purdy, *Sailing Directory*, ii. 61; Smith, *Voy. and Shipwreck*, p. 412).

[3] Εὐρακύλων, A, B, Sahid., Copt., Smith, p. 59. It was thus a "point wind." If anything is to be said for the very ill-supported Εὐροκλύδων of the Syriac, we can only regard the word as *surfrappé* by Greek sailors (see *Language and Languages*, p. 119).

seized the wheat-ship in its grasp,[1] the condition of the vessel was practically hopeless. It was utterly impossible for her—it would have been impossible for the finest made vessel—to "look the wind in the face."[2] The suddenness and fury of the blow left the sailors not one moment to furl the mainsail, or to do anything but leave the ship to be driven madly forward before the gale,[3] until after a fearful run of twenty-three miles they neared the little island of Clauda,[4] and ran in under its lee. Happily the direction of the wind, and the fact—in which we see the clear hand of Providence—that the storm had burst on them soon after they had rounded Cape Matala, and not a little later on in their course, had saved them from being dashed upon the rocks and reefs, which lie more to the north-west between both Candia and Clauda; but their condition was, in other respects, already dangerous, if not quite desperate. The ships of the ancients had one mainmast and one mainsail; any other masts or rigging were comparatively small and insignificant. Hence the strain upon the vessel from the leverage of the mast was terrific, and it was impossible that the Alexandrian ship, however stoutly built, should have

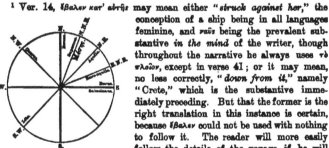

[1] Ver. 14, ἔβαλεν κατ' αὐτῆς may mean either "*struck against her*," the conception of a ship being in all languages feminine, and ναῦς being the prevalent substantive *in the mind* of the writer, though throughout the narrative he always uses τὸ πλοῖον, except in verse 41; or it may mean, no less correctly, "*down from it*," namely "Crete," which is the substantive immediately preceding. But that the former is the right translation in this instance is certain, because ἔβαλεν could not be used with nothing to follow it. The reader will more easily follow the details of the voyage, if he will compare the map with the directions indicated on this compass.

[2] ἀντοφθαλμεῖν. Eyes were painted on the prow (Eustath. *ad Il.* xiv. 717).

[3] One of the Cursives (137) adds συστείλαντες τὰ ἱστία.

[4] Clauda; B, Καυδᾶ; Plin. iv. 20; Gaudus, Gozzo.

scudded with her huge sail set in the grasp of a typhoon, without her timbers starting. It is evident that she had already sprung a serious leak. There was no available harbour in the little island, and therefore the captain, who seems to have shown the best seamanship which was possible in his age, took advantage of the brief and partial lull which was afforded them by the shelter of the island to do the two things which were most immediately necessary—namely, first to secure the means of escape, for some at any rate of the crew, in case the vessel foundered, and next to put off that catastrophe as long as possible. He therefore gave orders at once to hoist the boat on board, and so secure it from being staved in. But this was a task by no means easy. The boat, which they had so securely towed astern in what they meant to be a sort of gala trip to Port Phœnix, had now been hurled after them through twenty miles of their swirling wake, and must therefore have been sorely battered, and perhaps half water-logged; and though they were now in slightly smoother water, yet such was the violence of the gale that it was difficult to perform the simplest duty. They managed, however—and Luke was one of those who lent a hand in doing it[1]—to heave the boat on board as a last resource in the moment of peril; and then the sailors proceeded to adopt the rough and clumsy method in use among the ancients to keep a vessel together. This consisted in undergirding, or, to use the modern and technical term for a practice which is now but rarely resorted to, in "*frapping*" it, by passing stout hawsers several times

---

[1] The narrative of St. Luke is admirably brief and pregnant, and yet we can at once trace in it the tasks in which he and St. Paul and other passengers or prisoners were able to take their share. They helped, for instance, in getting hold of the boat (ver. 16), and in lightening the vessel (ver. 19, *leg. ἐρρίψαμεν*); but they could not help in such technical tasks as frapping the vessel, heaving the lead, dropping the anchors, &c.

under the prow, and tying them as tightly as possible round the middle of the vessel.[1] They had thus met the two most pressing dangers, but a third remained. There was no place into which they could run for shelter, nor could they long avail themselves of the partial protection which they derived from the weather-shore of the little island, and they knew too well that the wind was driving them straight towards the Goodwin Sands of the Mediterranean —the dreaded bay of the Greater Syrtis.[2] There was only one way to save themselves, which was not, as the English Version most erroneously expresses it, to "strike sail and so be driven"—since this would be certain destruction— but to lie to, by rounding the prow of the vessel on the starboard tack as near to the wind as possible, to send down the topsail and cordage, lower the ponderous yard to such a height as would leave enough of the huge mainsail to steady the vessel,[3] set the *artemo*, or storm-sail, and so— having made all as snug as their circumstances permitted —let her drift on, broadside to leeward, at the mercy of wind and wave. This they did, and so ended the miserable day, which had begun with such soft breezes and presumptuous hopes.[4]

All night long the storm blew, and, in spite of the undergirding, the vessel still leaked. Next day, therefore, they kept throwing over from time to time everything that could possibly be spared to lighten the ship;[5]

---

[1] ὑποζώματα, *mitrae*, Vitruv. x. 15, 6; Thuc. i. 29; Plato, *Rep.* x. 616; Hor. *Od.* i. 14, 6. "They [a Spanish man-of-war in a storm] were obliged to throw overboard all their upper-deck guns, and take six turns of the cable round the ship to prevent her opening" (Anson, *Voyage Round the World*). The *Albion* was frapped with iron chains after the battle of Navarino.

[2] Ver. 17, ἐκπέσωσι, not "fall into," but "be driven ashore on" (Hdt. viii. 13).

[3] χαλάσαντες τὸ σκεῦος, here "lowering the great yard" (Smith).

[4] Ver. 13, δόξαντες τῆς προθέσεως κεκρατηκέναι..

[5] Ver. 18, ἐκβολὴν ἐποιοῦντο, *jacturam faciebant*, whereas what they did the day after was an instantaneous act, ἔρριψαμεν.

A DISMANTLED HULK.

but even this was insufficient. The next night brought no relief; the vessel still leaked and leaked, and all labour at the pumps was in vain. The fate which most commonly befell ancient vessels—that of foundering at sea—was obviously imminent. On the third day, therefore, it became necessary to take some still more decisive step. This, in a modern vessel, would have been to cut down the masts by the board; in ancient vessels, of which the masts were of a less towering height, it consisted in heaving overboard the huge mainyard, which, as we see, was an act requiring the united assistance of all the active hands.[1] It fell over with a great splash, and the ship was indefinitely lightened. But now her violent rolling—all the more sensible from the loose nature of her cargo—was only counteracted by a trivial storm-sail. The typhoon, indeed, had become an ordinary gale, but the ship had now been reduced to the condition of a leaky and dismantled hulk, swept from stem to stern by the dashing spray, and drifting, no one knew whither, under leaden and moonless heavens. A gloomy apathy began to settle more and more upon those helpless three hundred souls. There were no means of cooking; no fire could be lighted; the caboose and utensils must long ago have been washed overboard; the provisions had probably been spoiled and sodden by the waves that broke over the ship; indeed, with death staring them in the face, no one cared

---

[1] Ver. 19, τὴν σκευὴν ἐῤῥίψαμεν. (This is the reading of G, H, most of the Cursives, both the Syriac versions, the Coptic, Æthiopic, &c. I agree with De Wette in thinking that the ἐῤῥιψαν of ℵ, A, B, C, *Vulg.*, is a mistaken alteration, due to the ἐποιοῦντο of the previous verse.) The meaning of the expression is disputed, but it has been universally overlooked that the aorist requires *some single act*. Hence Alford's notion that ἡ σκευὴ means beds, furniture, spare rigging, &c., and Wetstein's, that it means the baggage of the passengers, fall to the ground, and Smith's suggestion that the main spar is intended is much strengthened. He observes that the effect would be much the same as that produced in modern vessels by heaving the guns overboard.

to eat. They were famishing wretches in a fast-sinking ship, drifting, with hopes that diminished day by day, to what they regarded as an awful and a certain death.

But in that desperate crisis one man retained his calm and courage. It was Paul the prisoner, probably in physical health the weakest and the greatest sufferer of them all. But it is in such moments that the courage of the noblest souls shines with the purest lustre, and the soul of Paul was inwardly enlightened. As he prayed in all the peacefulness of a blameless conscience, it was revealed to him that God would fulfil the promised destiny which was to lead him to Rome, and that, with the preservation of his own life, God would also grant to him the lives of those unhappy sufferers, for whom, all unworthy as some of them soon proved to be, his human heart yearned with pity. While the rest were abandoning themselves to despair, Paul stood forth on the deck, and after gently reproaching them with having rejected the advice which would have saved them from all that buffeting and loss,[1] he bade them cheer up, for though the ship should be lost, and they should be wrecked on some island, not one of them should lose their lives. For they knew that he was a prisoner who had appealed to Cæsar; and that night an angel of the God, whose child and servant he was, had stood by him, and not only assured him that he should stand before Cæsar, but also that God had, as a sign of His grace, granted him the lives of all on board. He bade them, therefore, to cheer up, and to share his own conviction that the vision should come true.

Who shall say how much those calm undoubting words were designed by God to help in bringing about their own

---

[1] Ἄνδρες, "gentlemen," as in xiv. 15, xix. 25; not κύριοι, as in Acts xvi. 30.

fulfilment? Much had yet to be done; many a strong measure to avert destruction had yet to be taken; and God helps those only who will take the appointed means to help themselves. The proud words "Caesarem vehis"[1] may have inspired the frightened sailor to strenuous effort in the open boat on the coast of Illyria, and certainly it was Paul's undaunted encouragements which re-inspired these starving, fainting, despairing mariners to the exertions which ultimately secured their safety. For after they had drifted fourteen days, tossed up and down on the heaving waves of Adria,[2] a weltering plaything for the gale, suddenly on the fourteenth night the sailors, amid the sounds of the long-continued storm, fancied that they heard the roar of breakers through the midnight darkness. Suspecting that they were nearing some land, and perhaps even detecting that white phosphorescent gleam of a surf-beat shore which is visible so far through even the blackest night, they dropped the lead and found that they were in twenty fathom water. Sounding again, they found that they were in fifteen fathoms.[3] Their suspicions and fears were now turned to certainty, and here was the fresh danger of having their desolate hulk driven irresistibly upon some iron coast. In the face of this fresh peril the only thing to be done was to drop anchor. Had they anchored the vessel in the usual

---

[1] Plut. *Caes.* 38; *De Fort. Rom.* 6; Florus, iv. 2; Dion Cass. xli. 46. "Et fortunam Caesaris" is a later addition.

[2] The Mediterranean between Greece, Italy, and Africa. Strabo, ii. 123. Ἰόνιον πέλαγος, ὁ νῦν Ἀδρίας (Hesych.). διαφερόμενον, "tossed hither and thither." So it would appear to those on board, but probably they drifted in the E.N. Easter, 477 miles in thirteen days at the natural rate of one mile and a half an hour. (See Smith, p. 101.)

[3] Mr. Smith says that Captain Stewart's soundings "would alone have furnished a conclusive test of the truth of this narrative" (p. ix.); and that we are enabled by these and similar investigations "to identify the locality of a shipwreck which took place eighteen centuries ago" (p. xiii.).

manner, from the prow,[1] the ship might have swung round against a reef; nor could they suppose, as they heard the extraordinary loudness of the surf beating upon the shore, that they were at that moment a quarter of a mile from land. So they dropped four anchors[2] through the hawse-holes in which the two great paddle-rudders ordinarily moved; since these—having long been useless as they drifted before the gale—had been half lifted out of the water, and lashed to the stern.[3] Having done this, they could only yearn with intense desire for the dawn of day. All through the remaining hours of that long wintry night, they stood face to face with the agony of death. In its present condition, the leak constantly gaining on them, the waves constantly deluging them with spray, the vessel might at any moment sink, even if the anchors held. But they did not know, what we know, that those anchors had dropped into clay of extraordinary tenacity, which, indeed, was the sole circumstance between them and hopeless wreck.

Gradually through the murky atmosphere of rain and tempest, the grim day began to dawn upon the miserable crew. Almost as soon as they could see the dim outlines of their own faces, haggard and ghastly with so much privation and so many fears, they observed that they were anchored off a low point, over which the sea was curling with a huge and most furious surf. Ignorant that this was Point Koura, on the north-east side of Malta,[4] and not recognising a single landmark on the featureless shore, the only thought of the selfish heathen sailors was to abandon the hulk and crew to their fate, while they

---

[1] "Anchora de prorâ jacitur" (Virg. Æn. iii. 277). Lord Nelson, reading this chapter just before the battle of Copenhagen, ordered our vessels to be anchored by the stern.
[2] Cf. Caes. Bell. Civ. i. 25.
[3] As appears from xxvii. 40.
[4] Where the English frigate *Lively* was wrecked in 1810.

saved themselves in the boat which they had with such
trouble and danger hoisted on board. Pretending, therefore, that they could steady the pitching of the ship, and
therefore make her hold together for a longer time, if they
used more anchors, and laid them out at full length of the
cables [1] instead of merely dropping them from the prow,
they began to unlash the boat and lower her into the sea.
Had they succeeded in their plot, they would probably
have been swamped in the surf upon the point, and all
on board would inevitably have perished from inability to
handle the sinking vessel. From this danger alike the
crew and the sailors were once more saved by the prompt
energy and courage of St. Paul. Seeing through the base
design, he quietly observed to Julius, who was the person
of most authority on board, "If these sailors do not stay
in the ship, *ye* cannot be saved." He says "ye," not
"we." Strong in God's promise, he had no shadow of
doubt respecting his own preservation, but the promise of
safety to all the crew was conditional on their own performance of duty. The soldiers, crowded together in the
vessel with their prisoners, heard the remark of Paul, and—
since he alone at that wild moment of peril had kept calm,
and was therefore the virtual captain—without the smallest
scruple drew their swords and cut through the boat's ropes,
letting her fall away in the trough of the sea. It is not
likely that the sailors felt much resentment. Their plan
was distinctly base, and it offered at the best a very
forlorn and dubious hope of safety. But the daylight had
now increased, and the hour was approaching in which
everything would depend upon their skill and promptitude,
and on the presence of mind of all on board. Once more,
therefore, the Apostle encouraged them, and urged them
all to take some food. "This is the fourteenth day," he

---

[1] xxvii. 30, ἐκτείνειν, not "to cast out," as in E.V.

said, "on which you are continuing foodless, in constant anxiety and vigilance, without taking anything. I entreat you, then, all to join in a meal, which is indeed essential to that preservation, of which I assure you with confidence, for not a hair of the head of any one of you shall perish." And having given them this encouragement, he himself set the example. Making of the simplest necessity of life a religious and eucharistic act, he took bread, gave thanks to God in the presence of them all, broke it, and began to eat. Catching the contagion of his cheerful trust, the drenched, miserable throng of 276 souls, who had so long been huddled together in their unspeakable wretchedness and discomfort, as their shattered vessel lay rolling and tossing under the dismal clouds, took fresh courage, and shared with him in a hearty meal. Knowing that this was the last meal they could ever take in the dismasted vessel, and also that it would be impossible to save the cargo, they lightened and righted the vessel by flinging overboard the wheat, which in the long drift of 476 miles from Clauda in the storm must have shifted much to one side and made the vessel heel over in a dangerous manner. When the full daylight enabled them to examine the shore, they saw no recognisable landmark—since the present Valetta, the harbour of Malta, at which ships often touched, was seven miles E.S.E. of the point where they were wrecked; but they saw a bay, at one extremity of which the cliffs sank down into a flat beach, and the only thing which they could hope to do was to thrust the ship out of her direct course, and strand her at this spot. To make a tack athwart the wind with a disabled ship was a manœuvre by no means easy, but it was worth attempting. They therefore cut away the anchors, letting the ropes drop into the sea,[1] unlashed and

---

[1] Ver. 40, ἀγκύρας περιελόντες εἴων εἰς τὴν θάλασσαν, not "when they had taken up the anchors, they committed *themselves* unto the sea," E.V.

let down the paddle-rudders,[1] hoisted the *artemo*, or foresail[2]—which was all that was left them—to the wind, and steered straight for the beach. But their manœuvre, resolutely as it had been undertaken, was a failure. They had unconsciously anchored off Ras el Koura. The opposite point looked like another promontory, but was in reality the island of Salmonetta, separated from the mainland by a deep, narrow, and precipitous channel. Through this channel, about a hundred yards in width, ran a current, and in the stormy race where the waters of this current met the waters of the bay, the vessel[3] would not answer to the helm, and all they could do was to run her ashore. Happily for them she drove, not upon a rock, but deep into a bank of mud, such as still exists at that very spot. Here the prow stuck immovably fast, while the stern was free. The crew rushed to the prow, while the waves, which broke with fury over the unsupported stern, began instantly to batter it to pieces. Here, even at this extremity, there rose for Paul and the other prisoners a new, unexpected, and yet more terrible danger. It was the duty of the soldiers to be responsible with their own lives for their prisoners. The Roman law was stern, rigid, and unbending, nor did it admit of any extenuating plea. So long as death seemed imminent, and every hand on board might be useful in averting it, the prisoners must have been left unchained; but in such a crisis as this, what was there to prevent any one of them from taking a dive into the sea, and so escaping? It would have been a horrible thing that blood and butchery should stain the planks of a shipwrecked vessel

---

[1] Eur. *Hel.* 1536.
[2] "Levato artemone," Vulg.; "a litil sail," Wycl.; "Vestibus extensis, et quod superaverat unum Velo prora suo," Juv. xii. 68, Artemone Solo. Sch.
[3] So διθάλασσος is used of the *Bosphorus* by Strabo, 124.

at the very moment when safety seemed within reach, and that this human sacrifice of lives which God had rescued should be the only thanksgiving of the survivors. It was even more horrible that they who had fraternised with their fellows in the levelling communism of sympathy, as they huddled side by side, with death staring them in the face, should now thrust their swords into hearts with which their own had so long been beating in fearful sympathy. From this peril the prisoners were again indirectly saved by him whose counsel and encouragement had all along been the direct source of their preservation. If the prisoners were to be killed, equal justice, or injustice, must be dealt to all of them alike, and Julius felt that it would be dastardly ingratitude to butcher the man to whom, under God's providence, they all owed their rescued lives. He therefore forbade the design of the soldiers, and gave orders that every one who could swim should first fling himself overboard, and get to land.[1] The rest seized hold of planks and other fragments of the fast-dissolving wreck.[2] The wind threw them landwards, and at last by the aid of the swimmers all were saved, and—at a spot which, owing to the accurate fidelity of the narrative, can still be exactly identified—a motley group of nearly three hundred drenched, and shivering, and weather-beaten sailors and soldiers, and prisoners and passengers, stood on that chill and stormy November morning upon the desolate and surf-beat shore of the island of Malta. Some, we are sure, there were who joined with Paul in hearty thanks to the God who, though He had not made the storm to cease, so that the waves thereof were still, had yet brought them safe to land, through all the perils of that tempestuous month.

---

[1] Probably Paul was among these (2 Cor. xi. 25).
[2] Ver. 41 ,ἐλύετο, "was going to pieces." "Dissolutum navigium" (Cic. *Att.* xv. 11).

Book X.

ROME.

CHAPTER XLIV.

ST. PAUL'S ARRIVAL AT ROME.

"Paulus Romae, apex Evangelii."—BENGEL.

So ended St. Paul's fourth shipwreck. The sight of the vessel attracted the natives of the island,[1] a simple Punic race, mingled with Greek settlers, and under Roman dominion. There have been times far more recent, and coasts far nearer to the scenes of civilisation, in which the castaways of a derelict would have been more likely to be robbed and murdered than received with hospitality and compassion; but these Maltese Phœnicians, nearly two millenniums ago, welcomed the rescued crew with unusual kindness. Heavy showers had come on, and the shipwrecked men were half-benumbed with fatigue and cold. Pitying their condition, the natives lit a huge fire of fagots and brushwood, that they might dry their clothes, and gave them in all respects a friendly welcome. Paul,

---

[1] The notion that the island on which they were wrecked was not Malta, but the little Adriatic island of Meleda, off the coast of Dalmatia, was started by Constantine the Porphyrogenite. It was founded on mistakes about Adria (xxvii. 27), barbarians (xxviii. 2), and vipers (*id.* 3), combined with various nautical considerations; and was supported by Georgi of Meleda, Jacob Bryant, and Dr. Falconer, and lastly by Dr. J. Mason Neale, in his *Notes on Dalmatia*, p. 161. All that can be said for it may be found in Falconer's *Dissertation* (3rd edit., with additional notes, 1872).

with that indomitable activity and disregard of self which neither danger nor fatigue could check, was busy among the busiest collecting fuel. He had got together a large bundle of furze-roots,[1] and had just put it on the blazing fire, when a viper which had been lying torpid, being suddenly revived and irritated by the heat, darted out of the bundle and "fastened on Paul's hand." Seeing the creature hanging from his hand, and observing that he was a prisoner, the simple natives muttered to one another that he must be some murderer, rescued indeed from the waves, but pursued by just vengeance even on land. Paul, quite undisturbed, shook the creature off into the fire, and was none the worse.[2] The natives expected that he would suddenly drop dead.[3] For a long time they watched him with eager eyes, but when they observed that no unpleasant result of any kind followed, they, like the rude people of Lystra, gradually changed their minds, and said that he was a god.

For three months, until the beginning of February opened the sea to navigation, the crew lived in Malta; and during that time, owing once more to the influence of St. Paul, he and his associates received the utmost kindness. Not far from the scene of the shipwreck lay the town now called Alta Vecchia, the residence of Publius, the governor of the island, who was probably a legate of the Prætor of Sicily. Since Julius was a person of distinction, this Roman official, who bore the title of

---

[1] φρυγάνων (see Theophrast. *Hist. Plant.* 1, 4). Hence the objection that *Bosquetta*, some distance from St. Paul's Bay, is the only place where there is timber in Malta, drops to the ground, even if there were ever anything in it.

[2] The disappearance of the viper from Malta, if it *has* disappeared, is no more strange than its disappearance from Arran. There is a curious parallel to the incident in the Greek Anthology. ("Εκτανε) λυγρὸς ἔχις· τί μάτην πρὸς κύματ' ἐμόχθει τὴν ἐπὶ γῆς φεύγων μοῖραν ὀφειλομένην; (*Anthol.*)

[3] So when Charmian is bitten, "Trembling she stood, and on the sudden dropped," *Ant. and Cleop.* v. 2 (Humphry).

Protos ("First")—a local designation, the accuracy of which is supported by inscriptions[1]—offered to the centurion a genial hospitality, in which Paul and his friends were allowed to share. It happened that at that time the father of Publius was lying prostrated by feverish attacks complicated with dysentery. St. Luke was a physician, but his skill was less effectual than the agency of St. Paul, who went into the sick man's chamber, prayed by his bedside, laid his hands on him, and healed him. The rumour of the cure spread through the little island, and caused all the sick inhabitants to come for help and tendance. We may be sure that St. Paul, though we do not hear of his founding any Church, yet lost no opportunity of making known the Gospel. He produced a deep and most favourable impression, and was surrounded on all sides with respectful demonstrations. In the shipwreck the crew must have lost all, except what little money they could carry on their own persons; they were therefore in deep need of assistance,[2] and this they received abundantly from the love and gratitude of the islanders to whom their stay had caused so many benefits.

Another Alexandrian corn-ship, the *Castor and Pollux*—more fortunate than her shattered consort—had wintered in the harbour of Valetta; and when navigation was again possible, Julius and his soldiers embarked on board of her with their prisoners, and weighed anchor for Syracuse. It was but eighty miles distant, and during that day's voyage St. Paul would gaze for the first time on the giant cone of Etna, the first active volcano he had ever seen. At Syracuse they waited three days for a more favourable wind.

---

[1] Bochart, *Phaleg.* II. i. 26. Πρῶτος Μελιταίων, *Corp. Inscr. Graec.* 5754.

[2] τιμαῖς. Cf. Ecclus. xxxviii. 1; "honos," Cic. *ad Divv.* xvi. 9.

Since it did not come, they made a circuitous tack,[1] which brought them to Rhegium. Here again they waited for a single day, and as a south wind then sprang up, which was exactly what they most desired, they sped swiftly through the Straits of Messina, between the chains of snow-clad hills, and after passing on their left the huge and ever-flashing cone of Stromboli, anchored the next day, after a splendid run of 180 miles, in the lovely Bay of Puteoli. The unfurled topsail which marked the Alexandrian corn-ship would give notice of her arrival to the idlers of the gay watering-place, who gathered in hundreds on the mole to welcome with their shouts the vessels which brought the staff of life to the granaries of Rome. Here Paul had the unexpected happiness to find a little Christian Church, and the brethren begged him to stay with them seven days. This enabled them to spend together a Sabbath and a Sunday, and the privilege was granted by the kindly and grateful Julius. Here, then, they rested, in one of the loveliest of earthly scenes, when Vesuvius was still a slumbering volcano, clad to its green summit with vines and gardens. Paul could not have looked unmoved on the luxury and magnificence of the neighbouring towns. There was Baiæ, where, to the indignation of Horace, the Roman nobles built out their palaces into the sea; and where the Cæsar before whose judgment-seat he was going to stand had enacted the hideous tragedy of his mother's murder, and had fled, pursued by her Furies, from place to place along the shore.[2] In sight was Pandataria, and the other distant rocky islets, dense with exiles of the noblest rank, where Agrippa Postumus, the last of the genuine

---

[1] xxviii. 13. περιελθόντες, "fetched a compass," 2 Sam. v. 33; 2 Kings iii. 9.
[2] A.D. 59. Διὸ καὶ ἄλλοσε ᾔει καὶ ἐπειδὴ κἀνταῦθα τὰ αὐτὰ αὐτῷ συνέβαινε, ἄλλοσε διαπλήκτως μεθίστατο. Dion. lxi. 13, 14; Tac. Ann. xiv. 8; Suet. Nero. 34.

Cæsars, had tried to stop the pangs of famine by gnawing the stuffing of his own mattress, and where the daughter of the great Augustus had ended, in unutterable wretchedness, her life of infamy. Close by was Cumæ, with its Sibylline fame, and Pausilypus, with Virgil's tomb, and Capreæ, where twenty-three years before Tiberius had dragged to the grave his miserable old age. And within easy distance were the little towns of Pompeii and Herculaneum, little dreaming as yet, in their Greek-like gaiety and many-coloured brilliance, how soon they would be buried by the neighbouring mountain in their total and sulphurous destruction.

Here, free and among brethren, Paul passed seven peaceful days. On the eighth they started for Rome, which was only distant a hundred and forty miles. News of their arrival had reached the brethren, and when they had gone about a hundred miles, past Capua, and through the rich vineyards of Italy, and then through the Pomptine Marshes, Paul and Luke and Aristarchus, among the bargees and hucksters who thronged Appii Forum,[1] caught sight of a body of Christians, who had come no less than forty miles to welcome them. Farther than this they could not have come, since there were two ways of reaching Rome from Appii Forum, and the centurion might have preferred the less fatiguing journey by the canal. Ten miles further on, at Tres Tabernæ, they found another group of brethren awaiting them. Though there were a few who loved him at Rome, Paul knew the power, the multitude, and the turbulence of the vast assemblage of synagogues in the great city, and on their favour or opposition much of his future destiny must, humanly speaking, depend. It was natural, therefore, that when he saw the little throng of Christians he should

[1] Hor. Sat. I. v. 4.

thank God, and take courage from this proof of their affection. Nothing cheered and inspired him so much as human sympathy, and the welcome of these brethren must have touched with the brightness of a happy omen his approach to a city which, greatly as he had longed to see it, he was now to enter under circumstances far more painful than he had ever had reason to expect.

And so through scenes of ever-deepening interest, and along a road more and more crowded with stately memorials, the humble triumph of the Lord's slave and prisoner swept on. St. Paul had seen many magnificent cities, but never one which was approached by a road so regular and so costly in construction. As they passed each well-known object, the warm-hearted brethren would point out to him the tombs of the Scipios and Cæcilia Metella, and the thousands of other tombs with all their architectural beauty, and striking bas-reliefs and touching inscriptions; and the low seats for the accommodation of travellers at every forty feet; and the numberless statues of the Dei Viales; and the roadside inns, and the endless streams of carriages for travellers of every rank—humble birotae and comfortable rhedae, and stately carpenta—and the lecticae or palanquins borne on the necks of slaves, from which the occupants looked luxuriously down on throngs of pedestrians passing to and from the mighty capital of the ancient world.

> "What conflux issuing forth or passing in;
> Prætors, Proconsuls to their provinces
> Hasting, or on return, in robes of state,
> Lictors and rods, the ensigns of their power,
> Legions and cohorts, turms of horse and wings;
> Or embassies from regions far remote,
> In various habits, on the Appian road ..
> Dusk faces with white silken turbans wreathed."

How many a look of contemptuous curiosity would be darted at the chained prisoner and his Jewish friends as they passed along with their escort of soldiers! But Paul could bear all this while he felt that he would not be utterly lonely amid the vast and densely-crowded wilderness of human habitations, of which he first caught sight as he mounted the slope of the Alban hills.

Perhaps as they left the Alban hills on the right, the brethren would tell the Apostle the grim annals of the little temple which had been built beside

>   ——" that dim lake which sleeps
>   Beneath Aricia's trees,
>   The trees in whose dim shadow
>   The ghastly priest doth reign,
>   The priest who slew the slayer
>   And shall himself be slain."

And so through ever-lengthening rows of suburban villas, and ever-thickening throngs of people, they would reach the actual precincts of the city, catch sight of the Capitol and the imperial palace, pass through the grove and by the fountain of Egeria, with its colony of begging Jews,[1] march past the pyramid of C. Cestius, under the arch of Drusus, through the dripping Capenian gate,[2] leave the Circus Maximus on the left, and pass on amid temples, and statues, and triumphal arches, till they reached the *Excubitorium*, or barracks of that section of the Prætorian cohorts whose turn it was to keep immediate guard over the person of the Emperor. It was thus that the dream of Paul's life was accomplished, and thus that in March, A.D. 61, in the seventh year of the reign of Nero, under the consulship of Cæsennius Pætus and Petronius Turpilianus, he entered Rome.

---

[1] Juv. *Sat.* iii. 12.   [2] Porta di S. Sebastiano.

Here the charge of the centurion Julius ended, though we can hardly suppose that he would entirely forget and neglect henceforth his noble prisoner, to whom in God's providence he owed his own life and the safety of the other prisoners entrusted to him. Officially, however, his connexion with them was closed when he had handed them over to the charge of the Præfect of the Prætorian guards. From this time forward, and indeed previously, there had always been two Praefecti Praetorio, but during this year a single person held the power of that great office, the honest and soldierly Afranius Burrus.[1] So far, Paul was fortunate, for Burrus, as an upright and humane officer, was not likely to treat with needless severity a prisoner who was accused of no comprehensible charge— of none at any rate which a Roman would consider worth mentioning—and who had won golden opinions both from the Procurators of Judæa and from the centurion who had conducted him from Jerusalem. A vulgar and careless tyrant might have jumped to the conclusion that he was some fanatical Sicarius, such as at that time swarmed throughout Judæa, and so have thrust him into a hopeless and intolerable captivity. But the good word of Julius, and the kindly integrity of Burrus, were invaluable to him, and he was merely subjected to that kind of *custodia militaris* which was known as *observatio*. For the first three days he was hospitably received by some member of the Christian community,[2] and was afterwards allowed to hire a lodging of his own, with free leave to communicate with his friends both by letter and by personal intercourse. The trial of having a soldier chained to him indeed continued, but that was inevitable

---

[1] Acts xxviii. 16, τῷ στρατοπεδάρχῃ. Trajan *ap.* Plin. *Epp.* x. 65, "Vinctus mitti ad *praefectos praetorii* mei debet."

[2] xxviii. 23, εἰς τὴν ξενίαν. Cf. Philem. 22; Acts xxi. 16.

under the Roman system. It was in mitigation of this intolerable concomitant of his imprisonment that the goodwill of his Roman friends might be most beneficially exercised. At the best, it was an infliction which it required no little fortitude to endure, and for a Jew it would be far more painful than for a Gentile. Two Gentiles might have much in common; they would be interested in common topics, actuated by common principles; but a Jew and Gentile would be separated by mutual antipathies, and liable to the incessant friction of irritating peculiarities. That St. Paul deeply felt this annoyance may be seen from his allusions to his "bonds" or his "coupling-chain" in every Epistle of the captivity. When the first Agrippa had been flung into prison by Tiberius, Antonia, out of friendship for his family, had bribed the Prætorian Prefect Macro to place him under the charge of a kind centurion, and to secure as far as possible that the soldiers coupled to him should be good-tempered men. Some small measure of similar consideration may have been extended to Paul; but the service was irksome, and there must have been some soldiers whose morose and sullen natures caused to their prisoner a terrible torture. Yet even over these coarse, uneducated Gentiles, the courtesy, the gentleness, the "sweet reasonableness" of the Apostle, asserted its humanising control. If he was chained to the soldier, the soldier was also chained to him, and during the dull hours until he was relieved, many a guardsman might be glad to hear from such lips, in all their immortal novelty, the high truths of the Christian faith. Out of his worst trials the Apostle's cheerful faith created the opportunities of his highest usefulness, and from the necessities of his long-continued imprisonment arose a diffusion of Gospel truths throughout the finest regiment of that army which less than a century later was to number among its contingents a "thundering legion," and in less than three centuries was to supplant the silver eagles of the empire by the then detested badge of a slave's torture and a murderer's punishment.

It was one of the earliest cares of the Apostle to summon together the leading members of the Roman Ghetto, and explain to them his position. Addressing them as "brethren," he assured them he had neither opposed his people nor contravened their hereditary institutions. In spite of this he had been seized at Jerusalem, and handed over to the Roman power. Yet the Romans, after examining him, had declared him entirely innocent, and would have been glad to liberate him had not the opposition of the Jews compelled him to appeal to Cæsar. But he was anxious to inform them that by this appeal he did not intend in any way to set the Roman authorities against his own nation, and that the cause of the chain he wore was his belief in the fulfilment of that Messianic hope in which all Israel shared.

The reply of the Jews was very diplomatic. Differences within their own pale, connected as we have seen with the name of Christ, had kindled such anger and alarm against them, that less than ten years before this time they had suffered the ruinous indignity of being banished from Rome by an edict of Claudius. That edict had been tacitly permitted to fall into desuetude; but the Jews were anxious not to be again subjected to so degrading an infliction. They therefore returned a vague answer, declaring—whether truthfully or not we cannot say—that neither by letter nor by word of mouth had they received any charge against the Apostle's character. It was true that, if any Jews had been deputed to carry before Cæsar the accusation of the Sanhedrin, they could only have started at the same time as Julius, and would therefore have been delayed by the same storms. The Jews wished, however, to learn from Paul his particular opinions, for, as he was a professed Christian, they could only say that that *sect was everywhere spoken against*.[1] It is obvious that this answer was meant to say as little as possible. It is inconceivable that the Jews should never have heard anything said against St. Paul; but being keen observers of the political horizon, and seeing that Paul was favourably regarded by people of distinction, they did not choose to embroil themselves in any quarrel with him. Nor does their professed ignorance at all disprove the existence of a Christian community so important as that to which St. Paul had addressed his Epistle to the Romans.[2] The Jews could boast of one or two noble proselytes; and it is possible that Pomponia Græcina,[3] wife of Plautius, one of the conquerors of Britain, may have been a Christian. But if so she had long been driven into the deepest seclusion,[4] and the conversion of the Consular Flavius Clemens, and his wife, Flavia Domitilla, who were martyred by Domitian, did not take place till some time afterwards. The Christian Church was composed of the humblest elements, and probably its Jewish and Gentile members formed two almost

---

[1] This they might well say. See Tac. *Ann.* xv. 44, Suet. *Ner.* 16; and, doubtless the *graffiti* of the catacombs, are only successors of others still earlier, just as are the hideous calumnies against which the Christian apologists appeal (Tert. *Apol.* 16, &c.).

[2] In Rom. i. 8 St. Paul tells the Roman Christians that their faith is proclaimed in the whole world. No one familiar with his style would see more in this than the favourable mention of them in the scattered Christian Churches which he visited. To St. Paul, as to every one else, "the world" meant the world in the midst of which he lived, *i.e.*, the little Christian communities which he had founded. Renan remarks, that in reading Benjamin of Tudela, one would imagine that there was no one in the world but Jews; and in reading Ibn Batoutah that there was no one in the world but Moslim.

[3] On this lady see Tac. *Ann.* xiii. 32.

[4] She was privately tried by her husband, and acquitted, in A.D. 57.

distinct communities under separate presbyters.[1] Now, with uncircumcised Gentile Christians of the lowest rank the leading Jews would not be likely to hold any intercourse, even if they were aware of their existence. But is it remembered that Rome at this time was a city of more than two million inhabitants? Is there any improbability that, among so many myriads, a small and struggling sect might, to outsiders, remain utterly unknown? The immense weight of the Epistle to the Romans furnishes no proof that the Church to which it was addressed was one which the world would regard as of any importance. The Sandemanians or Glassites are a Christian body in London, and it is quite conceivable that some eminent member of their body, like the late Mr. Faraday, might address to them a letter of deep significance; would it be any sufficient reason to deny their existence if it was found that the Archdeacons and Rural Deans of London had barely so much as heard of their peculiar tenets?

Since, however, the Romish Jews professed a wish for further information, St. Paul begged them to fix their own day to hear what he had to set before them. They came to him in considerable numbers. That only the heads of their community can have been invited is clear. St. Paul's abode could only have accommodated an insignificant fraction of the Jewish residents, who at this time are believed to have amounted to 60,000. It is said that there were seven synagogues in Rome,[2] and the officers of these synagogues would probably be as many as Paul

---

[1] Lightfoot, *Philippians*, p. 219. It is at any rate a most remarkable fact that, when St. Paul wrote the Epistle to the Colossians, two only of the Judaic Christians showed him any countenance—namely, Mark and Jesus, whose surname of Justus, if it be intended as a translation of δ δίκαιος, shows that he, like "James the Just" was a faithful observer of the Law (Col. iv. 11.)

[2] Friedländer, iii. 510.

could hope to address at once. All day long, from dawn
till evening, he set before them his personal testimony and
his scriptural arguments. That they were not wholly
unimpressed, appears from the length of the discussion;
but while a few were convinced, others disbelieved. The
debate acquired towards its conclusion a somewhat stormy
emphasis; and before it broke up Paul addressed the dis-
sentients with something of his old fiery energy, applying
to them the passage of Isaiah once quoted by our Lord
Himself, which said that they should not see nor hear
because they *would* not, and that their blindness and
deafness were a penal consequence of the grossness of
their hearts. And then he sternly warned them that the
salvation of God was now sent to the Gentiles, and that
the Gentiles would listen to its gracious offer.[1]

Henceforth St. Paul took his own line, opening no
further communication with his obstinate fellow-countrymen. For two whole years he remained in Rome, a
fettered prisoner, but living in his own hired lodging,[2]
and cheered by the visits of the fellow-workers who were
truest and best beloved. The quiet and holy Timotheus
perhaps acted as his amanuensis, and certainly shewed
him all the tenderness of a son;[3] the highly-cultivated
Luke was his historiographer and his physician;[4] Aristarchus attended him so closely as to earn the designation
of his "fellow-prisoner;"[5] Tychicus brought him news
from Ephesus;[6] Epaphroditus warmed his heart by the
contributions which showed the generous affection of
Philippi;[7] Epaphras came to consult him about the

---

[1] Vs. 29 is not found in ℵ, A, B, E.
[2] Μίσθωμα, not "house," as in the E. V., but "lodging"—*meritorium conductum*.
[3] Phil. i. 1; ii. 19, *seqq*.; Col. i. 1; Philem. 1.
[4] Col. iv. 14; Philem. 24.   [6] Eph. vi. 21; Col. iv. 7.
[5] Col. iv. 10; Philem. 24.   [7] Phil. ii. 25; iv. 18.

heresies which were beginning to creep into the churches of Laodicea, Hierapolis, and Colossæ;[1] Mark, dear to the Apostle as the cousin of Barnabas, more than made up for his former defection by his present constancy;[2] and Demas had not yet shaken the good opinion which he at first inspired.[3] Now and then some interesting episode of his ministry, like the visit and conversion of Onesimus, came to lighten the tedium of his confinement.[4] Nor was his time spent fruitlessly, as, in some measure, it had been at Cæsarea. Throughout the whole period he continued heralding the kingdom of God, and teaching about the Lord Jesus Christ with all openness of speech "unmolestedly."

With that one weighty word ἀκωλύτως, we lose the help of the Acts of the Apostles. From the Epistles of the imprisonment we learn that, chained though he was in one room, even the oral teaching of the Apostle won many converts, of whom some at least were in positions of influence; and that—as soldier after soldier enjoyed the inestimable privilege of being chained to him—not his bonds only, but also his Gospel, became known throughout the whole body of Prætorian guards. But besides this, God overruled these two years of imprisonment in Rome for the benefit of the whole world. Two imprisonments, away from books, away from all public opportunities for preaching, each of two years long, with only a terrible shipwreck interpolated between them—how sad an interruption to most minds would these have seemed to be! Yet in the first of these two imprisonments, if nothing

---

[1] Col. i. 7; iv. 12.
[2] Col. iv. 10; Philem. 24; 2 Tim. iv. 11.
[3] Col. iv. 14; Philem. 24; 2 Tim. iv. 10.
[4] Col. iv. 9; Philem. 10.

else was achieved, we can perceive that his thoughts were ripening more and more in silent growth; and in that second imprisonment he wrote the letters which have enabled him to exercise a far wider influence on the Church of Christ throughout the world than though he had been all the while occupied in sermons in every synagogue and missionary journeys in every land.

CHAPTER XLV.

ST. PAUL'S SOJOURN IN ROME.

Πάλιν ἐπιτομὴν τῆς οἰκουμένης.—ATHEN. *Deipnos*, 1120.
Fumum et opes strepitumque Romae.—HOR.

St. Paul's arrival at Rome was in many respects the culminating point of his Apostolic career, and as he continued to work there for so long a time, it is both important and interesting to ascertain the state of things with which he came in contact during that long stay.

Of the city itself it is probable that he saw little or nothing until he was liberated, except such a glimpse of it as he may have caught on his way to his place of confinement. Although his friends had free access to him, he was not permitted to visit them, nor could a chained Jewish prisoner walk about with his guarding soldier. Yet on his way to the Prætorian barracks he must have seen something of the narrow and tortuous streets, as well as of the great open spaces of ancient Rome; something of the splendour of its public edifices, and the meanness of its lower purlieus; something of its appalling contrast between the ostentatious luxury of inexhaustible wealth, and the painful squalor of chronic pauperism.[1] And during his stay he must have seen or heard much of the dangers which beset those densely-crowded masses of human beings;[2] of

---

[1] Juv. *Sat.* iii. 126—189.
[2] Juv. *Sat.* iii. 235; Tac. *Ann.* xv. 38.

men injured by the clumsy carrucae rumbling along with huge stones or swaying pieces of timber;[1] of the crashing fall of houses raised on weak foundations to storey after storey of dangerous height;[2] of women and children trampled down amid the rush of an idle populace to witness the horrid butcheries of the amphitheatre; of the violence of nightly marauders; of the irresistible fury of the many conflagrations.[3] It is obvious that he would not have been allowed to seek a lodging in the Jewish quarter beyond the Tiber, since he would be obliged to consult the convenience of the successions of soldiers whose duty it was to keep guard over him. It is indeed possible that he might have been located near the Excubitorium, but it seems more likely that the Prætorians who were settled there were too much occupied with the duties thrown on them by their attendance at the palace to leave them leisure to guard an indefinite number of prisoners. We infer, therefore, that Paul's "hired apartment" was within close range of the Prætorian camp. Among the prisoners there confined he might have seen the Jewish priests who had been sent to Rome by Felix, and who won from their nation so much approval by the abstinence which they endured in the determination that they would not be defiled by any form of unclean meat.[4] Here, too, he may have seen Caradoc, the British prince whose heroic resistance and simple dignity extorted praise even from Roman enemies.[5] The fact that he was not in the crowded city precincts would enable him at less cost to get a better room than the stifling garrets which Juvenal so feelingly describes as at once ruinously expensive and distressingly inconvenient.

---

[1] Juv. *Sat.* iii. 254—261; Mart. v. 22.
[2] Juv. iii. 197, *seq.*
[3] *Id.* 239, *seq.*, 190—231
[4] Jos. *Vit.* 3.
[5] Tac. *Ann.* xii. 38; *H.* iii. 45.

Considering that he was a prisoner, his life was not dull. If he had to suffer from deep discouragements, he could also thank God for many a happy alleviation of his lot. He had indeed to bear the sickness of hope deferred, and put up with the bitterness of "the law's delays." His trial was indefinitely postponed—perhaps by the loss, during shipwreck, of the *elogium* of Festus; by the non-appearance of his accusers; by their plea for time to procure the necessary witnesses; or by the frivolous and inhuman carelessness of the miserable youth who was then the emperor of the world. He was saddened at the rejection of his teaching by his unconverted countrymen, and by the dislike and suspicion of Judaising Christians. He could not but feel disheartened that some should be preaching Christ with the base and contentious motive of adding affliction to his bonds.[1] His heart must have been sometimes dismayed by the growth of subtle heresies in the infant Church.[2] But, on the other hand, he was safe for the present from the incessant perils and tumults of the past twenty years; and he was deprived of the possibility, and therefore exempt from the hard necessity, of earning by incessant toil his daily bread. And again, if he was neglected by Jews and Judaisers, he was acceptable to many of the Gentiles; if his Gospel was mutilated by unworthy preachers, still Christ was preached; if his bonds were irksome, they inspired others with zeal and courage; if one form of activity had by God's will been restrained, others were still open to him, and while he was strengthening distant Churches by his letters and emissaries, he was making God's message known more and more widely in imperial Rome. He had preached with but small success in Athens, which had been pre-eminently the home of intellect; but he was daily reaping the fruit

---

[1] Phil. i. 16.   [2] Later Epistles, *passim*.

of his labours in the city of empire—the city which had snatched the sceptre from the decrepit hands of her elder sister—the capital of that race which represented the law, the order, and the grandeur of the world.

That many of the great or the noble resorted to his teaching is wholly improbable, nor is there a particle of truth in the tradition which, by the aid of spurious letters, endeavoured to represent the philosopher Seneca as one of his friends and correspondents. We have seen that Gallio prided himself on ignoring his very existence; and it is certain that Seneca would have shared, in this as in all other respects, the sentiments of his brother. In his voluminous writings he never so much as alludes to the Christians, and if he had done so he would have used exactly the same language as that so freely adopted many years later—and, therefore, when there was far less excuse for it—even by such enlightened spirits as Pliny, Tacitus, Epictetus, and M. Aurelius. Nothing can less resemble the inner spirit of Christianity than the pompous and empty vaunt of that dilettante Stoicism which Seneca professed in every letter and treatise, and which he belied by the whole tenor of his life. There were, indeed, some great moral principles which he was enabled to see, and to which he gave eloquent expression, but they belonged to the spirit of an age when Christianity was in the air, and when the loftiest natures, sick with disgust or with satiety of the universal vice, took refuge in the gathered experiences of the wise of every age. It is doubtful whether Seneca ever heard more than the mere name of the Christians; and of the Jews he only speaks with incurable disdain. The ordinary life of the wealthy and noble Roman of St. Paul's day was too much divided between abject terror and unspeakable depravity to be reached by anything short of a miraculous awakening.

> "On that hard Pagan world disgust
>   And secret loathing fell;
> Deep weariness and sated lust
>   Made human life a hell.
>
> In his cool hall, with haggard eyes,
>   The Roman noble lay;
> He drove abroad in furious guise
>   Along the Appian Way.
>
> He made a feast, drank fast and fierce,
>   And crowned his hair with flowers—
> No easier nor no quicker passed
>   The impracticable hours."

The condition of the lower classes rendered them more hopeful subjects for the ennobling influences of the faith of Christ. It is true that they also lived in the midst of abominations. But to them vice stood forth in all its bare and revolting hideousness, and there was no wealth to gild its anguishing reactions. Life and its temptations wore a very different aspect to the master who could lord it over the souls and bodies of a thousand helpless minions, and to the wretched slave who was the victim of his caprice and tyranny. As in every city where the slaves far outnumbered the free population, they had to be kept in subjection by laws of terrible severity. It is no wonder that in writing to a Church of which so many members were in this sad condition, St. Paul had thought it necessary to warn them of the duty of obedience and honour towards the powers that be.[1] The house of a wealthy Roman contained slaves of every rank, of every nation, and of every accomplishment, who could be numbered not by scores, but by hundreds. The master might kill or torture his slaves

---

[1] Rom. xiii., xiv.

with impunity, but if one of them, goaded to passionate revenge by intolerable wrong, ventured to raise a hand against his owner, the whole *familia*, with their wives and children, however innocent, were put to death.[1] The Roman lady looked lovely at the banquet, but the slave girl who arranged a curl wrong had been already branded with a hot iron.[2] The *triclinia* of the banquet might gleam with jewelled and myrrhine cups, but if a slave did but drop by accident one crystal vase he might be flung then and there to feed the lampreys in his master's fishpond. The senator and the knight might loll upon cushions in the amphitheatre, and look on luxuriously at the mad struggles of the gladiators, but to the gladiator this meant the endurance of all the detestable savagery of the *lanista*, and the taking of a horrible oath that, "like a genuine gladiator," he would allow himself to be bound, burned, beaten, or killed at his owner's will.[3] There were, doubtless, many kind masters at Rome; but the system of slavery was in itself irredeemably degrading, and we cannot wonder, but can only rejoice, that, from Cæsar's household downwards, there were many in this condition who found in Christian teaching a light and peace from heaven. However low their earthly lot, they thus attained to a faith so sure and so consolatory that in the very catacombs they surrounded the grim memorials of death with emblems of peace and beauty, and made the ill-

---

[1] The necessity for this law had been openly argued in the Senate, and it was put in force during this very year, A.D. 61, when Pedanius Secundus, the prefect of the city, was murdered by one of his slaves (Tac. *Ann.* xiv. 42). In consequence of that murder—itself caused by dreadful depravities—no less than four hundred slaves had been executed, and it is far from impossible that there may have been some Christians among them. On their numbers see Juv. iii. 141; viii. 180; xiv. 305. Mancipiorum *legiones*, Plin. H. M. xxxiii. 6, § 26.

[2] Juv. xiv. 24; Becker, *Charicles*, ii. 53; *Gallus*, ii. 124.

[3] Petron. *Satyr.* p. 117 (Sen. *Ep.* 7).

spelt jargon of their quaint illiterate epitaphs the expression of a radiant happiness and an illimitable hope.

From the Roman aristocracy, then, Paul had little to expect and little to fear; their whole life—physical, moral, intellectual—moved on a different plane from his. It was among the masses of the populace that he mainly hoped for converts from the Gentiles, and it was from the Jews, on the one hand, and the Emperor, on the other, that he had most to dread. The first terrible blow which was aimed at any Church among the Gentiles was dealt by the Emperor, and the hand of the Emperor was not improbably guided by the secret malice of the Jews. That blow, indeed—the outburst of the Neronian persecution—St. Paul escaped for a time by the guiding Providence which liberated him from his imprisonment just before the great fire of Rome; but since he escaped it for a time only, and since it fell on many whom he had taught and loved, we will conclude this chapter by a glance at these two forces of Antichrist in the imperial city.

1. The importance of the Jews at Rome began, as we have seen, with the days of Pompeius.[1] Julius Cæsar—who, as Philo informs us, felt an undisguised admiration for the manly independence with which they held themselves aloof from that all but idolatrous adulation into which the degenerate Romans were so ready to plunge—allowed them to settle in a large district beyond the Tiber, and yearly to send deputies and temple-tribute to their holy city. From that time forward they were the incessant butt for the half-scornful, half-alarmed wit and wrath of the Roman writers. The district assigned to them, being in the neighbourhood of the wharfs where

[1] Cic. pro Flacc. 28; Jos. c. Apion. i. 7; Tac. Ann. ii. 85; Philo, Leg. ad Galum, .p. 508

the barges from Ostia were accustomed to unlade, was particularly suitable for the retail trade in which they were mainly occupied.[1] They increased with almost incredible rapidity. Their wisp of hay and the basket, which were their sole belongings, and were adopted to secure them from the danger of unclean meats, were known in every quarter. Martial describes how Jewish hawkers broke his morning slumbers with their bawling, and Juvenal complains of the way in which their gipsy-like women got themselves smuggled into the boudoirs of rich and silly ladies to interpret their dreams.[2] Others of them, with a supple versatility which would have done credit to the Greeks themselves, thrust themselves into every house and every profession, flung themselves with perfect shamelessness into the heathen vices, and became the useful tools of wealthy rascality, and the unscrupulous confidants of the "gilded youth."[3] Some became the favourites of the palace, and made nominal proselytes of noble ladies, who, like Poppæa, had every gift except that of virtue.[4] But whatever their condition, they were equally detested by the mass of the population. If they were false to their religion they were flouted as renegades; if they were true to it, their Sabbaths, and their circumcision, and their hatred of pork, their form of oath, their lamp-lightings, and their solemn festivals were held up to angry ridicule,[5] as signs of the most abject superstition. If a Roman saw a knot of Jew beggars, he turned from them with a shudder of disgust; if he noticed the statue of a

---

[1] Jos. *Antt.* xvii. 11, § 1; Tac. *Ann.* ii. 85. See on the whole subject Friedländer, *Sittengesch. Roms*, iii. 500; Hausrath, p. 474, *seqq.*

[2] Mart. i. 41, 3; i. 5, 3; Juv. iv. 116, v. 8; xiv. 134.

[3] Mart. xi. 94; vii. 30.

[4] Tac. *Ann.* xiii. 44, "Huic mulieri cuncta alia fuere praeter honestum animum."

[5] See Pers. v. 180; Hor. *Sat.* ii. 3, 288.

Jewish king or Alabarch, he frowned at it as a proof of the degradation of the age. Whether successful or unsuccessful—whether he was an Herodian prince or a match-selling pedlar—the Jew was to the Latin races an object of abhorrence and disdain. They were regarded with the same feelings as those with which a citizen of San Francisco looks on the Chinese immigrant—as intruders, whose competition was dangerous—as aliens, whose customs were offensive. And yet they made their presence tremendously felt. Rome, so tolerant and so indifferent in her own religious beliefs, was sometimes startled into amazement by the raging violence of their internal disputes. Cicero, one hundred and twenty years before this period, prided himself on his courage in defending Flaccus against their charges, and was obliged to deliver his speech in a low tone of voice, for fear of exciting a riot among the thousands of them who besieged the court to denounce their enemy. Sober Quirites had listened with astonishment to their wild wailing round the funeral pile of their patron, Julius Cæsar.[1] Even poets and satirists imply that those who were attracted by feelings of superstition to adopt some of their customs were neither few in number nor insignificant in position.[2]

Under Augustus their condition was not materially altered. Tiberius, recognising them as a dangerous element in the population, made a ruthless attempt to keep down their numbers by conscriptions and deportations. Gaius, on the other hand, grossly as he behaved to their most venerable ambassadors, was so much attached to the elder Agrippa that he respected their religious and political immunities. The position of the Herodian princes in the imperial court was sufficient to protect them during the greater part of the reign of Claudius. During

[1] Sueton. *Caes.* 84.   [2] Hor. *Sat.* 1, ix. 20.

the reign of Nero, and therefore at the very time of St. Paul's Roman imprisonment, they enjoyed a secret influence of the most formidable kind, since Poppæa never hesitated to intercede for them, and had even given orders that after her death her body was—in accordance with the Jewish practice—to be buried and not burnt.

2. If Paul had little to hope from the Jewish community at Rome, he had still less reason to place any confidence in the justice, or mercy, or even the ordinary discernment of the Cæsar to whom he had appealed. The first three Cæsars had been statesmen and men of genius. For Gaius might have been urged the mitigating plea of congenital madness. Claudius was redeemed from contempt by a certain amount of learning and good nature. But Nero was in some respects worse than any who had preceded him. Incurably vicious, incurably frivolous, with no result of all his education beyond a smattering of ridiculous or unworthy accomplishments, his selfishness had been so inflamed by unlimited autocracy that there was not a single crime of which he was incapable, or a single degradation to which he could not sink. The world never entrusted its imperial absolutism to a more despicable specimen of humanity. He was a tenth-rate actor entrusted with irresponsible power. In every noble mind he inspired a horror only alleviated by contempt. The first five years of his reign—that "golden quinquennium" which was regarded as an ideal of happy government—were a mere illusion.[1] Their external success and happiness had been exclusively due to the wise counsels of Burrus and Seneca, which Nero—who was but seventeen when his stepfather Claudius had been poisoned by his mother Agrippina—was too ignorant, too careless, and too bent on personal pleasure to dispute. Yet in all that con-

[1] Nero succeeded Claudius on October 13, A.D. 54.

cerned the *personal* conduct of himself and of Agrippina even those five years had been thickly sown with atrocities and infamies, of which the worst are too atrocious and too infamous to be told. His very first year was marked not only by open ingratitude to his friends, but also by the assassination of Junius Silanus, and the poisoning of the young son of Claudius—Britannicus, a boy of fourteen, from whom he had usurped the throne. The second year was marked by the cowardly folly of his disguised nightly marauding among his peaceful subjects, after the fashion of the Mohawks in the reign of Queen Anne. From these he had descended, through every abyss of vice and crime, to the murder of his mother, his public displays in the theatre,[1] the flight from place to place in the restless terrors of a haunted conscience, and finally to the most abandoned wickedness when he found that even such crimes as his had failed to sicken the adulation or to shake the allegiance of his people. He was further encouraged by this discovery to throw off all shadow of control. Shortly after Paul's arrival Burrus had died, not without suspicion of being poisoned by his imperial master. Nero seized this opportunity to disgrace Seneca from his high position. To fill up the vacancy created by the death of Burrus, he returned to the old plan of appointing two Prætorian Præfects. These were Fenius Rufus, a man of no personal weight, but popular from his benevolent disposition,[2] and Sofonius Tigellinus, one of the worst characters of that bad age. Tigellinus was dear to Nero from the exceptional cruelty and infamy of his nature, and to him

[1] At the Juvenalia, which he instituted on the occasion of first shaving his beard, Gallio had to submit to the degradation of publicly announcing his appearance in the theatre, and Burrus and Seneca had to act as prompters and tutors, "with praises on their lips and anguish in their hearts" (Dion. lxi. 20, 19; Tac. *Ann.* xiv. 15).

[2] Tac. *Ann.* xiv. 51.

was practically entrusted the entire power.[1] The banishment and subsequent murder of Nero's wife Octavia, the unhappy daughter of Claudius, took place within a year of St. Paul's arrival at Rome.

Such are some of the events which must have been whispered to the Apostle from time to time by the Prætorians who guarded him; and if his condition was rendered less tolerable by the promotion of such a wretch as Tigellinus, he must also have felt that his hopes for the future had been rendered more precarious by the downfall of Seneca, and the now unchecked tyranny of the incestuous matricide before whose tribunal his appeal must soon be tried. But if deep fears as to the result of that appeal alternated with passing hopes, neither his natural fears nor his earthly hopes disturbed the serenity of his soul. He quietly continued the discharge of every duty which was still possible to him in his captivity, and for the rest he knew that his times were in God's hands, and that, whether life awaited him or death, all things were his, whether things present or things to come, and he was Christ's, and Christ was God's. Alike on the stage of stormy publicity and in the solitude of his sad imprisonment, his life was hid with Christ in God.

---

[1] Validior Tigellinus in animo Principis et intimis libidinibus assumptus (Tac. l. c.). Τιγελλῖνον δέ τινα Σοφόνιον ἀσελγείᾳ τε καὶ μιαιφονίᾳ πάντας τοὺς καθ' ἑαυτὸν ἀνθρώπους ὑπεραίροντα (Dion. lxii. 13).

CHAPTER XLVI.

EPISTLES OF THE CAPTIVITY.

> "That man is very strong and powerful who has no more hopes for himself, who looks not to be loved any more, to be admired any more, to have any more honour or dignity, and who cares not for gratitude; but whose sole thought is for others, and who only lives on for them."—HELPS.

THE history of St. Paul's first imprisonment, as well as the thoughts by which he was then occupied, can only be derived from the "Epistles of the captivity." The extant Epistles of St. Paul fall naturally into four connected groups, "separated from each other alike by chronological intervals and by internal characteristics." They are respectively the letters of the second missionary journey (1, 2 Thess.); those of the third missionary journey (1, 2 Cor., Gal., Rom.); those of the first imprisonment (Phil., Col., Philem., Eph.); and those of the second imprisonment (1, 2 Tim., Tit.). These groups may be respectively characterised as the Eschatological Epistles (1, 2 Thess.); the Epistles of the anti-Judaic controversy (1, 2 Cor., Gal., Rom.); the letters against incipient Gnosticism (Col., Eph.); and the Pastoral Epistles (1, 2 Tim., Tit.). The Epistles to the Philippians and to Philemon stand in most respects separate from the group to which they belong.

1. The two letters to the Thessalonians are the simplest of all in their matter and manner, and deal mainly (as we have seen) with the question of the shortly-expected return of Christ. They were written about A.D. 52.

2. The next great group of letters may be called in one of their aspects the letters of Judaic controversy. This group comprises the two Epistles to the Corinthians—which show St. Paul's method of dealing with questions of doctrine and discipline in a restless, intellectual, and partly disaffected Church; and those to the Galatians and Romans. They were written during the years A.D. 57 and A.D. 58, a period pre-eminently of storm and stress in the Apostle's life, of physical suffering and mental anxiety, which leave deep traces on his style.

Of these, the Epistles to the Corinthians are largely occupied with the personal question of Paul's Apostolate. His Jewish-Christian opponents had found it easier to impugn his position than to refute his arguments. It became a duty and a necessity to prove his claim to be a teacher of co-ordinate authority with the very chiefest of the Twelve.

The Epistles to the Galatians and the Romans contain the defence of his main position as regards the Law; a definition of the relations between Christianity and Judaism; and the statement and demonstration of the Gospel entrusted to him by special revelation. Of these, the latter is calmer, fuller, and more conciliatory in tone, and serves as the best commentary on the former.

The Epistle to the Philippians finds its main motive in an entirely different order of conceptions. In it we only hear the dying echoes of the great controversy, and if his one outburst of strong indignation against his opponents (ii. 3—6, 18) reminds us of the heat of the Epistle to the Galatians, on the other hand he here suppresses the natural sense of deep personal injuries, and even utters an expression of rejoicing that these very opponents, whatever may be their motives, are still preachers of the Gospel of Christ (i. 14—20).

3. The next two Epistles, those to the Colossians and Ephesians, mark the rise of a new phase of error. They are the controversy with incipient Gnosticism. Hence also they are the chief Christological and Ecclesiastical Epistles, the Epistles of Christian dogma, the Epistles of Catholicity. The idea and constitution of the Church of Christ was the destined bulwark against the prevalence of heresy, and the doctrine of Christ was the sole preservative against the victory of error. The dominant thought of the Colossians is Christ over all; that of the Ephesians the Universal Church in Christ.

The Epistle to Philemon, a sort of appendix to the Colossians, stands alone as a letter addressed solely to an individual friend, though it involves the statement of an immortal principle.

4. In the last group stand the three Pastoral Epistles, containing, as we should have expected, the proof that there had been a development of the Gnostic tendency on the one hand, and of Church organisation on the other. In the Second Epistle to Timothy we have the last words and thoughts of St. Paul before his martyrdom.[1]

May we go further, and attempt, in one or two words, a description of each separate Epistle, necessarily imperfect from its very brevity, and yet perhaps expres-

---

[1] Other classifications have been attempted—*e.g.*, that of Baur, who divides them into ὁμολογούμενα (four), ἀντιλεγόμενα (six), and νόθα (three).

Similarly, M. Renan classes the Epistles as follows:—1. Incontestable—Gal., 1, 2 Cor., Rom. 2. Authentic, though disputed—1, 2 Thess., Phil. 3. Probably authentic, though open to serious objection—Col. and Philem. 4. Doubtful—Eph. 5. Spurious—The Pastoral Epistles. (*St. Paul,* v.)

Lange classes the Epistles as—1. Eschatological (1, 2 Thess.). 2. Soteriological (Gal., Rom). 3. Ecclesiastical (1 Cor., *polemically*; 2 Cor. *apologetically*). 4. Christological (Col., Eph.). 5. Ethical (Philip.). 6. Pastoral Philem., 1, 2 Tim., Tit.). (*Introd. to Romans.*)

Olshausen's classification of them under the heads of—1. Dogmatic; 2. Practical; 3. Friendly—is unsuccessful.

sive of some one main characteristic? If so, we might perhaps say that the First Epistle to the Thessalonians is the Epistle of consolation in the hope of Christ's return; and the second, of the immediate hindrances to that return, and our duties with regard to it. The First Epistle to the Corinthians is the solution of practical problems in the light of eternal principles; the Second, an impassioned defence of the Apostle's impugned authority, his *Apologia pro vitâ suâ*. The Epistle to the Galatians is the Epistle of freedom from the bondage of the Law; that to the Romans of justification by faith. The Epistle to the Philippians is the Epistle of Christian gratitude and Christian joy in sorrow; that to the Colossians the Epistle of Christ the universal Lord; that to the Ephesians, so rich and many-sided, is the Epistle of "the heavenlies," the Epistle of grace, the Epistle of ascension with the ascended Christ, the Epistle of Christ in His One and Universal Church; that to Philemon, the Magna Charta of emancipation. The First Epistle to Timothy, and that to Titus, are the manuals of the Christian pastor; the Second Epistle to Timothy is the last message of a Christian ere his death.[1]

He must doubtless have written others besides these, but intense as would have been for us the theologic and psychologic interest of even the most trivial of his writings, we may assume, with absolute certainty, that those which we still possess have been preserved in accordance with God's special Providence, and were by far the most precious and important of all that he wrote.

That the four letters which we shall now examine were written at Rome, and not, as some critics have imagined, at Cæsarea, may be regarded as absolutely certain.

[1] See Excursus IV., "Distinctive Words, Keynotes, and Characteristics of the Epistles."

Although Rome is not mentioned in any of them, yet the facts to which they advert, and the allusions in which they abound, are such as exactly suit the ancient and unanimous tradition that they were penned during the Roman imprisonment,[1] while they agree far less with the novel and fantastic hypothesis that they were sent from Cæsarea.[2] If any confirmation for this certain tradition were required, it would be found, as far as the Epistle to the Philippians is concerned, in the salutation which St. Paul sends from the converts in "Cæsar's household." As regards the other three Epistles it is sufficient to say that internal evidence conclusively proves that all three were written at the same time, as they were despatched by the same messengers, and that whereas during his Cæsarean imprisonment St. Paul was looking forward to visit Rome,[3] he is, at the time of writing these letters, looking forward to visit, first Macedonia, then Colossæ.[4] Further than this, the allusions in these Epistles show that, prisoner though he was, he was enabled to exercise a powerful influence for the spread of the Gospel in a city of the highest importance.[5] Meyer, indeed—with that hypercritical ingenuity which, like vaulting ambition, so constantly overleaps itself and falls on the other side—argues that Onesimus is more likely to have fled from Colossæ to Cæsarea than to Rome; an argument of which we can only say that Cæsarea—a mere Procuratorial resi-

[1] Chrys., *Procem ad Epist. ad Ephes.*; Jerome, *ad Eph.* iii. 1, iv. 1, vi. 20; Theodoret, *Procem ad Epist. ad Eph.*, &c. If I do not mention Oeder's theory (?) that the Epistle to the Philippians was written from Corinth (see Schenkel, *Der Brief an die Philippier*, p. 110), it is because "it is not worth while," as Baur says, "to discuss vague hypotheses which have no support in history, and no coherence in themselves."

[2] I can only express my surprise that this theory should have commended itself not only to Schulz and Schneckenburger, but even to Holtzmann, Reuss, Schenkel, and Meyer. [4] Phil. ii. 24; Philem. 22.

[3] Acts xix. 21; xxiii. 11. [5] Eph. vi. 19, 20; Col. iv. 3, 4.

dence full of Jews—would be about the very last town which any one would naturally have dreamt of suggesting as a likely hiding-place for a runaway Asiatic slave. Meyer might as reasonably argue that a London pickpocket would be more likely to hide himself at Biarritz than at New York. His other arguments derived from the non-mention of the name of Onesimus in the Epistle to the Ephesians, and the incidental expression "you also" in that letter, are too trivial for serious discussion.

The question next arises, in what order these Epistles were written; and the *primâ facie* argument that the Epistle to the Philippians seems to have been written before the approaching crisis of his trial has been taken as a sufficient proof that it was written after the other three. On the other hand, there is the same expectation of approaching release in the Epistle to Philemon, so that on this circumstance no conclusion can be built. The notion that this Epistle shows traces of deeper depression than the others, and that this may be accounted for by the change wrought in his affairs through the influence of Tigellinus and Poppæa, is partly unsupported by fact, since a spirit of holy joy is the very keynote of the Epistle; and partly inconsistent with itself, since, if the hostile influences were at work at all appreciably, they were quite as much so within a few months after Paul's Roman imprisonment began, as they were at its close.[1] It is true that the letter could not have been written during the earliest months of the captivity at Rome, because time must be allowed for the news of Paul's arrival there to have reached the

[1] The death of Burrus and the appointment of Tigellinus took place very early in A.D. 62, some nine months after St. Paul's arrival. Nero's marriage with Poppæa took place about the time, and indeed bears very little on the matter, since her influence as Nero's mistress was probably even greater than that which she enjoyed as his wife.

Philippians; for the despatch of Epaphroditus with their contributions; for his illness at Rome; for the arrival of intelligence to that effect at Philippi; and for the return of their expressions of sorrow and sympathy.[1] Now a journey from Rome to Philippi—a distance of seven hundred miles — would, under ordinary circumstances, occupy about a month, and as we do not suppose that any of these letters were written during the first year of the imprisonment, ample time is allowed for these journeys, and no objection whatever to the traditional priority of the Epistle to the Philippians can be raised on this score.

Still less can any argument be urged from the absence of greetings from Luke and Aristarchus, or from the allusion to Timothy as the sole exception to the general selfishness which the Apostle was grieved to mark in those around him. The *presence* of particular names in the greetings of any letter may furnish a probable or even positive argument as to its date, but their *absence* is an indication of the most uncertain character. It needs no more than the commonest everyday experience to prove the utter fallaciousness of the "argument from silence;" and we know far too little of the incessant missions and movements, from church to church, and continent to continent, of the companions of St. Paul, to be able in any way to build upon the non-occurrence of the name of any one of them. Since, therefore, there are no adequate arguments *against* regarding the Epistle to the Philippians as the

---

[1] Dr. Lightfoot (*Philipp.*, p. 34) thinks that Aristarchus may have left St. Paul at Myra, and may have conveyed to Philippi the news of St. Paul's journey to Rome, as he was on his way home to Thessalonica; but I can see no sufficient reason for believing that Aristarchus, who was in some sense St. Paul's "fellow-prisoner" at Rome (Col. iv. 10), went home from Adramyttium (Acts xxvii. 2). In any case he could only have taken the news that St. Paul was *on his way* to Rome, not that he had arrived.

earliest of the four Epistles of the captivity—although it may have been written only a few months before the other three—full weight may be given to the internal evidence, which is in favour of that supposition. That internal evidence consists in the general resemblance of this Epistle to those of the earlier group—especially to the Epistle to the Romans—which enables us to regard it as an intermediate link between the Epistles of the captivity and those of the third Apostolic journey.[1] To the Epistle to the Romans it presents many and close parallels in thought and language, while its general tone and spirit, its comparative calmness, the spiritual joy which breathes through its holy resignation, the absence of impassioned appeal and impetuous reasoning, mark its affinity to the three by which it was immediately followed. Although not much more than four years had now elapsed since Paul, a free man and an active Apostle, elaborated at Corinth the great argument which he had addressed to the Gentiles and proselytes, who formed the bulk of the Church of Rome, his controversy with Judaism had to some extent faded into the background. Every Church that he had founded was now fully aware of his sentiments on the questions which were agitated between the advocates of Judaic rigour and Gospel freedom. In writing to the Philippians there was no need

---

[1] Lightfoot, *Philippians*, pp. 40—45, *e.g.*—

PHILIPPIANS.	ROMANS.	PHILIPPIANS.	ROMANS.
i. 3, 4, 7, 8	i. 8—11	iii. 4, 5	xi. 1
i. 10	ii. 18	iii. 9	x. 3
ii. 8, 9, 10, 11	xiv. 9, 11	iii. 21	viii. 29
ii. 4	xii. 10	iii. 19	xvi. 18

To these we may add Phil. iii. 3, Rom. xii. 1, and the use of φρονεῖν in Phil. i. 7, ii. 2, 5, iii. 15, with Rom. xii. 3, 16, xiv. 6. The Epistle also presents some interesting points of comparison with the last which he ever wrote:—
Phil. i. 23, ἐπιθυμίαν ἔχων εἰς τὸ ἀναλῦσαι, 2 Tim. iv. 6, καιρὸς τῆς ἐμῆς ἀναλύσεως ἐφέστηκεν. Phil. ii. 17, εἰ καὶ σπένδομαι, 2 Tim. iv. 6, ἐγὼ γὰρ ἤδη σπένδομαι. Phil. iii. 14, κατὰ σκοπὸν διώκω ἐπὶ τὸ βραβεῖον, 2 Tim. iv. 7, 8, τὸν δρόμον τετέλεκα, ἀπόκειταί μοι ὁ τῆς δικαιοσύνης στέφανος.

to dwell on these debates, for whatever dangers might yet await them—dangers sufficiently real to call forth one energetic outburst, which reminds us of his earlier tone—they had up to this time proved themselves faithful to his teaching, and were as yet unsophisticated by any tampering interference of emissaries from Jerusalem. The Judaisers of the party of James may have heard enough of the devotion of the Philippians for St. Paul to show them that it would be unadvisable to dog his footsteps through the Christian Churches of Macedonia. They might leave their view of the question with better policy in the hands of those unconverted Jews, who would never hesitate to use on its behalf the engines of persecution. Thus St. Paul had no need to enter on the debate which had so recently occupied the maturity of his powers; and in the Epistle to the Philippians we have only "the spent waves of this controversy." Nevertheless, as we have seen, his was a mind whose sensitive chords continued to quiver long after they had been struck by the plectrum of any particular emotion. He was reminded of past controversies by the coldness and neglect of a community in which some "preached Christ even of contention, supposing to add affliction to his bonds." If, then, he dwelt on doctrinal considerations at all in a letter of affectionate greetings to the community which was dearest to his heart, they would naturally be those on which he had last most deeply thought. By the time that he sat down to dictate the Epistle to the Colossians a fresh set of experiences had befallen him. His religious musings had been turned in an entirely different direction. The visit of Epaphras of Colossæ had made him aware of new errors, entirely different from those which he had already combated, and the Churches of Proconsular Asia evidently needed that his teaching should be directed to questions which lay far apart from the controversies of the last eight years. On the other hand, I regard it as psychologically certain that, had the Epistle to the Philippians been written, as so many critics believe, after those to the "Ephesians" and Colossians, it could not possibly have failed to bear upon its surface some traces of the controversy with that hybrid philosophy—that Judaic form of incipient Gnosticism—in which he had been so recently engaged. These considerations seem to me to have decided the true order of the Epistles of the Captivity, and to give its only importance to a question on which little would otherwise depend.

The Epistle to the Philippians [1] arose directly out of one of the few happy incidents which diversified the dreary uncertainties of St. Paul's captivity. This was the visit of Epaphroditus, a leading presbyter of the Church of Philippi, with the fourth pecuniary contribution by which that loving and generous Church had ministered to his necessities. At Rome, St. Paul was unable with his fettered hands to work for his livelihood, and it is possible that he found no opening for his special trade. One would have thought that the members of the Roman Church were sufficiently numerous and sufficiently wealthy to render it an easy matter for them to supply his necessities; but the unaccountable indifference which seems to have marked their relations to him, and

---

[1] The notion that the Epistle is really two and not one seems to have originated in Phil. iii. 1, and in a mistaken supposition that Polycarp, in his letter to the Philippians, mentions more than one letter of St. Paul to them (ὃς καὶ ἀπὼν ὑμῖν ἔγραψεν ἐπιστολάς, *ad Philip.* c. 3). That 'Επιστολάς, however, may only differ from ἐπιστολή in being a more important term, is *conclusively* proved by Thuc. viii. 51; Jos. *Antt.* xii. 4, § 10. That St. Paul wrote other letters to the Philippians during the ten years which had elapsed since he visited them, and that he may have written other letters after this, is not only possible, but probable; but if any such letters had survived till the time of Polycarp, it is wholly improbable that they should not have been subsequently preserved.

of which he complains both in this and in his later imprisonment, shows that much could not be hoped from their affection, and strangely belied the zealous respect with which they had come thirty or forty miles to meet and greet him. It is, of course, possible that they may have been willing to help him, but that he declined an assistance respecting which he was sensitively careful. But the Philippians knew and valued the privilege which had been accorded to them—and perhaps to them only—by their father in Christ—the privilege of helping him in his necessities. It was a custom throughout the Empire to alleviate by friendly presents the hard lot of prisoners,[1] and we may be sure that when once the Philippians had heard of his condition, friends like Lydia, and other converts who had means to spare, would seize the earliest opportunity to add to his comforts. Epaphroditus arrived about autumn, and flinging himself heartily into the service of the Gospel—which in a city like Rome must have required the fullest energies of every labourer—had succumbed to the unhealthiness of the season, and been prostrated by a dangerous and all but fatal sickness. The news of this illness had reached Philippi, and caused great solicitude to the Church.[2] Whatever gifts of healing were entrusted to the Apostles, they do not seem to have considered themselves at liberty to exercise them in their own immediate circle, or for any ends of personal happiness. No miracle was wrought, except one of those daily miracles which are granted to fervent prayer.[3] Paul had many trials to bear, and the

---

[1] Thus, the friends of Agrippa had helped him by providing him with better fare and accommodation when he was imprisoned by Tiberius; and Lucian relates the warmth and open-handedness with which the Christians diminished the hardships, and even shared night after night the confinement of Peregrinus. [2] Phil. ii. 26.

[3] Compare what Luther said of Melancthon's sickness and recovery.

death of "his brother, Epaphroditus," as he tenderly calls him, would have plunged him in yet deeper sadness. We cannot doubt that he pleaded with God for the life of his sick friend, and God had mercy on him. Epaphroditus recovered; and deeply as Paul in his loneliness and discouragement would have rejoiced to keep him by his side, he yielded with his usual unselfishness to the yearning of Epaphroditus for his home, and of the Christians of Philippi for their absent pastor. He therefore sent him back, and with him the letter, in which he expressed his thankfulness for that constant affection which had so greatly cheered his heart.

And thus it is that the Epistle to the Philippians is one of the least systematic, the least special in character, of all St. Paul's writings. But it is this which raises the genuineness of the letter, not indeed beyond cavil, but far beyond all reasonable dispute. The Tübingen school, in its earlier stages, attacked it with the monotonous arguments of their credulous scepticism. With those critics, if an Epistle touches on points which make it accord with the narrative of the Acts, it was forged to suit them; if it seems to disagree with them, the discrepancy shows that it is spurious. If the diction is Pauline, it stands forth as a proved imitation; if it is un-Pauline, it could not have proceeded from the Apostle. The notion that it was forged to introduce the name of Clement because he was confused with Flavius Clemens, and because Clement was a fellow-worker of St. Peter, and it would look well to place him in connexion with Paul—and the notion that in Phil. ii. 6 — 8 the words *form* and *shape* express Gnostic conceptions, and that the verses refer to the Valentinian Æon Sophia, who aimed at an equality with God—are partly founded on total misinterpretations of the text, and are partly the perversity of a criticism which has strained its eyesight to such an extent as to become utterly purblind.[1] This Epistle is genuine beyond the faintest shadow or suspicion of doubt. The Philippian Church was eminently free from errors of doctrine and irregularities of practice. No schism seems to have divided it; no heresies had crept into its faith; no false teachers had perverted its allegiance. One fault, and one alone, seems to have needed correction, and this was of so personal and limited a character that, instead of denouncing it, Paul only needs to hint at it gently and with affectionate entreaty. This was a want of unity between some of its female members, especially Euodia and Syntyche, whom Paul begs to become reconciled to each other, and whose feud, and any partisanship which it may have entailed, he tacitly and considerately rebukes by the constant iteration of the word "all" to those whom he can only regard as one united body. In fact, we may say that disunion and despondency were the main dangers to which they were exposed; hence "all" and "rejoice" are the two leading words and thoughts. But this absence of any special object makes the letter less doctrinally distinctive than those which are more controversial in character. It would, indeed, be colourless if it did not receive a colouring from the rich hues of the writer's individuality. It is not, like the First Epistle to the Thessalonians, a consolation to the afflicted, by reminding them of the near advent of their Lord;[2] or a series of re-

[1] Baur, *Paul.* ii. 50, *seqq.* Schwegler, *Nachapostol. Zeital.* ii. 133, *seqq.* The three arguments are: (1) Gnostic conceptions in ii. 6—9; (2) want of anything distinctively Pauline; (3) the questionableness of some of the historic data.

[2] The topic of "persecution" is prominent only in the Epistles to the Macedonian Churches. It had led the Philippians to despondency; the Thessalonians to a mistaken *form* of hope.

plies to questions, like the greater part of the First Epistle to the Corinthians; nor a trumpet note of defiance to powerful and aggressive opponents, like the Epistle to the Galatians; nor a treatise of theology, like the Epistle to the Romans: but it is the warm, spontaneous outpouring of a loving heart expressing itself with unreserved gratitude and tenderness towards the favourite children of his ministry. If it exhibits to us somewhat less than other Epistles of St. Paul's peculiar teaching, it has this high source of interest that it shows to us more of his character and feelings. In this respect it somewhat resembles the Second Epistle to the Corinthians, except that in it St. Paul is writing to those who were kindest and most faithful to him, whereas towards the Corinthians he had little cause for gratitude, and much need of forbearance. Amid the trials and suspense of a galling imprisonment it reveals to us, not directly, but as it were unconsciously, the existence of an unquenchable happiness—a peace as of the inmost heart of the ocean under the agitation of its surface storms. It was dictated by a worn and fettered Jew, the victim of gross perjury, and the prey of contending enmities; dictated at a time when he was vexed by hundreds of opponents, and consoled but by few who cared for him; and yet the substance of it all may be summed up in two words—$\chi\alpha\acute{\iota}\rho\omega$, $\chi\alpha\acute{\iota}\rho\epsilon\tau\epsilon$ ("I rejoice; rejoice ye"). If any one compare the spirit of the best-known classic writers in their adversity with that which was habitual to the far deeper wrongs and far deadlier sufferings of St. Paul—if he will compare the Epistle to the Philippians with the "Tristia" of Ovid, the letters of Cicero from exile, or the treatise which Seneca dedicated to Polybius from his banishment in Corsica—he may see, if he will, the difference which Christianity has made in the happiness of man.

CHAPTER XLVII.

THE EPISTLE TO THE PHILIPPIANS.

"Summa Epistolae—gaudeo, gaudete."—BENGEL.

THE greeting is from "Paul and Timotheus, slaves of Jesus Christ, to all the saints who are in Christ Jesus in Philippi, with the bishops and deacons." Timothy is naturally associated with him as one who had laboured at Philippi, but so little is he supposed to have any share in the authorship that St. Paul afterwards proceeds to speak of him in the third person. The "bishops" (*i.e.*, the presbyters) and deacons are specially greeted, perhaps because they had taken an active part in the collection of the contribution. He does not call himself an apostle, because to them no assertion of his authority was in any way needful.[1]

The thanksgiving which follows is unusually full. He tells them that he thanks God in *all* his remembrance of them, *always*, in *all* his supplication on behalf of them *all*, making his supplication with joy for their united work in furtherance of the Gospel from the first day when he had visited them—ten years ago—until now; and he is

---

[1] Phil. i. 1, 2. This Epistle may be thus summarised:—i. 1, 2, Greeting; i. 3—11, Thanksgiving and prayer; 12—26, Personal details; i. 27—ii. 16, Exhortation to unity by the example of Christ; ii. 17—30, Personal details; iii. 1, 2, Last injunction suddenly broken off by a digression in which he denounces Judaism and Antinomianism; iii. 3—iv. 1, Exhortation to unity iv. 2, 3, and to Christian joy; 4—9, Gratitude for their aid; iv. 10—20, Final greetings and benediction; 21—23, The unity of the Epistle (in spite of Heinrichs, Weisse, &c.) is generally admitted.

very sure that God, who began in them that sacred work of co-operation in a good cause, will carry it on to perfection until the day of Christ;[1] a conviction arising from his heartfelt sense that they were ALL of them partakers of the grace which God had granted to him, and which they had manifested by their sympathetic aid in his bondage, and in the defence and establishment of the Gospel. God knows how much he yearns for them in Christ; and his prayer for them is that their love may abound more and more in full knowledge of the truth, and all insight into its application, so that they may discriminate all that is best and highest,[2] and be pure towards God and blameless towards men, for the day of Christ, having been filled with the fruit of a righteousness attainable not by their own works but by Jesus Christ, for the glory and praise of God.[3]

They must not suppose, he tells them, that he is the Apostle of a ruined cause, or that his imprisonment is a sign that God's frown is on his work, and that it is coming to nought; on the contrary, he wants them to recognise that his misfortunes have been overruled by God to the direct furtherance of the Gospel. The necessity of his being coupled to guardsman after guardsman, day after day and night after night, had resulted in the notoriety of his condition as a prisoner for Christ among all the Prætorian cohorts,[4] and to everybody else; and

---

[1] "It is not God's way to do things by halves" (Neander).

[2] Ver. 10, δοκιμάζειν τὰ διαφέροντα, cf. Rom. ii. 18. "Non modo prae malis bona, sed ex malis optima" (Bengel). "Ut probetis potiora" (Vulg.).

[3] i. 3—11.

[4] Ver. 13, ἐν ὅλῳ τῷ πραιτωρίῳ. The word, though used of royal residences in the provinces (Mark xv. 16; Acts xxiii. 35), was purposely avoided at Rome, where the ostentation of a military despotism was carefully kept out of sight (Merivale, vi. 268, n.). The use of *Prætorium* (properly "General's tent") for the house of the Emperor on the Palatine would have been an insult to the Romans. The contrast with τοῖς λοιποῖς πᾶσιν shows that *persons* are meant (Lightfoot, pp. 97—99; Schleusner, s.v.).

the majority of the brethren had been stimulated by his bonds to a divine confidence, which had shown itself in a yet more courageous daring than before in preaching the word of God. Some of them preach Christ out of genuine good will, but some, alas! tell the story of Christ insincerely[1] out of mere envy and discord. The former are influenced by love to him, knowing that he is appointed for the defence of the Gospel; the latter announce Christ out of partisanship with base motives, thinking to make his bonds more galling.[2] Perhaps the day had been when Paul might have denounced them in tones of burning rebuke; but he is already Paul the prisoner, though not yet Paul the aged. He had learnt, he was learning more and more, that the wrath of man, even in a holy cause, worketh not the righteousness of God; he had risen, and was rising more and more, above every personal consideration. What mattered it whether these preachers meant only to insult him, and render his bondage yet more galling? After all, "in every way, whether with masked design or in sincerity, Christ is being preached, and therein I do—aye, and "—whatever angry feelings may try to rise within my heart—" I will rejoice."[3]

It is thus that the Apostle first tramples on the snake of any mere personal annoyance that may strive to hiss in his sad heart, and crushes it yet more vigorously with a determined effort if its hiss still tries to make itself heard. He has attained by this time to a holy resignation.

---

[1] i. 15, κηρύσσουσιν; 16, καταγγέλλουσιν. It is doubtful whether the change of word implies as much as Dean Blakesley seems to think (*Dict. of Bible*, *s.v.* Philippi). 'Εριθεία:—1, Working for hire; 2, Canvassing of hired partisans; 3, "Factiousness" (Arist. *Polit.* v. 3).

[2] *Leg. ἐγείρειν* (א, A, B, D, F, G).

[3] i. 12—18. Perhaps the χαρήσομαι implies, "I shall in the long-run have good cause to rejoice; for," &c.

"For I know that this trouble will turn to salvation by means of your prayer, and the rich outpouring[1] of the spirit of Jesus Christ, in accordance with my earnest desire[2] and hope that with all outspokenness, as always, so now"—he was going to say, "I may magnify Christ," but with his usual sensitive shrinking from any exaltation of himself, he substitutes the third person,[3] and says, "So now Christ shall be magnified in my body, whether by life or by death. For to me to live is Christ, and to die is gain.[4] But if life in the flesh means that I shall reap the fruit of labour . . . well, what to choose I cannot tell; but I am hard pressed by the alternatives. I desire to break up my earthly camp,[5] and be with Christ, for it is very far, far better;[6] but to abide by this earthly life is more necessary for your sakes. And I am confidently persuaded of this, that I shall bide and abide[7] with you all, for the advance and joy of your faith, that by a second stay of mine among you you may have in me some further subject for your Christian glorying."[8]

Only in any case he bids them play worthily the part, not only of Roman but of Christian citizens,[9] that, whether he came and saw their state, or only heard of it at a distance, he might know that they stood firm in one spirit, with one heart, fellow-wrestlers with the Faith in the Gospel, and not scared in anything by their adversaries—conduct which would be to those adversaries a proof of their ultimate perdition, and to themselves of salvation; an evidence from God Himself, since, thus, they were privileged not only to believe in Christ, but to suffer for Him, as sharers in a contest like that in which

---

[1] Ver. 19, ἐπιχορηγία; Gal. iii. 5; 2 Cor. ix. 10; Eph. iv. 16; 2 Pet. i. 5.

[2] Ver. 20, ἀποκαραδοκίαν; Rom. viii. 19; ἐπιτεταμένη προσδοκία, Chrys. (See Jos. B. J. iii. 7, § 26, and Schleusner, s.v.)

[3] Lightfoot, Phil. i. 20.

[4] "Quicquid vivo, Christum vivo . . . In Paulo non Paulus vivit, sed Jesus Christus" (Bengel).

[5] 2 Cor. v. 1; iv. 6—8. On the intermediate state of the dead, see 1 Cor. xv. 51, 52.

[6] Ver. 23, πολλῷ μᾶλλον κρεῖσσον.

[7] μενῶ καὶ παραμενῶ (Lightfoot, Phil. i. 25).

[8] i. 19—26. καύχημα, "a ground of boasting."

[9] Ver. 27, πολιτεύεσθε.

they saw Paul engaged when he was among them, and in which they know by rumour that he was at that moment engaged.[1]

And this brings him to one main object of his letter, which was to urge on them this earnest entreaty:—

"If, then, there be any appeal to you in Christ, if any persuasiveness in love, if any participation in the Spirit, if any one be heart and compassionateness,[2] complete my joy by thinking the same thing, having the same love, heart-united, thinking *one* thing. Nothing for partisanship, nor for empty personal vanity! but in lowliness of mind,[3] each of you thinking others his own superiors, not severally keeping your eye on your own interests, but, also severally, on the interests of others.[4]

"Be of the same mind in yourselves as Christ Jesus was in Himself, who existing in the form (μορφῇ) of God, deemed not equality with God a thing for eager seizure,[5] but emptied Himself, taking the form of a slave, revealing Himself in human semblance, and being found in shape (σχήματι) as a man,[6] humbled Himself, showing Himself obedient even to death, aye, and that death—the death of the Cross."

[1] i. 27—30.

[2] ii. 1, εἴ τις σπλάγχνα καὶ οἰκτιρμοί. This reading of א, A, B, C, D, E, F, G, K, has usually been treated as a mere barbarism. So it is grammatically; but the greatest writers, and those who most deeply stir the heart, constantly make grammar give way to the rhetoric of emotion; and if St. Paul in his eager rush of words really said it, the amanuensis did quite right to take it down. Possibly, too, the word σπλάγχνα had come to be used colloquially like a collective singular (cf. spoglia, dépouille, bible, &c.). How entirely it had lost its first sense we may see from the daring ἐνδύσασθε .. σπλάγχνα of Col. iii. 12.

[3] A word redeemed from the catalogue of vices (Col. ii. 18; Plato, *Legg.* iv., p. 774; Epict. i. 3) into that of virtues.

[4] ii. 1—4, *leg.* σκοποῦντες (א, A, B, F, G).

[5] This interpretation of the Greek Fathers is preferable to that of most of the Latin Fathers, followed by our E.V. It makes ἁρπαγμὸν ἡγεῖσθαι identical in meaning with the common phrase ἅρπαγμα ἡγ. = "to clutch at greedily." Besides, this sense is demanded by the whole context (μὴ τὰ ἑαυτῶν σκοπεῖν). This is the passage which is supposed to be borrowed from the conception of the Valentinian Æon *Sophia*, who showed an eccentric and passionate desire, προάλλεσθαι, "to dart forward;" κεκοινωνῆσθαι τῷ πατρὶ τῷ τελείῳ, "to be associated with the Perfect Father;" καταλαβεῖν τὸ μέγεθος αὐτοῦ, to grasp His greatness! (Iren. *Adv. Haer.* i. 2, 2.)

[6] Baur sees Docetism here, as he saw Valentinianism in ver. 6 (*Paul.* ii. 15—21); μορφή, abiding substantial form (Rom. viii. 29; Gal. iv. 19); σχῆμα, outward transitory fashion (iii. 21; Rom. xii. 2; 1 Cor. vii. 31).

Those words were the very climax; in striving to urge on the Philippians the example of humility and unselfishness as the only possible bases of unity, he sets before them the Divine lowliness which had descended step by step into the very abyss of degradation. He tells them of Christ's eternal possession of the attributes of God; His self-abnegation of any claim to that equality; His voluntary exinanition of His glory; His assumption of the essential attributes of a slave; His becoming a man in all external semblance; His display of obedience to His Father, even to death, and not only death, but—which might well thrill the heart of those who possessed the right of Roman citizenship, and were therefore exempt from the possibility of so frightful a degradation—death by crucifixion. Such were the elements of Christ's self-abasement! Yet that self-humiliation had purchased its own infinite reward, for—

"Because of it God also highly exalted Him, and freely granted Him the name above every name, that in the name of Jesus every knee should bend of heavenly and earthly and subterranean beings, and every tongue gratefully confess[1] that Jesus Christ is Lord, to the glory of the Father."[2]

Could they have a stronger incentive? In his absence, as in his presence, he exhorts them to maintain their obedience, and work out their own salvation with fear and trembling, since the will and the power to do so came alike from God.[3] Let them lay aside the murmurings and dissensions which were the main hindrance to their proving themselves blameless and sincere—children of

---

[1] ἐξομολογήσηται. Cf. Matt. xi. 25; Luke x. 21.
[2] ii. 9—11.
[3] Vers. 12, 13, κατεργάζεσθε . . . ὁ Θεὸς γάρ . . Here we see the correlation of Divine grace and human effort. Cf. 1 Cor. ix. 24, τρέχετε, ἵνα καταλάβητε. Rom. ix. 16, οὐδὲ τοῦ τρέχοντος, ἀλλὰ τοῦ ἐλεοῦντος Θεοῦ.

God, uncensured in the midst of a crooked and distorted generation, among whom they appeared as stars,[1] holding forth the word of life, so as to secure to him for the day of Christ a subject of boast that he neither ran his race nor trained for his contest to no purpose.

"Nay, even if I am poured out as a libation over the sacrifice and free offering of your faith,[2] I rejoice and congratulate you all; and likewise rejoice ye too, and congratulate me."[3]

Perhaps, then, he might never come to them himself.

"But I hope in the Lord Jesus speedily to send Timothy to you, that he in turn may be cheered by a knowledge of your fortunes. For I have no emissary like him—no one who will care for your affairs with so genuine an earnestness. For," he sadly adds, "one and all seek their own interests, not those of Jesus Christ. But ye remember how *he* stood the test, since as a son for a father he slaved with me for the Gospel. Him then, at any rate, I hope to send—as soon as I get a glimpse[4] of how it will go with me—at once. But I feel sure in the Lord that I myself too shall quickly come. I think it necessary, however, to send you Epaphroditus, my brother, and fellow-labourer, and fellow-soldier,[5] the messenger whom you sent to minister to my need, since he was ever yearning for you, and feeling despondent because you heard of his illness. Yes, he was indeed ill almost to death; but God pitied him, and not him only, but also me, that I may not have grief upon grief. With all the more eagerness, then, I send him, that you may once more rejoice on seeing him, and I may be less full of grief. Welcome him, then, in the Lord with all joy, and hold such as him in honour, because for the sake of the work he came near

---

[1] φωστῆρες. Gen. i. 14; Rev. xxi. 11. Bp. Wordsworth makes it mean "torches in the dark, narrow streets."

[2] Cf. 2 Tim. iv. 6. Compare the striking parallel in the death of Seneca, Tac. *Ann.* xv. 64. Some make ἐπί, not "over," but "in addition to," because Jewish libations were poured, not "on," but "round" the altar. (Jos. *Antt.* iii. 9, § 4.) But the allusion may be to Gentile customs.

[3] ii. 14—18. "We are reminded of the messenger who brought the tidings of the battle of Marathon expiring on the first threshold with these words on his lips: χαίρετε καὶ χαίρομεν (Plut. *Mor.*, p. 347)." (Lightfoot, *ad loc.*)

[4] ἀφίδω.

[5] 2 Tim. ii. 3; Philem. 2.

to death, playing the gambler with his life,[1] in order to fill up the necessary lack of your personal ministration towards me.[2]

"For the rest, my brethren, farewell, and indeed fare ye well in the Lord.[3] To write the same things to you is not irksome to *me*, and for *you* it is safe."[4]

Then came a sudden break.[5] It seems clear that the Apostle had intended at this point to close the letter, and to close it with a repetition of the oft-repeated exhortation—for which he half apologises—to greater peace and unity among themselves.[6] It is quite possible that these last words might have run on, as they do in the First Epistle to the Thessalonians, to a considerable length;[7] but here something occurred to break the sequence of the Apostle's thoughts. When he returned to his dictation he began a digression far more severe and agitated in its tone than the rest of his letter, and he does not resume the broken thread of his previous topic till the second verse of the fourth chapter, where, instead of any general exhortation, he makes a direct personal appeal.

As to the nature of the interruption we cannot even conjecture. It may have been merely a change of the soldier who was on guard; but in the exigencies of a life which, though that of a prisoner, was yet fully occupied, many circumstances may have caused a little delay before

---

[1] παραβολευσάμενος (א, A, B, D, E, F, G). It is used especially of one who endangers his life by attendance on the sick (*parabolani*). (Wetst. *ad loc.*)

[2] ii. 19—30.

[3] I have tried to keep up the two meanings of "farewell" and "rejoice."

[4] iii. 1.

[5] Ewald, *Sendschr.*, p. 438.

[6] This is the simplest and most reasonable explanation of τὰ αὐτὰ γράφειν, and accords with St. Paul's custom of a concluding warning (1 Cor. xvi. 22; Gal. vi. 15, &c.), or it may refer to the topic of joy (i. 18, 25; ii. 17; iv. 4). It has led to all sorts of hypotheses. St. Paul had doubtless written other letters to the Philippians (the natural though not the necessary inference from καὶ αὐτὸν ὑμῖν ἔγραψεν ἐπιστολάς—Polyc. *ad Phil.* 3), but these words do not show it. (*V. supra*, p. 419.)

[7] 1 Thess. iv. 1.

everything could be ready, and the amanuensis once more at his post. And meanwhile something had occurred which had ruffled the Apostle's soul—nay, rather which had disturbed it to its inmost dep'hs. That something can only have been a conflict, in some form or other, with Judaising teachers. Something must either have thrown him in contact with, or brought to his notice the character and doctrine of false Apostles, of the same class as he had encountered at Corinth, and heard of in the Churches of Galatia. Once more the thoughts and tone of the Epistle to the Galatians, the truths and arguments of the Epistle to the Romans, swept in a storm of emotion over his soul; and it is with a burst of indignation, stronger for the moment than he had ever before expressed, that, on once more continuing his letter, he bids Timothy write to the still uncontaminated Church:—

"Beware of the dogs!¹ Beware of the bad workers!² Beware of the concision party!"³

The words are intensely severe. He implies, "They call us dogs, but they, not we, are the veritable dogs; and we, not they, are the true circumcision. Their circumcision is but concision—a mere mutilation of the flesh. We serve by the Spirit of God⁴—they serve ordinances; we boast in Christ Jesus—they do but trust in the flesh." And why should they put themselves into rivalry with him? If the external were anything in which to place

---

[1] Generally used of Gentiles and Hellenising Jews (Matt. xv. 26), involving a coarse shade of reproach (Deut. xxiii. 18; Rev. xxii. 15). We cannot be sure of the allusion here.

[2] Cf. 2 Cor. xi. 13; Matt. xxiii. 15.

[3] περιτομή, κατατομή would be in Latin "circumcisi," "decisi" (*Curti*, Hor. *Sat.* i. 9, 70); in German, *Beschnittene, Zerschnittene*. "Concision" means circumcision regarded as a mere mutilation. Cf. Acts vii. 51; Rom. iii. 25—29; Col. ii. 11; Ezek. xliv. 7; Deut. x. 16.

[4] iii. 3, λατρεύοντες, *intr.* Luke ii. 37; Acts xxvi. 7.

confidence, he could claim it in even a greater degree than any one else. He had been circumcised when eight days old; he was an Israelite, and of one of the noblest tribes of Israel, and not a mere Hellenist, but a Hebrew—aye, and a Hebrew of Hebrews;[1] and—to pass from hereditary to personal topics of carnal boasting—as regards Law, he was a Pharisee; as regards Judaic enthusiasm, he had even persecuted the Church; as regards legal righteousness, he had proved himself above all reproach. Things like these were at one time the gains which he reckoned that life had brought him, but now for Christ's sake he had got to count them as a loss.

"Aye, and more than that, I even count all things to be a loss for the sake of the transcendence of the knowledge of Christ Jesus, my Lord, for whose sake I was mulcted of all things,[2] and I regard them as refuse flung to dogs,[3] that I may gain Christ, and may be found in Him, not having any righteousness of mine which is of Law, but that which is by means of faith in Christ, that which comes of God, which is based on faith,[4] that I may know Him, and the power of His resurrection, and the fellowship of His sufferings, being conformed to His death, if so be I may attain to the resurrection (I mean not the general resurrection, but the resurrection of those that are Christ's) from the dead."[5]

And yet, as he goes on to warn them—though he had all this pregnant ground for confidence in externalisms, though he had rejected it all for the sake of Christ as mere foul and worthless rubbish, though his whole trust was

---

[1] iii. 5. A proselyte, son of a proselyte, was called a *Ger ben-ger*, but Paul was עברי בן עברי. (*Pirke Abhoth*, v.)

[2] May this refer to some sudden loss of all earthly means of living at his conversion?

[3] Ver. 8, σκύβαλα. In derivation perhaps from root σκατ, but in usage = κυσίβαλα (Suid.). Some prefer the technical sense of the word = "excrementa" (Theodoret).

[4] Ver. 9, διὰ πίστεως . . . ἐκ Θεοῦ . . . ἐπὶ τῇ πίστει.

[5] iii. 2—11, *leg.* τὴν ἐκ νεκρῶν (א, A, B, D, E).

now in Christ's righteousness, and not in his own—so far was he even still from the secure and vaunting confidence of their adversaries, that he did not at all consider that he had grasped the prize, or had been already perfected:—

"But I press forward to see if I may even grasp—for which purpose[1] I too was grasped by Christ. Brothers, I do not reckon myself to have grasped; but one thing—forgetting the things behind, and leaning eagerly forward for the things before, I press forward to the goal for the prize of my heavenly calling of God in Christ Jesus."

He is like one of those eager charioteers of whom his guardsmen so often talked to him when they had returned from the contests in the Circus Maximus, and joined their shouts to those of the myriads who cheered their favourite colours—leaning forward in his flying car, bending over the shaken rein and the goaded steed, forgetting everything—every peril, every competitor, every circling of the meta in the rear, as he pressed on for the goal by which sat the judges with the palm garlands that formed the prize.[2]

"Let all, then, of us who are full grown in spiritual privileges have this mind; then if in any other respect ye think otherwise[3] than ye should, this shall God reveal to you; only walk in the same path to the point whereunto we once reached."[4]

And as a yet further warning against any danger of their abusing the doctrine of the free gift of grace by antinomian practices, he adds—

"Show yourselves, brethren, imitators of me, and mark those who walk as ye have us for an example. For many walk about whom I

---

[1] ἐφ' ᾧ may also mean "because" (2 Cor. v. 4); or there may be an ellipse of the accusative after καταλάβω, as in the E.V.

[2] "Non progredi est regredi" (Aug.).

[3] ἑτέρως, used euphemistically (= κακῶς, Od. i. 234, θάτερον = τὸ κακόν). So the Hebrew "*acheer*." The meaning is, If you have the heart of the matter, God will enlighten you in non-essentials.

[4] iii. 12—16, omit κανόνι, τὸ αὐτὸ φρονεῖν (א, A, B).

often used to tell you, and now tell you even with tears—the enemies of the cross of Christ, whose end is destruction, whose god their belly, and their glory in their shame, men minding earthly things. For our real citizenship is in heaven, whence also we anxiously await as a Saviour the Lord Jesus Christ, who shall change the fashion of the body of our abasement so as to be conformable to the body of His glory,[1] according to the efficacy of His power to subject also every existing thing unto Himself. So, my brethren, beloved and longed for, my joy and crown, so stand ye firm in the Lord, beloved."[2]

Then after this long digression, which, beginning in strong indignation, calms itself down to pathetic appeal, he once more takes up the exhortation to unity with which he had intended to conclude. He entreats two ladies, Euodia and Syntyche, to unity of mind in Christ, and he also affectionately asks Syzygus[3]—on whose name of "yokefellow" he plays, by calling him a genuine yokefellow—a yokefellow in heart as well as in name[4]—to assist these ladies in making up their quarrel, which was all the more deplorable because of the worth of them both, seeing that they wrestled with him in the Gospel, with Clement too, and the rest of his fellow-workers whose names are in the Book of Life.[5]

---

[1] Ver. 21, μετασχηματίσει . . . σύμμορφον; ii. 6.

[2] iii. 17—iv. 1.

[3] iv. 3, γνήσιε Σύζυγε. Clement of Alexandria seems to have taken the word to mean Paul's *wife*, οὐκ ὀκνεῖ τὴν αὐτοῦ προσαγορεύειν σύζυγον ἣν οὐ περιεκόμιζεν (*Strom.* iii. 6, 53), cf. Euseb. *H. E.* iii. 30. Renan (p. 145) thinks it was Lydia. Why is she not saluted? If Lydia be merely a Gentilic name she may be one of those two ladies, or she may have been dead.

[4] Schwegler thinks that this is intended to be taken as an allusion to the Apostle Peter! The play on names is quite in St. Paul's manner. The only difficulty is that Syzygus does not occur elsewhere as a name.

[5] iv. 2, 3. Baur's wild conjecture (?) about Clement—that the whole story of his Romish Episcopate is invented to give respectability to the early Christians, by insinuating his identity with the Consular Flavius Clemens, and that the whole of this Epistle is forged to lead up to this passing allusion—looks almost tame beside Volkmar's hypothesis (?) about Euodia and Syntyche—viz., that Euodia="orthodoxy," the Petrine party, and Syntyche, "the partner"=

"Fare ye well always; again I will say, fare ye well. Let your reasonableness be recognised by all men. Be anxious about nothing, but in everything, in your general and special prayers, with thanksgiving, let your requests be made known before God. Then shall the peace of God, which surpasseth all understanding, keep sentry over your hearts, and the devices of your hearts, in Christ Jesus.

"Finally, brethren, whatsoever things are real, whatsoever things are awful, whatsoever things are just, whatsoever things are pure, whatsoever things are amiable, whatsoever things are winning, if 'virtue,'[1] if 'honour,' have a real meaning for you, on these things meditate. The things which ye both learned and received, both heard and saw in me, these things do, and the God of peace shall be with you."[2]

Then comes the warm, yet delicate, expression of his heartfelt gratitude to them for the pecuniary contribution by which now, for the fourth time, they, and they only, had supplied the wants which he could no longer meet by manual labour.

"One word more:—I rejoiced in the Lord greatly, that now once more your thought on my behalf blossomed afresh.[3] In this matter ye were indeed bearing me in mind, but ye were without opportunity. Not that I speak with reference to deficiency, for I learnt to be always independent in existing circumstances. I know how both to be humiliated, and I know how to abound. In everything and in all things I have been initiated how both to be satisfied and to be hungry, both to abound and to be in need. I am strong for everything in Him who gives me power. Still ye did well in making yourselves partakers in my affliction. And ye know as well as I do, Philippians, that in the beginning of the Gospel, when I went forth from Macedonia, no Church communicated with me as regards giving and receiving, except ye only, for even in Thessalonica both once and twice ye sent to my need—not

the Pauline party! Clement, though a Philippian, *may possibly* be identical with "Clement of Rome" (Orig. *in Joann.* i. 29; Euseb. *H. E.* iii. 15, &c.); we cannot even say "probably," because the name is *exceedingly* common.

[1] iv. 8, ἀρετή, here alone in St. Paul.
[2] iv. 4—9.
[3] Ver. 10, ἀνεθάλετε, literally, "ye blossomed again to think on my behalf." Chrysostom says, ὅτι πρότερον ὄντες ἀνθηροὶ ἐξηράνθησαν, which is to touch the metaphor with an Ithuriel spear (*Repullulastis*, Aug.; *Refloruistis*, Vulg.).

THE CHURCH OF PHILIPPI. 437

that I am on the look-out for the gift, but I am on the look-out for the fruit which abounds to your account. Now, however, I have all things to the full,[1] and I abound. I have been fulfilled by receiving from Epaphroditus the gifts you sent, an odour of sweet fragrance, a sacrifice acceptable, well-pleasing to God.[2] But my God shall fulfil all your need according to His riches, in glory, in Christ Jesus. Now to our God and Father be glory for ever and ever. Amen.[3]

"Salute every saint in Christ Jesus. The brethren with me salute you. All the saints salute you, and especially[4] those of Cæsar's household.[5]

"The grace of our Lord Jesus Christ be with your spirit."

No great future awaited the Philippian Church. Half a century later, Ignatius passed through Philippi with his "ten leopards," on his way to martyrdom; and Polycarp wrote to the Church a letter which, like that of St. Paul, is full of commendations. Little more is heard of it. Its site is still occupied by the wretched village of Filibidjek, but in spite of the fair promise of its birth, "the Church of Philippi has," in the inscrutable counsel of God, "lived without a history, and perished without a memorial."[6]

[1] Ver. 18, ἀπέχω. (Matt. vi. 2.) The word is used for "giving receipt in full."
[2] Gen. viii. 21.
[3] iv. 10—20.
[4] Why especially? It is impossible to say.
[5] It should be borne in mind that these slaves would be counted by *thousands—atrienses, cubicularii, secretarii, lectores, introductores, nomenclatores, dispensatores, silentiarii* (to keep the others quiet), &c. &c., and even slaves to tell the master the names of his other slaves! We read of Romans who had 20,000 slaves. Four thousand was no very extraordinary number (Sen. *De Vit. Beat.* 17; Plin. *H. N.* xxxiii. 10; Athen. vi., p. 272).
[6] Lightfoot, p. 64.

CHAPTER XLVIII.

GNOSTICISM IN THE GERM.

Ο, καθάπερ ἄν τις εἰκάσειε, ἀνθρώποις ὑπηρέτην τινὰ πέμψας ἢ ἄγγελον ἀλλ᾽ αὐτὸν τὸν τεχνίτην καὶ δημιουργὸν τῶν ὅλων.—*Ep. ad Diognet.* 7.

THE remaining three of the Epistles of the Captivity were written within a short time of each other, and were despatched by the same messengers. Tychicus was the bearer of those to the Ephesians and Colossians. Onesimus, who naturally took the letter to Philemon, was sent at the same time with him, as appears from the mention of his name in the Epistle to the Colossians. In both of these latter Epistles there is also a message for Archippus.

There is nothing but internal evidence to decide which of these letters was written first. The letter to Philemon was, however, a mere private appendage to the Epistle to the Colossians, which may have been written at any time. The letter to this Church must claim the priority over the circular Epistle which is generally known as the Epistle to the Ephesians. The reason for this opinion is obvious — the Epistle to the Colossians was called forth by a special need, the other Epistle was not. It is in exact psychological accordance with the peculiarities of St. Paul's mind and style that if, after writing a letter which was evoked by particular circumstances, and led to the development of particular truths, he utilised the opportunity of its despatch to send another letter, which had no such immediate object, the tones of the first letter would still vibrate in the second. When he had discharged his immediate duty to the Church of Colossæ, the topics dwelt upon in writing to the neighbouring Churches would be sure to bear a close resemblance to those which had most recently been occupying his thoughts. Even apart from special information, St. Paul may have seen the desirability of warning Ephesus and its dependencies against a peril which was infusing its subtle presence within so short a distance from them; and it was then natural that his language to them should be marked by the very differences which separate the Epistle to the Colossians from that to the Ephesians. The former is specific, concrete, and polemical; the latter is abstract, didactic, general. The same words and phrases predominate in both; but the resemblances are far more marked and numerous in the practical exhortations than in the doctrinal statements. In the Epistle to the Colossians he is primarily occupied with the refutation of an error; in that to the Ephesians he is absorbed in the rapturous development of an exalted truth. The main theme of the Colossians is the Person of Christ; that of the Ephesians is the life of Christ manifested in the living energy of His Church.[1] In the former, Christ is the "Plenitude," the synthesis and totality of every attribute of God; in the latter, the ideal Church, as the body of Christ, is the Plenitude, the recipient of all the fulness of Him who filleth all things with all.[2] Christ's person is most prominent in the Colossians; Christ's body, the Church of Christ, in the Ephesians.

The genuineness of these two letters has been repeatedly and formidably assailed, and the grounds of the attack are not by any means so fantastic as those

[1] Col. ii. 19; Eph. iv. 16.
[2] Col. i. 19; ii. 9; Eph. i. 23; iii. 19; iv. 13. (John i. 14, 16.) German writers express the difference by saying that *Christlichkeit* is more prominent in the Colossians, *Kirchlichkeit* in the Ephesians.

on which other letters have been rejected as spurious. To dwell at length on the external evidence is no part of my scheme, and the grounds on which the internal evidence seems to me decisive in their favour, even after the fullest and frankest admission of all counter-difficulties, will best appear when we have considered the events out of which they spring, and which at once shaped, and are sufficient to account for, the peculiarities by which they are marked.

Towards the close of St. Paul's Roman imprisonment, when his approaching liberation seemed so all but certain that he even requests Philemon to be getting a lodging in readiness for him, he received a visit from Epaphras of Colossæ. To him, perhaps, had been granted the distinguished honour of founding Churches not only in his native town, but also in Laodicea and Hierapolis, which lie within a distance of sixteen miles from each other in the valley of the Lycus. That remarkable stream resembles the Anio in clothing the country through which it flows with calcareous deposits; and in some parts of its course, especially near Colossæ, it flowed under natural bridges of gleaming travertine deposited by its own waters, the course of which was frequently modified by this peculiarity, and by the terrific earthquakes to which the valley has always been liable. The traveller who followed the course of the Lycus in a south-eastward direction from the valley of the Mæander into which it flows, would first observe on a plateau, which rises high above its northern bank, the vast and splendid city of Hierapolis, famous as the birthplace of him who in Nicopolis

> "Taught Arrian when Vespasian's brutal son
> Cleared Rome of what most shamed him"—[1]

[1] Epictetus was a contemporary of the Apostle. As to the Christian tinge of his Stoic speculations, see my *Seekers after God*.

and famous also for the miraculous properties of the mephitic spring whose exhalations could be breathed in safety by the priests of Cybele alone. About six miles further, upon the southern bank of the river, he would see Laodicea, the populous and haughty metropolis of the "Cibyratic jurisdiction," which alone of the cities of proconsular Asia was wealthy and independent enough to rebuild its streets and temples out of its own resources, when, within a year of the time at which these letters were written, an earthquake had shaken it.[1] Passing up the valley about ten miles further, he might before sunset reach Colossæ, a town far more anciently famous than either, but which had fallen into comparative decay, and was now entirely eclipsed by its thriving and ambitious neighbours.[2]

This remarkable valley, and these magnificent cities, St. Paul, strange to say, had never visited. Widely as the result of his preaching at Ephesus had been disseminated throughout Asia, his labours for the Ephesian Church had been so close and unremitting as to leave him no leisure for wider missionary enterprise.[3] And although Jews abounded in these cities, the divinely guided course of his previous travels had not brought him into this neighbourhood. It is true that St. Luke vaguely tells us that in the second missionary journey, St. Paul had passed through "the Phrygian and Galatian country,"[4] and that in the shifting ethnological sense of the term the cities of the Lycus-valley might be regarded as Phrygian.

---

[1] Tac. *Ann.* xiv. 27, "propriis opibus revaluit." Rev. iii. 14. Cicero, who resided there as Proconsul of Cilicia, frequently refers to it in his letters.

[2] Now Chonos. Dr. Lightfoot calls it "the least important Church to which any Epistle of St. Paul was addressed" (*Col.* p. 16).

[3] Acts xx. 31.

[4] Acts xvi. 6. In Acts xviii. 23 the order is "the Galatian country and Phrygia." In the former instance he was travelling from Antioch in Pisidia to Troas; in the latter from Antioch in Syria to Ephesus.

But the expression seems rather to mean that the course of his journey lay on the ill-defined marches of these two districts, far to the north and east of the Lycus. In his third journey his natural route from the cities of Galatia to Ephesus would take him down the valleys of the Hermus and Cayster, and to the north of the mountain range of Messogis which separates them from the Lycus and Mæander. From St. Paul's own expression it seems probable that the Churches in these three cities had been founded by the labours of Epaphras, and that they had never "seen his face in the flesh" at the time when he wrote these Epistles, though it is not impossible that he subsequently visited them.[1]

And yet he could not but feel the deepest interest in their welfare, because, indirectly though not directly, he had been indeed their founder. Ephesus, as we have seen, was a centre of commerce, of worship, and of political procedure; and among the thousands "both Jews and Greeks" "almost throughout all Asia," who heard through his preaching the word of the Lord,[2] must have been Philemon,[3] his son, Archippus, and Epaphras, and Nymphas, who were leading ministers of the Lycus Churches.[4]

And there was a special reason why St. Paul should write to the Colossian Christians. Philemon, who resided there, had a worthless slave named Onesimus—a name which, under the circumstances, naturally lent itself to a satiric play of words; for instead of being "Beneficial," he had been very much the reverse, having first (apparently) robbed his master, and then run away from him. Rome was in ancient days the most likely place to furnish a secure refuge to a guilty fugitive, and thither, even more than to modern London, drifted inevitably the vice and misery of the

[1] Col. i. 4, 6, 9; ii. 1.   [2] Acts xix. 10—26.
[3] Philem. 1, 2.   [4] Col. iv. 12, 13, 15.

world. Philemon was a Christian, and some access of wretchedness, or danger of starvation, may have driven the runaway slave to fling himself on the compassion of the Christian teacher, whom he may have heard and seen when he attended his master on some great gala-day at Ephesus. The kind heart of Paul was ever open; he had a deep and ready sympathy for the very lowest and poorest of the human race, because in the very lowest and poorest he saw those "for whom Christ died." His own sufferings, too, had taught him the luxury of aiding the sufferings of others, and he took the poor dishonest fugitive to his heart, and was the human instrument by which that change was wrought in him which converted the "*non tressis agaso*" into a brother beloved. But Onesimus was still legally the debtor and the slave of Philemon; and Paul, ever obedient to the law, felt it a duty to send him back. He placed him under the protecting care of Tychicus of Ephesus, and sent with him a letter which could not fail to ensure his pardon. It was necessary, therefore, for him to write to a citizen of Colossæ, and another circumstance determined him to write also to the Colossian Church.

This was the strange and sad intelligence which he heard from Epaphras. They had many opportunities for intercourse, for, either literally or metaphorically, Epaphras shared his captivity, and did not at once return to his native city. In his conversations with St. Paul he told him of an insidious form of error unlike any which the Apostle had hitherto encountered. The vineyard of the Lord's planting seemed, alas! to resemble the vineyards of earth in the multiplicity of perils which it had to overcome before it could bring forth its fruit. Now it was the little foxes that spoiled its vines; now the wild boar which broke down its hedge; and now, under the blighting influence of neglect and infertile soil, its unpruned branches only brought forth the clusters of Gomorrah. An erroneous tendency, as yet germinant and undeveloped, but one of which the prescient eye of St. Paul saw all the future deadliness, had insensibly crept into these youthful Churches, and, although they only knew the Apostle by name, he felt himself compelled to exert the whole force of his authority and reasoning to check so perilous an influence. Doubtless Epaphras had expressly sought him for the sake of advice and sympathy, and would urge the Apostle to meet with distinct warnings and clear refutation the novel speculations with which he may have felt himself incompetent to cope.

The new form of error was partly Judaic, for it made distinctions in meats, attached importance to new moons and sabbaths,[1] and insisted upon the value of circumcision, if not upon its actual necessity.[2] Yet it did not, as a whole, resemble the Galatian Judaism, nor did it emanate, like the opposition at Antioch, from a party in Jerusalem, nor was it complicated, like the Corinthian schisms, with personal hostility to the authority of St. Paul. Its character was Judaic, not so much essentially as virtually; not, that is, from any special sympathy with national and Levitical Hebraism, but rather because there were certain features of Judaism which were closely analogous to those of other Oriental religions, and which commanded a wide sympathy in the Eastern world.

We must judge of the distinctive colour of the dawning heresy quite as much from the truths by which St. Paul strives to check its progress, as by those of its tenets on which he directly touches.[3] In warning the Colossians

---

[1] Col. ii. 16.   [2] Col. ii. 11.
[3] They were "Gnostic Ebionites," Baur; "Cerinthians," Mayerhoff; "Christian Essenism in its progress to Gnosticism," Lipsius; "A connecting

respecting it, he bids them be on their guard against allowing themselves to be plundered by a particular teacher, whose so-called philosophy and empty deceit were more in accordance with human traditions and secular rudiments than with the truth of Christ. The hollow and misguiding system of this teacher, besides the importance which it attached to a ceremonialism which at the best was only valuable as a shadow or a symbol, tried further to rob its votaries of the prize of their Christian race by representing God as a Being so far removed from them that they could only approach Him through a series of angelic intermediates. It thus ignored the precious truth of Christ's sole mediatorial dignity, and turned humility itself into a vice by making it a cloak for inflated and carnal intellectualism. In fact, it was nothing more nor less than pride which was thus aping humility; and, in endeavouring to enforce an ignoble self-abrogation of that direct communion with God through Christ which is the Christian's most imperial privilege, it not only thrust all kinds of inferior agencies between the soul and Him, but also laid down a number of rules and dogmas which were but a set of new Mosaisms without the true Mosaic sanctions. Those rules were, from their very nature, false, transient, and trivial. They paraded a superfluous self-abasement, and insisted on a hard asceticism, but at the same time they dangerously flattered the soul with a semblance of complicated learning, while they were found to be in reality valueless as any remedy against self-indulgence. That these ascetic practices and dreamy imaginations were accompanied by a pride which arrogated to itself certain mysteries as an exclusive possession from which the vulgar

link between Essenes and Corinthians," Nitzsch; "Ascetics and Theosophists of the Essene school," Holtzmann; "Precursors of the Christian Essenes," Ritschl. (Pfleiderer, ii. 98.)

intellect must be kept aloof; that, while professing belief in Christ, the Colossian mystic represented Him as one among many beings interposed between God and man; that he regarded matter in general and the body in particular as something in which evil was necessarily immanent,[1] seem to result from the Christology of the Epistle, which is more especially developed in one particular direction than we find it to be in any of St. Paul's previous writings. Already, in writing to the Corinthians, he had said that "if he had ever known Christ after the flesh, from henceforth he knew Him no more," and in this Epistle the Person of our Lord as the Eternal Coexistent Son is represented in that divine aspect the apprehension of which is a boon infinitely more transcendent than a human and external knowledge of Jesus in His earthly humiliation. And yet—as though to obviate beforehand any Cerinthian attempt to distinguish between Jesus the man of sorrows and Christ the risen Lord, between Jesus the crucified and Christ the Eternal Word—he is, even in this Epistle, emphatic in the statement that these are one.[2] To say that there is any change in St. Paul's fundamental conception of Christ would be demonstrably false, since even the juxtaposition of our Lord Jesus Christ with God the Father as the source of all grace, and the declaration that all things, and we among them, exist solely through Him, are statements of His divinity in St. Paul's earliest Epistles[3] as strong as anything which could be subsequently added. But hitherto the Apostle had been led to speak of Him mainly as the Judge of the quick and dead, in the Epistles

---

[1] So, too, Philo regarded the body as the Egypt of the soul. (*Ques. rer. div. haer.* 518.)

[2] i. 20, 22; ii. 6.

[3] 1 Thess. i. 1; v. 28; 1 Cor. viii. 6; 2 Cor. iv. 4; v. 19; Rom. ix. 5. Even Renan fully admits this (*St. Paul*, x. 274).

to the Thessalonians; as the invisible Head and Ruler of the Church in those to the Corinthians; as the Author of all spiritual freedom from ceremonial bondage, and the Redeemer of the world from the yoke of sin and death, as in those to the Romans and Galatians; as the Saviour, the Raiser from the dead, the Life of all life, the Source of all joy and peace, in that to the Philippians. A new phase of His majesty had now to be brought into prominence—one which was indeed involved in every doctrine which St. Paul had taught concerning Him as part of a Gospel which he had received by revelation, but which no external circumstance had ever yet led him to explain in all its clearness. This was the doctrine of Christ, as the Eternal, Pre-existing, yet Incarnate Word. He had now to speak of Him as One in whom and by whom the Universe—and that not only its existing condition but its very matter and its substance—are divinely hallowed, so that there is nothing irredeemable, nothing inherently antagonistic to Holiness, either in matter or in the body of man; as One in whom dwells the "plenitude" of the divine perfections, so that no other angelic being can usurp any share of God which is not found in Him; as One who is the *only* Potentate, the *only* Mediator, the *only* Saviour, the Head of the Body which is the Church, and the Source of its life through every limb. And the expression of this truth was rendered necessary by error. The Colossian teachers were trying to supplement Christianity, theoretically by a deeper wisdom, practically by a more abstentious holiness. It was the beautiful method of St. Paul to combat false doctrine as little as possible by denunciation and controversy (though these two have at times their necessary place), and as much as possible by the presentation of the counter truth. We are able, therefore, to find the theological errors of the Colossians reflected in the positive theology which is here developed in order to counteract them. In the moral and practical discussions of the Epistle we see the true substitute for that extravagant and inflating asceticism which had its origin partly in will-worship, ostentatious humility, and trust in works, and partly in mistaken conceptions as to the inherency of evil in the body of man. St. Paul points out to them that the deliverance from sin was to be found, not in dead rules and ascetic rigours, which have a fatal tendency to weaken the will, while they fix the imagination so intently on the very sins against which they are intended as a remedy, as too often to lend to those very sins a more fatal fascination —but in that death to sin which is necessarily involved in the life hid with Christ in God. From that new life—that resurrection from the death of sin—obedience to the moral laws of God, and faithfulness in common relations of life, result, not as difficult and meritorious acts, but as the natural energies of a living impulse in the heart which beats no longer with its own life but with the life of Christ.

Alike, then, from the distinct notices and the negative indications of the Epistle we can reproduce with tolerable clearness the features of the Colossian heresy, and we at once trace in it the influence of that Oriental theosophy, those mystical speculations, those shadowy cosmogonies and moral aberrations which marked the hydra-headed forms of the systems afterwards summed up in the one word Gnosticism. This very circumstance has been the main ground for impugning the genuineness of the Epistle. It is asserted that Gnosticism belongs to a generation later, and that these warnings are aimed at the followers of Cerinthus, who did not flourish until after Paul was dead, or even at those of Valentinus, the

founder of a Gnostic system in the second century.
In support of this view it is asserted that the Epistle
abounds in un-Pauline phrases, in words which occur in
no other Epistle, and in technical Gnostic expressions,
such as plenitude, mystery, wisdom, knowledge, powers,
light, darkness. Now, that Gnosticism as a well-developed
system belongs to a later period is admitted; but the belief
that the acceptance of the Epistle as genuine involves an
anachronism, depends solely on the assumption that
Gnostic expressions[1] may not have been prevalent, and
Gnostic tendencies secretly at work, long before they
were crystallised into formal heresies. As far as these
expressions are concerned, some of them are not technical
at all until a Gnostic meaning is read into them, and
others, like "knowledge" (*gnósis*), &c., "plenitude" (*pleróma*), though beginning to be technical, are used in a
sense materially different from that which was afterwards
attached to them. As for the asserted *traces* of doctrines
distinctly and systematically Gnostic, it is a matter of
demonstration that they are found, both isolated and
combined, during the Apostolic age, and before it, as
well as afterwards. The esoteric exclusiveness which
jealously guarded the arcana of its mysteries from general
knowledge; the dualism which became almost Manichæan
in the attempt to distinguish between the good and evil
impulses; the notion that God's "plenitude" could only
flow out in a multitude of imperfect emanations; the
consequent tendency to exalt and worship a gradation of
angelic hierarchies; the rules and purifications which were
designed to minimise all infection from the inevitable
contact with matter; the attempt to explain the inherency

[1] The use of these expressions is admirably illustrated by some remarks of Tertullian, *Adv. Praxeam.*, 8. He has used the word προβολή, and anticipating the objection that the word is tainted with Valentinianism, he replies that Heresy has taken that word from Truth to mould it after its own likeness.

of evil in matter by vain and fanciful cosmogonies; the multiplication of observances; the reduction of food and drink to the barest elements, excluding all forms of animal life; the suspicious avoidance or grudging toleration of marriage as a pernicious and revolting necessity; —these are found in various Oriental religions, and may be traced in philosophies which originated among the Asiatic Greeks. They find a distinct expression in the doctrines of the Essenes.[1] Their appearance in the bosom of a Christian community was indeed new; but there was nothing new in their existence; nothing in them with which, as *extraneous* forms of error, St. Paul's Jewish and Gentile studies—were it only his knowledge of Essene tenets and Alexandrian speculations—had not made him perfectly familiar. That they should appear in a Phrygian Church, powerfully exposed to Jewish influences, and yet consisting of Gentiles trained amid the mysteries of a ceremonial nature worship, and accustomed to the utterances of a speculative philosophy [2] must have been painful to St. Paul, but could not have been surprising. The proof that

---

[1] Neander (*Planting*, p. 323, seqq.) points out the Phrygian propensity to the mystical and magical as indicated by the worship of Cybele, by Montanism, by the tendencies condemned at the council of Laodicea, and by the existence of Athinganians in the ninth century, &c. Perhaps the incipient heresies of Asia might be most briefly characterised as the germ of Gnosticism evolved by Essene and Oriental speculations on the origin of evil. These speculations led to baseless angelologies injurious to the supremacy of Christ; to esoteric exclusiveness injurious to the universality of the Gospel; and to mistaken asceticism injurious to Christian freedom. Cloudy theories generated unwise practices. It is interesting to observe that some at least of the same tendencies are traceable in St. John's rebukes to the seven Churches. Compare Rev. iii. 14 and Col. i. 15—18; Rev. iii. 21 and Col. iii. 1, Eph. ii. 6. Some interesting Zoroastrian parallels are quoted from Bleeck by the Rev. J. Ll. Davies in his essay on traces of foreign elements in these Epistles (*Ephes*. pp. 141—9). He says "the decay and mixture of old creeds in the Asiatic intellect had created a soil of 'loose fertility—a footfall there sufficing to upturn to the warm air half-germinating' theosophies."

[2] Lightfoot, *Col*. pp. 114—179.

these forms of heresy might have been expected to appear is rendered yet more cogent by the knowledge that, within a very short period of this time, they actually *did* appear in a definite and systematic form, in the heresy of Cerinthus, with whom St. John himself is said to have come into personal collision.[1] And under these circumstances, so far from seeing a mark of spuriousness, we rather deduce an incidental argument in favour of the genuineness of the Epistle from the nature of the errors which we find that it is intended to denounce. Many critics have been eager to prove that St. Paul could not have written it, because they reject that fundamental doctrine of the Eternal Divinity of Christ, of which this group of Epistles is so impregnable a bulwark; yet this was so evidently the main article in the belief of St. Paul that the proof of its being so would hardly be weakened, even if these Epistles could be banished from the canon to which hostile criticism has only succeeded in showing more conclusively that they must still be considered to belong.

The Christology, then, of these Epistles is nothing more than the systematic statement of that revelation respecting the nature of Jesus, which is implicitly contained in all that is written of Him in the New Testament;[2] and the so-called "Gnosticism" with which these Epistles deal is nothing more than a form of error—a phase of the crafty working of systematic deception—which is common to the intellectual, moral, and spiritual aberrations of all ages and countries. It is found in the Zend Avesta; it is found in Philo; it is found in Neoplatonism; it is found in the Kabbala; it is found in Valentinus. Abject sacerdotalism, superstitious ritual, extravagant asceticism, the

---

[1] Neander, *Planting*, i. 325; *Ch. Hist.* ii. 42; Lightfoot, *Col.*, p. 107, seq

[2] "Les plus énergiques expressions de l'Epître aux Colossiens ne font qu'enchérir un peu sur celles des Epîtres antérieures" (Renan, *St. P.* x.).

faithlessness which leads men to abandon the privilege of immediate access to God, and to thrust between the soul and its One Mediator all sorts of human and celestial mediators; the ambition which builds upon the unmanly timidity of its votaries its own secure and tyrannous exaltation; the substitution of an easy externalism for the religion of the heart; the fancy that God cares for such barren self-denials as neither deepen our own spirituality nor benefit our neighbour; the elaboration of unreasonable systems which give the pompous name of Theology to vain and verbal speculations drawn by elaborate and untenable inferences from isolated expressions of which the antinomies are unfathomable, and of which the true exegetic history is deliberately ignored; the oscillating reactions which lead in the same sect and in even the same individual to the opposite extremes of rigid scrupulosity and antinomian licence:[1]—these are the germs not of one but of all the heresies; these are more or less the elements of nearly every false religion. The ponderous technicalities of the systematiser; the interested self-assertions of the priest; the dreamy speculations of the mystic; the Pharisaic conceit of the externalist; the polemical shibboleths of the sectarian; the spiritual pride and narrow one-sidedness of the self-tormentor; the ruinous identification of that saving faith which is a union with Christ and a participation of His life with the theoretic acceptance of a number of formulæ:—all these elements have from the earliest dawn of Christianity mingled in the tainted stream of heresy their elements of ignorance, self-interest, and error. In their dark features we detect a common resemblance.

"Facies non omnibus una
Nec diversa tanem, quales decet esse sororum."

There was Gnosticism in the days of St. Paul as there

[1] Clem. Alex. *Strom.* iii. 5; 2 Tim. iii. 1—7; Jude 8; Rev. ii. 14, 20—22.

is Gnosticism now, though neither then nor now is it recognised under that specific name.

We may, therefore, pass to the study of the Epistle with the strongest conviction that there is no expression in it which, on these grounds at any rate, disproves its genuineness. None but Paul could have written it. To say that it is un-Pauline in doctrine is to make an arbitrary assertion, since it states no single truth which is not involved in his previous teachings. The fact that it is a splendid development of those teachings, or rather an expansion in the statement of them, in order to meet new exigencies, is simply in its favour. Nor do I see how any one familiar with the style and mind of St. Paul can fail to recognise his touch in this Epistle. That the style should lack the fire and passion — the "*meras flammas*"—of the Epistle to the Galatians, and the easy, fervent outflowing of thought and feeling in those to the Thessalonians, Corinthians, and Philippians, is perfectly natural. Of all the converts to whom St. Paul had written, the Colossians alone were entire strangers to him. He had not indeed visited the Church of Rome, but many members of that Church were personally known to him, and he was writing to them on a familiar theme which had for years been occupying his thoughts. The mere fact that he had already written on the same topic to the Galatians would make his thoughts flow more easily. But in writing to the Colossians he was handling a new theme, combating a recent error with which, among Christians, he had not come into personal contact, and of which he merely knew the special characteristics at secondhand. When, in the Epistle to the Ephesians, he reverts to the same range of conceptions,[1] his sentences

[1] *V. infra*, pp. 481, seq. "These two letters are twins, singularly like one another in face, like also in character, but not so identical as to exclude a strongly-marked individuality" (J. Ll. Davies, *Eph. and Col.*, p. 7). He says

run with far greater ease. The style of no man is stereotyped, and least of all is this the case with a man so many-sided, so emotional, so original as St. Paul. His manner, as we have repeatedly noticed, reflects to an unusual degree the impressions of the time, the place, the mood, in which he was writing. A thousand circumstances unknown to us may have given to this Epistle that rigid character, that want of spontaneity in the movement of its sentences, which led even Ewald into the improbable conjecture that the words were Timothy's, though the subject and the thoughts belong to St. Paul. But the difference of style between it and other Epistles is no greater than we find in the works of other authors at different periods of their lives, or than we daily observe in the writings and speeches of living men who deal with different topics in varying moods.

that the style is laboured, but "the substance eminently genuine and strong." A forger would have copied phrases; who could copy the most "characteristic and inward conceptions of the Apostle?" Even critics who fail to admit the genuineness of the whole letter, see that its sentiments and much of its phraseology are so indisputably Pauline that they adopt the theory of interpolation (Hitzig, Weiss, Holtzman), or joint authorship of Paul and Timothy (Ewald).

CHAPTER XLIX.

THE EPISTLE TO THE COLOSSIANS.

"Per Me venitur, ad Me pervenitur, in Me permanetur."—AUG. *In Joann.* xii.

"'Ἐν αὐτῷ περιπατεῖτε. In eo ambulate; in illo solo. Hic Epistolae scopus est."—BENGEL.

"Viva, pressa, solida, nervis plena, mascula."—BÖHMER, *Isag.* lx.

"Brevis Epistola, sed nucleum Evangelii continens."—CALVIN.

AFTER a brief greeting "to the saints and faithful brethren in Christ which are in Colossæ,"[1] he enters on the usual "thanksgiving," telling them how in his prayers he ever thanked God our Father[2] on their behalf, on hearing of their faith in Christ and love to all the saints, because of the hope stored up for them in heaven. Of that hope they had heard when the Gospel was first preached to them in its true genuineness; and as that Gospel grew and bore fruit[3] in all the world, so it was doing in them, from the day when they heard of the grace of God, and recognised it in all its fulness, from the teaching of Epaphras, the Apostle's beloved fellow-prisoner

---

[1] Ver. 2, Κολοσσαῖς, κ, B, D, F, G, L; but probably πρὸς Κολοσσαεῖς in the later superscription.

[2] This, if the reading of B, D, Origen, &c., be correct, is the only instance where God the Father stands alone in the opening benediction. The briefest summary of the Epistle is as follows:—I. Introduction: i. 1, 2, Greeting; i. 3—8, Thanksgiving; i. 9—13, Prayer. II. Doctrinal: the person and office of Christ, i. 13—ii. 3. III. Polemical: warnings against error, and practical deductions from the counter truths, ii. 4—iii. 4. IV. Practical: general precepts, iii. 5—17; special precepts, iii. 18—iv. 6. V. Personal messages and farewell, iv. 7—18.

[3] Ver. 6, καρποφορούμενον, "*spontaneously* bearing fruit" (ver. 10, καρποφοροῦντας), and yet gaining progressive force in doing so (αὐξανόμενοι).

and their faithful pastor on the Apostle's behalf.[1] By Epaphras he has been informed of their spiritual charism of love, and from the day that he heard of their Christian graces it was his earnest and constant prayer that their knowledge of God's will might be fully completed in all spiritual wisdom and intelligence, in practical holiness, in fresh fruitfulness and growth, in increasing power to endure even suffering with joy, and in perpetual thanksgiving to God, who qualified us for our share in the heritage of the saints in light, and who rescued us from the power of darkness, and transferred us by baptism into the kingdom of the Son of His love, in whom we have our redemption, the remission of our sins.[2]

Of the nature of that Son of God, on whose redemption he has thus touched, he proceeds to speak in the next five verses. They form one of the two memorable passages which contain the theological essence of this Epistle. They are the full statement of those truths with respect to the person of Christ which were alone adequate to meet the errors, both of theory and practice, into which the Colossians were sliding under the influence of some Essene teacher. The doctrine of Christ as the Divine Word,— the Likeness of God manifested to men—the Pre-existent Lord of the created world—could alone divert them from the dualism and ascetic rigour which their Phrygian mysticism and mental proclivities had led them to introduce into the system of Christianity. And therefore having spoken of Christ, he shows "His absolute supremacy in relation to the universe, the *natural* creation (15—17), and

---

[1] Ver. 7, ὑπὲρ ἡμῶν, א, A, B, D, F, G. This can only mean that Epaphras preached on St. Paul's behalf—*i.e.*, in his stead—and, if it be the right reading, furnishes another decisive proof that St. Paul had never himself preached in these Churches.

[2] i. 9—14. The "by His blood" of the E. V. is a reading interpolated from Eph. i. 7.

in relation to the Church, the new *moral* creation (ver. 18)."[1]

"Who is the Image of the Unseen God, the First-born of all Creation, since in Him all things were created[2] in the heavens and upon the earth, the things seen and the things unseen,—whether 'thrones' or 'dominations,' 'principalities' or 'powers':[3] all things have been created[4] by Him and unto Him: and HE IS[5] before all things, and in Him all things cohere; and He is the head of the body —the Church; who is the origin, the first-born from the dead, that He and none other may become the Presiding Power in all things; because in Him God thought good that the whole Plenitude[6] should permanently

---

[1] Dr. Lightfoot, in his valuable note (p. 209), shows that Christ is spoken of *first* in relation to God—the word εἰκών involving the two ideas of Representation and Manifestation; and, *secondly*, in relation to created things— the words πρωτότοκος πάσης κτίσεως involving the idea of mediation between God and Creation, and πρωτότοκος being applied to the Logos by Philo, and to the Messiah in Ps. lxxxix. 27. It implies priority to, and sovereignty over, all creation. It seems as though there were already tendencies to find the cross an offence, and to distinguish between the crucified Jesus and the ascended Christ (i. 19, 20—22 ; ii. 6—9).

[2] Ver. 16, ἐκτίσθη, "created by one word."

[3] No definite angelology can be extracted from these words (cf. ii. 18; Eph. i. 21). The hierarchies of the pseudo-Dionysius are as entirely arbitrary as Milton's

"Thrones, dominations, virtues, princedoms, powers,
Warriors, the flower of heaven."

But to say that the passage is gnostic, &c., is absurd in the face of such passages as Rom. viii. 38; 1 Cor. xv. 24.

[4] Ver. 16, ἔκτισται, "have been created, and still continue."

[5] HE IS—ἔστιν, not ἐστιν (so Lightfoot), since the tense and the repetition of the pronouns imply pre-existence and personality (John viii. 58; Ex. iii. 14).

[6] This rendering "Plenitude"—in the sense of "completeness" and "completed fulfilment"—will be found to meet all the uses of the words in St. Paul, both in its ordinary sense (1 Cor. x. 26; Rom. xi. 12, 25; xiii. 10; xv. 29; Gal. iv. 4; Eph. i. 10), and in its later quasi-technical sense, as applied to the "totality of the Divine attributes and agencies" (Col. i. 19; ii. 9; Eph. i. 23; iii. 19; iv. 13). It is directly derived from the O. T. usage (Jer. viii. 16, &c.); and the later localised usage of Cerinthus and Valentinus is in turn derived from it. If it be derived from πληρόω, in the sense of "*fulfil*" rather than its sense to "fill," the difficulties of its usage by St. Paul are lessened; I cannot say that they disappear. Lightfoot, *Col.* 323—339. Those who wish to see other views may find them in Baur, *Paul.* ii. 93; Pfleiderer, ii. 172; Holtzmann, *Eph. Col.* 222, *seq.*; Fritzsche on Rom. x. 1. On the connexion of πλήρωμα with the Hebrew מלא there are some

dwell,[1] and by Him to reconcile all things to Himself, making peace by the blood of His cross;—by Him, whether the things on the earth or the things in the heavens. And you, who once were alienated and enemies in your purpose, in the midst of wicked works,—yet now were ye reconciled[2] in the body of His flesh by death, to present yourselves holy and unblemished and blameless before Him, if, that is, ye abide by the faith, founded and firm, and not being ever shifted from the hope of the Gospel which ye heard, which was proclaimed throughout this sublunary world—of which I became—I, Paul—a minister."[3]

The immense grandeur of this revelation, and the thought that it should have been entrusted to *his* ministry, at once exalts and humiliates him; and he characteristically[4] continues:—

"Now I rejoice in my sufferings on your behalf, and supplement the deficiencies of the afflictions of Christ in my flesh on behalf of His body, which is the Church,[5] of which I became a minister according to

valuable remarks in Taylor's *Pirque Aboth*, p. 54. *Makom*, "place"=186, and by Gematria was identified with Yehovah, because the squares of the letters of the Tetragrammaton $(10^2 + 5^2 + 6^2 + 5^2)$ give the same result (Buxt. *Lex. Chald.* 2001). So far from being exclusively gnostic, Philo had already said (*De Somniis*, 1.) that the word has three meanings, of which the third is *God*. Hence the interesting Alexandrianism in the LXX. of Ex. xxiv. 10, εἶδον τὸν τόπον οὗ εἱστήκει ὁ θεός. "God," said a celebrated Jewish proverb, "is not in Ha-Makom [the "Place," the "Universe"], but all Ha-Makom is in God."

[1] Ver. 19, κατοικῆσαι, not a παροικία or transient, but a κατοικία or permanent abode. Cf. Gen. xxxvi. 44, LXX.; κατοικεῖν, ישב; παροικεῖν, גור, &c.

[2] Ver. 21, ἀποκατηλλάγητε (B). The ἀπο, as in ἀπολαμβάνειν υἱοθεσίαν (Gal. iv. 5) and ἀποκατάστασις, points to the *restoration* of a lost condition.

[3] i. 15—23. At ver. 20 begins a sketch of Christ's work, first generally (20), then specially to the Colossians (21—23).

[4] Cf. Eph. iii. 2—9; 1 Tim. i. 11.

[5] τὰ ὑστερήματα. These latter words throw light on the former. Christ's sacrifice is, of course, "a full, perfect, and sufficient sacrifice, oblation, and satisfaction for the sins of the whole world," and the sufferings of saints *cannot*, therefore, be *vicarious*. But they *can* be *ministrative*, and *useful*— nay, even requisite for the continuance of Christ's work on earth; and in that sense St. Paul, and every "partaker of Christ's sufferings" (2 Cor. i. 7; Phil. iii. 10) can "personally supplement in Christ's stead (ἀνταναπληρῶ) what is lacking of Christ's afflictions on behalf of His body, the Church." Steiger, Maurice, Huth, &c., read "the sufferings of the Christ in my flesh;" but there can be no Χριστὸς in the σάρξ which Christ destroys.

the stewardship of God granted to me to you-ward, to develop fully the word of God, the mystery[1] which has lain hidden from the ages and the generations, but is now manifested to His saints, to whom God willed to make known what is the wealth of the glory of this mystery among the Gentiles, which mystery is Christ in you the hope of glory; whom we preach"—not to chosen *mystae*, not with intellectual exclusiveness, not with esoteric reserves, but absolutely and universally—"warning *every* man, and teaching *every* man in *all* wisdom, that we may present *every* man 'perfect' in Christ.[2] For which end also I toil, contending according to His energy, which works in me in power.[3]

"For I wish you to know how severe a contest[4] I have on behalf of you, and those in Laodicea, and all who have not seen my face in the flesh, that their hearts may be confirmed, they being compacted[5] in love, and so brought to all wealth of the full assurance of intelligence, unto the full knowledge of that mystery of God, which is Christ,[6] in whom are all the treasures of wisdom and knowledge—hid treasures,"—yet, as the whole passage implies, hidden no longer, but now brought to light.[7] "This I say"—*i.e.*, I tell you of this possibility of full knowledge for you all, of this perfect yet open secret of wisdom in Christ—"that no man may sophisticate you by plausibility of speech. For even though personally absent, yet in my spirit I am with you, rejoicing in and observing your military array, and the solid front of your faith in Christ. As, then, ye received the Christ—Jesus the Lord—walk in Him, rooted, and being built up in Him,[8] and being confirmed by your faith, even as ye were taught, abounding in that faith with thanksgiving."[9]

---

[1] The mystery of the equal admission of the Gentiles (i. 27; iv. 3; Eph. i. 10; iii. 3, 8, and *passim*).

[2] The repetition of the πάντα is a clear warning against esoteric doctrines, and the exclusive arrogance of intellectual spiritualism which is a germ of many heresies. It is naturally a favourite word of the Apostle who had to proclaim the universality of the Gospel (1 Cor. x. 1; xii. 29, 30, &c.). Τέλειος was used of those initiated into the mysteries.

[3] i. 24—29.

[4] Ver. 1. ἀγῶνα, referring back to ἀγωνιζόμενος, i. 29.

[5] Read συμβιβασθέντες.

[6] Ver. 2. Read τοῦ Θεοῦ, Χριστοῦ. (Lightfoot, *Col.*, p. 318.)

[7] Prov. ii. 4; Matt. xiii. 44; 1 Cor. ii. 7; iv. 5.

[8] Ver. 7. Notice the change from ἐρριζωμένοι, the permanent result of stability, to ἐποικοδομούμενοι, the continuous process of edification. Notice, too, the confusion of metaphor which is no confusion of thought: "walk," "rooted," "being built," "being strengthened."

[9] ii. 1—7.

He has thus given them a general warning against being dazzled by erroneous teaching. He has laid down for them, with firm hand and absolute definiteness, the truth that the Pleroma dwells permanently in Christ— the sole Lord of the created universe, and therefore the guarantee that there is in matter no inherent element of inextinguishable evil; the sole Head of the Church, the sole Redeemer of the world; the sole centre, and source, and revealer of wisdom to all alike, as they had all along been taught. But it is now time to come to more specific warnings—to the more immediate application of these great eternal principles; and he continues:—

"Look that there be no person [whom one might name][1] who is carrying you off as plunder by his 'philosophy,'[2] which is vain deceit in accordance with mere human traditions, and earthly rudiments,[3] and not in accordance with Christ. For in Him all the Plenitude of Godhead[4] has bodily its permanent abode, and ye are in Him, fulfilled with *His* Plenitude, who is the head of every 'principality' and 'power.'"[5]

From this great truth flow various practical consequences. For instance, the Essene mystic, who was making a prey of them by the empty and specious sophistry which he called philosophy, impressed on them the value of circumcision, though not, it would seem, with the same insistency as the Christian Pharisees who had intruded themselves into Galatia. But what possible good could circumcision do them? Their circumcision was spiritual, and had already been performed—not by human hands, but by Christ Himself; not as the partial mutila-

---

[1] Ver. 8, τις, indefinitely definite (cf. Gal. i. 7).
[2] Remarkable as being the only place where St. Paul uses the word "philosophy," just as he only uses "virtue" once (Phil. iv. 8). Both are superseded by loftier conceptions.
[3] See *supra*, p. 152. (Gal. iv. 3, 9).
[4] θεότης, *deitas*; stronger than θειότης, *divinitas*.
[5] ii 7—10.

tion of one member, but as the utter stripping away from them of the whole body of the flesh.[1] It was, in fact, their baptism, in which they had been buried with Christ, and also raised with Him through their faith in the power of God who raised Him from the dead.[2]

"You, too, dead by transgressions and the uncircumcision of your flesh, God quickened with Him, freely remitting to us all our transgressions, wiping out the bond which, by its decrees, was valid against us,[3] which was opposed to us—this bond He has taken away, nailing it to His cross. Stripping utterly away from Him the 'principalities' and 'powers' (of wickedness),[4] He made a show of them boldly, leading them in triumph on that cross"[5]—thus making the gibbet of the slave His *foretrum*, on which to carry the spoils of His triumph as an Eternal Conqueror, after deadly struggle with the clinging forces of spiritual wickedness.

Since, then, mere legal obligations are part of a dead compact, a torn and cancelled bond, which is now nailed to Christ's Cross—

"Let no one then judge you in eating and drinking,[6] and in the matter of a feast, or a new-moon, or Sabbath,[7] which things are a shadow

---

[1] Ver. 11, ἀπέκδυσις.

[2] Cf. Phil. iii. 10.

[3] Deut. xxvii. 14—26; Gal. ii. 19, iv. 9. ὀφειλέτης. The "ordinances" are those of the Mosaic and the natural law. The δόγμασιν is difficult; the rendering 'consisting in ordinances' would seem to require ἐν, as in Eph. ii. 15. Also the Greek fathers made it mean "wiping out *by the decrees of the Gospel*."

[4] Tearing himself free from the assaults of evil spirits, which would otherwise have invested Him as a robe (cf. 1 Pet. v. 5, ἐγκομβώσασθε; Heb. xii. 1, εὐπερίστατος; Isa. xi. 5, &c.), He carried away their spoils, as trophies, on His cross.

[5] ii. 11—15. For θριαμβεύσας, cf. 2 Cor. ii. 14, *supra*, vol. i., p. 636.

[6] "This is the path of the Thorah. A morsel with salt shalt thou eat; thou shalt drink also water by measure" (*Perek.* R. Meir).

[7] If after nineteen centuries the Christian Church has not understood the sacred freedom of this language, we may imagine what insight it required to utter it in St. Paul's day, and how the Jews would gnash their teeth when they heard of it. When "the Emperor" asked R. Akibba how he recognised the Sabbath day, he said, "The river Sambatyon (the so-called 'Sabbatic river') proves it; the necromancer proves it (who can do nothing on the Sabbath); thy father's grave proves it (which smokes, to show that its tenant is in hell,

of things to be, but the substance is Christ's. Let no one then snatch your prize from you, by delighting in abjectness,[1] and service of the angels,[2] treading the emptiness of his own visions[3] in all the futile inflation of his mere carnal understanding, and not keeping hold of Him who is "the Head," from whom supplied and compacted by its junctures and ligaments, the whole body grows the growth of God.[4] If ye died with Christ from mundane rudiments, why, as though living in the world, are ye ordinance-ridden with such rules as 'Do not handle,' 'Do not taste,' 'Do not even touch,' referring to things all of which are perishable in the mere consumption,[5] according to 'the commandments and teachings of men'? All these kinds of rules have a credit for wisdom in volunteered supererogation[6] and abasement—hard usage of the body—but have no sort of value as a remedy as regards the indulgence of the flesh."[7]

except on the Sabbath, on which day even hell rests").—*Sanhedrin*, f. 65, 2. Myriads of passages might be quoted to show that it was the very keystone of the whole Judaic system: see *Babha Kama*, f. 82, 1; *Abhoda Zara*, f. 64, 2, &c. The law of the Sabbath, as our Lord strove so often to convince the Jews, is a law of holy freedom, not of petty bondage.

[1] θέλων ἐν, ף יָפֵץ, 1 Sam. xviii. 22, &c. See Aug., Beng., Olsh., Lightf.

[2] Angelology of the most developed description existed in the Jewish Church long before Gnosticism was heard of. See Gfrörer, *Jahr. des Heils.* i. 124, *seq.* I have collected some of the facts in a paper on Jewish Angelology and Demonology (*Life of Christ*, ii. 465, *seq.*). Neander refers to the κήρυγμα Πέτρου, and Clem. Alex. *Strom.* vi. 635. Theodoret (ii. 18) mentions that even in his day there were oratories to the Archangel Michael.

[3] ἃ ἑόρακεν (א, A, B, D. Dr. Lightfoot and others make the very simple conjectural emendation, ἃ ἑόρακεν κενεμβατεύων, *aut s. a.* This does not indeed occur in any MS., but its disappearance would be easily explained—(i.) by the homœoteleuton; (ii.) by the rare verb. The verb κενεμβατεύω (not unlike the ἀεροβατῶ καὶ περιφρονῶ τὸν ἥλιον, " I tread the air and circumspect the sun," of Arist. *Nub.* 225, and the αἰθεροβατεῖτε of Philo, i. 465) might conceivably have been suggested by one of the heretical theosophic terms, if κένωμα had ever been used by some incipient Gnostic of that day (as afterwards) by way of antithesis to Pleroma. But may not ἃ ἑόρακεν ἐμβατεύων be taken (metaphorically) to mean "*dwelling upon* what He has seen"?

[4] The accordance of the passage with the highest scientific range of that age is remarkable, and may be due to St. Luke.

[5] Mark vii. 1—23.

[6] Ver. 23, ἐθελοθρησκεία, a happy coinage of St. Paul's, which Epiphanius expands into ἐθελοπερισσοθρησκεία (*Haer.* i. 16).

[7] ii. 16—23. This remarkable passage, which is very obscure in the E. V., is an argument *against*, not *for*, the worrying scrupulosities of exaggerated asceticism—on the ground that they are useless for the end in view. St. Paul

The *true* remedy, he proceeds to imply, is very different :—

"If then ye were raised with Christ, seek the things above, where Christ is sitting on the right hand of God. Think of the things above, not the things on the earth. For ye died" (to sin in baptism), "and your life has been hidden with Christ in God. When Christ, our life, is manifested, then ye also with Him shall be manifested in glory. Kill then at a blow"—not by regulated asceticisms, but by this outburst of a new life, which is in Christ, which *is* Christ—"your members that are on the earth—fornication, uncleanness, passion, evil desire, and, above all, covetousness, for that is idolatry—because of which things cometh the wrath of God.[1] In which things ye also walked once, when ye were living in them; but now put ye away also *all* vices, anger, wrath, malice, railing, foul calumny, out of your mouths. Lie not one to another, since ye utterly stripped off the old man with his deeds, and put on the new man, which is being ever renewed to full knowledge according to the image of his Creator, in a region wherein there is no room for Greek or Jew, circumcision or uncircumcision, barbarian, Scythian,[2] slave, free, but Christ is all things, and in all. Put on then, as elect of God, saints beloved, hearts of compassion, kindness, humbleness, meekness, long-suffering, forbearing one another, and forgiving one another, if any one have a complaint against any one. Even as the Lord forgave you, so also do ye. And over all these things put on love, for love is the girdle of perfection; and let the peace of Christ arbitrate in your hearts, unto which peace ye were even called in one body, and show yourselves thankful. Let the word of Christ dwell in you richly in all wisdom, teaching one another and admonishing one another in psalms, hymns,[3] spiritual songs in grace, singing in your hearts to God. And everything whatever ye do, in word or in deed, do all things in the name of the Lord Jesus, thanking God the Father by Him."[4]

might have gone even further; for the lives of hermits and monks show us that the virulence of temptation is intensified into insupportable agony by the morbid introspection which results from mistaken means of combating it.

[1] Ver. 6, our ἐπὶ τοὺς υἱοὺς τῆς ἀπειθείας, introduced probably from Eph. v. 6.

[2] Ver. 11. The Scythians were the lowest type of barbarians (Gal. iii. 28).

[3] Christian hymnology began very early, though the hymns were not necessarily metrical (Rev. xv. 3; Acts xvi. 25; Eph. v. 19, 20; Plin. *Ep.* 97; *Mart. S. Ign.* vii. ᾠδαὶ ἀπ' ἀρχῆς ὑπὸ πιστῶν γραφεῖσαι, Euseb. *H. E.* v. 28. Rhythmic passages are Eph. v. 14; 1 Tim. iii. 16; vi. 15, 16; 2 Tim. ii. 11—13 (*Dict. Christ. Antt.* s. v. Hymns).

[4] iii. 1—17.

Then follow various practical exhortations—to wives to love their husbands, as is eternally fit in the Lord;[1] to husbands to love their wives, and not behave bitterly towards them; to children to obey their parents; to fathers not to irritate their children, that they may not lose heart.[2] To slaves, of whose duties and position he must often have thought recently, from his interest in Onesimus, he gives the precept to obey earthly masters, working as ever in their Great Taskmaster's eye, looking for the reward of faithfulness to Him who would also send the retribution for wrong-doing. On masters he enjoins justice and equity towards their slaves, remarking that they too have a Lord in heaven.[3]

Then he tells them to be constant in watchful prayer and thanksgiving, and asks their prayers that God would grant an opening for that ministry for which he was a prisoner. To the outer world he bids them walk in wisdom, buying up every opportunity, and addressing each one to whom they spoke with pleasant and wholesome words—" in grace seasoned with salt."[4]

He sends no personal news, because that will be conveyed by Tychicus, his beloved brother, and a faithful minister and fellow-slave in the Lord, whom he sends for that purpose[5] to strengthen their hearts, with Onesimus,

---

[1] ὃς ἀνῆκεν, "as ever was, and ever is fitting" (cf. Acts xxii. 22). (See my *Brief Greek Syntax*, § 140.)

[2] Notice the *rare* originality of the exhortation. Should we expect to find it in a forger?

[3] iii. 18—25. From such passages as these were drawn such noble warning rules of feudalism as: "Entre toi vilain, et toi seigneur, il n'y a juge fors Dieu." "Le seigneur qui prend des droits injustes de son vilain, les prend au péril de son âme" (Beaumanoir). These humble practical rules might be all the more necessary for those who looked on outward family duties as vulgar, and obstructions to spiritual contemplation. (Maurice, *Unity*, 587.) How different this from οὐδὲ προσγελᾶν δούλοις Ἀριστοτέλης εἴα ποτε. (Clem. Alex. *Strom.* iii. 12, § 84.)

[4] iv. 1—6. [5] iv. 8, *leg.*, ἵνα γνῶτε τὰ περὶ ἡμῶν (A, B, D, F, G).

their fellow-citizen, and *now* their faithful and beloved brother, whatever he may have been before. He sends them greetings from Aristarchus, his fellow-prisoner;[1] from Mark, the cousin of Barnabas,[2] about whose possible visit they had received special injunctions; and Jesus surnamed Justus—the only three Jewish Christians who worked with him to further God's kingdom, and so became a source of consolation to him. Epaphras, also one of themselves, greets them—a slave of Christ Jesus, ever contending on their behalf in his prayers that they may stand perfect and entire in all God's will, and one who was deeply interested in their Churches. Luke the physician, the beloved, greets them, and Demas.[3] He begs them to greet the Laodicean brethren, and Nymphas, and the church in the house of him and his friends.[4] He orders his Epistle to be publicly read, not only in the Colossian, but also in the Laodicean Church, and bids them read the circular letter which they could procure from Laodicea.[5] "And say to Archippus, Take heed to the ministry which thou receivedst in the Lord, that thou fulfil it."[6] The letter concludes with his own autograph

---

[1] Ver. 10, συναιχμάλωτος. Properly, "a fellow-captive taken in war." So of Epaphras (Philem. 23), Andronicus, Junias (Rom. xvi. 7.) In none of these cases can we tell the exact allusion, or whether the word is literal or metaphorical.

[2] Barnabas was perhaps dead, and thus Mark would be free. Paul seems to have had a little misgiving about his reception.

[3] Perhaps Paul's insight into character is shown by his somewhat ominous silence about Demas. (2 Tim. iv. 10.)

[4] Ver. 15, αὐτῶν (א, A, C); αὐτῆς (B, Lachm.); αὐτοῦ (F, G, K, &c.).

[5] τὴν ἐκ Λαοδικείας, "written *to* Laodicea and coming to them from Thrace." Constructio praegnans. (*Brief Greek Syntax*, § 89; Winer, § lxvi. 6). There can be little doubt that this was the Epistle to the "Ephesians." The apocryphal Epistle to Laodicea is a miserable cento. (See Lightfoot, *Col.* 340—366; Westcott, *Canon*, p. 572.)

[6] Archippus is believed to be a son of Philemon, and chief presbyter of Laodicea. If so, Tychicus would see him on his way to Colossæ. It is at least curious that the lukewarmness, the lack of zeal which seems here to be

salutation, to which he briefly adds, "Remember my bonds. Grace be with you."[1]

It is no part of my present task to trace the subsequent history of the Churches of the Lycus. The followers of Baur in Germany, and of Renan in France, have tried to represent that St. Paul's teaching in Asia was followed by a reaction in which his name was calumniated and his doctrines ignored. The theory is very dubious. The doctrines and the warnings of St. John to the Seven Churches are closely analogous to, sometimes almost verbally identical with, those of St. Paul; and the essence of the teaching of both Apostles on all the most important aspects of Christianity is almost exactly the same. An untenable inference has been drawn from the supposed silence of Papias about St. Paul, so far as we can judge from the references of Eusebius. It was the object of Papias to collect *traditional* testimonies from various Apostles and disciples, and of these St. Paul *could* not have been one. Papias was Bishop of Hierapolis, in which St. Paul may never have set his foot. Even if he did, his visit was brief, and had taken place long before Papias wrote, whereas after the destruction of Jerusalem St. John resided for many years at Ephesus, and there were gathered around him Andrew, Philip, Aristion, and others who had known the Lord. These were the authorities to which Papias referred for his somewhat loose and credulous traditions, and he may have quoted St. Paul, just as Polycarp does, without its at all occurring to Eusebius to mention the fact. Not only is there no proof of a general apostasy from Pauline principles, but in the decrees of the Council held at Laodicea about the middle of the fourth century,

gently rebuked, is the distinguishing character of the Laodicean Church, as represented by its "angel" in Rev. iii. 15. (Trench, *Seven Churches*, 180.)

[1] This shorter form is characteristic of Paul's later Epistles—Col i., 2 Tim., Tit. The longer form is found in all up to this date.

we read the very same warnings against angelolatry, Judaism, and Oriental speculation, which find a place in these Epistles of the Captivity. Colossæ itself—liable as it was to constant earthquakes, which were rendered more ruinous by the peculiarities of the Lycus with its petrifying waters—was gradually deserted, and the churches of Asia finally perished under the withering blight of Islam with its cruelties, its degradation, and its neglect.

CHAPTER L.

THE EPISTLE TO PHILEMON.

"Quasi vero curent divina de servis!"—MACROB. *Sat.* i. 11.

"In servos superbissimi, crudelissimi, contumeliosissimi sumus."—SEN. *Ep.* xlvii.

"Aequalitas naturae et fidei potior est quam differentia statuum."—BENGEL.

"Through the vista of history we see slavery and its Pagan theory of two races fall before the holy word of Jesus, 'All men are the children of God.'"—MAZZINI, *Works*, vi. 99.

"'The story is too rare to be true.' Christian faith has answered that. 'It is too suggestive to be true.' Christian science has answered that."—LANGE, *Apostol. Zeitalt.* i. 134.

IN the Epistle to the Colossians, St. Paul had sent no greeting to Philemon—who was a prominent member of that Church—because he purposed to write him a separate letter. A man like St. Paul, whose large and loving heart had won for him so many deeply-attached friends, must have often communicated with them by brief letters, but the Epistle to Philemon is the only private letter of this correspondence which has been preserved for us—the only private letter in the canon of the New Testament, with the exception of the brief letter of St. John to the well-beloved Gaius.[1] We cannot but regret the loss. Hundreds of letters of Cicero, of Seneca, and of Pliny have come down to us, and, though some of them are models of grace and eloquence, how gladly would we resign them all for even one or two of those written by the Apostle! In style, indeed, his letter is quite careless

---

[1] The "elect lady" of 2 John i. 1 is believed to be, not an individual, but Church.

and unpolished; but whereas the letters of the great Romans, with all their literary skill and finish, often leave on us an involuntary impression of the vanity, the insincerity, even in some instances the entire moral instability of their writers, on the other hand, this brief letter of St. Paul reveals to us yet another glimpse of a character worthy of the very noblest utterances which we find in his other Epistles. These few lines, at once so warm-hearted and so dignified, which theological bigotry was once inclined to despise as insignificant, express principles of eternal applicability which even down to the latest times have had no small influence in the development of the world's history. With all the slightness of its texture, and the comparative triviality of the occasion which called it forth, the letter is yet a model of tact, of sympathy, and of high moral nobleness. This little "idyl of the progress of Christianity"[1] shows that under the worn and ragged gabardine of the wandering missionary there beat the heart of a true gentleman, whose high-bred manners would have done honour to any court.[2]

We have seen that during his imprisonment St. Paul was, by "that unseen Providence which men nickname Chance," brought into contact with a runaway slave from Colossæ, whose name was Onesimus, or "Profitable." He had fled to Rome—to Rome, the common *sentina* of the world[3]—to hide himself from the consequences of crimes for which a heathen master might without compunction have consigned him to the *ergastulum* or the cross; and

[1] Davies.
[2] Even Baur seems to blush for the necessity which made him declare this Epistle spurious. He only does so because it is more or less involved with the other three, and stands or falls with them. "What has criticism to do with this short, attractive, friendly, and graceful letter, inspired as it is by the noblest Christian feeling, and which has never yet been touched by the breath of suspicion?" (*Paul.* ii. 80.)
[3] Sall. *Cat.* xxxvii. 5.

in the basement of one of the huge Roman *insulae*, or in the hovel of some fellow-child of vice and misery in that seething mass of human wretchedness which weltered like gathered scum on the fringe of the glittering tide of civilisation, he was more secure than anywhere else of remaining undetected. What it was that rescued him from the degradations which were the sole possible outcome of such an ill-begun career we cannot tell. He would soon exhaust what he had stolen from his master; and as Rome was full to overflowing of slaves and idlers —as the openings for an honest maintenance even in the barest poverty were few—it is hard to see what resource was left to him except a life of villany. Perhaps in this condition he was met by his fellow-Colossian, Epaphras, who as a Presbyter of Colossæ would be well known to Philemon. Perhaps Aristarchus, or any other of those who had been St. Paul's companions at Ephesus, had come across him, and recognised him as having been in attendance on Philemon at the time of his conversion by St. Paul. Perhaps he had himself been present at some of those daily addresses and discussions in the school of Tyrannus, which, though at the time they had not touched his heart, had at the least shown him the noble nature of the speaker, and revealed to the instinctive sense of one who belonged to an oppressed class, the presence of a soul which could sympathise with the suffering. How this may have been we do not know, but we do know that his hopes were not deceived. The Apostle received him kindly, sympathetically, even tenderly. The Rabbis said, "It is forbidden to teach a slave the Law."[1] "As though Heaven cared for slaves!" said the ordinary Pagan, with a sneer.[2] Not so thought St.

---

[1] *Ketubhoth*, f. 28, 1.
[2] Macrob. *Saturn.* i. 11. The better Stoics furnish a noble exception to this tone.

Paul. In Christianity there is nothing esoteric, nothing exclusive. Onesimus became a Christian. The heart which was hard as a diamond against Pharisaism and tyranny, was yet tender as a mother's towards sorrow and repentant sin. Paul had learnt in the school of Him who suffered the penitent harlot to wash His feet with her tears and wipe them with the hair of her head; of Him who had said to the convicted adulteress, "Neither do I condemn thee; go, and sin no more." Paul in no wise shared the anti-Christian respect of persons which made some people in St. Jerome's days[1] argue that it was beneath his dignity to trouble himself about a runaway slave. He understood better than the Fathers that the religion of Christ is the Magna Charta of humanity. The drag-net of His "fishers of men" was dropped to the very depths of the social sea. Here was one whose position was the lowest that could be conceived. He was a slave; a slave of the country whose slaves were regarded as the worst there were; a slave who had first robbed a kind master, and then run away from him; a slave at whom current proverbs pointed as exceptionally worthless,[2] amenable only to blows, and none the better even for them.[3] In a word, he was a slave; a Phrygian slave; a thievish Asiatic runaway slave, who had no recognised rights, and towards whom no one had any recognised duties. He was a mere "live chattel;"[4] a mere "implement with a voice;"[5] a thing which had no rights, and towards which there were no duties. But St. Paul converted him, and the slave became a Christian, a brother beloved and serviceable, an heir of immortality, a son of the kingdom,

---

[1] *In Ep. ad Philem.*
[2] Μυσῶν ἔσχατος. Menand. *Androg.* 7; Plat. *Theaet.* 209, B.
[3] Cic. *pro Flacc.* 27.
[4] Arist. *Pol.* i. 4, ἔμψυχον ὄργανον.
[5] Varro, *de Re Rust.* i. 17. "Instrumenti genus . . . vocale."

one of a royal generation, of a holy priesthood. The satirist Persius speaks with utter scorn of the rapid process by which a slave became a freeman and a citizen: "There stands Dama—a twopenny stable-boy, and a pilfering scoundrel; the Prætor touches him with his wand, and twirls him round, and

> "Momento turbinis, exit
> MARCUS Dama! . . . . Papae! Marco spondente recusas
> Credere tu nummos? Marco sub judice palles!"[1]

But the difference between Dama the worthless drudge and Marcus Dama the presumably worthy citizen was absolutely infinitesimal compared to the real and unsurpassable difference which separated Onesimus the good-for-nothing Phrygian fugitive from Onesimus the brother faithful and beloved.

And thus the Epistle to Philemon becomes the practical manifesto of Christianity against the horrors and iniquities of ancient and modern slavery.[2] From the very nature of the Christian Church—from the fact that it was "a kingdom not of this world"—it could not be revolutionary. It was never meant to prevail by physical violence, or to be promulgated by the sword. It was the revelation of eternal principles, not the elaboration of

---

[1] Pers. *Sat.* v. 76—80.
[2] "Omnia in servum licent" (Sen. *Clem.* i. 18). For an only too vivid sketch of what those horrors and iniquities were, see Döllinger, *Judenth. u. Heidenth.* ix. 1, § 2; Wallon, *Hist. de l'Esclavage dans l'Antiquité*. The difference between the wisdom which is of the world and the wisdom which is of God may be measured by the difference between the Epistle to Philemon and the sentiments of heathens even so enlightened as Aristotle (*Polit.* i. 3; *Eth. Nic.* viii. 13) and Plato (*Legg.* vi. 777, *seq.*; *Rep.* viii. 549). The difference between Christian morals and those of even such Pagans as passed for very models of virtue, may be estimated by comparing the advice of St. Paul to Christian masters, and the detestable greed and cruelty of the elder Cato in his treatment of his slaves (Plut. *Cat. Maj.* x. 21; Plin. *H. N.* xviii. 8, 3). See too Plautus, *passim*; Sec. *Ep.* xlvii.; Juv. *Sat.* vi. 219, *seq.*; Tac. *Ann.* xiv. 42—45; and Plut. *Apophthegm.* vi. 778 (the story of Vedius Pollio).

practical details. It did not interfere, or attempt to interfere, with the facts of the established order. Had it done so it must have perished in the storm of excitement which it would have inevitably raised. In revealing truth, in protesting against crime, it insured its own ultimate yet silent victory. It knew that where the Spirit of the Lord is there is liberty. It was loyal to the powers that be. It raised no voice, and refused no tribute even to a Gaius or a Nero. It did not denounce slavery, and preached no fatal and futile servile war. It did not inflame its Onesimi to play the parts of an Eunus or an Artemio. Yet it inspired a sense of freedom which has been in all ages the most invincible foe to tyranny, and it proclaimed a divine equality and brotherhood, which while it left untouched the ordinary social distinctions, left slavery impossible to enlightened Christian lands.[1]

This delicate relation to the existing structure of society is admirably illustrated by the Letter to Philemon. The tension always produced by the existence of a slave population, vastly preponderant in numbers, was at that moment exceptionally felt. Less than two years before St. Paul wrote to Philemon, a Consular, a Præfect of the city, named Pedanius Secundus, had been murdered by a slave under circumstances of infamy which characterised that entire epoch. In spite of the pity of the people, the Senate had decided that the old ruthless law, re-established by the Silanian decree under Augustus, should be carried out, and the entire *familia* of slaves be put to death. Regardless of the menaces of the populace, Nero ordered

[1] On the relation of Christianity to slavery see Lecky, *Hist. of Rationalism*, ii. 258; Troplong, *De l'Influence du Christ sur le Droit civil*, &c.; Gold. Smith, *Does the Bible sanction American Slavery?* De Broglie, *L'Eglise et L'Emp.* vi. 498, *seq.*; i. 162, 306; Wallon, *De l'Esclavage*, ii. *ad fin.*, &c. The feeling is indicated in Rev. xviii. 13.

the sentence to be executed by military force, and four hundred human beings of every age and of both sexes had been led through lines of soldiers to their slaughter in spite of the indubitable innocence of the vast majority. This horrible event, together with the thrilling debate to which it had given rise in the Senate, had made the subject of slavery a "burning question" at Rome, and deepened the general feeling which had long found proverbial expression, that "the more slaves the more enemies." In that memorable debate, it had been asserted by C. Cassius Longinus that the only way in which the rich could live in Rome—few amid multitudes, safe amid the terrified, or, at the worst, not unavenged among the guilty—would be by a rigid adherence to the old and sanguinary law.

Such, then, was the state of things in which St. Paul sat down to write his letter of intercession for the Phrygian runaway. He could not denounce slavery; he could not even emancipate Onesimus; but just as Moses, "because of the hardness of your hearts,"[1] could not overthrow the *lex talionis*, or polygamy, or the existence of blood-feuds, but rendered them as nugatory as possible, and robbed them as far as he could of their fatal sting, by controlling and modifying influences, so St. Paul established the truths that rendered slavery endurable, and raised the slave to a dignity which made emancipation itself seem but a secondary and even trivial thing. A blow was struck at the very root of slavery when our Lord said, "Ye all are brethren." In a Christian community a slave might be a "bishop," and his master only a catechumen; and St. Paul writes to bid the Corinthians pay due respect and subjection to the household of Stephanas, though some of the Corinthians were people of good posi-

[1] Matt. xix. 8.

tion, and these were slaves.¹ Onesimus repaid by gratitude, by affection, by active and cherished services to the aged prisoner, the inestimable boon of his deliverance from moral and spiritual death. Gladly would St. Paul, with so much to try him, with so few to tend him, have retained this warm-hearted youth about his person,—one whose qualities, however much they may have been perverted and led astray, were so naturally sweet and amiable, that St. Paul feels for him all the affection of a father towards a son.² And had he retained him, he felt sure that Philemon would not only have pardoned the liberty, but would even have rejoiced that one over whom he had some claim should discharge some of those kindly duties to the Apostle in his affliction which he himself was unable to render.³ But Paul was too much of a gentleman⁴ to presume on the kindness of even a beloved convert. And besides this, a fault had been committed, and had not yet been condoned. It was necessary to show by example that, where it was possible, restitution should follow repentance, and that he who had been guilty of a great wrong should not be irregularly shielded from its legitimate consequences. Had Philemon been a heathen, to send Onesimus to him would have been to consign the poor slave to certain torture, to possible

---

¹ See Hausrath, *Neut. Zeitg.* ii. 405.

² It is not said in so many words that Onesimus was young, but the language used respecting him seems clearly to show that this was the case (Philem. 10, 12, &c.). The expression σπλάγχνα, like the Latin *viscera*, is used of sons—οἱ παῖδες σπλάγχνα λέγονται (Artemid. *Oneirocr.* i. 44; cf. v. 57).

³ Philem. 13, ἵνα ὑπὲρ σοῦ μοι διακονῇ. It is unlikely that διακονῶ here implies religious assistance.

⁴ Many writers have felt that no word but "gentleman," in its old and truest sense, is suitable to describe the character which this letter reveals. (Stanley, *Cor.* 391; Newman, *Serm. on Various Occasions*, 133.) "The only fit commentator on Paul was Luther—not by any means such a *gentleman* as the Apostle was, but almost as great a genius" (Coleridge, *Table Talk*).

crucifixion.[1] He would, to a certainty, have become henceforth a "branded runaway," a *stigmatias*,[2] or have been turned into the slave-prison to work in chains. But Philemon was a Christian, and the "Gospel of Christ, by Christianising the master, emancipated the slave."[3] Paul felt quite sure that he was sending back the runaway—who had become his dear son, and from whom he could not part without a violent wrench—to forgiveness, to considerate kindness, in all probability to future freedom; and at any rate right was right, and he felt that he ought not to shrink from the personal sacrifice of parting with him. He therefore sent him back under the kind care of Tychicus, and—happily for us—with a "commendatory Epistle," which even Baur apologises for rejecting, and which all the world has valued and admired.[4] It has been compared by Grotius and others with the graceful and touching letter written by the younger Pliny to his friend Sabinianus to intercede for an offending freedman, who with many tears and entreaties had besought his aid. That exquisitely natural and beautifully-written letter does credit both to Pliny's heart and to his head, and yet polished as it is in style, while St. Paul's is written with a sort of noble carelessness of expression, it stands for beauty and value far below the letter to Philemon. In

[1] Juv. *Sat.* vi. 219; Plin. *Ep.* ix. 21, "Ne torseris illum."
[2] δραπέτης ἐστιγμένος (Ar. *Av.* 759). (Becker, *Charikles*, p. 370).
[3] Bp. Wordsworth.
[4] Baur's rejection of it is founded on un-Pauline expressions—*i.e.*, expressions which only occur in other Epistles which he rejects; on the assertion that the circumstances are improbable; and that the word σπλάγχνα—which he admits to be Pauline, and which might, he says, have occurred *twice*—is used *three* times! The Epistle is therefore to him an "*Embryo einer Christlichen Dichtung.*" *Admissi risum teneatis?* The "Vorwurf der Hyperkritik, eines übertriebenen Misstrauens, einer alles angreifenden Zweifelsucht" is, however, one which applies not only to his criticism of this Epistle, but to much of his general method; only in this instance, as Wiesinger says, it is not only *Hyperkritik* but *Unkritik*.

the first place, it is for a young freedman who had been deeply beloved, and not for a runaway slave. In the next place, it is purely individual, and wholly wanting in the large divine *principle* which underlies the letter of St. Paul. And there are other marked differences. Paul has no doubt whatever about the future good conduct of Onesimus; but Pliny thinks that the young freedman may offend again. Pliny assumes that Sabinianus is and will be angry; Paul has no such fear about Philemon. Paul pleads on the broad ground of Humanity redeemed in Christ; Pliny pleads the youth and the tears of the freedman, and the affection which his master had once felt for him. Paul does not think it necessary to ask Philemon to spare punishment; Pliny has to beg his friend not to use torture. Paul has no reproaches for Onesimus; Pliny severely scolded his young suppliant, and told him—without meaning to keep his word—that he should never intercede for him again. The letter of Pliny is the letter of an excellent Pagan; but the differences which separate the Pagan from the Christian stand out in every line.[1]

[1] A translation of Pliny's letter will be found in Excursus V. (*Ep.* ix. 21.)

CHAPTER LI.

THE EPISTLE TO PHILEMON.

"Servi sunt? immo conservi."—SEN.

"Evangelico decore conscripta est."—JER.

"Epistola familiaris, mire ἀστεῖος summae sapientiae praebitura specimen."—BENGEL.

"Ita modeste et suppliciter pro infimo homine se dimittit ut vix alibi usquam magis ad vivum sit expressa ingenii ejus mansuetudo."—CALVIN.

"PAUL, a prisoner of Christ Jesus, and Timothy the brother, to Philemon, our beloved and fellow-worker, and to Apphia the sister,[1] and to Archippus our fellow-soldier, and to the Church in thy house; grace to you, and peace from God our Father and the Lord Jesus Christ.

"I thank my God always, making mention of thee in my prayers—hearing thy love, and the faith thou hast towards the Lord Jesus and unto all the saints[2]—that the kindly exercise of thy faith may become effectual, in the full knowledge of every blessing we possess, unto Christ's glory. For I had much joy and consolation in thy love, because the hearts of the saints have been refreshed by thee, brother.

"Although, then, I feel much confidence in Christ to enjoin upon thee what is fitting, yet I rather entreat thee for love's sake, being such an one as Paul the aged,[3] and at this moment also a prisoner of Christ

---

[1] The reading is uncertain, but א, A, D, E, F, G (B is here deficient) read ἀδελφῇ, and we judge from Theodore of Mopsuestia that ἀγαπητῇ may in his age, and perhaps in the Apostle's, have given rise to coarse remarks from coarse minds.

[2] Ver. 5, πρὸς . . . εἰς.

[3] Ver. 9, τοιοῦτος ὢν ὡς is not unclassical, as Meyer asserts. (See instances in Lightfoot, *Col.*, p. 404.) St. Paul must at this time have been sixty years old, and people of that age, particularly when they have been battered, as he had been, by all the storms of life, naturally speak of themselves as old. I cannot think that this means "an ambassador" (Eph. vi. 20). To say nothing of the fact that the reading is πρεσβύτης, not πρεσβευτής, and allowing that the two might often have been confused (just as, indeed, πρεσβὺς and πρεσβευτὴς interchange the meanings of their plurals), yet would Paul have said "an ambassador" without saying of whom?

THE EPISTLE TO PHILEMON.

Jesus. I entreat thee about my child, whom I begot in my bonds—Onesimus—once to thee the reverse of his name—profitless[1] not 'profitable,' and no Christian, but now truly profitable[2] and a good Christian—whom I send back to thee. Him that is the son of my bowels,[3] whom I should have preferred to retain about my own person that he may on thy behalf minister to me in the bonds of the Gospel—but without thy opinion I decided to do nothing, that thy kindly deed may not be a matter of compulsion, but voluntary. For perhaps on this account he was parted for a season, that thou mayst have him back for ever, no longer as a slave, but above a slave, a brother beloved, especially to me, but how far more to thee, both naturally and spiritually. If, then, thou holdest me as a comrade, receive him like myself. But if he wronged thee in any respect, or is in thy debt, set that down to me. I Paul write it with my own hand, I will repay it[4]—not to say to thee that thou owest me even thyself besides. Yes, brother, may I 'profit' by thee in the Lord.[5] Refresh my heart in Christ. Confiding in thy

---

[1] ἀχρ. *Litotes;* erat enim noxius (Bengel).

[2] Ver. 11. There seems here, as Baur acutely observes, to be a *double paronomasia*, which I have endeavoured to indicate. For Χριστὸς and Χρηστὸς were confused with each other, and the Christians did not dislike this. Ἐκ τοῦ κατηγορουμένου ἡμῶν ὀνόματος χρηστότατοι ὑπάρχομεν χριστιανοί γὰρ εἶναι κατηγορούμεθα τὸν δὲ χρηστὸν μισεῖσθαι οὐ δίκαιον (Justin, *Apol.* i. 4). (Tert. *Apol.* 3.) *Supra*, i., p. 300.

[3] "Son of my bowels, Anselm!" (Browning, *The Bishop's Tomb*.) Σπλάγχνα = *corculum*, "my very heart;" "the very eyes of me;" רחמי. The elliptic form of the sentence, so characteristic of St. Paul, is filled up in some MSS. by Σὺ δὲ αὐτόν, τούτεστι τὰ ἐμὰ σπλάγχνα προσλαβοῦ.

[4] Ἀντὶ γραμματίου (a bond) τήνδε κατέχε τὴν ἐπιστολὴν πᾶσαν αὐτὴν γέγραφα (Theodoret). Some have supposed that Paul here took the pen from the amanuensis, and that this is the only autograph sentence. Oosterzee, &c., treat this as "a good-humoured jest;" and others think it unlike the delicacy which never once reminds the Judaisers of the *chaluka* which St. Paul had toiled to raise. But a slave was valuable, and something in the character of Philemon may have led to the remark. Bengel rightly says, "Vinctus scribit serio," as a father pays the debts of his son. Schrader, Lardner, Bleek, Hackett regard it as "no better than calumny" to say that Onesimus had stolen anything.

[5] Ver. 20, ὀναίμην. "I send you back an Onesimus now worthy of his name; will you be my Onesimus?" It is vain for critics to protest against these plays on names. They have been prevalent in all ages, and in all writers, and in all countries, as I have shown by multitudes of instances in *Chapters on Language*, ch. xxii. As a parallel to this play on Onesimus, compare Whitefield's personal appeal to the comedian Shuter, who had often played the character of Ramble—"And thou, poor Ramble, who hast so often rambled from Him. . . . . Oh, end thy ramblings and come to Jesus."

compliance I write to thee, knowing that even more than I say thou wilt do. But further than this, prepare for me a lodging, for I hope that by means of your prayers I shall be granted to you.

"There salute thee Epaphras, my fellow-prisoner in Christ Jesus, Marcus, Aristarchus, Demas, Luke, my fellow-labourers.

"The grace of the Lord Jesus Christ be with the spirit of you and yours."[1]

When Pliny interceded with Sabinianus for the offending freedman, he was able to write shortly afterwards, "You have done well in receiving back your freedman to your house and heart. This will give you pleasure, as it certainly gives me pleasure; first, because it shows me your self-control, and secondly, because you esteem me sufficiently to yield to my authority, and make a concession to my entreaties." What was the issue of St. Paul's letter we are not told, but we may feel quite sure that the confidence of one who was so skilful a reader of human character was not misplaced; that Philemon received his slave as kindly as Sabinianus received his freedman; that he forgave him, and not merely took him into favour, but

---

[1] Paul had been trained as a Rabbi. To see what Christianity had taught him we have only to compare his teachings with those of his former masters. Contrast, for instance, the Rabbinic conception of a slave with that tender estimate of human worth—that high conception of the dignity of man as man —which stands out so beautifully in this brief letter. The Rabbis taught that on the death of a slave, whether male or female—and even of a Hebrew slave—the benediction was not to be repeated for the mourners, nor condolence offered to them. It happened that on one occasion a female slave of Rabbi Eliezer died, and when his disciples came to condole with him he retired from them from room to room, from upper chamber to hall, till at last he said to them, "I thought you would feel the effects of tepid water, but you are proof even against hot water. Have I not taught you that these signs of respect are *not* to be paid at the death of slaves?" "What, then," asked the disciples, "are pupils on such occasions to say to their masters?" "The same as is said when their oxen and asses die," answered the Rabbi—"May the Lord replenish thy loss." They were not even to be mourned for by their masters; Rabbi Jose only permitted a master to say—"Alas, a good and faithful man, and one who lived by his labour!" But even this was objected to as being too much (*Berachoth*, f. 16, 2; Maimonides, *Hilch. Aval.*, § 12; *Hal.* 12).

did what St. Paul does not ask, but evidently desired, namely, set him free.[1] We may be sure, too, that if St. Paul was ever able to carry out his intended visit to Colossæ, it was no mere "lodging" that Philemon prepared for him, but a home under his own and Apphia's roof, where they and the somewhat slack Archippus, and the church that assembled in their house, might enjoy his beloved society, and profit by his immortal words.

[1] The ecclesiastical traditions about Philemon's episcopate, martyrdom, &c., are too late and worthless to deserve mention; and the same may be said of those respecting Onesimus. As far as dates are concerned, he *might* be the Onesimus, Bishop of Ephesus, mentioned forty-four years later by St. Ignatius. A postscript in two MSS. says that he was martyred at Rome by having his legs broken on the rack.

CHAPTER LII.

THE EPISTLE TO "THE EPHESIANS."

Τῇ Ἐκκλησίᾳ τῇ ἀξιομακαρίστῳ τῇ οὔσῃ ἐν Ἐφέσῳ τῆς Ἀσίας.—IGNAT. *ad Eph.* i.

"Nulla Epistola Pauli tanta habet mysteria tam reconditis sensibus involuta."—JER. *in Eph.* iii.

Ἐν σῶμα καὶ ἓν πνεῦμα.—EPH. iv. 4.

THE polemical *speciality* of the Epistle to the Colossians, compared with the far more magnificent generality of the great truths which occupy the earlier chapters of the Epistle to "the Ephesians,"[1] seems (as we have already

---

[1] That the Epistle was meant for the Ephesians, *among others*, is generally admitted, and Alford points out the suitableness of "the Epistle of the grace of God" to a church where Paul had specially preached "the Gospel of the grace of God" (Acts xx. 24, 32). And the pathetic appeal contained in the words ὁ δέσμιος (iii. 1; iv. 1) would come home to those who had heard the prophecy of Acts xx. 22. Other points of parallel between this Epistle and that to the Ephesian elders are the rare use of βουλή (i. 11; Acts xx. 27), of περιποίησις (i. 14; cf. Acts xx. 28), and of κληρονομία (i. 14, 18; v. 5; Acts xx. 32; and Maurice, *Unity*, 512—514). But without going at length into the often-repeated argument, the mere surface-phenomena of the Epistle—not by any means the mere omission of salutations, and of the name of Timothy—but the want of intimacy and speciality, the generality of the thanksgiving, the absence of the word "brethren" (see vi. 10), the distance, so to speak, in the entire tone of address, together with the twice-repeated εἴγε (iii. 2; iv. 21), and the constrained absence of strong personal appeal in iii. 2—4, would alone be inexplicable, even if there were no external grounds for doubting the authenticity of the words ἐν Ἐφέσῳ. But when we find these words omitted for no conceivable reason in ℵ, B, and know, on the testimony of Basil, that he had been traditionally informed of their omission, and found them omitted, ἐν τοῖς παλαιοῖς τῶν ἀντιγράφων, as also did Marcion, Tertullian, and Jerome, we are led to the unhesitating conclusion that the letter was not addressed exclusively to the Ephesians. The view which regards it as an encyclical, sent, among other places, to Laodicea, is highly probable (Col. iv. 16). In Eph. vi. 21, καὶ ὑμεῖς is most easily explicable, on the supposition that the

GENUINENESS OF THE EPISTLE.

observed) to furnish a decisive proof that the latter, to some extent, sprang out of the former, and that it was written because the Apostle desired to utilise the departure of Tychicus with the letter which had been evoked by the heresies of Colossæ.

Of the genuineness of the Epistle, in spite of all the arguments which have been brought against it, I cannot entertain the shadow of a doubt. I examine the question without any conscious bias. If the arguments against its Pauline authorship appeared valid, I am aware of no prepossession which would lead me to struggle against their force, nor would the deepest truths of the Epistle appear to me the less profound or sacred from the fact that tradition had erred in assigning its authorship.[1]

To the arguments which endeavoured to show that the Phaedo had not been written by Plato it was thought almost sufficient to reply—

εἴ με Πλάτων οὐ γράψε δύω ἐγένοντο Πλάτωνες.

Certainly if St. Paul did not write the Epistle to "the

---

letter was to go to different cities. In any case, the absence of greetings, &c., is a clear mark of genuineness, for a forger would certainly have put them in. The Epistle is by no means deficient in external evidence. Irenæus (*Haer.* v. 2, 3), Clement of Alexandria (*Strom.* iv. 8), Polycarp (*ad Phil.* i., xii.), Tertullian (*adv. Marc.* v. 1, 17), and perhaps even Ignatius (*ad Eph.* vi.), have either quoted or alluded to it; and it is mentioned in the Muratorian Canon. Impugners of its authenticity must account for its wide and early acceptance, no less than for the difficulty of its forgery. It is a simple fact that the Epistle was accepted as unquestionably Pauline from the days of Ignatius to those of Schleiermacher. Renan sums up the objections to its authenticity under the heads of (i.) Recurrent phrases and ἅπαξ λεγόμενα; (ii.) style weak, diffused, embarrassed; (iii.) traces of advanced Gnosticism; (iv.) developed conception of the Church as a living organism; (v.) un-Pauline exegesis; (vi.) the expression "holy Apostles;" (vii.) un-Pauline views of marriage. I hope to show that these objections are untenable.

[1] That the Epistle to the Hebrews was *not* written by the Apostle is now almost universally believed, yet this conviction has never led the Church to underrate its value as a part of the sacred canon of the New Testament Scriptures.

Ephesians," there must have been two St. Pauls. Baur speaks contemptuously of such an objection;[1] but can any one seriously believe that a forger capable of producing the Epistle to the Ephesians could have lived and died unheard of among the holy, but otherwise very ordinary, men and mediocre writers who attracted notice in the Church of the first century? It is true that De Wette, and his followers,[2] treat the Epistle *de haut en bas* as a verbose and colourless reproduction, quite inferior to St. Paul's genuine writings, and marked by poverty of ideas and redundance of words. We can only reply that this is a matter of taste. The colour red makes no impression on the colour-blind; and to some readers this Epistle has seemed as little colourless as is the body of heaven in its clearness. Chrysostom—no bad judge surely of style and rhetoric—spoke of the lofty sublimity of its sentiments. Theophylact dwells on the same characteristics as suitable to the Ephesians. Grotius says St. Paul here equals the sublimity of his thoughts with words more sublime than any human tongue has ever uttered. Luther reckoned it among the noblest books of the New Testament. Witsius calls it a divine Epistle glowing with the flame of Christian love, and the splendour of holy light, and flowing with fountains of living water. Coleridge said of it, "In this, the divinest composition of man, is every doctrine of Christianity: first, those doctrines peculiar to Christianity; and secondly, those precepts common to it with natural religion." Lastly, Alford calls it "the greatest and most heavenly work of one whose very imagination is peopled with things in the heavens, and even his fancy rapt into the visions of God." Pflei-

---

[1] *Paul.* ii. 2.
[2] Dr. Davidson, *Introd.* ii. 388. In his earlier edition, Dr. Davidson thought "nothing more groundless" than such assertions, and he then said "The language is rich and copious, but it is everywhere pregnant with meaning." (See Gloag, *Introd.*, p. 313.)

derer, though he rejects the genuineness of the Epistle, yet says that "of all the forms which Paulinism went through in the course of its transition to Catholicism, that of the Epistle to the Ephesians is the most developed and the richest in dogma."

The close resemblance in expression, and in many of the thoughts, to the Epistle to the Colossians, when combined with the radical differences [1] which separate the two Epistles, appears to me an absolutely irresistible proof in favour of the authenticity of both, even if the external evidence were weaker than it is. Roughly speaking, we may say that the style of Colossians shows a "rich brevity;" that of Ephesians a diffuser fulness. Colossians is definite and logical; Ephesians is lyrical and Asiatic. In Colossians, St. Paul has the error more prominently in view; in Ephesians he has the counteracting truth. In Colossians he is the soldier; in Ephesians the builder. In Colossians he is arguing against a vain and deceitful philosophy; in Ephesians he is revealing a heavenly wisdom. Colossians is "his caution, his argument, his process, and his work-day toil;" Ephesians is instruction passing into prayer, a creed soaring into the loftiest of Evangelic Psalms. Alike the differences and the resemblances are stamped with an individuality of style which is completely beyond the reach of imitation.[2] A

[1] There is the *general* resemblance that in both (Col. iii.; Eph. iv. 1) the same transition leads to the same application—the humblest morality being based on the sublimest truths; and there are the *special* resemblances (α) in Christological views; (β) in phraseology—seventy-eight verses out of 155 being expressed in the same phrases in the two Epistles. On the other hand, there are marked differences—(α) there are ἅπαξ λεγόμενα in both; (β) the leading word τὰ ἐπουράνια is peculiar to Ephesians; (γ) Ephesians has deep thoughts and whole sections (i. 3—14; iv. 5—15; v. 7—14; 23—31; vi. 10—17) which are not found in Colossians; (δ) there are seven Old Testament allusions or quotations in Ephesians, and only one in Colossians (ii. 21).

[2] Hence the critics are quite unable to make up their minds whether the Epistles were written by two authors, or by one author; and whether St

forger might indeed have sat down with the deliberate purpose of borrowing words and phrases and thoughts from the Epistle to the Colossians, but in that case it would have been wholly beyond his power to produce a letter which, in the midst of such resemblances, conveyed so different an impression in a style so characteristic and so intensely emotional.[1] Even if we could regard it as probable that any one could have poured forth truths so exalted, and moral teaching so pure and profound, in an Epistle by which he deliberately intended to deceive the Church and the world,[2] it is *not* possible that one actuated by such a purpose should successfully imitate the glow and rush of feeling which marks the other writings of the

Paul was in part the author of either or of neither; and whether the Colossians was an abstract of the Ephesians, or the Ephesians an amplification of the Colossians.

[1] The similarity of expressions (Davidson, *Introd.* i. 384) often throws into more marked relief the *dissimilarity* in fundamental ideas. It is another amazing sign of the blindness which marred the keen insight of Baur in other directions, that he should say the contents of the Epistles " are so *essentially the same* that they cannot well be distinguished "! (*Paul.* ii. 6.) The metaphysical Christology, which is polemically dwelt upon in the Colossians, is only assumed and alluded to in the Ephesians; and the prominent conceptions of Predestination and Unity which mark the doctrinal part of the Ephesians find little or no place in the Colossians. The recurrence of any word ἥτις δειδόντεσσι νεωτάτη ἀμφιπέληται is a common literary phenomenon, and any careful student of Æschylus is aware that if he finds a startling word or metaphor he may find it again in the next hundred lines, even if it occurs in no other play. Nothing, therefore, was more natural than that there should be a close resemblance, especially of the moral parts of two Epistles, written perhaps within a few days of each other; and that even though the doctrinal parts had different objects, and were meant for different readers, we should find alternate expansions or abbreviations of the same thoughts and the repetition of phrases so pregnant as ὁ πλοῦτος τῆς δόξης (Eph. i. 18; Col. i. 27); τὸ πλήρωμα (Eph. i. 23; Col. i. 19;) περιτομὴ ἀχειροποιητός (Eph. ii. 11; Col. ii. 11); and ὁ παλαιὸς ἄνθρωπος (Eph. iv. 22; Col. iii. 9). When Schneckenburger talks of " a *mechanical* use of materials" he is using one of those phrases which betray a strong bias, and render his results less plausible than they might otherwise seem. " How can he have overlooked the memorable fact, which all readers of the Epistle have noticed, that the idea of catholicity is here first raised to dogmatic definiteness and predominant significance?" (Pfleiderer, ii. 164).

[2] iii. 1, 8, &c.

Apostle, and expresses itself in the to-and-fro-conflicting eddies of thought, in the one great flow of utterance and purpose. The style of St. Paul may be compared to a great tide ever advancing irresistibly towards the destined shore, but broken and rippled over every wave of its broad expanse, and liable at any moment to mighty refluences as it foams and swells about opposing sandbank or rocky cape.[1] With even more exactness we might compare it to a river whose pure waters, at every interspace of calm, reflect as in a mirror the hues of heaven, but which is liable to the rushing influx of mountain torrents, and whose reflected images are only dimly discernible in ten thousand fragments of quivering colour, when its surface is swept by ruffling winds. If we make the difficult concession that any other mind than that of St. Paul could have originated the majestic statement of Christian truth which is enshrined in the doctrinal part of the Epistle, we may still safely assert, on literary grounds alone, that no writer, desirous to gain a hearing for such high revelations, could have so completely merged his own individuality in that of another as to imitate the involutions of parentheses, the digressions at a word, the superimposition of a minor current of feeling over another that is flowing steadily beneath it, the unconscious recurrence of haunting expressions, the struggle and strain to find a worthy utterance for thoughts and feelings which burst through the feeble bands of language, the dominance of the syllogism of emotion over the syllogism of grammar—the many other minute characteristics which stamp so ineffaceable an impress on the Apostle's undisputed works.

[1] "Every one must be conscious of an overflowing fulness in the style of this Epistle, as if the Apostle's mind could not contain the thoughts that were at work in him, as if each one that he uttered had a luminous train before it and behind it, from which it could not disengage itself" (Maurice, *Unity of the New Testament*, p. 535).

This may, I think, be pronounced with some confidence to be a pyschological impossibility. The intensity of the writer's feelings is betrayed in every sentence by the manner in which great truths interlace each other, and are yet subordinated to one main and grand perception, Mannerisms of style may be reproduced; but let any one attempt to simulate the language of genuine passion, and every reader will tell him how ludicrously he fails. Theorists respecting the spuriousness of some of the Pauline Epistles have, I think, entirely underrated the immense difficulty of palming upon the world an even tolerably successful imitation of a style the most living, the most nervously sensitive, which the world has ever known. The spirit in which a forger would have sat down to write is not the spirit which could have poured forth so grand a eucharistic hymn as the Epistle to the Ephesians.[1] Fervour, intensity, sublimity, the unifying— or, if I may use the expression, *esemplastic*—power of the imagination over the many subordinate truths which strive for utterance; the eagerness which hurries the Apostle to his main end in spite of deeply important thoughts which intrude themselves into long parentheses and almost interminable paragraphs—all these must, from the very nature of literary composition, have been far beyond the reach of one who could deliberately sit down with a lie in his right hand to write a false superscription, and boast with trembling humility of the unparalleled spiritual privileges entrusted to him as the Apostle of the Gentiles.

A strong bias of prejudice against the doctrines of the Epistle may perhaps, in some minds, have overborne the sense of literary possibilities. But is there in reality anything surprising in the developed Christology of St. Paul's

[1] J. Ll. Davies, *Eph.*, p. 19.

later years? That his views respecting the supreme divinity of Christ never wavered will hardly, I think, be denied by any candid controversialist. They are as clearly, though more implicitly, present in the First Epistle to the Thessalonians as in the Second Epistle to Timothy. No human being can reasonably doubt the authenticity of the Epistle to the Romans; yet the Pauline evangel logically argued out in that Epistle is identical with that which is so triumphantly preached in this. They are not, as Reuss has observed, two systems, but two methods of exposition. In the Romans, Paul's point of view is *psychologic*, and his theology is built on moral facts—the universality of sin, and the insufficiency of man, and hence salvation by the grace of God, and union of the believer with the dead and risen Christ. But in the Ephesians the point of view is *theologic*—the idea of God's eternal plans realised in the course of ages, and the unity in Christ of redeemed humanity with the family of heaven. "The two great dogmatic teachers of the sixteenth century, both essentially disciples of St. Paul, have both, so to speak, divided between them the inheritance of their master. The manual of Melancthon attaches itself to the Epistle to the Romans; the 'Institutes' of Calvin follow the direction marked out in that to the Ephesians; party spirit will alone be able to deny that, in spite of this difference of method, the system of the two writers has, after all, been one and the same."[1] Is there a word respecting Christ's exaltation in the Epistle to the Ephesians which implies a greater or diviner Being than Him of whom St. Paul has spoken as the Final Conqueror in the 15th chapter of the First Epistle to the Corinthians?

We can imagine that when he began to dictate this

[1] Reuss, *Les Epîtres Paulin.* ii. 146.

circular letter to the churches of Asia, the one overwhelming thought in the mind of the Apostle was the ideal splendour and perfectness of the Church of Christ, and the consequent duty of holiness which was incumbent on all its members. The thought of Humanity regenerated in Christ by an eternal process, and the consequent duty of all to live in accordance with this divine enlightenment—these are the double wings which keep him in one line throughout his rapturous flight. Hence the Epistle naturally fell into two great divisions, doctrinal and practical; the idea and its realisation; pure theology and applied theology; the glorious unity of the Church in Christ its living head, and the moral exhortations which sprang with irresistible force of appeal from this divine mystery. But as he was in all his doctrine laying the foundations of practice, and throughout founded the rules of practice on doctrine, the two elements are not so sharply divided as not to intermingle and coalesce in the general design. The glory of the Christian's vocation is inseparably connected with the practical duties which result from it, and which it was directly intended to educe. Great principles find their proper issue in the faithful performance of little duties.

It is naturally in the first three chapters that St. Paul is most overpowered by the grandeur of his theme. Universal reconciliation in Christ as the central Being of the Universe is the leading thought both of the Ephesians and the Colossians, and it is a deeper and grander thought than that of the Epistle to the Hebrews, which only sees this unity in Christ's priesthood, or that of the Pseudo-Clementines, which sees it in Christ as the Prophet of Truth.[1] St. Paul is endeavouring to impress upon the

[1] Baur, *First Three Cent.* i. 126.

minds of all Christians that they have entered upon a new *æon* of God's dispensations—the *æon* of God's ideal Church, which is to comprehend all things in heaven and earth. Round this central conception, as round a nucleus of intense light, there radiate the considerations which he wishes them specially to bear in mind:—namely, that this perfected idea is the working out of a purpose eternally conceived; that the œconomy—*i.e.*, the Divine dispensation[1]—of all the past circumstances of history has been fore-ordained before all ages to tend to its completion; that it is a *mystery*—*i.e.*, a truth hidden from previous ages, but now revealed; that each Person of the Blessed Trinity has taken direct part therein; that this plan is the result of free grace; that it is unsurpassable in breadth and length, and height and depth, being the exhibition of a love of which the wealth is inexhaustible and passes knowledge; that the benefits of it extend alike to Jew and Gentile; that it centres in the person of the risen Christ; and that to the Apostle himself, unworthy as he is, is entrusted the awful responsibility of preaching it among the Gentiles.

The incessant recurrence of *leading words connected with these different thoughts* is a remarkable feature of the first three chapters.[2] Thus, in the endeavour to express that the whole great scheme of redemptive love is part of the Divine "Will" and "Purpose," those two words are frequently repeated. Grace ($\chi\acute{a}\rho\iota\varsigma$) is so prominent in the Apostle's mind that the word is used thirteen times, and may be regarded as the key-note of the entire Epistle.[3] The writer's thoughts are so completely with the risen and ascended Christ as the head, the centre, the life of

---

[1] οἰκονομία, Eph. i. 10; iii. 2.

[2] θέλημα, Eph. i. 1, 5, 9, 11 (v. 17; vi. 6); βουλή, i. 11; εὐδοκία, i. 9; πρόθεσις, iii. 11.

[3] χάρις, i. 2, 6 (*bis*), 7; ii. 5, 7, 8; iii. 2, 7, 8; iv. 7, 32; vi. 24.

the Church, that he six times uses the expression "the heavenlies" without any limitation of time or place.[1] He feels so deeply the necessity of spiritual insight to counteract the folly of fancied wisdom, that the work of the Spirit of God in the spirit of man is here peculiarly prominent.[2] The words "wealth,"[3] and "glory,"[4] and "mystery,"[5] and "plenitude,"[6] show also the dominant chords which are vibrating in his mind, while the frequent compounds in ὑπὲρ, πρὸ, and σύν,[7] show how deeply he is impressed with the loftiness, the fore-ordainment, and the result of this Gospel in uniting the Jew and Gentile within one great spiritual Temple, of which the middle wall has been for ever broken down. "It would, indeed," says Mr. Maurice, "amply repay the longest study to examine the order in which these details are introduced, in what relation they stand to each other, how they are all referred to one ground, the good pleasure

[1] τὰ ἐπουράνια, i. 3, 20; ii. 6; iii. 10; vi. 12. "The Apostle carries us into '*the heavenlies*' (not 'the heavenly *places*,' as our translators render it, so perverting the idea of a sentence from which place and time are carefully excluded), into a region of voluntary beings, of spirits, standing by a spiritual law, capable of a spiritual blessing" (Maurice, *Unity of the New Testament*, p. 523.)

[2] πνεῦμα and πνευματικὸς occurs thirteen times in this Epistle (i. 3, 13, 17; ii. 18, 22; iii. 5, 16; iv. 3, 4, 23, 30; v. 18; vi. 17, 18); and only once in the Colossians (i. 8, 9).—Baur, *Paul*, ii. 21.

[3] πλοῦτος, πλούσιος, i. 7, 18; ii. 4, 7; iii. 8, 16. This word is only used in this sense by St. James (ii. 5). See Paley, *Horae Paulinae*, Ephes. ii. But see 2 Cor. viii. 9; Phil. ii. 7.

[4] δόξα, i. 6, 12, 14, 17, 18; iii. 16, 21, &c.

[5] μυστήριον, Eph. i. 9; iii. 3, 4, 9 (v. 32); vi. 19. In no other Epistle, except that to the Colossians, and 1 Cor., does it occur more than twice.

[6] πλήρωμα, i. 23; iii. 19; iv. 10—13 (i. 10). In the quasi-technical sense it is only found in the Epistle to the Colossians, i. 19; ii. 9.

[7] ὑπέρβαλλον, i. 19; ὑπεράνω, 21. Cf. iii. 19, ὑπερεκπερισσοῦ; 20; iv. 10, &c. These compounds are characteristic of the emphatic energy of St. Paul's style.
Προορίσας, i. 5; προέθετο, i. 9; προητοίμασεν, ii. 10; πρόθεσις, iii. 11.
Συνεζωοποίησε, ii. 5; συνήγειρε, συνεκάθισεν, 6; συμπολῖται, ii. 19 (a late and bad word, Phryn., p. 172); συνοικοδομεῖσθε, 22; συγκληρόνομα, σύσσωμα, συμμέτοχα, iii. 6; σύνδεσμος, iv. 3; συμβιβαζόμενον, συναρμολογούμενον, 16.

of His will, and to one end, the gathering up of all things in Christ.[1] But however desirable the minute investigation is, after the road has been travelled frequently, the reader must allow the Apostle to carry him along at his own speed on his own wings, if he would know anything of the height from which he is descending and to which he is returning."[2]

After his usual salutation to the saints that are in —— (perhaps leaving a blank to be filled up by Tychicus at the places to which he carried a copy of the letter), he breaks into the rapturous sentence which is "not only the exordium of the letter, but also the enunciation of its design."

"Blessed be the God and Father of our Lord Jesus Christ, who blessed us with all spiritual blessings in the heavenlies in Christ, even as He chose us out in Him before the foundation of the world, that we should be holy and blameless before Him, in love; fore-ordaining us to adoption by Jesus Christ into Himself, according to the good pleasure of His will, *for the praise of the glory* of His grace wherewith He graced us in the beloved."[3]

This leads him to a passage in which the work of the Son in this great fore-ordained plan is mainly predominant.

"In whom we have our redemption through His blood, the remission of transgressions, according to the wealth of His grace, wherewith He abounded towards us, in all wisdom and discernment, making

---

[1] The Epistle may be thus briefly summarised:—Salutation (i. 1, 2). Thanksgiving for the election of the Church, and the unity wrought by Christ's redemption and calling of both Jews and Gentiles (i. 3—14). Prayer for their growth into the full knowledge of Christ (15—23). Unity of mankind in the heavenlies in Christ (ii. 1—22). Fuller explanation of the mystery, with prayer for the full comprehension of it, and doxology (iii. 1—21). Exhortation to live worthily of the ideal unity of the Catholic Church in love (iv. 1—16). Exhortation to the practical duties of the new life, in the conquest over sin (iv. 17—v. 21), and in social relations (v. 22—vi. 9). The armour of God (vi. 10—17). Final requests and farewell (vi. 10—24).

[2] *Unity of the New Testament*, p. 525. See Excursus V., "Phraseology and Doctrines of the Epistle to the Ephesians."

[3] i. 3—6. Notice the marvellous compression and exhaustive fulness of this great outline of theology.

known to us the mystery of His will, according to His good pleasure which He purposed in Himself, with a view to the dispensation of the fulness of the seasons—to sum up all things in Christ, both the things in the heavens and the things on the earth—in *Him*. In whom we also were made an inheritance, being fore-ordained according to the purpose of Him who worketh all things according to the counsel of His will, that we should be *to the praise of His glory* who have before hoped in Christ."[1]

This repetition of the phrase "to the praise of His glory," introduces the work of the Third Person of the blessed Trinity.

"In whom (Christ) ye also" (as well as the Jewish Christians who previously had hoped in Christ) "on hearing the word of truth, the Gospel of your salvation, in whom (I say), believing, ye too were sealed with the Holy Spirit of promise, who is the earnest of our inheritance, with a view to the redemption of the purchased possession *unto the praise of His glory*."[2]

Since, therefore, it is the fixed ordinance, from all eternity, of the Blessed God, that man should be adopted through the redemption of Christ to the praise of the glory of the Eternal Trinity, and should receive the seal of the Spirit as the pledge of full and final entrance into his heritage, St. Paul tells them that, hearing of their faith and love, he ceaselessly prayed that God—the God of our Lord Jesus Christ, the Father of the Glory—would grant them a full knowledge[3] of Himself, giving them "illuminated eyes in their hearts" to know what their calling means, and the wealth and glory of this heritage, and the surpassing greatness of the power which He had put forth in raising Christ from the dead, and seating

[1] i. 7—12.
[2] i. 13, 14.
[3] Ἐπίγνωσις, i. 17; iv. 13. I have already alluded to the importance attached to true knowledge in these Epistles, written as it was to counteract the incipient but already baneful influence of a "knowledge falsely called." Hence we have also γνῶσις, iii. 19; σύνεσις, iii. 4; φρόνησις, i. 8; σοφία, ib.; ἀποκάλυψις, iii. 3; φωτίζειν, iii. 9; &c. &c.

Him at His right hand in the heavenlies, as the Supreme Ruler now and for ever of every spiritual and earthly power, and as the Head over all things to the Church,—which is His body, "the Pleroma" (*i.e.*, the filled continent, the brimmed receptacle) "of Him who filleth all things with all things."[1]

But for whom were these great privileges predestined, and how were they bestowed? The full answer is contained in the second chapter. They were intended for all, both Jews and Gentiles, and were bestowed by free grace. In this section the leading conception is the unity of mankind, in the heavenlies, in Christ. The Gentiles had been dead in transgressions and sins, absorbed in the temporal and the external,[2] showing by their disobedience the influence of the Prince of the power of the air; and the Jews, too, had been occupied with the desires of the flesh, doing the determinations of the flesh and the thoughts, and were by nature children of wrath[3] even as the rest; but God in His rich love and mercy quickened both Jews and Gentiles together, while still dead in their transgressions, and raised them together, and seated them together in the heavenlies in Christ Jesus—a name that occurs in verse after verse, being at the very heart of the Apostle's thoughts. The instrumental cause of this great salvation is solely free grace, applied by faith, that this grace might be manifested to the coming ages in all its

---

[1] i. 15—23. See iv. 10. Cf. Xen. *Hell.* vi. 2, 14, τὰς ναῦς ἐπληροῦτε. On the different application of the word Pleroma here and in Col. i. 19, *v. supra*. The view that it here means "complement" like *parapleroma* seems to me much less probable. On the expression the "God of our Lord Jesus Christ," cf. ver. 3; John xx. 17. In the unique phrase, "the Father of the Glory," ὁ πατὴρ τῆς δόξης, Canon Barry sees an allusion to the Jewish identification of "the Word" with "the Shechinah." Compare the use of Δόξα in James ii. 1; Titus ii. 13; Heb. i. 3.

[2] ii. 2, κατὰ τὸν αἰῶνα τοῦ κόσμου τούτου.

[3] Mr. Maurice's rendering, "children *of impulse*," is untenable.

surpassing wealth of kindness; and that we, thus created anew in Christ, and so prevented from any boast[1] that we achieved by good works our own salvation, might still walk in good works, to which God predestined us.[2] The Gentiles, then, were to remember that their former uncircumcision, so far as it was of any importance, was that spiritual uncircumcision which consisted in utter alienation from Christ, His kingdom, and His promises. But now in Christ, by the blood of Christ, the once afar have been made near. For He is our Peace; He has broken down the separating partition—the enmity between the two members of His great human family—by doing away with the law of ordinances and decrees,[3] that He might create the two—Jew and Gentile—into one fresh human being, making peace; and might reconcile them both in one body to God by the cross, slaying thereby the enmity between them both, and between them and God. The result, then, of His advent is peace to the far-off and to

---

[1] ii. 9. The last appearance of the word "boast" in St. Paul.

[2] ii. 10. It is interesting to see how the epoch of *controversy* on the great topic of these verses is here assumed to be closed; ἐπ' ἔργοις ἀγαθοῖς, οἷς προητοίμασεν ὁ Θεὸς ἵνα 'ν αὐτοῖς περιπατήσωμεν. Certainly οἷς may be by attraction for ἅ; but it is surely a very awkward expression to say that "God created *good works* that we should walk in them," and although ἡμᾶς is not expressed, it is involved in περιπατήσωμεν. Alford, who adopts the E.V., compares it with John v. 38, which is, however, no parallel. Nowhere is the harmonising of good works with free grace more admirably illustrated than here. Good works are here included in the predestined purpose of grace, so that they are not a condition of salvation, but an aim set before us, and rendered practicable by God's unconditional favour. (See Pfleiderer, ii. 189.)

[3] Cf. Col. i. 20—22. The application of the word is somewhat different; but it is exactly the kind of difference which might be made by an author dealing independently with his own expressions, and one on which a forger would not have ventured. The breaking down of the Chel, "the middle wall of partition," was that part of Christ's work which it fell mainly to St. Paul to continue. The charge that he had taken Trophimus into the Court of Israel, literally false, was ideally most true. And Paul the Apostle was the most effectual uprooter of the "hedge," which Saul the Pharisee thought it his chief work to make around the Law.

the nigh; for through Him we both have access by one Spirit to the Father. The Gentiles are no longer aliens, but fellow-citizens with the saints, built on the corner-stone of Christ which the Apostles and prophets laid—like stones compaginated[1] into the ever-growing walls of the one spiritual House of God.[2]

Then follows a chapter of parentheses, or rather of thoughts leading to thoughts, and linked together, as throughout the Epistle, by relatival connexions.[3] Resuming the prayer (i. 17) of which the thread had been broken by the full enunciation of the great truths in which he desired them to be enlightened: "For this cause," he says—namely, because of the whole blessed mystery which he has been expounding, and which results in their corporate union in Christ—"I, Paul, the prisoner of the Lord, on behalf of you Gentiles"—and there once more the prayer is broken by a parenthesis which lasts through thirteen verses. For, remembering that the letter is to be addressed not only to the Ephesians, of whom the majority were so well known to him, but also to other Asiatic churches, some of which he had not even visited, and which barely knew more of him than his name,[4] he pauses to dwell on the exalted character of the mission entrusted to him, and to express at the same time his own sense of utter personal unworthiness. Having called himself "the prisoner of the Lord on behalf of you Gentiles," he breaks off to say—

"Assuming that you have heard of the dispensation of the grace of God given me towards you—that by revelation was made known to me

[1] This word, used by St. Jerome, may express the unusual συναρμολογουμένη.
[2] ii. 1—22.
[3] See Ellicott, ad iii. 5.
[4] Although undoubtedly the εἴγε ἠκούσατε, like the similar expression in iv. 21, Gal. iii. 4, &c., implies that the fact is *assumed*, yet it is certainly not an expression which would well accord with a letter addressed only to a church in which the writer had long laboured.

the mystery [of the calling of the Gentiles], as I previously wrote to you in brief,[1] in accordance with which you can, as you read it, perceive my understanding in the mystery of Christ—a mystery which in other generations was not made known to the sons of men as it is now revealed to His holy Apostles[2] and prophets by the Spirit—(namely) that the Gentiles are[3] co-heirs, and concorporate, and comparticipant[4] of the promise in Christ Jesus by the Gospel, of which I became a minister, according to the gift of the grace of God given to me according to the working of His power. To me, the less-than-least[5] of all saints, was given this grace, to preach among the Gentiles the untrackable[6] wealth of Christ; and to enlighten all on the nature of the dispensation of the mystery that has been hidden from the ages in God, who created all things; that now to the principalities and the powers in the heavenlies may be made known by the Church the richly-variegated wisdom of God,[7] according to the pre-arrangement of the ages which

---

[1] i. 9, *seq.*; ii. 13, *seq.*

[2] Serious objections have been made to this phrase, as proving that it could not have been written by the pen that wrote Gal. ii. The objection is groundless. Assuming the ἁγίοις to be correct (though not found in every MS.; cf. Col. i. 26)—i. It is perfectly *generic*, not individual; cf. ver. 8 and ii. 20; 1 Cor. xvi. 1, 15. ii. Apostles and prophets are bracketed, and the epithet "holy" means "sanctified," a title which they share with all "saints." iii. "Apostles" does not here necessarily bear its *narrower* sense.

[3] Not "should be," as in A.V.

[4] iii. 6, συγκληρόνομα, σύσσωμα, συμμέτοχα. The two parts—Jews and Gentiles—are to become one body, the body of Christ, the Christian Church (ii. 16). The strange English words may perhaps correspond to the strange Greek words which St. Paul invented to express this newly-revealed mystery in the strongest possible form, as though no words could be too strong to express his dominant conception of the reunion in Christ of those who apart from Him are separate and divided.

[5] iii. 8, ἐλαχιστοτέρῳ. Would a forger have made St. Paul write thus? The expression has been compared to 1 Cor. xv. 9, but expresses a far deeper humility, because it is used when the writer is alluding to a far loftier exaltation. Those who criticise the phrase as exaggerated must be destitute of the deepest spiritual experiences. The confessions of the holiest are ever the most bitter and humble, because their very holiness enables them to take the due measure of the heinousness of sin. The self-condemnation of a Cowper or a Fénelon is far stronger than that of a Byron or a Voltaire. "The greatest sinner, the greatest saint, are equi-distant from the goal where the mind rests in satisfaction with itself. With the growth in goodness grows the sense of sin. One law fulfilled shows a thousand neglected" (Mozley, *Essays*, i. 327).

[6] iii. 8, ἀνεξιχνίαστον. Job v. 9, אֵין חֵקֶר. Cf. Rom. xi. 33, ἀνεξερεύνητα τὰ κρίματα αὐτοῦ καὶ ἀνεξιχνίαστοι αἱ ὁδοί.

[7] πολυποίκιλος. Cf. στέφανου π. ἀνθέων. Eubulus, *Ath.* xv. 7, p. 679.

He made in Christ Jesus our Lord, in whom we have our confidence and our access by faith in Him: wherefore I intreat you not to lose heart in my afflictions on your behalf, seeing that this is your glory. For this cause, then" (and here he resumes the thread of the prayer broken in the first verse) "I bend my knees to the Father,[1] from whom every fatherhood[2] in heaven and on earth derives its name, that He would give you, according to the wealth of His glory, to be strengthened by power through His Spirit into spiritual manhood,[3] that Christ may dwell in your hearts by faith—ye having been rooted and founded in love, that ye may have strength to grasp mentally with all saints what is the length and breadth and depth and height, and to know (spiritually) the knowledge-surpassing love of Christ, that ye may be filled up to all the plenitude of God."[4]

"Now to Him that is able above all things to do superabundantly above[5] all that we ask or think, according to the power [of the Holy Spirit] which worketh in us, to Him be glory in the Church, in Christ Jesus, to all the generations of the age of the ages. Amen."[6]

With this prayer he closes the doctrinal part of the Epistle; the remaining half of it is strictly practical. St. Paul would have felt it no descent of thought to pass from the loftiest spiritual mysteries to the humblest moral duties. He knew that holiness was the essence of God's Being, and he saw in the holiness of Christians the beautiful result of that predestined purpose, which, after being wrought out to gradual completion in the dispensation of past *æons*, was now fully manifested and revealed in Christ. He knew that the loftiest principles were the necessary basis of the simplest acts of faithfulness, and that all which is most pure, lovely, and of good report, in the Christian life, is the sole result of all that is most sublime in the

---

[1] The addition "of our Lord Jesus Christ," however ancient, is probably spurious, as it is not found in א, A, B, C, the Coptic, the Æthiopic versions, &c.

[2] Not "the whole family," as in A.V.

[3] iii. 16, εἰς τὸν ἔσω ἄνθρωπον.

[4] iii. 1—19. In other words, "that ye may be filled with all the plenitude of goodness wherewith God is filled;" "omnes divinae naturae divitiae" (Fritzsche).

[5] Of twenty-eight compounds in ὑπὲρ in the New Testament, no less than twenty are found in St. Paul alone.   [6] iii. 20, 21.

Christian's faith. The lustre of the planets may be faint
and poor, but yet it is reflected from the common sun;
and so the goodness of a redeemed man, however pale
in lustre, is still sacred, because it is a reflexion from
the Sun of righteousness. The reflected light of morality
is nothing apart from the splendour of that religion
from which it is derived. There is little which is
admirable in the honesty which simply results from
its being the best policy; or in the purity which is
maintained solely by fear of punishment; or even in the
virtue which is coldly adopted out of a calculation that it
tends to the greatest happiness of the greatest number. It
was not in this way that St. Paul regarded morality.
Many of the precepts which he delivers in the practical
sections of his Epistles might also have been delivered, and
nobly delivered, by an Epictetus or a Marcus Aurelius; but
that which places an immeasurable distance between the
teachings of St. Paul and theirs, is the fact that in St.
Paul's view holiness is not the imperfect result of rare
self-discipline, but the natural outcome of a divine life,
imparted by One who is the common Head of all the
family of man, and in participation with whose plenitude
the humblest act of self-sacrifice becomes invested with a
sacred value and a sacred significance. And there are
these further distinctions (among many others) between
the lofty teachings of Stoicism and the divine exhortations
of Christianity. Stoicism made its appeal only to the noble-
hearted few, despising and despairing of the vulgar herd
of mankind in all ranks, as incapable of philosophic training
or moral elevation. Christianity, in the name of a God who
was no respecter of persons, appealed to the very weakest
and the very worst as being all redeemed in Christ. Again,
Stoicism was dimmed and darkened to the very heart's core
of its worthiest votaries by deep perplexity and incurable

sadness; Christianity breathes into every utterance the joyous spirit of victory and hope. Even the best of the Stoics looked on the life of men around them with a detestation largely mingled with contempt, and this contempt weakened the sense of reciprocity, and fed the fumes of pride. But St. Paul addresses a revelation unspeakably more majestic, more profound, more spiritual, than any which Stoicism could offer, to men whom he well knows to have lived in the trammels of the vilest sins of heathendom, and barely even yet to have escaped out of the snare of the fowler. He confidently addresses exhortations of stainless purity and sensitive integrity to men who had been thieves and adulterers, and worse ; and so far from any self-exaltation at his own moral superiority, he regards his own life as hid indeed with Christ in God, but as so little fit to inspire a feeling of satisfaction that he is lost in the conviction of his own unworthiness as contrasted with the wealth of God's compassion, and the unspeakable grandeur of the long-hidden mystery which now in due time he is commissioned to set forth. The mingled prayer and pæan of this magnificent Epistle is inspired throughout "by a sense of opposites—of the union of weakness and strength, of tribulation and glory, of all that had been and all that was to be, of the absolute love of God, of the discovery of that love to man in the Mediator, of the working of that love in man through the Spirit, of the fellowship of the poorest creature of flesh and blood on earth with the spirits in heaven, of a canopy of love above and an abyss of love beneath, which encompasses the whole creation." The Apostle would have delighted in the spirit of those words which a modern poet has learnt from the truths which it was his high mission to reveal :—

> " I say to thee, do thou repeat
> To the first man thou mayest meet

> In lane, highway, or open street,
> That he, and we, and all men move
> Under a canopy of love
> As broad as the blue sky above."[1]

"I then," continues the Apostle—and how much does that word "then" involve, referring as it does to all the mighty truths which he has been setting forth!—"I then, the prisoner in the Lord, exhort you to walk worthily of the calling in which ye were called." This is the keynote to all that follows. So little was earthly success or happiness worth even considering in comparison with the exceeding and eternal weight of glory which affliction was working out for them, that while he has urged them not to lose heart in his tribulations, he makes those very tribulations a ground of appeal, and feels that he can speak to them with all the stronger influence as "a prisoner in the Lord," and "an ambassador in a chain." And the worthy elevation to the grandeur of their calling was to be shown by virtues which, in their heathen condition, they would almost have ranked with abject vices—lowliness, meekness, endurance, the forbearance of mutual esteem. The furious quarrels, the mad jealousies, the cherished rancours, the frantic spirit of revenge which characterised their heathen condition, are to be fused by the heat of love into one great spiritual unity and peace. Oneness, the result of love, is the ruling thought of this section (iv. 3—13). "One body, and one spirit, even as also ye were called in one hope of your calling, one Lord, one Faith, one Baptism, one God and Father of all, who is above all, and through all, and in all."[2] Yet this unity is not a dead level of uniformity. Each has his separate measure of grace given by Him who, ascending in triumph, with Sin and Death bound to His chariot-wheels, "gave

---

[1] Archbishop Trench.   [2] Omit ἡμῶν, א, A, B, C, &c.

gifts for men,"[1] having first descended that by ascending "far above all heavens" He might fill all things. Apostles therefore, and Prophets, and Evangelists, and Pastors, and Teachers were all appointed by virtue of the gifts which He gave, with a view to perfect the saints, and so to build up the Church which is the body of Christ, until we all finally attain[2] to the unity of the faith, and the full knowledge of the Son of God, to perfect manhood, to the measure of the stature of the Plenitude of Christ." But to contribute to this perfect growth we must lay aside moral and spiritual childishness; we must keep the hand firmly on the helm that we may not be tossed like dismantled hulks by every wave and storm of doctrine, in that fraudful sleight and craft which many devote to further the deliberate system of error. To be true and to be loving is the secret of Christian growth.[3] Sincerity and charity are as the life-blood in the veins of that Church, of which Christ is the Head and Heart, "from whom the whole body being fitly framed and compacted by means of every joint of the vital supply, according to the proportional energy of each individual part, tends to the increase of the body, so as to build itself up in love."[4]

After this expansion of the duty of Unity, he returns to his exhortation; and, as before he had urged them to walk worthily of their vocation, he now urges them not to walk, as did the rest of the Gentiles, in the vanity of their

[1] On this singular reference to Ps. lxviii., and the change of the ἔλαβες δόματα ἐν ἀνθρώποις, see Davies, p. 44. It is at least doubtful whether there is the slightest allusion to the descent into hell. The point is the *identity* of Him who came to earth (*i.e.*, the historic Jesus) and Him who ascended, *i.e.*, of the Eternal and the Incarnate Christ.

[2] The omission of ἂν marks the certain result.

[3] iv. 15, ἀληθεύοντες δὲ ἐν ἀγάπῃ—not merely "*speaking* the truth," but '*being* true."

[4] iv. 1—16.

mind, having been darkened in their understanding, and utterly alienated from the life of God because of their ignorance and the callosity of their hearts,[1] seeing that they, having lost all sense of shame or sorrow for sin,[2] abandoned themselves to wantonness for the working of all uncleanness, in inordinate desire :[3]—

"But NOT so did ye learn Christ—assuming that ye heard Him, and were taught in Him as the truth is in Jesus,[4] that ye put off, as concerns your former conversation, the old man which is ever being corrupted according to the lusts of deceit, and undergo renewal by the spirit of your mind, and put on the new man which after God was created in righteousness and holiness of truth."[5]

Then follow the many practical applications which result from this clothing of the soul with the new-created humanity. Put away lying, because we are members of one another.[6] Let not just anger degenerate into chronic exasperation, neither give room to the devil. Let honest work, earning sufficient even for charity, replace thievishness. For corruption of speech[7] let there be such as is "good for edification of the need[8] that it may give grace

---

[1] τῶρος, "tufa-stone," is used, secondarily, for a hard tumour, or *callus* at the end of injured bones.

[2] ἀπηλγηκότες. "Qui postquam peccaverint, non dolent." "A sin committed a second time does not seem a sin" (*Moed Katon*, f. 27, 2).

[3] πλεονεξία.

[4] The form of expression might seem to point to a warning against any incipient docetic tendency (cf. 1 John iv. 2, 3) to draw a distinction between Christ and Jesus, between the Eternal Christ and the human Jesus.

[5] iv. 17—24.

[6] The necessity of the following moral exhortations will excite no astonishment in the minds of those who have studied the Epistle to the Corinthians, or who have sufficient knowledge of the human heart to be aware that the evil habits of a heathen lifetime were not likely to be cured in all converts by a moment of awakenment, or by an acceptance of Christian truths, which in many cases may have been mainly intellectual.

[7] iv. 29, σαπρός, "rotten" (Matt. vii. 17), the opposite of ὑγιής, "sound," in 2 Tim. i. 13, &c., and "seasoned with salt," Col. iv. 6.

[8] Not "for the use of edification," as in E.V., but for such edification as the occasion requires.

to the hearers," since unwholesome impurity is a chronic grief to that Holy Spirit who has sealed you as His own to the day of redemption. Then, returning to his main subject of unity, he says :—

"Let all bitterness, and wrath, and anger, and clamour, and railing be put away from you with all malice, and become kind to one another, compassionate, freely forgiving one another, as God also in Christ[1] freely forgave you. Become, then, imitators of God as children beloved, and walk in love, even as Christ loved us and gave Himself for us an offering and sacrifice to God for a savour of sweet smell."[2]

Then, proceeding to other practical duties, he forbids every form of impurity or obscenity, in word or deed, with the worldly polish[3] which was often nearly akin to it, since they are unsuitable to the Christian character, and they who are addicted to such things have no inheritance in the kingdom of God, and whatever men may say, such things are the abiding source of God's wrath.[4] Let thanksgiving take the place of indecency of speech. For though they *were* darkness, they are now light in the Lord. Walk as children of light. For the fruit of light[5] is in all goodness, and righteousness, and truth. Light is the prevalent conception here, as love was in the last

---

[1] iv. 32, ἐν Χριστῷ, not as in E.V., "for Christ's sake."

[2] iv. 25—v. 2.

[3] Ver. 4, εὐτραπελία. Aristotle defines it as "cultivated impertinence" (*Rhet.* ii. 12), and places the polished worldling (εὐτράπελος, *facetus*) midway between the boor (ἄγροικος) and the low flatterer (βωμολόχος) (*Eth. N.* ii. 7). The mild word, τὰ οὐκ ἀνήκοντα, is due, not to the comparatively harmless "polish" which has been last mentioned, but to *litotes*—the use of a soft expression (like Virgil's "*illaudati* Busiridis aras"), to be corrected by the indignant mental substitution of a more forcible word. See *supra*, i. 627.

[4] Ver. 6, ἔρχεται, is ever coming.

[5] This is the true reading (φωτὸς), not "fruit of the Spirit," as in the E.V. The reading was doubtless altered to soften the harshness of the metaphor; but St. Paul is as indifferent as Shakespeare himself to a mere verbal confusion of metaphors when the sense is clear. To see allusions here to Ormuzd and Ahriman is surely absurd.

chapter.¹ Let them not participate in the unfruitful infamies of secret darkness, "but rather even convict them, for all things on being convicted are illumined by the light, for all that is being illumined is light."² And this is the spirit of what is perhaps a Christian hymn:—

*Ἔγειρε ὁ καθεύδων
Ἀνάστα ἐκ τῶν νεκρῶν
Ἐπιφαύσει σοι ὁ Χριστός.*

("Awake thee, thou that sleepest,
And from the dead arise thou,
And Christ shall shine upon thee.") ³

"Take heed, then, how ye walk carefully, not as unwise but as wise, buying up the opportunity because the days are evil. Do not prove yourselves senseless, but understanding what is the will of the Lord."⁴

Thus, mingling special exhortation with universal principles, he proceeds to warn them against drunkenness, and recalling perhaps the thrill of emotion with which he and they have joined in such stirring words as those he has just quoted, he bids them seek rather the spiritual exaltations of that holy enthusiasm which finds vent in the melodies of Christian hymnology, and in the eucharistic music of the heart, while at the same time all are mutually submissive to each other in the fear of God.⁵

The duty of submissiveness thus casually introduced is then illustrated and enforced in three great social rela-

---

¹ Paley (*Hor. Paul.*) says that St. Paul here "goes off" at the word light; but this is not nearly so good an instance of this literary peculiarity as iv. 8, "ascended."

² Deeds of darkness must cease to be deeds of darkness when the light shines on them. The light *kills* them. Everything on which light is poured *is* light, because it reflects light. φανερούμενον cannot mean "that maketh manifest," as in the E.V.

³ Isa. lx. 1, 2. The versification is of the Hebrew type. On Christian hymnology, *v. supra*, on Col. iii. 16. Antiphonal congregational singing was very early introduced (Rev. xix. 1—4).

⁴ Vers. 3—17.

⁵ Vers. 18—21.

tions.[1] Wives are to be submissive to their husbands, as the Church is to Christ; and husbands to love their wives, as Christ loved the Church, to sanctify it into stainless purity, and to cherish it as a part of Himself in inseparable union. Children are to obey their parents, and parents not to irritate their children. Slaves are to render sincere and conscientious service, as being the slaves of their unseen Master, Christ, and therefore bound to fulfil all the duties of the state of life in which He has placed them; and masters are to do their duty to their slaves, abandoning threats, remembering that they too have a Master in whose sight they all are equal.[2]

Having thus gone through the main duties of domestic and social life as contemplated in the light of Christ, he bids them finally "grow strong in the Lord and in the might of His strength."[3] The exhortation brings up the image of armour with which the worn and aged prisoner was but too familiar. Daily the coupling-chain which bound his right wrist to the left of a Roman legionary clashed as it touched some part of the soldier's arms. The baldric, the military boot, the oblong shield, the cuirass, the helmet, the sword of the Prætorian guardsman were among the few things which he daily saw. But we cannot doubt that, with his kindly human interest in life and youth, the Apostle, who knew that heathendom too was redeemed in Christ,

---

[1] All commentators have felt a difficulty in seeing the connexion between singing and subjection. I believe that it lies in a reminiscence of the unseemly Babel of contentious vanities which St. Paul had heard of, perhaps even witnessed, at Corinth, where such disorder had been caused by the obtrusive vanity with which each person wished to display his or her particular χάρισμα. If so—or even if the association was something else—we have another inimitable mark of genuineness. No forger would dream of appending a most important section of his moral teaching to a purely accidental thought.

[2] Ver. 22—vi. 9.

[3] vi. 10. The ἀδελφοί is wanting in ℵ, B, D, E, and does not occur in Eph. or Col.

whose boyhood had been passed in a heathen city, who loved man as man because he saw a vision of all humanity in God—would have talked often to the weary soldiers who guarded him; would have tried by wholesome and courteous and profitable words to dissipate their tedium, until we can well imagine that the legionaries who had to perform the disagreeable task would, in spite of intense national repugnances, prefer to be chained to Paul the Jewish prisoner than to any whom caprice, or justice, or tyranny consigned to their military charge. Doubtless the soldiers would tell him in what countries they had been stationed, what barbarians they had helped to subdue. He would ask them in what tumult they had got that fracture in the helmet, in what battle that dint upon the shield, by what blow they had made that hack in the sword.[1] They would tell him of the deadly wrestle with foes who grappled with them in the *mêlée*, and of the *falaricae*,[2] the darts wrapped round with flaming tow, from which their shields had saved them in the siege. And thinking of the sterner struggle against deadlier enemies, even against the world-rulers of this darkness, against the spiritual powers of wickedness in the heavenlies,[3] in which all God's children are anxiously engaged, he bids the Christian converts assume, not "the straw-armour of reason," but the panoply of God, that they may be able to withstand in the evil day. Let spiritual truth be their baldric

---

[1] The *pilum*, or heavy javelin, which a soldier would not bring with him to the guard-room, is omitted.

[2] Or *malleoli* (Ps. vii. 13).

[3] The Rabbinical מזיקין. Similarly, in 2 Cor. iv. 4, St. Paul goes so far as to call "the Prince of the power of the air," ὁ θεὸς τοῦ αἰῶνος τούτου. (Cf. 1 John v. 19; John xiv. 30; xvi. 11.) "The spirituals of wickedness in the heavenlies" are the *Geisterchaft* of iniquity in the regions of space; but one would expect ἐπουρανίοις. The E.V. conceals the difficulty by its "high places;" but if ἐπουρανίοις be right, it can only be in a physical sense. As for mortal enemies: "vasa sunt, alius utitur; organa sunt, alius jungit" (Aug.).

or binding girdle;[1] moral righteousness their breastplate; zealous alacrity in the cause of the Gospel of Peace their *caligae* of war;[2] and in addition to these, let faith be taken up as their broad shield[3] against the darts of the evil one, however fiercely ignited. Their one weapon of offence is to be the sword of the Spirit, which is the Word of God.[4] Prayer and watchfulness is to be their constant attitude; and in their prayers for all saints he begs also for their prayers on his own behalf, not that his chains may be loosed, but that he may boldly and aptly make known the mystery of the Gospel, on behalf of which he is an ambassador—not inviolable, not splendid, but—"an ambassador in a coupling-chain."[5]

He sends no news or personal salutations because he is sending the faithful and beloved Tychicus, who will tell them, as well as other cities, all his affairs; but he concludes with a blessing of singular fulness:

"Peace to the brethren and love with faith from God the Father and the Lord Jesus Christ. Grace be with all who love our Lord Jesus Christ in incorruption."[7]

We have now examined all the Epistles of St. Paul except the last group of all—the three addressed to Timothy and

[1] "Veritas astringit hominem, mendaciorum magna est laxitas" (Grot.).
[2] Cf. Rom. iii. 17; x. 15; ἐτοιμασία may, however, mean "basis," "sole" (מָכוֹן, Ezra iii. 3; Ps. lxxxviii. 15, LXX.). The Gospel of *Peace* gives a secure foothold even in *war*.
[3] Faith, not merit, as in Wisd. v. 19. (Cf. Ps. xviii. 31, &c.) Notice the emphatic position of πεπυρωμένα.
[4] Dr. Davidson finds this a tedious and tasteless amplification of 1 Thess. v. 8, 2 Cor. x. 3, 4, and has many similar criticisms (*Introd.* i. 388, 390). It is impossible to argue against such criticisms as bearing on the question of genuineness. The general metaphor is not uncommon (Isa. lix. 16—19; 1 Thess. v. 8; Wisd. v. 17—20; Bleeck, *Zend Avesta*, p. 90; Davies, p. 61). (See the account of the arms in the Interpreter's House in *Pilgrim's Progress*, and Gurnall's *Christian Armour*.)
[5] vi. 10—20. In ver. 18 it is περὶ πάντων τῶν ἁγίων καὶ ὑπὲρ ἐμοῦ. "Paradoxon: mundus habet splendidos legatos" (Bengel). [6] vi. 21—24.

Titus. These are usually known as the Pastoral Epistles, because they sketch the duties of the Christian Pastor. Of the Epistle to the Hebrews I have said nothing, because I hope to speak of it hereafter, and because, for reasons which appear to me absolutely convincing, I cannot regard it as a work of St. Paul's. But even if the Epistle to the Hebrews be accepted as having been written by the Apostle, it adds nothing to our knowledge of his history. But for the preservation of the Pastoral Epistles, we should not know a single additional fact about him, except such as we can glean from vague and wavering traditions.

The Acts of the Apostles ends with the statement that Paul remained a period of two whole years in his own hired lodging, and received all who came in to visit him, preaching the kingdom of God and teaching the things concerning the Lord Jesus Christ with all confidence unmolestedly.[1] The question why St. Luke deliberately ended his sketch of the Apostle at that point, is one which can never receive a decisive answer. He only related circumstances of which he was an eyewitness, or which he knew from trustworthy information, and for that reason his narrative, in spite of its marked *lacunae*, is far more valuable than if it had been constructed out of looser materials. It may, however, be safely asserted that since he had been with St. Paul during at least a part of the Roman imprisonment, he brought down his story to the period at which he first wrote his book. A thousand circumstances may have prevented any resumption of his work as a chronicler, but it is inconceivable that St. Paul should have died almost immediately afterwards, by a martyr's

---

[1] The cadence is expressive of stability; of motion succeeded by rest; of action settled in repose. "An emblem of the history of the Church of Christ, and of the life of every true believer in Him" (Bishop Wordsworth).

death, and St. Luke have been aware of it before his book was published, and yet that he should not have made the faintest allusion to the subject.[1] The conjecture that Theophilus knew all the rest, so that it was needless to commit it to writing, is entirely valueless, for whoever Theophilus may have been, it is clear that St. Luke was not writing for him alone. It is also, to say the least, a probable conjecture that soon after the close of those two whole years some remarkable change took place in the condition of the prisoner. That such a change *did* take place is the almost unanimous tradition of the Church. However slight may be the grounds of direct testimony, it has been generally believed in all ages that (about the beginning of the year A.D. 64) St. Paul was tried, acquitted, and liberated; and that after some two years of liberty, during which he continued to prosecute his missionary labours, he was once more arrested, and was, after a second imprisonment, put to death at Rome. This would, at least, accord with the anticipations expressed in his own undoubted Epistles. Although he was still a prisoner when he wrote the letter to the Philippians, his trial was near at hand, and while promising to send Timothy to inquire about their fortunes, he adds, "But I am confident in the Lord that I myself too shall come speedily;" and this is so far from being a *casual* hope that he even asks Philemon "to get a lodging ready for him, for he hopes that he shall be granted to them by their prayers." It is, of course, quite possible that

[1] So far as anything can be said to be probable in the midst of such uncertainties, the probability is that the leisure of his attendance on St. Paul during the Roman imprisonment had enabled St. Luke to draw up the main part of his work; that he concluded it exactly at the point at which St. Paul was expecting immediate liberation, and that he either published it at the first favourable opportunity after that time, or was prevented—it may be even by death—from ever continuing or completing his task.

St. Paul's sanguine expectations may have been frustrated,[1] but he certainly would not have expressed them so distinctly without good grounds for believing that powerful friends were at work in his favour. Whether Festus, and Agrippa, and Lysias, and Publius had used their influence on his behalf, or whether he had reason to rely on any favourable impression which he may have made among the Prætorian soldiers, or whether he had received intelligence that the Jews had seen reason to abandon a frivolous and groundless prosecution, it is impossible to conjecture;[2] but his strong impression that he *would* be liberated at least helps to confirm the many arguments which lead us to believe that he actually was. If so, it must have been very soon after the close of that two years' confinement with which St. Luke so suddenly breaks off.

For in July, A.D. 64, there broke out that terrible persecution against the Christians, from which, had he

---

[1] For this reason I have not here laid any stress on his once-purposed visit to Spain (Rom. xv. 24, 28). It seems clear from Philem. 22 that he had either abandoned this intention, or at any rate postponed it till he had re-visited Asia.

[2] It is undesirable to multiply uncertain conjectures, but perhaps the Jews may have sent their documents, witnesses, &c., with Josephus when he went to Rome, A.D. 64. He tells us that, by the influence of the Jewish pantomimist Aliturus and of Poppæa, he was enabled to secure the release of some Jewish priests, friends of his own, whom Festus had, on grounds which Josephus calls trivial, sent bound to Rome. Josephus was doubtless one of a commission dispatched for this purpose, and it is conceivable that the prosecution of St. Paul's trial may have been a subordinate object of this commission, and that the trial may have broken down all the more completely from the loss of witnesses and evidence in the shipwreck which Josephus underwent. His vessel foundered on the voyage, and out of two hundred souls only eighty were picked up, by a ship of Cyrene, after they had swum or floated all night in the waves. Josephus then proceeded to Puteoli in another ship. He makes little more than a dry allusion to these events (*Vit.* 3), which contrasts singularly with the vivid minuteness of St. Luke; but the general incidents so far resemble those of St. Paul's shipwreck that some have conjectured that the two events were identical. Chronology and other considerations render this impossible, nor is there any great reason to suppose that Josephus is here introducing embellishments from the story of St. Paul.

been still at Rome, it is certain that he could not have
escaped. If, therefore, the Pastoral Epistles be forgeries,
we have heard the last words of St. Paul, and at the last
verse of the Acts the curtain rushes down in utter darkness upon the remainder of his life. Let us, then, consider
what tradition says, and whether we can still accept as
genuine the Epistles to Timothy and Titus. If the indications derived from these sources are in any degree trustworthy, we have still to hear some further thoughts and
opinions of the Apostle. We catch at least a misty glimpse
of his final movements, and attain to a sure knowledge
of his state of mind up to the moment of his death. If
tradition be mistaken, and if the Epistles are spurious, then
we must acquiesce in the fact that we know nothing more
of the Apostle, and that he perished among that "vast
multitude" whom, in the year 64, the vilest of Emperors,
nay, almost of human beings, sacrificed to the blind
madness which had been instigated against them by a
monstrous accusation. If, indeed, St. Paul perished amid
that crowd of nameless martyrs, there is but little probability that any regard would have been paid to his claim
as a Roman citizen. He may have perished, like them,
by crucifixion; or have been covered, like them, in the skins
of wild beasts, to be mangled by dogs; or, standing in his
tunic of ignited pitch, may with his dying glance have
caught sight of the wicked Emperor of triumphant
Heathendom, as the living torch of hideous martyrdom
cast a baleful glare across the gardens of the Golden House.[1]
From all this, however, we may feel a firm conviction
that, by the mercy of God, he was delivered for a time.[2]

It is true that, so far as direct evidence is concerned,

---

[1] Tac. *Ann.* xv. 44 (cf. Mart. x. 25; Juv. *Sat.* viii. 235); Sen. *Ep.* 14, 4
Schol. in *Juv.* i. 155; Tert. *Apol.* 15; *ad Nat.* i. 18; *ad Mart.* 5.
[2] See Excursus VIII., "Evidence as to the Liberation of St. Paul."

we can only say that St. Paul's own words render it probable that he was liberated, and that this probability finds some slight support in a common tradition, endorsed by the authority of some of the Fathers. But this tradition goes little further than the bare fact. If we are to gain any further knowledge of the biography of St. Paul, it must be derived from the Pastoral Epistles, and from them alone. If they be not genuine, we know no single further particular respecting his fortunes.

Now, it must be admitted that a number of critics, formidable alike in their unanimity and their learning, have come to the conclusion that the Epistles to Timothy and Titus were not written by St. Paul.[1] Their arguments are entitled to respectful attention, and they undoubtedly suggest difficulties, which our ignorance of all details in the history of those early centuries renders it by no means easy to remove. Nevertheless, after carefully and impartially weighing all that they have urged—of which some account will be found in the Excursus at the end of the volume—I have come to the decided conviction that the Epistles are genuine, and that the first two of them were written during the two years which intervened between St. Paul's liberation and his martyrdom at Rome.

[1] Schmidt, Schleiermacher, Eichhorn, Credner, De Wette, Baur, Zeller, Hilgenfeld, Schenkel, Ewald, Hausrath, Renan, Pfleiderer, Krenkel, Davidson, &c.

CHAPTER LIII.

THE FIRST EPISTLE TO TIMOTHY.

Ἐν ἀδήλῳ του σκότει φωλευόντων εἰσέτι τότε τῶν, εἰ καί τινες ὑπῆρχον, παραφθείρειν ἐπιχειρούντων τὸν ὑγιῆ κανόνα τοῦ σωτηρίου κηρύγματος.—HEGESIPPUS ap. Euseb. *H. E.* iii. 32.

I SHALL not attempt, by more than a few sentences, to dispel the obscurity of that last stage of the Apostle's life which began at the termination of his Roman imprisonment. We feel that our knowledge of his movements is plunged in the deepest uncertainty the moment that we lose the guidance of St. Luke. I cannot myself believe that he was able to carry out his intention of visiting Spain. The indications of his travels in the two later Pastoral Epistles seem to leave no room for such a journey; nor, if it had really taken place, can we imagine that no shadow of a detail respecting it should have been preserved. But even if he did accomplish this new mission, we cannot so much as mention a single church which he founded, or a single port at which he touched. To speak of his work in Spain could only therefore leave a fallacious impression. If he went at all, it must have been immediately after his imprisonment, since his original object had been merely to visit Rome on his way to the "limit of the West." In writing to the Romans he had expressed a hope that he would be furthered on his journey by their assistance. Judging by the indifference with which they treated him in both of his imprisonments, there is too much reason to fear that this hope was in any case doomed to disappointment. The next trace of his existence is the First Epistle to Timothy. That Epistle is less organic—that is, it has less structural unity—than any other of St. Paul's Epistles. The time and place at which it was written are wholly uncertain, because the only historic indication which it contains is that "on his way to Macedonia Paul had begged Timothy to remain at Ephesus."[1]

"Paul, an Apostle of Jesus Christ, according to the commandment of God our Saviour,[2] and Christ Jesus our hope, to Timothy my true child in the faith; grace, mercy, and peace from God the Father[3] and Christ Jesus our Lord."[4]

This salutation is remarkable for the title "Saviour" applied to God the Father, perhaps derived from some recent study of Psalm lxiii. 7, and continued throughout the Pastoral Epistles when once adopted; for the name "our Hope," applied to Christ, and not improbably borrowed from the same verse; and for the word "mercy" so naturally introduced by the worn and tried old man, between the usual greetings of "grace and peace."[5]

---

[1] The general outline of the Epistle is as follows:—Salutation (i. 1, 2). The object of the letter to encourage Timothy to resist false teachers, and hold fast the faith (3—11, 18—20), with the Apostle's thanks to God for the mercy which had made him a minister of the Gospel (12—17). The duty of praying for rulers, with rules about the bearing of women in public worship (ii.). The qualifications of "bishops" (presbyters) and deacons (iii.). Fresh warnings respecting the false teachers, and the way in which Timothy is to deal with them (iv.). His relations to elders (v. 1, 2); to the order of "widows" (3—16); and to presbyters, with rules as to their selection (17—25). Directions concerning slaves, especially with reference to the false teachers; warnings against covetousness; with final exhortations and benediction (vi.).

[2] Not, of course, "a Saviour." The spread of Christianity is naturally marked by the increasing anarthrousness (omission of the article) of its commonest terms. We mark this fact in the word Christ, which is an appellative in the Gospels (almost always "*the* Christ"—*i.e.*, the Messiah), but has become, in the Epistles, a proper name.

[3] Omit ἡμῶν, ℵ, A, D, F, G (B, deficient). [4] i. 1, 2. [5] Cf. Gal. vi. 16.

"As I begged thee to remain still in Ephesus, on my way to Macedonia, that thou mightest command some not to teach different doctrine, nor to give heed to myths and interminable genealogies,[1] seeing that these minister questions rather than the dispensation of God[2] which is in faith——"[3] The sentence, quite characteristically, remains unfinished; but St. Paul evidently meant to say, "I repeat the exhortation which then I gave."

In contrast with these false teachers he tells him that the purpose of the Gospel is love out of a pure heart, a good conscience, and faith unfeigned, failing of which some turned aside to vain jangling. They wanted to pass themselves off as teachers of the Jewish Law, but their teaching was mere confusion and ignorance.

The mention of the Law leads him to allude to its legitimate function.[4] To those who were justified by faith it was needless, being merged in the higher law of a life in unity with Christ; but its true function was to warn and restrain those who lived under the sway of mere passion in heathenish wickedness.[5] For these, though not for the regenerate, the thunders of Sinai are necessary, "according to the Gospel of the glory of the blessed God, wherewith I was entrusted."[6]

He then at once digresses into an expression of

---

[1] Though the Sephiroth of the Kabbala belong to a much later period, and the Zohar is probably a mediæval book, yet Judaic speculations of the same kind seem to have been the prototype of the Valentinian emanations with their successive intermarriages of æons.

[2] i. 4; leg. οἰκονομίαν (א, A, B, F, G, &c.). The questions do not further the divine scheme of God, which works, not in the sphere of misty uncertainties, but in the sphere of faith.

[3] 3, 4. For similar *anakoluth*ɪ, see Gal. ii. 4, 5; Rom. v. 12, &c.

[4] i. 8, 9, νόμος . . . νομίμως.

[5] For the true use of the Law, and the limitation to its validity, see Rom. vii. 12; Gal. iii. 19; Phil. iii. 9. It is idle to pretend that there is anything un-Pauline in this sentiment. With the list of crimes—which is, however, varied with perfect independence—cf. Rom. i. 29; 1 Cor. vi. 9; Gal. v. 19.

[6] i. 8—11.

heartfelt gratitude to God for that grace which superabounded over his former ignorant faithlessness, a faithlessness which had led him to outrage and insult, such as only his ignorance could palliate.

"Faithful is the saying,[1] and worthy of all acceptation, that Christ Jesus came into the world to save sinners, of whom I am chief.[2] But on this account I gained mercy, that in me first and foremost Christ Jesus might manifest His entire long-suffering as a pattern for those who were hereafter to believe on Him to life eternal. Now to the King of the Ages,[3] the incorruptible, invisible, only God,[4] honour and glory unto the ages of the ages. Amen.[5]

"This charge I commit to thee, son Timothy, in accordance with the prophecies which in time past were prophesied of thee,[6] that thou in them mayest war the good warfare,[7] having faith and a good conscience, which some rejecting have been wrecked as regards the faith; of whom is Hymenæus and Alexander, whom I handed over to Satan, that they may be trained not to blaspheme."[8]

It will be seen that in this section he begins with the

[1] This arresting formula would naturally arise with the rise of Christian axioms; cf. "These words are faithful and true" (Rev. xxi. 5; xxii. 6).

[2] Cf. "God be merciful to me the sinner" (Luke xviii. 13); πρῶτος, "non tempore sed malignitate" (Aug. *in Ps.* lxxi. 1).

[3] Not here in its technical sense of "the æons;" cf. Ps. cxlv. 13, "a kingdom of all ages."

[4] Omit σοφῷ (א, A, D, F, G, &c.).

[5] For similar personal digressions, see Gal. i. 12; 1 Thess. ii. 4; 2 Cor. iii. 6; iv. 1, &c.; and for the doxology (Rom. xv. 33; xvi. 27; 2 Cor. ii. 14; ix. 15; Phil. iv. 20, &c. The passage is intensely individual, for "all Paul's theology is in ultimate analysis, the reflex of his personal experience" (Reuss, *Les Epitres*, ii. 352).

[6] Perhaps a reference to his solemn ordination, as in iv. 14, when Silas, who was a prophet (Acts xv. 32), was present among others (Acts xiii. 3).

[7] στρατεία, not ἀγών, as in 2 Tim. iv. 7. It is St. Paul's favourite metaphor (Rom. xiii. 12; 2 Cor. x. 5; 1 Thess. v. 8, &c.).

[8] i. 12—20. It is impossible to know the exact circumstances referred to. For Hymenæus, see 2 Tim. ii. 17. For Alexander, 2 Tim. iv. 14; Acts xix. 33; but even the identifications are precarious. For "delivering to Satan," see 1 Cor. v. 5. Whether it was excommunication, or generally giving up from all Church influences, and leaving Satan to deal with them, or the delivery to præternatural corporal sufferings, the *intention*, we see, was merciful and disciplinary (παιδευθῶσι).

false teachers, and after two digressions—one suggested by the mention of the Law, the other by his personal commission to preach the Gospel—returns to them again.

The second chapter contains regulations for public worship, the duty of praying for those in authority, and the bearing and mutual relations of men and women in religious assemblies,—broken by brief and natural digressions on the universality of God's offered grace, and on his own Apostolic office. He directs that

"Petitions, prayers, supplications, and thanksgivings[1] should be made for all, and especially for kings,[2] and those in authority, that we may spend a calm and quiet life in all godliness and gravity. This is fair and acceptable before our Saviour, God, who wills all men to be saved, and to come to full knowledge of the truth. For there is one God and one Mediator between God and men, the man Christ Jesus,[3] who gave Himself a ransom for all—the testimony in its own seasons. For which testimony I was appointed an herald and an Apostle (I speak the truth;[4] I lie not,[5]) in faith and truth."[6]

After this double digression he expresses his wish that the men[7] should pray in every place, "uplifting holy

[1] The synonyms are mainly cumulative, though, perhaps δεήσεις means special, προσευχάς general, and ἐντεύξεις earnest prayers (see Phil. iv. 6).

[2] Baur sees in this plural an indication that the Epistle was written in the times of the Antonines, when Emperors took associates in the Empire. Can theorising be more baseless?—The word "kings" does not necessarily refer only to local viceroys, &c., like the Herods, but was in the provinces applied generically to the Emperors, as it constantly is in the Talmud. It was most important to both Jews and Christians that they should not be suspected of civic turbulence (Jos. B. J. ii. 10, § 4; Bingham, xv. 8, 14). Hence we see how baseless is the conjecture of Pfleiderer (*Protestanten bibel*) that it was written in the time of Hadrian, who befriended the Christians (Euseb. H. E. iv. 8, 9).

[3] The word μεσίτης as applied to Christ is new, but not the conception (Rom. v. 10; 2 Cor. v. 19). There may be a silent condemnation of incipient Docetism in ἄνθρωπος, as well as of the supposed mediation of angels in εἷς (Col. ii. 15, 18).

[4] Om. ἐν Χριστῷ (A, D, F, G, &c.).

[5] A natural reminiscence of the occasions when such asseverations had been so necessary that they had become habitual (2 Cor. xi. 31; Rom. ix. 1).

[6] ii. 1—7.

[7] τοὺς ἄνδρας (ii. 8).

hands,[1] without wrath and doubting; and that women, with shamefastness and sobriety, should adorn themselves, not with plaits of hair, and gold or pearls, or costly raiment, but, in accordance with their Gospel profession, with good works." Let them be silent and submissive, not obtrusive and didactic. This rule he supports by the narrative of the Fall, as illustrative of *generic* differences between the sexes,[2] adding, however, that in spite of the greater liability to deception and sin, woman "shall be saved through motherhood, if they abide in faith and love and sanctification with sobermindedness."[3]

The third chapter passes into the qualifications for office in the Church. It is introduced by a sort of Christian aphorism, "Faithful is the saying, If any man desires the office of the pastorate,[4] he desires a good work." The qualifications on which St. Paul insists are irreproachableness, faith-

---

[1] The ancient attitude of prayer (Bingham, *Antiq.* xiii. 8, 10; Ps. xxiv. 4; xxvi. 6); cf. Tennyson—

> "For what are men better than sheep or goats
> That nourish a blind life within the brain,
> If knowing God *they lift not hands* of prayer
> Both for themselves and those who call them friend."

[2] This is quite independent of, yet exactly analogous to, his reasoning in 1 Cor. xi. 8, 9 (cf. 2 Cor. xi. 3; Wisd. xxv. 24).

[3] ii. 8—15. It will be seen that he is here looking at the question from a wholly different point of view to that in 1 Cor. vii., which applies not to the whole sex, but to a chosen few. So, too, in the previous verses, he is considering concrete facts, not the abstract abolition of all sexual distinctions in Christ (Gal. iii. 28). The ἡ τεκνογονία is probably not specific ("*the* childbearing"—*i.e.*, the Incarnation—surely a most obscure allusion), but generic—*i.e.*, a holy married life, with the bearing and training of children, is, as a rule, the appointed path for women, and it will end in their salvation, in spite of their original weakness. if that path be humbly and faithfully pursued. Doubtless St. Paul was thinking of Gen. iii. 16.

[4] To translate this "the office of a bishop" is, as Alford says in his usual incisive way, "merely laying a trap for misunderstanding." Episcopacy proper was developed after the death of St. Paul, but before that of St. John, as a bulwark against heresy.

ful domestic life,[1] soberness, sobermindedness, decorousness, hospitable disposition, and aptitude to teach. He who is quarrelsome over wine, given to blows and covetousness, is unfit. Moderation, peacefulness, indifference to money, a well-ordered household, grave and obedient children, are signs that a man may aspire to the sacred work; but he must not be a neophyte,[2] that he may not, through the cloudy fumes of pride, fall into the devil's judgment.[3] He must be well thought of by his Pagan neighbours, that he may not fall into disrepute, and the devil's snare which such loss of character involves.[4]

Deacons, too, must be grave, straightforward, sober, not avaricious, sound in faith, and pure of conscience; and their freedom from reproach must be tested before they are appointed.[5]

Deaconesses[6] must be grave, not slanderers, sober,

---

[1] I am not persuaded that μιᾶς γυναικὸς ἄνδρα really implies more than this, with reference to the prevalence of divorce, &c. The early prejudice against second marriages naturally inclined the ancient commentators to take it exclusively in one way; but the remark of Chrysostom, τὴν ἀμετρίαν κωλύει, seems to me to be nearest the truth. St. Paul's opinion was not in the least that of Athenagoras, that a second marriage is "specious adultery," since in some cases he even recommends it (v. 14; 1 Cor. vii. 39; Rom. vii. 2, 3), but he would possibly have held with Hermas (Pastor. ii. 4), that though a second marriage is no sin, it is a better and nobler thing to avoid it. It is as Gregory of Nazianzus says, "a concession" (συγχώρησις—Orat. xxxi.).

[2] The first occurrence of the word "neophyte"—"newly-*planted*"—a recent convert. For the metaphor, see 1 Cor. iii. 6. At Ephesus there must have been a choice of presbyters who were not "neophytes." Perhaps the reason why this qualification is omitted in Tit. i. 6 is that there would have been greater difficulty in carrying it out in the more recent Churches of Crete.

[3] These Epistles are peculiar in the use of the word "devil." Elsewhere St. Paul uses "Satan," except in Eph. iv. 27; vi. 11. It is impossible to say whether "the devil's judgment" means "that which he has incurred" or "that which he inflicts."

[4] iii. 1—7.

[5] iii. 8—10. Besides the "Seven," deacons properly so called may be referred to in 1 Cor. xii. 28; Rom. xii. 7; 1 Pet. iv. 11; as well as in Phil. i. 1.

[6] Γυναῖκας must mean "deaconesses" (Rom. xvi. 1. "Ancillae quae ministrae

faithful. The domestic relations of deacons and deaconesses must be irreproachable; for an honourable diaconate secures an honourable position,[1] and boldness in the faith.[2]

"These things I write to thee, though I hope to come to you unexpectedly soon;[3] but in order that, if I am delayed, thou mayst know how to bear thyself in the house of God—seeing that it is the Church of God —as a pillar and basis of the truth.[4]

"And confessedly great is the mystery of godliness—who was[5]

> "Manifested in the flesh,
> Justified in the Spirit,
> Seen of angels,
> Preached among the Gentiles,
> Believed on in the world,
> Taken up in glory."[6]

dicebantur."—Plin. ix. 27), because the wives of deacons were certainly not selected by the Church.

[1] iii. 11—13.

[2] καλὸς βαθμὸς can only mean "a fair standing-point," "an honourable position," from which to discharge nobly his Christian duties. The notion that it means "earning preferment" would be an immense anachronism. Cf. vi. 19: καλὸν θεμέλιον.

[3] τάχιον—an untranslatable ellipse. John xiii. 27; Heb. xiii. 23.

[4] Apart from the awkwardness of the Church being, in the same verse, the house of God and also a pillar and base of the truth, the expression is one of the most difficult and surprising—one of the least obviously Pauline— in the whole Epistle. The separate metaphors occur in Gal. ii. 9 and Eph. ii. 20, but only of *persons*. There is, therefore, much to be said for attaching them to ἀναστρέφεσθαι, and making them apply to Timothy, as I have done. (See Dean Stanley, *Sermons on the Apostolic Age*, p. 115.) The words are applied to the martyr Attalus in the Epistle of the Church of Lyons, c. 5. Others attach them to the next sentence—which they would turn into a most awkward and unnatural anti-climax. If, however, they are applied to the Church, the meaning is clear enough—namely that apart from the Church the truth of the Gospel would be without that earthly institution on which, by Christ's ordinance, its stability and permanence depends.

[5] Ὅς is read by א, A, C, F, G. (The reading of A was once supposed to be ΘC, but Bishop Ellicott testifies that the apparent line across the O was originally due to the *sagitta* of the ε in the word εὐσεβείαν on the other side of the page. See his *Pastoral Epistles*, p. 103.) Besides this, it is so unquestionably supported by every canon of criticism that it may now be regarded as a certain reading.

[6] iii. 14—16. These last phrases are so rhythmic in their introverted parallelism with the varied order of their triple antitheses, that they have, with much probability, been supposed (like Eph. v. 14) to belong to some ancient hymn or

The true doctrine again recalls him to the subject of the false teachers. Beyond the present peril lies the prophecy of future apostasies, in which some shall give heed to deceitful spirits and doctrines of devils, by means of the hypocrisy of liars, whose consciences have been seared. This apostasy, partly present, partly future, is marked by dualistic tendencies. It hinders marriage,[1] and commands abstinence from meats,[2] forgetting that thankfulness and prayer sanctify everything. Another feature of the nascent heresy is a fondness for profane and anile myths. A third is mere bodily asceticism. This training may indeed have a partial advantage; but better is the gymnasium which trains for godliness, since godliness is profitable both for this life and the next ("faithful is the saying"): for with a view to this—because we have hope in the living God, who is the Saviour of all, specially of the faithful[3]—we are enabled to endure both toil and struggle.[4] These truths Timothy is to teach, showing himself an example to the faithful in speech, conversation, love, spirituality, faith, purity, so that none may despise his youth.[5] Till St. Paul arrives he is bidden to occupy

creed. The extreme antiquity of Christian hymns is proved by Eph. v. 19, and by Plin. *Epp.* x. 97. "Justified in the Spirit" means that Christ was manifested to be the Son of God (Rom. i. 4) by the workings of His higher spiritual life; "seen of angels" refers to the various angelic witnesses of scenes of His earthly life.

[1] Not yet "forbids," but somewhat "discourages." Cf. Jos. *B. J.* ii. 8, 2, and 13.
[2] Cf. Rom. xiv. 1—4; 1 Cor. viii. 8; x. 20.
[3] The universalism of expression is here even more remarkable than in ii. 4.
[4] *Leg.* ἀγωνιζόμεθα, ℵ, A, F, C, G, K.
[5] The sneers that Timothy "seems to have been endowed by Christian legend with the gift of immortal youth" are very groundless. If he were converted in A.D. 45, at the age of sixteen, he would now (A.D. 66) be only thirty-seven—a very youthful age for so responsible a position. The aged rector of one who has now become a very exalted ecclesiastic, and is long past sixty, still says of his first curate, "I always told you that young man was very ambitious;" and when M. Thiers was Prime Minister of France, and

himself in reading,[1] exhortation, teaching; securing progress by diligence, and not neglecting—which possibly Timothy, in his retiring character, was tempted to do—the grace which was solemnly bestowed on him at his ordination.[2]

Then he is advised how to behave towards various orders in his Church. He is not to use severe language to an elder, but to exhort them as fathers; the younger men as brothers, the elder women as mothers, the younger as sisters, in all purity.[3] Special directions are given about widows.[4] Those are true widows who rightly train their children or grandchildren, who do their duty to their parents, who devote themselves to constant prayer. But in a widow, a prurient, frivolous character is a living death; for, in a Christian, neglect of domestic duties and relations is worse than heathenism. No widow is therefore to be put on the list before sixty years of age, after one honourable marriage,[5] and after having acquired a character for motherliness, hospitality, kindly service, succour to the afflicted, and continuance in every good work. But Timothy is to have nothing to say to younger widows who want to marry again when they begin to wax restive against the yoke of Christ—and so are

called on his old schoolmaster, he found that he was only remembered as "the little Adolphus who played tricks."

[1] Perhaps the earliest allusion to the duty of reading Scripture.

[2] iv. 1—16. Acts xvi. 1, and 2 Tim. i. 6, where he receives a similar injunction.

[3] "Omnes puellas et virgines Christi aut aequaliter ignora aut aequaliter dilige" (Jer.). But how inferior to the direction of St. Paul!

[4] Acts ii. 44; vi. 1.

[5] Cf. Tit. i. 6. It is a remarkable sign of the position of widows in the Church that Polycarp calls them θυσιαστήριον Θεοῦ, "an altar of God" (ad Phil. 4). From the severity of some of St. Paul's remarks, Reuss thinks that he may have had in view the occasional second marriage of Christian widows with Pagans, which would be a disgraceful proceeding after they had received assistance from the Church. They might be "deaconesses" earlier than sixty, but not "widows."

convicted of setting at nought their first faith.[1] To avoid the danger of gadding idleness and unseemly gossiping, it is better that such should avoid all chance of creating scandal by quietly re-entering into married life. Hence all younger widows must be supported by their own relations, and not at the expense of the Church.[2]

Returning to the Presbyters, he quotes the passage of Deuteronomy, "Thou shalt not muzzle a threshing ox," and adds the maxim, "The labourer is worthy of his hire,"[3] to support his rule that "double honour" be paid to faithful and laborious pastors.[4] If they do wrong they must indeed be rebuked, but never on ill-supported accusations. "I solemnly charge thee before God, and the Lord Jesus Christ, and the elect angels,[5] to observe these rules without prejudice, and without doing anything by favour." He is not to ordain any one too hastily, lest he be involved in the responsibility for their sins; and this discrimination is the more necessary because there are flagrant sins which marshal men to judgment, and hidden sins which stealthily follow behind them; just as also there are some good works which are openly manifest, and others which are concealed, although ultimately all shall stand revealed in their true light.

---

[1] In their practical pledge not to marry again when they were placed on the official list of widows.

[2] v. 1—16.

[3] 1 Cor. ix. 9. Those who apply ἡ γραφή to both clauses must admit that the Gospel of St. Luke had been published, and had come to be regarded of Divine authority, before this Epistle (Luke x. 7). But the inference is most precarious, for our Lord often alluded to current proverbs, and ἡ γραφή may here only apply to the quotation from Deut. xxv. 4.

[4] διπλῆ τιμή is a perfectly general expression. The spirit of foolish literalism led to double rations for the Presbyters at the Agapæ.

[5] See 1 Cor. xi. 10; 1 Pet. i. 12. It is not possible to explain the exact shade of meaning in the word "elect." They are probably so called, as Calvin says, "excellentiae causâ." Cf. τοὺς ἱεροὺς ἀγγέλους in Agrippa's adjuration to the Jews not to rebel against Rome (Jos. B. J. ii. 16, and Tobit xii. 15).

In the very midst of these wise and serious directions are introduced two personal exhortations. One of them—"Keep thyself pure"—may naturally have been suggested by the passing thought that he whose duty it was to exercise so careful an oversight over others must be specially watchful to be himself free from every stain. The other, "Be no longer a water-drinker, but use a little wine because of thy stomach, and thy frequent infirmities,"[1] is so casual that, though we see at once how it may have occurred to St. Paul's thoughts—since otherwise the former rule might have led to a self-denial still more rigid,[2] and even injurious to health—it is far too natural and spontaneous, too entirely disconnected from all that precedes and follows it, to have occurred to any imitator. An imitator, if capable of introducing the natural play of thought to which the precept "Keep thyself pure" is due, would have been far more likely to add—and especially in an Epistle which so scrupulously forbids indulgence in wine to all Church officials—"And, in order to promote this purity, take as little wine as possible, or avoid it altogether."[3]

He then passes to the duties of slaves.[4] Their conversion is not to be made a plea for upsetting the social order, and giving any excuse for abusing the Gospel. Christian masters are still to be treated as masters, and to be served all the more heartily "because all who are partakers of this kindly service are faithful and beloved."

---

[1] These "frequent infirmities" perhaps explain the timidity of Timothy's character (1 Cor. xvi. 10, 11). Some have seen a reflex of this in the reproaches addressed, in the midst of praise, to "the angel of the Church of Ephesus."

[2] Rom. xiv. 2. Plutarch speaks of an ὅσιος ὑγρεία (*De Isid. et Osir*, § 6).

[3] Ver. 17—23.

[4] Some have fancied, with very little probability, that the topic is suggested by the mention of those whose good works cannot be *finally* hid, but are little likely to be noticed in this world.

Here again he reverts to the false teachers—who had perhaps perverted the truth of Christian equality into the falsehood of socialism [1]—to denounce their inflated ignorance and unwholesome loquacity as the source of the jealousies and squabbles of corrupt men, who look on religion as a source of gain. A source of gain indeed it is when accompanied with the contentment [2] arising from the sense of the nakedness of our birth and death, and the fewness of our real needs,[3] whereas the desire of wealth breeds the numerous forms of foolish desire which plunge men into destruction and perdition. For all evils spring from the root of covetousness,[4] which has led many into heresy as well as into manifold miseries. The Apostle appeals to his son in the faith to flee these things: to pursue[5] righteousness, godliness, faith, love, endurance, gentleness; to strive the good strife of faith; to grasp eternal life, " to which also thou wert called, and didst confess the good confession before many witnesses." He most solemnly adjures him, by Christ and His good confession before Pontius Pilate,[6] to keep the commandment without spot, without reproach, till the manifestation of our Lord Jesus Christ, which He shall show in His own seasons, who is the blessed and only Potentate, the King

[1] Gal. iii. 28. The recognition of the existing basis of society is found throughout the Epistles (1 Cor. vii. 21; Col. iii. 22, &c.).

[2] αὐτάρκεια, self-sufficing independence (2 Cor. ix. 8; Phil. iv. 11). Cf. Prov. xiv. 14, "The good man shall be satisfied from himself."

[3] Phil. iv. 11—13.

[4] ῥίζα need not be rendered "a root," for it is a word which does not require the article; but St. Paul does not, of course, mean that it is the only root from which all evils spring, but the root from which all evils *may* spring. So Diogenes Laertius calls it "the metropolis of all evils" (*Vit. Diogen.* vi. 50); and Philo, *De Spec. Legg.* 346, calls it ὁρμητήριον πάντων παρανομημάτων (cf. Luke xii. 15—21).

[5] δίωκε, ἐπιλαβοῦ.

[6] There is an obvious allusion in the καλὴ ὁμολογία of Christ to that of the previous verse, but in the latter instance it seems to mean the faithful performance of the will of God even to death.

of kings and Lord of lords, who alone hath immortality, dwelling in light unapproachable, whom no man ever saw, or can see—to whom honour and eternal strength. Amen.[1]

With this majestic description of the Divine attributes it might well have been thought that the Epistle would close. A forger might naturally desire a climax; but St. Paul is never influenced by such considerations of style. Filled with the thought of the perils of wealth in a city like wealthy Ephesus, he once more, in a sort of postscript,[2] advises Timothy to warn the rich "not to be highminded, nor to fix their hopes on the uncertainty of riches, but on the living God, who richly affords us all things for enjoyment," and to use their riches wisely and generously, "treasuring up for themselves a fair foundation for the future, that they may grasp that which is really life."[3]

Then, with one parting reference to the false teachers, the Epistle ends:—

"O Timothy, guard the trust committed to thee, turning away from these profane babblings, and "antitheses" of the knowledge which usurps the name; which some professing have gone astray as regards the faith. Grace be with thee."[4]

The "Amen"[5] is probably a pious addition, and the various superscriptions which tell us that the Epistle was written from Laodicea, "which is the metropolis of Phrygia Pacatiana," or "from Nicopolis," or "from Athens," "by the hands of his disciple Titus," or "from Macedonia," are idle guesses, of which the latter alone has any plausibility, though even this is only a precarious inference from the verse which suggested it.

[1] vi. 1—16.
[2] Reuss, *Les Epîtres*, ii. 378.
[3] vi. 17—19. Leg. ὄντως, A, D, E, F, G.
[4] א, A, F, G, read μεθ' ὑμῶν, as in 2 Tim. iv. 22; Tit. iii. 15.
[5] Omitted by א, A, D, F, G.

CHAPTER LIV.

THE EPISTLE TO TITUS.

"Lord Jesus, I am weary in Thy work, but not of Thy work. Let me go and speak for Thee once more . . . seal Thy truth, and then die."—Whitefield.

FROM St. Paul's message to Philemon we infer that as speedily as possible after he was set free he visited Ephesus and the cities of the Lycus. Even if he deferred this visit till he had carried out his once-cherished plan of visiting Spain, we know that the moment his destiny was decided he sent Timothy to Philippi, with the intention of following him at no long interval.[1] Hence when Timothy rejoined him, probably at Ephesus, he left him there as we have seen to finish the task of setting the Church in order, and himself set out on his promised journey to Macedonia. It is not likely that he felt any desire to revive the gloomy reminiscences of Jerusalem, and to incur a second risk of being torn to pieces by infuriated Pharisees. In that unhappy city a fresh outburst of the spirit of persecution had ended the year before (A.D. 63) in the murder of James the Lord's brother.[2] Soon after the accession of Gessius Florus to the post of Procurator, there were violent disturbances throughout Judæa. The war which culminated in the total destruction of the Jewish polity did not indeed break out till A.D. 66, but the general spirit of turbulence, the deeply

---

[1] Phil. ii. 19—23. [2] Jos. *Antt.* xx. 9, 1, 2; Acts xii. 1—11.

seated discontent with the government of Agrippa II., and the threatening multiplication of the Sicarii, showed that everything was ripening for the final revolt.[1] We may be sure that when the ship of Adramyttium sailed from Tyre, St. Paul had seen his last of the Holy Land. From Macedonia he doubtless went to Corinth, and he may then have sailed with Titus to Crete.

On the southern shores of that legendary island he had involuntarily touched in the disastrous voyage from Myra, which ended in his shipwreck at Malta. But a prisoner on his way to trial, in a crowded Alexandrian corn-vessel which only awaited the earliest opportunity to sail, could have had but little opportunity to preach the gospel even at the Fair Havens and Lasæa, and we may at once reject the idle suggestion that the Church of Crete had then first been founded. It is probable that the first tidings of Christianity had been carried to the island by those Cretan Jews who had heard the thrilling words of St. Peter at Pentecost; and the insufficiency of knowledge in these Churches may be accounted for in part by these limited opportunities, as well as by the inherent defects of the Cretan character. The stormy shores of Crete, and the evil reputation of its inhabitants even from mythical days, may well have tended to deter the evangelising visits of the early preachers of Christianity; and the indication that the nascent faith of the converts was largely tainted with Jewish superstition is exactly what we should have expected. St. Paul's brief sojourn in the island with Titus was probably the first serious effort to consolidate the young, struggling, and imperilled Churches; and we can easily imagine that it was the necessity of completing an anxious work, which reluctantly com-

[1] Jos. *B. J.* ii., xiv. 2.

pelled the Apostle to leave his companion behind him. The task could not have been left in wiser or firmer hands than those of one who had already made his influence felt and his authority respected among the prating and conceited sophists of turbulent Corinth. Those who argue that, because Paul had but recently parted with Titus, the advice contained in the letter would be superfluous, are starting a purely imaginary difficulty, and one of which the futility is demonstrated by the commonest experiences of daily life. Objections of this kind are simply astonishing, and when we are told that the instructions given are too vague and commonplace to render them of any value, and that "the pointlessness of the directions must have made them all but worthless to an evangelist,"[1] we can only reply that the Christian Church in all ages, in spite of the incessant tendency to exalt dogma above simple practice, has yet accepted the Pastoral Epistles as a manual which has never been surpassed.

From Crete, St. Paul may have returned by Ephesus and Troas to Macedonia, and thence to Dalmatia and Illyricum;[2] and we learn from the Epistle to Titus that he was accompanied by several friends, for whom he found the amplest employment in missions to various Churches. He intended to spend the winter at Nicopolis, which, beyond all question, must be the well-known and flourishing city of Epirus, built by Augustus to commemorate his victory at Actium. When he wrote the Epistle to Titus, he was about to send Artemas or Tychicus to him in Crete, to continue the work of organisation there, while Titus is directed to join the Apostle at Nicopolis before the winter comes on.

[1] Davidson, *Introd.* ii. 129; Reuss, *Les Epîtres*, ii. 333.
[2] Rom. xv. 19.

How little we really know about Titus will be best seen by the theories which attempt to identify him with Titus (or, Titius) Justus (Acts xviii. 7), with Silas, and even with Timothy! Though he is not mentioned in the Acts—probably because he never happened to be a companion of the Apostle at the same time that Luke was with him—he seems to have been one of the trustiest and most beloved members of the noble little band of St. Paul's friends and disciples. As he was a Greek by birth, St. Paul, whose convert he was, had chosen to take him to Jerusalem on that memorable visit, which ended in the recognition of Gentile emancipation from the yoke of Mosaism.[1] If we were right in the conjecture that the generous self-sacrifice of Titus on this occasion rescued Paul from a grievous struggle, if not from an immense peril, we may imagine how close would have been the personal bond between them. He had special connexions with Corinth, to which he had three times been sent by the Apostle during the troubles of that distracted Church.[2] The warm terms in which St. Paul always speaks of him as his brother, and associate, and fellow-labourer, and the yearning anxiety which made him utterly miserable when he failed to meet him in Troas, show that he was no ordinary man; and the absence from this Epistle of the personal warnings and exhortations which are found in those to Timothy, lead us to believe that Titus was the more deeply respected, even if Timothy were the more tenderly beloved. The last notice of him is his visit to Dalmatia during the second imprisonment, and we may feel the strongest confidence that this was undertaken as a special duty, and that he did not voluntarily desert his friend and teacher whom he had so long and faithfully served. The Epistle

---

[1] Gal. ii. 3; Tit. i. 4.   [2] 2 Cor. vii., viii.

which St. Paul addresses to him goes over much the same ground as that to Timothy, but with additional particulars, and in a perfectly independent manner. It excited the warm admiration of Luther, who says of it: "This is a short Epistle, but yet such a quintessence of Christian doctrine, and composed in such a masterly manner, that it contains all that is needful for Christian knowledge and life." The subjects are touched upon in the same easy and natural order as in the other Pastoral Epistles, and the incidental mention of people so entirely unknown in the circle of the Apostle's friends as Artemas and Zenas, the lawyer, together with the marked variations in the initial and final salutations, are among the many incidental circumstances which powerfully strengthen the argument in favour of its authenticity.

The greeting with which the Apostle opens is somewhat obscure and involved, owing to the uncertainty of the exact meaning of the various prepositions employed. It differs from all other salutations in the phrase "a slave of God," instead of "a slave of Jesus Christ," and it is marked by the prominence of the title Saviour, which is applied throughout this Epistle both to God and to Christ.[1]

"Paul, a slave of God, but an Apostle of Jesus Christ for the faith of the elect of God and the full knowledge of the truth which is according to godliness, (based) on the hope of eternal life, which God, who cannot lie, promised before eternal times, but manifested His word in His own seasons in the preaching with which I was entrusted according to the commandment of God our Saviour—to Titus, my true son after the common faith, grace and peace, from God our Father, and the Lord Jesus Christ our Saviour."

[1] If the idea of God the Father as a Saviour had not occurred both in the Old Testament and elsewhere in St. Paul, the expression might fairly have been called un-Pauline. But the idea is distinctly found in 1 Cor. i. 21.

After this solemn greeting he proceeds at once to the many practical directions which are the object of his writing. He left Titus in Crete to finish all necessary regulations, and especially to ordain presbyters in every city, who are to be men of irreproachable character, and well-ordered domestic positions, for a "bishop" must be blameless as God's steward, not self-willed, not passionate, and with the other positive and negative qualifications which he has already mentioned in the Epistle to Timothy —with the addition that he is to love what is good, and to hold fast the faithful word according to the instruction he has received that he may be able to exhort with healthy teaching and to refute the gainsayers.[1]

These opponents are described as being disorderly, prating, and self-deceiving Jewish Christians, who for the sake of filthy lucre turn whole families upside down. To these, as to the Cretans in general, St. Paul applies the stinging line of their fellow-countryman Epimenides—

"The Cretans are always liars, evil wild beasts, lazy gluttons,"[2]

—for which reason they must be sharply rebuked, that they may be healthy in the faith, ceasing to heed

---

[1] i. 5—9.

[2] The line is an hexameter from the poem on "Oracles" by Epimenides, the Cretan poet and philosopher. It was quoted by Callimachus, *Hymn to Zeus*, 8, and well known in antiquity because it gave rise to the syllogistic catch known as "the Liar."
They were among the three very bad K's of antiquity.

Κρῆτες, Καππάδοκαι, Κίλικες, τρία κάππα κάκιστα.

As for their lying, κρητίζειν meant "to tell lies;" of their ferocity, gluttony, drunkenness, and sensuality, and above all of their greed, ample testimonies are quoted—"Cretenses spem pecuniae secuti" (Liv. xliv. 45); τοῖς χρήμασιν, ὥσπερ κηρίοις μέλιτται, προσλιπαροῦντες (Plut. *Paul. Æmil.* 23); Polyb. vi. 46 &c., and a remarkable epigram of Leonides—

Αἰεὶ ληϊσταὶ καὶ ἀλιφθόροι οὔτε δίκαιοι
Κρῆτες· τίς Κρητῶν οἶδε δικαιοσύνην.

(See Meursius's *Creta*, and Wetstein *ad loc.*)

Jewish myths and the commandments of men who turn away from the truth.[1] Among these commandments there seem to have been many distinctions between things clean and unclean, all of which the Apostle sweeps aside in his clear decisive manner by the deep truth that to the pure all things are pure;—whereas nothing is or can be pure to men of defiled mind and conscience, such as these, who, professing knowledge of God, in deeds denied Him, being detestable, and disobedient, and to every good deed reprobate.[2]

"But speak thou the things which become the healthy teaching." The keynote of this wholesome teaching is sober-mindedness. *Aged men* are to be temperate, grave, sober-minded, sound in love, in faith, in endurance. *Aged women* are to show a sacred decorum in demeanour, free from slander and intemperance,[3] teachers of what is fair, that they may train the younger women, too, to be sober-minded, ennobling the estimate of their Christian profession by humble, diligent, submissive performance of their home duties. Titus must also exhort *young men* to be sober-minded, and in all respects he is to set them a pure example of dignity, and faithfulness to the truth. Slaves are to "adorn the doctrine of God our Saviour in all things," by silent obedience and cheerful honesty.

"For God's grace was manifested bringing salvation to all men, training us to the end that once for all rejecting impiety and all worldly desires, we should live in the present age soberly, and righteously, and godly, expecting the blessed hope and manifestation of the glory of the

---

[1] Possibly Titus had tried to regard these "myths" as harmless.
[2] i. 10—16.
[3] ii. 3, "Not enslaved by much wine." On the proverbial intemperance of women among the ancients, see *Antholog.* xi. 298; Aristoph. *Thesmr.* 735 and *passim*; Athen. x. 57.

great God and our Saviour Jesus Christ,[1] who gave Himself for us, that He might ransom us from all lawlessness, and purify for Himself a peculiar people, zealous of good works. These things speak, and rebuke and exhort with all authority. Let no man despise thee."[2]

After this swift and perfect summary of the Christian life, alike in its earthly and spiritual aspects, he reverts to necessary subjects for practical exhortation. Naturally turbulent, the Cretans are to be constantly reminded of the duty of submission in all things right and good. Naturally ferocious, they are to be exhorted to meekness of word and deed towards all men. For even so God showed gentleness to us when we were living in foolish and disobedient error, the slaves of various passions, in a bitter atmosphere of reciprocal hatred. "But when"—and

---

[1] The question as to whether these words should be rendered as in the text, or "*our great God and Saviour Jesus Christ*," is simply a critical question. The analogy of other passages throughout these and other Epistles (1 Tim. i. 1; v. 21; vi. 13; and, above all, ii. 3—5; 2 Peter i. 1; 2 Thess. i. 12; Jude 4, &c.), and the certainty that this translation is not required either by the anarthrous Σωτήρ, or by the word ἐπεφάνη, show that the view taken by our English Version, and the majority of Protestant and other versions, as well as by many of the ancient versions, is correct.

[2] Which of all the Fathers of the first or second century was in the smallest degree capable of writing so masterly a formula of Christian doctrine and practice as these verses (ii. 11—14), or the perfectly independent yet no less memorable presentation of Gospel truth—with a completeness only too many-sided for sects and parties—in iii. 5—7? Will any one produce from Clemens, or Hermas, or Justin Martyr, or Ignatius, or Polycarp, or Irenæus—will any one even produce from Tertullian, or Chrysostom, or Basil, or Gregory of Nyssa—any single passage comparable for terseness, insight, and mastery to either of these? Only the inspired wisdom of the greatest of the Apostles could have traced so divine a summary with so unfaltering a hand. If the single chorus of Sophokles was sufficient to acquit him of senility—if the thin unerring line attested the presence of Apelles—if the flawless circle of Giotto, drawn with one single sweep of his hand, was sufficient to authenticate his workmanship and prove his power—surely such passages as these ought to be more than adequate to defend the Pastoral Epistles from the charge of vapidity. Would it not be somewhat strange if all the great Christian Fathers of three centuries were so far surpassed in power and eloquence by the supposed *falsarii* who wrote the Epistles of the First and Second Captivity of St. Paul?

here follows another concentrated summary of Pauline doctrine unparalleled for beauty and completeness—

"But when the kindness and love towards man of God our Saviour was manifested, not in consequence of works of righteousness which we did, but according to His mercy He saved us, by means of the laver of regeneration, and renewal by the Holy Ghost, which He poured upon us richly through Jesus Christ our Saviour, that being justified by His grace we might become heirs, according to hope, of eternal life."

Faithful is the saying [1]—and in accordance with it he desires Titus to teach with due insistence, that all who have believed may live up to their profession. This teaching is fair and beneficent, but foolish speculations and discussions,[2] and genealogies and legalist disputes are vain and useless. But if, after one or two admonitions, a man would not give up his own depraved and wilful perversities, then Titus is to have nothing more to say to him.[3]

The brief letter closes with a few personal messages. Titus may soon expect the arrival of Artemas or Tychicus,[4]

---

[1] Π. ὁ λόγος here refers to what has gone before, and it is remarkable that this favourite formula is generally applied, as here, to expressions which have something solemn and almost rhythmic in the form of their expression (1 Tim. i. 15; iii. 1; 2 Tim. ii. 11—the analogous 1 Tim. iii. 16). Were the quotations from Lymus? The contrast between the regenerate present and the unregenerate past is common in St. Paul (1 Cor. vi. 11; Gal. iv. 3; Eph. ii., &c.). If any one were asked to fix on two passages which contained the essence of all Pauline theology he would surely select Rom. iii. 21—26 and Tit. iii. 5—7; and the latter, though less polemical, is in some respects more complete. Again I ask, Would it not be strange if the briefest yet fullest statement of his complete message should come from a spurious Epistle?

[2] St. Paul stigmatises these sophistic discussions as both κενοί and μάταιοι— i.e., empty in their nature, and void of all results.

[3] αἱρέσεις only occurs in 1 Cor. xi. 19; Gal. v. 20, and means, not "heresies," but "ecclesiastical divisions."

[4] "Artemas or Tychicus." Who was Artemas, or Artemidorus? That he, like Trophimus and Tychicus (Acts xx. 4; xxi. 29), was an Ephesian, we may perhaps conjecture from his name, and Paul may have met with him in his recent visit to Ephesus; but what could possibly have induced a forger to insert a totally unknown name like that of Artemas? or to imagine any uncertainty in the mind of Paul as to which of the two he should send? (On Tychicus, see Col. iv. 7; Eph. vi. 21.)

and on the arrival of either, to take up his work, he is with all speed to join Paul at Nicopolis for the winter. He is also asked to do anything he can to further the journey and meet the requirements of Zenas the jurist,[1] and Apollos. And St. Paul hopes that all *our people also* will learn to follow the example of these kindly services to all who require them, that they may not be unfruitful. "All who are with me salute thee. Salute those who love us in the faith. God's grace with you all."

These last three greetings have several points of interest. They show us that Paul, who was soon to be so sadly and unworthily deserted, was still carrying on his manifold missionary activities as one in a band of devoted friends. The fact that they differ in expression from every other closing salutation is a mark of authenticity, because a forger would have been sure to confine himself to a servile and unsuspicious repetition of one of the forms which occur elsewhere. But what does St. Paul mean by the remarkable expression, "let *our people also* learn to be forward in good works"? It is usually explained to mean "the other believers as well as thou;" but this is obviously unsatisfactory. On the other hand, we have no sufficient data to interpret it of the existence of converts of Apollos forming a different body from those of Paul. Its very obscurity is a sign that the allusion is to some fact which was known to the correspondent, but is unknown to us.

Titus here disappears from Christian history. The rest of his biography evaporates into the misty outlines of late ecclesiastical conjecture scarcely to be dignified by the name of tradition.

---

[1] Does this mean "a lawyer" in the same sense as νομοδιδάσκαλος in Luke v. 17? Was he a Jewish scribe, or a Greek or Roman legist? It is quite impossible to say; and who was this Zenas, or Zenodorus? What should put such a name and such an allusion into a forger's mind?

CHAPTER LV.

THE CLOSING DAYS.

"Christianus etiam extra carcerem saeculo renuntiavit, in carcere autem etiam carceri. . . . Ipsam etiam conversationen saeculi et carceris comparemus, si non plus in carcere spiritus acquirit, quam caro amittit."—TERT. *ad Mart.* 2.

"In a free state Gaius would have found his way to Bedlam, and Nero to Tyburn."—FREEMAN, *Essays*, ii. 337.

SOME of those critics who have been most hostile to the genuineness of the Pastoral Epistles have felt and expressed a certain reluctance to set down the Second Epistle to Timothy as the work of a forger, and to rob the world of this supremely noble and tender testament of the dying soldier of Christ. And some who have rejected the two other Epistles have made an exception in favour of this. For myself I can only express my astonishment that any one who is sufficiently acquainted with the Christian literature of the first two centuries to see how few writers there were who showed a power even distantly capable of producing such a letter, can feel any hesitation as to its having been written by the hand of Paul. The Tübingen critics argue that the three Epistles must stand or fall together, and think that the First Epistle to Timothy shows signs of spuriousness, which drags the other two letters into the same condemnation. Accepting the close relationship which binds the three letters together, and seeing sufficient grounds in the First Epistle to Timothy and the Epistle to Titus to furnish at least a very strong probability of their genuineness, it seems to me that the probability is raised to certainty by the undoubted genuineness of the Second Epistle to Timothy. If, indeed, St. Paul was never liberated from his first Roman imprisonment, then the Pastoral Epistles must be forgeries; for the attempts of Wieseler and others to prove that they might have been written during any part of the period covered by the narrative of the Acts—during the three years' stay at Ephesus, for instance, or the stay of eighteen months at Corinth—sink to the ground not only under the weight of their own arbitrary hypotheses, but even more from the state both of the Church and of the mind and circumstances of the Apostle, which these letters so definitely manifest. But as the liberation and second imprisonment of St. Paul are decidedly favoured by tradition, and give a most easy and natural explanation to every allusion in these and in earlier Epistles, and as no single valid objection can be urged against this belief, I believe that there would never have been any attempt to disprove its possibility except from the hardly concealed desire to get rid of these letters and the truths to which they bear emphatic witness.

The allusions in the Second Epistle, though too fragmentary and insignificant to have been imagined by an imitator, are only allusions, and it is quite possible that they may not supply us with sufficient data to enable us to arrive at any continuous narrative of events in the Apostle's history between his first and second imprisonment. To dwell on these events at any length would therefore be misleading; but it is perfectly allowable to construct an hypothesis which is simple in itself, and which fits in with every circumstance to which any reference is made. The probability of the hypothesis, and the natural manner in which it suits the little details to which St. Paul refers, is one more of the many indications that we are here dealing with genuine letters.

If, then, we piece together the personal notices of this Epistle, they enable us to trace the further fortunes of St. Paul after the winter which he spent at Nicopolis, in the society of Titus. At his age, and with his growing infirmities—conscious too, as he must have been, from those inward intimations which are rarely wanting, that his life was drawing to a close—it is most unlikely that he should have entered on new missions, and it is certain that he would have found more than sufficient scope for all his energies in the consolidation of the many Greek and Eastern Churches which he had founded, and in the endeavour to protect them from the subtle leaven of spreading heresies. The main part of his work was accomplished. At Jerusalem and at Antioch he had vindicated for ever the freedom of the Gentile from the yoke of the Levitic Law. In his letters to the Romans and Galatians he had proclaimed alike to Jew and Gentile that we are not under the Law, but under grace. He had rescued Christianity from the peril of dying away into a Jewish sect, only distinguishable from Judaism by the accepted fulfilment of Messianic hopes. Labouring as no other Apostle had laboured, he had preached the Gospel in the chief cities of the world, from Jerusalem to Rome, and perhaps even as far as Spain. During the short space of twenty years he had proclaimed Christ crucified to the simple Pagans of Lycaonia, the fickle fanatics of Galatia, the dreamy mystics of Phrygia, the vigorous colonists of Macedonia, the superficial dilettanti of Athens, the sensual and self-satisfied traders of Corinth, the semi-barbarous natives of Dalmatia, the ill-reputed islanders of Crete, the slaves and soldiers and seething multitudes of Rome. He had created the terminology, he had formulated the truths of Christianity. It had been his rare blessedness to serve the Gospel at once as an

active missionary and as a profound thinker. The main
part of his work was done. There was no further danger
to be apprehended from "them of the circumcision," or
from "certain who came from James." New dangers
were arising, but their worst developments lay far in
the future.[1] As Karl the Great burst into tears when,
after a life spent in subjugating Lombards and Saxons, he
saw in the offing the barques of the pirate Norsemen, and
knew that they would never give much trouble in his
own days, but wept to think of the troubles which they
would cause hereafter, so Paul felt the presentiment of
future perils from the Essenic elements which were
destined to ripen into Gnosticism, but he did not live to
witness their full development. His desire would be,
not to attempt the foundation of new Churches, but to
forewarn and to strengthen the beloved Churches which
he had already founded.

And therefore, after he left Nicopolis, he would
naturally travel back to Beroea, Thessalonica, Philippi,
and so by Neapolis to Troas, where he stayed in the house
of a disciple named Carpus. Here it was that the final
crisis of his fate seems to have overtaken him. It is at
least a fair conjecture that he would not have left at the
house of Carpus his precious books, and the cloak which
was so necessary to him, unless his departure had been
hasty and perhaps involuntary. His work and his success
in that town had been sufficiently marked to attract
general attention, and it was exactly the kind of town in
which he might have been liable to sudden arrest. Since
Nero's persecution of the Christians, they must have been
more or less the objects of hatred and suspicion throughout the Empire, and especially in the provincial towns
of Asia Minor, which were ever prone to flatter the

---

[1] 2 Tim. iii. 1, ἐνστήσονται καιροὶ χαλεποί.

Emperor, because their prosperity, and sometimes almost their existence, depended on his personal favour. Any officer eager to push himself into notice, any angry Jew, any designing Oriental, might have been the cause of the Apostle's arrest; and if it took place at Troas, especially if it were on some pretext suggested by Alexander the coppersmith, or connected with St. Paul's long and active work at Ephesus, he would, in the ordinary course of things, have been sent under guard to Ephesus to be judged by the Proconsul. While awaiting his trial there he would, of course, have been put in prison; and the fact that his place of imprisonment is still pointed out among the ruins of Ephesus, although no imprisonment at Ephesus is directly mentioned in Scripture, adds perhaps a slight additional probability to these conjectures. It was here that he experienced at the hands of Onesiphorus the kindness which was continued to him at Rome,[1] and to which he alludes with a gratitude all the more heartfelt, because very shortly afterwards Onesiphorus seems to have died.

From the trial at Ephesus, where his cause might have suffered from local prejudices, he may once more have found it necessary to appeal to Cæsar. Barea Soranus, the then Proconsul, may have been glad, as Pliny afterwards was in Bithynia, to refer the case to the highest tribunal. Timothy would naturally desire to accompany him, but at that time the Apostle—still sanguine, still accompanied by other friends, still inclined to believe that his life, which had long been valueless to himself, might be saved from human violence, however near might be its natural close—thought it necessary to

---

[1] 2 Tim. i. 18, ὅσα ἐν Ἐφέσῳ διηκόνησε, "how many acts of service he rendered" to Paul and others. Wieseler's inference that Onesiphorus was a deacon is hardly supported by so general a verb.

leave his friend at Ephesus to brave the dangers, and fulfil the duties of that chief pastorate, respecting which he had recently received such earnest instructions. It was natural that they should part with deep emotion at a time so perilous and under circumstances so depressing. St. Paul, sitting in his dreary and desolate confinement at Rome, recalls with gratitude the streaming tears of that farewell, which proved how deeply his affection was requited by the son of his heart. In all his wanderings, in all his sickness, in all his persecutions, in all his imprisonments, in all his many and bitter disappointments, the one spot invariably bright, the one permanent consolation, the one touch of earthly happiness, had been the gentle companionship, the faithful attendance, the clinging affection of this Lycaonian youth. For St. Paul's sake, for the Gospel's sake, he had left his mother, and his home, and his father's friends, and had cheerfully accepted the trying life of a despised and hunted missionary. By birth a Greek, he had thrown in his lot by circumcision with the Jew, by faith with the Christian; and his high reward on earth had been, not the shadow of an immortal honour, but the substance of lofty service in the cause of the truth which was to subdue the world. The affection between him and the Apostle began in the spiritual sonship of conversion, and was cemented by community of hopes and perils until it had become one of the strongest ties in life. For troubled years they had cheered each other's sorrows in the midst of painful toils. The very difference in their age, the very dissimilarity of their characters, had but made their love for each other more sacred and more deep. The ardent, impetuous, dominant character and intense purpose of the one, found its complement and its repose in the timid, yielding, retiring, character of the other. What Melancthon was to Luther, whom Luther felt that he could not spare, and for whose life when all hope seemed over he stormed heaven with passionate and victorious supplication,[1]— that and more than that was the comparatively youthful Timothy to the more tried and lonely Paul.

We may hope that the Apostle, now once more a prisoner, was not alone when he left Ephesus to cross the Mediterranean for the last time. Titus and Tychicus[2] had probably accompanied him from Nicopolis; Demas may have joined him at Thessalonica, Luke at Philippi; and Trophimus, undeterred by his past dangers at Jerusalem, volunteered to accompany him from the Ionian capital. But the kindly intentions of the latter were frustrated, for he fell ill at Miletus, and there the sad little band of Christians had to leave him when the vessel started.[3] Erastus, if he was with him at Ephesus, stayed behind when they reached his native Corinth.

Of the particulars of the voyage we know nothing. It may very possibly have been from Ephesus to Cenchreae, over the Diolkos to Lechaeum, and then along the Gulf of Corinth and across the Adriatic to Brundisium,

[1] "Allda musste mir unser Herr Gott herhalten. Denn ich rieb Ihm die Ohren mit allen promissionibus exaudiendarum precum." (Luther.)

[2] Hence we infer that Artemas, and not Tychicus, had been sent to replace Titus at Crete; and the mention of the name Artemas first in Tit. iii. 12 is yet another of the numberless subtle traces of genuineness.

[3] This incidental allusion (*most* unlike a forger) throws a valuable light, as also does the almost fatal illness of Epaphroditus at Rome, on the limitation which the Apostles put on the exercise of any supernatural gift of healing. It is, further, an insuperable stumblingblock in the way of every possible theory which denies the second imprisonment. Some have suggested a desperate alteration of the text to Μελίτη, and Schrader is content with the preposterous fiction of a Miletus in Crete! But why should St. Paul tell Timothy that Trophimus was sick at Miletus? For the same reason that a person writing to London might, even in these days of rapid communication, tell a correspondent that their common friend was ill at Southend. Miletus was more than thirty miles from Ephesus, and Trophimus might be ill for months without Timothy knowing of it.

whence the prisoner, his guards and his companions, would make their dreary way along the great Appian road to Rome. This time no disciples met them at the Appii Forum or the Three Taverns, nor could anything have well occurred to make Paul thank God and take courage. The horrible Neronian persecution had depressed, scattered, and perhaps decimated the little Christian community; and the Jews, who had received Paul at the time of his first imprisonment with an ostentatiously indifferent neutrality, had been transformed since then—partly, no doubt, by the rumours disseminated by emissaries from Jerusalem, and partly by the mutual recriminations after the fire of Rome—into the bitterest and most unscrupulous enemies. On the former occasion, after a short detention in the Prætorian camp, St. Paul had been allowed to live in his own lodging; and even if this had been in the humblest purlieus of the Trastevere, among the Jewish vendors of sulphur matches and cracked pottery,[1] it had still been his own, and had allowed him to continue, in a sphere however restricted, his efforts at evangelisation. But Christianity was now suspected of political designs, and was practically reduced to a *religio illicita*. This time he had no kindly-disposed Lysias to say a good word for him, no friendly testimonies of a Festus or an Agrippa to produce in his favour. The government of Nero, bad almost from the first, had deteriorated year by year with alarming rapidity, and at this moment it presented a spectacle of awful cruelty and abysmal degradation such as has been rarely witnessed by the civilised world. While an honest soldier like Burrus held the high post of Prætorian Præfect, a political prisoner was at least sure that he would not be treated with wanton severity; but with a Tigellinus in

---

[1] But see *supra*, II., p. 399.

that office—a Tigellinus whose foul hands were still dripping with Christian blood, and whose foul life was stained through and through with every form of detestable wickedness—what could be expected? We catch but one glimpse of this last imprisonment before the curtain falls, but that glimpse suffices to show how hard it was. Through the still blackened ruins of the city, and amid the squalid misery of its inhabitants—perhaps with many a fierce scowl turned on the hated Christian—Paul passed to his dungeon, and there, as the gate clanged upon him, he sat down, chained night and day, without further hope—a doomed man.

To visit him now was no longer to visit a man against whom nothing serious was charged, and who had produced a most favourable impression on the minds of all who had been thrown into relation with him. It was to visit the bearer of a name which the Emperor and his minions affected to detest; it was to visit the ringleader of those who were industriously maligned as the authors of a calamity more deadly than any which had ever afflicted the city since its destruction by the Gauls. Merely to be kind to such a man was regarded as infamous. No one could do it without rendering himself liable to the coarse insolence of the soldiers.[1] Nay, more, it was a service of direct political danger. Rome swarmed with spies who were ready to accuse any one of *laesa majestas* on the slightest possible occasion. Now who but a Christian would visit a Christian? What could any respectable citizen have to do with the most active propagandist of a faith which had at first been ignored as contemptible, but which even calm and cultivated men were beginning to regard as an outrage against humanity?[2]

[1] See Juv. *Sat.* xvi. 8—12.
[2] "Odio generis humani convicti sunt." (Tac. *Ann.* xv. 44; cf. *H.* v. 5.)

And if any Christian were charged with being a Christian on the ground of his having visited St. Paul, how could he deny the charge, and how, without denying it, could he be saved from incurring the extremest danger?

Under these circumstances the condition of the Apostle was very different from what it had been three years before. His friends had then the freest access to him, and he could teach Christ Jesus with all boldness undisturbed. Now there were few or no friends left to visit him; and to teach Jesus Christ was death. He knew the human heart too well to be unaware how natural it was that most men should blush to associate themselves with him and his chain. One by one his Asiatic friends deserted him.[1] The first to leave him were Phygellus and Hermogenes.[2] Then the temptations of the present course of things, the charm of free and unimperilled life, were too much for Demas, and he too—though he had long been his associate—now forsook him. Crescens departed, perhaps on some necessary mission, to the Churches of Galatia, and Titus to those of Dalmatia. He had dispatched Tychicus to Ephesus shortly before he wrote this letter. One friend alone was with him—the beloved physician, the faithful, unobtrusive, cultivated Luke.[3] Of hardship Paul recked nothing; he had spent a life of endless hardship, and had learnt a complete independence of the outward elements of comfort; but to one situated as he was, and liable to constant pain, to be utterly companionless would have been a trial too hard to bear.

---

[1] 2 Tim. i. 15.

[2] Nothing whatever is known of these two. In later days the Christians, under the stress of persecution, had learnt their lessons better, so that their tender faithfulness to one another in distress excited the envious astonishment of Pagans (Lucian, *De Morte. Peregr.* § 13).

[3] Where was Aristarchus (Acts xxvii. 2; Col. iv. 10; Phil. 24)? We cannot tell; but his name would not have been omitted by an ingenious imitator.

A single happy unexpected visit broke the continuity of his loneliness, and cheered him amid the sense of desertion. The good-hearted Ephesian Onesiphorus, who had already made himself conspicuous among the Christians of his native city by his active kindliness, came to Rome. He knew that St. Paul was somewhere in that city as a prisoner, and he rose above the timid selfishness of his fellow-countrymen. He set about searching for the captive Jew. In a city thronged with prisoners, and under a government rife with suspicions, upon which it acted with the most cynical unscrupulousness, it was by no means a safe or pleasant task to find an obscure, aged, and deeply implicated victim. Had Onesiphorus been less in earnest, it would have been easy for him to make an excuse to other Christians, and to his own conscience, that he had not known where Paul was, and that he had looked for him but could not find him. But he would not abandon his earnest search until it led him to the side of the Apostle.[1] Nor was he content with a single visit. Glad to face the shame and scorn of befriending one whose condition was now so abject, he came to the Apostle again and again, and refreshed his soul with that very consolation—the sense of human sympathy—for which most of all it yearned.[2] Probably the death of this true and warm-hearted Ephesian took place at Rome, for St. Paul utters a fervent wish that he may find mercy of the Lord in the great day, and in writing to Timothy he sends a greeting to his household, but not to him.[3] The tone of intense gratitude which breathes through the few verses in which the Apostle alludes to him makes us feel that the brave and loving friendliness

---

[1] 2 Tim. i. 17, σπουδαιότερον ἐζήτησέν με καὶ εὗρεν.
[2] 2 Tim. i. 16, πολλάκις με ἀνέψυξεν.
[3] 2 Tim. iv. 19.

of this true brother, contrasted as it was with the cowardly defection of the other Asiatics, was the brightest gleam of light which fell on the dense gloom of the second imprisonment.

At last the time came when the Apostle had to stand before the great Roman tribunal. What was called in Roman law the *prima actio* came on.[1] The Scriptures were written with other objects than to gratify our curiosity with the details of historic scenes, however memorable or however important. That which God has revealed to us in Scripture is rather the œconomy —the gradual unfolding and dispensation—of His eternal scheme for the salvation of mankind, than the full biography of those whose glory it was to be entrusted with the furtherance of His designs. Eagerly should we have desired to know the details of that trial, but St. Paul only tells us a single particular. His silence once more illustrates the immense difference between ancient and modern correspondence. A modern, in writing to a dear friend, would have been sure to give him some of the details, which could hardly fail to interest him. It may be said that these details might have been supplied by the bearer of the letter. It may be so; but if we judge St. Paul by his own writings, and by the analogy of other great and spiritually-minded men, we should infer that personal matters of this kind had but little interest for him. Accustomed to refer perpetually to his high spiritual privileges—digressing incessantly to the fact of his peculiar Apostolate—he yet speaks but little,

---

[1] Such certainly seems to be the natural meaning of πρώτη ἀπολογία (2 Tim. iv. 16), and it is not certain that this method of procedure and the *ampliatio* or *comperendinatio* had been entirely abandoned. In these matters the mere caprice of the Emperor was all that had to be consulted. It is, however, possible that the πρώτη ἀπολογία may refer to the first count of the indictment, since Nero had introduced the custom of hearing every count separately.

and never in detail, of the outward incidents of his life. *They* did but belong to the world's passing show, to the things which were seen and evanescent. Two vivid touches alone reveal to us the nature of the occasion. One is the deplorable fact that not a single friend had the courage to stand by his side. He had to defend himself single-handed. No *patronus* would encourage him, no *advocatus* plead his cause, no *deprecator* say a word in his favour. "No man took his place by my side to help me; all abandoned me; God forgive them." The other is that even at that supreme moment, with the face of the threatening tyrant fixed loweringly upon him, and the axed fasces of the lictors gleaming before his eyes, his courage did not quail. If man forsook him, God strengthened him. If even Luke left him to face the court alone, the Lord Himself stood by him. He spoke, and spoke in a manner worthy of his cause. How much heathen literature would we freely sacrifice for even a brief sketch of that speech such as Luke could so well have given us had he only been present! How supreme would have been the interest of a defence uttered by St. Paul in the Roman forum, or in a Roman basilica! Alas! the echoes of his words have died away for ever. We only know what he who uttered it tells us of it. But he was satisfied with it. He felt that the Lord had strengthened him in order that, through his instrumentality, the preaching of the Gospel might be fulfilled to the uttermost, and that all the Gentiles might hear it. And he was successful—successful, we cannot doubt, not merely that he might prolong his days in useless and hopeless misery, but for some high design, and perhaps among other reasons that he might leave us his last precious thoughts in the Second Epistle to his dearest convert. But the danger had been imminent, and the too-certain result was only postponed. "I was rescued," he says, "out of the lion's mouth." Each juror received three voting tablets—one marked with A., for *Absolvo;* another with C., for *Condemno;* and a third with N.L., for *Non liquet*, or "not proven." The majority of votes had been of the third description, and the result had been the *ampliatio*, or postponement of the trial for the production of further evidence. But St. Paul was not deceived by any false hopes. "I was rescued out of the lion's mouth. The Lord shall deliver me"—not necessarily from death or danger, but—"from every evil work,[1] and shall save me unto His heavenly kingdom." Death by martyrdom was no such "evil work;"[2] from *that* he did not expect to be saved—nay, he knew, and probably even hoped, that through that narrow gate an entrance might be ministered unto him abundantly into Christ's heavenly kingdom. But he must have passed through perilous and exciting hours, or he would have hardly used that metaphor of the lion's mouth,[3] prompted perhaps by a reminiscence of the powerful image of the shepherd prophet, "As the shepherd tears out of the mouth of a lion two legs and the piece of an ear."[4]

But who was the lion? Was it Satan?[5] or Helius, the Præfect of the city? or Nero?[6] or is the expression a

---

[1] From all that can be *really* called πονηρόν. "Liberabit me ne quid agam" (and we may add, *ne quid patiar*) "Christiano, ne quid Apostolo indignum" (Grot.).

[2] "Decollabitur? liberabitur, liberante Domino" (Bengel). It would be difficult for me to exaggerate my admiration for this truly great commentator. On the following words, "to whom be glory for ever and ever," he remarks, "Doxologiam parit spes, quanto majorem res."

[3] 2 Tim. iv. 17.

[4] Amos iii. 12. Cf. ἐνώπιον τοῦ λέοντος, referring to Xerxes (Apocr. Esth. xiv. 13).

[5] 1 Pet. v. 8.

[6] Λέοντα γὰρ τὸν Νέρωνά φησι διὰ τὸ θηριῶδες (Chrys.). τέθνηκεν ὁ λέων (of the death of Tiberius) (Jos. *Antt.* xviii. 6, § 10); but here λέοντος has no article.

merely general one? Even if so, it is not impossible that he may have pleaded his cause before Nero himself. The power of deciding causes had been one which the Roman Emperors had jealously kept in their own hands; and if the trial took place in the spring of A.D. 66, Nero had not yet started for Greece, and would have been almost certain to give personal attention to the case of one who had done more than any living man to spread the name of Christ. Nero had been intensely anxious to fix on the innocent Christians the stigma of that horrible conflagration, of which he himself had been dangerously suspected, and the mere suspicion of which, until averted into another channel, had gone far to shake even his imperial power. And now the greatest of the Christians—the very *coryphæus* of the hated sect—stood chained before him. He to whom popularity, forfeited in part by his enormous crimes, had become a matter of supreme importance, saw how cheaply it could be won by sacrificing a sick, deserted, aged, fettered prisoner, for whom no living soul would speak a word, and who was evidently regarded with intense hatred by Gentiles from Asia, by the dense rabble of the city, and by Jews from every quarter of the world. Cicero has preserved for us a graphic picture of the way in which, nearly a century and a half before this time, a screaming, scowling, gesticulating throng of Jews, undeterred by soldiers and lictors, surrounded with such threatening demonstrations the tribunal before which their oppressor, Flaccus, was being tried, that he, as his advocate, though he had been no less a person than a Roman Consul, and "father of his country," was obliged to plead in low tones for fear of their fury. If in B.C.

The metaphor is probably general, as in Ps. xxii. 21. Esther is said to have cried, "Save me from the lion's mouth," when she went to Ahasuerus (*Megillah*, f. 15, 2).

59 the Romish Jews could intimidate even a Cicero in their hatred to a Flaccus, is it likely that they would have abstained from hostile demonstrations against an enemy so detested and so perfectly defenceless as St. Paul?

Paul before Nero! if indeed it was so, what a contrast does the juxtaposition of two such characters suggest— the one the vilest and most wicked, the other the best and noblest of mankind! Here, indeed, we see two races, two civilisations, two religions, two histories, two *aeons* brought face to face. Nero summed up in his own person the might of legions apparently invincible; Paul personified that more irresistible weakness which shook the world. The one showed the very crown and flower of luxurious vice and guilty splendour; the other the earthly misery of the happiest saints of God. In the one we see the incarnate Nemesis of past degradation; in the other the glorious prophecy of Christian sainthood. The one was the deified autocrat of Paganism; the other the abject ambassador of Christ. The emperor's diadem was now confronted for the first time by the Cross of the Victim before which, ere three centuries were over, it was destined to succumb.

Nero, not yet thirty years of age, was stained through and through with every possible crime, and steeped to the very lips in every nameless degradation. Of all the black and damning iniquities against which, as St. Paul had often to remind his heathen converts, the wrath of God for ever burns, there was scarcely one of which Nero had not been guilty. A wholesale robber, a pitiless despot, an intriguer, a poisoner, a murderer, a matricide, a liar, a coward, a drunkard, a glutton, incestuous, unutterably depraved, his evil and debased nature—of which even Pagans had spoken as "a mixture of blood and mud"—had sought abnormal outlets to weary, if it could not sate, its insatiable proclivity to crime. He was that last worst specimen of human wickedness—a man who, not content with every existing form of vice and sin in which the taint of human nature had found a vent, had become "an inventor of evil things." He had usurped a throne; he had poisoned, under guise of affection, the noble boy who was its legitimate heir; he had married the sister of that boy, only to break her heart by his brutality, and finally to order her assassination; he had first planned the murder, then ordered the execution, of his own mother, who, however deep her guilt, had yet committed her many crimes for love of him; he had treacherously sacrificed the one great general whose victories gave any lustre to his reign; among other murders, too numerous to count, he had ordered the deaths of the brave soldier and the brilliant philosopher who had striven to guide his wayward and intolerable heart; he had disgraced imperial authority with every form of sickening and monstrous folly; he had dragged the charm of youth and the natural dignity of manhood through the very lowest mire; he had killed by a kick the worthless but beautiful woman whom he had torn from her own husband to be his second wife; he had reduced his own capital to ashes, and buffooned, and fiddled, and sung with his cracked voice in public theatres, regardless of the misery and starvation of thousands of its ruined citizens; he had charged his incendiarism upon the innocent Christians, and tortured them to death by hundreds in hideous martyrdoms; he had done his best to render infamous his rank, his country, his ancestors, the name of Roman—nay, even the very name of man.

And Paul had spent his whole life in the pursuit of truth and the practice of holiness. Even from boyhood a grave and earnest student of the Law of God, he surpassed in learning and faithfulness all the other "pupils of the wise" in the school of the greatest Doctor of the Law; and if the impetuous ardour of his nature, and that commonest infirmity of even noble minds—the pride of erroneous conviction which will not suffer itself to be convinced of error—had for a time plunged him into a course of violent intolerance, of which he afterwards repented with all the intensity of his nature, yet even this sin had been due to the blind fury of misdirected zeal in a cause which he took—or for a time thought that he took—to be the cause of God. Who shall throw the first stone at him? not even those learned and holy men whose daily lives show how hard it is to abdicate the throne of infallible ignorance, and after lives of stereotyped error to go back as humble learners to the school of truth. But, if for a moment he erred, how grandly—by what a life of heroic self-sacrifice—had he atoned for his fault! Did ever man toil like this man? Did ever man rise to a nobler superiority over the vulgar objects of human desire? Did ever man more fully and unmurmuringly resign his whole life to God? Has it ever been granted to any other man, in spite of all trials, obstructions, persecutions, to force his way in the very teeth of "clenched antagonisms" to so full an achievement of the divine purpose which God had entrusted to his care? Shrinking from hatred with the sensitive warmth of a nature that ever craved for human love, he had yet braved hatreds of the most intense description—the hatred not only of enemies, but of friends; not only of individuals, but of entire factions; not only of aliens, but of his own countrymen; not only of Jews, but even of those who professed the same faith with himself.[1] Shrinking from

---

[1] "They who hurt me most are my own dear children—my brethren—*fraterculi mei, aurei amiculi mei.*" (Luther, *Cochlearius,* 146.)

pain with nervous sensibility, he yet endured for twenty years together every form of agony with a body weakened by incessant hardship. The many perils and miseries which we have recounted are but a fragment of what he had suffered. And what had he done? He had secured the triumph, he had established the universality, he had created the language, he had co-ordinated the doctrines, he had overthrown the obstacles of that Faith which is the one source of the hope, the love, the moral elevation of the world.

And now these two men were brought face to face—imperial power and abject weakness; youth cankered with guilt, and old age crowned with holiness; he whose whole life had consummated the degradation, and he whose life had achieved the enfranchisement of mankind. They stood face to face the representatives of two races—the Semitic in its richest glory, the Aryan in its extremest degradation: the representatives of two trainings—the life of utter self-sacrifice, and the life of unfathomable self-indulgence: the representatives of two religions—Christianity in its dawning brightness, Paganism in its effete despair: the representatives of two theories of life—the simplicity of self-denying endurance ready to give up life itself for the good of others, the luxury of shameless Hedonism which valued no consideration divine or human in comparison with a new sensation: the representatives of two spiritual powers—the slave of Christ and the incarnation of Antichrist. And their respective positions showed how much, at this time, the course of this world was under the control of the Prince of the Power of the Air—for incest and matricide were clothed in purple, and seated on the curule chair, amid the ensigns of splendour without limit and power beyond control; and he whose life had exhibited all that was great and noble in the heart of man stood in peril of execution, despised, hated, fettered, and in rags.

But Roman Law was still Roman Law, and, except where passions of unusual intensity interfered, some respect was still paid to the forms of justice. For the time, at any rate, Paul was rescued out of the lion's mouth. There was some flaw in the indictment, some deficiency in the evidence; and though St. Paul well knew that it was but a respite which was permitted him, for the time at any rate he was remanded to his prison. And Nero, if indeed he were "the lion" before whom this first defence had been pleaded, had no further door for repentance opened to him in this life. Had he too trembled, as Paul reasoned before him of temperance, righteousness, and the judgment to come? Had he too listened in alarm as Herod Antipas had listened to the Baptist? Had he too shown the hue of passing shame on those bloated features so deformed by the furrows of evil passion—as, at the Council of Constance, the Emperor Sigismund blushed, when John Huss upbraided him with the breach of his pledged word? The Emperor, who stood nearest to Nero in abysmal depravity, and who, like him, being himself unutterably impure and bad, had the innermost conviction that all others were at heart the same, used to address grave men with the most insulting questions, and if the indignant blood mantled on their cheeks, he used to exclaim, "Erubuit, salva res est."[1] "He blushed; it is all right." But of Domitian we are expressly told that he *could not* blush; that his flushed cheeks were an impervious barrier against the access of any visible shame.[2] And in all probability Nero was infinitely too far gone to blush. It is far more probable that, like Gallio, he only listened to the defence of this worn

[1] Heliogabalus. [2] Tac. *Agric.* 45; Suet. *Dom.* 18; Plin. *Paneg.* 48.

and aged Jew with ill-concealed impatience and profound disdain. He would have regarded such a man as this as something more abject than the very dust beneath his feet. He would have supposed that Paul regarded it as the proudest honour of his life even to breathe the same atmosphere as the Emperor of Rome. His chance of hearing the words of truth returned no more. About this time he sailed on his frivolous expedition to Greece; and after outraging to an extent almost inconceivable the very name of Roman, by the public singings of his miserable doggrel, and the sham victories in which the supple and shameless Greeks fooled him to the very top of his bent, he returned to find that the revolt of Galba was making head, until he was forced to fly at night in disguise from his palace, to quench his thirst with ditch-water, to display a cowardice which made him contemptible to his meanest minions, and finally to let his trembling hand be helped by a slave to force a dagger into his throat.

But it is no wonder that when, over the ruins of streets which the fire had laid in ashes, St. Paul returned to his lonely prison, there was one earthly desire for the fulfilment of which he still yearned. It was once more to see the dear friend of earlier years—of those years in which, hard as were their sufferings, the hope of Christ's second coming in glory to judge the world seemed still so near, and in which the curtains of a neglected death and an apparently total failure had not yet been drawn so closely around his head. He yearned to see Timothy once more; to be refreshed by the young man's affectionate devotion; to be cheered and comforted by the familiar attendance of a true son in Christ, whose heart was wholly at one with his; who shared so fully in all his sympathies and hopes; who had learnt by long and familiar attendances how best to brighten his spirits and to supply his wants. It was this which made him write that second letter to Timothy, which is, as it were, his "cycnea oratio," and in which, amid many subjects of advice and exhortation, he urges his friend with reiterated earnestness to come, to come at once, to come before winter,[1] to come ere it is too late, and see him, and help him, and receive his blessing before he died.

[1] 2 Tim. iv. 9, 21.

CHAPTER LVI.

PAUL'S LAST LETTER.

Παῦλος δὲ ὁ τρισμακάριος τὴν κεφαλὴν ξίφει ἀπετμήθη ὁ ἀνεκδιήγητος ἄνθρωπος.
—Ps. Chrys. *Orat. Enam.*

"Testamentum Pauli et cycnea cantio est haec Epistola."—Bengel.

"Hoc praestat carcer Christiano, quod eremus Prophetis."—Tert. *ad Mart.* 3.

"Mortem habebat Paulus ante oculus. . . . Quaecunque igitur hic legimus de Christi regno, de spe vitae aeternae, de Christianâ militiâ, de fiduciâ confessionis, de certitudine doctrinae, non tanquam atramento scripta, sed ipsius Pauli sanguine accipere convenit. . . . Proinde haec Epistola quasi solennis quaedam est subscriptio Paulinae doctrinae, eaque ex repraesenti."—Calvin.

HE began much in his usual form—

"Paul, an Apostle of Jesus Christ by the will of God,[1] according to the promise of the life which is in Christ Jesus, to Timothy my beloved son, grace, mercy, and peace, from God our Father and Christ Jesus our Lord. I thank God, whom I serve from my forefathers in a pure conscience—as the remembrance which I have of thee night and day in my supplications is incessant, longing earnestly to see thee—remembering thy tears[2]—that I may be filled with joy.[3] [I thank God, I say] on being reminded[4] of the unfeigned faith which is in thee, which dwelt first in thy grandmother Lois, and in thy mother Eunice; yes, and I feel confident that it dwells also in thee."[5]

---

[1] διὰ θελήματος. The attempt to deduce some very special and recondite inference from the fact that he uses this phrase for the κατ' ἐπιταγὴν of the First Epistle, seems to me as arbitrary as Mack's argument that the use of ἀγαπητῷ for γνησίῳ in the next verse is a sign that this Epistle shows more affection but less confidence.

[2] Tears at parting. Cf. Acts xx. 37.

[3] Does not this involved sentence, with its tesselation of parenthetic thoughts, at once indicate the hand of Paul?

[4] How reminded? We do not know; but this is the proper meaning of ὑπόμνησις—ὅταν τις ὑφ' ἑτέρου εἰς μνήμην προαχθῇ.

[5] i. 1—5, πέπεισμαι δέ. To make the δέ imply "notwithstanding appearances," as Alford does, is too strong; but the adversative force of δέ, though unnoticed by most commentators, and missed in many versions, does seem to

Perhaps the sadness of Timothy's heart—the tears for his absent and imprisoned teacher—had hindered the activity of his work, and plunged him in a too indolent despondency; and so Paul, remembering all the hopes which had inaugurated his youthful ministry, continues—

"For which cause[1] I remind thee to fan aflame the gift of God which is in thee by the imposition of my hands; for God gave us not the spirit of cowardice, but of power and of love, and of moral influence.[2] Be not then ashamed of the testimony of our Lord, nor of me His prisoner, but rather share my sufferings for the Gospel in accordance with the power of God, who saved us and called us with a holy calling, not according to our works, but according to His own plans and the grace given us in Christ Jesus before eternal times, but now manifested by the appearing of our Saviour Jesus Christ, who did away with death, and brought life and immortality to light by the Gospel, whereunto I was appointed a herald, and an Apostle, and teacher of the Gentiles, for which reason also I suffer these things; but *I* am not ashamed. For I know on whom I have believed, and I feel confident that He is able to preserve the trust committed to me till that day."[3]

Then—having ended the double digression on the word Gospel, which suggests to him first what that word implies (9, 10), and then recalls to him his own mission —he returns to his exhortation—

"As a pattern of wholesome teachings,[4] take those which thou heardest from me, in faith and the love which is in Christ Jesus. That fair trust preserve, through the Holy Spirit which dwelleth in us."[5]

imply that passing shade of hesitation about the fervour of the faith of Timothy—at any rate as manifested in vigorous action—which I have tried to indicate in the "Yes, and I feel confident."

[1] This phrase—δι' ἣν αἰτίαν for διό—is peculiar to the Pastoral Epistles.
[2] σωφρονισμοῦ. The form of the word seems to imply not only "sober-mindedness," but the teaching others to be sober-minded.
[3] i. 6—12.
[4] This seems to me the real meaning, though Alford has something to urge for his view that it should be rendered, "Have (in what I have just said to you) a pattern of sound words, which," &c.
[5] i. 13, 14.

Then he touches for a moment on the melancholy circumstances of which we have already spoken—his abandonment by the Asiatic converts,[1] and the zealous refreshing kindness of Onesiphorus, for whom he breathes an earnest prayer.[2]

"Thou therefore, my child, be strengthened in the grace which is in Christ Jesus, and the things which thou heardest from me in the presence of many witnesses, these things extend to faithful men who shall be adequate also to teach others. Share my sufferings as a fair soldier of Christ Jesus."[3]

The conditions of this soldiership he illustrates by three similes, drawn from the life of the soldier, the athlete, and the labourer, and doubtless meant to suggest to Timothy the qualities of which at that depressed period he stood most in need. The soldier must abandon all business entanglements, and strive to please his captain. The athlete, if he wants the crown, must keep the rules. The *toiling* husbandman has the first claim to a share of the harvest.[4] It was a delicate way of suggesting to Timothy the duties of increased single-heartedness, attention to the conditions of the Christian life, and strenuous labour; and that he might not miss the bearing of these similitudes he adds, "Consider what I say, for the Lord will give you[5] understanding in all things." By the example of his own sufferings he reminds him that the cardinal truths of the Gospel are ample to inspire toil and endurance.

---

[1] The expression οἱ ἐν τῇ Ἀσίᾳ πάντες, "all those *in* Asia," is difficult. It seems to imply that they had abandoned St. Paul in Rome, and had now returned to Asia, so that they would be "in Asia" by the time this letter arrived.

[2] i. 15—18.

[3] The distinction between καλὸς and ἀγαθὸς can only be kept up by the old English word "fair," as in Tennyson's

"So that ye trust to our fair Father, Christ."

[4] ii. 1—6.   [5] ii. 7, *leg.* δώσει.

"Bear in mind," he says, "Jesus Christ, raised from the dead, of the seed of David, according to my Gospel—in the cause of which I suffer even to chains as a malefactor: but the word of God has not been chained. For this reason, for the sake of the elect, I am enduring all things, that they too may obtain the salvation which is in Christ Jesus with eternal glory. Faithful is the saying—

> 'If we died with, we shall also live with Him;[1]
> If we endure, we shall also reign with Him;
> If we deny, He also will deny us.
> If we are faithless, He abideth faithful,
> For He is not able to deny Himself.'"[2]

"These things call to their remembrance;" and from this verse to the end of the chapter he reverts to the false teachers among whom Timothy is labouring, and against whom he has warned him in the First Epistle, testifying to them before the Lord not to fight about "views"—a thing entirely useless—to the subversion of the hearers.[3] "Strive to present thyself approved to God, a workman unshamed, rightly dividing the word of truth."[4] He is to shun the vain babblings of men like Hymenæus and Philetus,[5] with their ever-advancing impiety and the spreading cancer of their doctrine, which identified the resurrection with spiritual deliverance from the death of sin, and denied that there was any other resurrection,[6] to the ruinous unsettle-

---

[1] Cf. 1 Cor. xv. 31; 2 Cor. iv. 18; Rom. vi. 8.

[2] ii. 7–13. The last words are rhythmical, perhaps liturgical.

[3] ii. 14. Logomachy is a sure mark of Sophistic teaching, and there is a resemblance of the Gnostics to the Sophists in several particulars.

[4] ὀρθοτομοῦντα, "rightly cutting," or "cutting straight." "Nihil praetermittere, nil adiicere, nil mutilare, discerpere, torquere" (Beza). But it is not clear whether the metaphor is from cutting roads, or victims, or furrows, or bread, or carpentry. It is better to regard it as general, "rightly handling," just as καινοτομεῖν came to mean merely "innovating." In patristic language ὀρθοτομία became another word for "orthodoxy."

[5] Nothing is known of them (1 Tim. i. 20).

[6] Since there is a trace of exactly the same heresy in 1 Cor. xv. 12, it is idle of Baur to assume any allusion to Marcion here. St. Paul's warning against thus making the resurrection a mere metaphor was all the more needful, because it was a distortion of his own expressions (Rom. vi. 4; Col. ii. 12, &c.).

ment of some. Fruitlessly, however, for God's firm foundation stands impregnable with the double inscription on it,[1] "The Lord knoweth them that are his," and "Let every one who nameth the name of Christ stand aloof from unrighteousness."[2] Yet there should be no surprise that such errors spring up in the visible Church. It is like a great house in which are vessels of wood and earth, as well as of gold and silver, and alike for honourable and mean purposes. What each one had to do then was to purge himself from polluting connexion with the mean and vile vessels, and strive to be "a vessel for honour, sanctified, serviceable to the master, prepared for every good purpose."[3] He is therefore to "fly" from the desires of youth,[4] and in union with all who call on the Lord from a pure heart to pursue righteousness, faith, love, peace, having nothing to do with those foolish and illiterate questions which only breed strifes unworthy of the gentle, enduring meekness of a slave of the Lord, whose aim it should be to train opponents with all mildness,[5] in the hope that God may grant them repentance, so that they may come to full knowledge of the truth, and "awake to soberness out of the snare of the devil, after having been taken alive by him—to do God's will."[6]

The third chapter continues to speak of these evil teachers and their future developments in the hard times

---

[1] Cf. Rev. xxi. 14.

[2] See Numb. xvi. 5, 26.

[3] 2 Tim. ii. 21. The general meaning of the passage is clear, though it is indistinctly expressed; on ἐκκαθάρῃ Melancthon remarks, "Haec mundatio non est desertio congregationis, sed conversio ad Deum."

[4] ἐπιθυμίας, not exclusively sensual passions.

[5] See Matt. xii. 19, 20.

[6] ii. 14—26. The devil has taken them captive in a snare while they were drunk; awaking, they use their recovered soberness (ἀνανήφω, crapulam excutio) to break the snare, and return to obedience to God's will. αὐτοῦ probably refers to Satan, ἐκείνου to God, although this explanation is not absolutely necessary.

to come. A stern sad picture is drawn of what men shall then be in their selfishness, greed, conceit, ingratitude, lovelessness, treachery, besotted atheism, and reckless love of pleasure. He bids Timothy turn away from such teachers with their sham religion, their creeping intrigues, their prurient influence, their feminine conquests,[1] resisting the truth just as the old Egyptian sorcerers, Jannes and Jambres[2] did, and destined to have their emptiness equally exposed.[3] But Timothy—who has followed all that Paul has been in the teaching, the purpose, and the sufferings of his life, and well knows how the Lord saved him out of many trials and persecutions in his first journey[4]—must expect persecution, and be brave and faithful, making his life a contrast to that of these deceived deceivers, in accordance with that training which from a babe he had

---

[1] Baur (*Pastoralbriefe*, p. 36) sees an allusion to the Gnostic prophetesses, Prisca, Maximilla, Quintilla, &c., and quotes Epiphan. *Haer*. xxvi. 11. But, on the one hand, these certainly did not deserve to be stigmatised as γυναικάρια (see Tert.), and on the other it is absurd to suppose that women would be any less susceptible to every phase of religious influence in the Apostle's days than they have been in all ages (cf. Jos. *Antt.* xvii. 2, § 4). Such a γυναικάριον was Helena whom Simon Magus took about with him (Justin, *Apol.* i. 26; Iren. *c. Haer.* i. 23). When Jerome speaks with such scorn and slander of Nicolas of Antioch (*choros duxit femineos*), Marcion and his female adherent, Apelles and Philumena, Arius and his sister, Donatus and Lucilla, Epidius and Agape, Priscillian and Galla, had he forgotten certain ladies called Paulla and Eustochium?

[2] Jannes and Jambres are mentioned by Origen, and even by Pliny (*H. N.* xxx. 1), who calls them Jannes and Jotapes, and Numenius (Orig. *c. Cels.* iv. 199). The names belong to the cycle of Jewish Hagadoth. They are mentioned in the Targum of Jonathan on Ex. vii. 11, and were said to be sons of Balaam.

[3] This is said to contradict ii. 16 and iii. 13. It only does so to an unintelligent literalism. Error will succeed, but its very success will end in its exposure. "Non proficient amplius, quamquam ipsi et eorum similes proficiant in pejus" (Bengel); or, as Chrysostom remarks, κἂν πρότερον ἀνθήσῃ τὰ τῆς πλάνης εἰς τέλος οὐ διαμενεῖ.

[4] It has been asked why he refers especially to these. Perhaps because they had come most heavily upon him, and affected him most severely as being the first of the kind which he had endured. Perhaps because Timothy was a Lycaonian, and Paul's memory of those old days is vividly awaked.

received in the Holy Scriptures, which were able to make him wise unto salvation through faith in Jesus Christ: since "every Scripture inspired by God is also profitable for teaching,[1] for reproof, for correction, for training in righteousness, that the man of God may be perfect, thoroughly equipped for every good work."[2]

The fourth chapter begins with a solemn appeal to him to do his duty as a pastor "in season, out of season,"[3] because the time would soon come when men would turn away from truth to the fantastic doctrines of teachers who would answer them according to their own lusts.

"Do *thou* then be sober in all things, endure sufferings. Do the work of an evangelist, fulfil thy ministry. For *I* am being already poured in libation, and the time of my departure[4] is close at hand. I have striven the good strife, I have finished my course, I have kept the faith. Henceforth there is laid up for me the crown of righteousness, which the Lord, the righteous Judge, shall give me in that day; and not to me only, but also to all who have loved His appearing."[5]

---

[1] This is almost certainly the true translation. It was so understood by Origen, Theodoret, by Erasmus and Grotius, by Whitby and Hammond, by Alford and Ellicott; is so translated in the Arabic, the Syriac, the Vulgate, Luther, the Dutch, and the Rhemish, and in the versions of Wiclif, Tyndale, Coverdale, and Cranmer. For the introduction of the predicate by καί see Gal. iv. 7, Luke i. 36, Rom. viii. 29, &c.

[2] iii. 1—17.

[3] iv. 2, εὐκαίρως, ἀκαίρως: "opportunè, importunè" (Aug.). The smallest element of literary sense is sufficient to save the verse from the fanatical abuse which has perverted so many passages of Scripture. If any antidote to its abuse is required, see Matt. vii. 6.

[4] ἀναλύσεως, "departure," not "dissolution" (Phil. i. 23). ἀναλύειν is "to set sail."

[5] iv. 1—8. "There is nothing better," says Chrysostom, "than this strife. There is no end to this crown. It is not a crown of price, nor is it assigned by any earthly arbiter, nor are men spectators of its bestowal; the theatre is filled with angel-witnesses." It is useless to argue with those who see a spirit of boasting here which contradicts 1 Cor. iv. 3; Phil. iii. 12; 1 Tim. i. 16. "*Distingue tempora et concordabit Scriptura.*" The same man may, at different moments, in different moods, and from different standpoints, say, "I am the chief of sinners," and "I have striven the good strife."

That is practically St. Paul's last word. The remainder of the letter is occupied with personal information, given in the natural, loose, accidental order of a letter, mingled with earnest entreaty to him that he would come at once. "Do your best to come to me quickly." Demas, Crescens, Titus, are all absent from him; Erastus did not come with him farther than Corinth; Trophimus was taken ill at Miletus; Luke only is left. Mark is useful to him for service—perhaps because he knew Latin—and therefore Timothy is to take him up somewhere on the way, and bring him.[1] Tychicus is already on the way to Ephesus,[2] so that he can take Timothy's place when he arrives. Timothy is to be on his guard against the pronounced hostility of Alexander the coppersmith.[3] Then follows the touching allusion to his first trial and deliverance, on which we have already dwelt. Greetings are sent to Prisca, Aquila, and the house of Onesiphorus. Once more, "Do your best to come before winter;"—if he comes after that

[1] Mark had been attached of late to the ministry of Peter. Perhaps—but all is here uncertain—St. Peter may have been already martyred. It is, at any rate, deeply interesting to observe how completely St. Mark had regained that high estimation in the mind of the Apostle which he had weakened by his early defection (Acts xv. 38).

[2] ἀπέστειλα. It is made a difficulty that St. Paul should mention this to Timothy, who is supposed to have been at Ephesus. But even if ἀπέστειλα cannot be an epistolary aorist, and so equivalent to "I am sending," Paul could not be sure that Timothy might not be visiting some of the neighbouring churches; and Tychicus may have gone by some longer route. Even apart from this, nothing is more common in letters than the mention of facts which must be perfectly well known to the person addressed; and, in any case, since Timothy could hardly leave without resigning his charge for a time into the hands of Tychicus, he might be glad of a personal assurance from Paul that he had sent him.

[3] The meaning of πολλά μοι κακὰ ἐνεδείξατο is not certain, but is probably nothing more than "exhibited very mischievous conduct towards me." The following words, "The Lord shall reward him (ἀποδώσει, א, A, C, D, E, F, G), according to his works," have been rebuked as a malediction. But the μὴ αὐτοῖς λογισθείη of verse 16 is sufficient to show that this was not the mood of Paul; and it is no malediction to say of an enemy, "I must leave God to deal with him," since God is infinitely more merciful than man.

time he may be too late. "Eubulus greets thee, and Pudens, and Linus, and Claudia, and all the brethren. The Lord Jesus Christ be with thy spirit. Grace be with you."[1]

I have purposely omitted the one simple, touching message, introduced so incidentally, and with such inimitable naturalness. "When you come, bring with you the cloak that I left at Troas, at Carpus' house, and the books, especially the parchments."[2] The verse has been criticised as trivial, as unworthy the dignity of inspiration. But men must take their notions of inspiration from facts, and not try to square the facts to their own

---

[1] iv. 9—22. Linus may be the traditional first Bishop of Rome (Iren. c. Haer. iii. 33; Euseb. H. E. iii. 4); but I am surprised that any one should accept the ingenious attempt to identify Pudens with the dissolute centurion of Martial's epigrams (iv. 18; xi. 53) and the Pudens who built a temple at Chichester to Neptune and Minerva; and Claudia with the British Claudia Rufina, whom he married, and with the daughter of the British king Cogidubnus or of Caractacus. The grounds of the identification were suggested by Archdeacon Williams in a pamphlet on Pudens and Claudia. No doubt the Pudens of Martial *may* be the Pudens of the Chichester inscription, since he married a British lady; and this Claudia *may* have been a daughter of Cogidubnus, and *may* have been sent to Rome as a hostage, or for education, and *may* have taken the name Rufina, because she *may* have been entrusted to the charge of Pomponia, the wife of Aulus Plautus, who had been a commander in Britain, and in whose family was a branch called Rufi. And it is possible that Pomponia *may* have been secretly a Christian (Tac. *Ann.* xiii. 32), and so this Claudia Rufina *may* have become a Christian too; but even if we grant the possibility of all these hypotheses, still nothing whatever remains to identify the Pudens and Claudia here separated from each other by another name with the Pudens and Claudia of whom we have been speaking. Claudia was the commonest of names, and the whole theory is an elaborate rope of sand.

[2] That φελόνης, if that be the true reading, means a cloak, seems to be nearly certain. It was the opinion of the Greek Fathers, who only mention alternatively the meaning γλωσσόκομον, or book-case. But had this been mea: t it would have been mentioned *after* the books, not before them. We may assume that the word is a transliteration of the Latin *poenula*, and meant a long thick cloak. The form of the transliteration might surprise us, but it is another incidental mark of genuineness, for it comes from the form which the word took in Syriac, פינו. Even if פינו be *pallium*, we see that in Syriac פ represents π. Modern ingenuity sees in it a sacrificial vestment—a chasuble!

theories. Even on these grounds the verse has its own value for all who would not obscure divine inspiration, nor obliterate the true meaning and sacredness of Scripture by substituting a dictated infallibility for the free play of human emotions in souls deeply stirred by the Holy Spirit of God. But even on other grounds how little could we spare this verse! What a light does it throw on the last sad days of the persecuted Apostle! The fact that these necessary possessions—perhaps the whole that the Apostle could call his own in this world—had been left at the house of Carpus, may, as we have seen, indicate his sudden arrest, either at Troas or on his way to it. A prisoner who is being hurried from place to place by unsympathising keepers is little able to look after his property. But now the Apostle is settled again, though his home is but a prison, and he feels that it will be his home for life. Winter is coming on, and winter in a Roman prison, as he knows by experience, may be very cold. He wants to get back his rough travelling cloak. It was one of those large sleeveless garments which we should call an "overall" or "dreadnought." Perhaps St. Paul had woven it himself of the black goat's hair of his native province. And, doubtless—for he was a poor man—it was an old companion—wetted many a time in the water-torrents of Asia, whitened with the dust of Roman roads, stained with the brine of shipwreck when Euroaquilo was driving the Adriatic into foam. He may have slept in its warm shelter on the chill Phrygian uplands, under the canopy of stars, or it may have covered his bruised and trembling limbs in the dungeon of Philippi. It is of little value; but now that the old man sits shivering in some gloomy cell under the palace or on the rocky floor of the Tullianum, and the winter nights are coming on, he bethinks him of the old cloak in the house of Carpus, and asks Timothy to bring it with him. "The cloke that I left at Troas with Carpus, bring with thee." "And the books, but especially the parchments."[1] The *biblia*—the papyrus books—few we may be sure, but old friends. Perhaps he had bought them when he was a student in the school of Gamaliel at Jerusalem; or they may have been given him by his wealthier converts.[2] The papyrus books, then, let Timothy bring, but especially the parchments—the vellum rolls. What were these? Perhaps among them was the *diploma* of his Roman franchise; or were they precious rolls of Isaiah and the Psalms, and the lesser Prophets, which father or mother had given him as a life-long treasure in the far-off happy days when, little dreaming of all that would befall him, he played, a happy boy, in the dear old Tarsian home? Dreary and long are the days—the evenings longer and drearier still—in that Roman dungeon; and it will be a deep joy to read once more how David and Isaiah, in *their* deep troubles, learnt, as *he* had learnt, to suffer and be strong. A simple message, then, about an old cloak and

---

[1] Many will recall the striking and pathetic parallel to this request in the letter written by the martyr William Tyndale, from the damp cells of Vilvorde, in the winter before his death, asking, for Jesus' sake, for a warmer cap, and something to patch his leggings, and a woollen shirt, and, *above all, his Hebrew Bible, Grammar, and Dictionary*: "Quamobrem tuam dominationem rogatum habeo, idque per Dominum Jesum, ut si mihi per hiemen hic manendum sit, solicites apud dominum commissarium, si forte dignari velit, de rebus meis quas habet mittere calidiorem birethum. Frigus enim patior in capite nimium . . . calidiorem quoque tunicam, nam haec, quam habeo, admodum tenuis est. Item pannum ad caligas deficiendas. *Duplois (sic) detrita est*, camiseae detritae sunt etiam. Camiseam laneam habet si mittere velit. . . . Maxime autem omnium tuam clementium rogo atque obsecro ut ex amino agere velit apud dominum commissarium quatenus dignari mihi velit *Bibl. Hebraicam, Grammaticam Hebraicam, et Vocabularium Hebraicam*, ut eo studio tempus conteram . . . W. Tindalus" (Life, by Demaus, p. 475).

[2] See Ewald, *Gesch.* iv. 626; vi. 391. Paul seems to have been a student all his life, as far as circumstances permitted. Acts xxvi. 24, τὰ πολλά σε γράμματα εἰς μανίαν περιτρέπει.

some books, but very touching. They may add a little comfort, a little relief, to the long-drawn tedium of these last dreary days. Perhaps he thinks that he would like to give them, as his parting bequest, to Timothy himself, or to the modest and faithful Luke, that their true hearts may remember him when the sea of life flows smooth once more over the nameless grave. It would be like that sheepskin cloak which centuries afterwards the hermit Anthony bequeathed to the Archbishop Athanasius —a small gift, but all he had. Poor inventory of a saint's possessions! not worth a hundredth part of what a buffoon would get for one jest in Cæsar's palace, or an acrobat for a feat in the amphitheatre; but would he have exchanged them for the jewels of the adventurer Agrippa, or the purple of the unspeakable Nero? No, he is much more than content. His soul is joyful in God. If he has the cloak to keep him warm, and the books and parchments to teach and encourage him, and Mark to help him in various ways, and if, above all, Timothy will come himself, then life will have shed on him its last rays of sunshine; and in lesser things, as well as in all greater, he will wait with thankfulness, even with exultation, the pouring out in libation of those last few drops of his heart's blood, of which the rich full stream has for these long years been flowing forth upon God's altar in willing sacrifice.[1]

But there are no complaints, no murmurs—there is nothing querulous or depressed in these last words of St. Paul. If the Pastoral Epistles, and above all this one, were not genuine, they must have been written by one who not only possessed the most perfect literary

---

[1] Cf. Phil. ii. 17. Seneca, when dying, sprinkled the bystanders with his blood, saying, "*Libare se* liquorem illum Jovi Liberatori" (Tac. *Ann.* xv. 64). So, too, Thrasea, "Libemus, inquit, Jovi Liberatori" (*Id.* xvi. 35).

skill, but who had also entered with consummate insight into the character and heart of Paul;—of Paul, but not of ordinary men, even of ordinary great men. The characteristic of waning life is disenchantment, a sense of inexorable weariness, a sense of inevitable disappointment. We trace it in Elijah and John the Baptist; we trace it in Marcus Aurelius; we trace it in Francis of Assisi; we trace it in Roger Bacon; we trace it in Luther. All is vain! We have lived, humanly speaking, to little or no purpose. "We are not better than our fathers." "Art thou He that should come, or do we look for another?" "I shall die, and people will say, 'We are glad to get rid of this schoolmaster.'" "My order is more than I can manage." "Men are not worth the trouble I have taken for them." "We must take men as we find them, and cannot change their nature." To some such effect have all these great men, and many others, spoken. They have been utterly disillusioned; they have been inclined rather to check the zeal, to curb the enthusiasm, to darken with the shadows of experience the radiant hopes of their younger followers. If in any man such a sense of disappointment—such a conviction that life is too hard for us, and that we cannot shake off the crushing weight of its destinies—could have ever been excusable, it would have been so in St. Paul. What visible success had he achieved?—the founding of a few Churches of which the majority were already cold to him; in which he saw his efforts being slowly undermined by heretical teachers; which were being subjected to the fiery ordeal of terrible persecutions. To the faith of Christ he saw that the world was utterly hostile. It was arraying against the Cross all its intellect and all its power. The Christ returned not; and what could His doves do among serpents, His sheep among wolves? The very name "Christian" had now come to be regarded as synonymous with criminal; and Jew and Pagan—like "water with fire in ruin reconciled," amid some great storm—were united in common hostility to the truths he preached. And what had he personally gained? Wealth?—He is absolutely dependent on the chance gifts of others. Power?—At his worst need there had not been one friend to stand by his side. Love?—He had learnt by bitter experience how few there were who were not ashamed even to own him in his misery. And now after all—after all that he had suffered, after all that he had done—what was his condition? He was a lonely prisoner, awaiting a malefactor's end. What was the sum-total of earthly goods that the long disease, and the long labour of his life, had brought him in? An old cloak and some books. And yet in what spirit does he write to Timothy? Does he complain of his hardships? Does he regret his life? Does he damp the courage of his younger friend by telling him that almost every earthly hope is doomed to failure, and that to struggle against human wickedness is a fruitless fight? Not so. His last letter is far more of a *paean* than a *miserere*. For himself the battle is over, the race run, the treasure safely guarded. The day's work in the Master's vineyard is well-nigh over now. When it is quite finished, when he has entered the Master's presence, then and there—not here or now—shall he receive the crown of righteousness and the unspeakable reward. And so his letter to Timothy is all joy and encouragement, even in the midst of natural sadness. It is the young man's heart, not the old man's, that has failed. It is Timotheus, not Paul, who is in danger of yielding to languor and timidity, and forgetting that the Spirit which God gave was one not of fear, but of power, and of love, and of a sound mind. "Bear, then, afflictions with me. Be strong in the grace of Jesus Christ. Fan up the flame in those whitening embers of zeal and courage. Be a good soldier, a true athlete, a diligent toiler. Do you think of my chains and of my hardships? They are nothing, not worth a word or a thought. Be brave. Be not ashamed. We are weak, and may be defeated; but nevertheless God's foundation-stone stands sure with the double legend upon it—one of comfort, one of exhortation. Be thou strong and faithful, my son Timothy, even unto death." So does he hand to the dear but timid racer the torch of truth which in his own grasp, through the long torch-race of his life, no cowardice had hidden, no carelessness had dimmed, no storm had quenched. "Glorious Apostle! would that every leader's voice could burst, as he falls, into such a trumpet-sound, thrilling the young hearts that pant in the good fight, and must never despair of final victory."[1] Yes, even so:

"Hopes have precarious life;
They are oft blighted, withered, snapped sheer off
In vigorous youth, and turned to rottenness;
*But faithfulness can feed on suffering,
And knows no disappointment.*"[2]

[1] Martineau, *Hours of Thought*, p. 89.   [2] "Spanish Gypsy."

CHAPTER LVII.

THE END.

"Bonum agonem subituri estis, in quo agonothetes Deus vivus est, xystarches Spiritus Sanctus, corona aeternitatis, bravium angelicae substantiae, politia in coelis, gloria in saecula saeculorum."—TERT. *ad Mart.* 3.

"Qui desiderat dissolvi et esse cum Christo, patienter vivit et delectabiliter moritur."—AUG.

"Lieblich wie der Iris Farbenfeuer
Auf der Donnerwolke duft'gem Thau
Schimmert durch der Wehmuth düstern Schleier
Hier der Ruhe heitres Blau."—SCHILLER.

DID Paul ever get that cloak, and the papyri and the vellum rolls? Did Timothy ever reach him?[1] None can tell us. With the last verse of the Second Epistle to Timothy we have heard Paul's last word. In some Roman basilica, perhaps before Helius, the Emperor's freedman, in the presence of some dense, curious, hostile crowd of Jews and Pagans, he must have been heard once more, in his second defence, or on the second count of the indictment against him; and on this occasion the majority of the assessors must have dropped the tablet C—the tablet of condemnation—into the voting urn, and the presiding judge must have pronounced sentence of decapitation on one who, though condemned of holding a dangerous and illegal superstition, was still a Roman citizen. Was he alone at his second trial as at his first? Did the Gentiles again hear of Jesus and the Resurrection? Did he to them, as to the

---

[1] That he did is a reasonable conjecture, and it not improbably led to that imprisonment the liberation from which is mentioned in the Epistle to the Hebrews (xiii. 23).

Athenians prove that the God whose Gospel he had been commissioned to proclaim was the same God after whom their fathers had ignorantly groped, if haply they might find him, in the permitted ages of ignorance, before yet, in the dispensation of the times, the shadow on the dial-plate of eternity had marked that the appointed hour had come? All such questions are asked in vain. Of this alone we may feel convinced—that he heard the sentence pronounced upon him with a feeling akin to joy—

> "For sure, no gladlier does the stranded wreck
> See, through the grey skirts of a lifting squall,
> The boat that bears the hope of life approach
> To save the life despaired of, than he saw
> Death dawning on him, and the end of all."

But neither respecting his bearing nor his fate do we possess any particulars. If any timid, disheartened, secret Christians stood listening in the crowded court —if through the ruined areas which marked the sites of what had once been shops and palaces before the conflagration had swept like a raging storm through the narrow ill-built streets—if from the poorest purlieus of the Trastevere or the gloomy haunts of the catacomb any converted slave or struggling Asiatic who believed in Jesus had ventured among the throng, no one has left a record, no one even told the story to his fellows so clearly as to leave behind him a floating tradition. We know nothing more. The last word has been spoken. The curtain has fallen on one of the noblest of human lives.

They who will may follow him in imagination to the possible scene of his martyrdom, but every detail must be borrowed from imagination alone. It may be that the legendary is also the real scene of his death. If so, accompanied by the centurion and the soldiers who were to see him executed, he left Rome by the gate now called by his name. Near that gate, close beside the English cemetery, stands the pyramid of C. Cestius, and under its shadow lie buried the mortal remains of Keats and Shelley, and of many who have left behind them beloved or famous names. Yet even amid those touching memorials the traveller will turn with deeper interest to the old pyramid, because it was one of the last objects on which rested the eyes of Paul. For nearly three miles the sad procession walked; and doubtless the dregs of the populace, who always delight in a scene of horror, gathered round them. About three miles from Rome, not far from the Ostian road, is a green and level spot, with low hills around it, known anciently as *Aquae Salviae*, and now as *Tre Fontane*. There the word of command to halt was given; the prisoner knelt down; the sword flashed, and the life of the greatest of the Apostles was shorn away.[1]

> " Dulce sonat æthere vox
> Hiems transiit, occidit nox,
> Imber abiit moestaque crux,
> Lucet io perpetua lux."—BALDE.

Earthly failure could hardly have seemed more absolute. No blaze of glory shone on his last hours. No multitudes of admiring and almost adoring brethren surrounded his last days with the halo of martyrdom. Near the spot where he was martyred it is probable that they laid him in some nameless grave—in some spot remembered only by the one or two who knew and loved him. How little did they know, how little did even he understand, that the apparent earthly failure would in reality

[1] I have not thought it desirable to trouble the reader with Mediæval legends of St. Paul's death, which may be seen, by those who list, in Fabricius, *Cod. Apocr.* iii. 632; Ordericus Vitalis, ii. 3.

be the most infinite success! Who that watched that obscure and miserable end could have dreamed that Rome itself would not only adopt the Gospel of that poor outcast, but even derive from his martyrdom, and that of his fellow Apostle, her chief sanctity and glory in the eyes of a Christian world; that over his supposed remains should rise a church more splendid than any ancient basilica; and that over a greater city than Rome the golden cross should shine on the dome of a mighty cathedral dedicated to his name?

How little did men recognise his greatness! Here was one to whom no single man that has ever lived, before or since, can furnish a perfect parallel. If we look at him only as a writer, how immensely does he surpass, in his most casual Epistles, the greatest authors, whether Pagan or Christian, of his own and succeeding epochs. The younger Pliny was famous as a letter-writer, yet the younger Pliny never produced any letter so exquisite as that to Philemon. Seneca, as a moralist stood almost unrivalled, yet not only is clay largely mingled with his gold, but even his finest moral aphorisms are inferior in breadth and intensity to the most casual of St. Paul's. Epictetus and Marcus Aurelius furnish us with the purest and noblest specimens of Stoic loftiness of thought, yet St. Paul's chapter on charity is worth more than all they ever wrote. If we look at the Christian world, the very greatest worker in each realm of Christian service does but present an inferior aspect of one phase only of Paul's many-sided pre-eminence. As a theologian, as one who formulated the doctrines of Christianity, we may compare him with St. Augustine or St. Thomas of Aquinum; yet how should we be shocked to find in him the fanciful rhetoric and dogmatic bitterness of the one, or the scholastic aridity of the other! If we look at him as a moral reformer, we may compare him with Savonarola; but in his practical control of even the most thrilling spiritual impulses—in making the spirit of the prophet subject to the prophet—how grand an exemplar might he not have furnished to the impassioned Florentine! If we consider him as a preacher we may compare him with St. Bernard; yet St. Paul would have been incapable of the unnatural ascetism and heresy-hunting hardness of the great Abbot of Clairvaux. As a reformer who altered the entire course of human history, Luther alone resembles him; yet how incomparably is the Apostle superior to Luther in insight, in courtesy, in humility, in dignity, in self-control! As a missionary we might compare him to Xavier, as a practical organiser to St. Gregory, as a fervent lover of souls to Whitefield, and to many other saints of God in many other of his endowments; but no saint of God has ever attained the same heights in so many capacities, or received the gifts of the Spirit in so rich an outpouring, or borne in his mortal body such evident brand-marks of the Lord. In his lifetime he was no whit behind the very chiefest of the Apostles, and he towers above the very greatest of all the saints who have since striven to follow the example of his devotion to his Lord.

"God buries his workmen, but carries on their work." It is not for any earthly rewards that God's heroes have sought—not even for the reward of hoping in the posthumous success of the cause to which they have sacrificed their lives. All questions of success or failure they have been content to leave in the hands of God. Their one desire has been to be utterly true to the best that they have known; their prayers have all been simplified to this alone—"Teach me to do the thing that pleaseth Thee, for Thou art my God; let Thy loving Spirit lead me into the land of righteousness." That God has seemed to be careless of their individual happiness they would be the last to complain; though He slay them, yet do they trust in Him. Failure was to St. Paul a word unknown. He knew that to fail—or seem to fail—in the cause of God, was to succeed beyond the dreams of earthly ambition.

His faith had never wavered amid life's severest trials, nor his hope grown dim amid its most bitter disappointments; and when he passed from the dungeon and the martyrdom to his crown of righteousness, he left the life which he had sown to be quickened by the power of God in the soil of the world's history, where it shall continue to bear fruit until the end of time, amid the ever-deepening gratitude of generations yet unborn. One who had lived with him, and knew his thoughts and hopes, and had himself preached the faith of Christ in days when to be a Christian was to suffer as a Christian, has written of God's heroes in words which St. Paul would have endorsed, and in which he would have delighted, "These all died in faith, not having received the promises, but having seen them afar off, and were persuaded of them, and embraced them, and confessed that they were strangers and pilgrims on the earth. For they that say such things declare plainly that they seek a country; and truly, if they had been mindful of that country whence they came out, they might have had opportunity to have returned. But now they desire a better country, that is, an heavenly; wherefore God is not ashamed to be called their God, for He hath prepared for them a city."

APPENDIX.

EXCURSUS I. (Vol. I., p. 612).

THE MAN OF SIN; OR, "THE LAWLESS."

"*Ego prorsus quid dixerit fateor me ignorare.*"—S. AUG.

THE various conjectures as to the "Man of Sin," and "that which withholdeth," may be classed under three heads—(i.) the nearly contemporary, (ii.) the distantly prophetic, and (iii.) the subjectively general. And in each of these classes the suggested antitypes are either (α) general and impersonal, or (β) individual and special.

(i.) The opinion adopted will, of course, depend greatly on the extent to which the destruction of Judaism in the overthrow of Jerusalem can be regarded as "a coming of the Lord." Those who, in accordance with most of the definite temporal prophecies of Scripture, think that St. Paul must have been alluding to something *nearly contemporary*—something which already loomed on the horizon, and therefore to something which would alone have a direct bearing on the lives of contemporary Christians, explain the Apostasy and the Man of Sin to represent, (α) generally, the Pharisees, or Gnosticism, or the growth of heresy; or (β) individually, Nero or some Roman Emperor, Simon Magus, or Simon the son of Gioras; and they see "the check" generally in the Roman Emperor, or the Jewish Law, or spiritual gifts,[1] or the time appointed by God;[2] or individually in some Emperor (*e.g.*, Claudius =qui claudit=ὁ κατέχει),[3] or James the Just,[4] or—in St. Paul himself!

(ii.) Those who have taken the *distantly prophetical* view of the passage explain the Apostasy of the Man of Sin to be, (α) generally, the Papacy, or the Reformation, or Rationalism, or something as yet undeveloped; or (β) individually, Mahomet, or Luther, or Napoleon, or some future

---

[1] Chrysostom.
[2] Theodoret (ὁ τοῦ Θεοῦ ὅρος).
[3] Hitzig—very precariously.
[4] Wieseler, *Chron.* 268—273.

personal Antichrist; while they see "the check" either, as above, in the Roman Empire, or in the German Empire, or, more generally still, in the fabric of human polity.

(iii.) Finally, those who take an entirely broad and subjective view of the passage, see in it only a vague forecast of that which finds its fulfilment in all Christian, and, indeed, in all secular, history, of the counter-working of two opposing forces, good and evil, Christ and Antichrist, the *Jetser tôbh* and the *Jetser-ha-râ*, a lawless violence and a restraining power.

Now, of all these interpretations one alone can be regarded as reasonably certain—namely, that which views "the check" as the Roman Empire,[1] and "the checker" as the Roman Emperor. This may be regarded as fairly established, and has received the widest acceptance, first, because it fulfils the conditions of being something present and intelligible; secondly, because we see an obvious reason why it should have been only hinted at, since to express it would have been a positive danger both to the writer and the community;[2] and, thirdly, because, as Bishop Wordsworth has pointed out, the Epistle was from the first publicly read, and the Thessalonians must have attached a meaning to it, and that meaning has been handed down to us traditionally from the earliest times.[3] Whatever may have been the wild vagaries of theological rancour, expressing itself in the form of Biblical commentary, the early Fathers, at least, were almost unanimous in regarding "the restraining power" as being the Roman Empire,[4] and the "restrainer" as being some Roman Emperor.[5] And it seems obvious that one main

---

[1] "Quis nisi Romanus status?" (Tert. *De Resurr. Carn.* 24). "Clausulam saeculi acerbitates horrendas comminentem Romani imperii commeatu scimus ratardari" (id. *Apol.* 32). This was all the more natural, because the Roman Empire was regarded as the Fourth Kingdom of Daniel. Prof. Jowett objects (1) that he could not have expected it to be so soon swept away; and (2) that it is not *in pari materiâ*. But for (1) see 1 Thess. i. 10; v. 4; 1 Cor. xvi. 22, &c.; and (2) St. Paul daily saw the bearing of the Empire on the spread and position of Christianity.

[2] St. Paul had already found this by experience, even though his conversation with the Thessalonians had been comparatively private. But when the Church grew, and heathens dropped not unfrequently into its meetings, it would have been most compromising to them to speak of the destruction of the Roman Empire contemplated as a near event.

[3] The Rabbis held a similar view. One of them said, "The Messiah will not come till the world *has become all white with leprosy* (Lev. xiii. 13) by the Roman Empire embracing Christianity." *Sanhedrin*, f. 97, 1; Soteh, f. 49, 2; (Amsterd. ed.).

[4] So Tert. *De Resurr. Carnis*, 24; Iren. v. 25, 26; Aug. *De Civ. Dei.* xx. 19; Jer. Qu. xi. *ad Algas;* Lact. vii. 15, &c.

[5] Claudius was Emperor when the Epistle was written, early in A.D. 54. Whether there is any allusion to his name in the word κατέχων I am not prepared to say. Kern believes that Nero is intended by "the Lawless," and therefore (seeing that the

feature in the blasphemous self-exaltation and opposition to God which is to be a mark of the Man of Sin is suggested by the insane and sacrilegious enormities of Caligula (A.D. 40) thirteen years earlier, as well as by the persecutions of Antiochus Epiphanes. Other traits may have been suggested by the pretensions and sorceries of Simon Magus and similar widely-accredited impostors. Nero became to the Christian Church some years afterwards the very impersonation of their ideal Antichrist.

But to form any conception as to St. Paul's meaning, besides being guided by his belief of the probable nearness of the Advent, and by the necessity that what he said should have some meaning and value to his hearers, we must consider (α) the views of the age; (β) the symbols he uses; and (γ) his own subsequent language when he alludes to any similar topic.

Turning, then, to these, we find that (α) St. Paul was fully aware that, in the then present dispensation, the triumph of Christ was not to be final or complete. He may well have heard of Christ's solemn question, "Nevertheless, when the Son of Man cometh, shall he find faith on the earth?"[1] Even thus early in his career his prescient eye may have observed the traces of that Judaic and Antichristian faction which was to undo so much of his work, and embitter so many years of his life, and to whom he applies the sternest language. Already he may have noticed the germs of the various forms of Gnosticism, of which, in his Epistle to Timothy, he describes the "devilish doctrines" in language which recalls some of his expressions in this place.[2] And the views of the early Christians, as expressed by other Apostles, were all founded on warnings which Christ had uttered, and all pointed in the same direction.[3] That St. Paul should have thrown his forebodings into the concrete was natural to one so familiar with Old Testament prophecy,[4] so given to personification, and so trained to the expectation of a Messiah who should be the personal victor over all iniquity in the person of the Arch-foe, the *Rashá*, the Antichrist. That this personification should

---

first five years of Nero were that "golden quinquennium," which Roman writers so highly praise) concludes that the Epistle is spurious. Rev. xvii. 10, 11, refers to a later time, and possibly to the strangely prevalent notion that Nero was not really dead, but would in due time re-appear. The expressions used are evidently coloured by the picture of Antiochus Epiphanes in Dan. xi. He is called "a man of sin" (ἀνὴρ ἁμαρτωλός) in 1 Macc. ii. 48, 62.

[1] Luke xviii. 8.
[2] 1 Tim. iv. 1—3 (cf. 2 Tim. i. 15; iii. 1—9; Col. ii. 8, 16—19; Acts xx. 29).
[3] Luke xviii. 8; 1 John iv. 3; 2 Pet. ii. 1, 2; iii. 3; Rev. xiii. and *passim;* and the Epistle of Jude.
[4] Ezek. xxxviii. 16, 17.

also in part have taken its colour from the monstrous wickedness and blasphemous follies of emperors like Tiberius and Caligula, was exactly what we should have expected; and, indeed, the hopes and fears of the Jews had acted on the world of heathendom, which in its turn reacted upon them. It is a most interesting confirmation of this fact that the Jews gave to Antichrist the name of *Armillus* (ארמילוס). Thus, in the Targum of Jonathan on Isa. xi. 4, we find, "With the breath of His lips shall He destroy the wicked Armillus;" and in the Jerusalem Targum on Numb. xi. 26, and Deut. xxxiv. 2, we are told of Armalgus the Impious. This seems to be an allusion to the bracelets (*armillæ*) which, with utter defiance of all public dignity, were worn in public by Caligula.[1] We see, then, what St. Paul's anticipations at this moment were. He thought that ere long the Roman Empire, so far at any rate as it was represented by the reigning Emperor, would be swept away; that thereupon the existing tendencies of iniquity and apostasy, whether in Judaism or in the Church itself, would be concentrated in the person of one terrible opponent, and that the destruction of this opponent would be caused by the personal Advent of the Lord. At this time portents and presages of the most direful character were in the air. The hideous secrets of the Imperial Court were darkly whispered among the people. There were rumours of monstrous births, of rains of blood, of unnatural omens.[2] Though Claudius had been the last to learn the infamous orgies of his wife Messalina, and perhaps the last to suspect the murderous designs of his wife and niece Agrippina, yet by this time even he was not unaware that his life hung on a thread. Little was as yet known of Nero in the provinces, but it might have been anticipated, before the illusive promise of the early part of his reign, that the son of such a father and such a mother could only turn out to be the monster which his father expected, and which he *did* ultimately turn out to be. If St. Paul anticipated that the present condition of the government would perish with Claudius, the reigning Emperor, and that his successor would be the Man of Sin, his anticipation was fulfilled. If he further anticipated that this representative of lawless and already working opposition to God and His Christ would be destroyed by the second Advent, he was then absolutely right so far as its Judaic elements were concerned, and so far as the second Advent was foreshadowed by the destruction of Jerusalem; and his anticipations were only mistaken *on a point*

---

[1] Suet. *Calig.* 52, "*Armil'latus* in publicum processit" (Hitzig., *Gesch. Is.* 583). The anniversary of his death was observed as a festival (Derenbourg, *Palest.* 208). Others, however, connect *Armillus* with ἐρημόλαος, or "Romulus" (Hamburger, *Talm. Wörterb.* s. v.).

[2] Tac. *Ann.* xii. 64; Suet. *Claud.* 43; Dion Cass. lx. 34, 35.

respecting which all knowledge was confessedly withheld—only in that ante-dating of the personal second Advent which was common to him with all Christians in the first century of Christianity. Nor need it be surprising to any one that he should mingle Jewish and heathen elements in the colours with which he painted the coming Antichrist. In doing this he was in full accord with that which must be the case, and with the dim expectations of paganism no less than with Rabbinic notions respecting the rival of the Messiah.[1]—Further than this we cannot go; and since we cannot—since all attempts at nearer indication have failed—since by God's express and declared Providence we are as far as the Thessalonians could have been from any accurate conception as to the times and seasons of the coming of Christ—it is clear that we lose no *vital* truth of the Gospel by our inability to find the exact interpretation of an enigma which has been hitherto insoluble, and of which, had it been necessary for us, the exact explanation would not have been withheld.[2]

---

[1] It was but a few years after this time that Balbillus, the Ephesian Jew, who professed a knowledge of astrology, used the prophecies of the Old Testament to assure Nero that he should be King at Jerusalem.

[2] The Thessalonians, says St. Augustine, knew what St. Paul meant, we do not. "Nos qui nescimus quod illi sciebant pervenire labore ad id quod sensit Apostolus cupimus, nec valemus."

APPENDIX.

EXCURSUS II.—CHIEF UNCIAL MANUSCRIPTS

	Century.	Acts of the Apostles.	Romans.	1 Cor.	2 Cor.
ℵ, Sinaiticus, at Petersburg (Imp. Library)	IV.	All	All.	All.	All.
A, Alexandrinus, at British Museum	V.	All.	All.	All.	(i. 1 to iv. 13) (xii. 7 to end)
B, Vaticanus, at Rome (Vatican Library)	IV.	All.	All.	All.	All.
C, Ephraemi, at Paris (Imperial Library), a Palimpsest MS.	V.	(i. 2 to iv. 3) (v. 35—x. 43) (xiii. 1—xvi. 37) (xx. 10—xxi. 31) (xxii. 21—xxiii. 18) (xxiv. 15—xxvi. 19) (xxvii. 17—xxviii. 5)	(i. 1—ii. 5) (iii. 21—ix. 6) (x. 15—xi. 31) (xiii. 10—end)	(i. 1—vii. 18) (ix. 7—xiii. 8) (xv. 40—end)	(i. 2—x. 18)
D₁, Bezae, at Cambridge (Univ. Library)	VI.	(i. 1—viii. 29) (x. 14—xxi. 2) (xxi. 10—16) (xxi. 18—xxii. 10) (xxii. 20—29)	......	......	......
D₂, Claromontanus, Paris (Imp. Lib.)	VI.	......	(i. 7—end)	All.	All.
E₁, Laudianus, Oxford (Bodleian)	VI.	(i. 1—xxvi. 29) (xxviii. 26—end)	......	......	......
E₂, Sangermanensis, Petersburg (Imperial Lib.). A transcript of D₂, mutilated	X.	......	......	......	......
F₂, Augiensis, Trinity College, Cambridge	IX.	......	(iii. 19—to end)	(i. 1—iii. 3) (iii. 16—vi. 7) (vi. 16—end)	All.
F₁, Coislinianus, Paris	VII.	......	Some fragments of the Epistles found in		
G₃, Angelicus, Rome (August. Monks)	IX.	(viii. 10—end) Same as L₂. See below.	The *Epistles of St. Paul* in this MS. are known as L₂.		
G₃, Boernerianus, Dresden (Royal Library)	IX.	......	(i. 1—onward)	This is a sister MS. to F₂.	
H₂, Mutinensis, Modena (Grand Ducal Library)	IX.	(v. 28—ix. 39) (x. 19—xiii. 36) (xiv. 3—xxvii. 4)	......	......	......
H₃, Coislinianus (twelve leaves at Paris, two leaves at Petersburg)	VI.	......	......	(x. 22—29) (xi. 9—17)	......
I, Fragments, Palimpsests Tischendorfiana. They are seven fragments, at Petersburg.	V.—VII.	(ii. 6—17) (xxvi. 7—18) (xxviii. 8—17)	......	(xv. 53—xvi. 9)	......
K₂, Mosquensis, at Moscow	IX.	......	(i. 1—x. 15)	(i. 13—viii. 7) (viii. 12—end)	All.
L₂, Angelicus, Rome. Same as G₂.	IX.	(viii. 10—end) See G₂ above.	All.	All.	All.
M₂, Ruber. Fragments at Hamburg and at British Museum	X.	......	......	(xv. 52—end)	(i. 1—15) (x. 13—xii. 6)
P, Porphyrianus. Published by Tischendorf. Monumenta sacra inedita. (See Alford, vol. 2.)	IX.	(ii. 14—end)	......	(i. 1—xii. 23) (xiii. 6—xiv. 23) (xiv. 39—end)	All.

This Table has kindly been drawn up for

[The general reader should notice (i.) that D and E mean different MSS. for the Acts and for the (iii.) that F (Augiensis) is in most instances

THE UNCIALS.

OF THE ACTS, AND EPISTLES OF ST. PAUL.

...l.	Eph.	Philip.	Coloss.	1 Thess.	2 Thess.	1 Tim.	2 Tim.	Titus.	Philem.
All.	All.	All.	All.	All.	All.	All.	All.	All.	All.
All.	All.	All.	All.	All.	All.	All.	All.	All.	All.
All.	All.	All.	All.	All.	All.	......	......	......	......
(i. 11—end)	(ii. 18–iv. 17)	(i. 23–iii. 5)	(i. 3—end)	(i. 3—ii. 9)	......	(iii. 9–v. 20)	(i. 3—end)	(i. 4—end)	(3 to end)
......	......	......	......	......	......	......	......	......	......
All.	All.	All.	All.	All.	All.	All.	All.	All.	All.
......	......	......	......	......	......	......	......	......	......
......	......	......	......	......	......	......	......	......	......
All.	All.	All.	{(i. 1—ii. 1) (ii. 8—end)}	All.	All.	All.	All.	All.	(1—21)

marginal notes to the great Septuagint Octateuch known as Cod. Coislinianus I.

supplying the commencement of Romans, and other deficiencies. It is considerably mutilated.

......	......	......	......	......	......	......	......	......	......
{(i. 4—10) (ii. 9—14)}	......	......	......	......	......	(iii. 7—14)	......	{(i. 1) (i. 15—ii. 5) (iii. 13 to end)}	...
......	......	......	......	......	......	......	......	(i. 1—15)	......
All.	All.	All.	All.	All.	All.	All.	All.	All.	All.
All.	All.	All.	All.	All.	All.	All.	All.	All.	All.
......	......	......	......	......	......	......	......	......	......
All.	All.	All.	{(i.1—iii.16) (iv.8—end)}	(i. 1—iii. 5) (iv. 17—end)	All.	All.	All.	All.	All.

me by the Rev. J. S. Northcote.

Epistles (ii.) that E (Sangermanensis) is a copy of the third corrector of D (Claromontanus); almost identical with G (Boernerianus).]

APPENDIX.

EXCURSUS III. (p. 82).

THEOLOGY AND ANTINOMIES OF ST. PAUL.

I HAVE treated so fully of the main outlines of St. Paul's theology in the sketch of the Epistle to the Romans that I need not here enter upon it, but it may be convenient to the reader to see at one glance two of his own most pregnant summaries of it. These are Rom. iii. 21—26; Tit. iii. 3—7, for further explanation of which I must refer to pp. 208, *seq.* 536.

Rom. iii. 21—26: "But now apart from Law, God's righteousness has been manifested, being witnessed to by the Law and the Prophets—even God's righteousness (I say) by means of faith in Jesus Christ unto all and upon all believers; for there is no difference. For all sinned and are falling short of the glory of God, being made righteous freely by His grace, by the means of the redemption which is in Christ Jesus, whom God set forth as "a propitiary" by means of faith in His blood for the manifestation of His righteousness, because of the praetermission of past sins by the long-suffering of God—with a view (I say) to the manifestation of His righteousness in the present season, so that He may be righteous and the giver of righteousness to him who is of faith in Jesus."

Tit. iii. 3—7: "For we were once ourselves also foolish, disobedient, wandering slaves to various lusts and pleasures, living in malice and envy, hateful, hating one another. But when the kindness and the love to man of our Saviour God appeared, not by works of righteousness which we did, but according to His mercy He saved us by means of the laver of regeneration and renewal of the Holy Ghost, which He poured forth upon us richly by means of Jesus Christ our Saviour, that being justified by His grace we should become heirs of eternal life according to hope."

By "antinomies" I mean the apparent contradictoriness to human reason of divine facts. Such antinomies must arise when Reason seeks to know something of the absolute, stepping beyond the limits of experience.

Among the apparent antinomies left without any attempt—because there is no possibility—of their reconciliation to our finite reason in the writings of St. Paul, are—

1. Predestination (Absolute dependence).   Rom. ix. (as explaining the rejection of Israel from the objective and theological point of view).

    Free Will (Moral self-determination).   Rom. ix. 30—x. 21 (as explaining the rejection of Israel from the moral and anthropological point of view).

2. Sin through Adam's fall; Rom. v. 12—21.
Sin as inherent in the flesh; 1 Cor. xv. 50, *seq.*

3. Christ judging *all Christians* at His Advent; Rom. ii. 16; xiv. 10; 1 Cor. iii. 13; 2 Cor. v. 10.
God finally judging *all men* through Christ; 1 Cor. iv. 5 (xv. 24, 25).

4. Recompense for ALL according to works; Rom. ii. 6—10; 2 Cor. v. 10.
Free forgiveness of the redeemed; Rom. iv. 4; ix. 11; xi. 6.

5. Universal Restoration and Blessedness; Rom. viii. 19—23; xi. 30—36.
A twofold end; Rom. ii. 5—12. "The perishing;" 2 Cor. ii. 15, &c.

6. Necessity of human effort; 1 Cor. ix. 24. "So run that ye may obtain."
Ineffectualness of human effort; Rom. ix. 16, "It is not of him that willeth, nor of him that runneth."
The two are brought together in Phil. ii. 12, 13, "Work out your own salvation ... For it is God which worketh in you."

To these others might perhaps be added, but none of them causes, or need cause, any trouble to the Christian. On the one hand, we know that *omnia exeunt in mysterium*, and that we cannot think for five minutes on any subject connected with the spiritual life without reaching a point at which the wings of the soul beat in vain as against a wall of adamant. On the other hand, we must bear in mind that Paul almost created the language of Christian theology; that he often enshrines in a single word a whole world of ideas; and that he always refuses to pursue the great saving truths of religion into mere speculative extremes. If we cannot live as yet in the realms of perfect and universal light, we have at any rate a lamp which throws a circle of radiance around our daily steps.

"Lead thou me on. I do not ask to see
The distant scene; one step enough for me."

EXCURSUS IV. (p. 413).

DISTINCTIVE WORDS, KEY-NOTES, AND CHARACTERISTICS OF THE EPISTLES.

It may perhaps serve to call attention to the individuality of the Epistles if I endeavour to point out how some of them may be roughly characterised by leading words or conceptions.

I.—*The Eschatological Group.*

1 THESSALONIANS.—This Epistle is marked by the extreme sweetness of its tone. Its key-note is Hope. Its leading words, παρουσία, θλίψις. Its main theme is Consolation from the near hope of the Second Advent, iv. 17, 18, ἡμεῖς οἱ ζῶντες ἁρπαγησόμεθα, κ. τ. λ. παρακαλεῖτε ἀλλήλους ἐν τοῖς λόγοις τούτοις.[1]

2 THESSALONIANS.—The key-note is ii. 1, 2, μὴ ταχέως σαλευθῆναι ... ὡς ὅτι ἐνέστηκεν ἡ ἡμέρα τοῦ κυρίου. Peculiar doctrinal section on the Man of Sin.

II.—*The Anti-Judaic Group.*

1 CORINTHIANS.—Love and unity amid divergent opinions. Little details decided by great principles. Life *in* the world, but not *of* it.

2 CORINTHIANS.—The Apostle's *Apologia pro vitâ suâ*. The leading words of i.—vi. "tribulation" and "consolation." In viii.—end, the leading conception "boasting not on merits but in infirmities."

GALATIANS.—The Apostle's independent authority. Christian liberty from the yoke of the Law. Circumcision nothing, and uncircumcision nothing, but——

ROMANS.—The Universality of sin, and the Universality of grace (πᾶς a leading word). Justification by faith. This Epistle is the sum of St. Paul's theology, and Rom. i. 16, 17 is the sum of the Epistle.

III.—*The Christological or Anti-Gnostic Group.*

PHILIPPIANS.—Joy in sorrow. "Summa Epistolæ, *gaudeo, gaudete*" (Bengel).

COLOSSIANS.—Christ all in all. The Pleroma. Leading conception, ii. 6, ἐν αὐτῷ περιπατεῖτε. "Hic epistolae scopus est" (Bengel).

PHILEMON.—Can a Christian master treat a brother as a slave? Leading conception, 12, προσλαβοῦ αὐτόν.

---

[1] "Habet haec epistola meram quandam dulcedinem, quae lectori dulcibus affectibus non assueto minus sapit quam ceterae severitate quadam palatum stringentes" (Bengel). "Im Ganzer ist es ein Trostbrief" (Hausrath, p. 290).

EPHESIANS.—Christ in His Church. The Epistle of the Ascension. The leading words are χάρις, τὰ ἐπουράνια, ἐν Χριστῷ.

IV.—The Pastoral Group.

1 TIMOTHY
TITUS
{ Manuals of the Christian pastor's dealing with the faithful and with false teachers. Leading conceptions, *sobriety* of conduct, *soundness* of faith.

2 TIMOTHY.—Last words. Be brave and faithful, as I have tried to be. Come quickly, come before winter; come before I die. iv. 6, ἐγὼ γὰρ ἤδη σπένδομαι.

EXCURSUS V. (p. 477).

LETTER OF PLINY TO SABINIANUS ON BEHALF OF AN OFFENDING FREEDMAN.

"C. Plinius Sabiniano suo S.

"Libertus tuus, cui succensere te dixeras, venit ad me advolutusque pedibus meis tanquam tuis haesit. Flevit multum, multum rogavit, multum etiam tacuit, in summa fecit mihi fidem paenitentiae. Vere credo emendatum, quia deliquisse se sentit. Irasceris, scio, et irasceris merito, id quoque scio: sed tunc praecipua mansuetudinis laus, cum irae caussa iustissima est. Amasti hominem et, spero, amabis: interim sufficit ut exorari te sinas. Licebit rursus irasci, si meruerit, quod exoratus excusatius facies. Remitte aliquid adulescentiae ipsius, remitte lacrimis, remitte indulgentiae tuae: ne torseris illum, ne torseris etiam te. Torqueris enim, cum tam lenis irasceris. Vereor ne videar non rogare, sed cogere, si precibus eius meas iunxero. Jungam tamen tanto plenius et effusius, quanto ipsum acrius severiusque corripui, districte minatus numquam me postea rogaturum. Hoc illi, quem terreri oportebat; tibi non idem. Nam fortasse iterum rogabo, impetrabo iterum: sit modo tale ut rogare me, ut praestare te deceat. Vale!"

TRANSLATION.

"C. Plinius to his Sabinianus, greeting :—

"Your freedman, with whom, as you had told me, you were vexed, came to me, and, flinging himself at my feet, clung to them as though they had been yours. He wept much, entreated much, yet at the same time left much unsaid, and, in short, convinced me that he was sincerely sorry. I believe that he is really reformed, because he is conscious of his delinquency. You are angry, I know; justly angry, that too I know; but gentleness is most praiseworthy exactly where anger is most justifiable. You loved the poor fellow, and I hope will love him again; meanwhile, it is enough to yield to intercession. Should he ever deserve it you may be angry again, and all the more excusably by yielding now. Make some allowance for his youth, for his tears, for your own kindly disposition. Do not torture him, lest you torture yourself as well, for it is a torture to you when one of your kindly nature is angry. I fear you will think that I am not asking but forcing you if I join my prayers to his; I will, however, do so, and all the more fully and unreservedly in proportion to the sharpness and severity with which I took him to task, sternly threatening that I would never say a word for him again. *That* I said to him because he needed to be well frightened; but I do not say it to you, for perhaps I shall say a word for him again, and again gain my point; provided only my request be such as it becomes me to ask and you to grant. Farewell!"

EXCURSUS VI. (I. 311, II. 352).

THE HERODS IN THE ACTS.

IF there be sufficient ground for the plausible conjecture which identifies Agrippa I. and Cypros with the king and queen who figure in the two following anecdotes of the Talmud, we shall see that the part he had to play was not always an easy one, and even led to serious complications.

i. The Talmud relates that on one occasion, at a festival, a lizard was found in the royal kitchen. It appeared to be dead, and if so the whole banquet would have become ceremonially unclean. The king referred the question to the queen, and the queen to Rabban Gamaliel. He asked whether it had been found in a warm or a cold place. "In a warm place," they said. "Then pour cold water over it." They did so. The lizard revived, and the banquet was pronounced clean. So that, the writer complacently adds, the fortune of the entire festival depended ultimately on Rabban Gamaliel.[1]

ii. The other story is more serious. It appears that at a certain

---

[1] *Pesachim*, f. 88, 2.

Passover the king and queen were informed by their attendants that two kinds of victims—a lamb and a kid—either of which was legal—had been killed for them, and they were in doubt as to which of the two was to be regarded as preferable. The king, who considered that the kid was preferable, and was less devoted to the Pharisees than his wife, sent to ask the high priest Issachar of Kephar-Barchaï, thinking that since he daily sacrificed victims, he would be sure to know. Issachar, who was of the same haughty, violent, luxurious temperament as all the numerous Sadducean high priests of the day, made a most contemptuous gesture in the king's face, and said that, if the kid was preferable, the lamb would not have been ordained for use in the daily sacrifice. Indignant at his rudeness, the king ordered his right hand to be cut off. Issachar, however, bribed the executioner, and got him to cut off the left hand. The king, on discovering the fraud, had the right hand cut off also.[1] It is thus that the story runs in the *Pesachim*, and further on it is said that when the doubt arose the king sent to the queen, and the queen to the Rabban Gamaliel, who gave the perfectly sensible answer that as either victim was legal, and as the king and queen had been perfectly indifferent in giving the order for the Paschal victims to be slain, they could eat of the one which had been first killed.[2]

As this story was not very creditable to Agrippa I., we find a sufficient reason for the silence of Josephus in passing over the name of Issachar in his notices of the High Priests.[3] His was not a name which could have sounded very agreeable in the ears of Agrippa II. The elder Agrippa seems to have been tempted in this instance into a violence which was not unnatural in one who had lived in the court of Tiberius, but which was a rude interruption of his plan of pleasing the priestly party, while Cypros took the Pharisees under her special patronage. Issachar seems to have come between Theophilus, son of Hanan, and Simon, son of Kanthera the Boethusian.[4] Whatever may have been the tendencies of Cypros, and his own proclivities, it was important to Agrippa that he should retain the support of the sacerdotal aristocrats; and they were well pleased to enjoy, in rapid succession, and as the appanage of half-a-dozen families, the burdensome dignity of Aaron's successor.

[1] *Pesachim*, f. 57, 1. In *Kerithôth*, f. 28, 2, it is told with some variations, and the king is called Jannæus. It is, however, a fashion of the Talmud to give this name to Asmonæan kings (Derenbourg, p. 211). May this wild story have been suggested by the indignation of the Jews against the first High Priest who wore gloves to prevent his hands from being soiled?

[2] *Id.* 88 *b.* When I was present at the Samaritan passover on the summit of Mount Gerizim, six lambs and one kid were sacrificed.

[3] *Antt.* xx. 10, 5.   [4] Herod the Great had married a daughter of Boethus.

The Pharisees, on the other hand, recounted with pleasure the fact that no sooner had Agrippa arrived at Jerusalem than he caused to be suspended on the columns of the *oulam*, or Temple portico, the chain of massive gold which he had received from Gaius as an indemnification for his captivity;[1] that he was most munificent in his presents to the nation; that he was a daily attendant at the Temple sacrifice; that he had called the attention of the Legate Petronius to the decrees of Claudius in favour of Jewish privileges, and had thereby procured the reprimand and punishment of the inhabitants of Dor,[2] who had insulted the Jews by erecting in their synagogue a statue of the emperor. They had also told with applause that he carried his basket of first-fruits to the Temple like any ordinary Israelite;[3] and that although every one had to give way in the streets to the king and his suite, yet Agrippa always yielded the right of road to a marriage or funeral procession.[4] There were two stories on which they dwelt with peculiar pleasure. One was that on a single day—perhaps that of his arrival at Jerusalem—he offered a thousand holocausts, and that when they had been offered, a poor man came with two pigeons. The priest refused this sacrifice, on the pretext that on that day he had been bidden to offer none but royal victims; but he yielded to the poor man's earnest solicitation on being told that the pigeons were brought in fulfilment of a vow that he would daily offer half the produce of his day's work; and Agrippa warmly approved of this disobedience to his orders.[5] On another occasion, at the Feast of Tabernacles, he received from the hands of the high priest the roll of the Law, and without seating himself, read the Lesson for the day, which was Deuteronomy xvii. 14–20. When he came to the words, "Thou mayest not set a stranger over thee which is not thy brother," the thought of his own Idumæan origin flashed across his mind, and he burst into tears. But the cry arose on all sides, "Fear not, Agrippa; thou art our brother, thou art our brother."[6]

[1] *Middôth*, iii. 7. Josephus (*Antt.* xix. 6, § 1) says that it was hung "over the treasury."

[2] Jos. *Antt.* xix. 6, § 3.

[3] *Bikkurim*, iii. 4; Derenbourg, p. 217.

[4] *Bab. Kethubhôth*, f. 17, 1; Munk, *Palest.* p. 571.

[5] *Vayyikra-rabba*, iii.

[6] *Sota*, f. 41, 1, 2. But, as Derenbourg points out, there were not wanting some stern Rabbis who unhesitatingly condemned this "flattery of the king." (See, too, Jost, *Gesch. d. Judenthums*, 420. It is not certain that the anecdote may not refer to Agrippa II.) In continuation of the story about Babha Ben Buta's advice to Herod the Great to rebuild the Temple, the Talmud adds that the Romans were by no means willing, but that the task was half done before the return of the messenger, who had been purposely told to spend three years in his mission.

THE HERODS IN THE ACTS.

There were other tendencies which would win for Agrippa the approval of the people no less than that of the Pharisees. Such, for instance, were his early abolition of a house-tax in Jerusalem, which had been felt to be particularly burdensome; and his construction of a new quarter of the Holy City, which was called Bezetha.[1] The Rabbis, indeed, refused to accord to the new district the sanctity of the old, because it had not been inaugurated by the presence of a king, a prophet, the Urim and Thummim, a Sanhedrin of seventy-one, two processions, and a choir.[2] It is far from improbable that this addition to Jerusalem was mainly intended to strengthen its natural defences, and that Agrippa had formed the secret intention of making himself independent of Rome. If so, his plans were thwarted by the watchful jealousy of Vibius Marsus,[3] who had succeeded Petronius as Praefect of Syria. He wrote and informed the Emperor of the suspicious proceedings of Agrippa, and an Imperial rescript commanded the suspension of these building operations. Petronius had been on terms of intimacy with Agrippa, but Marsus distrusted and bitterly offended him.[4] After the completion of the magnificent theatre, and other buildings which he had presented to Berytus, he was visited by a number of neighbouring princes—Antiochus, King of Commagene, Sampsigeramus of Emesa, Cotys of Lesser Armenia, Polemo of Pontus, and his brother Herod, King of Chalcis. It is probable that these royal visits were not of a purely complimentary character, but may have been the nucleus of a plot against the Roman power. If so, their machinations were scattered to the winds by the contemptuous energy of the Praefect, who felt a truly Roman indifference for the gilded impotence of these Oriental vassals. As the gathering took place at Tiberias, he went thither, and Agrippa, in whose character, as in that of all his family, there was a large vein of ostentation,[5] went seven furlongs out of the city to meet

---

Among other things the Romans said, "If thou hast succeeded by violence at home, we have the genealogy here. *Thou art neither a king, nor the son of a king, but a liberated slave*" (*Babha Bathra*, f. 3, 2).

[1] Josephus (*B. J.* v. 4, § 2) says that this word means "New City"; but elsewhere (*Antt.* xii. 10, § 2; xi. 1) he writes it *Bêth-Zêtho*, or "House of Olive-trees." In the Syriac version of Acts i, 12, ἐλαιών, *olive-yard*, is rendered *Bêth-Zêtho*; and in *B. J.* ii. 19, § 4, Josephus seems to draw a distinction between Bezetha and the New City (Munk, *Palest.*, p. 45). Derenbourg, however, holds that Bezetha is a transliteration of the Chaldaic *Beth Hadta*, and that Josephus is right (*Palest.*, p. 218).

[2] *Jer. Sanhedr.* i. 3; Jos. *B. J.* v. 4, § 2.

[3] Jos. *B. J.* ii. 11, § 6.

[4] Jos. *Antt.* xix. 6, § 2.

[5] Thus on a coin, engraved by Akerman, *Numism. Illustr.*, he is called βασιλεὺς μέγας.

him, with the five other kings in his chariot. Marsus did not like the look of this combination, and sent his servants to the kings with the cool order that they were all to make the best of their way at once to their respective homes. It was in consequence of this deliberate insult that, after the death of Agrippa, Claudius, in respect to his memory, and in consequence of a request which he had received from him, displaced Marsus, and sent C. Cassius Longinus in his place.[1]

AGRIPPA II. AND BERENICE.

Not a spark of true patriotism seems ever to have been kindled in the breast of Agrippa II. He was as complete a renegade as his friend Josephus,[2] but without his versatility and genius. He had passed all his early years in the poisoned atmosphere of such courts as those of Gaius and Claudius, and was now on excellent terms with Nero. The mere fact that he should have been a favourite with the Messallinas, and Agrippinas, and Poppæas, of a palace rife with the basest intrigues, is sufficient to condemn him. His appointments to the High-priesthood were as bad as those of his predecessors, and he incurred the displeasure of the Jews by the arbitrary rapidity of the constant changes which he made. Almost the only specific event which marked his period of royalty was a dispute about a view from a window. In a thoroughly unpatriotic and irreverent spirit he had built a banquet-hall in Herod's palace at Jerusalem, which overlooked the Temple courts. It was designed to serve the double purpose of gratifying the indolent curiosity of his guests as they lay at table, by giving them the spectacle of the Temple worship in its most sacred details, and also of maintaining a certain espionage over the movements of the worshippers, which would at any moment enable him to give notice to the Roman soldiers if he wished them to interfere. Indignant at this instance of contemptible curiosity and contemptible treachery, the Jews built up a counter wall to exclude his view. Agrippa, powerless to do anything himself, invoked the aid of the Procurator. The wall of the Jews excluded not only the view of Agrippa, but also that of the commandant in the tower of Antonia, and Festus ordered them to pull it down. The Jews resisted this demand with their usual determined fury, and Festus so far gave way that he allowed them to send an embassy to Rome to await the decision of the Cæsar. The Jews sent Ishmael Ben Phabi the high priest, Helkias the treasurer, and other

[1] Jos. *Antt.* xix. 8, § 1.
[2] For instance, he changed the name of Cæsarea Philippi to Neronias; stripped Judæa to ornament Berytus; and even stooped to take the surname *Marcus*, which is found on one of his coins (Jos. *Antt.* xx. 9, § 4, Eckhel, *Doct. Num. Vet.* iii. 498).

distinguished ambassadors, and astutely gaining the ear of Poppæa—who is believed to have been a proselyte, but if so, was a proselyte of whom the Jews ought to have been heartily ashamed—obtained a decision in their favour. Women like Poppæa, pantomimists like Aliturus— such were in these days the defenders of the Temple for the Jews against their hybrid kings! We hear little more of Agrippa II. till the breaking out of the war which ended in the destruction of Jerusalem. As might have been expected, he, like Josephus, like Tiberius Alexander, and other eminent renegades, was found in the ranks of the Roman invaders, waging war on the Holy City. He probably saw the Temple sink amid its consuming fires. Like Josephus he may have watched from a Roman window the gorgeous procession in which the victor paraded the sacred spoils of the Temple, while the wretched captives of his countrymen—

"Swelled, slow-pacing by the car's tall side,
The Stoic tyrant's philosophic pride."

After that he fell into merited obscurity, and ended a frivolous life by a dishonoured old age.

Such was the prince who came to salute Festus, and he was accompanied by his sister, who was unhappily notorious even among the too notorious ladies of rank in that evil time. Berenice was the Lucrezia Borgia of the Herodian family. She was beautiful, like all the princesses of her house. Before the age of sixteen she had been married to her uncle Herod of Chalcis, and being left a widow before she was twenty, went to live in Rome with her equally youthful brother. Her beauty, her rank, the splendour of her jewels, the interest and curiosity attaching to her race and her house, made her a prominent figure in the society of the capital; and a diamond, however lustrous and valuable, was enhanced in price if it was known that it had once sparkled on the finger of Berenice, and had been a present to her from her brother.[1] The relations between the two gave rise to the darkest rumours, which gained credence, because there was nothing to contradict them in the bearing or character of the defamed persons. So rife indeed did these stories become, that Berenice looked out for a new marriage. She contracted an alliance with Polemo II., King of Cilicia, insisting, however, that he should save her from any violation of the Jewish law by submitting to the rite of circumcision.[2] Circumcision, not conversion,

[1] "Adamas nottissimus, et Berenices
In digito factus pretiosior; hunc dedit olim
Barbarus incestae, dedit hunc Agrippa sorori."
Juv. Sat. vi. 156; Jos. Antt. xx. 6, 3.

[2] Jos. Antt. xx. 7, 3.

was all that she required. So true is the charge brought alike by St. Paul in his Epistles, and by the writers of the Talmud, that the reason why the Jews insisted upon circumcision was only that they might have whereof to glory in the flesh.[1] The lowering of the Gentile fasces in token of external respect was all that they cared for, and when that was done, the Ger might go his own vile way—not improbably to Gehenna.[2] Circumcision to them was greater than all affirmative precepts, and was therefore exalted above love to God or love to our neighbour.[3] No doubt it cost Polemo something to accept concision, in order to satisfy the orthodox scrupulosity of an abandoned Jewess; but her wealth was an inducement too powerful to resist. It was hardly likely that such a marriage could last. It was broken off very rapidly by the elopement of Berenice, after which Polemo immediately repudiated every shadow and semblance of allegiance to the Jewish religion, and Berenice returned to the house of her brother, until her well-preserved but elderly beauty, added to the munificence of her presents, first won the old Vespasian, and then his son Titus.[4] The conqueror of Judæa was so infatuated by his love for its dishonoured princess that he took her with him to Rome, and seriously contemplated making her a partner of his imperial throne.[5] But this was more than the Romans could stand, far gone as they were in servitude and adulation. The murmurs which the rumoured match stirred up were so wrathful in their indignation, that Titus saw how unsafe it would be to wed a Jewess whose name had been dragged through the worst infamy. He dismissed her—*invitus invitam*—and we hear of her no more. Thus in the fifth generation did the sun of the Herodian house set in obscure darkness, as it had dawned in blood; and with it set also the older and purer splendour of the Asmonæan princes. They had mingled the honourable blood of Judas the Maccabee with that of Idumæan adventurers, and the inheritors of the grandest traditions of Jewish patriotism were involved in a common extinction with the representatives of the basest intrigues of Jewish degradation.

[1] Gal. vi. 13. It was, of course, a Judaic triumph to make a king not only a *Ger Thoshabh*, or a proselyte of the gate, but even a *Ger hatsedek*, "a proselyte of righteousness," or "of the Covenant." These latter were despised alike by Jews and Gentiles (Suet. *Claud*. 25; *Domit*. 12; *Yebhamoth*, xlvii. 4; see Wetstein on Matt. xxiii. 15).

[2] See McCaul, *Old Paths*, pp. 63 *seqq*.

[3] *Nedarim*, f. 32, c. 2.

[4] Jos. *Antt*. xx. 7, 3.

[5] Suet. *Tit*. 7; Tac. *H*. ii. 81.

EXCURSUS VII. (p. 493).

PHRASEOLOGY AND DOCTRINES OF THE EPISTLE TO THE EPHESIANS.

IT is admitted that there are some new and rare expressions in this Epistle;[1] but they are sufficiently accounted for by the idiosyncrasy of the writer, and the peculiarity of the subjects with which he had to deal. It is monstrous to assume that, in the case of one so fresh and eager as St. Paul, the vocabulary would not widely vary in writings extending over nearly twenty years, and written under every possible variety of circumstances, to very different communities, and in consequence of very different controversies. The wide range of dissimilarity in thought and expression between Epistles of *admitted* authenticity ought sufficiently to demonstrate the futility of overlooking broad probabilities and almost universal testimony, because of peculiarities of which many are only discoverable by a minute analysis. It must be remembered that at this period the phraseology of Christianity was still in a plastic, it might almost be said in a fluid, condition. No Apostle, no writer of any kind, contributed one tithe so much to its ultimate cohesion and rigidity as St. Paul. Are we then to reject this Epistle, and that to the Colossians, on grounds so flimsy as the fact that in them for the first time he speaks of the remission (ἄφεσις, Eph. i. 7 ; Col. i. 14) instead of the prætermission (πάρεσις, Rom. iii. 25) of sins ; or that, writing to a Church predominantly Gentile, he says "Greeks and Jews" (Col. iii. 11) instead of "Jews and Greeks" (Rom. i. 16, &c.); or that he uses the word "Church" in a more abstract and generic sense than in his former writings ; or that he uses the rhetorical expression that the Gospel has been preached in all the world (Col. i. 6, 23) ? By a similar mode of reasoning it would be possible to prove in the case of almost every voluminous author in the world that half the works attributed to him have been written by some one else. Such arguments only encumber with useless *débris* the field of criticism. There is indeed one very unusual expression, the peculiarity of which has been freely admitted by all fair controversialists. It is the remark that the mystery of Christ is now revealed "to the holy Apostles and Prophets" (iii. 5). The Prophets (as in ii. 20 ; iv. 11) are doubtless those of the New Testament —those who had received from the Spirit His special gifts of illumination ; but the epithet is unexpected. It can only be accounted for by the general dignity and fulness (the σεμνότης) of the style in which the

---

[1] Such ἅπαξ λεγόμενα, or unusual expressions, as τὰ ἐπουράνια, κοσμοκράτορες πολυποίκιλος, περιποίησις, ἀφθαρσία, διάβολος.

Epistle is written; and the epithet, if genuine, is, it need hardly be said, official and impersonal.

It would be much more to the purpose if the adverse critics could produce even one decided instance of un-Pauline theology. The demonology of the Epistle is identical with that of Paul's Rabbinic training.[1] The doctrine of original sin, even if it were by any means necessarily deducible from Eph. ii. 3—which is not the case, since the word φύσει is not identical with "by birth"—is quite as clearly involved in the Epistles to the Romans and Galatians. The descent of Christ into Hades is not necessarily implied in iv. 8; and even if it were, the fact that St. Paul has not elsewhere alluded to it furnishes no shadow of a proof that he did not hold it. The method of quoting Scripture is that of all Jewish writers in the age of Paul, and the reminiscences of the Old Testament in iv. 8 and v. 14 (if the latter be a reminiscence) are scarcely more purely verbal than others which occur in the Epistles of which no doubt has ever been entertained. On the other hand, it is frankly admitted that in all *essential* particulars the views of the Epistle are distinctly Pauline. The relations of Christianity to Judaism; the universality of human corruption through sin; the merging of heathenism and Judaism in the higher unity of Christianity; the prominence given to faith and love; the unconditional freedom of grace; the unserviceableness and yet the moral necessity of good works; are in absolute accordance with the most fundamental conceptions of St. Paul's acknowledged writings. If some of these great truths of theology here receive a richer, more mature, and more original development, this is only what we should expect from the power of a mind which never ceased to grow in grace and wisdom, and which regarded growth in grace and wisdom as the natural privilege of a Christian soul. On the other hand, we might well be amazed if the first hundred years after the death of Christ produced a totally unknown writer who, assuming the name of Paul, treats the mystery which it was given him to reveal with a masterly power which the Apostle himself rarely equalled, and most certainly never surpassed. Let any one study the remains of the Apostolic Fathers, and he may well be surprised at the facility with which writers of the Tübingen school, and their successors, assume the existence of Pauls who lived unheard of and died unknown, though they were intellectually and spiritually the equals, if not the superiors, of St. Paul himself! In no single Epistle is the point of view so clear, so supreme, so final—in no other Epistle of the Homologoumena is the doctrine so obviously the outcome and issue of truths which before had been less fully

---

[1] *Thacksiphis*—an association of demons, and *Isbalgamith* (see *Berachôth*, f. 51, 1).

and profoundly enunciated—so undeniably the full consummate flower from germs of which we have, as it were, witnessed the planting. At supreme epochs of human enlightenment whole centuries of thought seem to separate the writings of a few years. The questions which occupy the Apostle in the Thessalonians and Galatians seem to lie indefinitely far behind the goal which his thoughts have now attained. In earlier Epistles he was occupied in maintaining the freedom of the Gentiles from the tyrannous narrowness of Jewish sacerdotalism; here, on the other hand, he is dwelling on the predestined grandeur of the equal and universal Church. In the Epistles to the Romans and the Galatians he has founded the claims of Christianity on "a philosophy of the history of religion," by showing that Christ is the Second Adam, and the promised seed of Abraham; here he contemplates a scheme predestined before the ages of earth began, and running through them as an increasing purpose, so that æon after æon revealed new forms and hues of the richly-varied wisdom, and the Gentiles (καὶ ὑμεῖς, i. 13) as well as the Jews are included in the predestined election (ἐκληρώθημεν, προορισθέντες, i. 11) to the purchased possession (περιποίησις, 14). And not to exhaust, which would be indeed impossible, the manifold aspects of this so-called "colourless" Epistle, the manner in which it expresses the conception of the quickening of spiritual death by union with the Risen Christ (ii. 1—6); the present realisation, the immanent consciousness of communion with God; the all-pervading supremacy of God in Christ; the importance of pure spiritual knowledge; the dignity given to the Church as the house (ii. 20—22), the body (iv. 12—16) and the bride (v. 25—27) of Christ,—all mark it out as the most sublime, the most profound, and, if I may use the expression, the most advanced and final utterance of that mystery of the Gospel which it was given to St. Paul for the first time to proclaim in all its fulness to the Gentile world.[1] It is not surprising that when these truths had once found utterance they should have had their influence on the teachings of the author of the Epistle to the Hebrews and upon St. Peter and St. John; nor is this any ground whatever, but rather the reverse, for looking with suspicion on the authenticity of the Epistle.[2]

[1] Entirely as I disagree with Pfleiderer, I have received great help from his *Paulinismus* (E. T. ii. 162—193) in the study of this Epistle.
[2] See 1 Pet. i. 14 (Eph. iv. 14); 1 Pet. i. 20 (Eph. i. 4); 1 Pet. i. 7 (Eph. i. 6); i. 5 (Eph. iii. 5); ii. 9 (Eph. i. 14); i. 3 (Eph. i. 17); ii. 11 (Eph. ii. 3); ii. 7 (Eph. iii. 6); v. 10 (Eph. iv. 2), &c. See Weiss, *Petrinisch. Lehrbegr.* 434.

EXCURSUS VIII (p. 513).

EVIDENCE AS TO THE LIBERATION OF ST. PAUL.

THE chief passages on the remaining life of St. Paul which have much historic importance are the following :—

I. Clemens Romanus, possibly a personal friend and fellow-worker of St. Paul, if he be the Clement mentioned in Phil. iv. 3,[1] but certainly a Bishop of Rome, and a writer of the first century, says that :—

"Because of envy, Paul also obtained the prize of endurance, having seven times borne chains, having been exiled, and having been stoned. After he had preached the Gospel both in the East and in the West, he won the noble renown of his faith, having taught righteousness to the whole world, and having come to the limit of the West, and borne witness[2] before the rulers. Thus he was freed from the world, and went into the holy place, having shown himself a pre-eminent example of endurance."[3]

II. The fragment of the Muratorian Canon (about A.D. 170), though obscure and corrupt, and only capable of uncertain conjectural emendation and interpretation, yet seems on the whole to imply the fact of "Paul's setting forth from the city on his way to Spain."[4]

III. Eusebius, in the fourth century, says :—

"Then, after his defence, there is a tradition that the Apostle again set forth to the ministry of his preaching, and having a second time entered the same city [Rome], was perfected by his martyrdom before him [Nero]."[5]

---

[1] We can only say that this is an ancient and not impossible tradition (see Lightfoot, *Philippians*, pp. 166—169).

[2] The word at this period did not *necessarily* mean "suffered martyrdom," but probably connoted it.

[3] Διὰ ζῆλον [καὶ ὁ] Παῦλος ὑπομονῆς βραβεῖον ὑπέσχεν, ἑπτάκις δεσμὰ φορέσας, φυγαδευθείς, λιθασθείς, κῆρυξ γενόμενος ἔν τε τῇ ἀνατολῇ καὶ [τῇ] δύσει, τὸ γενναῖον τῆς πίστεως αὐτοῦ κλέος ἔλαβεν, δικαιοσύνην διδάξας ὅλῳ τῷ κόσμῳ καὶ ἐπὶ τὸ τέρμα τῆς δύσεως ἐλθών, καὶ μαρτυρήσας ἐπὶ τῶν ἡγουμένων οὕτως ἀπηλλάγη τοῦ κόσμου καὶ εἰς τὸν ἅγιον τόπον ἐπορεύθη, ὑπομονῆς γενόμενος μέγιστος ὑπογραμμός.—*Ep*. 1 *ad Cor*. 5 (see Lightfoot, *Epistles of Clement*, pp. 46—52).

[4] "Lucas obtime Theophile comprindit quia sub praesentia ejus singula gerebantur, sicuti et semote passionem Petri evidenter declarat, sed profectionem Pauli ab urbe ad Spaniam proficiscentis . . . ."

[5] τότε μὲν οὖν ἀπολογησάμενον, αὖθις ἐπὶ τὴν τοῦ κηρύγματος διακονίαν λόγος ἔχει στείλασθαι τὸν ἀπόστολον, δεύτερον δ' ἐπιβάντα τῇ αὐτῇ πόλει τῷ κατ' αὐτὸν (Νέρωνα) τελειωθῆναι μαρτυρίῳ (Euseb. *H. E.* ii. 22, 25). He quotes Dionysius of Corinth to show that Peter and Paul had both been at Rome (*id. ib.* 25), which is also stated by Ignatius (*ad Rom.* iv.).

IV. Chrysostom (died A.D. 407) says :—

"After he had been in Rome, he again went into Spain. But whether he thence returned into those regions [the East] we do not know."[1]

V. St. Jerome (died A.D. 420) says that "Paul was dismissed by Nero, that he might preach Christ's Gospel also in the regions of the West."[2]

I take no notice of the inscription supposed to have been found in Spain (Gruter, pp. 238, 9), which gratefully records that Nero has purged the province of brigands, and of the votaries of a new superstition, because even on the assumption that it is genuine it has no necessary bearing on the question. Nor does any other writer of the least authority make any important contribution to the question, since it cannot be regarded as adding one iota of probability to the decision to quote the general assertions of Cyril of Jerusalem and Theodoret that St. Paul visited Spain; nor can it be taken as a counter-evidence that Origen does not mention Spain when he remarks 'that he carried the Gospel from Jerusalem to Illyricum, and was afterwards martyred in Rome in the time of Nero.' Even as late as the fourth century, no writer ventures to do more than allude distantly to the supposed fact in a manner which shows that not a single detail on the subject existed, and that tradition had nothing tangible to add to the data furnished by the New Testament, or the inferences to which it led. On the other hand, the testimony of the pseudo-Dionysius (A.D. 170) that St. Peter and St. Paul, after founding the Church of Corinth, went to Italy—apparently together (ὁμόσε)—and were there martyred about the same time, is, so far as it goes, somewhat unfavourable to the Spanish journey, and at any rate proves that even in the second century tradition had buried its ignorance in the shifting sand of erroneous generalities.

If we be asked what is the *historic value* of this evidence, we must answer that it is very small indeed. The testimony of Clement, assuming it to be genuine, would be important from his early date if it were not so entirely vague. It is a purely rhetorical passage, in which it seems not impossible that he means to compare St. Paul to the sun rising in the east and setting in the west. The expression that "he taught righteousness to the whole world" shows that we are here dealing with enthusiastic phrases rather than rigid facts. The expression

---

[1] Μετὰ τὸ γενέσθαι ἐν Ῥώμῃ πάλιν εἰς τὴν Σπανίαν ἀπῆλθεν εἰ δὲ ἐκεῖθεν πάλιν εἰς ταῦτα τὰ μέρη οὐκ ἴσμεν (Chrys. *ad* 2 *Tim.* iv. 20).

[2] "Sciendum est. . . . Paulum a Nerone dimissum ut evangelium Christi in occidentis quoque partibus praedicaret" (Jer., *Catal. Scrip.*). See also Tert. *Scorp.* 15, *De Praescr.* 36; Lactant. *De Mort. Persec.* 2.

"having *come* to the limit of the West" is unfavourable to a Spanish journey. "The limit of the West," though undoubtedly it would mean Spain to an author who was writing from Rome, if he were speaking in plain and lucid prose, has not necessarily any such meaning in a glowing comparison, least of all on the hypothesis that the native place of the writer was Philippi. If, however, Spain is intended, and if the word "bearing witness" (μαρτυρήσας) means martyrdom, then the author, taken *literally*, would imply that St. Paul perished in Spain. The argument that "before the rulers" must be a reference to Helius and Polycletus, or Tigellinus and Nymphidius Sabinus, or two other presidents left to act as regents during Nero's absence in Greece, is a mere gossamer thread of attenuated inference. The authority of St. Clement, then, must be set aside as too uncertain to be of decisive value.[1]

Nor is the sentence in the second-century Canon discovered by Muratori at Milan of any great value. The verb which is essential to the meaning has to be supplied, and it is even possible that the writer may have intended to quote Luke's silence as to any Spanish journey to prove that the tradition respecting it—which would have been naturally suggested by Rom. xv. 24—had no authority in its favour.

Eusebius, indeed, is more explicit, but, on the one hand, he lived so late that his testimony, unless supported by reference to more ancient authorities, is of no importance; and on the other hand, he is so far from following his usual habit of quoting any authority for his assertion, that he distinctly ascribes it to tradition. He merely observes that "it is said," and then proceeds to support the probability of this tradition by an extraordinary misconception of 2 Tim. iv. 16, 17, in which he founds an argument for the Apostle's second imprisonment on the grounds that he spoke of deliverance from the first when he said, "I was saved from the mouth of the lion." His testimony is rendered the more worthless because in his *Chronicon* he misdates by nearly ten years the time of the first imprisonment, and his erroneous inference from 2 Tim. seems to show that the floating rumour was founded on a mere hypothesis suggested by the Epistles themselves.[2] The real proofs of St. Paul's liberation are, as we have seen, of a different character

---

[1] See however Döllinger, *First Age*, 78, *seq.*; Westcott, *Hist. of Canon*, p. 479; and Lightfoot, *Ep. of Clement*, p. 508, who quotes Strabo, ii. 1, Vell. Paterc. i. 2, to show that Spain is probably meant.

[2] He makes Paul arrive at Rome A.D. 55.

EXCURSUS IX. (p. 514).

THE GENUINENESS OF THE PASTORAL EPISTLES.

As our knowledge of the life of St. Paul, after his first imprisonment, depends entirely on the decision as to the authenticity of the Pastoral Epistles, I will here briefly examine the evidences.

I. Turning first to the external evidence in their favour, we find an almost indisputable allusion to the First Epistle to Timothy in Clement of Rome.[1] That they were universally accepted by the Church in the second century is certain, since they are found in the Peshito Syriac, mentioned in the Muratorian Canon, and quoted by Ignatius, Polycarp, Hegesippus, Athenagoras, Irenæus, Clemens of Alexandria, Theophilus of Antioch, and perhaps by Justin Martyr. After the second century the testimonies are unhesitating and unbroken, and Eusebius, in the fourth century, reckons them among the homologomena or acknowledged writings of St. Paul. With the exception of Marcion, and Tatian, who rejected the two Epistles to Timothy, there seems to have been no doubt as to their genuineness from the first century down to the days of Schmidt and Schleiermacher. On what grounds Marcion rejected them we are not informed. It is possible that Baur may be right in the supposition that he was not aware of their existence.[2] But this would be no decisive argument against them, since the preservation and dissemination of purely private letters, addressed to single persons, must have been much more precarious and slow than that of letters addressed to entire Churches. But in such a case Marcion's authority is of small value. He dealt with the Scriptures on purely subjective grounds. His rejection of the Old Testament, and of all the New Testament except ten Epistles of St. Paul, and a mutilated Gospel of St. Luke, shows that he made no sort of scruple about excluding from his canon any book that militated against his peculiar dogmas. Nor is Tatian's authority of more weight. The only reason why he accepted as genuine the Epistle of Titus while he rejected those of Timothy, is conjectured to have been that in the Epistle to Titus the phase of incipient Gnosticism which meets with the condemnation of the Apostle is more distinctly identified with Jewish teaching.[3]

---

[1] "Let us then approach Him in holiness of soul, lifting to Him pure and unstained hands."—*Ep.* 1, *ad Cor.* 29; *cf.* 1 Tim. ii. 8.

[2] Baur, *Pastoralbriefe*, p. 138.

[3] Tit. i. 10, 14; iii. 9. Tatian founded a sect of Gnostic Encratites towards the close of the second century.

But perhaps it may be argued that the Pastoral Epistles were forged in the second century, and that the earlier passages which are regarded as allusions to them, or quotations from them, are in reality borrowed from Clemens, Polycarp, and Hegesippus, by the writer, who wished to enlist the supposed authority of St. Paul in condemnation of the spreading Gnosticism of the second century. No one would argue that there is a merely *accidental* connection between, "Avoiding profane and vain babblings, and oppositions [or antitheses] of the knowledge [Gnosis] which is falsely so called" in 1 Tim. vi. 20, and "the combination of impious error arose by the fraud of false teachers [ἑτεροδιδασκάλων, comp. 1 Tim i. 3, ἑτεροδιδασκαλεῖν] who henceforth attempted to preach their science falsely so called" in Hegesippus.[1] But Baur argues that the forger of the Epistle stole the term from Hegesippus, and that it was aimed at the Marcionites, who are especially indicated in the word "Antitheses" which is the name of a book written by Marcion to point out the contradiction between the Old and New Testament, and between those parts of the New Testament which he rejected and those which he retained.[2] Now, "antitheses" may mean simply "oppositions" as it is rendered in our version, and the injunction is explained by Chrysostom and Theophylact, and even by De Wette, to mean that Timothy is not to embroil himself in idle and fruitless controversies. But even, supposing that "antilogies" are meant, what shadow of proof is there that nothing of the kind existed among the "vain babblings" of Essenian speculation? "Hegesippus," says Baur,[3] "considering his Ebionite views, can scarcely have drawn from an Epistle supposed to be by Paul." It is difficult to believe that this remark is perfectly serious;[4] but if it be, I would ask, Is it not indefinitely more improbable that the *falsarius*[5] would instantly

---

[1] *Ap.* Euseb. *H. E.* iii. 32.

[2] Tert. Adv. *Marc.* i. 19; iv. &c. Baur also (*Paul.* ii. 111) dwells on the use of the word ὑγιής, "sound," "wholesome," by Hegesippus and in 1 Tim. i. 10.

[3] *Paul.* ii. 101.

[4] Davidson freely admits that "there is no great difficulty in supposing that he read the Pastoral Epistles written in Paul's name, and remembered some of their expressions" (*Introd.* ii. 181).

[5] Admitting that "pseudonymity and literary deception" were regarded in antiquity as very different things, I would willingly avoid the word "forger" if there were any other convenient word which could be substituted for it. I quite concede to De Wette, Schleiermacher, Baur, &c., that the word connotes much more than it ought to do, as applied to a writer of the first two centuries, and that "the forging of such Epistles must not be judged according to the modern standard of literary honesty, but according to the spirit of antiquity, which attached no such definite value as we do to literary property, and regarded the *thing* much more than the person" (Baur, *Paul.* ii. 110).

condemn his own work as spurious by interpolating marked passages from Clemens, Polycarp, and Hegesippus, which his instructed readers would be sure to recognise, and which would then be absolutely fatal to the success of his design?

II. Let us, then, pass to the internal evidence. It is argued that these three Epistles cannot have been written by St. Paul—(1) Because "they stand far below the originality, the wealth of thought, and the whole spiritual substance and value of the authentic Epistles;"[1] (2) Because they abound in un-Pauline words and phrases; (3) Because their theology differs from that of the Apostle; (4) Because they deal with conditions of ecclesiastical organisation which had no existence till long after the age of the Apostles; (5) Because they betray allusions to later developments of Gnostic heresy: and these objections we will briefly consider.

(1) Now as to the style of these Epistles, we admit at once that it is inferior to that of St. Paul's greatest productions. For eloquence, compression, depth, passion, and logical power, they cannot for one moment be compared to the letters to the Corinthians, Romans, Galatians, or Ephesians. St. Paul is not here at his best or greatest. "His restless energies," says Alford,[2] "are still at work; but those energies have changed their complexion; they have passed from the dialectic character of his earlier Epistles, from the wonderful capacity of intricate combined rationalism of his subsequent Epistles, to the urging, and repeating, and dilating upon truths which have been the food of his life; there is a resting on former conclusions, a constant citation of the *temporis acti*, which lets us into a most interesting phase of the character of the great Apostle. We see here rather the succession of brilliant sparks than the steady flame; burning words indeed and deep pathos, but not the flower of his firmness as in his discipline of the Galatians; not the noon of his bright, warm eloquence, as in the inimitable Psalm of Love."[3]

But in what way does this invalidate their authenticity? We entirely dissent from Baur's exaggerated depreciation of their value; if we admitted that they were as meagre of contents, as colourless in treatment, as deficient in motive and connexion, as full of monotony, repetition, and dependence, as he asserts—what then? Must a writer be always at his greatest? Does not the smallest knowledge of literary history prove at once that writers are liable to extraordinary variations of literary capacity? Do not their shorter and less important works offer in many cases a most singular contrast to their more elaborate compositions? Are all the works of Plato of equal value? Do we find

---

Baur, *Paul*. ii. 106. [2] *Greek Test*. iii. 83. [3] 1 Cor. xiii.

in the *Epinomis* the grandeur and profundity which mark the *Phaedo* and the *Theaetetus?* Is the *Leges* as rich in style as the *Phaedrus?* Is there no difference in manner between the *Annals of Tacitus* and the dialogue *De Oratoribus?* Was it the same hand which wrote *Love's Labour's Lost* and *Hamlet?* Would any one who read the more prosaic parts of the *Paradise Regained* recognise the poet of the first or sixth books of the *Paradise Lost?* Is the style of Burke in the *Essay on the Sublime and Beautiful* the same as his style in the *Essay on the French Revolution?* It would be quite superfluous to multiply instances. If it be asserted that the Pastoral Epistles are valueless, or unworthy of their author, we at once join issue with the objectors, and, independently of our own judgment, we say that, in that case, they would not have deceived the critical intuition of centuries of thinkers, of whom many were consummate masters of literary expression. If, on the other hand, it be merely contended that the style lacks the *verve* and passion of the earlier Epistles, we reply that this is exactly what we should expect. Granted that "it is not the object of this, as of preceding Epistles, to develop fully some essentially Pauline idea which has still to vindicate itself, and on which the Christian consciousness and life are to be formed, but rather to apply the contents of Christian doctrine to practical life in its varying circumstances," we reply that nothing could be more natural. Granted that, unlike all the other Epistles, they have no true organic development; that they do not proceed from one root-idea which penetrates the whole contents, and binds all the inner parts in an inner unity, because the deeper relations pervade the outward disconnectedness; that no one creative thought determines their contents and structure; that they exhibit no genuine dialectic movement in which the thought possesses sufficient inherent force to originate all the stages of its development;[1] granted, I say—and it is a needlessly large concession—that this depth of conception, this methodical development, this dialectic progress, are wanting in these three letters, we entirely refuse to admit that this want of structural growth belies their Pauline origin. It is little short of absurd to suppose that every one of St. Paul's letters —however brief, however casual, however private—must have been marked by the same features as the Epistles to the Romans or the Galatians. I venture to say that every objection of this kind falls at once to the ground before the simple observation of the fact that these were not grand and solemn compositions dealing with the great problems which were rending the peace of the assembled Churches before which they would be read, but ordinary private letters, addressed by an elder and a superior to friends whom he had probably known from early

[1] Baur, *Paul.* ii. 107.

boyhood, and who were absolutely familiar with the great main features of his teaching and belief. Add the three circumstances that one of them was written during the cruel imprisonment in which his life was drawing to its close; that they were probably written by his own hand, and not with the accustomed aid of an amanuensis;[1] and that they were certainly written in old age,—and we shall at once see how much there is which explains the general peculiarities of their style, especially in its want of cohesion and compression. There are in these Epistles inimitable indications that we are reading the words of an old man. There is neither senility nor garrulity, but there is the dignity and experience which marks the *jucunda senectus*.[2] The digressiveness becomes more diffuse, the generalities more frequent, the repetitions more observable.[3] Formulæ are reiterated with an emphasis which belongs less to the necessities of the present than to the reminiscences of the past. Divergences into personal matters, when he is writing to Timothy, who had so long been his bosom companion, become more numerous and normal.[4] And yet it is impossible not to feel that a Paul is still the writer. There are flashes of the deepest feeling, outbursts of the most intense expression. There is rhythmic movement and excellent majesty in the doxologies, and the ideal of a Christian pastor is drawn not only with an unfaltering hand, but with a beauty, fulness, and simplicity, which a thousand years of subsequent experience have enabled no one to equal, much less to surpass. In these Epistles direct logical controversy is to a great extent neglected as needless. All that the Apostle had to say in the way of such reasoning had probably been said to his correspondents, in one form or other, again and again. For them, as entrusted with the supervision of important Christian communities, it was needless to develop doctrines with which they were familiar. It was far more necessary to warn them respecting the fatal moral tendencies in which heresies originated, and the fatal moral aberrations in which they too often issued.

[1] The Epistle to the Galatians and the concluding doxology of the Epistle to the Romans were also autographic; and Dean Alford—than whom few men have ever been more closely acquainted with the style of the Apostle in all its peculiarities—has pointed out a series of resemblances between these writings and the Pastoral Epistles (*Greek Test.* iii. 86).

[2] Even when he wrote the Epistle to Philemon he calls himself Paul the Aged, and he had gone through much since then. Supposing him to have been converted at the age of thirty, he would now have been nearly sixty, and could hardly have seemed otherwise than aged, considering the illnesses and trials which had shattered a weak and nervous frame.

[3] 1 Tim. i. 15; ii. 4—6; iii. 16, &c.; 2 Tim. i. 9; ii. 11—13; Tit. i. 15; ii. 11; iii. 3, &c. &c.

[4] 1 Tim. i. 11, *seqq.*; 2 Tim. i. 11, *seqq.*; 15, *seqq.*; iv. 6, *seqq.*

And while we are on this subject of style, how much is there which we must at once see to be favourable to the authenticity of these writings! Take the First Epistle to Timothy alone, which is more seriously attacked than the other two, and which is supposed to drag down its companions by the evidence of its spuriousness. Do we not find in it abundant traces of a familiar style? Is it even conceivable that a forger would have actually begun with an *anakoluthon* or unfinished construction? Such sentences abound in the style of St. Paul, and to imitate them with perfect naturalness would be no easy task. But even supposing the possibility of imitation, would a forger have started off with one? Again, it would be very easy to caricature or clumsily imitate the digressive manner which we have attributed to familiarity and age; but to reproduce it so simply and naturally as it here appears would require supreme literary accomplishment. Would an imitator have purposely diverged from St. Paul's invariable salutation by the insertion of "mercy" between "grace" and "peace"? It is easy to understand on psychological grounds that St. Paul might call himself "the chief of sinners" (i. 15); but would a devoted follower have thus written of him? Would he *purposely* and *continually* have lost the main thread of his subject as at ii. 3, 7? A writer with a firm grasp of truths which he knows to be complementary to each other would never hesitate at any merely apparent contradiction of his previous opinions; still less would he hesitate to modify those opinions in accordance with circumstances; but would a forger have been so bold as apparently to contradict in ii. 15 what St. Paul had taught in 1 Cor. vii.? Would he be skilful enough to imitate the simple and natural manner in which, more than once, the Apostle has resumed his Epistle after seeming to be on the point of ending it, as at iii. 14, 15? St. Paul, like most supremely noble writers, is quite indifferent to confusion of metaphors; but would an imitator be likely to follow him with such lordly indifference as at vi. 19? In writing to familiar friends, nothing is more natural than the perfectly casual introduction of minute and unimportant particulars. There is nothing like this in St. Paul's other letters, not even in that to Philemon, and therefore a forger would have had no model to copy. How great a literary artist, then, must have been the forger who—writing with some theory of inspiration, and under the shadow of a great name, and with special objects in view—could furnish accidental minutiæ so natural, so interesting, and even so pathetic as that in 1 Tim. v. 23, or introduce, by way of precaution, such particulars—"unexampled in the Apostle's other writings, founded on no incident, tending to no result"—as the direction to Timothy to bring with him to

Rome "the cloak which I left at Troas with Carpus, and the books, especially the parchments." It seems to me that forgery, even under the dominant influence of one impressive personality and one supreme idea, is by no means the extraordinarily easy and simple thing which it appears to be to the adherents of the Tübingen criticism. It is a comparatively simple matter to pass off imitations of a Clemens Romanus or an Ignatius, but it is hardly likely that the world would be long deceived by writings palmed off upon it as those of a Milton—still less of a St. Paul.

(2) It is said they abound in unusual, isolated, and un-Pauline expressions. Among these are "It is a faithful saying,"[1] "piety," and "piously" (εὐσέβεια, εὐσεβῶς), found eight times in these Epistles, and nowhere else except in 2 Pet. ;[2] the metaphor of "wholesomeness" (ὑγιής, ὑγιαίνειν), applied to doctrines nine times in these Epistles, and not elsewhere ;[3] the use of δεσπότης "Lord" for κύριος "master;"[4] the use of ἀρνεῖσθαι "to deny" for the renunciation of true doctrine; and of παραιτεῖσθαι "to avoid," of which the latter is, however, used by Paul in his speech before Festus, and which, as well as προσέχειν, with a dative in the sense of "attend to," he very probably picked up in intercourse with St. Luke, to whom both words are familiar.[5] No one, I think, will be seriously startled by these unusual phrases, nor will they shake our belief in the genuineness of the Epistles when we recall that there is not a single Epistle of St. Paul in which these *hapax legomena*, or isolated expressions, do not abound. Critics who have searched minutely into the comparative terminology of the New Testament Scriptures, tell us that there are no less than 111 peculiar terms in the Epistle to the Romans, 186 in the two Epistles to the Corinthians, 57 and 54 respectively in the short Epistles to the Galatians and Philippians, 6 even in the few paragraphs addressed to Philemon. It is not therefore in the least degree surprising that there should be 74 in the First Epistle to Timothy, 67 in the Second, and 13 in that to Titus. Still less shall we be surprised when we examine them. St. Paul, it must be remembered, was the main creator of theological

---

[1] 1 Tim. i. 15; iii. 1; iv. 9; 2 Tim. ii. 11; Tit. iii. 8.

[2] 1 Tim. ii. 2; iii. 16; iv. 7; vi. 11; 2 Tim. iii. 5, 12; Tit. i. 1; ii. 12. Pfleiderer suggests that this word εὐσέβεια may have been taken as the fundamental idea of the Christian holy life as the word "faith" became gradually externalised.

[3] 1 Tim. i. 10; vi. 3, 4; 2 Tim. i. 13; iv. 3; Tit. i. 9, 13; ii. 1, 8. And, as a natural antithesis, γάγγραινα and νοσεῖν are applied to false doctrine.

[4] 1 Tim. vi. 1, 2; 2 Tim. ii. 21; Tit. ii. 9.

[5] Alford, *l.c.* Can the use of δεσπότης instead of κύριος be due to the literary inconvenience which was gradually felt to arise from the fact that the latter word was more and more incessantly employed as the title of our Lord Jesus Christ?

language. In the Pastoral Epistles he is dealing with new circumstances, and new circumstances would inevitably necessitate new terms. Any one who reads the list of unusual expressions in the Epistles to Timothy will see at once that the large majority of them are directly connected with the new form of error with which St. Paul had recently been called upon to deal. Men who are gifted with a vivid power of realisation are peculiarly liable to seize upon fresh phrases which embody their own thoughts and convictions, and these phrases are certain to occur frequently at particular periods of their lives, and to be varied from time to time.[1] This is simply a matter of psychological observation, and is quite sufficient to account for the expressions we have mentioned, and many more. We can have little conception of the plasticity of language at its creative epoch, and we must never forget that St. Paul had to find the correct and adequate expression for conceptions which as yet were extremely unfamiliar. Every year would add to the vocabulary, which must at first have been more or less tentative, and the harvest of new expressions would always be most rich where truths, already familiar, were brought into collision with heresies altogether new. The list of *hapax legomena* in the note [2] are all due, not to the difference of authorship, but to the exigencies of the times.

(3) It would be a much more serious—it would indeed be an all but fatal—objection to the authenticity of these Epistles, if it could be proved that their theology differs from that of Paul. But a very little examination will show that there is no such contradiction—nothing beyond the varying expression of truths which complement but do not contradict each other. Some, indeed, of the alleged discrepancies are too shadowy to grasp. If Christianity be described as "the doctrine" and as "sound doctrine";[3] if the word "faith" has acquired a more objective significance, so as sometimes almost to imply a body of truths as opposed to heresy;[4] if the name "Saviour"—rare in St. Paul—be

---

[1] I feel convinced that the Tübingen methods applied to the writings of Mr. Carlyle (for instance) or Mr. Ruskin, would prove in the most triumphant manner that some of their writings were forgeries (a) from their resemblance to, (β) from their dissimilarity from, their other writings. But as Dean Alford happily says, "In a fresh and vigorous style there will ever be (so to speak) *librations* over any rigid limits of habitude which can be assigned; and such are to be judged of, not by their mere occurrence or number, but by their subjective character being or not being in accordance with the writer's well-known characteristics" (*Test*. iii. 54).

[2] γενεαλογίαι, 1 Tim. i. 4, Tit. iii. 9; ματαιολόγος, 1 Tim. i. 6, Tit. i. 10; κενοφωνίαι, 1 Tim. vi. 20, 2 Tim. ii. 16; λογομαχίαι, παραθήκη, βέβηλος, ἀστοχεῖν, τυφοῦσθαι; &c.

[3] 1 Tim. i. 10; vi. 1.

[4] 1 Tim. i. 19; ii. 7; iii. 9; iv. 1—6, vi. 10, 21. Pfleiderer, *Paulinism*, ii. 201.

applied to God, and not to Christ;[1] if "Palingenesia" (regeneration) occurs only in the Epistle to Titus;[2] these are peculiarities of language, not differences of theology. There is a dominant practical tendency in these Epistles;—so there is, we reply, in all St. Paul's Epistles. The value and blessedness of good works is incessantly insisted on;[3]—is this, then, to be stigmatised as "utilitarianism and religious eudæmonism," and a decided pietistic attenuation of the Pauline doctrine? Are they not, then, insisted on even in the Epistles to the Romans and Galatians, though there he is developing a theory, and here he is professedly occupied with moral instructions? Will any one attempt to prove that St. Paul, either in these Epistles or elsewhere, held any other view of good works than this—that they are profitless to obtain salvation, but are morally indispensable?[4] De Wette's further objection, that St. Paul here makes an apology for the Law (1 Tim. i. 8), and his attempt to draw a subtle distinction between the universalism of these Epistles and of the other Pauline writings, deserve no serious refutation. St. Paul's method and object are here wholly unlike those of his Epistles to Churches composed of heterogeneous and often of hostile elements; but it may be asserted, beyond all fear of contradiction, that, bearing in mind the non-theoretical treatment of the points on which he here touches, and the fact that he is writing to friends and disciples already absolutely convinced of the main truths of his theology, there is not one word in these Epistles which either contradicts or seriously differs from the fundamental ideas of St. Paul. Even Baur —candid, with all his hypercritical prejudices—only sees in them "a certain *something* of the specific Pauline doctrine with a dominant practical tendency," an "applying of the contents of Christian doctrine to the various circumstances of practical life."[5]

(4) It is not, however, on the above grounds that the Pastoral Epistles have been most seriously attacked. The considerations which we have here seen to be untenable are really due to after-thoughts; and

---

[1] Pfleiderer says that in Tit. ii. 13 Christ is called "our great God and Saviour," and that "this goes beyond all the previous Christology of St. Paul." But there can be no doubt that the phrase is applied to God in this place, as also in 1 Tim. i. 1; ii. 3; iv. 10; Tit. i. 3; ii. 10. The anarthrousness of Σωτήρ is no valid grammatical objection.

[2] Tit. iii. 5.

[3] Baur, *Paul.* ii. 106; De Wette, *Pastoralbr.* 117, s.; Pfleiderer, *Paulinism*, 210; Reuss, *Les Epîtres*, ii. 314.

[4] Rom. ii. 6—10; xiii. 3; Gal. v. 6, &c.; Eph. ii. 8—10, &c.

[5] *Paul.* ii. 107. It is the view of some hostile critics that the Asiatic Epistles (Eph. and Col.) are Pauline with un-Pauline interpolations; and the Pastoral Epistles un-Pauline, yet containing Pauline matter.

the assaults on the genuineness of the Epistles have mainly risen from the belief that they are "tendency-writings," meant to serve the twofold object of magnifying ecclesiastical organisation and of covertly attacking a Gnosticism which was not prevalent till long after the Apostle's time. The two subjects are by no means disconnected. The Gnostics, it is said—as the first heretics properly so called—gave occasion for the episcopal constitution of the Church; and if there were no such heretics at that time, then these ecclesiastical arrangements will be devoid of any historical occasion or connexion! I have sought the strongest and fullest statements of these objections, and shall try to express the reasons why they appear to me to be most absolutely groundless. I quite freely admit that there are some remarkable peculiarities in these Epistles; I do not deny that they suggest some difficulties of which we can give no adequate explanation; I cannot go so far as to say that the objections brought against them are "not adequate even to raise a *doubt* on the subject of their authenticity;" but for these very reasons I can say, with all the deeper sincerity, that, whatever minor hesitations and doubts may remain unremoved, the main arguments of those who reject the Epistles have—even without regard to other elements of external testimony and internal evidence in their favour—been fairly met and fairly defeated all along the line.

(α) Let us first consider the question of ecclesiastical organisation. And here we are at once met with the preliminary and fundamental objection of Baur, that in the Epistles which supply us with the surest standard of St. Paul's principles he never betrays the slightest interest in ecclesiastical institutions, not even when they might be thought to lie directly in his way; and that this want of interest in such things is not merely accidental, but founded deep in the whole spirit and character of Pauline Christianity.

But this form of statement is invidious, and will not stand a moment's examination. In the minutiæ of ecclesiastical institutions, as affected by mere sectarian disputes, St. Paul would have felt no interest; and to that exaltation of human ministers which has received the name of sacerdotalism—feeling as he did the supreme sufficiency of one Mediator—he would have been utterly opposed. It is very probable that he would have treated the differences between Presbyterianism and Episcopacy as very secondary questions—questions of expediency, of which the settlement might lawfully differ in different countries and different times. But to say that he would have considered it superfluous to give directions about the consolidation of nascent Churches, and would have had no opinion to offer about the duties and qualifications of ministers, is surely preposterous. It is, moreover, contradicted by historic facts. His tours to confirm the Churches, his solemn

GENUINENESS OF THE PASTORAL EPISTLES. 617

appointment of presbyters with prayers and fastings in his very first missionary journey,[1] and his summons to the Ephesian presbyters, that they might receive his last advice and farewell, would be alone sufficient to prove that such matters did—as it was absolutely necessary that they should—occupy a large part of his attention. Are we to suppose that he gave no pastoral instructions to Timothy when he sent him to the Churches of Macedonia, or to Titus when he appointed him a sort of commissioner to regulate the disorders of the Church of Corinth?

It is true that the pseudo-Clementines, the Apostolical constitutions, parts of the letters of Ignatius, and in all probability other early writings, were forged, with the express object of giving early and lofty sanction to later ecclesiastical development, and above all to the supposed primacy of Rome. But what could be more unlike such developments than the perfectly simple and unostentatious arrangements of the Pastoral Epistles? In the rapid growth of the Christian Church, and the counter-growth of error, the establishment of discipline and government would almost from the first become a matter of pressing exigency. Even in the Epistles to the Corinthians and Romans we find terms that imply the existence of deacons, deaconesses, teachers, prophets, apostles, rulers, overseers or presbyters, and evangelists; and a comparison of the passages referred to will show that all these names, with the exception of the first,[2] were used vaguely, and to a certain extent even synonymously, or as only descriptive of different aspects of the same office.[3] If the imposition of hands is alluded to in the Epistles to Timothy, so it is in the Acts.[4] The notion that a formal profession of faith was required at ordination so little results from 2 Tim. i. 13 that the very next verse is sufficient to disprove such a meaning. If the Pastoral Epistles contained a clear defence of the episcopal system of the second century, this alone would be sufficient to prove their spuriousness; but the total absence of anything resembling it is one of the strongest proofs that they belong to the Apostolic age. Bishop and presbyter are still synonyms, as they are throughout the New Testament.[5] If ἐπίσκοπος,

---

[1] Acts xiv. 23.
[2] 1 Cor. xii. 28; xvi. 15; Rom. xii. 7; xvi. 1; Phil. i. 1; 1 Thess. v. 12; Eph. iv. 11; Acts xx. 17, 28.
[3] To a certain extent, indeed, the overseers, presbyters, and deacons, in their purely official aspect, corresponded to the *Sheliach*, the *Rosh ha-Keneseth*, the *Chazzan* of the synagogue.
[4] 1 Tim. iv. 14; v. 22; Acts vi. 6; viii. 17.
[5] Thus in 1 Tim. iii. St. Paul passes at once from "bishops" (1—7) to "deacons" (8—13), and afterwards speaks of these same bishops as "presbyters" (v. 17—19), and in Tit. i. 5—7 the identification is indisputable. No one is ignorant that "bishops" and "presbyters" are in the New Testament identical (Acts xx. 17—28; Phil. i. 1; 1 Pet. v. 2). The fact was well known to the Fathers, οἱ πρεσβύτεροι

"overseer," or "bishop" be used in the singular, this is partly an accident of language in the common generic use of the Greek article, and partly arises from the very nature of things as a transitional stage to the ultimate meaning of the word—since, even in a presbytery, it is inevitable that some one presbyter should take the lead. Timothy and Titus exercise functions which would be now called episcopal; but they are not called "bishops"; their functions were temporary; and they simply act as authoritative delegates of the Apostle of the Gentiles.[1] Nor is there any trace of exalted pretensions in the overseers whom they appoint. The qualifications required of them are almost exclusively moral. The directions given are " ethical, not hierarchical." And yet it is asserted that one main object of the First Epistle to Timothy is "to establish the primacy of the bishops as against the presbyters"![2] A more arbitrary statement could hardly be formulated. Let any one turn from the Epistle to the letters of St. Ignatius,[3] where he will read "Give heed to the bishop, that God also may give heed to you;" to the pseudo-Ignatius,[4] who tells us that " he who doeth anything without the knowledge of the bishop serveth the devil"; to the pseudo-Clementines, which say that "the bishop occupies the seat of Christ, and must be honoured as the image of God";[5] and he will see how glaring is the anachronism of supposing that it was written towards the middle of the second century to oppose the Marcionites; and how utterly different is the mild and natural authority which the Apostle assigns to a representative presbyterate from that " crushing despotism " of irresponsible authority for which the writers of the second century were willing to betray their Christian liberty.

We will consider the minor objections on this head when we come to the actual passages to which exception is taken, and especially the difficult expression in which the Church is apparently called " a pillar

---

τὸ παλαιὸν ἐκαλοῦντο ἐπίσκοποι . . . καὶ οἱ ἐπίσκοποι πρεσβύτεροι (Chrys. *ad Phil.* i. 1; Jer. *ad Tit.* i. 5). The more marked distinction of the two is first found in Ignatius *ad Polyc.* 6.

[1] 1 Tim. i. 3; iii. 14; 2 Tim. iv. 9, 21; Tit. i. 5; iii. 12.

[2] Pfleiderer, *Paulinism*, ii. 205. Yet he admits (p. 203) that in the second Epistle the remarks addressed to Timothy are " very far removed from the later conceptions of the exalted condition of a bishop," and that even in the first Epistle "the difference between bishops and presbyters does not appear to be any fixed difference of officers."

[3] *Ad Polyc.* 6. If the shorter form of the seven Ignatian Epistles be genuine, they show that, even at the beginning of the second century, the ecclesiastical development was so far in advance of the Pastoral Epistles as almost to demonstrate the genuineness of the latter.

[4] *Ad Smyrn.* 9.

[5] Clem. *Hom.* iii. 62, 66, 70. For these and other quotations see Dr. Lightfoot's essay on the Christian ministry (*Philippians*, p. 209, *seqq.*).

GENUINENESS OF THE PASTORAL EPISTLES. 619

and ground of the truth."[1] But another ground of objection is the rules about widows, which, as Baur asserts, "can only be successfully explained out of the ecclesiastical vocabulary of the second century," in which the term χῆραι is applied to an order consisting not only of bereaved persons but even of young virgins.[2] That this use of the word did not arise in the Apostle's time may be fairly assumed, but if there be not one single fact in the passage referred to which makes this necessary, the objection falls to the ground. Baur's only argument is that if χῆραι be actual widows, the Apostle gives two directly contradictory precepts about them, bidding the younger widows to marry again (1 Tim. v. 11—14), and yet ordering that a second marriage is to exclude them, should they again become widows, from the *viduatus* of the Church. But where is the contradiction? We learn from the Acts that the Church continued the merciful and, indeed, essential custom, which it had learnt from the synagogue, of maintaining those widows, who from the circumstances of Eastern and ancient society were its most destitute members, and whose helpless condition constituted a special appeal to pity. But it was only natural that each Church should try as far as possible to utilise this institution, and that the widows should themselves desire to be serviceable to the brethren to whom they owed their livelihood. Hence "the widows" became a recognised order, and acquired a semi-religious position. Into this order St. Paul wisely forbids the admission of widows who are still of an age to marry again. Of the female character in general and in the abstract he does not ordinarily speak in very exalted terms, and in this respect he only resembles most ancient writers, although, in spite of surrounding conditions of society, he sees the moral elevation of the entire sex in Christ. He regarded it as almost inevitable that the religious duties of the "order of widows," although they involved a sort of consecration to celibacy for the remainder of their lives, would never serve as a sufficient barrier to their wish to marry again; and he thought that moral degeneracy and outward scandal would follow from the intrusion of such motives into the fulfilment of sacred functions. There is here no contradiction, and not the shadow of a proof that in the language of the Epistle there must be any identification of widows with an order of female celibates or youthful nuns.[3]

(β) We now come to the last objection, which is by far the strongest and most persistent, as it is also the earliest. The spuriousness of the Pastoral Epistles is mainly asserted on the ground that they indicate

[1] 1 Tim. iii. 15.
[2] τὰς παρθένους τὰς λεγομένας χήρας (Ign. *ad Smyrn.* 13). The genuineness of the passage is far from certain.
[3] 1 Cor. xiv. 34; 1 Tim. ii. 12—14; 2 Tim. iii. 6; &c.

the existence of a Gnosticism which was not fully developed till after the death of St. Paul. A more extensive theory was never built on a more unstable foundation.[1] The one word *antitheseis* in 1 Tim. vi. 20, seems to Baur a clear proof that the first Epistle to Timothy is a covert polemic against Marcion in the middle of the second century. To an hypothesis so extravagant it is a more than sufficient answer that the heretical tendencies of the false teachers were distinctly Judaic, whereas there was not a single Gnostic system which did not regard Judaism as either imperfect or pernicious. Objections of this kind can only be regarded as fantastic until some proof be offered (1) that the germs of Gnosticism did not exist in the apostolic age; and (2) that the phrases of Gnosticism were not borrowed from the New Testament, nor those of the New Testament from the Gnostic systems. Knowing as we do that "Æon" was thus borrowed by Valentinus,[2] and that "Gnosis" was beginning to acquire a technical meaning even when St. Paul wrote his Epistle to the Corinthians,[3] we see that on the one hand Gnostic terms are no proof of allusion to Gnostic tenets, and on the other, that Gnostic tendencies existed undeveloped from the earliest epoch of the Christian Church. It would be far truer to say that the absence of anything like definite allusion to the really distinctive elements of Marcionite or Valentinian teaching is a decisive proof that these Epistles belong to a far earlier epoch, than to say that they are an attempt to use the great name of Paul to discountenance those subtle heresies. In the Epistle to the Colossians St. Paul had dealt formally with the pretended philosophy and vaunted insight, the incipient dualism, the baseless angelology, and the exaggerated asceticism of local heretics whose theosophic fancies were already prevalent.[4] In these Epistles he merely touches on them, because in private letters to beloved fellow-workers there was no need to enter into any direct controversy with their erroneous teachings. But he alludes to these elements with the distinct statement that they were of Judaic origin. Valentinus rejected the Mosaic law; Marcion was Antinomian; but these Ephesian and Cretan teachers, although their dualism is revealed by their ascetic discouragement of marriage, their denial of the resurrection, and their interminable "genealogies" and myths,[5]

[1] Apparently the use of the word ἑτεροδιδασκαλεῖν in 1 Tim. i. 3 as compared with ἑτεροδιδάσκαλοι in Hegesippus first led Schleiermacher to doubt the genuineness of the First Epistle.

[2] Hippolytus (*R. H.* vi. 20) tells us that Valentinus gave the name of Æons to the emanations which Simon Magus had called Roots.

[3] 1 Cor. viii. 1. The adjective "Gnostic" is ascribed to the Ophites, or to Carpocrates. (Iren. *Haer.* i. 25; Euseb. *H. E.* iv. 7, 9.)

[4] See Col. i. 16, 17; ii. 8, 18; and Mansel, *The Gnostic Heresies*, p. 54.

[5] 1 Tim. i. 4; iv. 4; 2 Tim. ii. 18.

are not only Jews, but founded their subtleties and speculations on the Mosaic law.[1] In dealing with these Paul has left far behind him the epoch of his struggle with the Pharisaic legalists of Jerusalem. Thought moves with vast rapidity; systems are developed into ever-varying combinations in an amazingly short space of time, at epochs of intense religious excitement, and as the incipient Gnosticism of the apostolic age shows many of the elements which would hereafter be ripened into later development, so it already shows the ominous tendency of restless speculation to degenerate into impious pride, and of over-strained asceticism to link itself with intolerable license.[2] These are speculations and tendencies which belong to no one country and no one age. Systems and ideas closely akin to Gnosticism are found in the religions and philosophies of Greece, Persia, India, China, Egypt, Phoenicia; they are found in Plato, in Zoroaster, in the Vedas, in the writings of the Buddhists, in Philo, in neo-Platonism, and in the Jewish Kabbalah. In all ages and all countries they have produced the same intellectual combinations and the same moral results. A writer of the second century could have had no possible object in penning a forgery which in his day was far too vague to be polemically effective.[3] On the other hand, an apostle of the year 65 or 66, familiar with Essene and Oriental speculations, a contemporary of Simon Magus the reputed founder of all Gnosticism, and of Cerinthus, its earliest heresiarch, might have had reason—even apart from divine guidance and prophetic inspiration—to warn the disciples to whom he was entrusting the care and constitution of his Churches against tendencies which are never long dormant, and which were already beginning to display a dangerous activity and exercise a dangerous fascination. If there is scarcely a warning which would not apply to the later Gnostics, it is equally true that there is not a warning which would not equally apply to errors distinctly reprobated in the Epistles to the Philippians, Corinthians,

[1] 1 Tim. i. 7; Tit. i. 10, 14; iii. 9.
[2] 1 Tim. i. 7, 19; iv. 2; 2 Tim. ii. 17; iii. 1—7; Tit. i. 11, 15, 16.
[3] The vagueness is due to the still wavering outlines of the heretical teachings. The "Gnosticism" aimed at has been by various critics identified with Kabbalism (Baumgarten); with Pharisaism (Wiesinger); with Essenism (Mangold); with Marcionism (Baur)—

"If shape it could be called which shape had none
Distinguishable in vesture, joint, or limb."

But whether Gnosticism be regarded as theological speculation (Gieseler), or an aristocratic and exclusive philosophy of religion (Neander), or allegorising dualism (Baur), if "it is still an accomplished task to seize amidst so much that is indefinite, vague, merely circumlocutory, and only partly true, those points that furnish a clear conception of it," then it is clearly idle to say that its undeveloped genius cannot have existed in the days of the Apostles.

and Colossians, as well as to the Churches addressed by St. Peter, St. Jude, and St. John.[1] Greek subtleties, Eastern imagination, Jewish mysticism—in one word, the inherent curiosity and the inherent Manicheism of unregenerate human nature—began from the very first to eat like a canker into the opening bud of Christian faith.

Those who wish to see every possible argument which can be adduced against the Pauline authorship of these Epistles, may find them marshalled together by Dr. Davidson in the later editions of his "Introduction to the Study of the New Testament."[2] To answer them point by point would be tedious, for many of them are exceedingly minute;[3] nor would it be convincing, for critics will make up their minds on the question on the broader and larger grounds which I have just examined. But to sum up, I would say that, although we cannot be as absolutely *certain* of their authenticity as we are of that of the earlier Epistles, yet that scarcely any difficulty in accepting their authenticity will remain if we bear in mind the following considerations. (1) In times like those of early Christianity, systems were developed and institutions consolidated with extraordinary rapidity. (2) These letters were written, not with the object of entering into direct controversy, but to guide the general conduct of those on whom that duty had devolved, and who were already aware of that fixed body of truth which formed the staple of the apostolic teaching. (3) They abound in unusual expressions, because new forms of error required new methods of stating truth. (4) Their unity is less marked and their style less logical, because they are the private and informal letters of an elder, written with the waning powers of a life which was rapidly passing beyond the sphere of earthly controversies. Pauline in much of their phraseology, Pauline in their fundamental doctrines, Pauline in their dignity and holiness of tone, Pauline alike in their tenderness and severity, Pauline in the digressions, the constructions, and the personality of their style, we may accept two of them with an absolute conviction of their authenticity, and the third—the First Epistle to Timothy, which is more open to doubt than the others—with at least a strong belief that in reading it we are reading the words of the greatest of the Apostles.[4]

[1] Phil. iii. 18; 1 Cor. xv.
[2] Vol. ii. pp. 137—195.
[3] I shall, however, touch on some of these in speaking of the Epistles separately. It has been said that Paley uses the discrepancies between the Acts and the Epistles to prove their independence, and the agreements to establish their truthfulness. It may certainly be said that the Tübingen school adduces un-Pauline expressions to prove non-authenticity, and Pauline expressions to prove forgery.
[4] Even Usteri, Lücke, Neander, and Bleek, are unconvinced of the authenticity

EXCURSUS X.

CHRONOLOGY OF THE LIFE AND EPISTLES OF ST. PAUL.

To enter fully into the chronology of this period would require a separate volume, and although there is now an increasing tendency to unanimity on the subject, yet some of the dates can only be regarded as approximate. As few definite chronological indications are furnished in the Acts or the Epistles, we can only frame our system by working backwards and forwards, with the aid of data which are often vague, from the few points where the sacred narrative refers to some distinct event in secular history. These, which furnish us with our *points de repère*, are—

> The Death of Herod Agrippa I., A.D. 44.
> The Expulsion of the Jews from Rome, A.D. 52.
> The Arrival of Festus as Procurator, A.D. 60.
> The Neronian Persecution, A.D. 64.

How widely different have been the schemes adopted by different chronologers may be seen from the subjoined table, founded on that given by Meyer.

of the First Epistle. Otto, Wieseler, and Reuss, have said all that is to be said in favour of a single captivity; but on the assumption that the Pastoral Epistles are genuine, such a theory forces us into a mass of impossibilities. The conviction at which I have arrived may be summed up thus:—If St. Paul was put to death at the end of his first imprisonment, the Pastoral Epistles must certainly be spurious. But there is the strongest possible evidence that two of them at least are genuine, and great probability in favour of the other. They therefore furnish us with a proof of the current tradition that his trial, as he had anticipated, ended in an acquittal, and that a period of about two years elapsed between his liberation and his subsequent arrest, imprisonment, and death.

APPENDIX.

EVENTS.	H. A. W. Meyer.	Eusebius.	Jerome.	Chronicon Paschale.	Baronius.	Petavius.	Usher.	Spanheim.	Pearson.	Tillemont.	Basnage.
Ascension of Christ	31	33	32	31	32	31	33	33	33	33	33
Stephen stoned	33 or 34	...	...	a. Claud. I.	32	31	33	38?	34	33	37
Paul's conversion	35	...	33	a. Claud. II.	34	33	35	40	35	34	37
Paul's first journey to Jerusalem	38	...	...	a. Claud. III.	37	36	38	43	38	37	40
Paul's arrival at Antioch	43	...	...	a. Claud. III.	41	40	43	43?	42	43	40
Death of James	44	...	...	...	42	41	44	...	44	44	44
The famine	44	41	44	...	42	42	44	44	44	44	42
Paul's second journey to Jerusalem	44	...	...	46	42	41	44	44	44	44	42
Paul's first missionary journey	45 to 51	...	...	a. Claud. V.	44 to 47	42	45 to 46	...	44 to 47	44 to 46	45 to 47
Paul's third journey to Jerusalem, to the Apostolic convention	52	...	...	...	49	49	52	53	49	51	50
Paul commences the second missionary journey	52	...	...	...	49	49	53	...	50	51	50
Banishment of the Jews from Rome	52	...	49	...	49	49	54	...	52	49 to 52	51
Paul arrives at Corinth	53	...	...	...	50	50	54	54?	52	52	51
Paul's fourth journey to Jerusalem (al. Cæsarea) and third miss. journey	55	...	...	...	52 Coss.	52	56	54?	54	54	53
Paul's abode at Ephesus	56 to 58	...	...	...	53 to 55	52 to 54	56 to 59	56 to 58	54 to 57	54 to 57	53 to 55
Paul's fifth journey to Jerusalem, and imprisonment	59	...	...	53 or 54	56	55	60	59	58	58	56
Paul is removed from Cæsarea to Rome	61	55	57	under Nero.	56	56	62	60	60	60	58
Paul's imprisonment of two years' in Rome	62 or 64	...	to a Ner. IV.	...	57 to 59	...	63 to 65	61 to 63	61 to 63	61 to 63	60 to 62

CHRONOLOGY OF THE LIFE OF ST. PAUL.

Bengel.	Michaelis.	Eichhorn.	Kuinoel.	Winer.	De Wette.	Schrader.	Olshausen.	Anger.	Sanclemente and Ideler.	Wieseler.	Ewald.	Lechler.	Wordsworth.	Alford.
30	33	32	33	30?	...	35	33	31	29 Id.	30	33	...	30	30
30	...	37	37 or 38	37?	...	35	...	37	...	39?	38	...	33	37
31	37?	37 or 38	40	38?	37 or 38	39	35	38	35 or 38	40	38	between 37 and 41	34	37
33	...	40 or 41	43	41	40 or 41	42	38	41	38 or 41	43	41	...	37	40
39	...	42	...	...	43 or 44	43	41	43 or 44 or 45?	...	44	44	...	43	41
42	about 44	44	43 or 44	44	44	44	...	43 or 44	...	44	44	...	...	44
44	44	44 or 45	44	44	...	...	...	44 or 45 or 46?	...	45	45 to 46	between 41 and 45	44	44
41 to 44	44	44	44	45	44 or 45	44	44		44	45	45 to 46	...	44	44
45 to 46	...	45 ff.	...	...	...	44 to 46	to 49	to about 48	...	45 to 47	48 to 51	46 to 48	45	45
47	...	52	52	51	50 or 51	47	52	51	52	about 50	52	...	49 to 50	50
47	...	53	...	...	51 or 52	47	52	51	...	about 50	52	...	51	51
...	54?	54?	52	52	between 52 and 54	49	...	51 or 52	...	52	52	...	...	...
48	54?	about 54	52	52	52 or 53	49	53	52	...	52	53	...	53	53
49	...	56	Coss	54	53 or 54	51	55	54	56	54	55	54 or 55	54	54
50 to 52	...	57 to 59	...	55 to 57	54 or 55ff	51 ff	56 and 57	54 to 57	...	54 to 57	to 58	55 to 57	54 to 57	55
53	60	60	57	58	58 or 59	59	60	58	60	58	59	58	58	58
55	62	62	59	60	60 or 61	61	62	60	62	60	61	60	61	61
56 to 58	63 to 65	63 to 65	60 to 62	61 to 63	62 to 64	62 to 64	63 to 65	61 to 63	63 to 65	61 to 64	62 to 64	63 to 64	61 to 63	61 to 63

I subjoin a separate list of the dates of the Epistles adopted in this volume. The reasons are stated *in loco*, but the reader will understand that the dates in some instances can only be *approximate*.

DATES OF THE EPISTLES.

EPISTLE.	WRITTEN AT	A.D.
1 Thessalonians.	Corinth.	52.
2 Thessalonians.	Corinth.	52.
1 Corinthians.	Ephesus.	57.
2 Corinthians.	Philippi (?).	58 (early).
Galatians.	Corinth.	58.
Romans.	Corinth.	58.
Philippians.	Rome.	61 or 62.
Colossians } Philemon }	Rome.	63.
Ephesians.	Rome.	63.
1 Timothy.	Macedonia (?).	65 or 66.
Titus.	Macedonia (?).	66.
2 Timothy.	Rome.	67.

The subjoined table will give the probable dates of the chief events in the Apostle's life, with those of the events in secular history with which they synchronised.

TABLE OF CONTEMPORARY RULERS, ETC.

	EMPERORS.	PROCURATORS.	LEGATES OF SYRIA.	KINGS.	HIGH PRIESTS.	EVENTS IN LIFE OF ST. PAUL.
14	TIBERIUS (sole Emperor).					
25					Caiaphas.	
26		Pontius Pilatus.				
29						
30						
31						
32	Retires to Capreæ					
33						
34	A Phœnix said to have been seen in Egypt.		Vitellius.			
35						
36						
37	GAIUS (Caligula) (March 16).	Marullus (Ἱππάρχης).			Jonathan	Martyrdom of Stephen. St. Paul's Conversion.
38			Petronius Turpilianus.	Herod Agrippa I.	Theophilus	First Visit to Jerusalem.
39						At Tarsus.
40	Orders his statue to be placed in the Temple. Embassy of Philo.					
41	CLAUDIUS (Jan. 24).				Simon Kanthera.	At Antioch.
42	Disciples called Christians at Antioch.		Vibuis Marsus.	Herod Agrippa I. (dominion extended).	Matthias.	

CHRONOLOGY OF THE LIFE OF ST. PAUL

TABLE OF CONTEMPORARY RULERS, ETC.—*continued.*

	EMPERORS.	PROCURATORS.	LEGATES OF SYRIA.	KINGS.	HIGH PRIESTS.	EVENTS IN LIFE OF ST. PAUL.
43	......	......	......	......	Elionæus, son of Kanthera.	
44	Famine (Jos. *Antt* xx. 5, 2).	Cuspius Fadus	Cassius Longinus.	Death of Herod Agrippa I.	......	Second Visit to Jerusalem.
45	......	......	......	......	Joseph Ben Kamhit.	First Mission Journey.
46	......	Tiberius Alexander.				
47	......	......		......	Ananias, son of Nebedæus.	
48	......	Ventidius Cumanus.	Ummidius Quadratus.			
49	Expulsion of Jews from Rome.	......	......	Agrippa II., King of Chalcis.		
50	Caractacus taken to Rome.					
51	......	......	......	......	......	Third Visit to Jerusalem, and Synod.
52	......	......	......	Agrippa II. (Batanæa and Trachonitis).	Ishmael Ben Phabi.	At Corinth. 1, 2 Thess.
53	......	Claudius Felix	......	......	......	Fourth Visit to Jerusalem.
54	NERO (Oct. 13)					
55						
56	Birth of Trajan.					
57	Trial of Pomponia Græcina (as a Christian ?).	......	......	......	......	Paul at Eph. 1 Cor.
58	......	......	......	......	......	Second Ep. to Corinthians. Epistle to Galatians.
59	Murder of Agrippina.					
60		Porcius Festus	Corbulo			
61	Revolt of Boadicea.	......	......	......	Joseph Cabi	At Rome.
62	Deaths of Burrus, Octavia, and Pallas. Nero marries Poppæa.	Albinus	......	......	Ananus	Epistle to Philippians.
63	Power of Tigellinus.	......	......	......	Jesus, son of Damnæus.	Ep. to Colossians, Philemon, and Ephesus. Paul liberated.
64	Great Fire of Rome. Persecution of Christians.					
65	Death of Seneca.	Gessius Florus	......	......	......	First Epistle to Timothy.
66	Beginnings of Jewish War. Nero in Greece.					Ep. to Titus.
67	Siege of Jotapata	......	......	......	......	Second Epistle to Timothy.
68	Suicide of Nero (June). GALBA.	Vespasian takes Jericho.	......	......	......	Martyrdom.

EXCURSUS XI.

TRADITIONAL ACCOUNTS OF ST. PAUL'S PERSONAL APPEARANCE.

THE traditional accounts of the personal appearance of the great Apostle are too late to have any independent value, but it is far from improbable that where they coincide they preserve with accuracy a few particulars. Such as they are, the reader may perhaps care to see them translated; but he must bear in mind the sad probability that there were periods of St. Paul's career at which, owing to the disfigurement wrought by the ravages of his affliction, we should not have liked to gaze upon his face.

In the sixth century John of Antioch, commonly called Malala,[1] writes that "Paul was in person round-shouldered (τῇ ἡλικίᾳ κονδοειδής), with a sprinkling of grey on his head and beard, with an aquiline nose, greyish eyes, meeting eyebrows,[2] with a mixture of pale and red in his complexion, and an ample beard. With a genial expression of countenance, he was sensible, earnest, easily accessible, sweet, and inspired with the Holy Spirit."

Nicephorus,[3] writing in the fifteenth century, says, "Paul was short, and dwarfish in stature, and, as it were, crooked in person and slightly bent. His face was pale, his aspect winning. He was bald-headed, and his eyes were bright. His nose was prominent and aquiline, his beard thick and tolerably long, and both this and his head were sprinkled with white hairs."

In the Acts of Paul and Thekla, a romance of the third century, he is described as "short, bald, bow-legged, with meeting eyebrows, hook-nosed, full of grace."[4]

Lastly, in the Philopatris of the pseudo-Lucian,[5] a forgery of the fourth century,[6] he is contemptuously alluded to as "the bald-headed, hook-nosed Galilæan who trod the air into the third heaven, and learnt the most beautiful things."

The reader must judge whether any rill of truth may have trickled into these accounts through centuries of tradition. As they do not contradict, but are rather confirmed by, the earliest portraits which

---

[1] X. 257.
[2] This σύνοφρυωμα, and the expression ἀτενίσας, may be the sole ground for fancying that the eyes of St. Paul were grey and bright.
[3] H. E. ii. 37.
[4] I can make nothing of the εὔκνημος following the ἀγκύλος ταῖς κνήμαις.
[5] Philopatr. 12.
[6] Such is the opinion of Gesner in his dissertation De Aetate et Auctore Philopatridis.

have been preserved to us, we may perhaps assume from them thus much, that St. Paul was short—a fact also mentioned by the pseudo-Chrysostom,[1] and to which he may himself allude with somewhat bitter touches of irony in his Second Epistle to the Corinthians[2]—that he had a slight stoop, if not a positive bend, in the shoulders; that his nose was aquiline, and that his thin hair was early "sable-silvered." We may also conjecture from these notices that his face was pale, and liable to a quick flush and change of expression, and that when he was not absolutely disfigured by his malady, or when he was able to throw off the painful self-consciousness by which it was accompanied, the grace and sweetness of his address, the dignity and fire of his bearing, entirely removed the first unfavourable impression caused by the insignificance of his aspect. We may conclude that this was the case from many of the circumstances of his intercourse with men and churches, and also from the fact that the rude inhabitants of Lystra take him—before he had yet attained to middle age, and before his body had been so rudely battered as it was by many subsequent miseries—for an incarnation of the young and eloquent Hermes.

[1] ὁ τρίπηχυς ἄνθρωπος.   [2] 2 Cor. x. 10—16, especially verse 14.

INDEX.

Abennerig, King—Ananias' influence over his family, ii. 136. (*See* Ananias.)

Abhôda Zara, Quotations from, ii. 176, 177.

Abraham—his wives as types, i. 56.

Acts of Apostles—The intention and genuineness of, i. 7, 8; not a perfect history, 8, 9; chief uncial MSS. of, ii. 588, 589; its abrupt termination not explained, 510.

Adiabene—Province of, i. 307; Royal family of, how entangled by Judaisers, ii. 135.

Adrian VI.—his remark on the statuary of the Vatican, i. 527.

Advent, Nearness of final Messianic, i. 605.

Æneas healed, i. 263.

Agabus—his prophecy, i. 305, ii. 289.

Agapæ—Institution of, i. 90; held with closed doors, 176; in reference to the circumcision of Titus, 418; abuse of, at Corinth, ii. 56.

Agrippa I. and II., ii. 595.

Agrippa II.—his desire to hear Paul, ii. 353; Paul brought before, 353 *et seq.*; his use of the word "Christian," i. 299, ii. 359.

Agrippa, Herod. (*See* Herod.)

Akiba—33 rules of, i. 59.

Alexandria, The learning of the Jews of, i. 124, 128.

Altar, Altars—built by advice of Epimenides, i. 531; Paul's view of the altar at Athens to the Unknown God, 532.

Ananias and Sapphira—their sin and death, i. 106.

Ananias (of Damascus)—his doubts about Paul, i. 200; his intercourse with Paul, 201.

Ananias (Jewish merchant)—his ascendancy over King Abennerig and his family, ii. 136.

Ananias (the high priest)—his outrage on Paul, ii. 323.

Andrew—Andrew and Philip, though Hellenic names, yet common among the Jews, i. 130.

Annas—his treatment of Peter and John, i. 106.

Antichrist—Jewish and heathen influences in Rome, ii. 404—409.

Antinomies of Paul, ii. 590, 591.

Antioch (in Pisidia)—Description of, i. 364; Paul and Barnabas at, 365; synagogue and worship, 365, 366; Paul preaches in synagogue, 367.

Antioch (in Syria)—Mission of Paul and Barnabas, A.D. 44, i. 288; description of, 289; earthquake at, A.D. 37, 293; Christians first so called at, 296; early Church and religious feelings at, 323; state of Church in, 398; false brethren in Church, 399; Peter and Paul at, 437 *et seq.*

Antoninus (Emperor) and Rabbi Juda Hakadosh, ii. 137; circumcised, 138.

Apollonius Tyaneus at Ephesus, ii. 17.

Apollos—as regards authorship of the Epistle to the Hebrews, i. 10; at Ephesus—journey to Corinth—his preaching there, ii. 19, 20; unintentional cause of division in the Church at Corinth, 20; his report of the Corinthian Church to Paul, 45; results of his teaching at Corinth, 52.

Apostle—of love, John, i. 1; of the foundation stone, Simon, 1; of progress, Paul, 2; of the Gentiles, Paul, 3; the source and vindication of Paul's authority as an Apostle, ii. 97 *et seq.*; term of authority first used by Paul in his Epistle to the Galatians, 140.

Apostles—their antecedents compared with those of Paul, i. 5; bold after weakness, 83; their Lord's intercourse with them after His Resurrection, and the power of His Resurrection on them, 84; the regenerators of the world, 84; their last inquiry of their Lord as to the promised kingdom, 85; their feelings after their Lord's Ascension, 86; Jews still, only with belief in Christ, 87; the holy women joining with them in prayer, 87; fill up vacancy of Judas Iscariot, 87—89; as witnesses of their Lord's Resurrection, 88; their hope between Ascension and Pentecost, 89; the promise of the Holy Ghost fulfilled, 94; speaking with tongues, 95, 96; limit of the gift of tongues, 98; different views of the gift, 98, 99; charge of intoxication refuted, 103; miracles and signs done by them, 104, 105, 106, 263, 341, 354, 380; conduct under persecution, and strength of their position, 105; scourged, though defended by Gamaliel, 108; their early failing to grasp the truth, 141; their perception that the Mosaic Law was to be superseded, 142; their failure to understand the teaching of their Lord, 143; remain in Jerusalem when others fly from Saul's persecuting zeal, 173; tradition of twelve years as the limit fixed by their Lord for their abode in Jerusalem, 320; Greece and Rome in their time, 331; showing the superiority of Christianity over Stoicism, 333; convinced by Paul on circumcision, 408; letter after their decision on circumcision, 429; genuineness of this encyclical letter, 434.

Apostolical Journeys of Paul—The first, A.D. 45—46, Antioch in Syria, Seleucia, Cyprus, Perga in Pamphylia, Antioch in Pisidia, Iconium, Lystra, Derbe, Lystra, Iconium, Antioch in Pisidia, Perga, Attalia, Antioch in Syria, i. 334—390; the second, A.D. 53—56, Antioch in Syria, Derbe, Lystra, Phrygia, Galatia, Mysia, Troas, Samothrace, Neapolis, Philippi, Thessalonica, Beroea, Athens, Corinth, Ephesus, Cæsarea, Jerusalem, 454—ii. 4; the third, A.D. 56—60, Jerusalem, Antioch in Syria, Galatia, Phrygia, Ephesus, Troas, Macedonia, Illyricum, Corinth, Troas, Assos, Mitylene, Chios, Trogyllium, Miletus, Cos, Rhodes, Patara, Tyre, Ptolemais, Cæsarea, Jerusalem, ii. 6—291.

Apotheosis of Roman Emperors, i. 664.

Aquila and Priscilla—their relation to Paul, i. 560.

Arabia, the scene of Paul's retirement on his conversion, i. 206, 212, 213.

Aramaic—Paul's knowledge of, i. 17; in relation to the gift of tongues, 101; decay and advance of among Jews, 125.

Aratus, poet, of Cicilia, quoted by Paul, i. 543.

Aretas, Emir of Petra, i. 179.

Aristarchus, Paul's companion on his voyage to Rome, ii. 364.

Art—its relation to Christianity, i. 528.

Artemas—Artemidorus, ii. 537.

Artemis—Temple at Ephesus, ii. 10—14; worship at Ephesus, 15—18.

Ascension of our Lord, i. 85.

Athens—Associations and description, i. 522; the statuary of, 525; Paul at, 531; philosophers of, 533—535; Paul's preaching and its results, 536 *et seq.*; Paul questioned by the Athenians, 540; Athenian view of the Resurrection and judgment to come, 548; later growth of the Church at Athens, 551; Paul leaves Athens, 553.

Augustus Cæsar—his protection of the Jews, ii. 261.

Aurelius Antoninus, Marcus, on Christianity, i. 671.

B.

Baptism of the Ethiopian eunuch and its results, i. 261, 285.

Bar-Jesus the sorcerer. (*See* Elymas.)

Barnabas, St.—with Paul at Lystra, i. 19; his early relations with Paul, 236; his influence with the Apostles in Paul's favour, 237, 238; twice secured Paul's services for the work of Christianity, 237, 288; his need of help, 287; his view of the admission of the Gentiles to the Christian covenant, 287; his view of Paul's character, 288; commencement of their joint work, 288; separated jointly with Paul by the Holy Spirit for the work of converting the world, 334; dispute with Paul as to the companionship of Mark, 449; their separation, 449; friendship with Paul not broken, but mutual loss owing to the separation, 451. (*See* Paul.)

Basil, St.—his Christian education at Athens, i. 551.

Berenice—Paul before her, ii. 353; her character, 599.

Beroeans compared with the Thessalonians as to gladness in receiving the word of God, i. 518.

Bethany, the scene of our Lord's Ascension, i. 85.

Books and parchments of Paul at Troas, i. 36; ii. 569 *et seq.*, 576.

Burdens laid on proselytes, i. 666.

Burrus, Afranius—his character, ii. 392; in charge of Paul, 392; as formerly Prætorian Prefect, 546.

INDEX. 633

C.

Cæsar. (*See* distinctive names.)
Caiaphas—Peter and John before, i. 106; as guilty of the blood of Christ, 165.
Caligula. (*See* Gaius.)
Captivity, Paul's Epistles in, ii. 417.
Carpus of Troas, Paul's cloak, books, and parchments left with, i. 36; ii. 569, 576.
Castor and Pollux, ship in which Paul sailed from Melita, ii. 385 *et seq.*
Cenchreæ, Church at, i. 565.
Cephas. (*See* Peter.)
Chamber of the Last Supper and of assembly of the Apostles, i. 86, 320.
Charity, ii. 77.
Chastity, ii. 68 *et seq.*
Chief Priests. (*See* Priests.)
Chosen People. (*See* Jews.)
Chrestian and Christian, i. 301.
Christ. (*See* Jesus.)
Christendom founded by St. Paul, i. 3.
Christian, Christians—Origin of the name, and where first used, i. 298, 299; "Christian" and "Nazarene," 299, 300; Christian character as opposed to Jewish character, ii. 97; contrast brought out in Paul's Epistles to the Corinthians, 97; the life of the Christian a life in Christ, 266; Christian and Chrestian, i. 301; Christian unity (*see* Unity); at first not in disfavour with the Pharisees, but used by them against the Sadducees, i. 139; their observances and their position, 140; charged with blasphemy rather than with idolatry, 171; first so called at Antioch in Syria, 296, 298; their endurance under persecution, 330; living sacrifice required of, ii. 258; dangers dreaded by Paul for the Christians of Rome, 259.
Christianity—Conditions of, to the Jews, i. 328; views of, by Pliny, Tacitus, and Suetonius, 330; compared with Stoicism, 333; relation of, to art, 528; judgments of early Pagan writers on, 669 *et seq.*; its introduction into Rome, ii. 164 *et seq.*; right and wrong interpretations of, 546, 547.
Chronology of the life and Epistles of St. Paul, ii. 623.
Chrysostom, St.—his estimate of St. Paul, i. 6, 619.
Church, The—Its vitality from early times, i. 83; the early days of, 105 *et seq.*; results of its increase, 145 *et seq.*; Paul twice secured for work of, by Barnabas, 237; rest and progress, 256 *et seq.*; extension of, 283; work begun by Stephen, advanced by Philip, completed by Paul, 286; the early Church at Antioch in Syria, 323; false brethren in the Church at Antioch in Syria, 399; peril to, from the difference on circumcision, 404; growth of, at Athens, 551; Church founded by Paul at Corinth, 563; Church at Cenchreæ, 565; danger to, at Corinth, ii. 47; the heathen not judges in Church questions, 67; qualifications for office in, 520 *et seq.*; regulations for rulers in, 524 *et seq.* (*See* names of the several Churches.)
Cicero—his views of Athenian philosophy, i. 534.
Circumcision — disputed point at the Church at Antioch in Syria, i. 400 *et seq.*; disputes dangerous to the Church 404; question submitted to Church at Jerusalem, and especially to the Apostles as having known the Lord Jesus Christ, 404, 405; decision and encyclical letter of the Apostles, 429; of Timothy and Titus, 461; absence of necessity for, the key-note of Paul's Epistle to the Galatians, ii. 134; Defence of, by Judaisers, 134; its use to Judaisers, 138; as required by the Jews, 599, 600.
Civil Governors. (*See* Governors.)
Claudius—his accession, and consideration for the Jews, i. 255; his attempt to eject the Jews from Rome, ii. 163; his persecution of the Jews, 261.
Clement, St.—writing of Paul, i. 9.
Clementines, Attacks on Paul in the, i. 675 *et seq.*
Cloak, Paul's, books, and parchments left at Troas, i. 36; ii. 569, 576.
Coleridge, Opinion of, on Paul's Epistle to the Romans, ii. 180.
Colossæ, Account of, ii. 440—442.
Colossians—Paul's Epistle to, ii. 440 *et seq.*; causes of, 442 *et seq.*; state of Church described to Paul by Epaphras, 443 *et seq.*; false teachers in Church at Colossæ, 447 *et seq.*; objects of Epistle to, 448 *et seq.*; genuineness of Epistle to, 453, 454; account of Epistle to, 454; Jesus the remedy against the Phrygian mysticism of, 456; warning to, against false teachers, 459; future of the Church, 466, 467.
Conscience, Happiness of clear, ii. 267.
Corinth—Paul visits, i. 553; description of, 554, 555; Church founded at, by Paul, 563; Paul's pain at the immorality of Corinth, 567; dangers to Church, ii. 47; results of Apollos' teaching at, 52; false teachers in Church at, 53; further division in

Church at, 54 ; disputes in Church at, 55, 56 ; incest in Church at, 57 ; here Paul wrote Epistles to Galatians and Romans, 125 ; Paul's rejoicing in Church of, 125.

Corinthian, Corinthians—Epistles to, i. 605; wherein different from rest in plan and divisions, 605 ; relapse of Corinthian Christians into sensuality, ii. 48; causes of Paul's First Epistle to, 49—51 ; sins at the Lord's Supper, 57. Account of 1 Corinthians, 60—87 ; Paul's warnings against false teachers and divisions in Church, 63—65 ; Paul's dealing with cases of incest, 66, 67 ; on charity, meat offered to idols, and resurrection from the dead, 68 et seq. ; selfishness the origin of disorders in Church, 81 ; Paul's self-defence to, 91 ; restoration of Mark, 93 ; punishments for profanation of the Lord's Supper, 93. Account of 2 Corinthians, 90—118 ; Paul's self-vindication not self-commendation, 100—103 ; Church behind Macedonian Church, which, thou poor, collected for necessities of the saints, 109.

Cornelius and his friends converted to the Christian faith, i. 281.

Covering of the head for women, ii. 75, 76.

Cretans, Account of, by Epimenides, ii. 535.

Crispus baptised by Paul, i. 562.

Cyprus, Paul and Barnabas at—its share in the propagation of Christianity, i. 347 ; the Jews of, 348.

D.

Damaris, i. 549.

Damascus—State of feeling between Jews and Christians, i. 223 ; Paul's escape from, 227 ; under Hareth, 650.

David, poetry of Psalms of, compared with St. Paul's Epistles, i. 18.

Deacons—Cause for and appointment of, i. 131—134 ; their names, 133 ; results of their appointment, 135.

Death overcome by life, ii. 215—217.

Denys, St., of France, i. 549.

Derbe, Paul and Barnabas at, i. 388.

Diana. (*See* Artemis.)

Diaspora. (*See* Dispersion.)

Dionysius the Areopagite and St. Denys, i. 549.

Disciples. (*See* Apostles.)

Dispersion of the Chosen People, i. 115, 116; results of, on Jews, Greeks, and Romans, 117 et seq.

Dorcas raised from the dead, i. 263.

Drusilla with Felix hearing Paul, ii. 341.

E.

Earthquake at Antioch, A.D. 37, i. 293.

Ebionites and Nazarenes, i. 676.

Effort, Human, necessary but ineffectual, ii. 591.

Elymas—his blindness, i. 341, 354 ; his resistance of Paul, 353.

Emperors, Roman, Apotheosis of, i. 664 et seq.

Epaphras of Colossæ Visit to Paul, and its results, ii. 418 ; his messages to Paul on the Church at Colossæ, ii. 443.

Epaphroditus of Philippi—Visit to Paul, and its results, ii. 419 ; his work at Rome: illness, recovery, return to Philippi, 420, 421.

Ephesus—Ephesians—visited by Paul, ii. 3 ; description of, 7 ; A development of Christianity at, 7 ; sketch of its history, ii. 8—10 ; reputation of its inhabitants, 10 ; Temple of Artemis at, 10—14 ; superstition of, 16 ; Christians burn magical books, as the result of Paul's labours, 26, 27 ; outbreak which occasioned Paul's departure, 28—42 ; Sketch of Church at, 43, 44 ; Paul's Epistle to the Romans probably also sent to Ephesus, 170, 171 ; Paul's interview with elders of the Church at Miletus, 280—284; sketch of Paul's Epistle to the Ephesians, 493 et seq. ; phraseology and doctrines of the Epistle, 601—603.

Epictetus on Christianity, i. 670.

Epicureans, i. 535.

Epimenides—Altars built by his direction, i. 531 ; Paul's quotation from, in Epistle to Titus, ii. 534.

Epistle — Epistles — Paul's — Value and power of, i. 3, 4 ; Genuineness of, 7, 9, 10 ; to Hebrews as work of Apollos, 10 ; undesigned coincidences in, 11 ; compared with poetry of Psalms of David, 18 ; their testimony to Paul's "stake in the flesh," 218 ; Paul's Epistles to the Thessalonians, 510 ; 1 Thess., account of, 574 et seq.; Paul's Epistles compared with our Lord's Sermon on the Mount, 576 ; Paul's intense feelings conveyed in his Epistles, 576 ; their character, 577 ; salutation and opening, 578, 579 ; characteristics of 1 Thess., 581 et seq. ; 2 Thess., account of, 559 et seq.; object of this Epistle, 604 ; difference of the plan and division of 1 and 2 Cor. from Paul's other Epistles, 605 ; explanation of 2 Thess. 1—12, 610 et seq.; 1 Cor. written during latter part of stay at Ephesus, ii. 45 ; cause of this Epistle, 49 et

INDEX. 635

seq.; account of ditto, 60 *et seq.*; subjects of several, 90; 2 Cor., account of, 96 *et seq.*; Epistles to Galatians and Romans written at Corinth, 125; cause of the Epistle to the Galatians, 130; object, viz. to prove circumcision unnecessary, 133, 134; lasting results of the Epistle to the Galatians, 139; account of ditto, 140 *et seq.*; cause of Epistle to the Romans, 161; account of ditto, 162 *et seq.*; conclusion of, as probably intended originally, 269; actual conclusion of, 270; Epistles written at Corinth made the subject of Paul's preaching in that city, 273; their bearing on Paul's life—division into groups, 410 *et seq.*; order in which written, 415; of the Captivity, 417 *et seq.*; to Colossians, 438 *et seq.*; to Philemon, 442 *et seq.*; the Christology of the epistles of the captivity, 451—453; to Ephesians, 482 *et seq.*; causes of this Epistle; its genuineness, subject, style, compared with Epistle to Colossians, 483 *et seq.*; pastoral, 510 *et seq.*; 1 Timothy, 515 *et seq.*; to Titus, 529 *et seq.*; genuineness of the Pastoral Epistles, 540, 607 *et seq.*; Paul's account to Timothy of his loneliness in prison; the support of him by his God, and his Roman trial; his approaching end, 546 *et seq.*; 2 Timothy, account of, 561 *et seq.*; chief uncial MSS. of, 588, 589; Paul's Epistles, division into groups of— Eschatological, Anti-Judaic, Christological or Anti-Gnostic, Pastoral, 592—593; phraseology and diction of Epistle to the Ephesians, 601—603; chronology of Paul's Epistles, 623—625; dates of ditto, 626.

Etesian winds, ii. 366, 368.

Eunice and Lois visited by Paul, i. 457.

Eunuch, Ethiopian, baptised by Philip, i. 261; results of baptism to infant church, 285.

Euodia and Syntyche as Christian women of Macedonia, i. 488; exhorted to unity by Paul in Epistle to Ephesians, ii. 422.

Euroaquilo—Euroclydon, ii. 371.

Eutychus, fall and restoration to life, ii. 276—279.

Evodius, Bishop of Antioch, tradition of, as inventor of the name of "Christian," i. 300.

F.

Faith—revived by writings of Paul, i. 3, 4; Justification by, first taught by Paul, 3; Power of justification by, ii. 188, 194, 209 *et seq.*, 213; difference between justification by faith and justification by the Law, 231; relation of hope to, 238.

Feasts, Love Feasts, i. 90. (*See* Agapæ.)

Felix, his judicial impartiality, i. 570, ii. 261; made Procurator of Judæa A.D. 52, ii. 306; his estimation among the Jews, 337; deferred completion of Paul's trial for evidences of Lysias, 340; trembles at Paul's reasoning, 341; his attempts to procure bribes for Paul's release, 342 *et seq.*; cause of his disgrace—his last act of injustice to Paul, 343 *et seq.*

Festus—his judicial impartiality, i. 570, ii. 261; succeeds Felix as Procurator of Judæa A.D. 60, 346; brings Paul before Agrippa, 353 *et seq.*; his treatment of Paul, 347—350.

Flaccus, Governor of Alexandria, arrest and death, i. 249, 250.

Food, Paul's rules as to use of, ii. 264.

Forgiveness of the redeemed, Paul's view of, ii. 591.

Foundation stone, Peter the Apostle of, i. 1.

Free will, Paul's view of, ii. 590.

G.

Gaius (Caligula) — succeeded Tiberius as Emperor of Rome, i. 244; friend of Herod Agrippa, 245; intended profanation of the Temple at Jerusalem, and death, 252—254.

Gaius (convert of St. Paul) baptized by Paul, i. 565.

Galatia—Galatians—Paul's visit to, i. 464 *et seq.*; their kindness to Paul, 471; Churches in, founded by Paul, 474.

Galatians, Paul's Epistle to—Cause of, ii. 130; object, to prove circumcision unnecessary, 133, 134; lasting results of, 139; account of, 140 *et seq.*; apostolic authority in the opening salutation first assumed in this Epistle, 140, 141; sense of wrong in the mind of the writer — abrupt plainness — charge of perverting the Gospel—vindication of the Apostolic character — commission and labours—recognition by the other Apostles—dispute with Peter, 142—147; who are sons of Abraham—from what Christ has ransomed us—use of the law, 148—150; concord of Law and Promise—all free in Christ, and Abraham's seed—difference between old and new covenants—old covenant fulfilled its office, 150 — 153; allegory of Sarah and Hagar and their sons—Galatians can combine neither Law and Gospel nor flesh and spirit—the question not of circumcision or uncircumcision, but of a new creature, 154—156.

Galen on Christians, i. 671.

Gallio, Lucius Junius Annæus, brother of Seneca, uncle of Lucan, made Proconsul of Asia, i. 566; character (generally misunderstood) among his friends, 567; his indifference when Paul is brought before him, 568; his reason for refusing to commit Paul, 569; his judicial impartiality, 570; result of his justice to Paul while in Corinth, ii. 1; protecting Paul by his disdainful justice, 261.

Gamaliel—as instructor of Paul, i. 5, 25, 44; his views of the wisdom of the Greeks, 37; Rabbi, Rabban—his parentage—liberality of his views, 44; his character, 45; as a Pharisee, 46; value of his teaching to Paul, 48; defence of Paul, 108, 109; Gamaliel and the school of Tübingen, 644, 646.

Gentiles—Deliverance and admission of, to the Church of Christ, i. 258; commencement of their reception into the Church, 285, 286; their generous help of Jewish Christians, 306; Simeon's prophecy, 325; of Pisidia gladly accept Gospel preached by Paul on its rejection by the Jews, 375; Paul's future care, 396; moderation of the Gentile Christians of Rome towards Jewish Christians when Paul wrote the Epistle to the Romans, ii. 174; their sin of denying and abandoning God, their punishment, 195, 196; Gentiles and Jews equally guilty before God, and equally redeemed, 205.

Ghost, Holy. (See Holy Ghost.)

Glossolalia, i. 52, 99, 100, 101. (See Tongues.)

God—Peace only in his love, i. 70; his dealings with men, 91; visions from, 194; his warnings, 198; universal worship prophesied by Zephaniah, 325; only giver of blessing on ministerial labours, ii. 63; effect of His righteousness on man, 188; truth to His promises proved by Paul, 206—288; manifestation of his righteousness, 209; His infinite love the solution of predestinarian difficulties, 244; His grace, wisdom, judgments, 256; kingdom of God defined, 266; God working in man, and judging through Christ, 591. (See Unknown God.)

Gospel—Witness to our Lord, i. 326; women's part in dissemination of, 488; the power of, ii. 186; for Jews and Gentiles alike, 195.

Governors, Civil—Duties to, ii. 260; Functions of, 260; Paul's teachings of obedience to, 262.

Grace—Relation to sin, ii. 219, 220; abundance of, above sin, 245; wisdom, and judgments, 256; source of grace, mercy, and pity, 257.

Greece—Character of, in time of the Apostles, i. 331.

Greeks—their "wisdom," i. 37; results on, of the dispersion of the Jews, 117; contact with Jews, 118; conversion of Greek proselytes, 286; their violent treatment of Sosthenes before Gallio, 571.

Gregory, Nazianzus—his Christian education at Athens, i. 551.

H.

Habakkuk, quoted by Paul, ii. 198.
Hagada and Hagadist, i. 58 et seq.
Halacha and Halachist, i. 58 et seq.
Hallel studied by Paul when a boy, i. 43.
Heathendom in the time of the Apostles, i. 331.
Hebraism and Hellenism, i. 115 et seq.
Hebrew—Paul's knowledge of, used by our Lord in Paul's conversion, i. 17.
Hebrews, Epistle to, as work of Apollos, i. 10.
Helena, Queen — her protracted vows, ii. 135, 136.
Hellenism and Hebraism, i. 115 et seq.
Herod Agrippa—his character, i. 246, 247; imprisoned by Tiberius, released by Gaius on his accession to the Empire, and appointed successor as Tetrarch to Herod Philip and Lysanias, 246; beginning of his reign, reception at Alexandria, 247; his influence and promotion, 309; observance of the Mosaic Law, 311; slays James—arrests Peter, 311 et seq.; his death, 314 et seq.
Herods in the Acts, ii. 594 et seq.
Hillel—grandfather of Gamaliel, i. 44, 45, 46, 47, 129; the seven rules of, 59; dealing with burdensome Mosaic regulations, 69.
Holy Ghost, Holy Spirit—Promise of, to Apostles, i. 84; gift of, at Pentecost, 93, 94; effects of gift, 94, 95.
Hope—its power unto salvation, its relation to faith, ii. 238, 239.
Hope and Peace the result of justification by faith, ii. 213, 214.

Hymn at first Pentecost after gift of tongues, i. 101.

I.

Iconium (Konieh) visited by Paul and Barnabas, i. 375.
Idolatry—Influence of, on Jewish and other communities, i. 122.
Idols—Meats offered to, ii. 68 *et seq.*
Incest in Corinthian Church—Paul's dealing with, ii. 66, 67.
Inspiration. (*See* Verbal Inspiration.)
Ishmael—Thirteen rules of, i. 59.
Israel—The dispersion of, ii. 255. (*See* Jews.)
Issachar, High Priest, ii. 595.
Izates, son of Abennerig, circumcised, i. 207, 308; ii. 136, 137.

J.

James the Greater, his death, i. 312.
James the Less, error in his view of Paul's work, i. 131; cause for his respect by the people, 142; compared with Paul, 232; convinced by Paul as to circumcision, 408; description of, 424; on circumcision, 426 *et seq.;* with elders of the Church receives Paul at Jerusalem, 292.
Jason—Name identical with Jesus, i. 25; charge against Jason by Jews of Thessalonica, 514.
Jerome, St.—Fragments of traditions of Paul, i. 15, 16; on Paul, 619; compared with Paul, ii. 247.
Jerusalem—Crowd at first Pentecost, i. 102; birthplace of Christianity, ii. 7; its dangers to Paul, 160; state of feeling among Jews at time of proposal of James and elders to Paul, 302 *et seq.*
Jesus Christ the Lord—Speaking to Paul in Hebrew at his conversion, i. 17; his notice of beauties of nature not the subject of Paul's language, 20; name identical with Jason, 25; love manifested in His death, risen, glorified, known to Paul by revelation, 74; intercourse with disciples after resurrection not continuous, 84; promise of Holy Spirit to Apostles; power of His resurrection, 84; His ascension, 85; His mission to found a kingdom, 143; His purposes to supersede the Law not seen in His observance of it, 143; significance not seen at the time of His teaching on the Sabbath, 143; universality of spiritual worship, &c., 143; fulfilled the Law in spiritualising it, 144; as Messiah, an offence to the Jews, but still that which Stephen undertook to prove, 148; why He declared Himself to Paul as "Jesus of Nazareth," 196; all in all to Paul, 202; second special revelation to Paul, 239; deeper meaning underlying many of His words, 267; tradition that twelve years was the limit laid down by Him for abode of His disciples in Jerusalem, 320; light to Gentiles, 325; erroneous view of Him by Suetonius, 330; His mission to send not peace but a sword, 572; the fundamental conception of all Christianity in John and Paul, 675; undivided, ii. 61; object of all preaching, 62; the only foundation, 63; common foundation for Jew and Gentile, 180; bond of human society, 180; this is the basis of all Paul's Epistles, 180; Power of life in, 237; His sacrifice and exaltation, 429; the Divine Word the remedy for Phrygian mysticism, &c., in the Colossian Christians, 456; as judge, 591.
Jews—as persecutors of Paul, i. 9; their care for youths as to "dubious reading," 37; marriage customs, 43, 84; value of the Scriptures among them, 51; their literature, 57 *et seq.;* vows, 71; as originators of discord among Christians, 74; underrating the apostolic dignity of Paul, 74; customs in synagogues, 87; persecuting the apostles, 107 *et seq.;* The dispersion of, 115 *et seq.;* result of the dispersion on themselves and on Greeks and Romans, 117, 120; result of contact on the Greeks, 117; violent outbreaks, 119; causes which led to their commercial character, 123; of Alexandria, their learning, advance in literature, more enlightened than the Rabbis of Jerusalem as to the purposes of of God's gifts, 124, 128; change of language on dispersion, and results of contact with Aryan race, 125; ordinances to prohibit relations with heathen, and bloodshed resulting from them, 129, 130; their Greek names, 133; their Messianic hopes, 148; their reverence for Moses, 151; infuriated at Stephen's view of the Law of Moses, 152; not naturally persecutors, 170; the forbearance of the Christian Jews of Rome to Gentiles when Paul wrote his Epistle to the Romans, 174; of Damascus—their feeling towards Christians—their reception of Paul's

preaching, 223—225; their scourgings of Paul, 226; relief at death of Tiberius, 245; allegiance to Gaius, 245; how regarded in Alexandria—barbarities practised on them, 247—251; contributions for brethren in Judæa, 305; Jewish Christians helped by Gentiles in return for spiritual wealth, 306; of Antioch in Syria, 322; conditions on which alone they could accept Christianity, 323; two Jews (Paul and Barnabas) on a journey for the conversion of the world, 324; of Cyprus, and of Salamis, 348; their lectionary, 369; jealousy of the Jews at Antioch in Pisidia, against the Gentiles at Paul's preaching, 374; Paul stoned at Lystra by Jews of Antioch and Iconium, 385; their hatred of Paul, 388; their hatred of Paul and Christ, 512; disturbance caused by them against Paul at Thessalonica, 513 *et seq.*; belief of Jews of Berœa, 518; Paul's intercourse with, and teaching of the Jews of Athens, 532; Paul's complaints of the Jews of Corinth, 566; their animosity against Christians, even to bringing false accusations against them, 570; of Thessalonica, 583; their calumnies against Paul, 583; their persecution of Paul, 585; scourgings, 661; Hatred of, in classical antiquity, 667; their opposition to Paul, ii. 19; introduced into Rome by Pompey, 162; his treatment of them, 162; useless as slaves, 162; consequent emancipation, 162; multiply and flourish, 162; cause of their position in the world, 162; attempts of Sejanus and Claudius to eject them from Rome, 163; Seneca's account of the Jews in Rome, 164; convicted by Paul of the same sin as the Gentiles, in forsaking and denying their God, 198 *et seq.*; equally redeemed with the Gentiles, but their hope vain while on wrong foundation, 240; Rejection of, from privileges, 246, 247; Love of Paul for, 248; not naturally, but spiritually alone, heirs of the promises, 249; their want of faith in rejection of the Gospel, 252, 253; their rejection by their God neither entire nor final, 254; their restoration, 255; their protection by Roman law, 261; their plot against Paul's life, 272; causes of their plot, 273; its discovery and prevention, 274; customs as to Nazarite vows, and proposal of elders at Jerusalem to Paul, 295, 296; disposition at time of Paul's fifth visit to Jerusalem, various outbreaks, 302 *et seq.*; of Ephesus, outbreak against Paul, 308 *et seq.*; charge against Paul of defiling the temple, 309 *et seq.*; Division among, at Paul's answer as to the resurrection, 328, 329; contest with Greeks in market-places of Cæsarea, 343, 347; edict of banishment by Claudius, 392; their reply to Paul's appeal to Cæsar, 392; Number of, in Rome,—they hear Paul, 384, 395; influence and trade at Rome, 404—406.

Joel, Fulfilment of prophecy of, at Pentecost, i. 1.

John—as a "son of thunder," i. 1; impress of individuality on Church, 1; martyrdom of life, 2; his miracles, 105; description of Rome in Apocalypse, 331; convinced by Paul on circumcision, 408; compared with Paul, 673 *et seq.*

John and Peter—two chief apostles, i. 2; before the chief priests, 106; their knowledge of the mind of Christ, 675.

John Mark. (*See* Mark.)

Jonathan, High Priest at death of Stephen, i. 156, 165.

Joseph, the Levite of Cyprus—his early relations with Paul, i. 235.

Joseph Barsabus, surnamed Justus—chosen with Matthias at election of an apostle, i. 88.

Josephus—his allusion to death of Herod Agrippa, i. 317.

Journeys—Apostolical, of Paul. (*See* Apostolical.)

Juda Hakkadosh, Rabbi, and the Emperor Antoninus, ii. 137.

Judaisers, Judaising teachers—Judaism—Paul's controversy with, in 2 Corinthians, Galatians, and Romans, ii. 96; success in undoing Paul's work in Antioch, Corinth, and Galatia, hence Epistle to Galatians, 129, 130; their charges against Paul, 132; circumcision the ground of their contention with Paul, 134; their motive in defending circumcision, 138; their hostility at Jerusalem dangerous to Paul, 160.

Judas Iscariot—his fall by sin and his end, i. 87; antitype of Ahitophel, 88.

Jude, misapprehension of his Epistle, i. 678.

Judgment, Paul on, ii. 591.

Julian, attempt to substitute the term "Nazarene" for "Christian," i. 299, 300.

Julius (Centurion)—his judicial impartiality, i. 570; placed in charge of Paul to take him to Rome, ii. 362 *et seq.*; gives up his charge of Paul, 390.

Julius Cæsar, his protection of the Jews, ii. 261.
Justification by faith. (*See* Faith.)
Juvenal, his description of Rome, i. 331.

K.

Kephas. (*See* Peter.)
Kingdom of God—erroneous ideas of, i. 65; foundation of, Christ's mission, 143; definition of, ii. 266.
Konieh. (*See* Iconium.)

L.

Languages. (*See* Tongues.)
Last Supper, Upper room of, i. 86, 320.
Law—The righteousness of, and what depended on it, i. 65; its 285 commands and 365 prohibitions, 65; Oral, nullity of, 66; its traditions and glosses injurious, 66; requirements before God, 68; requirements impossible for man to satisfy, 69; Hypocrisy in observance of, 69; of Moses, our Lord's explanation of its destiny, 151; Use, objects, and end of, ii. 217, 218, 517; its position in the scheme of salvation, 221, 222; why not justifying, 223; multiplying transgressions, 224—226; difference between justification by the Law and justification by faith, 230; position further defined, 233; illustration from marriage, 233; its relation to sin, 234, 236.
Lectionary, Jewish, i. 369.
Levanter, ii. 371.
Lex Porcia, i. 41.
Life—overcoming death, ii. 215—217; in Christ, 237; its power, 237.
Lois and Eunice visited by Paul, i. 457.
Longinus on the style of Paul, i. 26, 619.
Lord. (*See* Jesus.)
Love—John, the Apostle of, i. 1; infinite love of God the solution of predestinarian difficulties, ii. 244; the debt of all, ii. 263. (*See* Charity.)
Love Feasts, i. 90; held with closed doors, 176. (*See* Agapæ.)
Lucan—his relation to Gallio, i. 567.
Lucian on Christianity, i. 671.
Luke—possible errors and minute exactness, i. 113; not professing to give a complete biography of Paul, 205; Paul's companion from Troas on second Apostolic journeys, 479; his fidelity to him, 479; antecedents and history —his character as physician, and in his relation to Paul, 480, 481; with Paul at Philippi, ii. 275; his companion on his voyage to Rome, 364; as historian of the Apostles, 510; abrupt ending of the Acts not explained, 510 *et seq.*; his faithfulness to Paul in his imprisonment, 546.
Luther, Martin, compared with Paul, i. 4, ii. 139, 247; Opinion of, Epistle to the Romans, ii. 180.
Lydia—baptised, i. 487; entertains Paul, 488; and friends at Philippi, their care for Paul in his imprisonment at Rome, ii. 420.
Lysias—his judicial impartiality, i. 570; protecting Paul by his soldier-like energy, ii. 261; rescues Paul from the Jews in the Temple, 311; his error about Paul, 312; permits Paul to speak to the Jews, 313; informed by Paul's nephew of plot of the Jews to take Paul's life—rescues him — and sends him from Jerusalem to Cæsarea, 311 *et seq.*
Lystra—visited by Paul and Barnabas, i. 380; Paul's sufferings there rewarded by his conversion of Timothy, 386; visited again by Paul, 457.

M.

Macedonia—Influx of Jew and Greeks, but without mixing with each other, i. 118; visited by Paul on second apostolic journey, 482; position of women in, 488.
Malta, in connexion with Paul's shipwreck, ii. 378, 382.
Man—Three great epochs in the religious history of, ii. 214; Four phases of, 226; not under the law but under grace, 226.
"Man of Sin," ii. 583 *et seq.*
Manaen, (Menahem) foster-brother of Herod Antipas, i. 323.
Manuscripts—Chief uncial MSS. of the Acts of the Apostles and the Epistles of St. Paul, ii. 588, 589.
Marcus Aurelius Antoninus on Christianity, i. 671.
Mark—interpreter to St. Peter, i. 98; companion of Paul and Barnabas, 320, 345; relationship to Barnabas, 358; leaves Paul and Barnabas at Perga, 359; as the cause of separation between Paul and Barnabas, 449; result to him of the difference between Paul and Barnabas, 452; again welcomed by Paul as a fellow-labourer, 453.
Marriage—Age for, and customs among Jews, i. 43, 81; Rabbinical injunction

to marry young, 81; in reference to Paul, 81; Paul's view of marriage and virginity as given to the Corinthian Church, ii. 70.
Mary, the mother of our Lord—Worship of, in Cyprus, i. 350.
Mary, owner of the house in which was the upper chamber in which the Apostles met, and possibly in which the Last Supper had taken place, i. 320.
Masters and servants—Mutual duties, ii. 527.
Matthias chosen an Apostle, i. 88, 89.
Meat and other food, Paul's rules as to use of, ii. 264.
Melancthon's opinion of Paul's Epistle to the Romans, ii. 181.
Melita. (See Malta.)
Menahem. (See Manaen.)
Mercy, Vessels of, ii. 251.
Messiah—Rabbinical idea of conditions of His coming, i. 66; fulfilling many prophecies, 150.
Miletus, Paul's interview at, with elders of the Church of Ephesus, ii. 280 et seq.
Miracles wrought by Apostles, i. 105, 106, 137, 263, 341, 354, 380.
Mishna—rules for marriages, i. 81; marriage the first of its 613 precepts, 81.
Missionary journeys of Paul. (See Apostolical.)
Mnason entertains Paul at Jerusalem, ii. 291.
Monastic life compared with Pharisaism, i. 64.
Monobazus, King of Adiabene, and his family, i. 307.
Monobazus, son of Abennerig and Helena, circumcised, ii. 136, 137.
Mosaic Law. (See Law.)
Moses—Jewish reverence for, i. 151; his claim on mankind, 151, 152; Relation of Paul to, before and after his conversion respectively, 213; his marriage, 325.
Mount of Olives, scene of our Lord's ascension, i. 85.

N.

"Nazarene"—Julian's attempt to get this word substituted for "Christian," i. 299, 300.
Nazarenes and Ebionites, i. 676.
Nazarite vows, Jewish customs as to, and proposal of elders at Jerusalem to Paul, ii. 295, 296.
Nero—Points with, in Paul's favour, ii. 360, 361; persecution, 404, 546; the direction of his influence at Rome, 407—409; his government, 546; Paul before Nero, 553 et seq.; his character, 554, 555.
New Testament. (See Testament.)
Nicodemus as a Pharisee, i. 46.
Nicolas—Significance of his appointment as a deacon, i. 133; evidence connecting him with the Nicolaitans insufficient, 133.

O.

Offertory, Paul on the, ii. 109, 117, 120, 122, 160.
Old Testament. (See Testament.)
Olives, Mount of. (See Mount of Olives.)
Onesimus—Visit to Paul and conversation, ii. 396; subject of Paul's Epistle to Philemon, 442, 443; his offence and its legal consequences, 469 et seq.
Onesiphorus—his search for Paul and visits to him in prison at Rome, ii. 549; his kindness to Paul, 563.
Oral Law. (See Law.)
Our Lord—our Redeemer—our Saviour. (See Jesus.)

P.

Paganism and its results, ii. 197.
Paphos, Soothsayers of, i. 353.
Paraclete. (See Holy Ghost.)
Parchments and books of Paul at Troas, i. 36; ii. 569 et seq., 576.
Parthenon dedicated to Virgin Mary, i. 552.
Pascal, Antecedents of, and compared with Paul, i. 4.
Passover, Upper room of, i. 86, 320.
Pastoral Epistles, Paul's, Genuineness of, ii. 607, et seq.
Paul—Apostolical journeys of (see Apostolical); Apostle of Progress, i. 2; "in deaths oft," 2; Apostle of the Gentiles, i. 3; teacher of justification by faith, 3; under God the founder of Christendom, 3; value of his Epistles, 3; power of his writings, 3, 4; his character, 3, 6; antecedents and life, compared with those of Luther, Wesley, and others, 4; antecedents compared with those of other Apostles, 5, 12; his education, 5, 12; his history gathered from the Acts and the Epistles but fragmentary, 7 et seq.; genuineness of his Epistles, 7, 9, 10; his account of his own sufferings, compulsory, 9; sufficiency for materials of his life and character, 11; undesigned coincidences in his Epistles, 11; "Paul the aged," 13; birthplace and boyhood, 13, et seq.; parentage and descent, 16,

34; power in his nationality, 16, 34; languages known to him, 16, 17; languages in which he spoke, 18; his inner life, 19; unobservant of such beauties of nature as were frequently mentioned by our Lord, 20; early impressions at Tarsus, 22; influencing causes of his trade, 23; influences of his trade on his character, 24; his parents, 24; their privileges as Roman citizens inherited by him, 24; his kinsmen, 25; his education under Gamaliel, 25; a Hebraist, though writing in Greek, 26; Longinus' criticisms on his style, 26; Cilicisms in his style, 27; influence on him of his residence in Tarsus, 27 et seq.; his preference of folly with God over the wisdom of heathendom, 33; not of Hellenic culture, his style peculiar and his Greek provincial, his thoughts Syriac, his dialectic method Rabbinic, 35, 36; his books and parchments at Troas, 36, ii. 569 et seq., 576; those books, &c., not Greek literature, 37; acquaintance with Greek literature, 38; classic quotations and allusions, 39; Roman citizenship, 40 et seq.; scourgings, 41, 42; Roman citizenship not inconsistent with Jewish descent, 42; early studies, 43; claims to be a Pharisee, 46; knowledge of the Old Testament, quoting the LXX., 47; value to him of Gamaliel's teaching, 48; his views of inspiration, 49; use of the Old Testament and of Scriptures generally, 50 et seq.; his style of argument to Jews, 51; as Hebrew and Hellenist, 58; endeavours to keep the Law, 65; misconception of the Oral Law, 66; extent of his obedience to the Law, 67; early anxieties, 70; compared with Luther, Bunyan, and John Newton, 71; early inward struggles, 72; saw the Lord Jesus Christ, 73—75; knowledge of the Lord Jesus Christ by faith, 75; not at Jerusalem at the time of our Lord's ministry and crucifixion—influence on him of Stephen's dying words. 77, 83; his marriage, 79, 80; early dealing with the infant Church, 83; cause for his hatred by the people, 142; his part in the dispute with Stephen in the Synagogue of the Libertines, 146; his feelings on listening to him, 146; holding the clothes of those who stoned Stephen, 167; aged thirty years at Stephen's martyrdom, 169; member of the Sanhedrin, and so a married man, 169; his fury against Christians, 170; even underrated as a persecutor, 172; 173; his confession of erring obstinacy in persecuting the Church, 174; under persecution, 175, 176; his commission for Damascus, 177 et seq.; reflections on his way to Damascus—conversion, 180, 191; inward struggles, 185; knowledge that he had been spoken to by his God, 192; result of having seen the Lord Jesus Christ, 193; his blindness, 193; the two accounts of his conversion, 197; immediately after his conversion led blind into Damascus, 199; entry into and departure from Damascus, 199, 200; original mission to Damascus, 202; his conversion as an evidence of Christianity, 202; Christ all in all to him, and his witness to Christ, 202; a preacher of the cross and the crucified, 203; a Nazarene, 205; the training necessary for his great work, 205; retirement into Arabia—his need of retirement, 206—208; source of his Apostleship, 210; frame of mind after his conversion, 211 et seq.; his relation to Moses and Mosaism, 213; his "thorn in the flesh" here called "stake in the flesh," 214 et seq.; traces of his "stake in the flesh," 215 et seq.; object of his "stake in the flesh," 221; return to and preaching at Damascus, 222 et seq.; how his preaching was received by the Jews of Damascus, 225; scourged by the Jews, 226; escape from Damascus, 227; journey from Damascus to Jerusalem, and reception there, 228; meeting with Peter at Jerusalem, 231; compared with James, 232; early relations with Joseph, Mark and Barnabas, 235, 236; early trials, 236; twice secured by Barnabas for the work of Christianity 237, 288; his recognition by the Apostles through Barnabas, 237, 288; early ministry, perils, escapes — second vision of a mission from the Lord Jesus to the Gentiles, 239 et seq.; again at Tarsus, 241; shipwrecks, 242; as Apostle of the Gentiles, 259; influence in Church, advancement of Paul, Stephen, and Philip respectively, 286; supplying the help need by Barnabas—with Barnabas at Antioch in Syria—their joint work begun, 287, 288; preaching at Antioch in Syria and its results, 295 et seq.; separated with Barnabas by the Holy Spirit for the work of converting the world, 334; Apostle of the Gentiles, 334; first Apostolic journey, 334 — 390; description of Paul, 341; strikes Elymas blind, 341; his miracles, 341, 354,

380; a widower and childless, 342; defects more than counterbalanced by his gifts, 342; at Cyprus, 347; at Salamis, 348; reason for change in his name, 355, 356; Mark leaves Paul and Barnabas at Perga, 359; at Antioch in Pisidia, 365; preaches there, 367; results, 367 *et seq.;* there also, on rejection of the Gospel by the Jews, turns to the Gentiles, 375; at Iconium, 378; preaches at Iconium, 378; results, 378 *et seq.;* at Lystra, 380; Paul preaches, 380; heals a cripple, 380; taken for gods, 381; disclaim the honours offered to them, 381; stoned by Jews at Lystra, 385; converts Timothy, 386; with Barnabas leaves Lystra, 387; at Derbe, 388; work and success, 388; Gaius and other friends and converts, 388; return from Derbe to Antioch in Syria, completing first Apostolic journey, 390; results of first Apostolic journey, 392; convictions after first Apostolic journey, 393; conscious of special mission to Gentiles, 398; with Barnabas goes to Jerusalem on question of circumcision, 405; converts Titus who goes with him to Jerusalem, 407; convinces John, Peter, and James on circumcision as unnecessary, 408; zeal for poor of Church at Jerusalem, 410; circumcises Timothy, 412; Nazarite vow, 417; with Peter at Antioch in Syria, 437 *et seq.;* his prominence as a guide of the Church, 438; influence at Antioch, where he is joined by Silas, 438; rebukes Peter for change of bearing towards Gentiles, 442 *et seq.;* result of rebuke on Peter, 447 *et seq.;* dispute with Barnabas as to the companionship of Mark, 449; separation, 449; mutual loss to Paul and Barnabas, though friendship not broken, 451; the welcome of Mark again as fellow-labourer, 453, ii. 568; second Apostolic journey, i. 454—ii. 4; visits Churches of Syria and Cilicia, Tarsus, Derbe, and Lystra, i. 445 *et seq.;* love for Timothy, 458; love for his churches, 459; circumcision of Timothy and Titus, 461; goes through Phrygia and Galatia, 463; visits Iconium, 463; Antioch in Pisidia, 463, 464; visits Jews on Euxine, Galatia, and results, 464, 465; illness in Galatia, 467 *et seq.;* cause of illness, 470; kindness of Galatians, 471; founds churches in Galatia, 474; visits Bithynia, Troas, Alexandria, 475 *et seq.;* meets with Luke, 479; Luke's fidelity to him, 479; takes Luke with him from Troas, 479; in his relations with Luke, 481; at Philippi, 482 *et seq.;* ministry at Philippi, 487; baptises Lydia of Thyatira, 487; lodges with Lydia, 488; reason for accepting pecuniary aid from Philippi *only* of all his churches, 488; his fellow-workers at Philippi, 488; casts out spirit of divination from possessed damsel, 490; anger of owners, 490; charge against Paul and Silas, 490; imprisoned and scourged, 490; conversion and baptism of jailor, 490; fear of the magistrates, 490; Paul and Silas leave Philippi, 490; leave Luke behind them, 490 *et seq.;* at Thessalonica, 504; poverty when there, 507; ministry there, 508; preaches Christ in synagogue, 508; believers chiefly among the Gentiles, 508; Epistles to the Thessalonians, 508, *et seq.;* dangers, 512; hatred of Paul by the Jews, 512; in concealment, 515; escape from Thessalonica, 515, 516; with Silas leaves Thessalonica for Berœa, 517; Athens, 519 *et seq.;* his feelings at Athens, 523, 530; intercourse with the Jews of Athens, 532; altar to the Unknown God, 532; preaches at Athens, 537; result, 537 *et seq.;* view of, in society, 540; answers questions of the Athenians, 541; declares true God and the resurrection of the dead, 543; tact in addressing Athenians, 543, 544; leaves Athens, 550; apparent failure, 550; germ of victory in all his apparent failures, 551; at Corinth, 553; Epistles to the Corinthians and Thessalonians, 556; grief at the wickedness of Corinth, 557 *et seq.;* will accept nothing from the Corinthians lest it be used as a handle, 559; relation to Aquila and Priscilla, 560; works as a tent-maker, 561; joined by Silas and Timotheus, 561; receives contributions from Philippian Christians, 561; founds Church at Corinth, 563; complaints of Paul by Jews of Corinth, 566; not allowed by Gallio to defend himself, 568; dismissed by Gallio, 569; his supposed correspondence with Seneca, spurious, 572; writes 1 Thess., probably his earliest Epistle, 574; account of 1 Thess., 574 *et seq.;* his intense feelings conveyed in his writings, 576; anxiety as to reception and result of his Epistles, 577; salutation and introduction in Epistles, 578; thankfulness on behalf of Thessalonian Christians in 1 Thess., 581; dangers at Thessalonica and Philippi, 383; calumnies from Jews and Gentiles,

583; answer to Thessalonian calumnies in his life and disinterestedness, 584; taking nothing from them, 584; persecution by the Jews, 585; joy in the Christians of Thessalonica, 586; visit of Timothy to Thessalonica, 589; his report of the faith which he finds there, 589 et seq.; enjoins practical Christian duties on the Thessalonians, 589; on the resurrection of the dead, 591 et seq.; corrects error and sloth caused by idea of day of the Lord as near at hand, 599; account of 2 Thess., 559 et seq.; view of day of the Lord, 601; object in 2 Thess., 604; style illustrative of writer's character, 619; various writers in testimony of, 619 et seq.; Rhetoric of, 625; classic quotations and allusions, 630; a Hagadist, 638; Paul and Philo, 638 et seq.; in Arabia, 651; "stake in the flesh," 652; Paul and John, 673 et seq.; attacks on Paul in the Clementines, 675 et seq.; stay at Corinth, ii. 1; at Ephesus, 1 et seq.; in his character as a Jew, 2; his temporary Nazarite vow and its conditions, 2; preaches Christ at Ephesus, 4; goes to Jerusalem for fourth time, 4; his four visits enumerated, 4; end of second Apostolic journey, 4; reception at Jerusalem, 5; third Apostolic journey, 6—291; goes again to Antioch and again visits Churches of Phrygia and Galatia, 6 et seq.; peril at Ephesus, 17; testimony to Apollos, 20; labours at Ephesus, 21; withdraws his disciples from Jews of Ephesus, and disputes daily in the school of Tyrannus, 22; success at Ephesus, 23; perils—outbreak at Ephesus from worshippers of Diana, 28 et seq.; leaves Ephesus, 43; joined by two Ephesians, Tychicus and Trophimus, 43; care for Corinthian Churches, 46; distress at news of Church from Corinth, 51; begins 1 Corinthians, 59; declaration to the Corinthians of purpose of his mission, 61; declares doctrine of crucified Saviour, 62; exhorts to unity in Christ, 63; condemns divisions in the Church, 63; warns against false teachers, 63 et seq.; case of incest in Corinthian Church, 66, 67; on charity, 68; meat offered to idols, 68; resurrection of the dead, 68 et seq.; on marriage and virginity, 70; his own struggles, 73; examples of those who have fallen through want of self-discipline, 73; on the head covered or uncovered at prayer, 75; condemnation of practices in Corinth at the Lord's Supper, 75; on charity, 75 et seq.; leaves Ephesus for Troas, and goes thence (in consequence of a vision) to Macedonia, 88; subjects of several Epistles, 90; self-defence to the Corinthians, 91 et seq., 100 et seq.; controversy (in three phases) with Judaism in 2 Corinthians, Galatians, and Romans, 96; source and vindication of his authority as an Apostle, 97 et seq.; character of his preaching described by himself, 104 et seq.; his ministry a ministry of reconciliation, 107; himself an ambassador for Christ, 107; no burden to the Corinthians, 109; the plainness of speech, indignation and irony, and yet meekness and gentleness of 2 Corinthians, from end of chapter ix., 110 et seq.; warning against false teachers, 114; his own labours and perils, 114 et seq.; visions and revelations, 116 et seq.; not burdensome to Corinthian Church, but caught them with guile, 117; route and work in Macedonia, 120 et seq.; pledge to the Apostles at Jerusalem, 122; leaves Macedonia and returns to Corinth, 123; his companions, 124; absence of information as to his intercourse with the Church at Corinth on his return thither, 127; ground for inferring his success in dealing with Corinthian difficulties, 127; his inmost thoughts revealed in Galatians and Romans, 128; grief at success of Judaising teachers at Antioch and Corinth, and in Galatia, 129, 130; hence Epistle to the Galatians, 129, 130; charges against him by Judaising teachers, and his replies, 132, 133; resistance of those who advocate the necessity for circumcision, 134; compared with Luther, 139; Apostolic authority first vindicated in Epistle to Galatians, 140; determination to go to Jerusalem through whatever danger, and afterwards to Rome, 159, 160; his faith in his God, 161; doubts as to accounts of his martyrdom, 166; in his character of deserter of Judaism, and defender of the spiritual seed of Abraham *only* as the true Israel of God, 175; interpretation of Habakkuk on life by faith, 193; cause of some logical defects in his statements, 215; objections to his arguments in Romans, 227; his use of different methods in argument, 228; apparent contradictions in his writings, 229; only jealous for the truth, 232 indifference to apparently illogical reasonings in his teaching, 232; method in enforcing truth compared with that of Luther, Jerome, and others, 247; grief for hardness of heart, 248; love for the Jews, 248; protected by the Roman impartiality of Gallio, Lysias, Felix, and Festus, 261; plot of Jews against his life, 272 *et seq.*; Sosipater, Aristarchus, Secundus, Gaius, Timotheus, Tychicus, Trophimus, and Luke, his companions, 274; at Philippi, 275; at Troas, 275; voyage by Lesbos, Chios, Samos, and Trogyllium to Miletus, 280; interview with the elders of the Ephesian Church at Miletus, 280—284; voyage from Miletus by Cos, Cnidus, Rhodes, Patara, and Cyprus, to Tyre, 284—286; at Tyre, 287; visits Philip the Evangelist at Cæsarea, 288; fifth visit to Jerusalem, and end of the third Apostolic journey, 291; reception by James and elders of the Church at Jerusalem —their proposal to him, 294, 295; does as James and elders proposed to him as to Nazarite vows, 308; outbreak of the Jews in the Temple against him, 308; charged by the Jews with defiling the Temple, 309 *et seq.*; rescued by Lysias from the Jews in the Temple, 311; address to the Jews after their outrage on him in the Temple, 313 *et seq.*; order to scourge him—declares himself a Roman citizen, 317 *et seq.*; before the Sanhedrin—his treatment by the High Priest—his protest—his defence, 325 *et seq.*; encouraged by a vision, 329; saved by his nephew from a conspiracy of Jews against his life, 331 *et seq.*; sent by Lysias to Cæsarea under escort, 332; the conduct of Lysias, 333; letter of Lysias to Felix, 334; preparations for his trial before Felix, 336 *et seq.*; defence before Felix, 338, 339; trial not concluded, but again summoned before Felix, 341; power of his arguments with Felix, 341; attempts of Felix to procure bribes for Paul's release, 342 *et seq.*; before Festus—appeal to Cæsar, 347 *et seq.*; before Festus and Agrippa, 354; his defence, 355 *et seq.*; sent in charge of Julius the centurion to Rome with Luke and Aristarchus as his fellow-voyagers, 362; voyage to Rome by Sidon, Cyprus, Myra, Cnidus, Fair Havens, where they waited long—his courage in danger—Melita, 365 *et seq.*; shipwreck at Melita, 378 *et seq.*; the viper at Melita, 384; declared a god, 384; heals Publius' father, 385; voyage and journey to Rome from Melita by Syracuse, Rhegium, Puteoli, Baiæ, Capua, Appii Forum, Three Taverns, 385—389; treatment at Rome, 390; his bonds, 391; appeal to Cæsar, 392; addresses the Jews at Rome, 394, 395; his companions and friends in Rome—Timotheus, Luke, Aristarchus, Tychicus, Epaphroditus, Epaphras, Mark, Demas, 395, 396; two years of sojourn and unhindered preaching in Rome, 396, 397; his abode, 398; discouragements, 398; postponement of his trial, 398; means of living, 398; success of his preaching, 398 *et seq.*; position at Rome, 404; varying characteristics of his Epistles, 410 *et seq.*; Epistles of the Captivity, 417 *et seq.*; loving care for him of Lydia and other Philippian friends when a prisoner at Rome, 420; indifference of the Roman Christians, 420; his own account of himself to the Philippians, 426; humility in his ministry and warning to the Colossian Church against false teachers, 458, 459; probable trial, acquittal, release, and course of events till death, 511 *et seq.*; his intended visit to Spain, 515; visit to Crete, 530; founds the Cretan Church, 531; closing days, 539 *et seq.*; fear of Gnosticism, 542; desire to strengthen the Churches against it, 542; relations between Paul and Timothy, 544, 545; companions in his last imprisonment, 545; writes to Timothy of his loneliness in prison, the support of his God, his trial, 546; hardships of second imprisonment in Rome, and change in his position, 547; left in his loneliness by friend after friend, Luke only faithful to him, 548; kindness of Onesiphorus in searching him out and visiting him in prison — gratitude to him, 549; his last trial — the little that he says of it — strengthened by his God, 550; his desire once more to see Timothy, 559, 560; last letter, 561 *et seq.*; farewell of Timothy, 567; personal matters, 568; significance of his request for his cloak, books, and parchments from Troas, 569, 576; final trial, condemnation, death, 577, 578; apparent failure—real greatness and success, 578; lasting results of his life and work, 578; crown of righteousness, 578 *et seq.*; theology and antinomies of, 590, 591; evidence as to liberation, 604 *et seq.*; chronology of his life and Epistles, 623; dates of his Epistles, 626; traditional account of his personal appearance, 628, 629.

INDEX.

Paulus, Sergius, Proconsul of Cyprus, i. 351, 671.
Peace and Hope, results of justification by faith, ii. 213, 214.
Pentecost, The first, after the Resurrection of our Lord, i. 83, 90; beginning of final phase of God's dealings with men, 91; crowded state of Jerusalem at, 95, 102; events of, 95, 102.
People, Chosen. (See Jews.)
Perishing, Paul's view of the, ii. 591.
Persecutions and results, i. 105 et seq., 284.
Peter, as Cephas, Apostle of the Foundation Stone, i. 1; impress of individuality on Church, 1; Peter and first Pentecost, 83 et seq.; discourse at first Pentecost and its effect, 103, 104; miracles, 105, 263; his reception of Paul at Jerusalem, 231; his admission of Gentiles into the Church, 258; rebukes Simon Magus, 260; lodging with Simon the tanner at Joppa, 264; vision at Joppa and its significance, 272; sent for by Cornelius to Cæsarea, 277; address to the Gentiles at Cæsarea and its results, 280, 281; address at Jerusalem and its results, 282, 283; in prison, 311, 313; released from prison by an angel, 314; convinced by Paul on circumcision, 408; his address on circumcision, 422; independence of Judaism, and free intercourse with Gentiles, 439; rebuked by Paul for change of bearing towards Gentiles, 440 et seq.; spirit in which he received Paul's rebuke, 447 et seq.; stoned, 647; doubts as to accounts of his martyrdom, ii. 166; not the founder of the Roman Church, 167.
Peter and John—Two chief Apostles, i. 2; before the chief priests, 106 et seq.; knowledge of the mind of Christ, 675.
Peter and Paul at Antioch in Syria, i. 437.
Pharaoh—his hardness of heart explained, ii. 242.
Pharisaism—its various aspects, i. 45, 46; compared with the monastic life, 64.
Pharisees, Life and observances of, i. 62 et seq.; minute points of observance, 68; scrupulous observance of Sabbath, 69; baptised, but understand Christ less than the Sadducees, who had handed him over to the secular arm, 151.
Philemon, Causes of Paul's Epistle to, ii. 442, 443; account, subject of, &c., 438, 468 et seq.
Philip (Apostle) and Andrew — Hellenic names, but still common among the Jews, i. 130.
Philip (Evangelist) appointed deacon, i. 132; evangelist as well as deacon, 138; ministry, 188; baptises Simon Magus, 260; baptises the Ethiopian eunuch, 261; the respective influence in Church advancement of Philip, Stephen, and Paul, 286; work in the Church, 286; Paul's visit to him at Cæsarea, ii. 288.
Philippi, Description of, i. 484 et seq.; Church of, alone ministering to Paul's necessities, 488; Paul's fellow-workers at, 488.
Philippians—ministering to Paul's necessities at Corinth, i. 56; Epistle to, ii. 417 et seq.; causes of, 419; loving care for Paul and his necessities, 420.
Philippians, Epistle to—Exhortation to unity in, ii. 422; characteristics of, 422, 423; account of, 424 et seq.; writer's encouragements to Philippians, 427; digression of special warnings, 431 et seq.; conclusion, 435; gratitude for help in necessities, 435; future of Philippian Church, 435 et seq.
Philosophers of Athens, i. 533 et seq.
Pilate—his judicial impartiality, 570.
Pliny—on tests of Christians, i. 330; his account of Christians in Bithynia, 330; letter to Sabinianus, ii. 593, 594.
Pliny the Younger on Christianity, i. 670.
Pompeii, Morals of, typical of those of Tarsus, Ephesus, Corinth, and Miletus, i. 36.
Pompey—introduction of Jews into Rome, ii. 162; his treatment of them and its results, 162.
Pontius Pilate. (See Pilate.)
Pope Adrian (See Adrian VI.)
Porcia, Lex, i. 41.
Porcius Festus. (See Festus.)
Predestination — Definition of, ii. 242; consistent with man's free will, 243; difficulties of, solved by the infinity of God's love, 244; Paul's view of, 590.
Priests, Chief, in judgment on Peter and John, i. 106; many Jewish, "obedient to the faith" of Christ, 135.
Priscilla and Aquila, their relation to Paul, i. 559.
Progress, Paul the Apostle of, i. 2.
Prophecy fulfilled in Messiah, i. 150.
Prophets foretold the calling of the Gentiles, i. 267.
Proselytes, Greek—their conversion, i. 286; burdens laid on, 666.
Psalms—The poetry of the, compared with Paul's Epistles, i. 18.
Public Worship. (See Worship.)
Publius' father healed by Paul at Melita, ii. 385.
Punishments, Capital, i. 647.

R.

Rabban, Rabbi, i. 4, 44.
Rabbi, Rabbis—School of the, i. 40 *et seq.*; misconception of the oral law, 66; "strain out gnats and swallow camels," 69; of Jerusalem, their ignorance of the intent of God's gifts, 124.
Rahab an ancestress of our Lord, i. 325
Recompense, Paul's view of, ii. 591.
Redeemed, Paul's view of the forgiveness of the, ii. 591.
Redeemer. (*See* Jesus.)
Restoration, Universal, Paul's view of, ii. 591.
Resurrection—Power of Christ's, i. 84; and Judgment, Athenian view of, 548; faith in the, confirmed, ii. 82 *et seq.*; Paul on, to Corinthian Church, 68 *et seq.*
Righteousness of God—its effect on man, i. 188 *et seq.*; of the Law and what depended on it, 65. (*See* God.)
Rome—Character of, in the time of the Apostles, described by St. John, Seneca, and Juvenal, i. 331; Jews introduced into, by Pompey, ii. 162; Introduction of Christianity into, 164; Jewish and Gentile elements in early Church of, 167, 168; impartiality of its law favourable to Paul, 261; Paul's confidence in the Christians of, 268; Paul at, 389 *et seq.*; its social condition—its early Christians—Paul's immunity, 402 *et seq.*; Prevailing influences in, during Paul's residence there, 404 *et seq.*; Indifference of the Christians of, to Paul and his necessities compared with the kindness of the Philippians, 419, 420, 515.
Roman, Romans—Result to, of the dispersion of the Jews, i. 117; their early views of Christianity, 569; their judicial impartiality when Christians were brought before them, 570; apotheosis of their emperors, 664 *et seq.*; Paul's position among, as a deserter of Judaism, and asserter of spiritual seed of Abraham as alone the true Israel of God, 175; Superiority of Paul's Epistle to, above the frivolity of the *Abhóda Zara*, 176; Paul's confidence, 185; trials, votes in, given by tablets, 552, 576.
Romans, Paul's Epistle to—cause of, ii. 161; account of Epistle, 162; addressed to both Jews and Gentiles, 168, 169; probably copied and sent to other Churches, as Ephesus and Thessalonica, 170, 171; object of, 171 *et seq.*; character and style of, 172 *et seq.*; character of Church when Paul wrote Epistle, 173; causes of, 174; spirit in which written, 174; how probably originated, 178, 179; deductions thence in writer's mind, 178, 179; Jesus Christ as common foundation for the Jew and Gentile the basis of this and of every one of Paul's Epistles, 180; opinions of Luther, Melancthon, Coleridge, and Tholuck, 180, 181; outline of, 181 *et seq.*; salutation and introduction, 184; comprehensiveness, 185; thanksgiving for faith of, 185; Roman Christians, 185; God's righteousness revealed in the Gospel of the Cross to Jew and Gentile alike, 187; justification by faith the one means of attaining to holiness—the great subject of the Epistle, 189; God's righteousness—the various sources and revelations of, 189 *et seq.*; the sins of Paganism, 196, 197; Jews equally guilty with Gentiles, 199; uselessness of circumcision, 203, 204; justification God's free gift, 211; justification establishing the Law, 213; universality of sin and of justification, 214, 215; by one, sin—by one, justification, 214, 215; purpose of the Law, 218; relations of sin and grace, 219; why the Law was inefficacious to justify, 223; the Law gave its strength to sin, 225, 226; Christians not under the Law, but under grace, history of man under four phases, 226; writer's style of argument justified against those who censure it, 228; Christian dead to past moral condition, risen to new one, because Christ in His crucified body has destroyed the power of sin, 233; predestination and free-will not inconsistent with each other, 242 *et seq.*; Jews, their fall, 246 *et seq.*; their hopes of restoration, 254 *et seq.*; obedience to the civil power enjoined, 260; Paul's respect for the civil power from his own experience, 260, 261; dues, 263; observances as to fasting and use of food, 263; the weak and the strong, 263 *et seq.*; Paul's defence of his Epistles, 268, 269; probable end of Epistle as originally intended, 269; its actual conclusion, 270.
Room, Upper. (*See* Upper Room.)
Rulers contemporary with Paul, Table of, ii. 626, 627.
Running so as to obtain, ii. 591.
Ruth, ancestress of Christ, i. 325.

S.

Sabbath observances of Pharisees and Sadducees, i. 69.

INDEX.

Sabbatic year, observances of, i. 69.
Sabinianus, Letter of Pliny to, ii. 593, 594.
Sacrifice, Living, required of all Christians, ii. 258.
Sadducees, scrupulous observances of Sabbath, i. 69.
St. Denys. (*See* Denys.)
St. Paul. (*See* Paul.)
Saint. (*In each case see Saint's name*).
Sakya Mouni, Antecedents of, i. 4.
Salamis—Jews of, i. 348; Paul and Barnabas at, 348.
Salvation through fear, ii. 591.
Sanhedrin—not afraid of the Lord Jesus, afraid of two of his disciples, i. 108; rage of at Stephen's discourse, i. 164; charged with laxity at the time of Stephen's martyrdom, 169; marriage a condition of membership, 169; Paul had been a member of, 169 *et seq.*
Sapphira. (*See* Ananias.)
Sardanapalus, Statue of, at Anchiale, i. 29.
"Saul the Pharisee," i. 62 *et seq.*
"Saul the persecutor," i. 169. (*See* Paul.)
Saviour. (*See* Jesus.)
Sceva, of Ephesus—sons overcome by evil spirit while using the holy name of Jesus, ii. 25 *et seq.*
School of the Rabbi, i. 40 *et seq.*
Scourging, Jewish, i. 661 *et seq.*
Scripture, Paul's use of, i. 50.
Sejanus—his attempt to eject the Jews from Rome, ii. 163; persecution of the Jews, 261.
Seneca—his description of Rome, i. 331; relation to Gallio, 567; his supposed correspondence with Paul spurious, 572; account of Jews in Rome, ii. 164; his disgrace by Nero, 408.
Septuagint, the work of the most learned men of the Jewish Dispersion, i. 128.
Sergius Paulus, Proconsul of Cyprus, i. 351, 671.
Sermon on the Mount compared with Paul's Epistles, i. 576.
Servants and masters, mutual duties of, ii. 527.
Shammai, the school of, i. 44; his descent, 325; view of the oral law, 401.
Shema in studies of Paul as a boy, i. 43.
Shipwreck, Paul's, ii. 378 *et seq.*
Silas—joins Paul at Antioch in Syria, i. 438; Paul's companion in his travels, 454 *et seq.* (*See* Paul.)
Silvanus. (*See* Silas.)
Simeon—his prophecy of our Lord as a Light to the Gentiles, i. 325.
Simeon Niger—position in Church at Antioch in Syria, i. 323.
Simon Magus, i. 260, 352.
Simon Peter. (*See* Peter.)

Sin, Relation of grace to, ii. 219, 220; relation of law to, 234 *et seq.*; Man of, 583 *et seq.*; Paul's views of, 591.
Sobermindedness, key-note of Paul's Epistle to Titus, ii. 535.
Sosthenes beaten before Gallio, ii. 571.
South-west and north-west explained, ii. 369.
Spinoza, Antecedents of, and compared with Paul, i. 4.
Spirit, Holy. (*See* Holy Ghost.)
"Stake in the flesh," Paul's, i. 214 *et seq.* (*See* Paul.)
Stephen—influence of his last words on Paul, i. 77; Stephen and the Hellenists, 115 *et seq.*; appointed one of the seven deacons, 132; influence on Paul, 134; more his teacher than Gamaliel, 134; what he must have been had he lived, 134; had probably heard the truth from the Lord Jesus, though the tradition that he was one of the seventy disciples is valueless, 137; elected deacon for his faith, 137; the most prominent of the seven, 137; equal with the Apostles in working wonders among the people, 137; his great part in the history of the Church, 138; evangelist as well as deacon, 138; compared with the twelve Apostles, 138; his dispute in the synagogue of the Libertines, 145; his triumph in argument, 147; its result, 147; his view of the law of Moses blasphemy to the Jews, 152; taken by violence before the Sanhedrin, 153; his view of the oral law, 154; charges against him by false witnesses, 154, 155; his reply a concise history of the Jewish nation down to their own murder of Christ, 162 *et seq.*; his vision of glory, 164; martyrdom, 165 *et seq.*; prays for his murderers, 167; burial, 171; respective influence of Stephen, Philip, and Paul in Church advancement, 286.
Stoics, stoicism, i. 335, ii. 14.
Suetonius—his error as to our Lord, i. 330; his view of Christianity, 330, 669.
Supper, Last, Upper room of, i. 86, 320.
Sword, The, as the result of our Lord's mission, i. 573.
Syntyche and Euodia, Christian women of Macedonia, i. 488. (*See* Enodia.)

T.

Tabitha raised from the dead, i. 263.
Tablets, Voting. (*See* Roman.)
Tacitus—his view of Christianity, i. 330, 669.

Talmud, Noble characters in, i. 46; its direction of observances, 64; allegories, 66; stories from, ii. 594, 595.

Tarsus—birthplace of Paul, i. 14; description and natural features, 17; commercial and political advantages of situation, 21; commercial prosperity, 22; resisting Brutus and Cassius, 22; conquered by Lucius Rufus, 22; scene of meetings of Antony and Cleopatra, 23; its moral condition in Paul's youth, 31; morals of Tarsus and other cities judged from evidence of Pompeii, 36.

Temperance. (*See* Sobermindedness.)

Temple at Jerusalem—scene of the great events of the first Pentecost after our Lord's resurrection, i. 90; destruction of, 604; Paul charged by Jews with defiling, ii. 309 *et seq.*

Terah, Legend of, i. 325.

Tertius, scribe of Paul's Epistle to Romans, ii. 174.

Tertullus accuses Paul to Felix, ii. 337.

Theology of Paul, ii. 590, 591.

Theophilus, High Priest, i. 180.

Thessalonica, Description of, i. 505; Famine at time of Paul's visit, 507; Paul's ministry at, 508 *et seq.*

Thessalonians—sent to stir up Bereans against Paul, i. 519; Paul's Epistles to, 510. 1 Thess.: Account of, 574; their faith and Christian spirit commended, 582; characteristics of, 583, 584; Paul's joy in, 586; their faith reported to Paul by Timothy, 587; expected to advance in Christian course, 588; brotherly love and quietness commended, 589; second coming of Christ, and judgment, 592 *et seq.*; results of 1 Thess., 595, 596; disturbed by idea of day of the Lord as very near, 599 *et seq.* 2 Thess.: Object of 2 Thess., i. 604; most important passage of 2 Thess., 608; explanation of 2 Thess. ii. 1—12.

Thessalonica—Paul's Epistle to Romans probably sent to Thessalonica also, ii. 170, 171; Tholuck, his account of Paul's Epistle to the Romans, 181; "thorn in the flesh," Paul's, i. 214. (*See* Paul; Stake.)

Tiberius, Death of, i. 244.

Tigellinus, Prætorian Prefect, his character, ii. 546, 547.

Timotheus. (*See* Timothy.)

Timothy—converted by Paul at Lystra, i. 386; circumcised, 46, 412; Paul's love for him, 458; Paul's Epistles to, 459; with Paul at Ephesus, 459; places at which he is mentioned as having been with Paul — character of Timothy, 459, 460; goes with Paul on his travels, 461; returns with Silas to Paul at Corinth from Thessalonica, 575; sent by Paul to Thessalonica, 587; his report of the faith of the Thessalonians, 587; Paul's personal advice to, ii. 526; his relation to Paul, 544 *et seq.*; Paul's account to him (in 2 Timothy) of his loneliness in prison, 546; of the support of his God, 546; of his trial, 546 *et seq.*

Timothy—1 Timothy: Account of, ii. 515 *et seq.*; object of Epistle, 516; warning against false teachers, 517; injunctions to prayer, quietness, sobriety, 519 *et seq.*; qualifications for offices in the Church, 521; of pastors and deacons, 521 *et seq.*; rules as to discipline of the body, 523; marriage, 523; widowhood, 523; ordination of presbyters, &c., 523 *et seq.* 2 Timothy: Account of, 561 *et seq.*; gratitude for the kindness of Onesiphorus, 562, 563; again warned against false teachers, of whom a picture is drawn, 564 *et seq.*; personal exhortations—appeal to him, as a pastor, to earnest duty, 565, 566; entreaty to come to him—Paul's cloak, books, parchments — conclusion, 569 *et seq.*, 576.

Titus—converted by Paul at Cyprus, i. 407; went with Paul and Barnabas to conference at Jerusalem on circumcision, 407; the question of his circumcision, 412, 461; rejoins Paul in Macedonia, ii. 88; Paul's Epistle to, Account of, 529, 532; leading subject of, temperance, sober-mindedness, 535.

Tongue "understood" of people commended for use, ii. 80.

Tongues—Speaking with unknown, i. 96 design of gift of, at Pentecost, 97; different view of this gift, 98, 99; at Jerusalem and Corinth respectively, 99, 100; power of, as used by Apostles, 101.

Tradition of twelve years as the limit laid down by our Lord for His disciples to remain in Jerusalem, i. 320.

Trials. (*See* Roman.)

Troas—Paul's cloak, books, and parchments left at with Carpus, i. 36; ii. 569, 576.

Trophimus of Ephesus joins Paul, ii. 43; ill at Miletus, 545.

Truth of God. (*See* God.)

Twelve years. (*See* Tradition.)

Tychicus of Ephesus joins Paul, ii. 43; Paul's companion, 587, 588.

Types, i. 56, 57.

U.

Unbelievers not to judge in church matters, ii. 67.
Uncial MSS. of Acts of Apostles and Paul's Epistles, ii. 588, 589.
Uncleanness, Test of, in Talmud, ii. 594.
Unity, Paul's exhortations to, chief subject of Epistle to Philippians, ii. 422, 428, 429.
Universal Restoration, Paul's view of, ii. 591.
Unknown God, Altars to, i. 524, 531; Paul's view of altar to, 532; Paul preaches on, 542.
Unknown tongues, Speaking in, condemned, ii. 80. (*See* Tongues.)
Upper room of Last Supper, and of assembly of Apostles in house of Mary, i. 86, 320.

V.

Verbal inspiration, i. 600.
Vessels of wrath and mercy, ii. 251.
Virginity and marriage, Paul writes on, to Corinthian Church, ii. 70 *et seq.*
Vision of man of Macedonia to Paul, ii. 88.
Visions, i. 193, 194.

Voting tablets. (*See* Roman.)
Vows, i. 71; Nazarite, ii., 295, 296.
Voyage, Paul's, to Rome, ii. 365 *et seq.* (*See* Paul.)

W.

Warnings, God's, i. 198.
Wesley, John, compared with Paul, i. 4.
Whitefield compared with Paul, i. 4.
Whit-Sunday, i. 90.
Will. (*See* Free will.)
Winds—of Paul's voyage to Rome, Etesian, &c., ii. 366.
Witness of Gospel to our Lord, i. 326.
Women—their part in the dissemination of the Gospel, i. 488.
Worship, Public, Regulations for, ii. 519.
Wrath, Vessels of, ii. 251.
Wreck. (*See* Shipwreck.)

Y.

Years, Twelve. (*See* Tradition.)

Z.

Zephaniah—Prophecy of universal worship of Jehovah, i. 325.

PASSAGES OF SCRIPTURE QUOTED OR REFERRED TO.

GENESIS.

i.		Vol. I.,	p.	638
14		,, II.		430
ii. 25		,,		225
iii. 15		,, I.		54
16		,, II.		520
iv. 25		,, I.		54
v. 2		,,		81
ix. 4		,,		427, 434
xii. 3		,,		325
21		,,		543
xiii. 15		,,		53
xv. 6		,, II.		148
13		,,		149
xvi. 13		,, I.		150
xviii. 16		,,		661
xxvi. 5		,, II.		212
xxvii. 39		,, I.		396
xxviii. 20		,, II.		3
xxix. 31		,,		249
xxxii. 25–32		,, I.		27
xxxvi.		,,		37
37		,,		26
44		,, II.		458
xl. 8		,,		63
xliv. 7, 17		,,		146
22		,,		101
xlv. 14		,,		283
xlvi. 2		,, I.		194
10		,,		25
29		,, II.		283

EXODUS.

iii. 2,		Vol. I.,	p.	192, 607
14		,, II.		457
iv. 26		,,		212
vi. 15		,, I.		25
vii. 11		,, II.		566
48		,,		137
xii. 1		,, I.		89
xiv. 31		,, I.		430
xv. 5		,, II.		115
xvi. 10		,,		248
xviii. 21		,,		170
xix. 1		,, I.		89
4		,,		368
16		,,		591
19		,, II.		176
xx. 7		,,		71
14		,,		600
19		,,		150
xxii. 18		,,		25
28		,,		323
xxiv. 8		,,		125

EXODUS (continued).

xxv. 8,		Vol. II.,	p.	209
xxxi. 18		,,		103
xxxii. 16		,,		129
32		,,		243
xxxiv. 33		,,		104
xxxix. 15		,,		72

LEVITICUS.

iv. 25,		Vol. II.,	p.	237
xi. 7		,, I.		274
xiii. 13		,,		185
		,, II.		584
xvi. 5		,,		237
8		,, I.		89
10		,, II.		210
xvii. 4		,, I.		434
8		,, II.		92
8–16		,, I.		430
xviii. 5		,,		186
		,, II.		148
26		,, I.		430
29		,,		664
30		,,		65
xix. 4		,,		582
18		,, II.		156
19		,,		108
xx. 6		,, I.		491
11		,, II.		92
xxi. 8		,, I.		506
43		,, I.		89
xxiv. 14		,,		647
xxv.		,,		123
xxvi. 26		,,		515
xxvii. 29		,, II.		87

NUMBERS.

v. 18,		Vol. I.,	p.	170
vi. 3, 5		,, II.		301
9, 10		,,		296
25, 26		,,		135
xi. 26		,,		586
xii. 12		,,		82
xv. 37–41		,, I.		48
xvi. 5, 26		,, II.		565
xxi. 17		,, I.		640
2, 3		,, II.		87
xxiv. 25		,, I.		88
9		,, II.		50
		,,		78
xxvi. 13		,, I.		25
52		,,		86
xxxiii. 55		,,		664
xxxv. 5		,,		86

DEUTERONOMY.

i. 13–16,		Vol. I.,	p.	170
31		,,		368
38		,,		368
i.–iii. 29		,,		350
vi. 4–9		,,		48
vii. 3		,,		645
25		,, II.		203
46		,,		248
ix. 6		,, I.		162
x. 12		,,		404
16		,,		162
		,, II.		432
xi. 13–27		,,		48
xiii. 8, 9		,,		171
xiv. 8		,,		274
xvi. 11		,,		108
16, 17		,,		122
22, 23		,,		646
xvii. 7		,,		647, 648
15		,,		310
xviii. 18		,, II.		256
xxi. 23		,, I.		140
		,, II.		77, 148
xxii. 10		,,		108
xxiii. 1		,, I.		322
2		,, II.		153
19		,,		483
xxv. 2		,, I.		108
2, 4		,,		663
3		,,		663
4		,, II.		535
6		,, I.		162
xxvii. 14–26		,, II.		461
20		,,		92
26		,,		148
xxviii. 25		,, I.		115
58, 59		,,		662
xxix. 9		,,		662
28		,,		449
xxxii. 15		,,		195
43		,, II.		203
xxxiii. 2		,, I.		162
		,, II.		149, 176
4		,, I.		309
xxxiv. 2		,, II.		586

JOSHUA.

ii. 15,		Vol. I.,	p.	227
vi. 17		,, II.		87
vii. 11		,, I.		34
14		,,		86
x. 26		,, II.		148
xv. 59		,, I.		226

PASSAGES OF SCRIPTURE

JOSHUA (*continued*).
xxiii. 13 Vol. I., p. 654
xxiv. 2 ,, 325
15 ,, 640

JUDGES.
iii. 31, Vol. I., p. 196
ix. 27 ,, II. 71
54 ,, I. 86
xviii. 21 ,, II. 290

I. SAMUEL.
iv. 22, Vol. II., p. 248
v. 22 ,, I. 404
viii. 15 ,, 53
x. 10, 11 ,, 106
11 ,, 102
20 ,, 88
xii. 18 ,, 430
xviii. 10 ,, 102, 106
22 ,, II. 290, 462
xix. 11 ,, I. 227
23, 24 ,, 102
xxi. 5 ,, 588
xxviii. 3, 9 ,, II. 25

II. SAMUEL.
v. 23, Vol. II., p. 396
vii. 14, 8 ,, 109
xx. ,, I. 607
xxii. 48 ,, 607
xxiv. 1 ,, 587

I. KINGS.
ii. 28, Vol. I., p. 214
v. 9 ,, 315
vi. 1 ,, 370
vii. 13, 14 ,, 24
viii. 27 ,, 160
xii. 2 ,, 23
xiv. 4 ,, II. 141
xvii. 21 ,, 278
xviii. 26 ,, 40
xix. 4 ,, 58
11 ,, I. 92
14 ,, 273
xx. 35 ,, 591
xxii. 11 ,, II. 289
24 ,, 115

II. KINGS.
ii. 3, Vol. I., p. 45
iii. 9 ,, II. 286
iv. 34 ,, 278
38 ,, I. 45
xix. 37 ,, II. 71
xxiii. 13 sq. ,, 202

I. CHRONICLES.
xxi. 1 Vol. I., p. 587
xxix. 10 ,, 160

II. CHRONICLES.
vi. 22, 23, Vol. I., p. 545

EZRA.
ii. 36—39, Vol. I., p. 136
iii. 3 ,, II. 509
7 ,, I. 315
vi. 16 ,, 116

NEHEMIAH.
iii. 16, Vol. I., p. 262
ix. 16 ,, 162

JOB.
i. 6, Vol. II., p. 114
v. 9 ,, 496
10 ,, I. 19
13 ,, 33
24 ,, 81
xii. 21 ,, 545
26 ,, 543
xiii. 7, 8 ,, II. 212
27 ,, I. 497
xiv. 2 ,, II. 249
xxv. 4 ,, 132
xxxii. 11 ,, I. 497
19 ,, 27
xxxviii. 36 ,, 645
xli. 11 ,, 546

PSALMS.
ii. Vol. I., p. 149
3 ,, II. 177
7 ,, I. 371
12 ,, 257
vii. 14 ,, II. 508
xiv. ,, I. 50
xvi. 10 ,, 150
xviii. 31 ,, II. 509
49 ,, 268
xix. 8 ,, I. 88
xxii. 19 ,, 89
21 ,, II. 553
31 ,, I. 428
xxiv. 4 ,, II. 590
xxvi. 6 ,, 590
xxxix. 6 ,, I. 587
xl. 7 ,, II. 237
xli. 10 ,, I. 150
xlviii. 12 ,, II. 61
l. 11, 12 ,, I. 546
liii. ,, 50
lviii. 8 ,, II. 52
lxiv. 6 ,, 516
lxvi. 18 ,, 208
lxviii. ,, 508
11 ,, I. 375
12 ,, 162
,, II. 149
18 ,, I. 182
19 ,, II. 249
31 ,, I. 261
lxxi. 1 ,, II. 518
lxxviii. 2 ,, 150
38, 39 ,, 632, 633
lxxix. 14 ,, 172
lxxxi. 12 ,, II. 210
lxxxii. 6 ,, 50
lxxxiv. 7 ,, I. 196
lxxxvi. 9 ,, 426
lxxxix. 6 ,, 587
15 ,, II. 509
28 ,, 457
xci. 7 ,, I. 639
xciv. 11 ,, 33
xcv. 7 ,, 605
ci. ,, II. 219
18 ,, I. 496
civ. 15 ,, 19
cv. 15 ,, 302
cvi. 28 ,, II. 50
cvii. 28 ,, I. 128
cix. 8 ,, 66
cx. 1 ,, 180
cxiii.—cxviii. ,, 46

PSALMS (*continued*).
cxvii. 1, Vol. II., p. 268
cxviii. 3 ,, I. 150
cxxxviii. 1 ,, II. 76
cxliii. 2 ,, 146
cxliv. 13 ,, 518
cxlvii. 2 ,, I. 116
8, 9 ,, 19

PROVERBS.
ii. 4, Vol. II., p. 459
17 ,, I. 81
iii. 3 ,, II. 108, 109
v. 18 ,, I. 81
vi. 12 ,, II. 108
vii. 3 ,, 108
viii. 30 ,, 102
xi. 24 ,, 110
xiii. 24 ,, I. 279
xvi. 20 ,, II. 197
33 ,, I. 88
xx. 25 ,, II. 323
xxi. 18 ,, 65
xxii. 9 ,, 110
xxiii. 6 ,, I. 471
xxiv. 18 ,, II. 259
xxv. 19 ,, I. 451

ECCLESIASTES.
v. 18, Vol. I., p. 536
vi. 6 ,, 88
vii. 20 ,, 196
ix. 18 ,, 607
x. 8 ,, 112, 322
xi. 6 ,, 31
xxxviii. 25 ,, 196

CANTICLES.
iii. 7, 8, Vol. I., p. 639
vii. 12 ,, 454

ISAIAH.
i. 1—22, Vol. I., p. 369
2 ,, 306
3 ,, 668
9 ,, II. 251
11—15 ,, I. 60
ii. 2, 3 ,, 223
iii. 10 ,, 494
v. 24 ,, 92
viii. 14 ,, 37
,, II. 252
23 ,, I. 150
ix. 1 ,, 150
12 ,, 193
x. 22 ,, II. 251
26 ,, 290
xi. 4 ,, I. 609
,, II. 596
5 ,, 461
10 ,, 268
xiv. 1 ,, I. 403
xx. 1 ,, II. 269
xxiv. 18 ,, I. 149
xxvi. 12 ,, 471
xxviii. 4 ,, I. 79
11 ,, II. 52
16 ,, 57
,, II. 219, 252
xxix. 14 ,, I. 33
xxx. 7 ,, 599
xxxi. 2 ,, 196
xxxii. 12 ,, 194
19 ,, 22
,, II. 61, 62

QUOTED OR REFERRED TO.   653

ISAIAH (continued).
xl. 3, Vol. I., p. 150
xliii. 6 ,, II. 108
    7 ,, I. 428
    9 ,, II. 176
xliv. 18 ,, I. 33
xlv. 9 ,, II. 250
    14 ,, I. 261
xlix. 6 ,, 322
lii. 10 ,, 325, 375
    14 ,, 185
    15 ,, II. 62
liii. ,, I. 150
    4 ,, 185
    5 ,, 605
    6 ,, 185
    7, 8 ,, 261
    9 ,, 150
lvi. 3, 8 ,, 262
lvii. 20 ,, II. 196
lviii. 3 ,, I. 167
    5—7 ,, 60
lix. 10 ,, 542
    16—19 ,, II. 509
    20 ,, 255
lx. 1, 2 ,, 506
    3, 9 ,, I. 326
lxi. 1 ,, 150
lxiii. 9 ,, 369
lxiv. 4 ,, II. 62
lxv. 4 ,, I. 275
    17 ,, II. 62
lxvi. 1, 2 ,, I. 160
    3 ,, 275
    16 ,, 383

JEREMIAH.
i. 6, Vol. I., p. 273
vii. 21 ,, 60
    22, 23 ,, II. 239
    9 ,, I. 53
    16 ,, II. 457
ix. 23, 24 ,, 62
    26 ,, I. 163
xiii. 1 ,, II. 239
xvii. 16 ,, 64
xviii. 6 ,, 250
xix. 13 ,, I. 269
xxiii. 6 ,, II. 190
xxix. 7 ,, I. 689
    26 ,, 427
xxxi. 3—33 ,, II. 108
    29 ,, 228
    31—36 ,, 108
xxxiii. 16 ,, 190
    25 ,, L. 401
        ,, 135
xxxvii. 7 ,, 261
xxxix. 16 ,, I. 261

EZEKIEL.
i. 24, Vol. I., p. 92
xi. 19 ,, II. 108
xvi. 13 ,, I. 536
xviii. 2 ,, II. 238
xx. 25 ,, I. 402
    ,, II. 238
xxiv. 6 ,, I. 80
xxvii. 17 ,, 315
xxviii. 24 ,, 654
xxxiii. 4 ,, 562
xxxvi. 21—28 ,, II. 203
    29 ,, 108
xxxviii. 16, 17 ,, I. 617
    ,, II. 585
xliii. 2 ,, I. 92
xliv. 6 ,, II. 309

EZEKIEL (continued).
xliv. 7, Vol. I., p. 162
    ,, II. 432
xlv. 7 ,, I. 434

DANIEL.
i. Vol. I., p. 617
    8 ,, 427
    8—12 ,, 424
    12 ,, 53
v. 19 ,, II. 63
vii. 9 ,, I. 607
    10, 11 } ,, 617
    23—26 }
ix. 23 ,, 194
    24 ,, 526
x. 7 ,, 192
xi. ,, II. 585
    31—36 ,, I. 617
xii. 10 ,, 614

HOSEA.
i. 9, 10, Vol. II., p. 251
ii. 6 ,, I. 654
    23 ,, II. 251
iv. 14 ,, I. 170
vi. 6 ,, 404
    ,, II. 229
xii. 8 ,, I. 122
xiii. 14 ,, II. 256

AMOS.
ii. 10, Vol. I., p. 366
iii. 12 ,, II. 552
viii. 4—6 ,, I. 122
ix. 11, 12 ,, 427

JONAH.
i. 3, Vol. I., p. 270
    7 ,, 89
iv. 1, 9 ,, 273

MICAH.
iv. 2, Vol. I., p. 232
v. 12 ,, II. 95
vi. 8 ,, I. 404
    12 ,, II. 227

HABAKKUK.
i. 5, Vol. I., p. 372
ii. 4 ,, 51
    ,, II. 148, 180
iii. 3 ,, 176
ix. 37 ,, I. 497

ZEPHANIAH.
i. 5, Vol. I., p. 269
ii. 11 ,, 325
iii. 10 ,, 261

HAGGAI.
ii. 8, Vol. II., p. 176

ZECHARIAH.
xi. 7, Vol. I., p. 425
    12 ,, 150
xii. 10 ,, 140
    16 ,, 150
xiv. 11 ,, II. 248
    16 ,, 176
    21 ,, I. 122

MALACHI.
i. 2, 3, Vol. II., p. 249
    7 ,, 427
    8 ,, II. 202
iii. 1 ,, I. 150
    8—10 ,, II. 202

TOBIT.
i. 10—14, Vol. II., p. 50
    12 ,, I. 424
v. 18 ,, II. 65
xi. 14 ,, I. 196, 201
xii. 12 ,, II. 76

ESTHER (Apocr.).
xiv. 13, Vol. II., p. 552

WISDOM OF SOLOMON.
i. 13—16, Vol. II., p. 217
ii. 7—9 ,, L. 536
    24 ,, 632, 642
    10 ,, II. 102
    14, 15 ,, I. 256
v. 4 ,, II. 358
    17 ,, L. 632
    18 ,, 562
    19 ,, II. 509
    22 ,, 118
vii. 22 sq. ,, I. 139
ix. 15 ,, 643
    ,, II. 105
x.—xii. ,, L. 128
xi., xvi. }
—xviii. } ,, 58
xi. 20 ,, 617
    ,, II. 585
    20, 21 ,, L. 609
    23—26 ,, 643
xiii.— }
xix. } ,, 129
xiv. 15 ,, 582
xv. 7 ,, 632
    ,, II. 250
xxv. 24 ,, 590

ECCLESIASTICUS.
vii. 26, Vol. L., p. 81
xiv. 6 ,, II. 471
xxv. 22 ,, II. 109
xxx. 1 ,, L. 547
xxxvi. 7 ,, II. 250
    29 ,, I. 568
xxxviii. 1 ,, II. 385
xliii. 9 ,, I. 81

BARUCH.
v. 12, Vol. I., p. 592
vi. 43 ,, 435

I. MACCABEES.
i. 8, Vol. I., p. 467
    15 ,, 127
    ,, II. 69, 208
ii. 48, 62 ,, 585
    52 ,, 212
iii. 27 ,, I. 298
v. ,, 427
    2 ,, 467
x. 36 ,, 470

II. MACCABEES.
i. 27, Vol. I., p. 116
iii. 10 ,, 131

II. MACCABEES (continued).

iii. 15,	Vol. I., p.	654	
iv. 7–9, 33	"	293	
10, 15	"	126	
12	"	126	
12 sq.	"	127	
33	"	294	
40	" II.	92	
v. 9	" I.	318	
21	"	293	
vi. 1	" II.	320	
18, 19	" I.	275	
19	"	126	
vii. 27	"	308	
31	" II.	197	
xi. 36	" I.	293	
xiv. 35	"	546	

III. MACCABEES.
(Extra-Apocryphal Book.)
Vol. I., p. 249

ST. MATTHEW.

iii. 10,	Vol. II., p.	63	
iv. 13	" I.	150	
v. 10–12	" II.	214	
14	" I.	310	
17	"	265	
18	"	142, 266	
32	"	142	
37	" II.	100	
39	"	115	
47	"	146	
vi. 3	" I.	63	
5	"	63	
7	" II.	40	
13	"	142	
24	"	249	
vii. 6	"	567	
17	"	504	
viii. 4	" I.	265	
ix. 10, 11	" II.	146	
13	" I.	143, 267	
30	"	144	
x. 7	" II.	249	
13	" I.	377	
14	"	376	
17	"	175	
23	"	173	
27	"	268	
xi. 3	"	415	
10	"	150	
25	" II.	429	
27	"	246	
29, 30	" I.	422	
xii. 7	"	143, 144, 267	
10	"	267	
19, 20	" II.	565	
39	" I.	170	
40	"	150	
46	"	86, 222	
55	"	86	
xiii. 35	"	150	
44	" II.	459	
52	" I.	532	
xiv. 2	"	471	
xv. 2–6	"	155	
13	"	110	
17	"	267	
20	"	267	
22	"	432	
xvi. 4	" I.	170	
27	"	587	
xvii. 24	"	121	

ST. MATTHEW (continued).

xviii. 8,	Vol. II., p.	69	
17	" I.	279	
xix. 3, 6, 8,	"	142	
8	"	267	
	" II.	202, 474	
xx. 21	" I.	675	
xxi. 13	" II.	202	
xxii. 4	"	67	
17	"	262	
21	"	260	
27	" I.	64	
28	" II.	325	
40	" I.	267	
	" II.	156	
xxiii. 5	" I.	63	
6	"	266	
13–25,	" II.	202	
15	" I.	63, 78, 329	
	" II.	432	
25, 27	"	327	
27	"	322	
27–29	" I.	586	
37	"	650	
xxiv. 6, 15	"	586	
17	"	268	
23, 24	"	352	
29, 30, 34	"	608	
31	"	591, 608	
37	"	562	
xxvi. 15	"	150	
24	" II.	69	
28	" I.	654	
40	" II.	283	
74	"	87	
xxvii. 9, 10	" I.	150	
13	" II.	297	
25	" I.	586	

ST. MARK.

i. 3,	Vol. I., p.	150	
44	"	265	
ii. 23	"	267	
27	"	142	
iii. 31	"	222	
iv. 16	" II.	103	
vi. 3	" I.	86	
vii. 1–23	" II.	462	
3, 5, 8, 9, 13	" I.	155	
4–8	"	63	
14, 16	"	276	
19	"	267, 276	
ix. 14	"	404	
x. 5–9	"	267	
xii. 33	"	267	
xiii. 9	"	175	
xiv. 15	"	86	
52	"	76	
xv. 7	"	404	
16	" II.	425	
21	"	269	
41	"	362	
xvi. 15	" I.	326	
17	"	96	

ST. LUKE.

i. 3,	Vol. I., p.	353	
9	"	88	
22	"	194	
36	" II.	567	
52	" I.	368	
ii. 23	"	324	
34	"	57, 150	
37	" II.	432	

ST. LUKE (continued).

iii. 22,	Vol. I., p.	92	
iv. 8	"	150	
20	"	132, 345, 367, 69*	
	" II.	390	
23	" I.	480	
v. 17	" II.	528	
vi. 29	"	322	
32, 33	"	146	
vii. 45	"	269	
viii. 3	"	362	
19	" I.	222	
27	"	391	
ix. 53	" II.	305	
54	" I.	675	
x. 1	"	89	
7	" II.	525	
21	"	429	
39	"	70	
xii. 15–21	"	527	
32	"	398	
50	" I.	562	
xiii. 2	"	299	
14	"	267	
xiv. 1–6	"	267	
34	" II.	249	
xvi. 17	"	266	
22	"	273	
xvii. 31	"	269	
xviii. 8	" II.	585	
11	" I.	64	
13	" II.	518	
xix. 23	" I.	132	
xx. 9	"	391	
47	"	64	
xxi. 9	"	599	
xxii. 26	"	133	
41	" II.	284	
44	" I.	480	
56	"	660	
64	" II.	115	
xxiii. 18	"	312	
19	" I.	404	
34	" I.	404	
34–46	"	69	
41	"	611	
43	"	116	
xxiv. 28	" I.	194	
25	"	104	
	" II.	147	
26	" I.	140	
45	"	84	
47	"	222	
48	"	84	
53	"	90	

ST. JOHN.

i. 11,	Vol. I., p.	396	
14	"	91	
14, 16	" I.	439	
46	" I.	299	
47	"	16	
iii. 8	"	102	
26	" II.	290	
30	"	267	
iv. 21–23	" I.	91	
22	"	142, 222	
	" I.	186	
v. 10	" I.	267	
17	"	142	
24	" II.	220	
vi. 63	"	103	
vii. 5	" I.	222	
12–47	"	203	
15	"	106	
35	"	116	
49	"	65	

QUOTED OR REFERRED TO. 655

St. John (continued).

viii. 43,	Vol. II., p. 208		
58	,,		457
59	,,		650
ix. 14	,,	I.	267
16	,,		203
41	,,	II.	63
x. 16	,,		258, 267
20	,,		203
28	,,		219
31–33	,,	I.	650
34	,,	II.	80
xi. 25	,,		220
52	,,	L.	608
xii. 9	,,		130
20	,,		126, 296
29	,,		192
31	,,	II.	262
42	,,	I.	125
43	,,	II.	327
xiii. 8	,,	I.	273
18	,,		150
27	,,	II.	522
xiv. 19	,,		219
20	,,		320
30	,,		104, 508
xv. 4–10	,,		219
5	,,		219
22	,,	I.	468
xvi. 7	,,		409
11	,,	II.	508
xvii. 12	,,	I.	609
18	,,		334
xviii. 7	,,		279
12	,,	II.	322
xix. 11	,,	I.	468, 654
26	,,	II.	77
37	,,	I.	150
40	,,		271
xx. 5, 6	,,	II.	284
17	,,		465
19, 26	,,	I.	86

Acts.

i. 2,	Vol. I., p. 89		
3	,,		84
4	,,		84
6	,,		85
7	,,		85
8	,,		86, 326
	,,	II.	186
10	,,	I.	660
15	,,		135
17	,,		89
19	,,		206, 480
20	,,		206
21	,,		206
22	,,		84
25	,,		87
ii. 1	,,		140
2	,,		90, 102
2, 3	,,		92
6	,,		102
9	,,		559
	,,	II.	167
14	,,	I.	103
15	,,		105
16	,,		104
17	,,		104
26	,,		150
27	,,		371
32	,,		84
44	,,		594
	,,	II.	488
46	,,	L.	90
47	,,		375
iii. 1	,,		90, 140

Acts (continued).

iii. 2–4,	Vol. I., p. 480		
7	,,		660
15	,,		84
16	,,		591
19	,,		65
19–21	,,	II.	251
21	,,		244
26	,,	I.	229
iv. 2	,,		492
8	,,		106
11	,,		150
29	,,		492
33	,,		84
v. 1	,,	II.	534
14	,,	I.	209
21	,,		106
26	,,		650
32	,,		84
34	,,		44
41	,,		167
	,,	II.	214
vi. 1	,,	I.	16, 126
2	,,		132
5	,,		126, 127
5, 10	,,		132
8	,,		137
9	,,		146, 404
	,,	I.	167
12	,,	I.	153
13, 14	,,		153
14	,,		154
15	,,		156, 660
56	,,		156
vii. 2	,,		163
	,,	II.	313
5–8	,,	I.	163
6	,,	II.	149
21	,,		432
43	,,		35
48	,,	I.	543
48, 51	,,		163
50	,,		164
52	,,		162
	,,	II.	315
53	,,	I.	162, 166
	,,	II.	140
55	,,	I.	660
56	,,		164
57	,,		165
58	,,		13, 646
viii. 1	,,		177
2	,,		172
3	,,		172
9	,,		352
11	,,		391
16	,,		173
21	,,		89
26	,,		261
30	,,		629
33	,,		261
ix. 1, 2	,,		178
3	,,		191
5	,,		76, 192
7	,,		192
8	,,		196
10–12	,,		194
13	,,		178
15	,,		324
	,,	II.	105
15, 16	,,	I.	324
17	,,		196
18	,,		480
19, 20	,,		205
20, 21	,,		224
21	,,		173
22	,,		585
23	,,		225
24	,,		227, 460

Acts (continued).

ix. 26,	Vol. I., p. 230, 232,		
			290, 405
27	,,		196, 237,
			539
29	,,		126, 127,
			229
30	,,		77, 337
31	,,		243
34	,,		300
x. 1	,,	II.	190
2	,,	I.	190, 196,
			404
4	,,	II.	390
9	,,	L.	140
9, 10	,,		480
10	,,		271
12	,,		271
13	,,	II.	57
14, 30	,,	L.	140
23	,,		278
28	,,		279
30	,,		140
36	,,		350
38	,,		300
40	,,		84
45	,,		96
xi. 2	,,		262
3	,,		126
4	,,		278
5	,,		194
12	,,		282
15	,,		96, 422
17	,,		422
18	,,		283
20	,,		126, 265,
			347, 480
	,,		77, 337
26	,,		290, 410
29	,,		
30	,,		405
xii. 1	,,		311
2	,,		312
3–6	,,		319
5	,,		348
9	,,		194, 314
12	,,	II.	330
13	,,	L.	332
17	,,		337
21	,,	II.	37
23	,,	L.	480
25	,,		480
xiii. 2	,,		324
	,,	II.	185
2, 3	,,	L.	140
3	,,		334
5	,,		345
9	,,		660
11	,,		354
12	,,		355
13–22	,,		371
16	,,		16
16–22	,,		370
17	,,		368
18	,,		368
19	,,		368
20	,,		370
20, 21	,,		638
22–31	,,		370
25	,,		369
26	,,		369
27	,,		369
32	,,		369
33–41	,,		370, 373
33	,,		371
33, 34	,,		369
35–37	,,		371
38, 39, 46	,,		222
39	,,		369

656 PASSAGES OF SCRIPTURE

Acts (continued).			Acts (continued).			Acts (continued).		
xiii. 41,	Vol. I.,	p. 150	xvi. 17,	Vol. I.,	p. 500	xix. 22,	Vol. I.,	p. 459
42	,,	874	18	II.	275	25	II.	376
43	,,	190, 74	19	,,	26	29	I.	368, 508
45	,,	375	19, 20	I.	468	32	II.	369
46	,,	375	20	,,	465	33	,,	518
48	,,	375	20, 21	,,	464	35	,,	10, 12
49	,,	375	20, 7	,,	465	36, 37	,,	41, 208
50	,,	560	21	,,	501	37	,,	14
51	,,	577	24	,,	497	xx.	I.	405
xiv. 1	,,	286	25	II.	465	1, 2	,,	477
2	,,	390	26	I.	466	1, 31	II.	45
3	,,	391	30	,,	500	3	,,	272, 274
4	,,	394	32	,,	878	4	,,	I. 313, 458, 460, 508
	II.	269	33	I.	500		II.	27, 537
6	I.	302	34, 35	,,	500	5	,,	I. 479, 508
9	,,	390	37	,,	501	6	,,	I. 274, 275
14	,,	345	39	,,	502			I. 386, 477, 482
15	,,	7, 288	40	,,	466, 502		II.	275
16	II.	376	xvii. 1	,,	479	6, 16	I.	140
	I.	383	2, 3	,,	508	9	,,	278
17	II.	210	4	,,	509	11, 12	,,	278
	I.	19, 382, 652	5	,,	158, 512	12	,,	278
19	,,	560	9	,,	515	13	I.	375
22	,,	389	11	,,	518		,,	279
	II.	617	13	,,	519, 560	16	,,	280
xv.	I.	405	14	,,	459, 502, 519, 562	17-38	,,	617
	II.	166	14, 15	,,	661	18-35	,,	27, 51, 283—288
1	I.	399, 400, 402	15	,,	523	19	,,	28
2	,,	408, 405, 406, 414	16	,,	524, 528	19, 31, 37	,,	283
4	,,	406	17	,,	532	20, 31, 34	,,	281
5	II.	396	18	,,	537	21	I.	450
6	I.	406	19	,,	539	26, 27, 32, 33	II.	482
7	,,	406	21	,,	548			
7-11	,,	422	22	,,	549			
11	,,	416	23	II.	352	33	I.	369, 374
19	,,	488		I.	524, 531, 542	34, 35	II.	482
20	,,	497	24	,,	18, 163	35	,,	281
23	,,	490, 457	26	,,	550	36	,,	281
22, 23, 27	,,	579	27	,,	632	37	,,	280
23, 41	,,	242	28	,,	680	38	,,	617
24	,,	420	30	,,	383, 547	30	I.	27, 441
24	,,	447		II.	210	33	I.	568
24	II.	146	32	I.	546	34	,,	367, 561
25	I.	345	xviii. 1	,,	506	37	,,	561
29	,,	437	2	,,	463	39	,,	264
32	II.	518		I.	22	xxi. 1	,,	264
34	I.	438	4	,,	296	2	II.	242
37	,,	449	5	,,	522	3	,,	206
38	,,	356	7	II.	522	4	,,	267, 654
	II.	546	8	I.	500, 565		,,	275
39	I.	405, 440	9	,,	74, 194	1, 4, 5	,,	267
40	,,	337, 456	12	,,	269	5	I.	467
xvi. 1	,,	610	13, 15	I.	568	8	,,	122
	,,	386	14	,,	569	8, 9	,,	268
	II.	524	17	,,	195, 570	15	I.	290
1, 2	I.	458		II.	80	16	I.	347, 462
3	,,	459	18, 21	I.	140		II.	290
	,,	417	18, 26	,,	560	18	,,	440, 479
	II.	518	19	,,	502	19	II.	294
6	I.	392, 427	22	,,	405	20	,,	517
	II.	441, 464	23	,,	464	20, 24	II.	140
6, 7	I.	587		II.	441	21	II.	229, 294
7	,,	475, 656	25	,,	19	25	,,	301
8	,,	476	27	,,	19	26	,,	126
9	,,	194, 479	xix. 6	I.	96		II.	274, 537, 595
10	,,	477, 478	9, 23	,,	299	30	,,	310
	II.	275	10	,,	464	33, 37	,,	311
12	I.	485, 487	10-20	II.	442	38	,,	312
14	,,	487	11	,,	23	39	,,	314
15	,,	500	14	,,	24	40	I.	17, 347
16	,,	120, 362	15, 16	,,	25	40	II.	315
	,,	491	19	I.	352			
16, 17			21	,,	478			
18, 19	,,	492		II.	41, 224			

QUOTED OR REFERRED TO. 657

Acts (continued).	Acts (continued).	Romans (continued).

Acts (continued).
xxii. 1, Vol. I., p. 162
2 „ 45
3 „ 15, 43, 44, 69, 140
 II. 314
4 „ I. 174
6 „ 66, 191
8 „ 76
10 „ 660
12 „ 283
14, 15 „ 202
16, 17 „ 206
17 „ 74, 194, 239, 656
17–21 „ 240
19 „ 373
21 „ 193, 394
 II. 315
22 „ I. 48
 II. 316
23 „ 464
24 „ 317
25 „ I. 466
 II. 317
25, 26, 29, 30 „ 319
30 „ 318
xxiii. 1 „ I. 354
 II. 390
1, 6 „ I. 66
2 „ II. 115
3 „ 322
5 „ I. 600
 II. 223
6 „ 4, 25
 II. 393
11 „ 414
12 „ 67
16 „ I. 85
26–30 „ II. 384
29 „ I. 570
35 „ II. 485
xxiv. 2 „ 327
4 „ 138
5 „ 209
6–8 „ II. 336
8, 10 „ 336
22 „ 338
10 „ I. 627
17 „ 410
 II. 202
21 „ II. 269
 II. 223
22, 26 „ 340
25 „ I. 340
 II. 342
xxv. 4 „ I. 414
8 „ II. 343
9 „ 343
11 „ 290
14 „ 145
15 „ I. 106
19 „ 570
 II. 352
22 „ 353
24 „ 347
xxvi. 1 „ I. 327
2, 3 „ 627
4, 5 „ 5
5 „ 46, 62
 II. 314
7 „ I. 116, 460
 II. 429
 „ 263
10 „ I. 169
11 „ 175, 177
14 „ 39, 196

Acts (continued).
xxvi. 15, Vol. I., p. 76
16 „ 196
17 „ 334
17, 18 „ 193
19 „ 194
20 „ 293
 II. 396
23 „ I. 149
24 „ II. 106, 571
24–27 „ 358
26 „ 355
28 „ I. 299
28, 29 „ 359
xxvii. 1 „ I. 479
2 „ 362
3 „ 274, 543
3 „ 5, 242
4 „ 365
7 „ 366
7 „ 367
10 „ II. 370, 376
12 „ 379, 371
13, 17, 18 „ 374
14 „ 372
16, 19 „ 373
17 „ 373
19 „ 275
24 „ I. 180
27 „ II. 353
29 „ 379
34, 40 „ 380
40 „ 376
41 „ 382
xxviii. 2, 3 „ I. 611
6 „ 480
8 „ II. 336
13 „ 560
14 „ 167, 275
15 „ I. 560
16, 23 „ II. 390
20 „ 263
24 „ I. 138
29 „ 404
30, 30 „ II. 395

ROMANS.
i. 1, Vol. I., p. 394, 492
 II. 156
1–7 „ 125
4 „ I. 360
 II. 185
5, 6 „ 168
7, 15 „ 171
8 „ I. 591
 II. 396
8–11 „ 417
8–15 „ 196
11, 12 „ 185
12, 14 „
13 „ 193, 168
14 „ I. 192, 222
15 „ II. 39
16 „ I. 126
 II. 601
16, 17 „ 196, 592
16–22 „ 197
16–iii. 20 „ 181
17 „ I. 51
18 „ 478, 596
18, 19, 20 „ II. 195
i. 18–32 „ I. 31
19 „ 626
19, 20 „ 392

Romans (continued).
i. 20, Vol. I., p. 383, 542, 635, 632
21 „ 543
21, 22 „ 33
21–32 „ 558
22 „ 626
24 „ 47, 547
 II. 196
24, 26, 28 „ 196
25 „ 240
27 „ 196
27, 28, 29–31 „ 197
28 „ I. 627, 629
 II. 196
29 „ I. 628
 II. 517
30 „ I. 628
30, 32 „ II. 197
ii. 1 „ 192, 327
 I. 629
 II. 196
1–16 „ 209
6 „ 199
6, 10 „ 230, 243
6, 10 „ I. 627
14, 15 „ 230
6–10 „ II. 231, 391, 615
6–12 „ 237
6–15 „ 267
7–10 „ I. 633
8 „ 27
 II. 465
9 „ I. 126
12 „ II. 200
13 „ 230
13, 14 „ 230
14 „ 200
15 „ I. 382
16 „ 243
 II. 200, 591
17, 18, 19 „ 201
17–21 „ I. 622
17–24 „ II. 203
18 „ 417
21 „ 202
22 „ 203
24 „ I. 46
 II. 203, 204
25–29 „ 206
iii. 1–4 „ I. 34, 46
2 „ II. 205
3–20 „ 206–208
4, 9, 21 „ 206
5 „ 208
5–8 „ 207
6 „ I. 47
9 „ I. 193, 627
 II. 207
9–20 „ 208
10–18 „ II. 509
15 „ I. 627
20 „ II. 208, 291, 293, 300
21–26 „ 209, 248, 597
21 „ 168
21–26 „
21–30 „ 181

ROMANS (continued).

iii. 22, Vol. II., p. 193
22–27 ,, 210
24 ,, 210
25 ,, I. 388
 ,, II. 106, 209, 601
25–29 ,, 482
27–30 ,, 211
28 ,, 211
31 ,, 211, 232
iii. 31–} ,, 181
iv. 25 }
iii. 31–} ,, 211–213
v. 21 }
iv. ,, 196
1 ,, 212
1–25 ,, 213
4 ,, 227, 591
5 ,, 226
6, 13 ,, I. 640
11 ,, 158
 ,, II. 212
12 ,, I. 640
12, 16,} ,, 54
18 }
15 ,, II. 103, 225
16 ,, 174
17 ,, I. 47
18 ,, II. 191
24, 28 ,, 192
25 ,, 213
v., vii., xi. ,, 296
v. 1 ,, 213
1–11 ,, 181, 214
1–12 ,, 214
3–5 ,, I. 628
6 ,, 206
7, 11 ,, II. 214
9 ,, I. 369
10 ,, II. 519
11 ,, I. 591
 ,, II. 237
12 ,, I. 648
 ,, II. 215, 517
12–20 ,, 517
12–21 ,, 181, 215–217, 237, 591
13 ,, 225
13, 14 }
15–18 } ,, 216
18, 19 }
14 ,, 216
15–20 ,, 201
16, 18 ,, 217
20 ,, 84, 149, 213, 203, 224
20, 21 ,, 218, 245
vi. ,, 182, 211, 219–221
vi.–viii. ,, I. 72
vi. 1 ,, II. 206
1–15 ,, 219, 220
1–23 ,, 237
2, 15 ,, 206, 222
3–23 ,, 148
4 ,, 564
4, 9 ,, I. 203
4, 11 ,, II. 103
5 ,, 219, 220
7 ,, I. 369
8 ,, II. 219, 564
9 ,, I. 369
12, 16 ,, II. 220
14 ,, 221, 226
15–23 ,, 219, 221
19 ,, 221

ROMANS (continued).

vi. 23, Vol. II., p. 210
vii. ,, 206
1–6 ,, 233
1–6,} ,, 237
7–25 }
1–11 ,, 146
vii. 1–} ,, 182
viii. 11 }
vii. 2 ,, I. 635
2, 3 ,, II. 591
6, 7,} ,, 103
10, 11 }
7 ,, 149, 206, 225, 232
7 sq. ,, 213
7, 13 ,, 206
7–12 ,, 225
vii. 7– } ,, 225–229
viii. 39 }
8–10 ,, I. 181
vii. 10–13 ,, II. 226
12 ,, 517
13 ,, I. 206
 ,, II. 100
vii. 13– } ,, 227
viii. 11 }
vii. 14 ,, 205
21 ,, 206
22 ,, 206
24 ,, I. 633
25 ,, 634
 ,, II. 236
viii. ,, 206
1 ,, I. 72
 ,, II. 237
2, 10 ,, 103
3 ,, I. 3, 206, 369
4 ,, II. 211
6 ,, 149, 237
11 ,, I. 206
12–30 ,, II. 182
18–25 ,, 238
19–23 ,, 94, 238, 248, 591
19–24 ,, 244
23–24 ,, 251
28 ,, 101
24 ,, I. 369
26–30 ,, II. 238
27 ,, I. 299
29 ,, II. 417, 488, 567
29, 30 ,, I. 628
31–39 ,, II. 238
34 ,, I. 698
36 ,, II. 30, 121
38 ,, I. 609
 ,, II. 142, 457
39 ,, 239
ix. ,, I. 34, 419
 ,, II. 500
ix.–xi. ,, 166, 122, 240
ix. 1 ,, 168
1–6 ,, I. 290
1–5 ,, 35, 595, 627
 ,, II. 248
1–31 ,, 248–250
3 ,, I. 25, 35, 196
4 ,, 16
4, 5 ,, II. 205
5 ,, I. 205
 ,, II. 445
5–13 ,, 591
6–9 ,, 249

ROMANS (continued).

ix. 8, Vol. I., p. 54
9 ,, 640
11 ,, II. 591
14 ,, 206
14, 30 ,, 206
15–18 ,, 250
16 ,, 429, 591
18 ,, 250
19–21 ,, 250
19–30 ,, 251
ix. 22–x. 21 ,, 251–252
26 ,, I. 333
28 ,, II. 251
30 ,, I. 628
 ,, II. 146
ix. 30–x. 4 ,, 252
ix. 30–x. 21 ,, 590
ix. 33 ,, 47, 57, 151
34 ,, II. 252
36 ,, I. 213
x. ,, 634
1 ,, 35
 ,, II. 168
2 ,, 417
3 ,, 252
4–19 ,, 252
5 ,, I. 69, 126
6 ,, 208
6–8 ,, 548
6–9 ,, 46
9 ,, II. 191
11 ,, 252
12 ,, 201
14, 15 ,, I. 698
15 ,, II. 509
15–21 ,, I. 46
16–21 ,, II. 252
18 ,, I. 47, 344
 ,, II. 168
xi. ,, 417, 519
1 ,, 254
1–10 ,, 254
4, 11 ,, 206
1–15 ,, 253–254
2 ,, I. 66
3 ,, ,, 208
6 ,, I. 591
8 ,, I. 47
13, 25 ,, II. 457
13 ,, 168
15–36 ,, 246
16–24 ,, 254–255
16–25 ,, I. 211
17 ,, ,, 628
22 ,, II. 113
23 ,, 498
24–27 ,, I. 608
25 ,, ,, 186
26 ,, 174
26, 32 ,, 245
30–36 ,, 84, 591
31 ,, 256
32 ,, I. 648
 ,, II. 84, 24
36 ,, 244
xii. ,, 188
xii.–xiv. ,, 270
xii. 1 ,, 267
1, 10 ,, 417
1–21 ,, 269
2 ,, 429
2, 3 ,, 268
3 ,, I. 630
 ,, II. 192
3, 16 ,, 417
5 ,, 219
6 ,, 268
7 ,, 261, 61

QUOTED OR REFERRED TO. 659

ROMANS (*continued*).

xii. 9, 10,}
11, 12,} Vol. II., p. 259
14, 16,}
19, 20,}
11   I. 589, 626
      II. 19
12   „ 157
xiii.   „ 182
xiii., xiv.   „ 402
xiii. 1—7   „ 260
3   „ 615
4   „ 160
5, 6,} „ 260
7, 8}
8   „ 156
10   „ 211, 457
11—14   I. 592
12   „ 85
      II. 240, 262, 518
13   I. 4
14   II. 230
xiv.   „ 481
xiv.–xv.} „ 183
12
xiv.–xv. „ 111
xiv. 1   I. 396
1–4   II. 523
1–12   „ 266
xiv. 1–xv. 13 „ 265–268
xiv. 2   „ 526
5   I. 44, 140
      II. 276, 417
6   „ 263, 417
9, 11   „ 417
10   „ 280, 591
13–21   „ 267
15   I. 205
21   „ 673
22, 23 „ II. 267
23   „ 145, 170
24   „ 170
xv.–xvi.   „ 270
xv. 1   I. 463
3   „ 267
1–8   „ 268
3   „ 208
4   „ 362
      II. 147
5   „ 470
9, 10, 11 „ 267
9–33   II. 269
14–34 „ 183
15, 16 „ 166
15–20 „ 170
16   I. 324, 326
      II. 268
18   I. 342, 344
19   II. 89, 531
20–33 „ 265, 269
22   I. 586
23   „ 478
      II. 193
23–29 „ 32
24   I. 661
      II. 186, 269
24, 26 „ 511
24, 33 „ 128
25   „ 299
25–32 „ II. 122
25, 26 „ 6
26   „ 512
26, 27 „ I. 305
27   „ 410
29   II. 427
31   „ 292
32   „ 269
33   „ 170

ROMANS (*continued*).

xvi., Vol. II., p. 269
1   I. 565
    II. 521, 617
1, 2   I. 568
    „ II. 170
    „   559, 560
    II. 2
3–20   „ 48
4   „ 37, 269
5   „ I. 562
5, 14, } II. 165
15 }
5, 7, 13, } „ 269
14, 16, }
22 }
7   „ I. 24, 560
    II. 465
7, 9, } „ 170
12, 13 }
14, 22, } „ 185
27, 33 }
16   „ I. 564
17   „ II. 141
17–20 „ 170, 173
17–20) „
19, 20, } „ 270
24, 27 }
18   „ 417
20, 24 „ 170
21   I. 506, 562
    II. 124, 274
22   „ 398
    II. 32, 37
24   „ I. 595
25   „ 211
    II. 171
25–27 „ I. 626
    II. 267
27   „ 170, 518

I. CORINTHIANS.

i.–iii. Vol. I., p. 624
i. 1 „ 344, 565
1–3 „ II. 60
2 „ I. 558
4–9,} II. 61
10, 20 }
7 „ I. 608
8 „ 597
10 „ II. 62
12 „ 447
13, 14 „ 63
12–17 „ I. 345
14 „ 368, 458, 562
16 „ 500
17 „ 564
18–25 „ 33
21 „ 33, 531
    II. 588
21, 22,} „ 62
24 }
22, 23 „ I. 126
23 „ 208, 564
23, 24 „ 629
27, 28 „ 334
28 „ II. 104
29 „ 627
30 „ 190
ii. 1–5 „ I. 564
2 „ 208, 564
3 „ 218, 556, 342, 5
6 „ II. 104
6–16 „ 63
7 „ 459
12 „ I. 628

I. CORINTHIANS (*continued*)

ii. 14, Vol. I., p. 32
15   II. 62
iii. 1–4 „ 64
2 „ I. 80, 628
2, 4 „ II. 63
6 „ 20, 521
8 „ 243
9 „ I. 587
10 „ 344
11 „ 555
12 „ II. 68, 192, 591
17 „ I. 627
18–20 „ 83
18–27 „ 38
19 „ 17, 33
22 „ 609
23 „ II. 249
iv. „ I. 688
3 „ 27
  II. 587
3, 4 „ 64
5 „ 104, 459, 591
6 „ 64, 154, 236
6–21 „ 66
7, 9,} „ 65
13, 15 }
8 „ I. 624
8–10 „ 585
8–11 „ 627
9 „ 112
9–13 „ 30
9 „ I. 517, 557
    II. 39
10 „ I. 33, 219
11, 12 „ 561
12, 13 „ 623
15 „ 80, 343
17 „ 459
18, 19 „ II. 65
v. 1 „ I. 435, 558
1, 2 „ 559, 627
1–9 „ II. 67
2 „ 641
    II. 65
5 „ 653
    II. 87, 518
6 „ 66
7 „ I. 203
    II. 67, 72
9 „ 574
9, 10 „ 559
10, 11 „ 67
9–13 „ II. 67
10 „ 591
11 „ 58
12–21 „ I. 564
vi. 1–20 „ II. 68
2 „ I. 47, 587, 623, 645
2–8 „ II. 112
7 „ 267
9 „ 634
    II. 517
9, 10 „ I. 343
9–11 „ 558
9–20 „ 558
11 „ 303
    II. 67, 587
13 „ 104
14 „ 605
15 „ II. 206, 232
15–18 „ 58
17 „ 191
vii. „ 520, 612
1 „ 60

I Corinthians (continued).				I. Corinthians (continued).				I. Corinthians (continued).			
vii. 1-40,	Vol. II., p. 71			x. 4,	Vol. I., p. 640			xiv. 16,	Vol. II., p. 80		
2	"	I.	211, 588	"	"	II.	222	18	"	I.	97
3,5,7,9 }	"	II.	60	4, 11	"	I.	57	21	"	"	48, 58
18, 19 }				6	"	"	58			II.	80
7, 8, 9	"	I.	637	7	"	II.	67	22	"	I.	97
8	"	"	79, 170	7, 8	"	I.	673, 674	26-40	"	II.	80
9, 36	"	"	82	8	"	II.	58, 73	32	"	I.	103
10	"	II.	71	11	"	"	58	39	"	"	564
10-24 }	"	"	70	15	"	"	219	xv.		"	203
(17-24) }				16	"	"	203			II.	489, 692
12	"	"	26	17	"	II.	243	1-12	"	"	82
12	"	I.	209, 611	20	"	"	523	3	"	I.	562
14	"	"	80	20, 21	"	I.	432	4	"	II.	112
18	"	"	127	26	"	II.	457	7	"	I.	86
19	"	"	633	33	"	I.	196	8	"	"	193, 196
21	"	II.	70, 527	xi. 1-17	"	II.	76			II.	82, 106
25	"	"	71	2	"	"	49	9	"	L.	76, 174
26	"	"	69	7, 8	"	I.	558				219
29, 31	"	"	70	8, 9	"	II.	590	10	"	"	219, 374
29-31	"	I.	633	10	"	I.	57, 638, 639			I.	98, 498
31	"	"	699, 634					10-29	"	"	183
		II.	486			II.	525	12	"	II.	564
36	"	I.	80	14	"	I.	557	12-35, }			
39	"	"	531			II.	2	35-50 }	"	"	83
viii.	"	I.	451	17	"	I.	611	19	"	"	31
		II.	78	17-34	"	II.	77	20	"	"	496
1	"	"	49, 699	19	"	"	537	21	"	"	606
1-13	"	"	72	21	"	I.	559	22	"	"	565
6	"	I.	613	22	"	"	211, 627, 638			II.	180, 243
		II.	246, 249, 446					23	"	"	587
				23	"	"	407	24	"	II.	104, 497
8	"	"	65, 523	24-33	"	"	9	24, 25	"	"	591
10	"	I.	87, 628	24, 27 }	"	"	77	25-28	"	"	246
13	"	"	674	29 }				26	"	"	249
		II.	267	29	"	I.	629	28	"	L.	57
ix.	"	"	157			"	633			II.	201
1	"	"	73, 196, 196, 410	xii.	"	"	96	30-39	"	"	143
				xii.-xiv. 33	"	II.	186	31	"	I.	2, 213
		II.	97, 98	xii. 1	"	"	78			"	564
1, 3, 7	"	"	447	1-31	"	"	56, 243	32	"	I.	29, 527
1-16	"	II.	112	3	"	"	143			"	39
1-27	"	"	78	4-6	"	II.	78	33	"	I.	630
2, 15	"	L.	34	8-10	"	"	78	33, 34	"	II.	58
4	"	"	561	9, 10	"	I.	471, 594	36	"	I.	57
5	"	"	79, 237, 424, 447	12, 13, }	"	"	219	36, 45	"	"	641
				27 }				39	"	"	53
6	,	"	452	12-27	"	"	258	41	"	"	18
7	"	II.	47	13	"	"	78	43	"	"	698
8	"	"	72	28	"	I.	323	45	"	"	47, 48
		"	527			I.	521, 617			II.	215
8-10, }				29, 30	"	"	459	47, 52	"	I.	638
11, 12, }	"	"	72	31	"	"	100	50 sq.	"	II.	501
13, 14 }				xii. 31-xiii. 13	"	"	78	50-58	"	"	84
9	"	I.	57	xi·i.	"	"	609	51	"	I.	605
		II.	222, 525	1	"	I.	100			II.	78
10	"	I.	443			II.	192	51, 52	"	"	427
		I.	427	2	"	"	78	52	"	"	84
12	"	I.	561	3, 4	"	I.	623	54	"	"	203
12, 13	"	II.	70	4	"	"	27	56	"	"	149, 225
15	"	I.	583			II.	65, 79	58	"	"	227
16	"	"	344	4, 5 }	"	"	79	xvi. 1-4	"	"	94
17	"	"	211	7, 8 }				2	"	"	6
		II.	192	5	"	I.	524	3	"	I.	410
19	"	I.	343, 396	8	"	II.	104, 249	3, 4	"	II.	274
20	"	"	469	9	"	"	142	5-7	"	"	33
21	"	"	393, 468	9-12	"	"	304	5, 8	"	"	37
		II.	147	10	"	"	268	5-19	"	I.	477
24	"	I.	634	xiv. 1-26	"	"	80	9	"	II.	19, 83
		II.	429, 591	3, 4	"	I.	100	10	"	I.	489
26, 27	"	I.	557	2, 19, }	"	"	100			II.	66
24-27	"	"	635	23, 27 }				10, 11	"	I.	536
26	"	"	557	4, 13, }	"	"	96	11	"	"	490
		II.	227	14, 27 }				12	"	"	627
x. 1	"	"	186, 459	7	"	"	100			II.	20, 86
1, 2	"	"	222	8	"	"	100	15	"	"	563
1-4	"	I.	48	9, 11, 17, }	"	"	100			II.	617
1-14	"	II.	48	20-23, 26- }				20	"	"	499
x. 1-xi. 1	"	"	76	28, 33, 40 }						II.	28, 170

QUOTED OR REFERRED TO. 661

I. Corinthians (continued).
xvi. 20, Vol. I., p. 594
22 ,, 85
,, II. 248, 481, 584
23 ,, I. 595

II. Corinthians.
i. Vol. I., p. 638
i.-vi. ,, II. 592
i. 1 ,, 195
1-11 ,, 100
i. 3 ,, 249
4, 6, 8 ,, 90
5 ,, I. 203, 591
6 ,, II. 99
7 ,, 458
8 ,, 30, 100, 186
8, 15 ,, 99
11, 12, } ,, I. 74
13-17 }
12 ,, II. 100, 102
14 ,, 100
15 ,, 288
15, 16 ,, 29
15, 23 ,, I. 216
16-23 ,, II. 39
17 ,, I. 217
,, II. 89
18 ,, 564
22 ,, 22
23 ,, II. 101
ii. ,, I. 638
1 ,, II. 101
1, 12 } ,, 99
13 }
2 ,, I. 217
4 ,, 220, 578
,, II. 90, 228
5 ,, I. 468
5-10 ,, II. 89
6, 10 ,, 102
7 ,, 125
11 ,, 102
12 ,, I. 477
12, 13 ,, II. 89
12-17 ,, 103
13 ,, I. 346
,, II. 276
14 ,, I. 192, 624
,, II. 96, 104, 461, 518
14-16 ,, I. 557, 624, 636
,, II. 31
15 ,, II. 591
16 ,, I. 641
,, II. 191
17 ,, I. 22, 217, 583
,, II. 103, 228
iii. 1 ,, I. 447, 624
,, II. 19, 89, 108, 113
1-3 ,, 103
1-18 ,, 97
2 ,, 629
,, II. 98
3 ,, 104
4 ,, 105
6 ,, 108, 174, 223, 518
7 ,, 104
7-18 ,, 222
10, 11 ,, 104
16, 18 ,, 104

II. Corinthians (continued).
iii. 18, Vol. II., p.193, 220
iv. 1 ,, 518
1-7 ,, 228
2 ,, I. 22, 217, 583
,, II. 104, 113
,, 223, 249
,, 446, 508
6 ,, I. 193
,, II. 105
6, 7 ,, I. 141
6-8 ,, II. 427
7 ,, I. 219, 342, 588
,, II. 107
8 ,, 629
,, II. 90, 100
8, 9 ,, 30
8-10 ,, I. 218
8-12 ,, II. 90
10 ,, I. 654, 655
,, II. 30, 104
11 ,, I. 218
14 ,, 603, 604
17 ,, II. 100
18 ,, 564
v. 1 ,, 427
1-4 ,, 84
2 ,, I. 641
3 ,, II. 105
4 ,, I. 218, 643
,, II. 315, 238, 434
5 ,, 99
5, 13 ,, 94
10 ,, 557
,, 48, 192, 230, 591
10, 11 ,, 104
11 ,, 89
11, 13 ,, 106
11, 15, 21 ,, 125
12 ,, 113
13 ,, 358
14 ,, I. 562
,, II. 74
15 ,, 201
15-21 ,, 146
16 ,, I. 73, 394
,, II. 106
17 ,, 125, 219
19 ,, 446, 519
19, 21 ,, 106
21 ,, 190
vi. 1 ,, I. 624
,, 374, 587
3-11 ,, 623
3-16 ,, 627
7 ,, II. 220
9, 10 ,, I. 623
10 ,, 623, 629
,, II. 107
vi. 11- } ,, 109
vii.16 }
vi. 14 ,, 558, 674
,, II. 72
vi. 14- } ,, 108
vii. 1 }
vi. 15, 18 ,, 108
16 ,, I. 416
18 ,, II. 248
vii., viii. ,, 532
1 ,, I. 558
,, II. 72
2 ,, I. 561, 627
2, 3 ,, II. 89
5 ,, I. 342, 590
,, II. 90

II. Corinthians (continued)
vii. 6-11,13 } Vol. II., p. 99
14, 15 }
8 ,, I. 576
,, II. 87
11 ,, I. 589, 627
11, 12 ,, II. 92
12 ,, 104, 108
viii.-end ,, 592
1 ,, 89, 99
viii. 1- } ,, 110
ix. 15 }
viii. 2 ,, I. 628
,, II. 90, 100
6 ,, 89, 110, 125
13 ,, 90
15 ,, I. 17
17 ,, II. 89
18 ,, I. 479
18, 23 ,, II. 89
19 ,, I. 389
20 ,, II. 65, 109, 221
21 ,, I. 611
22 ,, 626
23 ,, II. 141, 269
24 ,, 123
ix. ,, I. 638
1 ,, 599, 627
2 ,, II. 89
6 ,, 110, 125
8 ,, I. 628
8, 11 ,, 585
10 ,, II. 100
11, 13 ,, 100
12 ,, I. 894
12-15 ,, II. 125
14 ,, 125
x.-xii. ,, 96
x.-xiii. ,, 625
x. 1 ,, II. 99, 108, 111
1, 2 ,, I. 216
1-10 ,, 563
1-11 ,, II. 113
2 ,, 112
2, 7, }
10, 11, } ,, 111
12, 18 }
3, 4 ,, 509
5 ,, 518
7 ,, I. 447
7, 10, } ,, I. 657
11, 18 }
7, 10, } ,, II. 113
11, 12 }
8 ,, 112
9 ,, I. 574
10 ,, 217, 342, 469
,, II. 89
10-16 ,, 629
12-18 ,, 111, 112
12, 16, } ,, 112
17, 18 }
14 ,, 629
15 ,, 112, 192
20-23 ,, 96
xi. ,, I. 624
,, II. 33
1 ,, 94, 112
1, 14, } ,, 115
19, 20 }
1, 16, }
17, 19, } ,, 112
21 }
1-28 ,, 116

PASSAGES OF SCRIPTURE

II. CORINTHIANS (continued).

xi. 2, Vol. I., p. 344
" II. 283
2, 20 " 125
3 " 100, 112, 520
4 " 112, 113, 125, 143
4, 20 " I. 657
5 " 219
" II. 114
6 " I. 216, 342, 623
" II. 104, 111, 114
6–21 " 114
7 " I. 217, 368
8 " 583, 622, 657
" II. 119
9 " I. 27, 216, 584, 561
10 " II. 114
13 " I. 583
" II. 103, 297, 432
14 " I. 640, 57
16–19 " 38, 219
16, 17, 19 } " II. 112
18–20 " I. 624
18–20 " II. 80
20 " 270, 322
20, 21 " 112
22 " I. 16, 66
" II. 114
22–23 " I. 627
25 " 2, 218
" II. 30
23–33 " I. 339
" II. 114
25 " 383
26 " 28
27 " 65
27, 29 " 29
28 " 115
29 " I. 673
29–34 " II. 83
31 " 249, 519
32 " I. 178, 227
33 " 227
xii. 1 " 74, 192, 194
1–3, 12–16 } " 624
1–10 " 653
" II. 114
1, 5, 6, 11 } " 112
1–11 " 117
2 " I. 57
3, 4 " 641
5, 9 " II. 297
6, 11 " II. 113
6, 16 " 94
7 " I. 214, 220
9 " II. 117
10 " I. 628
10, 11 " I. 214
11 " I. 219
" II. 125
11, 12 " 114
12 " I. 565
13 " 27
13, 14 " II. 112
xii. 13– xiii. 10 } " 118
xii. 14 " I. 583

II. CORINTHIANS (continued).

xii. 14, Vol. II.. p. 117
16 " I. 217
18 " II. 110
20 " 52, 197
20, 21 " 125
21 " I. 558
" II. 58
29 " I. 3 9
xiii. 1 " II. 29, 99, 101, 113
2 " I. 74
3–9 " 342
5 " II. 125
11–13 " 118
12 " I. 594
14 " 595

GALATIANS.

I., ii., Vol. II., p. 269
1 " I. 210, 324
" II. 229
1–5 " 142
1, 6, 10 " 125
1–10 " 143
4 " I. 609
" II. 142
6 " I. 629
6–9 " II. 298
6–10 " 143
7 " I. 400
8 " 343
" L. 143
8, 9 " I. 110
" II. 87, 248
9 " I. 657
10 " 78, 392, 395, 415
11 " 209
11–ii. 21 " II. 144–146
11–24 " 144
12 " 518
13 " I. 140, 174
" II. 100, 144
13, 14 " L. 40
14 " 5, 62, 638
15 " 181, 344
15, 16 " 193
" II. 106
16 " I. 74, 206
17 " 206
" II. 232
17, 18 " 140
18 " L. 213, 231, 237
18, 19 " II. 140
19 " I. 237, 238, 424
21 " 77, 241, 337
" II. 286
21–24 " I. 241
22 " 228
24 " 74
ii. " 405
" II. 496
1 " I. 320, 405
1–6 " 414
1–10 " 405
" II. 145
2 " L. 656
3–6 " 406
2, 7 " 211
3 " 126
" II. 592
4 " L. 299
" II. 297

GALATIANS (continued).

ii. 4, 5, Vol.II., p. 517
6 " I. 219, 627
" II. 145
6, 20 " 125
7 " I. 405, 409
" II. 200, 322
7, 8 " I. 238
7–9 " 406
9 " 1, 219, 409, 452
" II. 55, 106
9, 10 " 140
9, 11, 14 " I. 237
10 " 410
11 " 219, 406, 430, 441, 442
" II. 70, 145, 166
11–21 " 140, 147
12 " I. 126, 439, 440, 447,
" II. 103, 146
13 " I. 464
14 " 439, 442
14, 16, 18 } " II. 298
15 " 198
15–21 " I. 444
16 " II. 192, 299
16, 20 " I. 628
17 " 468
" II. 206
19 " 461
20 " I. 8, 446, 654, 655
" II. 191
20 " 219, 290
21 " 222
iii. " 206, 226, 265
iii., iv. " 298
iii. 1 " I. 219, 432, 470, 657
" II. 147
1–5 " 140
1–14 " 147, 148
2 " 192
3, 13 " 125
4 " I. 628
" II. 147, 497
5 " I. 471
" II. 109, 427
6–18 " 140
6–29 " 126
10 " I. 69
" II. 103, 224
11 " I. 51, 369
12 " 196
14 " 325
15 " 636
" II. 148
15–18 " 149
15, 19 " 149
15–, iv.11 } " 148–152
iii. 16 " I. 48, 58
17 " 163
17, 18 " 635
18 " 34
19 " 57, 162, 163, 638
" II. 149, 294, 517
19, 20 " 150, 151
19–22 " 141
21 " 206, 222, 232

GALATIANS (continued).			GALATIANS (continued).			EPHESIANS (continued).		
iii. 21-29,	Vol II.,	p. 151	v. 16-26,	Vol. II.,	p. 156	i. 13, Vol. II.,		p. 486
22-26	,,	211	v. 16- }			19, 21	,,	492
24	,,	151	vi. 10 }	,,	141	20-22	,,	246
26	,,	192	v. 17	,,	224	21	I.	638
27	I.	475	19	,,	197		II.	457
	II.	220, 263	20	,,	25, 537	22	,,	439, 457,
28	, I.	87, 283,	21	,,	6			486, 492
		613	vi. 1	,, I.	628	ii.	,,	537
	II.	483, 520,	1-5	,, II.	157	1-6	,,	603
		527	1, 4 }			1-22	,,	485, 497
28, 29	,, I.	54	3, 15 }	,,	125	2	,, I.	638
iv. 1, 2	,,	635	1-18	,,	157, 158		II.	104, 262,
1, 3	,,	636	2	,,	157			495
1-11	,, II.	141, 152	5	,,	157	4, 7	,,	602, 603
2	,, I.	219	6, 7	,, I.	474	4, 7	,,	492
3	,, II.	152, 174,	6-10	,, II.	157	5, 7, 8	,,	491
		537	7	,,	227, 230	5, 6, }		
3, 9	,,	460	7, 10	,, I.	657	19, 22 }	,,	492
4	,,	249, 457	11	,,	26	6	,, I.	208, 362
4, 5	,,	151	11-18	,, II.	158		II.	450, 492
7	,,	567	12	,, I.	175, 475,	8-10	,,	615
8	,, I.	475, 582			623	9, 10	,,	496
9	,,	2	12, 13	,, II.	265	10	,,	492
10	,,	44, 140	13	,, I.	446	11	,,	496
11	,,	415, 626,		II.	600	12	,, I.	208
		461	14	,,	232	12 sq.	,, II.	496
12	,,	342, 448	15	,, I.	34, 662	14	,, I.	641
12-14	,,	468		II.	431		II.	136, 309
12-16	,,	653	16	,,	516	15	,,	461
	II.	153	17	,, I.	392, 632,	16	,,	452, 496
12-20	,,	153, 154			654, 655	18, 29	,,	492
14	,, I.	218, 219,		II.	30, 143	19-22	,,	219
		658	18	,, I.	585	20	,, I.	151
	II.	153	19	,,	203		II.	496, 522,
16	,, I.	447		II.	517			601, 603
	II.	6				20-22	,,	608
17	,, I.	219, 415,				21	,,	396
		634	EPHESIANS.			iii.	,,	459
	II.	125, 154	i.	Vol. I.,	p. 633	1	,,	111, 482
17-20	,,	154	1	,,	209	1-19	,,	499
19	,, I.	220, 343	1, 2	,, II.	496	1-21	,,	493, 497-9
	II.	428	1, 5, }			2	,,	482, 491
21-31	,,	155	9, 11 }	,,	491	2-4	,,	492
22	,,	73	2, 6, 7	,,	491	2, 7, 8,	,,	491
24	,,	222	3	,,	495	2-9	,,	458
24-31	,, I.	48	3-6	,,	493	3	,, I.	211, 470,
iv. 24- }	,, II.	154-156	3-14	,,	485, 498		II.	147, 359
v. 26 }			3, 13, }			3-6	,, I.	210
25	,, I.	652	17 }	,,	492	3, 8	,, II.	459
29	,,	57, 640	3, 20	,,	492	3, 9	,,	494
v. 1-6	,, II.	155	4	,, I.	610	3, 4, 9,	,,	492
1-9	,,	265		II.	603	4	,,	494
1-12	,,	141	5	,, I.	636	5	,, I.	447
1, 13, }			5, 9	,,	607		II.	497, 601,
14 }	,, I.	446		II.	492			603
2	,,	140, 432,	6	,,	459, 603	5, 16	,,	492
		475	6, 12 }			6	,, I.	396
	II.	108, 111	14, 17 }	,,	492		II.	219, 492
		422	18 }					496, 603
3, 6 }	,,		7	,,	458, 601	8	,,	496
12-14 }			7-12	,,	494	8, 16	,,	492
6	,, I.	581, 632	7, 18	,,	492	10	,, I.	638
6	,, II.	615	8	,,	494		II.	76, 492
7-12	,,	155	9	,,	491, 492	11	,,	491, 492
8	,, I.	581	9 sq.	,,	496	16	,,	492
10	,, II.	155	10	,, I.	89	16-21, }		
11	,, I.	398		II.	457, 491,	&c.	,,	498
	II.	143			492	17, 18, }		
11-18	,,	141	11	,,	491, 603	20, &c. }	,,	I. 581
12	,, I.	417, 624	11, 14, }			18	,, II.	494
	II.	139, 299	18 }	,,	482	19	,,	439, 457,
12-15	,,	156	13	,, I.	22			492
13-18	,,	141	13, 14	,, II.	494, 603	19, 20	,,	492
14	,,	156	14	,,	603	20, 21	,,	271, 499
15	,,		15, 18	,, I.	581	iv. 1	,,	432, 495
20, 21 }	,,	125	15-23	,, II.	493, 495	1-16	,,	493, 508
15, 21 }			17	,,	249, 494,	2	,,	603
26	,, I.	474			603	3-13	,,	503

EPHESIANS (continued).

iv. 3, 16,	Vol. II.,	p.	492
4, 30, 33	„		492
5	„	I.	613
5–15	„	II.	485
6	„		109, 249
7, 32	„		491
8	„	I.	57
		II.	249, 506, 602
8–11	„	I.	624
10	„		641
		II.	492, 495
10–13	„		492
11	„	I.	323
		II.	601
12	„	I.	393
12–16	„	II.	608
13	„		439, 457, 494
14	„		606
15	„		506
16	„		219, 427, 439
iv. 17–v. 21	„		493
iv. 17–24, 29	„		504
iv. 20–24	„		504
21	„		482, 497
22	„		496
24	„		290
25–v. 2	„		505
27	„	I.	587
		II.	521
31–v. 2	„		505
32	„		505
v.		I.	657
2	„	II.	197
3, 12	„	I.	589
3–17	„	II.	506
4	„	I.	627
4, 6	„	II.	505
5	„		63, 483
7–14, 22–31	„		485
9	„		491
11	„		617
12–15	„	I.	624
14	„	II.	463, 522, 601
14, 15–17	„		506
17	„		491
18	„	I.	103
		II.	492
18–21	„		506
19, 20	„		463
v. 22–vi. 9	„		498
v. 24	„		69
25	„	I.	299
		II.	233, 503
25–27	„		
26	„	I.	568
32	„	II.	492
vi. 1, 9	„		507
4	„		491
5	„		290
10	„		492
10–17	„		485, 496
10–20	„		509
10–24	„		488
11	„	I.	587
		II.	541
12	„	I.	628
12–17	„		502
15	„		628
17, 18	„	II.	492
18	„		509
19	„	I.	211, 594

EPHESIANS (continued).

vi. 19,	Vol. II.,	p.	492
19, 20	„		414
20	„	I.	13
		II.	478
21	„		395, 482, 587
21–24	„		509
23	„		507
23, 24	„		509
24	„	I.	595, 612
		II.	491

PHILIPPIANS.

i. 1,	Vol. I.,	p.	429
		II.	395, 521, 617
1, 2	„		424
3, 4, 7, 8, 10	„		417
3–11	„		424, 425
4	„		2–1
7	„		417
10	„		282, 425
11	„		219
12–18	„		426
12–26	„		424
13	„		425
14–20	„		411
15, 16	„		426
15, 17	„	I.	447
16	„	II.	173, 400
18, 25	„		431
19	„	I.	471
		II.	458
19–26	„		497
19, 20, 23, 27	„		427
20–23	„	I.	608
21	„	II.	191
23	„		417, 567
25	„		282
27	„	I.	429
		II.	320
27–30	„		428
i. 27–	„		
ii. 16	„		424
i. 28–30	„	I.	502
ii. 1	„		627
		II.	428
1–4	„		428
1–8	„		428
2, 5, 15	„		417
3	„		425
3–6, 18	„		411
4, 8, 9, 10, 11	„		417
6	„		249, 258, 428, 435
6–8	„		421
6–9	„		422
7	„	I.	27
8	„		431, 628
8–11	„	II.	483
9–11, 12, 13	„		429
11	„		433
12, 13	„	I.	591
14	„	I.	400
14–18	„	II.	430
16	„	I.	414
		II.	145, 282
17	„		430, 431, 573
17–30	„		424
18–30	„	I.	460

PHILIPPIANS (continued).

ii. 19,	Vol. I.,	p.	579
19–23	„	II.	529
19–30	„		431
19–	„		430–1
iii. 1	„		
ii. 20	„	I.	346, 459
22	„		458
24	„	II.	282, 414
25	„		141, 395, 430
26	„		29
30	„	I.	334
iii. 1	„		439
		II.	419, 431
1, 2	„		494
2	„	I.	140, 431, 634
		II.	173, 297, 299, 432
2, 3	„	I.	639
		II.	156
2, 18	„		270
3	„		432
3, 4, 5, 9, 19, 21	„		427
iii. 3– iv. 1	„		424
iii. 5	„	I.	4, 16
		II.	433
6	„	I.	174
8	„		507
8, 9	„	II.	433
10	„	I.	655
		II.	458, 461
12	„	I.	180, 228, 430
		II.	215, 567
12–14	„	I.	635
		II.	434
12–16	„		434
13	„		622
14	„	I.	459, 694
		II.	327
14, 17	„		417
15, 16	„		434
17–iv. 1	„		434, 435
19	„	I.	609
		II.	517
20	„	I.	362, 459
21	„	II.	428, 435
iv. 2, 3	„		424
3	„	I.	79, 689, 568, 629
		II.	435
4	„		424, 426
4, 9	„	I.	85
5	„	I.	519
6	„	I.	627
8	„		460
8, 10	„		436
10	„		215
10–20	„		424, 436
10–23	„		436–7
11	„		527
11, 12	„	I.	508
11–13	„	I.	527
11–18	„	I.	535
12	„	II.	267
15	„	I.	422, 561
15, 16	„		507
16	„		433
18	„	II.	395, 426
19, sq.	„		395
20	„		518
21–23	„		424
23	„	I.	595

QUOTED OR REFERRED TO. 665

COLOSSIANS.		
i. 1, Vol. II., p.	395
1, 2 ,,	455
2, 6, } ,,	455
10 }	
3-8 ,,	455
4 ,, I.	581
4, 6 ,,	463
4, 6, 9 ,, II.	442
5 ,, I.	208
6, 23 ,, II.	601
7 ,,	23, 396
7, 9- } ,,	456
14 }	
8, 9 ,,	462
9-13 ,,	455
11 ,,	281
13-ii. 3 ,,	455
14 ,,	601
15 ,,	249
15-18 ,,	450
15-23 ,,	457, 458
16 ,, I.	638
16, 17 ,, II.	246, 630
18 ,,	219, 455, 457
19 ,,	439, 457, 486, 492, 495
19, 20- } ,,	457
23 }	
20, 22 ,,	446
20-22 ,,	496
20, 21- } ,,	458
23 }	
21 ,,	458
24 ,, I.	654, 655
,, II.	458
24-29 ,,	459
i. 24-ii. 7 ,,	458, 459
i. 25 ,, I.	210
27 ,, II.	459
29 ,,	459
ii. 1 ,, I.	463
,, II.	442, 459
1-7 ,,	459
2 ,,	281
ii. 4-iii. 4 ,,	455
ii. 6 ,, I.	694
,, II.	446, 592
6-9 ,,	457
7 ,,	459
7-11 ,,	460
8 ,,	152, 460
8, 12 ,,	620
8, 16-19 ,,	585
9 ,,	249, 439, 457, 460
11 ,,	432, 461
11, 16 ,,	444
11-16 ,,	461
12 ,,	504
12-15 ,,	461
14 ,, I.	420
,, II.	106
15 ,, I.	638
15, 18 ,, II.	519
16 ,, I.	44
,, II.	152
16, 18 ,,	457
16-23 ,,	461-2
17 ,, I.	268
18 ,,	27
,, II.	65, 94, 498
19 ,,	450
21 ,,	455
23 ,, I.	451

COLOSSIANS (continued).		
ii. 23, Vol. II , p.	462
27 ,,	486
iii. ,,	485
1 ,, I.	203
,, II.	450
1, 3, &c. ,,	496
1-18 ,,	463
2 ,,	428
3 ,,	219
4 ,,	230
5 ,,	67
iii. 5-iv. 6 ,,	455
iii. 6 ,,	63
6, 11 ,,	463
10 ,,	220
11 ,,	201, 601
12 ,,	464
iii. 12-iv. 6 ,,	455
iii. 19 ,,	486
22 ,,	70, 527
24 ,,	243
24, 25 ,,	230
iv. 2 ,, I.	504
,, II.	281
3 ,, I.	211
,, II.	259
3, 4 ,,	414
4 ,, I.	479
5 ,,	433
6 ,, II.	504
7 ,,	395, 537
7, 10, } ,,	395
14 }	
7-18 ,,	455
9, 10, } ,,	396
14 }	
10 ,, I.	236, 320, 452-3, 506
,, II.	37, 416, 465, 506, 548
10, 11 ,,	170
10, 11, 14 ,,	480
11 ,,	173, 394
12, 13, } ,,	442
15 }	
13-16 ,,	26
15 ,, I.	636
15, 17 ,, II.	465
16 ,,	462
17 ,, I.	638
18 ,,	595
I. THESSALONIANS.	
i. 1, Vol. I., p.	429
,, II.	446
1-10 ,, I.	582
2 ,,	582, 633
2, 3, } ,,	511
6-8 }	
5 ,,	511
6 ,,	511, 576, 628
6, 8, 10 ,,	582
6, 10 ,,	596
8 ,,	506
9 ,,	388, 510
9, 10 ,,	608
10 ,, II.	584
ii. 1, 2 ,, I.	511
1-12 ,,	585
2 ,,	495, 508
2, 4, 7, } ,,	584
8, 9 }	
3 ,,	582, 657
3-5 ,,	217
3-6 ,,	511

THESSALONIANS (continued).		
ii. 4, Vol. II., p.	518
5, 7, 9 ,, I.	488
5, 9, 10 ,,	583
6 ,,	511, 579
6, 9 ,,	24
7 ,,	80
7, 11 ,,	343
8 ,,	27
9 ,,	480, 504, 511, 561
10-12 ,,	511
11 ,,	585
12 ,,	514, 596
14 ,,	510, 511
14-16 ,,	586, 586
15 ,,	239
17 ,,	586, 587
18 ,,	515, 518
19 ,,	597, 634
iii. 1 ,,	346, 661
1, 6 ,,	579
2 ,,	550
4 ,,	511
4, 7 ,,	557
5 ,,	414, 587
10 ,,	480, 584
11 ,,	611
13 ,,	587, 597
iv. 1-8 ,,	590
1 ,, II.	481
3, 17 ,, I.	596
4 ,,	588
6 ,,	589, 627
7 ,,	588
9 ,,	627, 633
11 ,,	611, 628
11, 12 ,,	589
12 ,, II.	157
13 ,,	185
13-18 ,, I.	592
14 ,,	211, 591
15 ,,	210, 597, 600, 601
15-17 ,,	608
16 ,,	57, 587, 633
16, 17 ,,	85
17 ,,	608
17, 18 ,, II.	592
v. 1 ,, I.	627, 633
1, 2, 4 ,,	592
1-11 ,,	592
3 ,,	80
4 ,, II.	584
5, 15 } ,, I.	596
16 }	
8 ,, II.	518
9 ,, I.	610
12 ,,	588
,, II.	617
12-15 ,, I.	593, 594
15 ,,	596
21 ,, II.	209
22 ,, I.	594
23 ,,	594, 597
27 ,, II.	144
28 ,,	595
,, I.	446
II. THESSALONIANS.	
i. 1, Vol. I., p.	429
2 ,,	579
3-12 ,,	608
4 ,,	606
4, 5 ,,	511
5 ,,	414

CPSIA information can be obtained
at www.ICGtesting.com
Printed in the USA
BVHW021927040623
665346BV00021B/61